OPERATING SYSTEMS

THREE EASY PIECES

REMZI H. ARPACI-DUSSEAU
ANDREA C. ARPACI-DUSSEAU
UNIVERSITY OF WISCONSIN–MADISON

To Vedat S. Arpaci, a lifelong inspiration

Preface

To Everyone

Welcome to this book! We hope you'll enjoy reading it as much as we enjoyed writing it. The book is called **Operating Systems: Three Easy Pieces** (available at `http://ostep.org`), and the title is obviously an homage to one of the greatest sets of lecture notes ever created, by one Richard Feynman on the topic of Physics [F96]. While this book will undoubtedly fall short of the high standard set by that famous physicist, perhaps it will be good enough for you in your quest to understand what operating systems (and more generally, systems) are all about.

The three easy pieces refer to the three major thematic elements the book is organized around: **virtualization**, **concurrency**, and **persistence**. In discussing these concepts, we'll end up discussing most of the important things an operating system does; hopefully, you'll also have some fun along the way. Learning new things is fun, right? At least, it (usually) should be.

Each major concept is divided into a set of chapters, most of which present a particular problem and then show how to solve it. The chapters are short, and try (as best as possible) to reference the source material where the ideas really came from. One of our goals in writing this book is to make the paths of history as clear as possible, as we think that helps a student understand what is, what was, and what will be more clearly. In this case, seeing how the sausage was made is nearly as important as understanding what the sausage is good for[1].

There are a couple devices we use throughout the book which are probably worth introducing here. The first is the **crux** of the problem. Anytime we are trying to solve a problem, we first try to state what the most important issue is; such a **crux of the problem** is explicitly called out in the text, and hopefully solved via the techniques, algorithms, and ideas presented in the rest of the text.

In many places, we'll explain how a system works by showing its behavior over time. These **timelines** are at the essence of understanding; if you know what happens, for example, when a process page faults, you are on your way to truly understanding how virtual memory operates. If

[1]Hint: eating! Or if you're a vegetarian, running away from.

you comprehend what takes place when a journaling file system writes a block to disk, you have taken the first steps towards mastery of storage systems.

There are also numerous **asides** and **tips** throughout the text, adding a little color to the mainline presentation. Asides tend to discuss something relevant (but perhaps not essential) to the main text; tips tend to be general lessons that can be applied to systems you build. An index at the end of the book lists all of these tips and asides (as well as cruces, the odd plural of crux) for your convenience.

We use one of the oldest didactic methods, the **dialogue**, throughout the book, as a way of presenting some of the material in a different light. These are used to introduce the major thematic concepts (in a peachy way, as we will see), as well as to review material every now and then. They are also a chance to write in a more humorous style. Whether you find them useful, or humorous, well, that's another matter entirely.

At the beginning of each major section, we'll first present an **abstraction** that an operating system provides, and then work in subsequent chapters on the mechanisms, policies, and other support needed to provide the abstraction. Abstractions are fundamental to all aspects of Computer Science, so it is perhaps no surprise that they are also essential in operating systems.

Throughout the chapters, we try to use **real code** (not **pseudocode**) where possible, so for virtually all examples, you should be able to type them up yourself and run them. Running real code on real systems is the best way to learn about operating systems, so we encourage you to do so when you can. We are also making code available for your viewing pleasure[2].

In various parts of the text, we have sprinkled in a few **homeworks** to ensure that you are understanding what is going on. Many of these homeworks are little **simulations** of pieces of the operating system; you should download the homeworks, and run them to quiz yourself. The homework simulators have the following feature: by giving them a different random seed, you can generate a virtually infinite set of problems; the simulators can also be told to solve the problems for you. Thus, you can test and re-test yourself until you have achieved a good level of understanding.

The most important addendum to this book is a set of **projects** in which you learn about how real systems work by designing, implementing, and testing your own code. All projects (as well as the code examples, mentioned above) are in the **C programming language** [KR88]; C is a simple and powerful language that underlies most operating systems, and thus worth adding to your tool-chest of languages. Two types of projects are available (see the online appendix for ideas). The first are **systems programming** projects; these projects are great for those who are

[2] `https://github.com/remzi-arpacidusseau/ostep-code`

new to C and UNIX and want to learn how to do low-level C programming. The second type are based on a real operating system kernel developed at MIT called xv6 [CK+08]; these projects are great for students that already have some C and want to get their hands dirty inside the OS. At Wisconsin, we've run the course in three different ways: either all systems programming, all xv6 programming, or a mix of both.

We are slowly making project descriptions, and a testing framework, available. See our repository[3] for more information. If not part of a class, this will give you a chance to do these projects on your own, to better learn the material. Unfortunately, you don't have a TA to bug when you get stuck, but not everything in life can be free (but books can be!).

[3] `https://github.com/remzi-arpacidusseau/ostep-projects`

To Educators

If you are an instructor or professor who wishes to use this book, please feel free to do so. As you may have noticed, they are free and available on-line from the following web page:

`http://www.ostep.org`

You can also purchase a printed copy from `http://lulu.com` or `http://amazon.com`. Look for it on the web page above.

The (current) proper citation for the book is as follows:

Operating Systems: Three Easy Pieces
Remzi H. Arpaci-Dusseau and Andrea C. Arpaci-Dusseau
Arpaci-Dusseau Books
August, 2018 (Version 1.00) or July, 2019 (Version 1.01)
`http://www.ostep.org`

The course divides fairly well across a 15-week semester, in which you can cover most of the topics within at a reasonable level of depth. Cramming the course into a 10-week quarter probably requires dropping some detail from each of the pieces. There are also a few chapters on virtual machine monitors, which we usually squeeze in sometime during the semester, either right at end of the large section on virtualization, or near the end as an aside.

One slightly unusual aspect of the book is that concurrency, a topic at the front of many OS books, is pushed off herein until the student has built an understanding of virtualization of the CPU and of memory. In our experience in teaching this course for nearly 20 years, students have a hard time understanding how the concurrency problem arises, or why they are trying to solve it, if they don't yet understand what an address space is, what a process is, or why context switches can occur at arbitrary points in time. Once they do understand these concepts, however, introducing the notion of threads and the problems that arise due to them becomes rather easy, or at least, easier.

As much as is possible, we use a chalkboard (or whiteboard) to deliver a lecture. On these more conceptual days, we come to class with a few major ideas and examples in mind and use the board to present them. Handouts are useful to give the students concrete problems to solve based on the material. On more practical days, we simply plug a laptop into the projector and show real code; this style works particularly well for concurrency lectures as well as for any discussion sections where you show students code that is relevant for their projects. We don't generally use slides to present material, but have now made a set available for those who prefer that style of presentation.

If you'd like a copy of any of these materials, please drop us an email. We have already shared them with many others around the world, and others have contributed their materials as well.

One last request: if you use the free online chapters, please just **link** to them, instead of making a local copy. This helps us track usage (over 1 million chapters downloaded in the past few years!) and also ensures students get the latest (and greatest?) version.

To Students

If you are a student reading this book, thank you! It is an honor for us to provide some material to help you in your pursuit of knowledge about operating systems. We both think back fondly towards some textbooks of our undergraduate days (e.g., Hennessy and Patterson [HP90], the classic book on computer architecture) and hope this book will become one of those positive memories for you.

You may have noticed this book is free and available online[4]. There is one major reason for this: textbooks are generally too expensive. This book, we hope, is the first of a new wave of free materials to help those in pursuit of their education, regardless of which part of the world they come from or how much they are willing to spend for a book. Failing that, it is one free book, which is better than none.

We also hope, where possible, to point you to the original sources of much of the material in the book: the great papers and persons who have shaped the field of operating systems over the years. Ideas are not pulled out of the air; they come from smart and hard-working people (including numerous Turing-award winners[5]), and thus we should strive to celebrate those ideas and people where possible. In doing so, we hopefully can better understand the revolutions that have taken place, instead of writing texts as if those thoughts have always been present [K62]. Further, perhaps such references will encourage you to dig deeper on your own; reading the famous papers of our field is certainly one of the best ways to learn.

[4] A digression here: "free" in the way we use it here does not mean open source, and it does not mean the book is not copyrighted with the usual protections – it is! What it means is that you can download the chapters and use them to learn about operating systems. Why not an open-source book, just like Linux is an open-source kernel? Well, we believe it is important for a book to have a single voice throughout, and have worked hard to provide such a voice. When you're reading it, the book should kind of feel like a dialogue with the person explaining something to you. Hence, our approach.

[5] The Turing Award is the highest award in Computer Science; it is like the Nobel Prize, except that you have never heard of it.

Acknowledgments

This section will contain thanks to those who helped us put the book together. The important thing for now: **your name could go here!** But, you have to help. So send us some feedback and help debug this book. And you could be famous! Or, at least, have your name in some book.

The people who have helped so far include: Aaron Gember (Colgate), Aashrith H Govindraj (USF), Abhinav Mehra, Abhirami Senthilkumaran*, Adam Drescher* (WUSTL), Adam Eggum, Aditya Venkataraman, Adriana Iamnitchi and class (USF), Ahmad Jarara, Ahmed Fikri*, Ajaykrishna Raghavan, Akiel Khan, Alex Curtis, Alex Wyler, Alex Zhao (U. Colorado at Colorado Springs), Ali Razeen (Duke), Alistair Martin, AmirBehzad Eslami, Anand Mundada, Andrei Bozântan, Andrew Mahler, Andrew Moss, Andrew Valencik (Saint Mary's), Angela Demke Brown (Toronto), Antonella Bernobich (UoPeople)*, Arek Bulski, B. Brahmananda Reddy (Minnesota), Bala Subrahmanyam Kambala, Bart Miller, Ben Kushigian (U. Mass), Benita Bose, Bill Yang, Biswajit Mazumder (Clemson), Bobby Jack, Björn Lindberg, Brandon Harshe (U. Minn), Brennan Payne, Brian Gorman, Brian Kroth, Caleb Sumner (Southern Adventist), Cara Lauritzen, Charlotte Kissinger, Cheng Su, Chien-Chung Shen (Delaware)*, Christian Stober, Christoph Jaeger, C.J. Stanbridge (Memorial U. of Newfoundland), Cody Hanson, Constantinos Georgiades, Dakota Crane (U. Washington-Tacoma), Dan Soendergaard (U. Aarhus), Dan Tsafrir (Technion), Danilo Bruschi (Universita Degli Studi Di Milano), Darby Asher Noam Haller, David Hanle (Grinnell), David Hartman, Dawn Flood, Deepika Muthukumar, Demir Delic, Dennis Zhou, Dheeraj Shetty (North Carolina State), Diego Oleiarz (FaMAF UNC), Dorian Arnold (New Mexico), Dominic White, Dustin Metzler, Dustin Passofaro, Dylan Kaplan, Eduardo Stelmaszczyk, Emad Sadeghi, Emil Hessman, Emily Jacobson, Emmett Witchel (Texas), Eric Freudenthal (UTEP), Eric Kleinberg, Eric Johansson, Erik Turk, Ernst Biersack (France), Ethan Wood, Fangjun Kuang (U. Stuttgart), Feng Zhang (IBM), Finn Kuusisto*, Gavin Inglis (Notre Dame), Giovanni Lagorio (DIBRIS), Glenn Bruns (CSU Monterey Bay), Glen Granzow (College of Idaho), Greggory Van Dycke, Guilherme Baptista, Hamid Reza Ghasemi, Hao Chen, Hao Liu, Henry Abbey, Hilmar Gústafsson (Aalborg University), Hrishikesh Amur, Huanchen Zhang*, Huseyin Sular, Hugo Diaz, Hyrum Carroll (Columbus State), Ilya Oblomkov, Itai Hass (Toronto), Jackson "Jake" Haenchen (Texas), Jaeyoung Cho (SKKU), Jagannathan Eachambadi, Jake Gillberg, Jakob Olandt, James Earley, James Perry (U. Michigan-Dearborn)*, Jan Reineke (Universität des Saarlandes), Jason MacLafferty (Southern Adventist), Jason Waterman (Vassar), Jay Lim, Jerod Weinman (Grinnell), Jhih-Cheng Luo, Jiao Dong (Rutgers), Jia-Shen Boon, Jiawen Bao, Jidong Xiao (Boise State), Jingxin Li, Joe Jean (NYU), Joel Kuntz (Saint Mary's), Joel Sommers (Colgate), John Brady (Grinnell), John Komenda, John McEachen (NPS), Jonathan Perry (MIT), Joshua Carpenter (NCSU), Jun He, Justinas Petuchovas, Karl Wallinger, Kartik Singhal, Katherine Dudenas, Katie Coyle (Georgia Tech), Kaushik Kannan, Kemal Bıçakcı, Kevin Liu*, KyoungSoo Park (KAIST), Lanyue Lu, Laura Xu, Lei Tian (U. Nebraska-Lincoln), Leonardo Medici (U. Milan), Leslie Schultz, Liang Yin, Lihao Wang, Looserof, Louie Lu, Manav Batra (IIIT-Delhi), Manu Awasthi (Samsung), Marcel van der Holst, Marco Guazzone (U. Piemonte Orientale), Marco Pedrinazzi (Universita Degli Studi Di Milano), Marius Rodi, Mart Oskamp, Martha Ferris, Masashi Kishikawa (Sony), Matt Reichoff, Matthias St. Pierre, Mattia Monga (U. Milan), Matty Williams, Meng Huang, Michael Machtel (Hochschule Konstanz), Michael Walfish (NYU), Michael Wu (UCLA), Mike Griepentrog, Ming Chen (Stonybrook), Mohammed Alali (Delaware), Mohamed Omran (GUST), Muhammad Yasoob Ullah Khalid, Murugan Kandaswamy, Nadeem Shaikh, Nan Xiao, Natasha

Eilbert, Natasha Stopa, Nathan Dipiazza, Nathan Sullivan, Neeraj Badlani (N.C. State), Neil Perry, Nelson Gomez, Nghia Huynh (Texas), Nicholas Mandal, Nick Weinandt, Nishin Shouzab, Patel Pratyush Ashesh (BITS-Pilani), Patricio Jara, Patrizio Palmisano, Pavle Kostovic, Perry Kivolowitz, Peter Peterson (Minnesota), Pieter Kockx, Radford Smith, Riccardo Mutschlechner, Ripudaman Singh, Rita Pia Folisi, Robert Ordóñez and class (Southern Adventist), Roger Wattenhofer (ETH), Rohan Das (Toronto)*, Rohan Pasalkar (Minnesota), Rohan Puri, Ross Aiken, Ruslan Kiselev, Ryland Herrick, Sam Kelly, Sam Noh (UNIST), Sameer Punjal, Samer Al-Kiswany, Sandeep Ummadi (Minnesota), Sankaralingam Panneerselvam, Satish Chebrolu (NetApp), Satyanarayana Shanmugam*, Scott Catlin, Scott Lee (UCLA), Seth Pollen, Sharad Punuganti, Shawn Ge, Shivaram Venkataraman, Shreevatsa R., Simon Pratt (Waterloo), Sivaraman Sivaraman*, Song Jiang (Wayne State), Spencer Harston (Weber State), Srinivasan Thirunarayanan*, Stefan Dekanski, Stephen Bye, Stephen Schaub, Suriyhaprakhas Balaram Sankari, Sy Jin Cheah, Teri Zhao (EMC), Thanumalayan S. Pillai, Thomas Griebel, Thomas Scrace, Tianxia Bai, Tobi Popoola (Boise State), Tong He, Tongxin Zheng, Tony Adkins, Torin Rudeen (Princeton), Tuo Wang, Tyler Couto, Varun Vats, Vikas Goel, Waciuma Wanjohi, William Royle (Grinnell), Xiang Peng, Xu Di, Yifan Hao, Yuanyuan Chen, Yubin Ruan, Yudong Sun, Yue Zhuo (Texas A&M), Yufeng Zhang (UCLA), Yufui Ren, Zef RosnBrick, Zeyuan Hu (Texas), ZiHan Zheng (USTC), Zuyu Zhang. Special thanks to those marked with an asterisk above, who have gone above and beyond in their suggestions for improvement.

In addition, a hearty thanks to Professor Joe Meehean (Lynchburg) for his detailed notes on each chapter, to Professor Jerod Weinman (Grinnell) and his entire class for their incredible booklets, to Professor Chien-Chung Shen (Delaware) for his invaluable and detailed reading and comments, to Adam Drescher (WUSTL) for his careful reading and suggestions, to Glen Granzow (College of Idaho) for his incredibly detailed comments and tips, Michael Walfish (NYU) for his enthusiasm and detailed suggestions for improvement, Peter Peterson (UMD) for his many bits of useful feedback and commentary, Mark Kampe (Pomona) for detailed criticism (we only wish we could fix all suggestions!), and Youjip Won (Hanyang) for his translation work into Korean(!) and numerous insightful suggestions. All have helped these authors immeasurably in the refinement of the materials herein.

Also, many thanks to the hundreds of students who have taken 537 over the years. In particular, the Fall '08 class who encouraged the first written form of these notes (they were sick of not having any kind of textbook to read — pushy students!), and then praised them enough for us to keep going (including one hilarious "ZOMG! You should totally write a textbook!" comment in our course evaluations that year).

A great debt of thanks is also owed to the brave few who took the xv6 project lab course, much of which is now incorporated into the main 537 course. From Spring '09: Justin Cherniak, Patrick Deline, Matt Czech, Tony Gregerson, Michael Griepentrog, Tyler Harter, Ryan Kroiss, Eric Radzikowski, Wesley Reardan, Rajiv Vaidyanathan, and Christopher Waclawik. From Fall '09: Nick Bearson, Aaron Brown, Alex Bird, David Capel, Keith Gould, Tom Grim, Jeffrey Hugo, Brandon Johnson, John Kjell, Boyan Li, James Loethen, Will McCardell, Ryan Szaroletta, Simon

Tso, and Ben Yule. From Spring '10: Patrick Blesi, Aidan Dennis-Oehling, Paras Doshi, Jake Friedman, Benjamin Frisch, Evan Hanson, Pikkili Hemanth, Michael Jeung, Alex Langenfeld, Scott Rick, Mike Treffert, Garret Staus, Brennan Wall, Hans Werner, Soo-Young Yang, and Carlos Griffin (almost).

Although they do not directly help with the book, our graduate students have taught us much of what we know about systems. We talk with them regularly while they are at Wisconsin, but they do all the real work — and by telling us about what they are doing, we learn new things every week. This list includes the following collection of current and former students and post-docs with whom we have published papers; an asterisk marks those who received a Ph.D. under our guidance, and two asterisks are for those who did a post-doctorate with us: Abhishek Rajimwale, Aishwarya Ganesan, Andrew Krioukov, Ao Ma, Brian Forney, Chris Dragga, Deepak Ramamurthi, Dennis Zhou, Edward Oakes, Florentina Popovici*, Hariharan Gopalakrishnan, Haryadi S. Gunawi*, James Nugent, Jing Liu, Joe Meehean*, John Bent*, Jun He*, Kan Wu, Kevin Houck, Lanyue Lu*, Lakshmi Bairavasundaram*, Laxman Visampalli, Leo Arulraj*, Leon Yang, Meenali Rungta, Muthian Sivathanu*, Nathan Burnett*, Nitin Agrawal*, Ram Alagappan, Samer Al-Kiswany**, Scott Hendrickson, Sriram Subramanian*, Stephen Todd Jones*, Stephen Sturdevant, Sudarsun Kannan**, Suli Yang*, Swaminathan Sundararaman*, Swetha Krishnan, Thanh Do*, Thanumalayan S. Pillai*, Timothy Denehy*, Tyler Harter*, Venkat Venkataramani, Vijay Chidambaram*, Vijayan Prabhakaran*, Yiying Zhang*, Yupu Zhang*, Yuvraj Patel, Zev Weiss*.

Our graduate students have largely been funded by the National Science Foundation (NSF), the Department of Energy Office of Science (DOE), and by industry grants. We are especially grateful to the NSF for their support over many years, as our research has shaped the content of many chapters herein.

We thank Thomas Griebel, who demanded a better cover for the book. Although we didn't take his specific suggestion (a dinosaur, can you believe it?), the beautiful picture of Halley's comet would not be found on the cover without him.

A final debt of gratitude is also owed to Aaron Brown, who first took this course many years ago (Spring '09), then took the xv6 lab course (Fall '09), and finally was a graduate teaching assistant for the course for two years or so (Fall '10 through Spring '12). His tireless work has vastly improved the state of the projects (particularly those in xv6 land) and thus has helped better the learning experience for countless undergraduates and graduates here at Wisconsin. As Aaron would say (in his usual succinct manner): "Thx."

Final Words

Yeats famously said "Education is not the filling of a pail but the lighting of a fire." He was right but wrong at the same time[6]. You do have to "fill the pail" a bit, and these notes are certainly here to help with that part of your education; after all, when you go to interview at Google, and they ask you a trick question about how to use semaphores, it might be good to actually know what a semaphore is, right?

But Yeats's larger point is obviously on the mark: the real point of education is to get you interested in something, to learn something more about the subject matter on your own and not just what you have to digest to get a good grade in some class. As one of our fathers (Remzi's dad, Vedat Arpaci) used to say, "Learn beyond the classroom".

We created these notes to spark your interest in operating systems, to read more about the topic on your own, to talk to your professor about all the exciting research that is going on in the field, and even to get involved with that research. It is a great field(!), full of exciting and wonderful ideas that have shaped computing history in profound and important ways. And while we understand this fire won't light for all of you, we hope it does for many, or even a few. Because once that fire is lit, well, that is when you truly become capable of doing something great. And thus the real point of the educational process: to go forth, to study many new and fascinating topics, to learn, to mature, and most importantly, to find something that lights a fire for you.

Andrea and Remzi
Married couple
Professors of Computer Science at the University of Wisconsin
Chief Lighters of Fires, hopefully[7]

[6]If he actually said this; as with many famous quotes, the history of this gem is murky.

[7]If this sounds like we are admitting some past history as arsonists, you are probably missing the point. Probably. If this sounds cheesy, well, that's because it is, but you'll just have to forgive us for that.

References

[CK+08] "The xv6 Operating System" by Russ Cox, Frans Kaashoek, Robert Morris, Nickolai Zeldovich. From: `http://pdos.csail.mit.edu/6.828/2008/index.html`. *xv6 was developed as a port of the original* UNIX *version 6 and represents a beautiful, clean, and simple way to understand a modern operating system.*

[F96] "Six Easy Pieces: Essentials Of Physics Explained By Its Most Brilliant Teacher" by Richard P. Feynman. Basic Books, 1996. *This book reprints the six easiest chapters of Feynman's Lectures on Physics, from 1963. If you like Physics, it is a fantastic read.*

[HP90] "Computer Architecture a Quantitative Approach" (1st ed.) by David A. Patterson and John L. Hennessy . Morgan-Kaufman, 1990. *A book that encouraged each of us at our undergraduate institutions to pursue graduate studies; we later both had the pleasure of working with Patterson, who greatly shaped the foundations of our research careers.*

[KR88] "The C Programming Language" by Brian Kernighan and Dennis Ritchie. Prentice-Hall, April 1988. *The C programming reference that everyone should have, by the people who invented the language.*

[K62] "The Structure of Scientific Revolutions" by Thomas S. Kuhn. University of Chicago Press, 1962. *A great and famous read about the fundamentals of the scientific process. Mop-up work, anomaly, crisis, and revolution. We are mostly destined to do mop-up work, alas.*

Contents

List of Figures

1

A Dialogue on the Book

Professor: *Welcome to this book! It's called* **Operating Systems in Three Easy Pieces***, and I am here to teach you the things you need to know about operating systems. I am called "Professor"; who are you?*

Student: *Hi Professor! I am called "Student", as you might have guessed. And I am here and ready to learn!*

Professor: *Sounds good. Any questions?*

Student: *Sure! Why is it called "Three Easy Pieces"?*

Professor: *That's an easy one. Well, you see, there are these great lectures on Physics by Richard Feynman...*

Student: *Oh! The guy who wrote "Surely You're Joking, Mr. Feynman", right? Great book! Is this going to be hilarious like that book was?*

Professor: *Um... well, no. That book was great, and I'm glad you've read it. Hopefully this book is more like his notes on Physics. Some of the basics were summed up in a book called "Six Easy Pieces". He was talking about Physics; we're going to do Three Easy Pieces on the fine topic of Operating Systems. This is appropriate, as Operating Systems are about half as hard as Physics.*

Student: *Well, I liked physics, so that is probably good. What are those pieces?*

Professor: *They are the three key ideas we're going to learn about:* **virtualization, concurrency***, and* **persistence***. In learning about these ideas, we'll learn all about how an operating system works, including how it decides what program to run next on a CPU, how it handles memory overload in a virtual memory system, how virtual machine monitors work, how to manage information on disks, and even a little about how to build a distributed system that works when parts have failed. That sort of stuff.*

Student: *I have no idea what you're talking about, really.*

Professor: *Good! That means you are in the right class.*

Student: *I have another question: what's the best way to learn this stuff?*

Professor: *Excellent query! Well, each person needs to figure this out on their own, of course, but here is what I would do: go to class, to hear the professor introduce the material. Then, at the end of every week, read these notes, to help the ideas sink into your head a bit better. Of course, some time later (hint: before the exam!), read the notes again to firm up your knowledge. Of course, your professor will no doubt assign some homeworks and projects, so you should do those; in particular, doing projects where you write real code to solve real problems is the best way to put the ideas within these notes into action. As Confucius said...*

Student: *Oh, I know! 'I hear and I forget. I see and I remember. I do and I understand.' Or something like that.*

Professor: *(surprised) How did you know what I was going to say?!*

Student: *It seemed to follow. Also, I am a big fan of Confucius, and an even bigger fan of Xunzi, who actually is a better source for this quote*[1].

Professor: *(stunned) Well, I think we are going to get along just fine! Just fine indeed.*

Student: *Professor – just one more question, if I may. What are these dialogues for? I mean, isn't this just supposed to be a book? Why not present the material directly?*

Professor: *Ah, good question, good question! Well, I think it is sometimes useful to pull yourself outside of a narrative and think a bit; these dialogues are those times. So you and I are going to work together to make sense of all of these pretty complex ideas. Are you up for it?*

Student: *So we have to think? Well, I'm up for that. I mean, what else do I have to do anyhow? It's not like I have much of a life outside of this book.*

Professor: *Me neither, sadly. So let's get to work!*

[1] According to `http://www.barrypopik.com` (on, December 19, 2012, entitled "Tell me and I forget; teach me and I may remember; involve me and I will learn") Confucian philosopher Xunzi said "Not having heard something is not as good as having heard it; having heard it is not as good as having seen it; having seen it is not as good as knowing it; knowing it is not as good as putting it into practice." Later on, the wisdom got attached to Confucius for some reason. Thanks to Jiao Dong (Rutgers) for telling us!

2

Introduction to Operating Systems

If you are taking an undergraduate operating systems course, you should already have some idea of what a computer program does when it runs. If not, this book (and the corresponding course) is going to be difficult — so you should probably stop reading this book, or run to the nearest bookstore and quickly consume the necessary background material before continuing (both Patt & Patel [PP03] and Bryant & O'Hallaron [BOH10] are pretty great books).

So what happens when a program runs?

Well, a running program does one very simple thing: it executes instructions. Many millions (and these days, even billions) of times every second, the processor **fetches** an instruction from memory, **decodes** it (i.e., figures out which instruction this is), and **executes** it (i.e., it does the thing that it is supposed to do, like add two numbers together, access memory, check a condition, jump to a function, and so forth). After it is done with this instruction, the processor moves on to the next instruction, and so on, and so on, until the program finally completes[1].

Thus, we have just described the basics of the **Von Neumann** model of computing[2]. Sounds simple, right? But in this class, we will be learning that while a program runs, a lot of other wild things are going on with the primary goal of making the system **easy to use**.

There is a body of software, in fact, that is responsible for making it easy to run programs (even allowing you to seemingly run many at the same time), allowing programs to share memory, enabling programs to interact with devices, and other fun stuff like that. That body of software

[1] Of course, modern processors do many bizarre and frightening things underneath the hood to make programs run faster, e.g., executing multiple instructions at once, and even issuing and completing them out of order! But that is not our concern here; we are just concerned with the simple model most programs assume: that instructions seemingly execute one at a time, in an orderly and sequential fashion.

[2] Von Neumann was one of the early pioneers of computing systems. He also did pioneering work on game theory and atomic bombs, and played in the NBA for six years. OK, one of those things isn't true.

THE CRUX OF THE PROBLEM:
HOW TO VIRTUALIZE RESOURCES

One central question we will answer in this book is quite simple: how does the operating system virtualize resources? This is the crux of our problem. *Why* the OS does this is not the main question, as the answer should be obvious: it makes the system easier to use. Thus, we focus on the *how*: what mechanisms and policies are implemented by the OS to attain virtualization? How does the OS do so efficiently? What hardware support is needed?

We will use the "crux of the problem", in shaded boxes such as this one, as a way to call out specific problems we are trying to solve in building an operating system. Thus, within a note on a particular topic, you may find one or more *cruces* (yes, this is the proper plural) which highlight the problem. The details within the chapter, of course, present the solution, or at least the basic parameters of a solution.

is called the **operating system** (**OS**)[3], as it is in charge of making sure the system operates correctly and efficiently in an easy-to-use manner.

The primary way the OS does this is through a general technique that we call **virtualization**. That is, the OS takes a **physical** resource (such as the processor, or memory, or a disk) and transforms it into a more general, powerful, and easy-to-use **virtual** form of itself. Thus, we sometimes refer to the operating system as a **virtual machine**.

Of course, in order to allow users to tell the OS what to do and thus make use of the features of the virtual machine (such as running a program, or allocating memory, or accessing a file), the OS also provides some interfaces (APIs) that you can call. A typical OS, in fact, exports a few hundred **system calls** that are available to applications. Because the OS provides these calls to run programs, access memory and devices, and other related actions, we also sometimes say that the OS provides a **standard library** to applications.

Finally, because virtualization allows many programs to run (thus sharing the CPU), and many programs to concurrently access their own instructions and data (thus sharing memory), and many programs to access devices (thus sharing disks and so forth), the OS is sometimes known as a **resource manager**. Each of the CPU, memory, and disk is a **resource** of the system; it is thus the operating system's role to **manage** those resources, doing so efficiently or fairly or indeed with many other possible goals in mind. To understand the role of the OS a little bit better, let's take a look at some examples.

[3]Another early name for the OS was the **supervisor** or even the **master control program**. Apparently, the latter sounded a little overzealous (see the movie Tron for details) and thus, thankfully, "operating system" caught on instead.

```
#include <stdio.h>
#include <stdlib.h>
#include <sys/time.h>
#include <assert.h>
#include "common.h"

int
main(int argc, char *argv[])
{
    if (argc != 2) {
        fprintf(stderr, "usage: cpu <string>\n");
        exit(1);
    }
    char *str = argv[1];
    while (1) {
        Spin(1);
        printf("%s\n", str);
    }
    return 0;
}
```

Figure 21: **Simple Example: Code That Loops And Prints (cpu.c)**

2.1 Virtualizing The CPU

Figure 21 depicts our first program. It doesn't do much. In fact, all it does is call `Spin()`, a function that repeatedly checks the time and returns once it has run for a second. Then, it prints out the string that the user passed in on the command line, and repeats, forever.

Let's say we save this file as `cpu.c` and decide to compile and run it on a system with a single processor (or **CPU** as we will sometimes call it). Here is what we will see:

```
prompt> gcc -o cpu cpu.c -Wall
prompt> ./cpu "A"
A
A
A
A
^C
prompt>
```

Not too interesting of a run — the system begins running the program, which repeatedly checks the time until a second has elapsed. Once a second has passed, the code prints the input string passed in by the user (in this example, the letter "A"), and continues. Note the program will run forever; by pressing "Control-c" (which on UNIX-based systems will terminate the program running in the foreground) we can halt the program.

```
prompt> ./cpu A & ./cpu B & ./cpu C & ./cpu D &
[1] 7353
[2] 7354
[3] 7355
[4] 7356
A
B
D
C
A
B
D
C
A
...
```

Figure 22: **Running Many Programs At Once**

Now, let's do the same thing, but this time, let's run many different instances of this same program. Figure 22 shows the results of this slightly more complicated example.

Well, now things are getting a little more interesting. Even though we have only one processor, somehow all four of these programs seem to be running at the same time! How does this magic happen?[4]

It turns out that the operating system, with some help from the hardware, is in charge of this **illusion**, i.e., the illusion that the system has a very large number of virtual CPUs. Turning a single CPU (or a small set of them) into a seemingly infinite number of CPUs and thus allowing many programs to seemingly run at once is what we call **virtualizing the CPU**, the focus of the first major part of this book.

Of course, to run programs, and stop them, and otherwise tell the OS which programs to run, there need to be some interfaces (APIs) that you can use to communicate your desires to the OS. We'll talk about these APIs throughout this book; indeed, they are the major way in which most users interact with operating systems.

You might also notice that the ability to run multiple programs at once raises all sorts of new questions. For example, if two programs want to run at a particular time, which *should* run? This question is answered by a **policy** of the OS; policies are used in many different places within an OS to answer these types of questions, and thus we will study them as we learn about the basic **mechanisms** that operating systems implement (such as the ability to run multiple programs at once). Hence the role of the OS as a **resource manager**.

[4]Note how we ran four processes at the same time, by using the `&` symbol. Doing so runs a job in the background in the `zsh` shell, which means that the user is able to immediately issue their next command, which in this case is another program to run. If you're using a different shell (e.g., `tcsh`), it works slightly differently; read documentation online for details.

```
#include <unistd.h>
#include <stdio.h>
#include <stdlib.h>
#include "common.h"

int
main(int argc, char *argv[])
{
    int *p = malloc(sizeof(int));                          // a1
    assert(p != NULL);
    printf("(%d) address pointed to by p: %p\n",
           getpid(), p);                                   // a2
    *p = 0;                                                // a3
    while (1) {
        Spin(1);
        *p = *p + 1;
        printf("(%d) p: %d\n", getpid(), *p);              // a4
    }
    return 0;
}
```

Figure 23: **A Program That Accesses Memory (mem.c)**

2.2 Virtualizing Memory

Now let's consider memory. The model of **physical memory** presented by modern machines is very simple. Memory is just an array of bytes; to **read** memory, one must specify an **address** to be able to access the data stored there; to **write** (or **update**) memory, one must also specify the data to be written to the given address.

Memory is accessed all the time when a program is running. A program keeps all of its data structures in memory, and accesses them through various instructions, like loads and stores or other explicit instructions that access memory in doing their work. Don't forget that each instruction of the program is in memory too; thus memory is accessed on each instruction fetch.

Let's take a look at a program (in Figure 23) that allocates some memory by calling `malloc()`. The output of this program can be found here:

```
prompt> ./mem
(2134) address pointed to by p: 0x200000
(2134) p: 1
(2134) p: 2
(2134) p: 3
(2134) p: 4
(2134) p: 5
^C
```

```
prompt> ./mem &; ./mem &
[1] 24113
[2] 24114
(24113) address pointed to by p: 0x200000
(24114) address pointed to by p: 0x200000
(24113) p: 1
(24114) p: 1
(24114) p: 2
(24113) p: 2
(24113) p: 3
(24114) p: 3
(24113) p: 4
(24114) p: 4
...
```

Figure 24: **Running The Memory Program Multiple Times**

The program does a couple of things. First, it allocates some memory (line a1). Then, it prints out the address of the memory (a2), and then puts the number zero into the first slot of the newly allocated memory (a3). Finally, it loops, delaying for a second and incrementing the value stored at the address held in `p`. With every print statement, it also prints out what is called the process identifier (the PID) of the running program. This PID is unique per running process.

Again, this first result is not too interesting. The newly allocated memory is at address `0x200000`. As the program runs, it slowly updates the value and prints out the result.

Now, we again run multiple instances of this same program to see what happens (Figure 24). We see from the example that each running program has allocated memory at the same address (`0x200000`), and yet each seems to be updating the value at `0x200000` independently! It is as if each running program has its own private memory, instead of sharing the same physical memory with other running programs[5].

Indeed, that is exactly what is happening here as the OS is **virtualizing memory**. Each process accesses its own private **virtual address space** (sometimes just called its **address space**), which the OS somehow maps onto the physical memory of the machine. A memory reference within one running program does not affect the address space of other processes (or the OS itself); as far as the running program is concerned, it has physical memory all to itself. The reality, however, is that physical memory is a shared resource, managed by the operating system. Exactly how all of this is accomplished is also the subject of the first part of this book, on the topic of **virtualization**.

[5]For this example to work, you need to make sure address-space randomization is disabled; randomization, as it turns out, can be a good defense against certain kinds of security flaws. Read more about it on your own, especially if you want to learn how to break into computer systems via stack-smashing attacks. Not that we would recommend such a thing...

2.3 Concurrency

```
#include <stdio.h>
#include <stdlib.h>
#include "common.h"

volatile int counter = 0;
int loops;

void *worker(void *arg) {
    int i;
    for (i = 0; i < loops; i++) {
        counter++;
    }
    return NULL;
}

int main(int argc, char *argv[]) {
    if (argc != 2) {
        fprintf(stderr, "usage: threads <value>\n");
        exit(1);
    }
    loops = atoi(argv[1]);
    pthread_t p1, p2;
    printf("Initial value : %d\n", counter);

    Pthread_create(&p1, NULL, worker, NULL);
    Pthread_create(&p2, NULL, worker, NULL);
    Pthread_join(p1, NULL);
    Pthread_join(p2, NULL);
    printf("Final value   : %d\n", counter);
    return 0;
}
```

Figure 25: **A Multi-threaded Program (`threads.c`)**

Another main theme of this book is **concurrency**. We use this conceptual term to refer to a host of problems that arise, and must be addressed, when working on many things at once (i.e., concurrently) in the same program. The problems of concurrency arose first within the operating system itself; as you can see in the examples above on virtualization, the OS is juggling many things at once, first running one process, then another, and so forth. As it turns out, doing so leads to some deep and interesting problems.

Unfortunately, the problems of concurrency are no longer limited just to the OS itself. Indeed, modern **multi-threaded** programs exhibit the same problems. Let us demonstrate with an example of a **multi-threaded** program (Figure 25).

Although you might not understand this example fully at the moment (and we'll learn a lot more about it in later chapters, in the section of the book on concurrency), the basic idea is simple. The main program creates two **threads** using `Pthread_create()`[6]. You can think of a thread as a function running within the same memory space as other functions, with more than one of them active at a time. In this example, each thread starts running in a routine called `worker()`, in which it simply increments a counter in a loop for `loops` number of times.

Below is a transcript of what happens when we run this program with the input value for the variable `loops` set to 1000. The value of `loops` determines how many times each of the two workers will increment the shared counter in a loop. When the program is run with the value of `loops` set to 1000, what do you expect the final value of `counter` to be?

```
prompt> gcc -o thread thread.c -Wall -pthread
prompt> ./thread 1000
Initial value : 0
Final value   : 2000
```

As you probably guessed, when the two threads are finished, the final value of the counter is 2000, as each thread incremented the counter 1000 times. Indeed, when the input value of `loops` is set to N, we would expect the final output of the program to be $2N$. But life is not so simple, as it turns out. Let's run the same program, but with higher values for `loops`, and see what happens:

```
prompt> ./thread 100000
Initial value : 0
Final value   : 143012    // huh??
prompt> ./thread 100000
Initial value : 0
Final value   : 137298    // what the??
```

In this run, when we gave an input value of 100,000, instead of getting a final value of 200,000, we instead first get 143,012. Then, when we run the program a second time, we not only again get the *wrong* value, but also a *different* value than the last time. In fact, if you run the program over and over with high values of `loops`, you may find that sometimes you even get the right answer! So why is this happening?

As it turns out, the reason for these odd and unusual outcomes relate to how instructions are executed, which is one at a time. Unfortunately, a key part of the program above, where the shared counter is incremented,

[6]The actual call should be to lower-case `pthread_create()`; the upper-case version is our own wrapper that calls `pthread_create()` and makes sure that the return code indicates that the call succeeded. See the code for details.

THE CRUX OF THE PROBLEM:
HOW TO BUILD CORRECT CONCURRENT PROGRAMS

When there are many concurrently executing threads within the same memory space, how can we build a correctly working program? What primitives are needed from the OS? What mechanisms should be provided by the hardware? How can we use them to solve the problems of concurrency?

takes three instructions: one to load the value of the counter from memory into a register, one to increment it, and one to store it back into memory. Because these three instructions do not execute **atomically** (all at once), strange things can happen. It is this problem of **concurrency** that we will address in great detail in the second part of this book.

2.4 Persistence

The third major theme of the course is **persistence**. In system memory, data can be easily lost, as devices such as DRAM store values in a **volatile** manner; when power goes away or the system crashes, any data in memory is lost. Thus, we need hardware and software to be able to store data **persistently**; such storage is thus critical to any system as users care a great deal about their data.

The hardware comes in the form of some kind of **input/output** or **I/O** device; in modern systems, a **hard drive** is a common repository for long-lived information, although **solid-state drives** (**SSDs**) are making headway in this arena as well.

The software in the operating system that usually manages the disk is called the **file system**; it is thus responsible for storing any **files** the user creates in a reliable and efficient manner on the disks of the system.

Unlike the abstractions provided by the OS for the CPU and memory, the OS does not create a private, virtualized disk for each application. Rather, it is assumed that often times, users will want to **share** information that is in files. For example, when writing a C program, you might first use an editor (e.g., Emacs[7]) to create and edit the C file (`emacs -nw main.c`). Once done, you might use the compiler to turn the source code into an executable (e.g., `gcc -o main main.c`). When you're finished, you might run the new executable (e.g., `./main`). Thus, you can see how files are shared across different processes. First, Emacs creates a file that serves as input to the compiler; the compiler uses that input file to create a new executable file (in many steps — take a compiler course for details); finally, the new executable is then run. And thus a new program is born!

[7] You should be using Emacs. If you are using vi, there is probably something wrong with you. If you are using something that is not a real code editor, that is even worse.

```
#include <stdio.h>
#include <unistd.h>
#include <assert.h>
#include <fcntl.h>
#include <sys/types.h>

int main(int argc, char *argv[]) {
    int fd = open("/tmp/file", O_WRONLY|O_CREAT|O_TRUNC,
                  S_IRWXU);
    assert(fd > -1);
    int rc = write(fd, "hello world\n", 13);
    assert(rc == 13);
    close(fd);
    return 0;
}
```

Figure 26: **A Program That Does I/O (`io.c`)**

To understand this better, let's look at some code. Figure 26 presents code to create a file (`/tmp/file`) that contains the string "hello world".

To accomplish this task, the program makes three calls into the operating system. The first, a call to `open()`, opens the file and creates it; the second, `write()`, writes some data to the file; the third, `close()`, simply closes the file thus indicating the program won't be writing any more data to it. These **system calls** are routed to the part of the operating system called the **file system**, which then handles the requests and returns some kind of error code to the user.

You might be wondering what the OS does in order to actually write to disk. We would show you but you'd have to promise to close your eyes first; it is that unpleasant. The file system has to do a fair bit of work: first figuring out where on disk this new data will reside, and then keeping track of it in various structures the file system maintains. Doing so requires issuing I/O requests to the underlying storage device, to either read existing structures or update (write) them. As anyone who has written a **device driver**[8] knows, getting a device to do something on your behalf is an intricate and detailed process. It requires a deep knowledge of the low-level device interface and its exact semantics. Fortunately, the OS provides a standard and simple way to access devices through its system calls. Thus, the OS is sometimes seen as a **standard library**.

Of course, there are many more details in how devices are accessed, and how file systems manage data persistently atop said devices. For performance reasons, most file systems first delay such writes for a while, hoping to batch them into larger groups. To handle the problems of system crashes during writes, most file systems incorporate some kind of intricate write protocol, such as **journaling** or **copy-on-write**, carefully

[8]A device driver is some code in the operating system that knows how to deal with a specific device. We will talk more about devices and device drivers later.

THE CRUX OF THE PROBLEM:
HOW TO STORE DATA PERSISTENTLY

The file system is the part of the OS in charge of managing persistent data. What techniques are needed to do so correctly? What mechanisms and policies are required to do so with high performance? How is reliability achieved, in the face of failures in hardware and software?

ordering writes to disk to ensure that if a failure occurs during the write sequence, the system can recover to reasonable state afterwards. To make different common operations efficient, file systems employ many different data structures and access methods, from simple lists to complex b-trees. If all of this doesn't make sense yet, good! We'll be talking about all of this quite a bit more in the third part of this book on **persistence**, where we'll discuss devices and I/O in general, and then disks, RAIDs, and file systems in great detail.

2.5 Design Goals

So now you have some idea of what an OS actually does: it takes physical **resources**, such as a CPU, memory, or disk, and **virtualizes** them. It handles tough and tricky issues related to **concurrency**. And it stores files **persistently**, thus making them safe over the long-term. Given that we want to build such a system, we want to have some goals in mind to help focus our design and implementation and make trade-offs as necessary; finding the right set of trade-offs is a key to building systems.

One of the most basic goals is to build up some **abstractions** in order to make the system convenient and easy to use. Abstractions are fundamental to everything we do in computer science. Abstraction makes it possible to write a large program by dividing it into small and understandable pieces, to write such a program in a high-level language like C[9] without thinking about assembly, to write code in assembly without thinking about logic gates, and to build a processor out of gates without thinking too much about transistors. Abstraction is so fundamental that sometimes we forget its importance, but we won't here; thus, in each section, we'll discuss some of the major abstractions that have developed over time, giving you a way to think about pieces of the OS.

One goal in designing and implementing an operating system is to provide high **performance**; another way to say this is our goal is to **minimize the overheads** of the OS. Virtualization and making the system easy to use are well worth it, but not at any cost; thus, we must strive to provide virtualization and other OS features without excessive overheads.

[9]Some of you might object to calling C a high-level language. Remember this is an OS course, though, where we're simply happy not to have to code in assembly all the time!

These overheads arise in a number of forms: extra time (more instructions) and extra space (in memory or on disk). We'll seek solutions that minimize one or the other or both, if possible. Perfection, however, is not always attainable, something we will learn to notice and (where appropriate) tolerate.

Another goal will be to provide **protection** between applications, as well as between the OS and applications. Because we wish to allow many programs to run at the same time, we want to make sure that the malicious or accidental bad behavior of one does not harm others; we certainly don't want an application to be able to harm the OS itself (as that would affect *all* programs running on the system). Protection is at the heart of one of the main principles underlying an operating system, which is that of **isolation**; isolating processes from one another is the key to protection and thus underlies much of what an OS must do.

The operating system must also run non-stop; when it fails, *all* applications running on the system fail as well. Because of this dependence, operating systems often strive to provide a high degree of **reliability**. As operating systems grow evermore complex (sometimes containing millions of lines of code), building a reliable operating system is quite a challenge — and indeed, much of the on-going research in the field (including some of our own work [BS+09, SS+10]) focuses on this exact problem.

Other goals make sense: **energy-efficiency** is important in our increasingly green world; **security** (an extension of protection, really) against malicious applications is critical, especially in these highly-networked times; **mobility** is increasingly important as OSes are run on smaller and smaller devices. Depending on how the system is used, the OS will have different goals and thus likely be implemented in at least slightly different ways. However, as we will see, many of the principles we will present on how to build an OS are useful on a range of different devices.

2.6 Some History

Before closing this introduction, let us present a brief history of how operating systems developed. Like any system built by humans, good ideas accumulated in operating systems over time, as engineers learned what was important in their design. Here, we discuss a few major developments. For a richer treatment, see Brinch Hansen's excellent history of operating systems [BH00].

Early Operating Systems: Just Libraries

In the beginning, the operating system didn't do too much. Basically, it was just a set of libraries of commonly-used functions; for example, instead of having each programmer of the system write low-level I/O handling code, the "OS" would provide such APIs, and thus make life easier for the developer.

Usually, on these old mainframe systems, one program ran at a time, as controlled by a human operator. Much of what you think a modern OS would do (e.g., deciding what order to run jobs in) was performed by this operator. If you were a smart developer, you would be nice to this operator, so that they might move your job to the front of the queue.

This mode of computing was known as **batch** processing, as a number of jobs were set up and then run in a "batch" by the operator. Computers, as of that point, were not used in an interactive manner, because of cost: it was simply too expensive to let a user sit in front of the computer and use it, as most of the time it would just sit idle then, costing the facility hundreds of thousands of dollars per hour [BH00].

Beyond Libraries: Protection

In moving beyond being a simple library of commonly-used services, operating systems took on a more central role in managing machines. One important aspect of this was the realization that code run on behalf of the OS was special; it had control of devices and thus should be treated differently than normal application code. Why is this? Well, imagine if you allowed any application to read from anywhere on the disk; the notion of privacy goes out the window, as any program could read any file. Thus, implementing a **file system** (to manage your files) as a library makes little sense. Instead, something else was needed.

Thus, the idea of a **system call** was invented, pioneered by the Atlas computing system [K+61,L78]. Instead of providing OS routines as a library (where you just make a **procedure call** to access them), the idea here was to add a special pair of hardware instructions and hardware state to make the transition into the OS a more formal, controlled process.

The key difference between a system call and a procedure call is that a system call transfers control (i.e., jumps) into the OS while simultaneously raising the **hardware privilege level**. User applications run in what is referred to as **user mode** which means the hardware restricts what applications can do; for example, an application running in user mode can't typically initiate an I/O request to the disk, access any physical memory page, or send a packet on the network. When a system call is initiated (usually through a special hardware instruction called a **trap**), the hardware transfers control to a pre-specified **trap handler** (that the OS set up previously) and simultaneously raises the privilege level to **kernel mode**. In kernel mode, the OS has full access to the hardware of the system and thus can do things like initiate an I/O request or make more memory available to a program. When the OS is done servicing the request, it passes control back to the user via a special **return-from-trap** instruction, which reverts to user mode while simultaneously passing control back to where the application left off.

The Era of Multiprogramming

Where operating systems really took off was in the era of computing beyond the mainframe, that of the **minicomputer**. Classic machines like the PDP family from Digital Equipment made computers hugely more affordable; thus, instead of having one mainframe per large organization, now a smaller collection of people within an organization could likely have their own computer. Not surprisingly, one of the major impacts of this drop in cost was an increase in developer activity; more smart people got their hands on computers and thus made computer systems do more interesting and beautiful things.

In particular, **multiprogramming** became commonplace due to the desire to make better use of machine resources. Instead of just running one job at a time, the OS would load a number of jobs into memory and switch rapidly between them, thus improving CPU utilization. This switching was particularly important because I/O devices were slow; having a program wait on the CPU while its I/O was being serviced was a waste of CPU time. Instead, why not switch to another job and run it for a while?

The desire to support multiprogramming and overlap in the presence of I/O and interrupts forced innovation in the conceptual development of operating systems along a number of directions. Issues such as **memory protection** became important; we wouldn't want one program to be able to access the memory of another program. Understanding how to deal with the **concurrency** issues introduced by multiprogramming was also critical; making sure the OS was behaving correctly despite the presence of interrupts is a great challenge. We will study these issues and related topics later in the book.

One of the major practical advances of the time was the introduction of the UNIX operating system, primarily thanks to Ken Thompson (and Dennis Ritchie) at Bell Labs (yes, the phone company). UNIX took many good ideas from different operating systems (particularly from Multics [O72], and some from systems like TENEX [B+72] and the Berkeley Time-Sharing System [S+68]), but made them simpler and easier to use. Soon this team was shipping tapes containing UNIX source code to people around the world, many of whom then got involved and added to the system themselves; see the **Aside** (next page) for more detail[10].

The Modern Era

Beyond the minicomputer came a new type of machine, cheaper, faster, and for the masses: the **personal computer**, or **PC** as we call it today. Led by Apple's early machines (e.g., the Apple II) and the IBM PC, this new breed of machine would soon become the dominant force in computing,

[10]We'll use asides and other related text boxes to call attention to various items that don't quite fit the main flow of the text. Sometimes, we'll even use them just to make a joke, because why not have a little fun along the way? Yes, many of the jokes are bad.

ASIDE: THE IMPORTANCE OF UNIX

It is difficult to overstate the importance of UNIX in the history of operating systems. Influenced by earlier systems (in particular, the famous **Multics** system from MIT), UNIX brought together many great ideas and made a system that was both simple and powerful.

Underlying the original "Bell Labs" UNIX was the unifying principle of building small powerful programs that could be connected together to form larger workflows. The **shell**, where you type commands, provided primitives such as **pipes** to enable such meta-level programming, and thus it became easy to string together programs to accomplish a bigger task. For example, to find lines of a text file that have the word "foo" in them, and then to count how many such lines exist, you would type: `grep foo file.txt|wc -l`, thus using the `grep` and `wc` (word count) programs to achieve your task.

The UNIX environment was friendly for programmers and developers alike, also providing a compiler for the new **C programming language**. Making it easy for programmers to write their own programs, as well as share them, made UNIX enormously popular. And it probably helped a lot that the authors gave out copies for free to anyone who asked, an early form of **open-source software**.

Also of critical importance was the accessibility and readability of the code. Having a beautiful, small kernel written in C invited others to play with the kernel, adding new and cool features. For example, an enterprising group at Berkeley, led by **Bill Joy**, made a wonderful distribution (the **Berkeley Systems Distribution**, or **BSD**) which had some advanced virtual memory, file system, and networking subsystems. Joy later co-founded **Sun Microsystems**.

Unfortunately, the spread of UNIX was slowed a bit as companies tried to assert ownership and profit from it, an unfortunate (but common) result of lawyers getting involved. Many companies had their own variants: **SunOS** from Sun Microsystems, **AIX** from IBM, **HPUX** (a.k.a. "H-Pucks") from HP, and **IRIX** from SGI. The legal wrangling among AT&T/Bell Labs and these other players cast a dark cloud over UNIX, and many wondered if it would survive, especially as Windows was introduced and took over much of the PC market...

as their low-cost enabled one machine per desktop instead of a shared minicomputer per workgroup.

Unfortunately, for operating systems, the PC at first represented a great leap backwards, as early systems forgot (or never knew of) the lessons learned in the era of minicomputers. For example, early operating systems such as **DOS** (the **Disk Operating System**, from **Microsoft**) didn't think memory protection was important; thus, a malicious (or perhaps just a poorly-programmed) application could scribble all over mem-

ASIDE: AND THEN CAME LINUX

Fortunately for UNIX, a young Finnish hacker named **Linus Torvalds** decided to write his own version of UNIX which borrowed heavily on the principles and ideas behind the original system, but not from the code base, thus avoiding issues of legality. He enlisted help from many others around the world, took advantage of the sophisticated GNU tools that already existed [G85], and soon **Linux** was born (as well as the modern open-source software movement).

As the internet era came into place, most companies (such as Google, Amazon, Facebook, and others) chose to run Linux, as it was free and could be readily modified to suit their needs; indeed, it is hard to imagine the success of these new companies had such a system not existed. As smart phones became a dominant user-facing platform, Linux found a stronghold there too (via Android), for many of the same reasons. And Steve Jobs took his UNIX-based **NeXTStep** operating environment with him to Apple, thus making UNIX popular on desktops (though many users of Apple technology are probably not even aware of this fact). Thus UNIX lives on, more important today than ever before. The computing gods, if you believe in them, should be thanked for this wonderful outcome.

ory. The first generations of the **Mac OS** (v9 and earlier) took a cooperative approach to job scheduling; thus, a thread that accidentally got stuck in an infinite loop could take over the entire system, forcing a reboot. The painful list of OS features missing in this generation of systems is long, too long for a full discussion here.

Fortunately, after some years of suffering, the old features of minicomputer operating systems started to find their way onto the desktop. For example, Mac OS X/macOS has UNIX at its core, including all of the features one would expect from such a mature system. Windows has similarly adopted many of the great ideas in computing history, starting in particular with Windows NT, a great leap forward in Microsoft OS technology. Even today's cell phones run operating systems (such as Linux) that are much more like what a minicomputer ran in the 1970s than what a PC ran in the 1980s (thank goodness); it is good to see that the good ideas developed in the heyday of OS development have found their way into the modern world. Even better is that these ideas continue to develop, providing more features and making modern systems even better for users and applications.

2.7 Summary

Thus, we have an introduction to the OS. Today's operating systems make systems relatively easy to use, and virtually all operating systems you use today have been influenced by the developments we will discuss throughout the book.

Unfortunately, due to time constraints, there are a number of parts of the OS we won't cover in the book. For example, there is a lot of **networking** code in the operating system; we leave it to you to take the networking class to learn more about that. Similarly, **graphics** devices are particularly important; take the graphics course to expand your knowledge in that direction. Finally, some operating system books talk a great deal about **security**; we will do so in the sense that the OS must provide protection between running programs and give users the ability to protect their files, but we won't delve into deeper security issues that one might find in a security course.

However, there are many important topics that we will cover, including the basics of virtualization of the CPU and memory, concurrency, and persistence via devices and file systems. Don't worry! While there is a lot of ground to cover, most of it is quite cool, and at the end of the road, you'll have a new appreciation for how computer systems really work. Now get to work!

References

[BS+09] "Tolerating File-System Mistakes with EnvyFS" by L. Bairavasundaram, S. Sundararaman, A. Arpaci-Dusseau, R. Arpaci-Dusseau. USENIX '09, San Diego, CA, June 2009. *A fun paper about using multiple file systems at once to tolerate a mistake in any one of them.*

[BH00] "The Evolution of Operating Systems" by P. Brinch Hansen. In 'Classic Operating Systems: From Batch Processing to Distributed Systems.' Springer-Verlag, New York, 2000. *This essay provides an intro to a wonderful collection of papers about historically significant systems.*

[B+72] "TENEX, A Paged Time Sharing System for the PDP-10" by D. Bobrow, J. Burchfiel, D. Murphy, R. Tomlinson. CACM, Volume 15, Number 3, March 1972. *TENEX has much of the machinery found in modern operating systems; read more about it to see how much innovation was already in place in the early 1970's.*

[B75] "The Mythical Man-Month" by F. Brooks. Addison-Wesley, 1975. *A classic text on software engineering; well worth the read.*

[BOH10] "Computer Systems: A Programmer's Perspective" by R. Bryant and D. O'Hallaron. Addison-Wesley, 2010. *Another great intro to how computer systems work. Has a little bit of overlap with this book — so if you'd like, you can skip the last few chapters of that book, or simply read them to get a different perspective on some of the same material. After all, one good way to build up your own knowledge is to hear as many other perspectives as possible, and then develop your own opinion and thoughts on the matter. You know, by thinking!*

[G85] "The GNU Manifesto" by R. Stallman. 1985. `www.gnu.org/gnu/manifesto.html`. *A huge part of Linux's success was no doubt the presence of an excellent compiler,* `gcc`*, and other relevant pieces of open software, thanks to the GNU effort headed by Stallman. Stallman is a visionary when it comes to open source, and this manifesto lays out his thoughts as to why.*

[K+61] "One-Level Storage System" by T. Kilburn, D.B.G. Edwards, M.J. Lanigan, F.H. Sumner. IRE Transactions on Electronic Computers, April 1962. *The Atlas pioneered much of what you see in modern systems. However, this paper is not the best read. If you were to only read one, you might try the historical perspective below [L78].*

[L78] "The Manchester Mark I and Atlas: A Historical Perspective" by S. H. Lavington. Communications of the ACM, Volume 21:1, January 1978. *A nice piece of history on the early development of computer systems and the pioneering efforts of the Atlas. Of course, one could go back and read the Atlas papers themselves, but this paper provides a great overview and adds some historical perspective.*

[O72] "The Multics System: An Examination of its Structure" by Elliott Organick. MIT Press, 1972. *A great overview of Multics. So many good ideas, and yet it was an over-designed system, shooting for too much, and thus never really worked. A classic example of what Fred Brooks would call the "second-system effect" [B75].*

[PP03] "Introduction to Computing Systems: From Bits and Gates to C and Beyond" by Yale N. Patt, Sanjay J. Patel. McGraw-Hill, 2003. *One of our favorite intro to computing systems books. Starts at transistors and gets you all the way up to C; the early material is particularly great.*

[RT74] "The UNIX Time-Sharing System" by Dennis M. Ritchie, Ken Thompson. CACM, Volume 17: 7, July 1974. *A great summary of* UNIX *written as it was taking over the world of computing, by the people who wrote it.*

[S68] "SDS 940 Time-Sharing System" by Scientific Data Systems. TECHNICAL MANUAL, SDS 90 11168, August 1968. *Yes, a technical manual was the best we could find. But it is fascinating to read these old system documents, and see how much was already in place in the late 1960's. One of the minds behind the Berkeley Time-Sharing System (which eventually became the SDS system) was Butler Lampson, who later won a Turing award for his contributions in systems.*

[SS+10] "Membrane: Operating System Support for Restartable File Systems" by S. Sundararaman, S. Subramanian, A. Rajimwale, A. Arpaci-Dusseau, R. Arpaci-Dusseau, M. Swift. FAST '10, San Jose, CA, February 2010. *The great thing about writing your own class notes: you can advertise your own research. But this paper is actually pretty neat — when a file system hits a bug and crashes, Membrane auto-magically restarts it, all without applications or the rest of the system being affected.*

Homework

Most (and eventually, all) chapters of this book have homework sections at the end. Doing these homeworks is important, as each lets you, the reader, gain more experience with the concepts presented within the chapter.

There are two types of homeworks. The first is based on **simulation**. A simulation of a computer system is just a simple program that pretends to do some of the interesting parts of what a real system does, and then report some output metrics to show how the system behaves. For example, a hard drive simulator might take a series of requests, simulate how long they would take to get serviced by a hard drive with certain performance characteristics, and then report the average latency of the requests.

The cool thing about simulations is they let you easily explore how systems behave without the difficulty of running a real system. Indeed, they even let you create systems that cannot exist in the real world (for example, a hard drive with unimaginably fast performance), and thus see the potential impact of future technologies.

Of course, simulations are not without their downsides. By their very nature, simulations are just approximations of how a real system behaves. If an important aspect of real-world behavior is omitted, the simulation will report bad results. Thus, results from a simulation should always be treated with some suspicion. In the end, how a system behaves in the real world is what matters.

The second type of homework requires interaction with **real-world code**. Some of these homeworks are measurement focused, whereas others just require some small-scale development and experimentation. Both are just small forays into the larger world you should be getting into, which is how to write systems code in C on UNIX-based systems. Indeed, larger-scale projects, which go beyond these homeworks, are needed to push you in this direction; thus, beyond just doing homeworks, we strongly recommend you do projects to solidify your systems skills. See this page (`https://github.com/remzi-arpacidusseau/ostep-projects`) for some projects.

To do these homeworks, you likely have to be on a UNIX-based machine, running either Linux, macOS, or some similar system. It should also have a C compiler installed (e.g., **gcc**) as well as Python. You should also know how to edit code in a real code editor of some kind.

Part I

Virtualization

3

A Dialogue on Virtualization

Professor: *And thus we reach the first of our three pieces on operating systems:* ***virtualization****.*

Student: *But what is virtualization, oh noble professor?*

Professor: *Imagine we have a peach.*

Student: *A peach? (incredulous)*

Professor: *Yes, a peach. Let us call that the* **physical** *peach. But we have many eaters who would like to eat this peach. What we would like to present to each eater is their own peach, so that they can be happy. We call the peach we give eaters* ***virtual*** *peaches; we somehow create many of these virtual peaches out of the one physical peach. And the important thing: in this illusion, it looks to each eater like they have a physical peach, but in reality they don't.*

Student: *So you are sharing the peach, but you don't even know it?*

Professor: *Right! Exactly.*

Student: *But there's only one peach.*

Professor: *Yes. And...?*

Student: *Well, if I was sharing a peach with somebody else, I think I would notice.*

Professor: *Ah yes! Good point. But that is the thing with many eaters; most of the time they are napping or doing something else, and thus, you can snatch that peach away and give it to someone else for a while. And thus we create the illusion of many virtual peaches, one peach for each person!*

Student: *Sounds like a bad campaign slogan. You are talking about computers, right Professor?*

Professor: *Ah, young grasshopper, you wish to have a more concrete example. Good idea! Let us take the most basic of resources, the CPU. Assume there is one physical CPU in a system (though now there are often two or four or more). What virtualization does is take that single CPU and make it look like many virtual CPUs to the applications running on the system. Thus, while each application* *thinks it has its own CPU to use, there is really only one. And thus the OS has created a beautiful illusion: it has virtualized the CPU.*

Student: *Wow! That sounds like magic. Tell me more! How does that work?*

Professor: *In time, young student, in good time. Sounds like you are ready to begin.*

Student: *I am! Well, sort of. I must admit, I'm a little worried you are going to start talking about peaches again.*

Professor: *Don't worry too much; I don't even like peaches. And thus we begin...*

4

The Abstraction: The Process

In this chapter, we discuss one of the most fundamental abstractions that the OS provides to users: the **process**. The definition of a process, informally, is quite simple: it is a **running program** [V+65,BH70]. The program itself is a lifeless thing: it just sits there on the disk, a bunch of instructions (and maybe some static data), waiting to spring into action. It is the operating system that takes these bytes and gets them running, transforming the program into something useful.

It turns out that one often wants to run more than one program at once; for example, consider your desktop or laptop where you might like to run a web browser, mail program, a game, a music player, and so forth. In fact, a typical system may be seemingly running tens or even hundreds of processes at the same time. Doing so makes the system easy to use, as one never need be concerned with whether a CPU is available; one simply runs programs. Hence our challenge:

> THE CRUX OF THE PROBLEM:
> HOW TO PROVIDE THE ILLUSION OF MANY CPUS?
>
> Although there are only a few physical CPUs available, how can the OS provide the illusion of a nearly-endless supply of said CPUs?

The OS creates this illusion by **virtualizing** the CPU. By running one process, then stopping it and running another, and so forth, the OS can promote the illusion that many virtual CPUs exist when in fact there is only one physical CPU (or a few). This basic technique, known as **time sharing** of the CPU, allows users to run as many concurrent processes as they would like; the potential cost is performance, as each will run more slowly if the CPU(s) must be shared.

To implement virtualization of the CPU, and to implement it well, the OS will need both some low-level machinery and some high-level intelligence. We call the low-level machinery **mechanisms**; mechanisms are low-level methods or protocols that implement a needed piece of functionality. For example, we'll learn later how to implement a **context**

> TIP: USE TIME SHARING (AND SPACE SHARING)
> **Time sharing** is a basic technique used by an OS to share a resource. By allowing the resource to be used for a little while by one entity, and then a little while by another, and so forth, the resource in question (e.g., the CPU, or a network link) can be shared by many. The counterpart of time sharing is **space sharing**, where a resource is divided (in space) among those who wish to use it. For example, disk space is naturally a space-shared resource; once a block is assigned to a file, it is normally not assigned to another file until the user deletes the original file.

switch, which gives the OS the ability to stop running one program and start running another on a given CPU; this **time-sharing** mechanism is employed by all modern OSes.

On top of these mechanisms resides some of the intelligence in the OS, in the form of **policies**. Policies are algorithms for making some kind of decision within the OS. For example, given a number of possible programs to run on a CPU, which program should the OS run? A **scheduling policy** in the OS will make this decision, likely using historical information (e.g., which program has run more over the last minute?), workload knowledge (e.g., what types of programs are run), and performance metrics (e.g., is the system optimizing for interactive performance, or throughput?) to make its decision.

4.1 The Abstraction: A Process

The abstraction provided by the OS of a running program is something we will call a **process**. As we said above, a process is simply a running program; at any instant in time, we can summarize a process by taking an inventory of the different pieces of the system it accesses or affects during the course of its execution.

To understand what constitutes a process, we thus have to understand its **machine state**: what a program can read or update when it is running. At any given time, what parts of the machine are important to the execution of this program?

One obvious component of machine state that comprises a process is its *memory*. Instructions lie in memory; the data that the running program reads and writes sits in memory as well. Thus the memory that the process can address (called its **address space**) is part of the process.

Also part of the process's machine state are *registers*; many instructions explicitly read or update registers and thus clearly they are important to the execution of the process.

Note that there are some particularly special registers that form part of this machine state. For example, the **program counter** (**PC**) (sometimes called the **instruction pointer** or **IP**) tells us which instruction of the program will execute next; similarly a **stack pointer** and associated **frame**

> TIP: SEPARATE POLICY AND MECHANISM
> In many operating systems, a common design paradigm is to separate high-level policies from their low-level mechanisms [L+75]. You can think of the mechanism as providing the answer to a *how* question about a system; for example, *how* does an operating system perform a context switch? The policy provides the answer to a *which* question; for example, *which* process should the operating system run right now? Separating the two allows one easily to change policies without having to rethink the mechanism and is thus a form of **modularity**, a general software design principle.

pointer are used to manage the stack for function parameters, local variables, and return addresses.

Finally, programs often access persistent storage devices too. Such *I/O information* might include a list of the files the process currently has open.

4.2 Process API

Though we defer discussion of a real process API until a subsequent chapter, here we first give some idea of what must be included in any interface of an operating system. These APIs, in some form, are available on any modern operating system.

- **Create:** An operating system must include some method to create new processes. When you type a command into the shell, or double-click on an application icon, the OS is invoked to create a new process to run the program you have indicated.
- **Destroy:** As there is an interface for process creation, systems also provide an interface to destroy processes forcefully. Of course, many processes will run and just exit by themselves when complete; when they don't, however, the user may wish to kill them, and thus an interface to halt a runaway process is quite useful.
- **Wait:** Sometimes it is useful to wait for a process to stop running; thus some kind of waiting interface is often provided.
- **Miscellaneous Control:** Other than killing or waiting for a process, there are sometimes other controls that are possible. For example, most operating systems provide some kind of method to suspend a process (stop it from running for a while) and then resume it (continue it running).
- **Status:** There are usually interfaces to get some status information about a process as well, such as how long it has run for, or what state it is in.

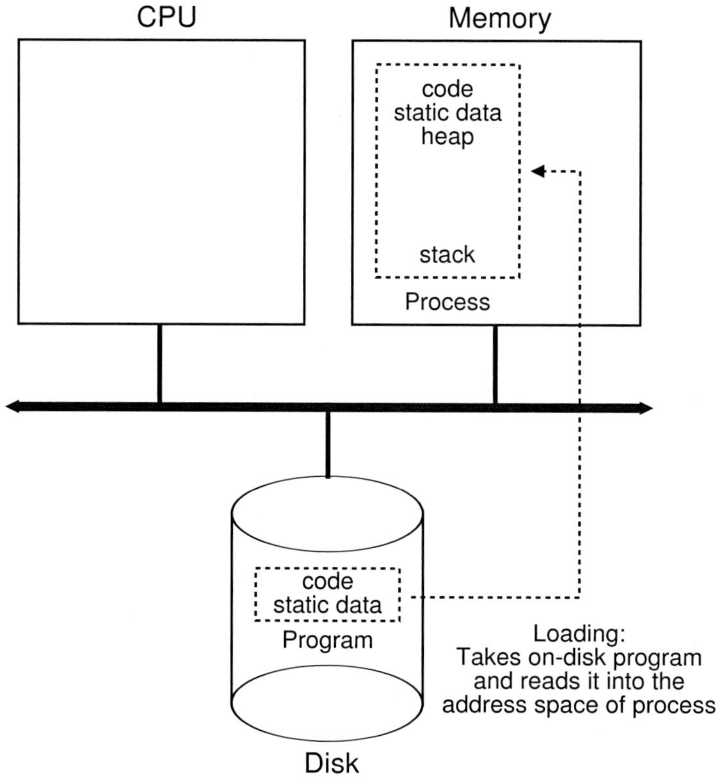

Figure 41: **Loading: From Program To Process**

4.3 Process Creation: A Little More Detail

One mystery that we should unmask a bit is how programs are transformed into processes. Specifically, how does the OS get a program up and running? How does process creation actually work?

The first thing that the OS must do to run a program is to **load** its code and any static data (e.g., initialized variables) into memory, into the address space of the process. Programs initially reside on **disk** (or, in some modern systems, **flash-based SSDs**) in some kind of **executable format**; thus, the process of loading a program and static data into memory requires the OS to read those bytes from disk and place them in memory somewhere (as shown in Figure 41).

In early (or simple) operating systems, the loading process is done **eagerly**, i.e., all at once before running the program; modern OSes perform the process **lazily**, i.e., by loading pieces of code or data only as they are needed during program execution. To truly understand how lazy loading of pieces of code and data works, you'll have to understand more about the machinery of **paging** and **swapping**, topics we'll cover in the future when we discuss the virtualization of memory. For now, just remember that before running anything, the OS clearly must do some work to get the important program bits from disk into memory.

Once the code and static data are loaded into memory, there are a few other things the OS needs to do before running the process. Some memory must be allocated for the program's **run-time stack** (or just **stack**). As you should likely already know, C programs use the stack for local variables, function parameters, and return addresses; the OS allocates this memory and gives it to the process. The OS will also likely initialize the stack with arguments; specifically, it will fill in the parameters to the `main()` function, i.e., `argc` and the `argv` array.

The OS may also allocate some memory for the program's **heap**. In C programs, the heap is used for explicitly requested dynamically-allocated data; programs request such space by calling `malloc()` and free it explicitly by calling `free()`. The heap is needed for data structures such as linked lists, hash tables, trees, and other interesting data structures. The heap will be small at first; as the program runs, and requests more memory via the `malloc()` library API, the OS may get involved and allocate more memory to the process to help satisfy such calls.

The OS will also do some other initialization tasks, particularly as related to input/output (I/O). For example, in UNIX systems, each process by default has three open **file descriptors**, for standard input, output, and error; these descriptors let programs easily read input from the terminal and print output to the screen. We'll learn more about I/O, file descriptors, and the like in the third part of the book on **persistence**.

By loading the code and static data into memory, by creating and initializing a stack, and by doing other work as related to I/O setup, the OS has now (finally) set the stage for program execution. It thus has one last task: to start the program running at the entry point, namely `main()`. By jumping to the `main()` routine (through a specialized mechanism that we will discuss next chapter), the OS transfers control of the CPU to the newly-created process, and thus the program begins its execution.

4.4 Process States

Now that we have some idea of what a process is (though we will continue to refine this notion), and (roughly) how it is created, let us talk about the different **states** a process can be in at a given time. The notion that a process can be in one of these states arose in early computer systems [DV66,V+65]. In a simplified view, a process can be in one of three states:

- **Running**: In the running state, a process is running on a processor. This means it is executing instructions.
- **Ready**: In the ready state, a process is ready to run but for some reason the OS has chosen not to run it at this given moment.

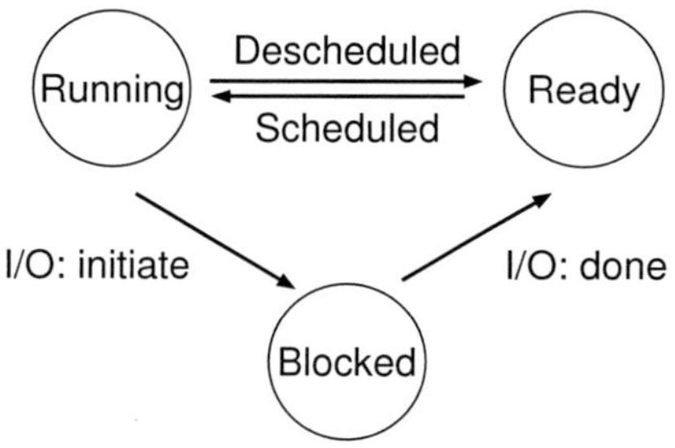

Figure 42: **Process: State Transitions**

- **Blocked**: In the blocked state, a process has performed some kind of operation that makes it not ready to run until some other event takes place. A common example: when a process initiates an I/O request to a disk, it becomes blocked and thus some other process can use the processor.

If we were to map these states to a graph, we would arrive at the diagram in Figure 42. As you can see in the diagram, a process can be moved between the ready and running states at the discretion of the OS. Being moved from ready to running means the process has been **scheduled**; being moved from running to ready means the process has been **descheduled**. Once a process has become blocked (e.g., by initiating an I/O operation), the OS will keep it as such until some event occurs (e.g., I/O completion); at that point, the process moves to the ready state again (and potentially immediately to running again, if the OS so decides).

Let's look at an example of how two processes might transition through some of these states. First, imagine two processes running, each of which only use the CPU (they do no I/O). In this case, a trace of the state of each process might look like this (Figure 43).

Time	Process_0	Process_1	Notes
1	Running	Ready	
2	Running	Ready	
3	Running	Ready	
4	Running	Ready	Process_0 now done
5	–	Running	
6	–	Running	
7	–	Running	
8	–	Running	Process_1 now done

Figure 43: **Tracing Process State: CPU Only**

Time	$Process_0$	$Process_1$	Notes
1	Running	Ready	
2	Running	Ready	
3	Running	Ready	$Process_0$ initiates I/O
4	Blocked	Running	$Process_0$ is blocked,
5	Blocked	Running	so $Process_1$ runs
6	Blocked	Running	
7	Ready	Running	I/O done
8	Ready	Running	$Process_1$ now done
9	Running	–	
10	Running	–	$Process_0$ now done

Figure 44: **Tracing Process State: CPU and I/O**

In this next example, the first process issues an I/O after running for some time. At that point, the process is blocked, giving the other process a chance to run. Figure 44 shows a trace of this scenario.

More specifically, $Process_0$ initiates an I/O and becomes blocked waiting for it to complete; processes become blocked, for example, when reading from a disk or waiting for a packet from a network. The OS recognizes $Process_0$ is not using the CPU and starts running $Process_1$. While $Process_1$ is running, the I/O completes, moving $Process_0$ back to ready. Finally, $Process_1$ finishes, and $Process_0$ runs and then is done.

Note that there are many decisions the OS must make, even in this simple example. First, the system had to decide to run $Process_1$ while $Process_0$ issued an I/O; doing so improves resource utilization by keeping the CPU busy. Second, the system decided not to switch back to $Process_0$ when its I/O completed; it is not clear if this is a good decision or not. What do you think? These types of decisions are made by the OS **scheduler**, a topic we will discuss a few chapters in the future.

4.5 Data Structures

The OS is a program, and like any program, it has some key data structures that track various relevant pieces of information. To track the state of each process, for example, the OS likely will keep some kind of **process list** for all processes that are ready and some additional information to track which process is currently running. The OS must also track, in some way, blocked processes; when an I/O event completes, the OS should make sure to wake the correct process and ready it to run again.

Figure 45 shows what type of information an OS needs to track about each process in the xv6 kernel [CK+08]. Similar process structures exist in "real" operating systems such as Linux, Mac OS X, or Windows; look them up and see how much more complex they are.

From the figure, you can see a couple of important pieces of information the OS tracks about a process. The **register context** will hold, for a

```
// the registers xv6 will save and restore
// to stop and subsequently restart a process
struct context {
  int eip;
  int esp;
  int ebx;
  int ecx;
  int edx;
  int esi;
  int edi;
  int ebp;
};

// the different states a process can be in
enum proc_state { UNUSED, EMBRYO, SLEEPING,
                  RUNNABLE, RUNNING, ZOMBIE };

// the information xv6 tracks about each process
// including its register context and state
struct proc {
  char *mem;                  // Start of process memory
  uint sz;                    // Size of process memory
  char *kstack;               // Bottom of kernel stack
                              // for this process
  enum proc_state state;      // Process state
  int pid;                    // Process ID
  struct proc *parent;        // Parent process
  void *chan;                 // If !zero, sleeping on chan
  int killed;                 // If !zero, has been killed
  struct file *ofile[NOFILE]; // Open files
  struct inode *cwd;          // Current directory
  struct context context;     // Switch here to run process
  struct trapframe *tf;       // Trap frame for the
                              // current interrupt
};
```

Figure 45: **The xv6 Proc Structure**

stopped process, the contents of its registers. When a process is stopped, its registers will be saved to this memory location; by restoring these registers (i.e., placing their values back into the actual physical registers), the OS can resume running the process. We'll learn more about this technique known as a **context switch** in future chapters.

You can also see from the figure that there are some other states a process can be in, beyond running, ready, and blocked. Sometimes a system will have an **initial** state that the process is in when it is being created. Also, a process could be placed in a **final** state where it has exited but

ASIDE: DATA STRUCTURE — THE PROCESS LIST

Operating systems are replete with various important **data structures** that we will discuss in these notes. The **process list** (also called the **task list**) is the first such structure. It is one of the simpler ones, but certainly any OS that has the ability to run multiple programs at once will have something akin to this structure in order to keep track of all the running programs in the system. Sometimes people refer to the individual structure that stores information about a process as a **Process Control Block (PCB)**, a fancy way of talking about a C structure that contains information about each process (also sometimes called a **process descriptor**).

has not yet been cleaned up (in UNIX-based systems, this is called the **zombie** state[1]). This final state can be useful as it allows other processes (usually the **parent** that created the process) to examine the return code of the process and see if the just-finished process executed successfully (usually, programs return zero in UNIX-based systems when they have accomplished a task successfully, and non-zero otherwise). When finished, the parent will make one final call (e.g., `wait()`) to wait for the completion of the child, and to also indicate to the OS that it can clean up any relevant data structures that referred to the now-extinct process.

4.6 Summary

We have introduced the most basic abstraction of the OS: the process. It is quite simply viewed as a running program. With this conceptual view in mind, we will now move on to the nitty-gritty: the low-level mechanisms needed to implement processes, and the higher-level policies required to schedule them in an intelligent way. By combining mechanisms and policies, we will build up our understanding of how an operating system virtualizes the CPU.

[1]Yes, the zombie state. Just like real zombies, these zombies are relatively easy to kill. However, different techniques are usually recommended.

ASIDE: KEY PROCESS TERMS

- The **process** is the major OS abstraction of a running program. At any point in time, the process can be described by its state: the contents of memory in its **address space**, the contents of CPU registers (including the **program counter** and **stack pointer**, among others), and information about I/O (such as open files which can be read or written).
- The **process API** consists of calls programs can make related to processes. Typically, this includes creation, destruction, and other useful calls.
- Processes exist in one of many different **process states**, including running, ready to run, and blocked. Different events (e.g., getting scheduled or descheduled, or waiting for an I/O to complete) transition a process from one of these states to the other.
- A **process list** contains information about all processes in the system. Each entry is found in what is sometimes called a **process control block** (**PCB**), which is really just a structure that contains information about a specific process.

References

[BH70] "The Nucleus of a Multiprogramming System" by Per Brinch Hansen. Communications of the ACM, Volume 13:4, April 1970. *This paper introduces one of the first* ***microkernels*** *in operating systems history, called Nucleus. The idea of smaller, more minimal systems is a theme that rears its head repeatedly in OS history; it all began with Brinch Hansen's work described herein.*

[CK+08] "The xv6 Operating System" by Russ Cox, Frans Kaashoek, Robert Morris, Nickolai Zeldovich. From: https://github.com/mit-pdos/xv6-public. *The coolest real and little OS in the world. Download and play with it to learn more about the details of how operating systems actually work. We have been using an older version (2012-01-30-1-g1c41342) and hence some examples in the book may not match the latest in the source.*

[DV66] "Programming Semantics for Multiprogrammed Computations" by Jack B. Dennis, Earl C. Van Horn. Communications of the ACM, Volume 9, Number 3, March 1966 . *This paper defined many of the early terms and concepts around building multiprogrammed systems.*

[L+75] "Policy/mechanism separation in Hydra" by R. Levin, E. Cohen, W. Corwin, F. Pollack, W. Wulf. SOSP '75, Austin, Texas, November 1975. *An early paper about how to structure operating systems in a research OS known as Hydra. While Hydra never became a mainstream OS, some of its ideas influenced OS designers.*

[V+65] "Structure of the Multics Supervisor" by V.A. Vyssotsky, F. J. Corbato, R. M. Graham. Fall Joint Computer Conference, 1965. *An early paper on Multics, which described many of the basic ideas and terms that we find in modern systems. Some of the vision behind computing as a utility are finally being realized in modern cloud systems.*

Homework (Simulation)

This program, `process-run.py`, allows you to see how process states change as programs run and either use the CPU (e.g., perform an add instruction) or do I/O (e.g., send a request to a disk and wait for it to complete). See the README for details.

Questions

1. Run `process-run.py` with the following flags: `-l 5:100,5:100`. What should the CPU utilization be (e.g., the percent of time the CPU is in use?) Why do you know this? Use the `-c` and `-p` flags to see if you were right.

2. Now run with these flags: `./process-run.py -l 4:100,1:0`. These flags specify one process with 4 instructions (all to use the CPU), and one that simply issues an I/O and waits for it to be done. How long does it take to complete both processes? Use `-c` and `-p` to find out if you were right.

3. Switch the order of the processes: `-l 1:0,4:100`. What happens now? Does switching the order matter? Why? (As always, use `-c` and `-p` to see if you were right)

4. We'll now explore some of the other flags. One important flag is `-S`, which determines how the system reacts when a process issues an I/O. With the flag set to SWITCH_ON_END, the system will NOT switch to another process while one is doing I/O, instead waiting until the process is completely finished. What happens when you run the following two processes (`-l 1:0,4:100 -c -S SWITCH_ON_END`), one doing I/O and the other doing CPU work?

5. Now, run the same processes, but with the switching behavior set to switch to another process whenever one is WAITING for I/O (`-l 1:0,4:100 -c -S SWITCH_ON_IO`). What happens now? Use `-c` and `-p` to confirm that you are right.

6. One other important behavior is what to do when an I/O completes. With `-I IO_RUN_LATER`, when an I/O completes, the process that issued it is not necessarily run right away; rather, whatever was running at the time keeps running. What happens when you run this combination of processes? (Run `./process-run.py -l 3:0,5:100,5:100,5:100 -S SWITCH_ON_IO -I IO_RUN_LATER -c -p`) Are system resources being effectively utilized?

7. Now run the same processes, but with `-I IO_RUN_IMMEDIATE` set, which immediately runs the process that issued the I/O. How does this behavior differ? Why might running a process that just completed an I/O again be a good idea?

8. Now run with some randomly generated processes: `-s 1 -l 3:50,3:50` or `-s 2 -l 3:50,3:50` or `-s 3 -l 3:50,3:50`. See if you can predict how the trace will turn out. What happens when you use the flag `-I IO_RUN_IMMEDIATE` vs. `-I IO_RUN_LATER`? What happens when you use `-S SWITCH_ON_IO` vs. `-S SWITCH_ON_END`?

5

Interlude: Process API

> **ASIDE: INTERLUDES**
> Interludes will cover more practical aspects of systems, including a particular focus on operating system APIs and how to use them. If you don't like practical things, you could skip these interludes. But you should like practical things, because, well, they are generally useful in real life; companies, for example, don't usually hire you for your non-practical skills.

In this interlude, we discuss process creation in UNIX systems. UNIX presents one of the most intriguing ways to create a new process with a pair of system calls: `fork()` and `exec()`. A third routine, `wait()`, can be used by a process wishing to wait for a process it has created to complete. We now present these interfaces in more detail, with a few simple examples to motivate us. And thus, our problem:

> **CRUX: HOW TO CREATE AND CONTROL PROCESSES**
> What interfaces should the OS present for process creation and control? How should these interfaces be designed to enable powerful functionality, ease of use, and high performance?

5.1 The `fork()` System Call

The `fork()` system call is used to create a new process [C63]. However, be forewarned: it is certainly the strangest routine you will ever call[1]. More specifically, you have a running program whose code looks like what you see in Figure 51; examine the code, or better yet, type it in and run it yourself!

[1] Well, OK, we admit that we don't know that for sure; who knows what routines you call when no one is looking? But `fork()` is pretty odd, no matter how unusual your routine-calling patterns are.

```
#include <stdio.h>
#include <stdlib.h>
#include <unistd.h>

int main(int argc, char *argv[]) {
  printf("hello world (pid:%d)\n", (int) getpid());
  int rc = fork();
  if (rc < 0) {
    // fork failed
    fprintf(stderr, "fork failed\n");
    exit(1);
  } else if (rc == 0) {
    // child (new process)
    printf("hello, I am child (pid:%d)\n", (int) getpid());
  } else {
    // parent goes down this path (main)
    printf("hello, I am parent of %d (pid:%d)\n",
           rc, (int) getpid());
  }
  return 0;
}
```

Figure 51: **Calling `fork()` (`p1.c`)**

When you run this program (called `p1.c`), you'll see the following:

```
prompt> ./p1
hello world (pid:29146)
hello, I am parent of 29147 (pid:29146)
hello, I am child (pid:29147)
prompt>
```

Let us understand what happened in more detail in `p1.c`. When it first started running, the process prints out a hello world message; included in that message is its **process identifier**, also known as a **PID**. The process has a PID of 29146; in UNIX systems, the PID is used to name the process if one wants to do something with the process, such as (for example) stop it from running. So far, so good.

Now the interesting part begins. The process calls the `fork()` system call, which the OS provides as a way to create a new process. The odd part: the process that is created is an (almost) *exact copy of the calling process*. That means that to the OS, it now looks like there are two copies of the program `p1` running, and both are about to return from the `fork()` system call. The newly-created process (called the **child**, in contrast to the creating **parent**) doesn't start running at `main()`, like you might expect (note, the "hello, world" message only got printed out once); rather, it just comes into life as if it had called `fork()` itself.

```
#include <stdio.h>
#include <stdlib.h>
#include <unistd.h>
#include <sys/wait.h>

int main(int argc, char *argv[]) {
  printf("hello world (pid:%d)\n", (int) getpid());
  int rc = fork();
  if (rc < 0) {          // fork failed; exit
    fprintf(stderr, "fork failed\n");
    exit(1);
  } else if (rc == 0) { // child (new process)
    printf("hello, I am child (pid:%d)\n", (int) getpid());
  } else {               // parent goes down this path (main)
    int rc_wait = wait(NULL);
    printf("hello, I am parent of %d (rc_wait:%d) (pid:%d)\n",
           rc, rc_wait, (int) getpid());
  }
  return 0;
}

```

Figure 52: **Calling `fork()` And `wait()` (`p2.c`)**

You might have noticed: the child isn't an *exact* copy. Specifically, although it now has its own copy of the address space (i.e., its own private memory), its own registers, its own PC, and so forth, the value it returns to the caller of **fork()** is different. Specifically, while the parent receives the PID of the newly-created child, the child receives a return code of zero. This differentiation is useful, because it is simple then to write the code that handles the two different cases (as above).

You might also have noticed: the output (of `p1.c`) is not **deterministic**. When the child process is created, there are now two active processes in the system that we care about: the parent and the child. Assuming we are running on a system with a single CPU (for simplicity), then either the child or the parent might run at that point. In our example (above), the parent did and thus printed out its message first. In other cases, the opposite might happen, as we show in this output trace:

```
prompt> ./p1
hello world (pid:29146)
hello, I am child (pid:29147)
hello, I am parent of 29147 (pid:29146)
prompt>
```

The CPU **scheduler**, a topic we'll discuss in great detail soon, determines which process runs at a given moment in time; because the scheduler is complex, we cannot usually make strong assumptions about what it will choose to do, and hence which process will run first. This **non-determinism**, as it turns out, leads to some interesting problems, particularly in **multi-threaded programs**; hence, we'll see a lot more non-determinism when we study **concurrency** in the second part of the book.

5.2 The `wait()` System Call

So far, we haven't done much: just created a child that prints out a message and exits. Sometimes, as it turns out, it is quite useful for a parent to wait for a child process to finish what it has been doing. This task is accomplished with the `wait()` system call (or its more complete sibling `waitpid()`); see Figure 52 for details.

In this example (`p2.c`), the parent process calls `wait()` to delay its execution until the child finishes executing. When the child is done, `wait()` returns to the parent.

Adding a `wait()` call to the code above makes the output deterministic. Can you see why? Go ahead, think about it.

(waiting for you to think .... and done)

Now that you have thought a bit, here is the output:

```
prompt> ./p2
hello world (pid:29266)
hello, I am child (pid:29267)
hello, I am parent of 29267 (rc_wait:29267) (pid:29266)
prompt>
```

With this code, we now know that the child will always print first. Why do we know that? Well, it might simply run first, as before, and thus print before the parent. However, if the parent does happen to run first, it will immediately call `wait()`; this system call won't return until the child has run and exited[2]. Thus, even when the parent runs first, it politely waits for the child to finish running, then `wait()` returns, and then the parent prints its message.

5.3 Finally, The `exec()` System Call

A final and important piece of the process creation API is the `exec()` system call[3]. This system call is useful when you want to run a program that is different from the calling program. For example, calling `fork()`

[2]There are a few cases where `wait()` returns before the child exits; read the man page for more details, as always. And beware of any absolute and unqualified statements this book makes, such as "the child will always print first" or "UNIX is the best thing in the world, even better than ice cream."

[3]On Linux, there are six variants of `exec()`: `execl`, `execlp()`, `execle()`, `execv()`, `execvp()`, and `execvpe()`. Read the man pages to learn more.

```
#include <stdio.h>
#include <stdlib.h>
#include <unistd.h>
#include <string.h>
#include <sys/wait.h>

int main(int argc, char *argv[]) {
  printf("hello world (pid:%d)\n", (int) getpid());
  int rc = fork();
  if (rc < 0) {          // fork failed; exit
    fprintf(stderr, "fork failed\n");
    exit(1);
  } else if (rc == 0) { // child (new process)
    printf("hello, I am child (pid:%d)\n", (int) getpid());
    char *myargs[3];
    myargs[0] = strdup("wc");   // program: "wc" (word count)
    myargs[1] = strdup("p3.c"); // argument: file to count
    myargs[2] = NULL;           // marks end of array
    execvp(myargs[0], myargs);  // runs word count
    printf("this shouldn't print out");
  } else {              // parent goes down this path (main)
    int rc_wait = wait(NULL);
    printf("hello, I am parent of %d (rc_wait:%d) (pid:%d)\n",
            rc, rc_wait, (int) getpid());
  }
  return 0;
}
```

Figure 53: **Calling `fork()`, `wait()`, And `exec()` (`p3.c`)**

in `p2.c` is only useful if you want to keep running copies of the same program. However, often you want to run a *different* program; `exec()` does just that (Figure 53).

In this example, the child process calls `execvp()` in order to run the program `wc`, which is the word counting program. In fact, it runs `wc` on the source file `p3.c`, thus telling us how many lines, words, and bytes are found in the file:

```
prompt> ./p3
hello world (pid:29383)
hello, I am child (pid:29384)
      29      107     1030 p3.c
hello, I am parent of 29384 (rc_wait:29384) (pid:29383)
prompt>
```

The `fork()` system call is strange; its partner in crime, `exec()`, is not so normal either. What it does: given the name of an executable (e.g., `wc`), and some arguments (e.g., `p3.c`), it **loads** code (and static data) from that

> TIP: GETTING IT RIGHT (LAMPSON'S LAW)
> As Lampson states in his well-regarded "Hints for Computer Systems Design" [L83], "**Get it right**. Neither abstraction nor simplicity is a substitute for getting it right." Sometimes, you just have to do the right thing, and when you do, it is way better than the alternatives. There are lots of ways to design APIs for process creation; however, the combination of `fork()` and `exec()` are simple and immensely powerful. Here, the UNIX designers simply got it right. And because Lampson so often "got it right", we name the law in his honor.

executable and overwrites its current code segment (and current static data) with it; the heap and stack and other parts of the memory space of the program are re-initialized. Then the OS simply runs that program, passing in any arguments as the `argv` of that process. Thus, it does *not* create a new process; rather, it transforms the currently running program (formerly `p3`) into a different running program (`wc`). After the `exec()` in the child, it is almost as if `p3.c` never ran; a successful call to `exec()` never returns.

5.4 Why? Motivating The API

Of course, one big question you might have: why would we build such an odd interface to what should be the simple act of creating a new process? Well, as it turns out, the separation of `fork()` and `exec()` is essential in building a UNIX shell, because it lets the shell run code *after* the call to `fork()` but *before* the call to `exec()`; this code can alter the environment of the about-to-be-run program, and thus enables a variety of interesting features to be readily built.

The shell is just a user program[4]. It shows you a **prompt** and then waits for you to type something into it. You then type a command (i.e., the name of an executable program, plus any arguments) into it; in most cases, the shell then figures out where in the file system the executable resides, calls `fork()` to create a new child process to run the command, calls some variant of `exec()` to run the command, and then waits for the command to complete by calling `wait()`. When the child completes, the shell returns from `wait()` and prints out a prompt again, ready for your next command.

The separation of `fork()` and `exec()` allows the shell to do a whole bunch of useful things rather easily. For example:

```
prompt> wc p3.c > newfile.txt
```

[4] And there are lots of shells; `tcsh`, `bash`, and `zsh` to name a few. You should pick one, read its man pages, and learn more about it; all UNIX experts do.

In the example above, the output of the program `wc` is **redirected** into the output file `newfile.txt` (the greater-than sign is how said redirection is indicated). The way the shell accomplishes this task is quite simple: when the child is created, before calling `exec()`, the shell closes **standard output** and opens the file `newfile.txt`. By doing so, any output from the soon-to-be-running program `wc` are sent to the file instead of the screen.

Figure 5.4 (page 48) shows a program that does exactly this. The reason this redirection works is due to an assumption about how the operating system manages file descriptors. Specifically, UNIX systems start looking for free file descriptors at zero. In this case, STDOUT_FILENO will be the first available one and thus get assigned when `open()` is called. Subsequent writes by the child process to the standard output file descriptor, for example by routines such as `printf()`, will then be routed transparently to the newly-opened file instead of the screen.

Here is the output of running the `p4.c` program:

```
prompt> ./p4
prompt> cat p4.output
      32      109      846 p4.c
prompt>
```

You'll notice (at least) two interesting tidbits about this output. First, when `p4` is run, it looks as if nothing has happened; the shell just prints the command prompt and is immediately ready for your next command. However, that is not the case; the program `p4` did indeed call `fork()` to create a new child, and then run the `wc` program via a call to `execvp()`. You don't see any output printed to the screen because it has been redirected to the file `p4.output`. Second, you can see that when we `cat` the output file, all the expected output from running `wc` is found. Cool, right?

UNIX pipes are implemented in a similar way, but with the `pipe()` system call. In this case, the output of one process is connected to an in-kernel **pipe** (i.e., queue), and the input of another process is connected to that same pipe; thus, the output of one process seamlessly is used as input to the next, and long and useful chains of commands can be strung together. As a simple example, consider looking for a word in a file, and then counting how many times said word occurs; with pipes and the utilities `grep` and `wc`, it is easy; just type `grep -o foo file | wc -l` into the command prompt and marvel at the result.

Finally, while we just have sketched out the process API at a high level, there is a lot more detail about these calls out there to be learned and digested; we'll learn more, for example, about file descriptors when we talk about file systems in the third part of the book. For now, suffice it to say that the `fork()/exec()` combination is a powerful way to create and manipulate processes.

```
#include <stdio.h>
#include <stdlib.h>
#include <unistd.h>
#include <string.h>
#include <fcntl.h>
#include <sys/wait.h>

int main(int argc, char *argv[]) {
  int rc = fork();
  if (rc < 0) {
    // fork failed
    fprintf(stderr, "fork failed\n");
    exit(1);
  } else if (rc == 0) {
    // child: redirect standard output to a file
    close(STDOUT_FILENO);
    open("./p4.output", O_CREAT|O_WRONLY|O_TRUNC, S_IRWXU);

    // now exec "wc"...
    char *myargs[3];
    myargs[0] = strdup("wc");   // program: wc (word count)
    myargs[1] = strdup("p4.c"); // arg: file to count
    myargs[2] = NULL;           // mark end of array
    execvp(myargs[0], myargs);  // runs word count
  } else {
    // parent goes down this path (main)
    int rc_wait = wait(NULL);
  }
  return 0;
}
```

Figure 54: **All Of The Above With Redirection (`p4.c`)**

5.5 Process Control And Users

Beyond `fork()`, `exec()`, and `wait()`, there are a lot of other interfaces for interacting with processes in UNIX systems. For example, the `kill()` system call is used to send **signals** to a process, including directives to pause, die, and other useful imperatives. For convenience, in most UNIX shells, certain keystroke combinations are configured to deliver a specific signal to the currently running process; for example, control-c sends a `SIGINT` (interrupt) to the process (normally terminating it) and control-z sends a `SIGTSTP` (stop) signal thus pausing the process in mid-execution (you can resume it later with a command, e.g., the `fg` built-in command found in many shells).

The entire signals subsystem provides a rich infrastructure to deliver external events to processes, including ways to receive and process those signals within individual processes, and ways to send signals to individual processes as well as entire **process groups**. To use this form of com-

ASIDE: RTFM — READ THE MAN PAGES

Many times in this book, when referring to a particular system call or library call, we'll tell you to read the **manual pages**, or **man pages** for short. Man pages are the original form of documentation that exist on UNIX systems; realize that they were created before the thing called **the web** existed.

Spending some time reading man pages is a key step in the growth of a systems programmer; there are tons of useful tidbits hidden in those pages. Some particularly useful pages to read are the man pages for whichever shell you are using (e.g., **tcsh**, or **bash**), and certainly for any system calls your program makes (in order to see what return values and error conditions exist).

Finally, reading the man pages can save you some embarrassment. When you ask colleagues about some intricacy of `fork()`, they may simply reply: "RTFM." This is your colleagues' way of gently urging you to Read The Man pages. The F in RTFM just adds a little color to the phrase...

munication, a process should use the `signal()` system call to "catch" various signals; doing so ensures that when a particular signal is delivered to a process, it will suspend its normal execution and run a particular piece of code in response to the signal. Read elsewhere [SR05] to learn more about signals and their many intricacies.

This naturally raises the question: who can send a signal to a process, and who cannot? Generally, the systems we use can have multiple people using them at the same time; if one of these people can arbitrarily send signals such as `SIGINT` (to interrupt a process, likely terminating it), the usability and security of the system will be compromised. As a result, modern systems include a strong conception of the notion of a **user**. The user, after entering a password to establish credentials, logs in to gain access to system resources. The user may then launch one or many processes, and exercise full control over them (pause them, kill them, etc.). Users generally can only control their own processes; it is the job of the operating system to parcel out resources (such as CPU, memory, and disk) to each user (and their processes) to meet overall system goals.

5.6 Useful Tools

There are many command-line tools that are useful as well. For example, using the `ps` command allows you to see which processes are running; read the **man pages** for some useful flags to pass to `ps`. The tool `top` is also quite helpful, as it displays the processes of the system and how much CPU and other resources they are eating up. Humorously, many times when you run it, `top` claims it is the top resource hog; perhaps it is a bit of an egomaniac. The command `kill` can be used to send arbitrary

> ASIDE: THE SUPERUSER (ROOT)
>
> A system generally needs a user who can **administer** the system, and is not limited in the way most users are. Such a user should be able to kill an arbitrary process (e.g., if it is abusing the system in some way), even though that process was not started by this user. Such a user should also be able to run powerful commands such as `shutdown` (which, unsurprisingly, shuts down the system). In UNIX-based systems, these special abilities are given to the **superuser** (sometimes called **root**). While most users can't kill other users processes, the superuser can. Being root is much like being Spider-Man: with great power comes great responsibility [QI15]. Thus, to increase **security** (and avoid costly mistakes), it's usually better to be a regular user; if you do need to be root, tread carefully, as all of the destructive powers of the computing world are now at your fingertips.

signals to processes, as can the slightly more user friendly `killall`. Be sure to use these carefully; if you accidentally kill your window manager, the computer you are sitting in front of may become quite difficult to use.

Finally, there are many different kinds of CPU meters you can use to get a quick glance understanding of the load on your system; for example, we always keep **MenuMeters** (from Raging Menace software) running on our Macintosh toolbars, so we can see how much CPU is being utilized at any moment in time. In general, the more information about what is going on, the better.

5.7 Summary

We have introduced some of the APIs dealing with UNIX process creation: `fork()`, `exec()`, and `wait()`. However, we have just skimmed the surface. For more detail, read Stevens and Rago [SR05], of course, particularly the chapters on Process Control, Process Relationships, and Signals; there is much to extract from the wisdom therein.

While our passion for the UNIX process API remains strong, we should also note that such positivity is not uniform. For example, a recent paper by systems researchers from Microsoft, Boston University, and ETH in Switzerland details some problems with `fork()`, and advocates for other, simpler process creation APIs such as **`spawn()`** [B+19]. Read it, and the related work it refers to, to understand this different vantage point. While it's generally good to trust this book, remember too that the authors have opinions; those opinions may not (always) be as widely shared as you might think.

ASIDE: KEY PROCESS API TERMS

- Each process has a name; in most systems, that name is a number known as a **process ID (PID)**.
- The **fork()** system call is used in UNIX systems to create a new process. The creator is called the **parent**; the newly created process is called the **child**. As sometimes occurs in real life [J16], the child process is a nearly identical copy of the parent.
- The **wait()** system call allows a parent to wait for its child to complete execution.
- The **exec()** family of system calls allows a child to break free from its similarity to its parent and execute an entirely new program.
- A UNIX **shell** commonly uses `fork()`, `wait()`, and `exec()` to launch user commands; the separation of fork and exec enables features like **input/output redirection**, **pipes**, and other cool features, all without changing anything about the programs being run.
- Process control is available in the form of **signals**, which can cause jobs to stop, continue, or even terminate.
- Which processes can be controlled by a particular person is encapsulated in the notion of a **user**; the operating system allows multiple users onto the system, and ensures users can only control their own processes.
- A **superuser** can control all processes (and indeed do many other things); this role should be assumed infrequently and with caution for security reasons.

References

[B+19] "A fork() in the road" by Andrew Baumann, Jonathan Appavoo, Orran Krieger, Timothy Roscoe. HotOS '19, Bertinoro, Italy. *A fun paper full of `fork()`ing rage. Read it to get an opposing viewpoint on the UNIX process API. Presented at the always lively HotOS workshop, where systems researchers go to present extreme opinions in the hopes of pushing the community in new directions.*

[C63] "A Multiprocessor System Design" by Melvin E. Conway. AFIPS '63 Fall Joint Computer Conference, New York, USA 1963. *An early paper on how to design multiprocessing systems; may be the first place the term `fork()` was used in the discussion of spawning new processes.*

[DV66] "Programming Semantics for Multiprogrammed Computations" by Jack B. Dennis and Earl C. Van Horn. Communications of the ACM, Volume 9, Number 3, March 1966. *A classic paper that outlines the basics of multiprogrammed computer systems. Undoubtedly had great influence on Project MAC, Multics, and eventually UNIX.*

[J16] "They could be twins!" by Phoebe Jackson-Edwards. The Daily Mail. March 1, 2016.. *This hard-hitting piece of journalism shows a bunch of weirdly similar child/parent photos and is frankly kind of mesmerizing. Go ahead, waste two minutes of your life and check it out. But don't forget to come back here! This, in a microcosm, is the danger of surfing the web.*

[L83] "Hints for Computer Systems Design" by Butler Lampson. ACM Operating Systems Review, Volume 15:5, October 1983. *Lampson's famous hints on how to design computer systems. You should read it at some point in your life, and probably at many points in your life.*

[QI15] "With Great Power Comes Great Responsibility" by The Quote Investigator. Available: `https://quoteinvestigator.com/2015/07/23/great-power`. *The quote investigator concludes that the earliest mention of this concept is 1793, in a collection of decrees made at the French National Convention. The specific quote: "Ils doivent envisager qu'une grande responsabilité est la suite inséparable d'un grand pouvoir", which roughly translates to "They must consider that great responsibility follows inseparably from great power." Only in 1962 did the following words appear in Spider-Man: "...with great power there must also come–great responsibility!" So it looks like the French Revolution gets credit for this one, not Stan Lee. Sorry, Stan.*

[SR05] "Advanced Programming in the UNIX Environment" by W. Richard Stevens, Stephen A. Rago. Addison-Wesley, 2005. *All nuances and subtleties of using UNIX APIs are found herein. Buy this book! Read it! And most importantly, **live it.***

ASIDE: CODING HOMEWORKS

Coding homeworks are small exercises where you write code to run on a real machine to get some experience with some basic operating system APIs. After all, you are (probably) a computer scientist, and therefore should like to code, right? If you don't, there is always CS theory, but that's pretty hard. Of course, to truly become an expert, you have to spend more than a little time hacking away at the machine; indeed, find every excuse you can to write some code and see how it works. Spend the time, and become the wise master you know you can be.

Homework (Code)

In this homework, you are to gain some familiarity with the process management APIs about which you just read. Don't worry – it's even more fun than it sounds! You'll in general be much better off if you find as much time as you can to write some code, so why not start now?

Questions

1. Write a program that calls `fork()`. Before calling `fork()`, have the main process access a variable (e.g., `x`) and set its value to something (e.g., `100`). What value is the variable in the child process? What happens to the variable when both the child and parent change the value of `x`?

2. Write a program that opens a file (with the `open()` system call) and then calls `fork()` to create a new process. Can both the child and parent access the file descriptor returned by `open()`? What happens when they are writing to the file concurrently, i.e., at the same time?

3. Write another program using `fork()`. The child process should print "hello"; the parent process should print "goodbye". You should try to ensure that the child process always prints first; can you do this *without* calling **wait()** in the parent?

4. Write a program that calls `fork()` and then calls some form of `exec()` to run the program `/bin/ls`. See if you can try all of the variants of `exec()`, including (on Linux) `execl()`, `execle()`, `execlp()`, `execv()`, `execvp()`, and `execvpe()`. Why do you think there are so many variants of the same basic call?

5. Now write a program that uses `wait()` to wait for the child process to finish in the parent. What does `wait()` return? What happens if you use `wait()` in the child?

6. Write a slight modification of the previous program, this time using `waitpid()` instead of `wait()`. When would `waitpid()` be useful?

7. Write a program that creates a child process, and then in the child closes standard output (`STDOUT_FILENO`). What happens if the child calls `printf()` to print some output after closing the descriptor?

8. Write a program that creates two children, and connects the standard output of one to the standard input of the other, using the `pipe()` system call.

6

Mechanism: Limited Direct Execution

In order to virtualize the CPU, the operating system needs to somehow share the physical CPU among many jobs running seemingly at the same time. The basic idea is simple: run one process for a little while, then run another one, and so forth. By **time sharing** the CPU in this manner, virtualization is achieved.

There are a few challenges, however, in building such virtualization machinery. The first is *performance*: how can we implement virtualization without adding excessive overhead to the system? The second is *control*: how can we run processes efficiently while retaining control over the CPU? Control is particularly important to the OS, as it is in charge of resources; without control, a process could simply run forever and take over the machine, or access information that it should not be allowed to access. Obtaining high performance while maintaining control is thus one of the central challenges in building an operating system.

> THE CRUX:
> HOW TO EFFICIENTLY VIRTUALIZE THE CPU WITH CONTROL
>
> The OS must virtualize the CPU in an efficient manner while retaining control over the system. To do so, both hardware and operating-system support will be required. The OS will often use a judicious bit of hardware support in order to accomplish its work effectively.

6.1 Basic Technique: Limited Direct Execution

To make a program run as fast as one might expect, not surprisingly OS developers came up with a technique, which we call **limited direct execution**. The "direct execution" part of the idea is simple: just run the program directly on the CPU. Thus, when the OS wishes to start a program running, it creates a process entry for it in a process list, allocates some memory for it, loads the program code into memory (from disk), locates its entry point (i.e., the `main()` routine or something similar), jumps to it, and starts running the user's code. Figure 61 shows this basic direct

OS	Program
Create entry for process list	
Allocate memory for program	
Load program into memory	
Set up stack with argc/argv	
Clear registers	
Execute **call** main()	
	Run main()
	Execute **return** from main
Free memory of process	
Remove from process list	

Figure 61: **Direct Execution Protocol (Without Limits)**

execution protocol (without any limits, yet), using a normal call and return to jump to the program's `main()` and later back into the kernel.

Sounds simple, no? But this approach gives rise to a few problems in our quest to virtualize the CPU. The first is simple: if we just run a program, how can the OS make sure the program doesn't do anything that we don't want it to do, while still running it efficiently? The second: when we are running a process, how does the operating system stop it from running and switch to another process, thus implementing the **time sharing** we require to virtualize the CPU?

In answering these questions below, we'll get a much better sense of what is needed to virtualize the CPU. In developing these techniques, we'll also see where the "limited" part of the name arises from; without limits on running programs, the OS wouldn't be in control of anything and thus would be "just a library" — a very sad state of affairs for an aspiring operating system!

6.2 Problem #1: Restricted Operations

Direct execution has the obvious advantage of being fast; the program runs natively on the hardware CPU and thus executes as quickly as one would expect. But running on the CPU introduces a problem: what if the process wishes to perform some kind of restricted operation, such as issuing an I/O request to a disk, or gaining access to more system resources such as CPU or memory?

> THE CRUX: HOW TO PERFORM RESTRICTED OPERATIONS
> A process must be able to perform I/O and some other restricted operations, but without giving the process complete control over the system. How can the OS and hardware work together to do so?

> **ASIDE: WHY SYSTEM CALLS LOOK LIKE PROCEDURE CALLS**
>
> You may wonder why a call to a system call, such as `open()` or `read()`, looks exactly like a typical procedure call in C; that is, if it looks just like a procedure call, how does the system know it's a system call, and do all the right stuff? The simple reason: it *is* a procedure call, but hidden inside that procedure call is the famous trap instruction. More specifically, when you call `open()` (for example), you are executing a procedure call into the C library. Therein, whether for `open()` or any of the other system calls provided, the library uses an agreed-upon calling convention with the kernel to put the arguments to `open()` in well-known locations (e.g., on the stack, or in specific registers), puts the system-call number into a well-known location as well (again, onto the stack or a register), and then executes the aforementioned trap instruction. The code in the library after the trap unpacks return values and returns control to the program that issued the system call. Thus, the parts of the C library that make system calls are hand-coded in assembly, as they need to carefully follow convention in order to process arguments and return values correctly, as well as execute the hardware-specific trap instruction. And now you know why you personally don't have to write assembly code to trap into an OS; somebody has already written that assembly for you.

One approach would simply be to let any process do whatever it wants in terms of I/O and other related operations. However, doing so would prevent the construction of many kinds of systems that are desirable. For example, if we wish to build a file system that checks permissions before granting access to a file, we can't simply let any user process issue I/Os to the disk; if we did, a process could simply read or write the entire disk and thus all protections would be lost.

Thus, the approach we take is to introduce a new processor mode, known as **user mode**; code that runs in user mode is restricted in what it can do. For example, when running in user mode, a process can't issue I/O requests; doing so would result in the processor raising an exception; the OS would then likely kill the process.

In contrast to user mode is **kernel mode**, which the operating system (or kernel) runs in. In this mode, code that runs can do what it likes, including privileged operations such as issuing I/O requests and executing all types of restricted instructions.

We are still left with a challenge, however: what should a user process do when it wishes to perform some kind of privileged operation, such as reading from disk? To enable this, virtually all modern hardware provides the ability for user programs to perform a **system call**. Pioneered on ancient machines such as the Atlas [K+61,L78], system calls allow the kernel to carefully expose certain key pieces of functionality to user programs, such as accessing the file system, creating and destroying processes, communicating with other processes, and allocating more

> TIP: USE PROTECTED CONTROL TRANSFER
> The hardware assists the OS by providing different modes of execution. In **user mode**, applications do not have full access to hardware resources. In **kernel mode**, the OS has access to the full resources of the machine. Special instructions to **trap** into the kernel and **return-from-trap** back to user-mode programs are also provided, as well as instructions that allow the OS to tell the hardware where the **trap table** resides in memory.

memory. Most operating systems provide a few hundred calls (see the POSIX standard for details [P10]); early Unix systems exposed a more concise subset of around twenty calls.

To execute a system call, a program must execute a special **trap** instruction. This instruction simultaneously jumps into the kernel and raises the privilege level to kernel mode; once in the kernel, the system can now perform whatever privileged operations are needed (if allowed), and thus do the required work for the calling process. When finished, the OS calls a special **return-from-trap** instruction, which, as you might expect, returns into the calling user program while simultaneously reducing the privilege level back to user mode.

The hardware needs to be a bit careful when executing a trap, in that it must make sure to save enough of the caller's registers in order to be able to return correctly when the OS issues the return-from-trap instruction. On x86, for example, the processor will push the program counter, flags, and a few other registers onto a per-process **kernel stack**; the return-from-trap will pop these values off the stack and resume execution of the user-mode program (see the Intel systems manuals [I11] for details). Other hardware systems use different conventions, but the basic concepts are similar across platforms.

There is one important detail left out of this discussion: how does the trap know which code to run inside the OS? Clearly, the calling process can't specify an address to jump to (as you would when making a procedure call); doing so would allow programs to jump anywhere into the kernel which clearly is a **Very Bad Idea**[1]. Thus the kernel must carefully control what code executes upon a trap.

The kernel does so by setting up a **trap table** at boot time. When the machine boots up, it does so in privileged (kernel) mode, and thus is free to configure machine hardware as need be. One of the first things the OS thus does is to tell the hardware what code to run when certain exceptional events occur. For example, what code should run when a hard-disk interrupt takes place, when a keyboard interrupt occurs, or when a program makes a system call? The OS informs the hardware of the

[1] Imagine jumping into code to access a file, but just after a permission check; in fact, it is likely such an ability would enable a wily programmer to get the kernel to run arbitrary code sequences [S07]. In general, try to avoid Very Bad Ideas like this one.

OS @ boot (kernel mode)	**Hardware**
initialize trap table	
	remember address of... syscall handler

OS @ run (kernel mode)	**Hardware**	**Program (user mode)**
Create entry for process list Allocate memory for program Load program into memory Setup user stack with argv Fill kernel stack with reg/PC **return-from-trap**		
	restore regs (from kernel stack) move to user mode jump to main	
		Run main() ... Call system call **trap** into OS
	save regs (to kernel stack) move to kernel mode jump to trap handler	
Handle trap Do work of syscall **return-from-trap**		
	restore regs (from kernel stack) move to user mode jump to PC after trap	
		... return from main **trap** (via `exit()`)
Free memory of process Remove from process list		

Figure 62: **Limited Direct Execution Protocol**

locations of these **trap handlers**, usually with some kind of special instruction. Once the hardware is informed, it remembers the location of these handlers until the machine is next rebooted, and thus the hardware knows what to do (i.e., what code to jump to) when system calls and other exceptional events take place.

TIP: BE WARY OF USER INPUTS IN SECURE SYSTEMS

Even though we have taken great pains to protect the OS during system calls (by adding a hardware trapping mechanism, and ensuring all calls to the OS are routed through it), there are still many other aspects to implementing a **secure** operating system that we must consider. One of these is the handling of arguments at the system call boundary; the OS must check what the user passes in and ensure that arguments are properly specified, or otherwise reject the call.

For example, with a `write()` system call, the user specifies an address of a buffer as a source of the write call. If the user (either accidentally or maliciously) passes in a "bad" address (e.g., one inside the kernel's portion of the address space), the OS must detect this and reject the call. Otherwise, it would be possible for a user to read all of kernel memory; given that kernel (virtual) memory also usually includes all of the physical memory of the system, this small slip would enable a program to read the memory of any other process in the system.

In general, a secure system must treat user inputs with great suspicion. Not doing so will undoubtedly lead to easily hacked software, a despairing sense that the world is an unsafe and scary place, and the loss of job security for the all-too-trusting OS developer.

To specify the exact system call, a **system-call number** is usually assigned to each system call. The user code is thus responsible for placing the desired system-call number in a register or at a specified location on the stack; the OS, when handling the system call inside the trap handler, examines this number, ensures it is valid, and, if it is, executes the corresponding code. This level of indirection serves as a form of **protection**; user code cannot specify an exact address to jump to, but rather must request a particular service via number.

One last aside: being able to execute the instruction to tell the hardware where the trap tables are is a very powerful capability. Thus, as you might have guessed, it is also a **privileged** operation. If you try to execute this instruction in user mode, the hardware won't let you, and you can probably guess what will happen (hint: adios, offending program). Point to ponder: what horrible things could you do to a system if you could install your own trap table? Could you take over the machine?

The timeline (with time increasing downward, in Figure 62) summarizes the protocol. We assume each process has a kernel stack where registers (including general purpose registers and the program counter) are saved to and restored from (by the hardware) when transitioning into and out of the kernel.

There are two phases in the limited direct execution (**LDE**) protocol. In the first (at boot time), the kernel initializes the trap table, and the CPU remembers its location for subsequent use. The kernel does so via a privileged instruction (all privileged instructions are highlighted in bold).

In the second (when running a process), the kernel sets up a few things (e.g., allocating a node on the process list, allocating memory) before using a return-from-trap instruction to start the execution of the process; this switches the CPU to user mode and begins running the process. When the process wishes to issue a system call, it traps back into the OS, which handles it and once again returns control via a return-from-trap to the process. The process then completes its work, and returns from `main()`; this usually will return into some stub code which will properly exit the program (say, by calling the `exit()` system call, which traps into the OS). At this point, the OS cleans up and we are done.

6.3 Problem #2: Switching Between Processes

The next problem with direct execution is achieving a switch between processes. Switching between processes should be simple, right? The OS should just decide to stop one process and start another. What's the big deal? But it actually is a little bit tricky: specifically, if a process is running on the CPU, this by definition means the OS is *not* running. If the OS is not running, how can it do anything at all? (hint: it can't) While this sounds almost philosophical, it is a real problem: there is clearly no way for the OS to take an action if it is not running on the CPU. Thus we arrive at the crux of the problem.

> THE CRUX: HOW TO REGAIN CONTROL OF THE CPU
> How can the operating system **regain control** of the CPU so that it can switch between processes?

A Cooperative Approach: Wait For System Calls

One approach that some systems have taken in the past (for example, early versions of the Macintosh operating system [M11], or the old Xerox Alto system [A79]) is known as the **cooperative** approach. In this style, the OS *trusts* the processes of the system to behave reasonably. Processes that run for too long are assumed to periodically give up the CPU so that the OS can decide to run some other task.

Thus, you might ask, how does a friendly process give up the CPU in this utopian world? Most processes, as it turns out, transfer control of the CPU to the OS quite frequently by making **system calls**, for example, to open a file and subsequently read it, or to send a message to another machine, or to create a new process. Systems like this often include an explicit **yield** system call, which does nothing except to transfer control to the OS so it can run other processes.

Applications also transfer control to the OS when they do something illegal. For example, if an application divides by zero, or tries to access memory that it shouldn't be able to access, it will generate a **trap** to the

OS. The OS will then have control of the CPU again (and likely terminate the offending process).

Thus, in a cooperative scheduling system, the OS regains control of the CPU by waiting for a system call or an illegal operation of some kind to take place. You might also be thinking: isn't this passive approach less than ideal? What happens, for example, if a process (whether malicious, or just full of bugs) ends up in an infinite loop, and never makes a system call? What can the OS do then?

A Non-Cooperative Approach: The OS Takes Control

Without some additional help from the hardware, it turns out the OS can't do much at all when a process refuses to make system calls (or mistakes) and thus return control to the OS. In fact, in the cooperative approach, your only recourse when a process gets stuck in an infinite loop is to resort to the age-old solution to all problems in computer systems: **reboot the machine**. Thus, we again arrive at a subproblem of our general quest to gain control of the CPU.

> THE CRUX: HOW TO GAIN CONTROL WITHOUT COOPERATION
> How can the OS gain control of the CPU even if processes are not being cooperative? What can the OS do to ensure a rogue process does not take over the machine?

The answer turns out to be simple and was discovered by a number of people building computer systems many years ago: a **timer interrupt** [M+63]. A timer device can be programmed to raise an interrupt every so many milliseconds; when the interrupt is raised, the currently running process is halted, and a pre-configured **interrupt handler** in the OS runs. At this point, the OS has regained control of the CPU, and thus can do what it pleases: stop the current process, and start a different one.

As we discussed before with system calls, the OS must inform the hardware of which code to run when the timer interrupt occurs; thus, at boot time, the OS does exactly that. Second, also during the boot sequence, the OS must start the timer, which is of course a privileged

> TIP: DEALING WITH APPLICATION MISBEHAVIOR
> Operating systems often have to deal with misbehaving processes, those that either through design (maliciousness) or accident (bugs) attempt to do something that they shouldn't. In modern systems, the way the OS tries to handle such malfeasance is to simply terminate the offender. One strike and you're out! Perhaps brutal, but what else should the OS do when you try to access memory illegally or execute an illegal instruction?

operation. Once the timer has begun, the OS can thus feel safe in that control will eventually be returned to it, and thus the OS is free to run user programs. The timer can also be turned off (also a privileged operation), something we will discuss later when we understand concurrency in more detail.

Note that the hardware has some responsibility when an interrupt occurs, in particular to save enough of the state of the program that was running when the interrupt occurred such that a subsequent return-from-trap instruction will be able to resume the running program correctly. This set of actions is quite similar to the behavior of the hardware during an explicit system-call trap into the kernel, with various registers thus getting saved (e.g., onto a kernel stack) and thus easily restored by the return-from-trap instruction.

Saving and Restoring Context

Now that the OS has regained control, whether cooperatively via a system call, or more forcefully via a timer interrupt, a decision has to be made: whether to continue running the currently-running process, or switch to a different one. This decision is made by a part of the operating system known as the **scheduler**; we will discuss scheduling policies in great detail in the next few chapters.

If the decision is made to switch, the OS then executes a low-level piece of code which we refer to as a **context switch**. A context switch is conceptually simple: all the OS has to do is save a few register values for the currently-executing process (onto its kernel stack, for example) and restore a few for the soon-to-be-executing process (from its kernel stack). By doing so, the OS thus ensures that when the return-from-trap instruction is finally executed, instead of returning to the process that was running, the system resumes execution of another process.

To save the context of the currently-running process, the OS will execute some low-level assembly code to save the general purpose registers, PC, and the kernel stack pointer of the currently-running process, and then restore said registers, PC, and switch to the kernel stack for the soon-to-be-executing process. By switching stacks, the kernel enters the call to the switch code in the context of one process (the one that was interrupted) and returns in the context of another (the soon-to-be-executing one). When the OS then finally executes a return-from-trap instruction,

> TIP: USE THE TIMER INTERRUPT TO REGAIN CONTROL
> The addition of a **timer interrupt** gives the OS the ability to run again on a CPU even if processes act in a non-cooperative fashion. Thus, this hardware feature is essential in helping the OS maintain control of the machine.

TIP: REBOOT IS USEFUL

Earlier on, we noted that the only solution to infinite loops (and similar behaviors) under cooperative preemption is to **reboot** the machine. While you may scoff at this hack, researchers have shown that reboot (or in general, starting over some piece of software) can be a hugely useful tool in building robust systems [C+04].

Specifically, reboot is useful because it moves software back to a known and likely more tested state. Reboots also reclaim stale or leaked resources (e.g., memory) which may otherwise be hard to handle. Finally, reboots are easy to automate. For all of these reasons, it is not uncommon in large-scale cluster Internet services for system management software to periodically reboot sets of machines in order to reset them and thus obtain the advantages listed above.

Thus, next time you reboot, you are not just enacting some ugly hack. Rather, you are using a time-tested approach to improving the behavior of a computer system. Well done!

the soon-to-be-executing process becomes the currently-running process. And thus the context switch is complete.

A timeline of the entire process is shown in Figure 63. In this example, Process A is running and then is interrupted by the timer interrupt. The hardware saves its registers (onto its kernel stack) and enters the kernel (switching to kernel mode). In the timer interrupt handler, the OS decides to switch from running Process A to Process B. At that point, it calls the `switch()` routine, which carefully saves current register values (into the process structure of A), restores the registers of Process B (from its process structure entry), and then **switches contexts**, specifically by changing the stack pointer to use B's kernel stack (and not A's). Finally, the OS returns-from-trap, which restores B's registers and starts running it.

Note that there are two types of register saves/restores that happen during this protocol. The first is when the timer interrupt occurs; in this case, the *user registers* of the running process are implicitly saved by the *hardware*, using the kernel stack of that process. The second is when the OS decides to switch from A to B; in this case, the *kernel registers* are explicitly saved by the *software* (i.e., the OS), but this time into memory in the process structure of the process. The latter action moves the system from running as if it just trapped into the kernel from A to as if it just trapped into the kernel from B.

To give you a better sense of how such a switch is enacted, Figure 64 shows the context switch code for xv6. See if you can make sense of it (you'll have to know a bit of x86, as well as some xv6, to do so). The `context` structures `old` and `new` are found in the old and new process's process structures, respectively.

OS @ boot (kernel mode)	**Hardware**
initialize trap table	
	remember addresses of... syscall handler timer handler
start interrupt timer	
	start timer interrupt CPU in X ms

OS @ run (kernel mode)	**Hardware**	**Program (user mode)**
		Process A ...
	timer interrupt save regs(A) → k-stack(A) move to kernel mode jump to trap handler	
Handle the trap Call `switch()` routine save regs(A) → proc_t(A) restore regs(B) ← proc_t(B) switch to k-stack(B) **return-from-trap (into B)**		
	restore regs(B) ← k-stack(B) move to user mode jump to B's PC	
		Process B ...

Figure 63: **Limited Direct Execution Protocol (Timer Interrupt)**

6.4 Worried About Concurrency?

Some of you, as attentive and thoughtful readers, may be now thinking: "Hmm... what happens when, during a system call, a timer interrupt occurs?" or "What happens when you're handling one interrupt and another one happens? Doesn't that get hard to handle in the kernel?" Good questions — we really have some hope for you yet!

The answer is yes, the OS does indeed need to be concerned as to what happens if, during interrupt or trap handling, another interrupt occurs. This, in fact, is the exact topic of the entire second piece of this book, on **concurrency**; we'll defer a detailed discussion until then.

To whet your appetite, we'll just sketch some basics of how the OS handles these tricky situations. One simple thing an OS might do is **disable interrupts** during interrupt processing; doing so ensures that when

```
# void swtch(struct context **old, struct context *new);
#
# Save current register context in old
# and then load register context from new.
.globl swtch
swtch:
  # Save old registers
  movl 4(%esp), %eax  # put old ptr into eax
  popl 0(%eax)        # save the old IP
  movl %esp, 4(%eax)  # and stack
  movl %ebx, 8(%eax)  # and other registers
  movl %ecx, 12(%eax)
  movl %edx, 16(%eax)
  movl %esi, 20(%eax)
  movl %edi, 24(%eax)
  movl %ebp, 28(%eax)

  # Load new registers
  movl 4(%esp), %eax  # put new ptr into eax
  movl 28(%eax), %ebp # restore other registers
  movl 24(%eax), %edi
  movl 20(%eax), %esi
  movl 16(%eax), %edx
  movl 12(%eax), %ecx
  movl 8(%eax), %ebx
  movl 4(%eax), %esp  # stack is switched here
  pushl 0(%eax)       # return addr put in place
  ret                 # finally return into new ctxt
```

Figure 64: **The xv6 Context Switch Code**

one interrupt is being handled, no other one will be delivered to the CPU. Of course, the OS has to be careful in doing so; disabling interrupts for too long could lead to lost interrupts, which is (in technical terms) bad.

Operating systems also have developed a number of sophisticated **locking** schemes to protect concurrent access to internal data structures. This enables multiple activities to be on-going within the kernel at the same time, particularly useful on multiprocessors. As we'll see in the next piece of this book on concurrency, though, such locking can be complicated and lead to a variety of interesting and hard-to-find bugs.

6.5 Summary

We have described some key low-level mechanisms to implement CPU virtualization, a set of techniques which we collectively refer to as **limited direct execution**. The basic idea is straightforward: just run the program you want to run on the CPU, but first make sure to set up the hardware so as to limit what the process can do without OS assistance.

ASIDE: HOW LONG CONTEXT SWITCHES TAKE

A natural question you might have is: how long does something like a context switch take? Or even a system call? For those of you that are curious, there is a tool called **lmbench** [MS96] that measures exactly those things, as well as a few other performance measures that might be relevant.

Results have improved quite a bit over time, roughly tracking processor performance. For example, in 1996 running Linux 1.3.37 on a 200-MHz P6 CPU, system calls took roughly 4 microseconds, and a context switch roughly 6 microseconds [MS96]. Modern systems perform almost an order of magnitude better, with sub-microsecond results on systems with 2- or 3-GHz processors.

It should be noted that not all operating-system actions track CPU performance. As Ousterhout observed, many OS operations are memory intensive, and memory bandwidth has not improved as dramatically as processor speed over time [O90]. Thus, depending on your workload, buying the latest and greatest processor may not speed up your OS as much as you might hope.

This general approach is taken in real life as well. For example, those of you who have children, or, at least, have heard of children, may be familiar with the concept of **baby proofing** a room: locking cabinets containing dangerous stuff and covering electrical sockets. When the room is thus readied, you can let your baby roam freely, secure in the knowledge that the most dangerous aspects of the room have been restricted.

In an analogous manner, the OS "baby proofs" the CPU, by first (during boot time) setting up the trap handlers and starting an interrupt timer, and then by only running processes in a restricted mode. By doing so, the OS can feel quite assured that processes can run efficiently, only requiring OS intervention to perform privileged operations or when they have monopolized the CPU for too long and thus need to be switched out.

We thus have the basic mechanisms for virtualizing the CPU in place. But a major question is left unanswered: which process should we run at a given time? It is this question that the scheduler must answer, and thus the next topic of our study.

ASIDE: KEY CPU VIRTUALIZATION TERMS (MECHANISMS)

- The CPU should support at least two modes of execution: a restricted **user mode** and a privileged (non-restricted) **kernel mode**.
- Typical user applications run in user mode, and use a **system call** to **trap** into the kernel to request operating system services.
- The trap instruction saves register state carefully, changes the hardware status to kernel mode, and jumps into the OS to a pre-specified destination: the **trap table**.
- When the OS finishes servicing a system call, it returns to the user program via another special **return-from-trap** instruction, which reduces privilege and returns control to the instruction after the trap that jumped into the OS.
- The trap tables must be set up by the OS at boot time, and make sure that they cannot be readily modified by user programs. All of this is part of the **limited direct execution** protocol which runs programs efficiently but without loss of OS control.
- Once a program is running, the OS must use hardware mechanisms to ensure the user program does not run forever, namely the **timer interrupt**. This approach is a **non-cooperative** approach to CPU scheduling.
- Sometimes the OS, during a timer interrupt or system call, might wish to switch from running the current process to a different one, a low-level technique known as a **context switch**.

References

[A79] "Alto User's Handbook" by Xerox. Xerox Palo Alto Research Center, September 1979. Available: `http://history-computer.com/Library/AltoUsersHandbook.pdf`. *An amazing system, way ahead of its time. Became famous because Steve Jobs visited, took notes, and built Lisa and eventually Mac.*

[C+04] "Microreboot — A Technique for Cheap Recovery" by G. Candea, S. Kawamoto, Y. Fujiki, G. Friedman, A. Fox. OSDI '04, San Francisco, CA, December 2004. *An excellent paper pointing out how far one can go with reboot in building more robust systems.*

[I11] "Intel 64 and IA-32 Architectures Software Developer's Manual" by Volume 3A and 3B: System Programming Guide. Intel Corporation, January 2011. *This is just a boring manual, but sometimes those are useful.*

[K+61] "One-Level Storage System" by T. Kilburn, D.B.G. Edwards, M.J. Lanigan, F.H. Sumner. IRE Transactions on Electronic Computers, April 1962. *The Atlas pioneered much of what you see in modern systems. However, this paper is not the best one to read. If you were to only read one, you might try the historical perspective below [L78].*

[L78] "The Manchester Mark I and Atlas: A Historical Perspective" by S. H. Lavington. Communications of the ACM, 21:1, January 1978. *A history of the early development of computers and the pioneering efforts of Atlas.*

[M+63] "A Time-Sharing Debugging System for a Small Computer" by J. McCarthy, S. Boilen, E. Fredkin, J. C. R. Licklider. AFIPS '63 (Spring), May, 1963, New York, USA. *An early paper about time-sharing that refers to using a timer interrupt; the quote that discusses it: "The basic task of the channel 17 clock routine is to decide whether to remove the current user from core and if so to decide which user program to swap in as he goes out."*

[MS96] "lmbench: Portable tools for performance analysis" by Larry McVoy and Carl Staelin. USENIX Annual Technical Conference, January 1996. *A fun paper about how to measure a number of different things about your OS and its performance. Download lmbench and give it a try.*

[M11] "Mac OS 9" by Apple Computer, Inc.. January 2011. `http://en.wikipedia.org/wiki/Mac_OS_9` . *You can probably even find an OS 9 emulator out there if you want to; check it out, it's a fun little Mac!*

[O90] "Why Aren't Operating Systems Getting Faster as Fast as Hardware?" by J. Ousterhout. USENIX Summer Conference, June 1990. *A classic paper on the nature of operating system performance.*

[P10] "The Single UNIX Specification, Version 3" by The Open Group, May 2010. Available: `http://www.unix.org/version3/`. *This is hard and painful to read, so probably avoid it if you can. Like, unless someone is paying you to read it. Or, you're just so curious you can't help it!*

[S07] "The Geometry of Innocent Flesh on the Bone: Return-into-libc without Function Calls (on the x86)" by Hovav Shacham. CCS '07, October 2007. *One of those awesome, mind-blowing ideas that you'll see in research from time to time. The author shows that if you can jump into code arbitrarily, you can essentially stitch together any code sequence you like (given a large code base); read the paper for the details. The technique makes it even harder to defend against malicious attacks, alas.*

Homework (Measurement)

> ASIDE: MEASUREMENT HOMEWORKS
>
> Measurement homeworks are small exercises where you write code to run on a real machine, in order to measure some aspect of OS or hardware performance. The idea behind such homeworks is to give you a little bit of hands-on experience with a real operating system.

In this homework, you'll measure the costs of a system call and context switch. Measuring the cost of a system call is relatively easy. For example, you could repeatedly call a simple system call (e.g., performing a 0-byte read), and time how long it takes; dividing the time by the number of iterations gives you an estimate of the cost of a system call.

One thing you'll have to take into account is the precision and accuracy of your timer. A typical timer that you can use is `gettimeofday()`; read the man page for details. What you'll see there is that `gettimeofday()` returns the time in microseconds since 1970; however, this does not mean that the timer is precise to the microsecond. Measure back-to-back calls to `gettimeofday()` to learn something about how precise the timer really is; this will tell you how many iterations of your null system-call test you'll have to run in order to get a good measurement result. If `gettimeofday()` is not precise enough for you, you might look into using the `rdtsc` instruction available on x86 machines.

Measuring the cost of a context switch is a little trickier. The lmbench benchmark does so by running two processes on a single CPU, and setting up two UNIX pipes between them; a pipe is just one of many ways processes in a UNIX system can communicate with one another. The first process then issues a write to the first pipe, and waits for a read on the second; upon seeing the first process waiting for something to read from the second pipe, the OS puts the first process in the blocked state, and switches to the other process, which reads from the first pipe and then writes to the second. When the second process tries to read from the first pipe again, it blocks, and thus the back-and-forth cycle of communication continues. By measuring the cost of communicating like this repeatedly, lmbench can make a good estimate of the cost of a context switch. You can try to re-create something similar here, using pipes, or perhaps some other communication mechanism such as UNIX sockets.

One difficulty in measuring context-switch cost arises in systems with more than one CPU; what you need to do on such a system is ensure that your context-switching processes are located on the same processor. Fortunately, most operating systems have calls to bind a process to a particular processor; on Linux, for example, the `sched_setaffinity()` call is what you're looking for. By ensuring both processes are on the same processor, you are making sure to measure the cost of the OS stopping one process and restoring another on the same CPU.

7

Scheduling: Introduction

By now low-level **mechanisms** of running processes (e.g., context switching) should be clear; if they are not, go back a chapter or two, and read the description of how that stuff works again. However, we have yet to understand the high-level **policies** that an OS scheduler employs. We will now do just that, presenting a series of **scheduling policies** (sometimes called **disciplines**) that various smart and hard-working people have developed over the years.

The origins of scheduling, in fact, predate computer systems; early approaches were taken from the field of operations management and applied to computers. This reality should be no surprise: assembly lines and many other human endeavors also require scheduling, and many of the same concerns exist therein, including a laser-like desire for efficiency. And thus, our problem:

> THE CRUX: HOW TO DEVELOP SCHEDULING POLICY
>
> How should we develop a basic framework for thinking about scheduling policies? What are the key assumptions? What metrics are important? What basic approaches have been used in the earliest of computer systems?

7.1 Workload Assumptions

Before getting into the range of possible policies, let us first make a number of simplifying assumptions about the processes running in the system, sometimes collectively called the **workload**. Determining the workload is a critical part of building policies, and the more you know about workload, the more fine-tuned your policy can be.

The workload assumptions we make here are mostly unrealistic, but that is alright (for now), because we will relax them as we go, and eventually develop what we will refer to as ... *(dramatic pause)* ...

a **fully-operational scheduling discipline**[1].

We will make the following assumptions about the processes, sometimes called **jobs**, that are running in the system:

1. Each job runs for the same amount of time.
2. All jobs arrive at the same time.
3. Once started, each job runs to completion.
4. All jobs only use the CPU (i.e., they perform no I/O)
5. The run-time of each job is known.

We said many of these assumptions were unrealistic, but just as some animals are more equal than others in Orwell's *Animal Farm* [O45], some assumptions are more unrealistic than others in this chapter. In particular, it might bother you that the run-time of each job is known: this would make the scheduler omniscient, which, although it would be great (probably), is not likely to happen anytime soon.

7.2 Scheduling Metrics

Beyond making workload assumptions, we also need one more thing to enable us to compare different scheduling policies: a **scheduling metric**. A metric is just something that we use to *measure* something, and there are a number of different metrics that make sense in scheduling.

For now, however, let us also simplify our life by simply having a single metric: **turnaround time**. The turnaround time of a job is defined as the time at which the job completes minus the time at which the job arrived in the system. More formally, the turnaround time $T_{turnaround}$ is:

$$T_{turnaround} = T_{completion} - T_{arrival} \tag{7.1}$$

Because we have assumed that all jobs arrive at the same time, for now $T_{arrival} = 0$ and hence $T_{turnaround} = T_{completion}$. This fact will change as we relax the aforementioned assumptions.

You should note that turnaround time is a **performance** metric, which will be our primary focus this chapter. Another metric of interest is **fairness**, as measured (for example) by **Jain's Fairness Index** [J91]. Performance and fairness are often at odds in scheduling; a scheduler, for example, may optimize performance but at the cost of preventing a few jobs from running, thus decreasing fairness. This conundrum shows us that life isn't always perfect.

7.3 First In, First Out (FIFO)

The most basic algorithm we can implement is known as **First In, First Out (FIFO)** scheduling or sometimes **First Come, First Served (FCFS)**.

[1] Said in the same way you would say "A fully-operational Death Star."

FIFO has a number of positive properties: it is clearly simple and thus easy to implement. And, given our assumptions, it works pretty well.

Let's do a quick example together. Imagine three jobs arrive in the system, A, B, and C, at roughly the same time ($T_{arrival} = 0$). Because FIFO has to put some job first, let's assume that while they all arrived simultaneously, A arrived just a hair before B which arrived just a hair before C. Assume also that each job runs for 10 seconds. What will the **average turnaround time** be for these jobs?

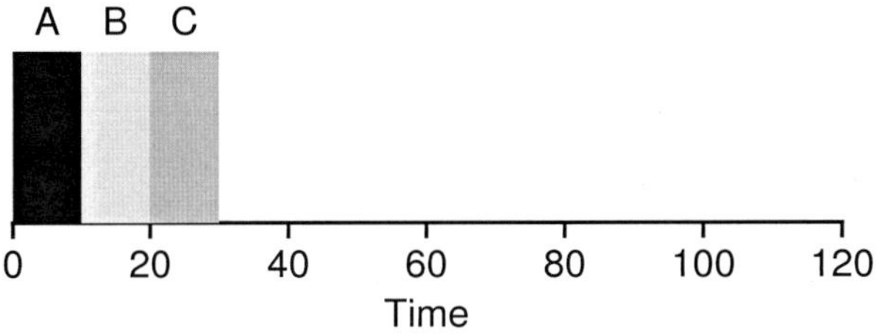

Figure 71: **FIFO Simple Example**

From Figure 71, you can see that A finished at 10, B at 20, and C at 30. Thus, the average turnaround time for the three jobs is simply $\frac{10+20+30}{3} =$ 20. Computing turnaround time is as easy as that.

Now let's relax one of our assumptions. In particular, let's relax assumption 1, and thus no longer assume that each job runs for the same amount of time. How does FIFO perform now? What kind of workload could you construct to make FIFO perform poorly?

(think about this before reading on ... keep thinking ... got it?!)

Presumably you've figured this out by now, but just in case, let's do an example to show how jobs of different lengths can lead to trouble for FIFO scheduling. In particular, let's again assume three jobs (A, B, and C), but this time A runs for 100 seconds while B and C run for 10 each.

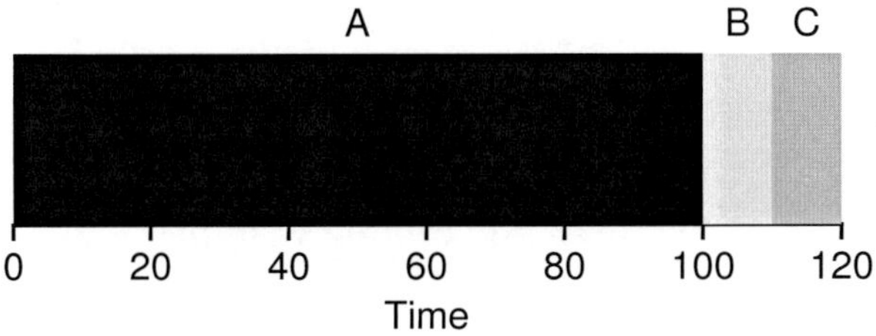

Figure 72: **Why FIFO Is Not That Great**

As you can see in Figure 72, Job A runs first for the full 100 seconds before B or C even get a chance to run. Thus, the average turnaround time for the system is high: a painful 110 seconds ($\frac{100+110+120}{3} = 110$).

This problem is generally referred to as the **convoy effect** [B+79], where a number of relatively-short potential consumers of a resource get queued

TIP: THE PRINCIPLE OF SJF

Shortest Job First represents a general scheduling principle that can be applied to any system where the perceived turnaround time per customer (or, in our case, a job) matters. Think of any line you have waited in: if the establishment in question cares about customer satisfaction, it is likely they have taken SJF into account. For example, grocery stores commonly have a "ten-items-or-less" line to ensure that shoppers with only a few things to purchase don't get stuck behind the family preparing for some upcoming nuclear winter.

behind a heavyweight resource consumer. This scheduling scenario might remind you of a single line at a grocery store and what you feel like when you see the person in front of you with three carts full of provisions and a checkbook out; it's going to be a while[2].

So what should we do? How can we develop a better algorithm to deal with our new reality of jobs that run for different amounts of time? Think about it first; then read on.

7.4 Shortest Job First (SJF)

It turns out that a very simple approach solves this problem; in fact it is an idea stolen from operations research [C54,PV56] and applied to scheduling of jobs in computer systems. This new scheduling discipline is known as **Shortest Job First (SJF)**, and the name should be easy to remember because it describes the policy quite completely: it runs the shortest job first, then the next shortest, and so on.

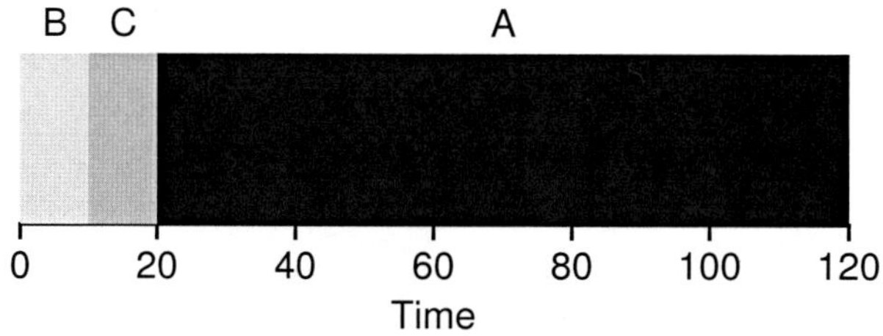

Figure 73: **SJF Simple Example**

Let's take our example above but with SJF as our scheduling policy. Figure 73 shows the results of running A, B, and C. Hopefully the diagram makes it clear why SJF performs much better with regards to average turnaround time. Simply by running B and C before A, SJF reduces average turnaround from 110 seconds to 50 ($\frac{10+20+120}{3} = 50$), more than a factor of two improvement.

[2] Recommended action in this case: either quickly switch to a different line, or take a long, deep, and relaxing breath. That's right, breathe in, breathe out. It will be OK, don't worry.

> ASIDE: PREEMPTIVE SCHEDULERS
> In the old days of batch computing, a number of **non-preemptive** schedulers were developed; such systems would run each job to completion before considering whether to run a new job. Virtually all modern schedulers are **preemptive**, and quite willing to stop one process from running in order to run another. This implies that the scheduler employs the mechanisms we learned about previously; in particular, the scheduler can perform a **context switch**, stopping one running process temporarily and resuming (or starting) another.

In fact, given our assumptions about jobs all arriving at the same time, we could prove that SJF is indeed an **optimal** scheduling algorithm. However, you are in a systems class, not theory or operations research; no proofs are allowed.

Thus we arrive upon a good approach to scheduling with SJF, but our assumptions are still fairly unrealistic. Let's relax another. In particular, we can target assumption 2, and now assume that jobs can arrive at any time instead of all at once. What problems does this lead to?

(Another pause to think ... are you thinking? Come on, you can do it)

Here we can illustrate the problem again with an example. This time, assume A arrives at $t = 0$ and needs to run for 100 seconds, whereas B and C arrive at $t = 10$ and each need to run for 10 seconds. With pure SJF, we'd get the schedule seen in Figure 74.

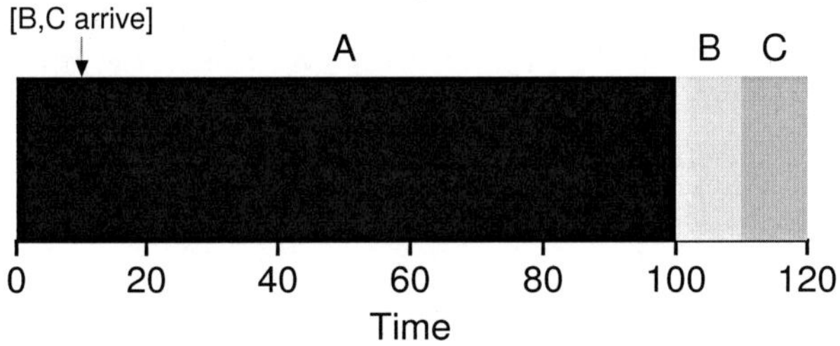

Figure 74: **SJF With Late Arrivals From B and C**

As you can see from the figure, even though B and C arrived shortly after A, they still are forced to wait until A has completed, and thus suffer the same convoy problem. Average turnaround time for these three jobs is 103.33 seconds ($\frac{100+(110-10)+(120-10)}{3}$). What can a scheduler do?

7.5 Shortest Time-to-Completion First (STCF)

To address this concern, we need to relax assumption 3 (that jobs must run to completion), so let's do that. We also need some machinery within the scheduler itself. As you might have guessed, given our previous discussion about timer interrupts and context switching, the scheduler can

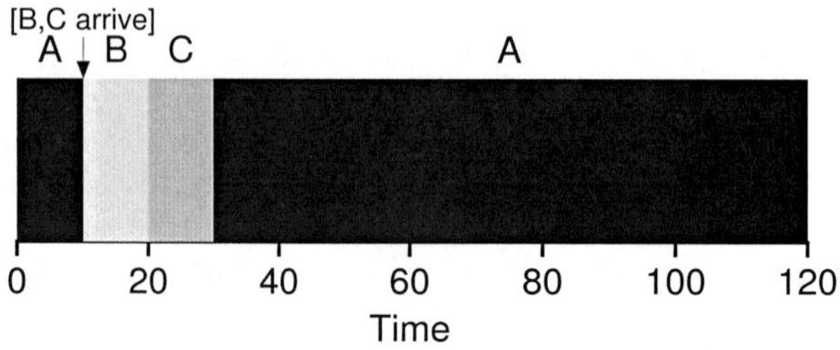

Figure 75: **STCF Simple Example**

certainly do something else when B and C arrive: it can **preempt** job A and decide to run another job, perhaps continuing A later. SJF by our definition is a **non-preemptive** scheduler, and thus suffers from the problems described above.

Fortunately, there is a scheduler which does exactly that: add preemption to SJF, known as the **Shortest Time-to-Completion First** (**STCF**) or **Preemptive Shortest Job First** (**PSJF**) scheduler [CK68]. Any time a new job enters the system, the STCF scheduler determines which of the remaining jobs (including the new job) has the least time left, and schedules that one. Thus, in our example, STCF would preempt A and run B and C to completion; only when they are finished would A's remaining time be scheduled. Figure 75 shows an example.

The result is a much-improved average turnaround time: 50 seconds ($\frac{(120-0)+(20-10)+(30-10)}{3}$). And as before, given our new assumptions, STCF is provably optimal; given that SJF is optimal if all jobs arrive at the same time, you should probably be able to see the intuition behind the optimality of STCF.

7.6 A New Metric: Response Time

Thus, if we knew job lengths, and that jobs only used the CPU, and our only metric was turnaround time, STCF would be a great policy. In fact, for a number of early batch computing systems, these types of scheduling algorithms made some sense. However, the introduction of time-shared machines changed all that. Now users would sit at a terminal and demand interactive performance from the system as well. And thus, a new metric was born: **response time**.

We define response time as the time from when the job arrives in a system to the first time it is scheduled[3]. More formally:

$$T_{response} = T_{firstrun} - T_{arrival} \tag{7.2}$$

[3]Some define it slightly differently, e.g., to also include the time until the job produces some kind of "response"; our definition is the best-case version of this, essentially assuming that the job produces a response instantaneously.

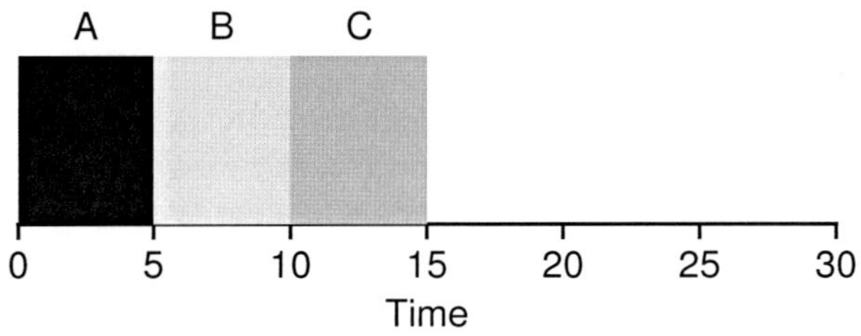

Figure 76: **SJF Again (Bad for Response Time)**

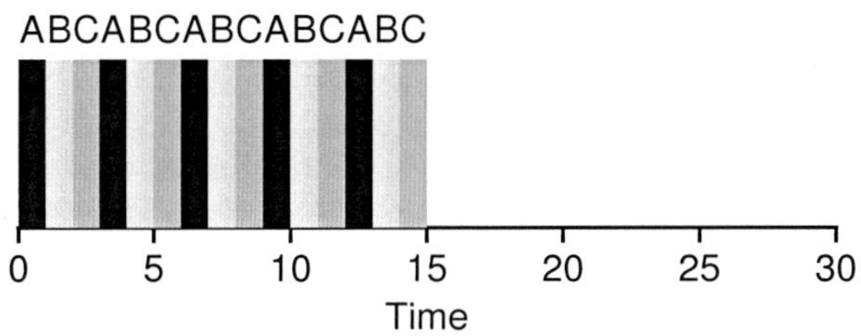

Figure 77: **Round Robin (Good For Response Time)**

For example, if we had the schedule above (with A arriving at time 0, and B and C at time 10), the response time of each job is as follows: 0 for job A, 0 for B, and 10 for C (average: 3.33).

As you might be thinking, STCF and related disciplines are not particularly good for response time. If three jobs arrive at the same time, for example, the third job has to wait for the previous two jobs to run *in their entirety* before being scheduled just once. While great for turnaround time, this approach is quite bad for response time and interactivity. Indeed, imagine sitting at a terminal, typing, and having to wait 10 seconds to see a response from the system just because some other job got scheduled in front of yours: not too pleasant.

Thus, we are left with another problem: how can we build a scheduler that is sensitive to response time?

7.7 Round Robin

To solve this problem, we will introduce a new scheduling algorithm, classically referred to as **Round-Robin (RR)** scheduling [K64]. The basic idea is simple: instead of running jobs to completion, RR runs a job for a **time slice** (sometimes called a **scheduling quantum**) and then switches to the next job in the run queue. It repeatedly does so until the jobs are finished. For this reason, RR is sometimes called **time-slicing**. Note that the length of a time slice must be a multiple of the timer-interrupt period; thus if the timer interrupts every 10 milliseconds, the time slice could be 10, 20, or any other multiple of 10 ms.

To understand RR in more detail, let's look at an example. Assume three jobs A, B, and C arrive at the same time in the system, and that

TIP: AMORTIZATION CAN REDUCE COSTS

The general technique of **amortization** is commonly used in systems when there is a fixed cost to some operation. By incurring that cost less often (i.e., by performing the operation fewer times), the total cost to the system is reduced. For example, if the time slice is set to 10 ms, and the context-switch cost is 1 ms, roughly 10% of time is spent context switching and is thus wasted. If we want to *amortize* this cost, we can increase the time slice, e.g., to 100 ms. In this case, less than 1% of time is spent context switching, and thus the cost of time-slicing has been amortized.

they each wish to run for 5 seconds. An SJF scheduler runs each job to completion before running another (Figure 76). In contrast, RR with a time-slice of 1 second would cycle through the jobs quickly (Figure 77).

The average response time of RR is: $\frac{0+1+2}{3} = 1$; for SJF, average response time is: $\frac{0+5+10}{3} = 5$.

As you can see, the length of the time slice is critical for RR. The shorter it is, the better the performance of RR under the response-time metric. However, making the time slice too short is problematic: suddenly the cost of context switching will dominate overall performance. Thus, deciding on the length of the time slice presents a trade-off to a system designer, making it long enough to **amortize** the cost of switching without making it so long that the system is no longer responsive.

Note that the cost of context switching does not arise solely from the OS actions of saving and restoring a few registers. When programs run, they build up a great deal of state in CPU caches, TLBs, branch predictors, and other on-chip hardware. Switching to another job causes this state to be flushed and new state relevant to the currently-running job to be brought in, which may exact a noticeable performance cost [MB91].

RR, with a reasonable time slice, is thus an excellent scheduler if response time is our only metric. But what about our old friend turnaround time? Let's look at our example above again. A, B, and C, each with running times of 5 seconds, arrive at the same time, and RR is the scheduler with a (long) 1-second time slice. We can see from the picture above that A finishes at 13, B at 14, and C at 15, for an average of 14. Pretty awful!

It is not surprising, then, that RR is indeed one of the *worst* policies if turnaround time is our metric. Intuitively, this should make sense: what RR is doing is stretching out each job as long as it can, by only running each job for a short bit before moving to the next. Because turnaround time only cares about when jobs finish, RR is nearly pessimal, even worse than simple FIFO in many cases.

More generally, any policy (such as RR) that is **fair**, i.e., that evenly divides the CPU among active processes on a small time scale, will perform poorly on metrics such as turnaround time. Indeed, this is an inherent trade-off: if you are willing to be unfair, you can run shorter jobs to completion, but at the cost of response time; if you instead value fairness,

> TIP: OVERLAP ENABLES HIGHER UTILIZATION
> When possible, **overlap** operations to maximize the utilization of systems. Overlap is useful in many different domains, including when performing disk I/O or sending messages to remote machines; in either case, starting the operation and then switching to other work is a good idea, and improves the overall utilization and efficiency of the system.

response time is lowered, but at the cost of turnaround time. This type of **trade-off** is common in systems; you can't have your cake and eat it too[4].

We have developed two types of schedulers. The first type (SJF, STCF) optimizes turnaround time, but is bad for response time. The second type (RR) optimizes response time but is bad for turnaround. And we still have two assumptions which need to be relaxed: assumption 4 (that jobs do no I/O), and assumption 5 (that the run-time of each job is known). Let's tackle those assumptions next.

7.8 Incorporating I/O

First we will relax assumption 4 — of course all programs perform I/O. Imagine a program that didn't take any input: it would produce the same output each time. Imagine one without output: it is the proverbial tree falling in the forest, with no one to see it; it doesn't matter that it ran.

A scheduler clearly has a decision to make when a job initiates an I/O request, because the currently-running job won't be using the CPU during the I/O; it is **blocked** waiting for I/O completion. If the I/O is sent to a hard disk drive, the process might be blocked for a few milliseconds or longer, depending on the current I/O load of the drive. Thus, the scheduler should probably schedule another job on the CPU at that time.

The scheduler also has to make a decision when the I/O completes. When that occurs, an interrupt is raised, and the OS runs and moves the process that issued the I/O from blocked back to the ready state. Of course, it could even decide to run the job at that point. How should the OS treat each job?

To understand this issue better, let us assume we have two jobs, A and B, which each need 50 ms of CPU time. However, there is one obvious difference: A runs for 10 ms and then issues an I/O request (assume here that I/Os each take 10 ms), whereas B simply uses the CPU for 50 ms and performs no I/O. The scheduler runs A first, then B after (Figure 78).

Assume we are trying to build a STCF scheduler. How should such a scheduler account for the fact that A is broken up into 5 10-ms sub-jobs,

[4] A saying that confuses people, because it should be "You can't *keep* your cake and eat it too" (which is kind of obvious, no?). Amazingly, there is a wikipedia page about this saying; even more amazingly, it is kind of fun to read [W15]. As they say in Italian, you can't *Avere la botte piena e la moglie ubriaca.*

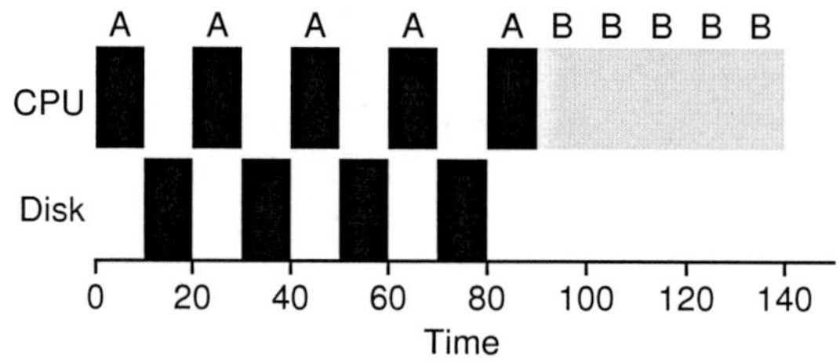

Figure 78: **Poor Use Of Resources**

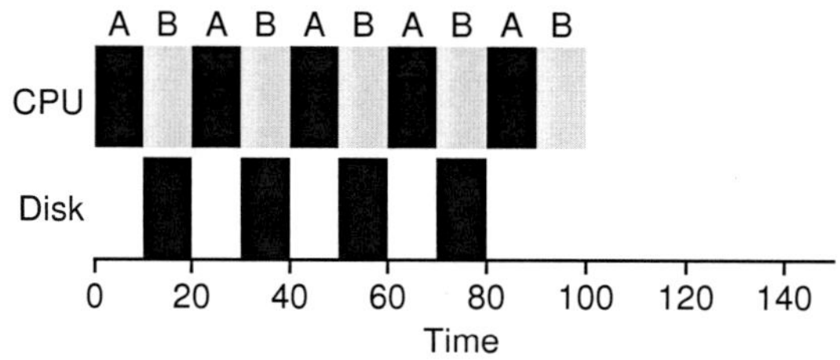

Figure 79: **Overlap Allows Better Use Of Resources**

whereas B is just a single 50-ms CPU demand? Clearly, just running one job and then the other without considering how to take I/O into account makes little sense.

A common approach is to treat each 10-ms sub-job of A as an independent job. Thus, when the system starts, its choice is whether to schedule a 10-ms A or a 50-ms B. With STCF, the choice is clear: choose the shorter one, in this case A. Then, when the first sub-job of A has completed, only B is left, and it begins running. Then a new sub-job of A is submitted, and it preempts B and runs for 10 ms. Doing so allows for **overlap**, with the CPU being used by one process while waiting for the I/O of another process to complete; the system is thus better utilized (see Figure 79).

And thus we see how a scheduler might incorporate I/O. By treating each CPU burst as a job, the scheduler makes sure processes that are "interactive" get run frequently. While those interactive jobs are performing I/O, other CPU-intensive jobs run, thus better utilizing the processor.

7.9 No More Oracle

With a basic approach to I/O in place, we come to our final assumption: that the scheduler knows the length of each job. As we said before, this is likely the worst assumption we could make. In fact, in a general-purpose OS (like the ones we care about), the OS usually knows very little about the length of each job. Thus, how can we build an approach that behaves like SJF/STCF without such *a priori* knowledge? Further, how can we incorporate some of the ideas we have seen with the RR scheduler so that response time is also quite good?

7.10 Summary

We have introduced the basic ideas behind scheduling and developed two families of approaches. The first runs the shortest job remaining and thus optimizes turnaround time; the second alternates between all jobs and thus optimizes response time. Both are bad where the other is good, alas, an inherent trade-off common in systems. We have also seen how we might incorporate I/O into the picture, but have still not solved the problem of the fundamental inability of the OS to see into the future. Shortly, we will see how to overcome this problem, by building a scheduler that uses the recent past to predict the future. This scheduler is known as the **multi-level feedback queue**, and it is the topic of the next chapter.

References

[B+79] "The Convoy Phenomenon" by M. Blasgen, J. Gray, M. Mitoma, T. Price. ACM Operating Systems Review, 13:2, April 1979. *Perhaps the first reference to convoys, which occurs in databases as well as the OS.*

[C54] "Priority Assignment in Waiting Line Problems" by A. Cobham. Journal of Operations Research, 2:70, pages 70–76, 1954. *The pioneering paper on using an SJF approach in scheduling the repair of machines.*

[K64] "Analysis of a Time-Shared Processor" by Leonard Kleinrock. Naval Research Logistics Quarterly, 11:1, pages 59–73, March 1964. *May be the first reference to the round-robin scheduling algorithm; certainly one of the first analyses of said approach to scheduling a time-shared system.*

[CK68] "Computer Scheduling Methods and their Countermeasures" by Edward G. Coffman and Leonard Kleinrock. AFIPS '68 (Spring), April 1968. *An excellent early introduction to and analysis of a number of basic scheduling disciplines.*

[J91] "The Art of Computer Systems Performance Analysis: Techniques for Experimental Design, Measurement, Simulation, and Modeling" by R. Jain. Interscience, New York, April 1991. *The standard text on computer systems measurement. A great reference for your library, for sure.*

[O45] "Animal Farm" by George Orwell. Secker and Warburg (London), 1945. *A great but depressing allegorical book about power and its corruptions. Some say it is a critique of Stalin and the pre-WWII Stalin era in the U.S.S.R; we say it's a critique of pigs.*

[PV56] "Machine Repair as a Priority Waiting-Line Problem" by Thomas E. Phipps Jr., W. R. Van Voorhis. Operations Research, 4:1, pages 76–86, February 1956. *Follow-on work that generalizes the SJF approach to machine repair from Cobham's original work; also postulates the utility of an STCF approach in such an environment. Specifically, "There are certain types of repair work, ... involving much dismantling and covering the floor with nuts and bolts, which certainly should not be interrupted once undertaken; in other cases it would be inadvisable to continue work on a long job if one or more short ones became available (p.81)."*

[MB91] "The effect of context switches on cache performance" by Jeffrey C. Mogul, Anita Borg. ASPLOS, 1991. *A nice study on how cache performance can be affected by context switching; less of an issue in today's systems where processors issue billions of instructions per second but context-switches still happen in the millisecond time range.*

[W15] "You can't have your cake and eat it" by Authors: Unknown.. Wikipedia (as of December 2015). `http://en.wikipedia.org/wiki/You_can't_have_your_cake_and_eat_it`. *The best part of this page is reading all the similar idioms from other languages. In Tamil, you can't "have both the moustache and drink the soup."*

Homework (Simulation)

This program, `scheduler.py`, allows you to see how different schedulers perform under scheduling metrics such as response time, turnaround time, and total wait time. See the README for details.

Questions

1. Compute the response time and turnaround time when running three jobs of length 200 with the SJF and FIFO schedulers.
2. Now do the same but with jobs of different lengths: 100, 200, and 300.
3. Now do the same, but also with the RR scheduler and a time-slice of 1.
4. For what types of workloads does SJF deliver the same turnaround times as FIFO?
5. For what types of workloads and quantum lengths does SJF deliver the same response times as RR?
6. What happens to response time with SJF as job lengths increase? Can you use the simulator to demonstrate the trend?
7. What happens to response time with RR as quantum lengths increase? Can you write an equation that gives the worst-case response time, given N jobs?

8

Scheduling: The Multi-Level Feedback Queue

In this chapter, we'll tackle the problem of developing one of the most well-known approaches to scheduling, known as the **Multi-level Feedback Queue (MLFQ)**. The Multi-level Feedback Queue (MLFQ) scheduler was first described by Corbato et al. in 1962 [C+62] in a system known as the Compatible Time-Sharing System (CTSS), and this work, along with later work on Multics, led the ACM to award Corbato its highest honor, the **Turing Award**. The scheduler has subsequently been refined throughout the years to the implementations you will encounter in some modern systems.

The fundamental problem MLFQ tries to address is two-fold. First, it would like to optimize *turnaround time*, which, as we saw in the previous note, is done by running shorter jobs first; unfortunately, the OS doesn't generally know how long a job will run for, exactly the knowledge that algorithms like SJF (or STCF) require. Second, MLFQ would like to make a system feel responsive to interactive users (i.e., users sitting and staring at the screen, waiting for a process to finish), and thus minimize *response time*; unfortunately, algorithms like Round Robin reduce response time but are terrible for turnaround time. Thus, our problem: given that we in general do not know anything about a process, how can we build a scheduler to achieve these goals? How can the scheduler learn, as the system runs, the characteristics of the jobs it is running, and thus make better scheduling decisions?

> THE CRUX:
> HOW TO SCHEDULE WITHOUT PERFECT KNOWLEDGE?
> How can we design a scheduler that both minimizes response time for interactive jobs while also minimizing turnaround time without *a priori* knowledge of job length?

> TIP: LEARN FROM HISTORY
> The multi-level feedback queue is an excellent example of a system that learns from the past to predict the future. Such approaches are common in operating systems (and many other places in Computer Science, including hardware branch predictors and caching algorithms). Such approaches work when jobs have phases of behavior and are thus predictable; of course, one must be careful with such techniques, as they can easily be wrong and drive a system to make worse decisions than they would have with no knowledge at all.

8.1 MLFQ: Basic Rules

To build such a scheduler, in this chapter we will describe the basic algorithms behind a multi-level feedback queue; although the specifics of many implemented MLFQs differ [E95], most approaches are similar.

In our treatment, the MLFQ has a number of distinct **queues**, each assigned a different **priority level**. At any given time, a job that is ready to run is on a single queue. MLFQ uses priorities to decide which job should run at a given time: a job with higher priority (i.e., a job on a higher queue) is chosen to run.

Of course, more than one job may be on a given queue, and thus have the *same* priority. In this case, we will just use round-robin scheduling among those jobs.

Thus, we arrive at the first two basic rules for MLFQ:

- **Rule 1:** If Priority(A) > Priority(B), A runs (B doesn't).
- **Rule 2:** If Priority(A) = Priority(B), A & B run in RR.

The key to MLFQ scheduling therefore lies in how the scheduler sets priorities. Rather than giving a fixed priority to each job, MLFQ *varies* the priority of a job based on its *observed behavior*. If, for example, a job repeatedly relinquishes the CPU while waiting for input from the keyboard, MLFQ will keep its priority high, as this is how an interactive process might behave. If, instead, a job uses the CPU intensively for long periods of time, MLFQ will reduce its priority. In this way, MLFQ will try to *learn* about processes as they run, and thus use the *history* of the job to predict its *future* behavior.

If we were to put forth a picture of what the queues might look like at a given instant, we might see something like the following (Figure 81). In the figure, two jobs (A and B) are at the highest priority level, while job C is in the middle and Job D is at the lowest priority. Given our current knowledge of how MLFQ works, the scheduler would just alternate time slices between A and B because they are the highest priority jobs in the system; poor jobs C and D would never even get to run — an outrage!

Of course, just showing a static snapshot of some queues does not really give you an idea of how MLFQ works. What we need is to under-

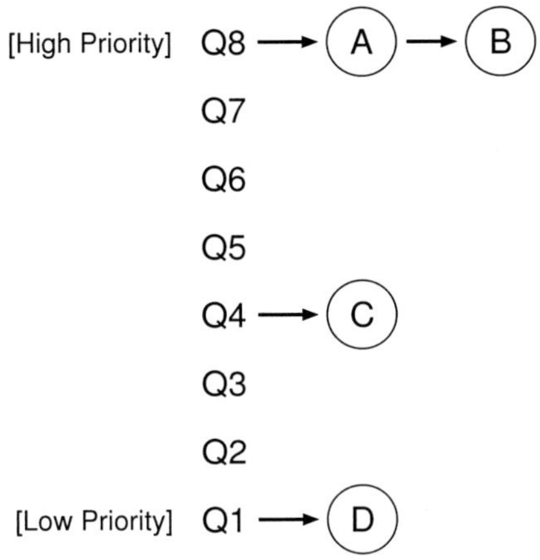

Figure 81: **MLFQ Example**

stand how job priority *changes* over time. And that, in a surprise only to those who are reading a chapter from this book for the first time, is exactly what we will do next.

8.2 Attempt #1: How To Change Priority

We now must decide how MLFQ is going to change the priority level of a job (and thus which queue it is on) over the lifetime of a job. To do this, we must keep in mind our workload: a mix of interactive jobs that are short-running (and may frequently relinquish the CPU), and some longer-running "CPU-bound" jobs that need a lot of CPU time but where response time isn't important. Here is our first attempt at a priority-adjustment algorithm:

- **Rule 3:** When a job enters the system, it is placed at the highest priority (the topmost queue).
- **Rule 4a:** If a job uses up an entire time slice while running, its priority is *reduced* (i.e., it moves down one queue).
- **Rule 4b:** If a job gives up the CPU before the time slice is up, it stays at the *same* priority level.

Example 1: A Single Long-Running Job

Let's look at some examples. First, we'll look at what happens when there has been a long running job in the system. Figure 82 shows what happens to this job over time in a three-queue scheduler.

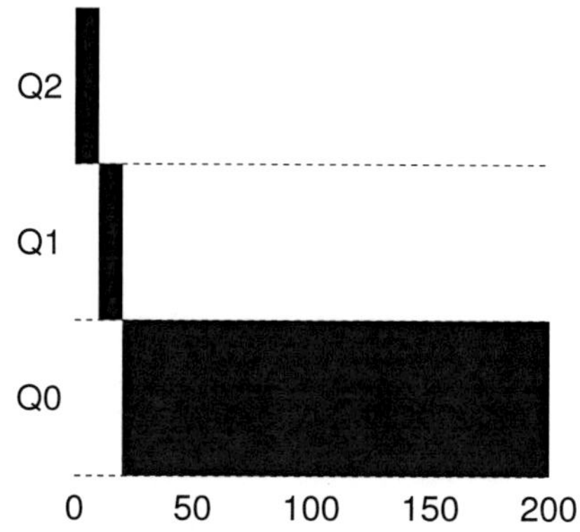

Figure 82: **Long-running Job Over Time**

As you can see in the example, the job enters at the highest priority (Q2). After a single time-slice of 10 ms, the scheduler reduces the job's priority by one, and thus the job is on Q1. After running at Q1 for a time slice, the job is finally lowered to the lowest priority in the system (Q0), where it remains. Pretty simple, no?

Example 2: Along Came A Short Job

Now let's look at a more complicated example, and hopefully see how MLFQ tries to approximate SJF. In this example, there are two jobs: A, which is a long-running CPU-intensive job, and B, which is a short-running interactive job. Assume A has been running for some time, and then B arrives. What will happen? Will MLFQ approximate SJF for B?

Figure 83 plots the results of this scenario. A (shown in black) is running along in the lowest-priority queue (as would any long-running CPU-intensive jobs); B (shown in gray) arrives at time $T = 100$, and thus is

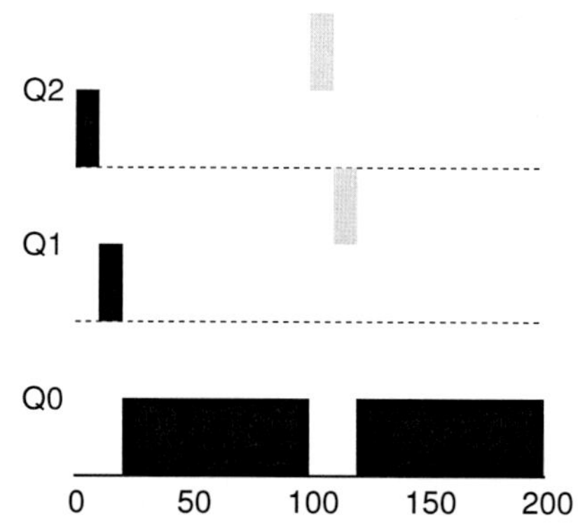

Figure 83: **Along Came An Interactive Job**

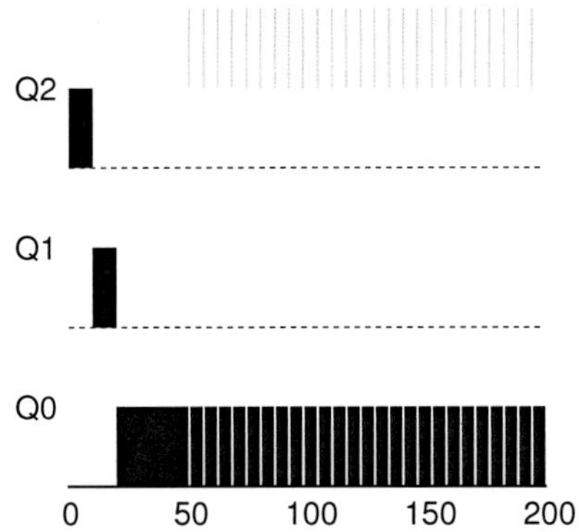

Figure 84: **A Mixed I/O-intensive and CPU-intensive Workload**

inserted into the highest queue; as its run-time is short (only 20 ms), B completes before reaching the bottom queue, in two time slices; then A resumes running (at low priority).

From this example, you can hopefully understand one of the major goals of the algorithm: because it doesn't *know* whether a job will be a short job or a long-running job, it first *assumes* it might be a short job, thus giving the job high priority. If it actually is a short job, it will run quickly and complete; if it is not a short job, it will slowly move down the queues, and thus soon prove itself to be a long-running more batch-like process. In this manner, MLFQ approximates SJF.

Example 3: What About I/O?

Let's now look at an example with some I/O. As Rule 4b states above, if a process gives up the processor before using up its time slice, we keep it at the same priority level. The intent of this rule is simple: if an interactive job, for example, is doing a lot of I/O (say by waiting for user input from the keyboard or mouse), it will relinquish the CPU before its time slice is complete; in such case, we don't wish to penalize the job and thus simply keep it at the same level.

Figure 84 shows an example of how this works, with an interactive job B (shown in gray) that needs the CPU only for 1 ms before performing an I/O competing for the CPU with a long-running batch job A (shown in black). The MLFQ approach keeps B at the highest priority because B keeps releasing the CPU; if B is an interactive job, MLFQ further achieves its goal of running interactive jobs quickly.

Problems With Our Current MLFQ

We thus have a basic MLFQ. It seems to do a fairly good job, sharing the CPU fairly between long-running jobs, and letting short or I/O-intensive interactive jobs run quickly. Unfortunately, the approach we have developed thus far contains serious flaws. Can you think of any?

(This is where you pause and think as deviously as you can)

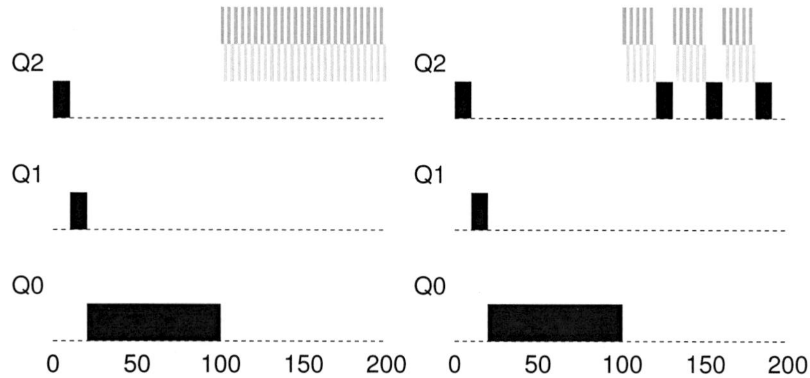

Figure 85: **Without (Left) and With (Right) Priority Boost**

First, there is the problem of **starvation**: if there are "too many" interactive jobs in the system, they will combine to consume *all* CPU time, and thus long-running jobs will *never* receive any CPU time (they **starve**). We'd like to make some progress on these jobs even in this scenario.

Second, a smart user could rewrite their program to **game the scheduler**. Gaming the scheduler generally refers to the idea of doing something sneaky to trick the scheduler into giving you more than your fair share of the resource. The algorithm we have described is susceptible to the following attack: before the time slice is over, issue an I/O operation (to some file you don't care about) and thus relinquish the CPU; doing so allows you to remain in the same queue, and thus gain a higher percentage of CPU time. When done right (e.g., by running for 99% of a time slice before relinquishing the CPU), a job could nearly monopolize the CPU.

Finally, a program may *change its behavior* over time; what was CPU-bound may transition to a phase of interactivity. With our current approach, such a job would be out of luck and not be treated like the other interactive jobs in the system.

> TIP: SCHEDULING MUST BE SECURE FROM ATTACK
> You might think that a scheduling policy, whether inside the OS itself (as discussed herein), or in a broader context (e.g., in a distributed storage system's I/O request handling [Y+18]), is not a **security** concern, but in increasingly many cases, it is exactly that. Consider the modern datacenter, in which users from around the world share CPUs, memories, networks, and storage systems; without care in policy design and enforcement, a single user may be able to adversely harm others and gain advantage for itself. Thus, scheduling policy forms an important part of the security of a system, and should be carefully constructed.

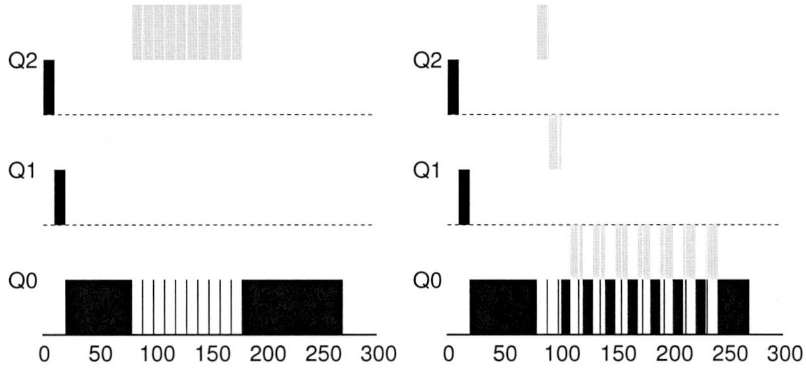

Figure 86: **Without (Left) and With (Right) Gaming Tolerance**

8.3 Attempt #2: The Priority Boost

Let's try to change the rules and see if we can avoid the problem of starvation. What could we do in order to guarantee that CPU-bound jobs will make some progress (even if it is not much?).

The simple idea here is to periodically **boost** the priority of all the jobs in system. There are many ways to achieve this, but let's just do something simple: throw them all in the topmost queue; hence, a new rule:

- **Rule 5:** After some time period S, move all the jobs in the system to the topmost queue.

Our new rule solves two problems at once. First, processes are guaranteed not to starve: by sitting in the top queue, a job will share the CPU with other high-priority jobs in a round-robin fashion, and thus eventually receive service. Second, if a CPU-bound job has become interactive, the scheduler treats it properly once it has received the priority boost.

Let's see an example. In this scenario, we just show the behavior of a long-running job when competing for the CPU with two short-running interactive jobs. Two graphs are shown in Figure 85 (page 90). On the left, there is no priority boost, and thus the long-running job gets starved once the two short jobs arrive; on the right, there is a priority boost every 50 ms (which is likely too small of a value, but used here for the example), and thus we at least guarantee that the long-running job will make some progress, getting boosted to the highest priority every 50 ms and thus getting to run periodically.

Of course, the addition of the time period S leads to the obvious question: what should S be set to? John Ousterhout, a well-regarded systems researcher [O11], used to call such values in systems **voo-doo constants**, because they seemed to require some form of black magic to set them correctly. Unfortunately, S has that flavor. If it is set too high, long-running jobs could starve; too low, and interactive jobs may not get a proper share of the CPU.

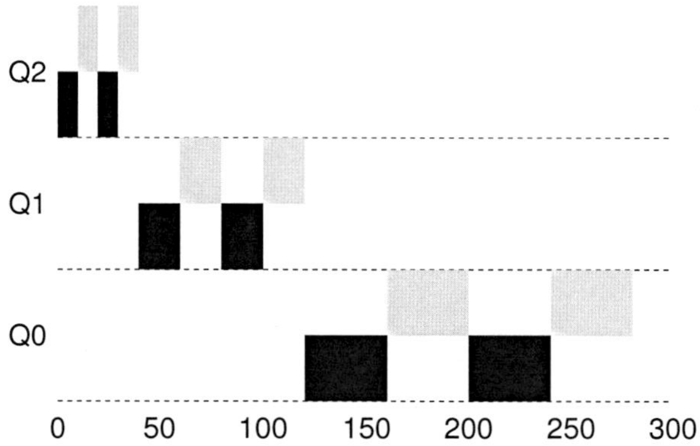

Figure 87: **Lower Priority, Longer Quanta**

8.4 Attempt #3: Better Accounting

We now have one more problem to solve: how to prevent gaming of our scheduler? The real culprit here, as you might have guessed, are Rules 4a and 4b, which let a job retain its priority by relinquishing the CPU before the time slice expires. So what should we do?

The solution here is to perform better **accounting** of CPU time at each level of the MLFQ. Instead of forgetting how much of a time slice a process used at a given level, the scheduler should keep track; once a process has used its allotment, it is demoted to the next priority queue. Whether it uses the time slice in one long burst or many small ones does not matter. We thus rewrite Rules 4a and 4b to the following single rule:

- **Rule 4:** Once a job uses up its time allotment at a given level (regardless of how many times it has given up the CPU), its priority is reduced (i.e., it moves down one queue).

Let's look at an example. Figure 86 (page 91) shows what happens when a workload tries to game the scheduler with the old Rules 4a and 4b (on the left) as well the new anti-gaming Rule 4. Without any protection from gaming, a process can issue an I/O just before a time slice ends and thus dominate CPU time. With such protections in place, regardless of the I/O behavior of the process, it slowly moves down the queues, and thus cannot gain an unfair share of the CPU.

8.5 Tuning MLFQ And Other Issues

A few other issues arise with MLFQ scheduling. One big question is how to **parameterize** such a scheduler. For example, how many queues should there be? How big should the time slice be per queue? How often should priority be boosted in order to avoid starvation and account for changes in behavior? There are no easy answers to these questions, and thus only some experience with workloads and subsequent tuning of the scheduler will lead to a satisfactory balance.

TIP: AVOID VOO-DOO CONSTANTS (OUSTERHOUT'S LAW)

Avoiding voo-doo constants is a good idea whenever possible. Unfortunately, as in the example above, it is often difficult. One could try to make the system learn a good value, but that too is not straightforward. The frequent result: a configuration file filled with default parameter values that a seasoned administrator can tweak when something isn't quite working correctly. As you can imagine, these are often left unmodified, and thus we are left to hope that the defaults work well in the field. This tip brought to you by our old OS professor, John Ousterhout, and hence we call it **Ousterhout's Law**.

For example, most MLFQ variants allow for varying time-slice length across different queues. The high-priority queues are usually given short time slices; they are comprised of interactive jobs, after all, and thus quickly alternating between them makes sense (e.g., 10 or fewer milliseconds). The low-priority queues, in contrast, contain long-running jobs that are CPU-bound; hence, longer time slices work well (e.g., 100s of ms). Figure 87 (page 92) shows an example in which two jobs run for 20 ms at the highest queue (with a 10-ms time slice), 40 ms in the middle (20-ms time slice), and with a 40-ms time slice at the lowest.

The Solaris MLFQ implementation — the Time-Sharing scheduling class, or TS — is particularly easy to configure; it provides a set of tables that determine exactly how the priority of a process is altered throughout its lifetime, how long each time slice is, and how often to boost the priority of a job [AD00]; an administrator can muck with this table in order to make the scheduler behave in different ways. Default values for the table are 60 queues, with slowly increasing time-slice lengths from 20 milliseconds (highest priority) to a few hundred milliseconds (lowest), and priorities boosted around every 1 second or so.

Other MLFQ schedulers don't use a table or the exact rules described in this chapter; rather they adjust priorities using mathematical formulae. For example, the FreeBSD scheduler (version 4.3) uses a formula to calculate the current priority level of a job, basing it on how much CPU the process has used [LM+89]; in addition, usage is decayed over time, providing the desired priority boost in a different manner than described herein. See Epema's paper for an excellent overview of such **decay-usage** algorithms and their properties [E95].

Finally, many schedulers have a few other features that you might encounter. For example, some schedulers reserve the highest priority levels for operating system work; thus typical user jobs can never obtain the highest levels of priority in the system. Some systems also allow some user **advice** to help set priorities; for example, by using the command-line utility `nice` you can increase or decrease the priority of a job (somewhat) and thus increase or decrease its chances of running at any given time. See the man page for more.

> TIP: USE ADVICE WHERE POSSIBLE
>
> As the operating system rarely knows what is best for each and every process of the system, it is often useful to provide interfaces to allow users or administrators to provide some **hints** to the OS. We often call such hints **advice**, as the OS need not necessarily pay attention to it, but rather might take the advice into account in order to make a better decision. Such hints are useful in many parts of the OS, including the scheduler (e.g., with `nice`), memory manager (e.g., `madvise`), and file system (e.g., informed prefetching and caching [P+95]).

8.6 MLFQ: Summary

We have described a scheduling approach known as the Multi-Level Feedback Queue (MLFQ). Hopefully you can now see why it is called that: it has *multiple levels* of queues, and uses *feedback* to determine the priority of a given job. History is its guide: pay attention to how jobs behave over time and treat them accordingly.

The refined set of MLFQ rules, spread throughout the chapter, are reproduced here for your viewing pleasure:

- **Rule 1:** If Priority(A) > Priority(B), A runs (B doesn't).
- **Rule 2:** If Priority(A) = Priority(B), A & B run in round-robin fashion using the time slice (quantum length) of the given queue.
- **Rule 3:** When a job enters the system, it is placed at the highest priority (the topmost queue).
- **Rule 4:** Once a job uses up its time allotment at a given level (regardless of how many times it has given up the CPU), its priority is reduced (i.e., it moves down one queue).
- **Rule 5:** After some time period S, move all the jobs in the system to the topmost queue.

MLFQ is interesting for the following reason: instead of demanding *a priori* knowledge of the nature of a job, it observes the execution of a job and prioritizes it accordingly. In this way, it manages to achieve the best of both worlds: it can deliver excellent overall performance (similar to SJF/STCF) for short-running interactive jobs, and is fair and makes progress for long-running CPU-intensive workloads. For this reason, many systems, including BSD UNIX derivatives [LM+89, B86], Solaris [M06], and Windows NT and subsequent Windows operating systems [CS97] use a form of MLFQ as their base scheduler.

References

[AD00] "Multilevel Feedback Queue Scheduling in Solaris" by Andrea Arpaci-Dusseau. Available: http://www.ostep.org/Citations/notes-solaris.pdf. *A great short set of notes by one of the authors on the details of the Solaris scheduler. OK, we are probably biased in this description, but the notes are pretty darn good.*

[B86] "The Design of the UNIX Operating System" by M.J. Bach. Prentice-Hall, 1986. *One of the classic old books on how a real UNIX operating system is built; a definite must-read for kernel hackers.*

[C+62] "An Experimental Time-Sharing System" by F. J. Corbato, M. M. Daggett, R. C. Daley. IFIPS 1962. *A bit hard to read, but the source of many of the first ideas in multi-level feedback scheduling. Much of this later went into Multics, which one could argue was the most influential operating system of all time.*

[CS97] "Inside Windows NT" by Helen Custer and David A. Solomon. Microsoft Press, 1997. *The NT book, if you want to learn about something other than UNIX. Of course, why would you? OK, we're kidding; you might actually work for Microsoft some day you know.*

[E95] "An Analysis of Decay-Usage Scheduling in Multiprocessors" by D.H.J. Epema. SIGMETRICS '95. *A nice paper on the state of the art of scheduling back in the mid 1990s, including a good overview of the basic approach behind decay-usage schedulers.*

[LM+89] "The Design and Implementation of the 4.3BSD UNIX Operating System" by S.J. Leffler, M.K. McKusick, M.J. Karels, J.S. Quarterman. Addison-Wesley, 1989. *Another OS classic, written by four of the main people behind BSD. The later versions of this book, while more up to date, don't quite match the beauty of this one.*

[M06] "Solaris Internals: Solaris 10 and OpenSolaris Kernel Architecture" by Richard McDougall. Prentice-Hall, 2006. *A good book about Solaris and how it works.*

[O11] "John Ousterhout's Home Page" by John Ousterhout. `www.stanford.edu/~ouster/`. *The home page of the famous Professor Ousterhout. The two co-authors of this book had the pleasure of taking graduate operating systems from Ousterhout while in graduate school; indeed, this is where the two co-authors got to know each other, eventually leading to marriage, kids, and even this book. Thus, you really can blame Ousterhout for this entire mess you're in.*

[P+95] "Informed Prefetching and Caching" by R.H. Patterson, G.A. Gibson, E. Ginting, D. Stodolsky, J. Zelenka. SOSP '95, Copper Mountain, Colorado, October 1995. *A fun paper about some very cool ideas in file systems, including how applications can give the OS advice about what files it is accessing and how it plans to access them.*

[Y+18] "Principled Schedulability Analysis for Distributed Storage Systems using Thread Architecture Models" by Suli Yang, Jing Liu, Andrea C. Arpaci-Dusseau, Remzi H. Arpaci-Dusseau. OSDI '18, San Diego, California. *A recent work of our group that demonstrates the difficulty of scheduling I/O requests within modern distributed storage systems such as Hive/HDFS, Cassandra, MongoDB, and Riak. Without care, a single user might be able to monopolize system resources.*

Homework (Simulation)

This program, `mlfq.py`, allows you to see how the MLFQ scheduler presented in this chapter behaves. See the README for details.

Questions

1. Run a few randomly-generated problems with just two jobs and two queues; compute the MLFQ execution trace for each. Make your life easier by limiting the length of each job and turning off I/Os.
2. How would you run the scheduler to reproduce each of the examples in the chapter?
3. How would you configure the scheduler parameters to behave just like a round-robin scheduler?
4. Craft a workload with two jobs and scheduler parameters so that one job takes advantage of the older Rules 4a and 4b (turned on with the `-S` flag) to game the scheduler and obtain 99% of the CPU over a particular time interval.
5. Given a system with a quantum length of 10 ms in its highest queue, how often would you have to boost jobs back to the highest priority level (with the `-B` flag) in order to guarantee that a single long-running (and potentially-starving) job gets at least 5% of the CPU?
6. One question that arises in scheduling is which end of a queue to add a job that just finished I/O; the `-I` flag changes this behavior for this scheduling simulator. Play around with some workloads and see if you can see the effect of this flag.

9

Scheduling: Proportional Share

In this chapter, we'll examine a different type of scheduler known as a **proportional-share** scheduler, also sometimes referred to as a **fair-share** scheduler. Proportional-share is based around a simple concept: instead of optimizing for turnaround or response time, a scheduler might instead try to guarantee that each job obtain a certain percentage of CPU time.

An excellent early example of proportional-share scheduling is found in research by Waldspurger and Weihl [WW94], and is known as **lottery scheduling**; however, the idea is certainly older [KL88]. The basic idea is quite simple: every so often, hold a lottery to determine which process should get to run next; processes that should run more often should be given more chances to win the lottery. Easy, no? Now, onto the details! But not before our crux:

> CRUX: HOW TO SHARE THE CPU PROPORTIONALLY
>
> How can we design a scheduler to share the CPU in a proportional manner? What are the key mechanisms for doing so? How effective are they?

9.1 Basic Concept: Tickets Represent Your Share

Underlying lottery scheduling is one very basic concept: **tickets**, which are used to represent the share of a resource that a process (or user or whatever) should receive. The percent of tickets that a process has represents its share of the system resource in question.

Let's look at an example. Imagine two processes, A and B, and further that A has 75 tickets while B has only 25. Thus, what we would like is for A to receive 75% of the CPU and B the remaining 25%.

Lottery scheduling achieves this probabilistically (but not deterministically) by holding a lottery every so often (say, every time slice). Holding a lottery is straightforward: the scheduler must know how many total tickets there are (in our example, there are 100). The scheduler then picks

TIP: USE RANDOMNESS

One of the most beautiful aspects of lottery scheduling is its use of **randomness**. When you have to make a decision, using such a randomized approach is often a robust and simple way of doing so.

Random approaches have at least three advantages over more traditional decisions. First, random often avoids strange corner-case behaviors that a more traditional algorithm may have trouble handling. For example, consider the LRU replacement policy (studied in more detail in a future chapter on virtual memory); while often a good replacement algorithm, LRU attains worst-case performance for some cyclic-sequential workloads. Random, on the other hand, has no such worst case.

Second, random also is lightweight, requiring little state to track alternatives. In a traditional fair-share scheduling algorithm, tracking how much CPU each process has received requires per-process accounting, which must be updated after running each process. Doing so randomly necessitates only the most minimal of per-process state (e.g., the number of tickets each has).

Finally, random can be quite fast. As long as generating a random number is quick, making the decision is also, and thus random can be used in a number of places where speed is required. Of course, the faster the need, the more random tends towards pseudo-random.

a winning ticket, which is a number from 0 to 99[1]. Assuming A holds tickets 0 through 74 and B 75 through 99, the winning ticket simply determines whether A or B runs. The scheduler then loads the state of that winning process and runs it.

Here is an example output of a lottery scheduler's winning tickets:

```
63 85 70 39 76 17 29 41 36 39 10 99 68 83 63 62 43  0 49
```

Here is the resulting schedule:

```
A     A  A     A  A  A  A  A  A     A     A  A  A  A  A
   B        B                    B     B
```

As you can see from the example, the use of randomness in lottery scheduling leads to a probabilistic correctness in meeting the desired proportion, but no guarantee. In our example above, B only gets to run 4 out of 20 time slices (20%), instead of the desired 25% allocation. However, the longer these two jobs compete, the more likely they are to achieve the desired percentages.

[1]Computer Scientists always start counting at 0. It is so odd to non-computer-types that famous people have felt obliged to write about why we do it this way [D82].

> TIP: USE TICKETS TO REPRESENT SHARES
> One of the most powerful (and basic) mechanisms in the design of lottery (and stride) scheduling is that of the **ticket**. The ticket is used to represent a process's share of the CPU in these examples, but can be applied much more broadly. For example, in more recent work on virtual memory management for hypervisors, Waldspurger shows how tickets can be used to represent a guest operating system's share of memory [W02]. Thus, if you are ever in need of a mechanism to represent a proportion of ownership, this concept just might be ... (wait for it) ... the ticket.

9.2 Ticket Mechanisms

Lottery scheduling also provides a number of mechanisms to manipulate tickets in different and sometimes useful ways. One way is with the concept of **ticket currency**. Currency allows a user with a set of tickets to allocate tickets among their own jobs in whatever currency they would like; the system then automatically converts said currency into the correct global value.

For example, assume users A and B have each been given 100 tickets. User A is running two jobs, A1 and A2, and gives them each 500 tickets (out of 1000 total) in A's currency. User B is running only 1 job and gives it 10 tickets (out of 10 total). The system converts A1's and A2's allocation from 500 each in A's currency to 50 each in the global currency; similarly, B1's 10 tickets is converted to 100 tickets. The lottery is then held over the global ticket currency (200 total) to determine which job runs.

```
User A -> 500 (A's currency) to A1 ->  50 (global currency)
       -> 500 (A's currency) to A2 ->  50 (global currency)
User B ->  10 (B's currency) to B1 -> 100 (global currency)
```

Another useful mechanism is **ticket transfer**. With transfers, a process can temporarily hand off its tickets to another process. This ability is especially useful in a client/server setting, where a client process sends a message to a server asking it to do some work on the client's behalf. To speed up the work, the client can pass the tickets to the server and thus try to maximize the performance of the server while the server is handling the client's request. When finished, the server then transfers the tickets back to the client and all is as before.

Finally, **ticket inflation** can sometimes be a useful technique. With inflation, a process can temporarily raise or lower the number of tickets it owns. Of course, in a competitive scenario with processes that do not trust one another, this makes little sense; one greedy process could give itself a vast number of tickets and take over the machine. Rather, inflation can be applied in an environment where a group of processes trust one another; in such a case, if any one process knows it needs more CPU time, it can boost its ticket value as a way to reflect that need to the system, all without communicating with any other processes.

```
// counter: used to track if we've found the winner yet
int counter = 0;

// winner: use some call to a random number generator to
//         get a value, between 0 and the total # of tickets
int winner = getrandom(0, totaltickets);

// current: use this to walk through the list of jobs
node_t *current = head;
while (current) {
    counter = counter + current->tickets;
    if (counter > winner)
        break; // found the winner
    current = current->next;
}
// 'current' is the winner: schedule it...
```

Figure 91: **Lottery Scheduling Decision Code**

9.3 Implementation

Probably the most amazing thing about lottery scheduling is the simplicity of its implementation. All you need is a good random number generator to pick the winning ticket, a data structure to track the processes of the system (e.g., a list), and the total number of tickets.

Let's assume we keep the processes in a list. Here is an example comprised of three processes, A, B, and C, each with some number of tickets.

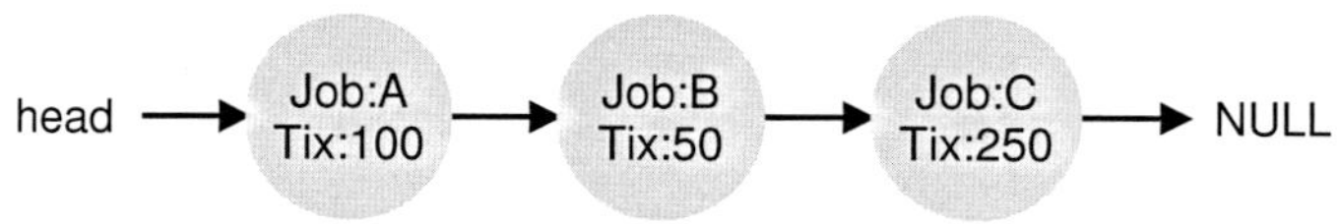

To make a scheduling decision, we first have to pick a random number (the winner) from the total number of tickets (400)[2] Let's say we pick the number 300. Then, we simply traverse the list, with a simple counter used to help us find the winner (Figure 91).

The code walks the list of processes, adding each ticket value to `counter` until the value exceeds `winner`. Once that is the case, the current list element is the winner. With our example of the winning ticket being 300, the following takes place. First, `counter` is incremented to 100 to account for A's tickets; because 100 is less than 300, the loop continues. Then `counter` would be updated to 150 (B's tickets), still less than 300 and thus again we continue. Finally, `counter` is updated to 400 (clearly greater than 300), and thus we break out of the loop with `current` pointing at C (the winner).

[2]Surprisingly, as pointed out by Björn Lindberg, this can be challenging to do correctly; for more details, see `http://stackoverflow.com/questions/2509679/how-to-generate-a-random-number-from-within-a-range`.

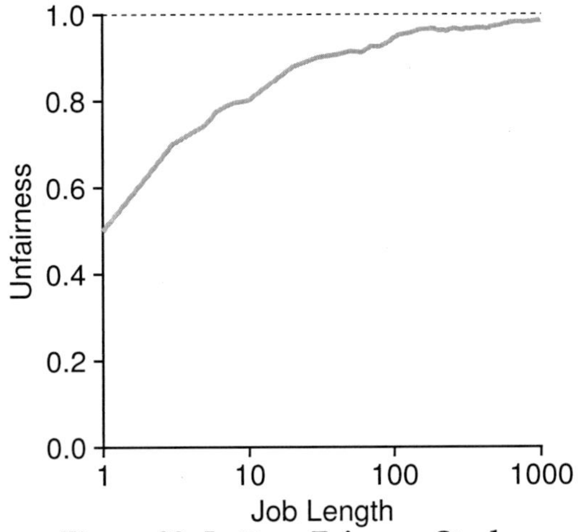

Figure 92: **Lottery Fairness Study**

To make this process most efficient, it might generally be best to organize the list in sorted order, from the highest number of tickets to the lowest. The ordering does not affect the correctness of the algorithm; however, it does ensure in general that the fewest number of list iterations are taken, especially if there are a few processes that possess most of the tickets.

9.4 An Example

To make the dynamics of lottery scheduling more understandable, we now perform a brief study of the completion time of two jobs competing against one another, each with the same number of tickets (100) and same run time (R, which we will vary).

In this scenario, we'd like for each job to finish at roughly the same time, but due to the randomness of lottery scheduling, sometimes one job finishes before the other. To quantify this difference, we define a simple **unfairness metric**, U which is simply the time the first job completes divided by the time that the second job completes. For example, if $R = 10$, and the first job finishes at time 10 (and the second job at 20), $U = \frac{10}{20} = 0.5$. When both jobs finish at nearly the same time, U will be quite close to 1. In this scenario, that is our goal: a perfectly fair scheduler would achieve $U = 1$.

Figure 92 plots the average unfairness as the length of the two jobs (R) is varied from 1 to 1000 over thirty trials (results are generated via the simulator provided at the end of the chapter). As you can see from the graph, when the job length is not very long, average unfairness can be quite severe. Only as the jobs run for a significant number of time slices does the lottery scheduler approach the desired outcome.

9.5 How To Assign Tickets?

One problem we have not addressed with lottery scheduling is: how to assign tickets to jobs? This problem is a tough one, because of course how the system behaves is strongly dependent on how tickets are allocated. One approach is to assume that the users know best; in such a case, each user is handed some number of tickets, and a user can allocate tickets to any jobs they run as desired. However, this solution is a non-solution: it really doesn't tell you what to do. Thus, given a set of jobs, the "ticket-assignment problem" remains open.

9.6 Why Not Deterministic?

You might also be wondering: why use randomness at all? As we saw above, while randomness gets us a simple (and approximately correct) scheduler, it occasionally will not deliver the exact right proportions, especially over short time scales. For this reason, Waldspurger invented **stride scheduling**, a deterministic fair-share scheduler [W95].

Stride scheduling is also straightforward. Each job in the system has a stride, which is inverse in proportion to the number of tickets it has. In our example above, with jobs A, B, and C, with 100, 50, and 250 tickets, respectively, we can compute the stride of each by dividing some large number by the number of tickets each process has been assigned. For example, if we divide 10,000 by each of those ticket values, we obtain the following stride values for A, B, and C: 100, 200, and 40. We call this value the **stride** of each process; every time a process runs, we will increment a counter for it (called its **pass** value) by its stride to track its global progress.

The scheduler then uses the stride and pass to determine which process should run next. The basic idea is simple: at any given time, pick the process to run that has the lowest pass value so far; when you run a process, increment its pass counter by its stride. A pseudocode implementation is provided by Waldspurger [W95]:

```
curr = remove_min(queue);    // pick client with min pass
schedule(curr);              // run for quantum
curr->pass += curr->stride; // update pass using stride
insert(queue, curr);         // return curr to queue
```

In our example, we start with three processes (A, B, and C), with stride values of 100, 200, and 40, and all with pass values initially at 0. Thus, at first, any of the processes might run, as their pass values are equally low. Assume we pick A (arbitrarily; any of the processes with equal low pass values can be chosen). A runs; when finished with the time slice, we update its pass value to 100. Then we run B, whose pass value is then set to 200. Finally, we run C, whose pass value is incremented to 40. At this point, the algorithm will pick the lowest pass value, which is C's, and

Pass(A) (stride=100)	Pass(B) (stride=200)	Pass(C) (stride=40)	Who Runs?
0	0	0	A
100	0	0	B
100	200	0	C
100	200	40	C
100	200	80	C
100	200	120	A
200	200	120	C
200	200	160	C
200	200	200	...

Figure 93: **Stride Scheduling: A Trace**

run it, updating its pass to 80 (C's stride is 40, as you recall). Then C will run again (still the lowest pass value), raising its pass to 120. A will run now, updating its pass to 200 (now equal to B's). Then C will run twice more, updating its pass to 160 then 200. At this point, all pass values are equal again, and the process will repeat, ad infinitum. Figure 93 traces the behavior of the scheduler over time.

As we can see from the figure, C ran five times, A twice, and B just once, exactly in proportion to their ticket values of 250, 100, and 50. Lottery scheduling achieves the proportions probabilistically over time; stride scheduling gets them exactly right at the end of each scheduling cycle.

So you might be wondering: given the precision of stride scheduling, why use lottery scheduling at all? Well, lottery scheduling has one nice property that stride scheduling does not: no global state. Imagine a new job enters in the middle of our stride scheduling example above; what should its pass value be? Should it be set to 0? If so, it will monopolize the CPU. With lottery scheduling, there is no global state per process; we simply add a new process with whatever tickets it has, update the single global variable to track how many total tickets we have, and go from there. In this way, lottery makes it much easier to incorporate new processes in a sensible manner.

9.7 The Linux Completely Fair Scheduler (CFS)

Despite these earlier works in fair-share scheduling, the current Linux approach achieves similar goals in an alternate manner. The scheduler, entitled the **Completely Fair Scheduler** (or **CFS**) [J09], implements fair-share scheduling, but does so in a highly efficient and scalable manner.

To achieve its efficiency goals, CFS aims to spend very little time making scheduling decisions, through both its inherent design and its clever use of data structures well-suited to the task. Recent studies have shown that scheduler efficiency is surprisingly important; specifically, in a study of Google datacenters, Kanev et al. show that even after aggressive optimization, scheduling uses about 5% of overall datacenter CPU time. Reducing that overhead as much as possible is thus a key goal in modern scheduler architecture.

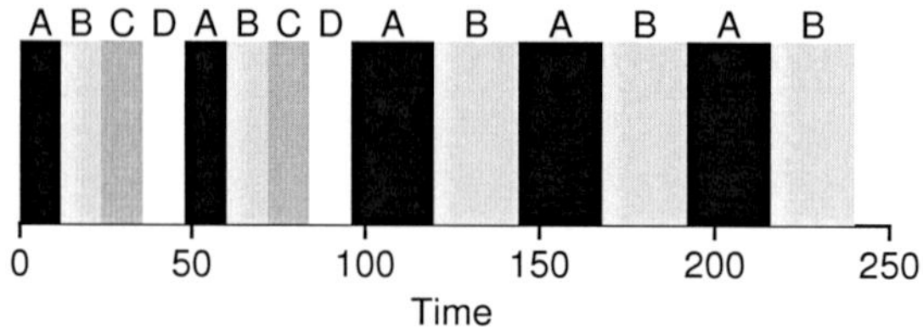

Figure 94: **CFS Simple Example**

Basic Operation

Whereas most schedulers are based around the concept of a fixed time slice, CFS operates a bit differently. Its goal is simple: to fairly divide a CPU evenly among all competing processes. It does so through a simple counting-based technique known as **virtual runtime (`vruntime`)**.

As each process runs, it accumulates `vruntime`. In the most basic case, each process's `vruntime` increases at the same rate, in proportion with physical (real) time. When a scheduling decision occurs, CFS will pick the process with the *lowest* `vruntime` to run next.

This raises a question: how does the scheduler know when to stop the currently running process, and run the next one? The tension here is clear: if CFS switches too often, fairness is increased, as CFS will ensure that each process receives its share of CPU even over miniscule time windows, but at the cost of performance (too much context switching); if CFS switches less often, performance is increased (reduced context switching), but at the cost of near-term fairness.

CFS manages this tension through various control parameters. The first is **`sched_latency`**. CFS uses this value to determine how long one process should run before considering a switch (effectively determining its time slice but in a dynamic fashion). A typical `sched_latency` value is 48 (milliseconds); CFS divides this value by the number (n) of processes running on the CPU to determine the time slice for a process, and thus ensures that over this period of time, CFS will be completely fair.

For example, if there are $n = 4$ processes running, CFS divides the value of `sched_latency` by n to arrive at a per-process time slice of 12 ms. CFS then schedules the first job and runs it until it has used 12 ms of (virtual) runtime, and then checks to see if there is a job with lower `vruntime` to run instead. In this case, there is, and CFS would switch to one of the three other jobs, and so forth. Figure 94 shows an example where the four jobs (A, B, C, D) each run for two time slices in this fashion; two of them (C, D) then complete, leaving just two remaining, which then each run for 24 ms in round-robin fashion.

But what if there are "too many" processes running? Wouldn't that lead to too small of a time slice, and thus too many context switches? Good question! And the answer is yes.

To address this issue, CFS adds another parameter, **`min_granularity`**, which is usually set to a value like 6 ms. CFS will never set the time slice of a process to less than this value, ensuring that not too much time is spent in scheduling overhead.

For example, if there are ten processes running, our original calculation would divide sched_latency by ten to determine the time slice (result: 4.8 ms). However, because of min_granularity, CFS will set the time slice of each process to 6 ms instead. Although CFS won't (quite) be perfectly fair over the target scheduling latency (sched_latency) of 48 ms, it will be close, while still achieving high CPU efficiency.

Note that CFS utilizes a periodic timer interrupt, which means it can only make decisions at fixed time intervals. This interrupt goes off frequently (e.g., every 1 ms), giving CFS a chance to wake up and determine if the current job has reached the end of its run. If a job has a time slice that is not a perfect multiple of the timer interrupt interval, that is OK; CFS tracks vruntime precisely, which means that over the long haul, it will eventually approximate ideal sharing of the CPU.

Weighting (Niceness)

CFS also enables controls over process priority, enabling users or administrators to give some processes a higher share of the CPU. It does this not with tickets, but through a classic UNIX mechanism known as the **nice** level of a process. The nice parameter can be set anywhere from -20 to +19 for a process, with a default of 0. Positive nice values imply *lower* priority and negative values imply *higher* priority; when you're too nice, you just don't get as much (scheduling) attention, alas.

CFS maps the nice value of each process to a weight, as shown here:

```
static const int prio_to_weight[40] = {
    /* -20 */ 88761, 71755, 56483, 46273, 36291,
    /* -15 */ 29154, 23254, 18705, 14949, 11916,
    /* -10 */  9548,  7620,  6100,  4904,  3906,
    /*  -5 */  3121,  2501,  1991,  1586,  1277,
    /*   0 */  1024,   820,   655,   526,   423,
    /*   5 */   335,   272,   215,   172,   137,
    /*  10 */   110,    87,    70,    56,    45,
    /*  15 */    36,    29,    23,    18,    15,
};
```

These weights allow us to compute the effective time slice of each process (as we did before), but now accounting for their priority differences. The formula used to do so is as follows:

$$\texttt{time\_slice}_k = \frac{\texttt{weight}_k}{\sum_{i=0}^{n-1} \texttt{weight}_i} \cdot \texttt{sched\_latency} \tag{9.1}$$

Let's do an example to see how this works. Assume there are two jobs, A and B. A, because it's our most precious job, is given a higher priority by assigning it a nice value of -5; B, because we hates it[3], just has the default priority (nice value equal to 0). This means $\texttt{weight}_A$ (from the table) is 3121, whereas $\texttt{weight}_B$ is 1024. If you then compute the time slice of each job, you'll find that A's time slice is about $\frac{3}{4}$ of `sched_latency` (hence, 36 ms), and B's about $\frac{1}{4}$ (hence, 12 ms).

In addition to generalizing the time slice calculation, the way CFS calculates `vruntime` must also be adapted. Here is the new formula, which takes the actual run time that process i has accrued ($\texttt{runtime}_i$) and scales it inversely by the weight of the process. In our running example, A's `vruntime` will accumulate at one-third the rate of B's.

$$\texttt{vruntime}_i = \texttt{vruntime}_i + \frac{\texttt{weight}_0}{\texttt{weight}_i} \cdot \texttt{runtime}_i \tag{9.2}$$

One smart aspect of the construction of the table of weights above is that the table preserves CPU proportionality ratios when the difference in nice values is constant. For example, if process A instead had a nice value of 5 (not -5), and process B had a nice value of 10 (not 0), CFS would schedule them in exactly the same manner as before. Run through the math yourself to see why.

Using Red-Black Trees

One major focus of CFS is efficiency, as stated above. For a scheduler, there are many facets of efficiency, but one of them is as simple as this: when the scheduler has to find the next job to run, it should do so as quickly as possible. Simple data structures like lists don't scale: modern systems sometimes are comprised of 1000s of processes, and thus searching through a long-list every so many milliseconds is wasteful.

CFS addresses this by keeping processes in a **red-black tree** [B72]. A red-black tree is one of many types of balanced trees; in contrast to a simple binary tree (which can degenerate to list-like performance under worst-case insertion patterns), balanced trees do a little extra work to maintain low depths, and thus ensure that operations are logarithmic (and not linear) in time.

CFS does not keep *all* process in this structure; rather, only running (or runnable) processes are kept therein. If a process goes to sleep (say, waiting on an I/O to complete, or for a network packet to arrive), it is removed from the tree and kept track of elsewhere.

Let's look at an example to make this more clear. Assume there are ten jobs, and that they have the following values of `vruntime`: 1, 5, 9, 10, 14, 18, 17, 21, 22, and 24. If we kept these jobs in an ordered list, finding the next job to run would be simple: just remove the first element. However, when placing that job back into the list (in order), we would have to scan

[3]Yes, yes, we are using bad grammar here on purpose, please don't send in a bug fix. Why? Well, just a most mild of references to the Lord of the Rings, and our favorite anti-hero Gollum, nothing to get too excited about.

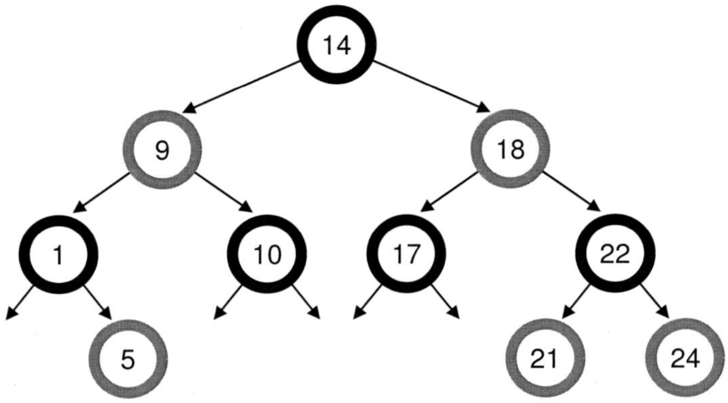

Figure 95: **CFS Red-Black Tree**

the list, looking for the right spot to insert it, an $O(n)$ operation. Any search is also quite inefficient, also taking linear time on average.

Keeping the same values in a red-black tree makes most operations more efficient, as depicted in Figure 95. Processes are ordered in the tree by `vruntime`, and most operations (such as insertion and deletion) are logarithmic in time, i.e., $O(\log n)$. When n is in the thousands, logarithmic is noticeably more efficient than linear.

Dealing With I/O And Sleeping Processes

One problem with picking the lowest `vruntime` to run next arises with jobs that have gone to sleep for a long period of time. Imagine two processes, A and B, one of which (A) runs continuously, and the other (B) which has gone to sleep for a long period of time (say, 10 seconds). When B wakes up, its `vruntime` will be 10 seconds behind A's, and thus (if we're not careful), B will now monopolize the CPU for the next 10 seconds while it catches up, effectively starving A.

CFS handles this case by altering the `vruntime` of a job when it wakes up. Specifically, CFS sets the `vruntime` of that job to the minimum value found in the tree (remember, the tree only contains running jobs) [B+18]. In this way, CFS avoids starvation, but not without a cost: jobs that sleep for short periods of time frequently do not ever get their fair share of the CPU [AC97].

Other CFS Fun

CFS has many other features, too many to discuss at this point in the book. It includes numerous heuristics to improve cache performance, has strategies for handling multiple CPUs effectively (as discussed later in the book), can schedule across large groups of processes (instead of treating each process as an independent entity), and many other interesting features. Read recent research, starting with Bouron [B+18], to learn more.

TIP: USE EFFICIENT DATA STRUCTURES WHEN APPROPRIATE

In many cases, a list will do. In many cases, it will not. Knowing which data structure to use when is a hallmark of good engineering. In the case discussed herein, simple lists found in earlier schedulers simply do not work well on modern systems, particular in the heavily loaded servers found in datacenters. Such systems contain thousands of active processes; searching through a long list to find the next job to run on each core every few milliseconds would waste precious CPU cycles. A better structure was needed, and CFS provided one by adding an excellent implementation of a red-black tree. More generally, when picking a data structure for a system you are building, carefully consider its access patterns and its frequency of usage; by understanding these, you will be able to implement the right structure for the task at hand.

9.8 Summary

We have introduced the concept of proportional-share scheduling and briefly discussed three approaches: lottery scheduling, stride scheduling, and the Completely Fair Scheduler (CFS) of Linux. Lottery uses randomness in a clever way to achieve proportional share; stride does so deterministically. CFS, the only "real" scheduler discussed in this chapter, is a bit like weighted round-robin with dynamic time slices, but built to scale and perform well under load; to our knowledge, it is the most widely used fair-share scheduler in existence today.

No scheduler is a panacea, and fair-share schedulers have their fair share of problems. One issue is that such approaches do not particularly mesh well with I/O [AC97]; as mentioned above, jobs that perform I/O occasionally may not get their fair share of CPU. Another issue is that they leave open the hard problem of ticket or priority assignment, i.e., how do you know how many tickets your browser should be allocated, or to what nice value to set your text editor? Other general-purpose schedulers (such as the MLFQ we discussed previously, and other similar Linux schedulers) handle these issues automatically and thus may be more easily deployed.

The good news is that there are many domains in which these problems are not the dominant concern, and proportional-share schedulers are used to great effect. For example, in a **virtualized** data center (or **cloud**), where you might like to assign one-quarter of your CPU cycles to the Windows VM and the rest to your base Linux installation, proportional sharing can be simple and effective. The idea can also be extended to other resources; see Waldspurger [W02] for further details on how to proportionally share memory in VMWare's ESX Server.

References

[AC97] "Extending Proportional-Share Scheduling to a Network of Workstations" by Andrea C. Arpaci-Dusseau and David E. Culler. PDPTA'97, June 1997. *A paper by one of the authors on how to extend proportional-share scheduling to work better in a clustered environment.*

[B+18] "The Battle of the Schedulers: FreeBSD ULE vs. Linux CFS" by J. Bouron, S. Chevalley, B. Lepers, W. Zwaenepoel, R. Gouicem, J. Lawall, G. Muller, J. Sopena. USENIX ATC '18, July 2018, Boston, Massachusetts. *A recent, detailed work comparing Linux CFS and the FreeBSD schedulers. An excellent overview of each scheduler is also provided. The result of the comparison: inconclusive (in some cases CFS was better, and in others, ULE (the BSD scheduler), was. Sometimes in life there are no easy answers.*

[B72] "Symmetric binary B-Trees: Data Structure And Maintenance Algorithms" by Rudolf Bayer. Acta Informatica, Volume 1, Number 4, December 1972. *A cool balanced tree introduced before you were born (most likely). One of many balanced trees out there; study your algorithms book for more alternatives!*

[D82] "Why Numbering Should Start At Zero" by Edsger Dijkstra, August 1982. Available: `http://www.cs.utexas.edu/users/EWD/ewd08xx/EWD831.PDF`. *A short note from E. Dijkstra, one of the pioneers of computer science. We'll be hearing much more on this guy in the section on Concurrency. In the meanwhile, enjoy this note, which includes this motivating quote: "One of my colleagues — not a computing scientist — accused a number of younger computing scientists of 'pedantry' because they started numbering at zero." The note explains why doing so is logical.*

[K+15] "Profiling A Warehouse-scale Computer" by S. Kanev, P. Ranganathan, J. P. Darago, K. Hazelwood, T. Moseley, G. Wei, D. Brooks. ISCA '15, June, 2015, Portland, Oregon. *A fascinating study of where the cycles go in modern data centers, which are increasingly where most of computing happens. Almost 20% of CPU time is spent in the operating system, 5% in the scheduler alone!*

[J09] "Inside The Linux 2.6 Completely Fair Scheduler" by M. Tim Jones. December 15, 2009. `http://ostep.org/Citations/inside-cfs.pdf`. *A simple overview of CFS from its earlier days. CFS was created by Ingo Molnar in a short burst of creativity which led to a 100K kernel patch developed in 62 hours.*

[KL88] "A Fair Share Scheduler" by J. Kay and P. Lauder. CACM, Volume 31 Issue 1, January 1988. *An early reference to a fair-share scheduler.*

[WW94] "Lottery Scheduling: Flexible Proportional-Share Resource Management" by Carl A. Waldspurger and William E. Weihl. OSDI '94, November 1994. *The landmark paper on lottery scheduling that got the systems community re-energized about scheduling, fair sharing, and the power of simple randomized algorithms.*

[W95] "Lottery and Stride Scheduling: Flexible Proportional-Share Resource Management" by Carl A. Waldspurger. Ph.D. Thesis, MIT, 1995. *The award-winning thesis of Waldspurger's that outlines lottery and stride scheduling. If you're thinking of writing a Ph.D. dissertation at some point, you should always have a good example around, to give you something to strive for: this is such a good one.*

[W02] "Memory Resource Management in VMware ESX Server" by Carl A. Waldspurger. OSDI '02, Boston, Massachusetts. *The paper to read about memory management in VMMs (a.k.a., hypervisors). In addition to being relatively easy to read, the paper contains numerous cool ideas about this new type of VMM-level memory management.*

Homework (Simulation)

This program, `lottery.py`, allows you to see how a lottery scheduler works. See the README for details.

Questions

1. Compute the solutions for simulations with 3 jobs and random seeds of 1, 2, and 3.

2. Now run with two specific jobs: each of length 10, but one (job 0) with just 1 ticket and the other (job 1) with 100 (e.g., `-l 10:1,10:100`). What happens when the number of tickets is so imbalanced? Will job 0 ever run before job 1 completes? How often? In general, what does such a ticket imbalance do to the behavior of lottery scheduling?

3. When running with two jobs of length 100 and equal ticket allocations of 100 (`-l 100:100,100:100`), how unfair is the scheduler? Run with some different random seeds to determine the (probabilistic) answer; let unfairness be determined by how much earlier one job finishes than the other.

4. How does your answer to the previous question change as the quantum size (`-q`) gets larger?

5. Can you make a version of the graph that is found in the chapter? What else would be worth exploring? How would the graph look with a stride scheduler?

10

Multiprocessor Scheduling (Advanced)

This chapter will introduce the basics of **multiprocessor scheduling**. As this topic is relatively advanced, it may be best to cover it *after* you have studied the topic of concurrency in some detail (i.e., the second major "easy piece" of the book).

After years of existence only in the high-end of the computing spectrum, **multiprocessor** systems are increasingly commonplace, and have found their way into desktop machines, laptops, and even mobile devices. The rise of the **multicore** processor, in which multiple CPU cores are packed onto a single chip, is the source of this proliferation; these chips have become popular as computer architects have had a difficult time making a single CPU much faster without using (way) too much power. And thus we all now have a few CPUs available to us, which is a good thing, right?

Of course, there are many difficulties that arise with the arrival of more than a single CPU. A primary one is that a typical application (i.e., some C program you wrote) only uses a single CPU; adding more CPUs does not make that single application run faster. To remedy this problem, you'll have to rewrite your application to run in **parallel**, perhaps using **threads** (as discussed in great detail in the second piece of this book). Multithreaded applications can spread work across multiple CPUs and thus run faster when given more CPU resources.

ASIDE: ADVANCED CHAPTERS

Advanced chapters require material from a broad swath of the book to truly understand, while logically fitting into a section that is earlier than said set of prerequisite materials. For example, this chapter on multiprocessor scheduling makes much more sense if you've first read the middle piece on concurrency; however, it logically fits into the part of the book on virtualization (generally) and CPU scheduling (specifically). Thus, it is recommended such chapters be covered out of order; in this case, after the second piece of the book.

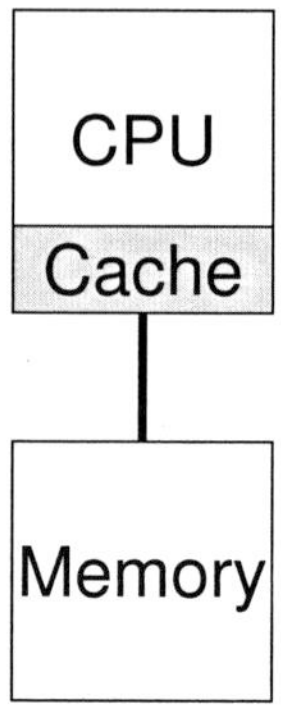

Figure 101: **Single CPU With Cache**

Beyond applications, a new problem that arises for the operating system is (not surprisingly!) that of **multiprocessor scheduling**. Thus far we've discussed a number of principles behind single-processor scheduling; how can we extend those ideas to work on multiple CPUs? What new problems must we overcome? And thus, our problem:

> CRUX: HOW TO SCHEDULE JOBS ON MULTIPLE CPUS
> How should the OS schedule jobs on multiple CPUs? What new problems arise? Do the same old techniques work, or are new ideas required?

10.1 Background: Multiprocessor Architecture

To understand the new issues surrounding multiprocessor scheduling, we have to understand a new and fundamental difference between single-CPU hardware and multi-CPU hardware. This difference centers around the use of hardware **caches** (e.g., Figure 101), and exactly how data is shared across multiple processors. We now discuss this issue further, at a high level. Details are available elsewhere [CSG99], in particular in an upper-level or perhaps graduate computer architecture course.

In a system with a single CPU, there are a hierarchy of **hardware caches** that in general help the processor run programs faster. Caches are small, fast memories that (in general) hold copies of *popular* data that is found in the main memory of the system. Main memory, in contrast, holds *all* of the data, but access to this larger memory is slower. By keeping frequently accessed data in a cache, the system can make the large, slow memory appear to be a fast one.

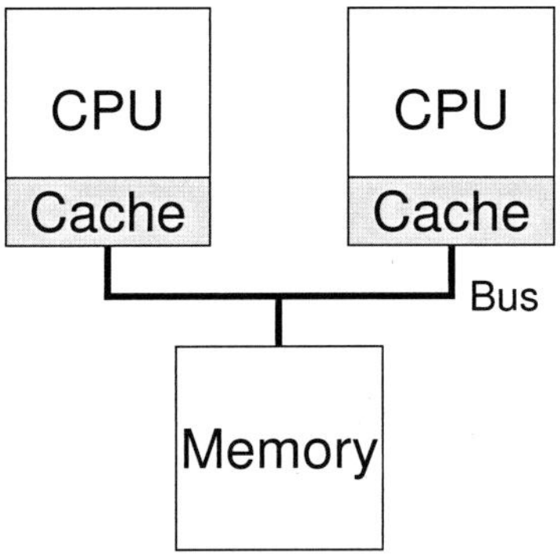

Figure 102: **Two CPUs With Caches Sharing Memory**

As an example, consider a program that issues an explicit load instruction to fetch a value from memory, and a simple system with only a single CPU; the CPU has a small cache (say 64 KB) and a large main memory. The first time a program issues this load, the data resides in main memory, and thus takes a long time to fetch (perhaps in the tens of nanoseconds, or even hundreds). The processor, anticipating that the data may be reused, puts a copy of the loaded data into the CPU cache. If the program later fetches this same data item again, the CPU first checks for it in the cache; if it finds it there, the data is fetched much more quickly (say, just a few nanoseconds), and thus the program runs faster.

Caches are thus based on the notion of **locality**, of which there are two kinds: **temporal locality** and **spatial locality**. The idea behind temporal locality is that when a piece of data is accessed, it is likely to be accessed again in the near future; imagine variables or even instructions themselves being accessed over and over again in a loop. The idea behind spatial locality is that if a program accesses a data item at address x, it is likely to access data items near x as well; here, think of a program streaming through an array, or instructions being executed one after the other. Because locality of these types exist in many programs, hardware systems can make good guesses about which data to put in a cache and thus work well.

Now for the tricky part: what happens when you have multiple processors in a single system, with a single shared main memory, as we see in Figure 102?

As it turns out, caching with multiple CPUs is much more complicated. Imagine, for example, that a program running on CPU 1 reads a data item (with value D) at address A; because the data is not in the cache on CPU 1, the system fetches it from main memory, and gets the value D. The program then modifies the value at address A, just updating its cache with the new value D'; writing the data through all the way to main memory is slow, so the system will (usually) do that later. Then assume the OS decides to stop running the program and move it to CPU 2. The program then re-reads the value at address A; there is no such data CPU 2's cache, and thus the system fetches the value from main memory, and gets the old value D instead of the correct value D'. Oops!

This general problem is called the problem of **cache coherence**, and there is a vast research literature that describes many different subtleties involved with solving the problem [SHW11]. Here, we will skip all of the nuance and make some major points; take a computer architecture class (or three) to learn more.

The basic solution is provided by the hardware: by monitoring memory accesses, hardware can ensure that basically the "right thing" happens and that the view of a single shared memory is preserved. One way to do this on a bus-based system (as described above) is to use an old technique known as **bus snooping** [G83]; each cache pays attention to memory updates by observing the bus that connects them to main memory. When a CPU then sees an update for a data item it holds in its cache, it will notice the change and either **invalidate** its copy (i.e., remove it from its own cache) or **update** it (i.e., put the new value into its cache too). Write-back caches, as hinted at above, make this more complicated (because the write to main memory isn't visible until later), but you can imagine how the basic scheme might work.

10.2 Don't Forget Synchronization

Given that the caches do all of this work to provide coherence, do programs (or the OS itself) have to worry about anything when they access shared data? The answer, unfortunately, is yes, and is documented in great detail in the second piece of this book on the topic of concurrency. While we won't get into the details here, we'll sketch/review some of the basic ideas here (assuming you're familiar with concurrency).

When accessing (and in particular, updating) shared data items or structures across CPUs, mutual exclusion primitives (such as locks) should likely be used to guarantee correctness (other approaches, such as building **lock-free** data structures, are complex and only used on occasion; see the chapter on deadlock in the piece on concurrency for details). For example, assume we have a shared queue being accessed on multiple CPUs concurrently. Without locks, adding or removing elements from the queue concurrently will not work as expected, even with the underlying coherence protocols; one needs locks to atomically update the data structure to its new state.

To make this more concrete, imagine this code sequence, which is used to remove an element from a shared linked list, as we see in Figure 103. Imagine if threads on two CPUs enter this routine at the same time. If

```
1  typedef struct __Node_t {
2      int              value;
3      struct __Node_t *next;
4  } Node_t;
5
6  int List_Pop() {
7      Node_t *tmp = head;         // remember old head ...
8      int value   = head->value;  // ... and its value
9      head        = head->next;   // advance head to next pointer
10     free(tmp);                  // free old head
11     return value;               // return value at head
12 }
```

Figure 103: **Simple List Delete Code**

Thread 1 executes the first line, it will have the current value of `head` stored in its `tmp` variable; if Thread 2 then executes the first line as well, it also will have the same value of `head` stored in its own private `tmp` variable (`tmp` is allocated on the stack, and thus each thread will have its own private storage for it). Thus, instead of each thread removing an element from the head of the list, each thread will try to remove the same head element, leading to all sorts of problems (such as an attempted double free of the head element at Line 10, as well as potentially returning the same data value twice).

The solution, of course, is to make such routines correct via **locking**. In this case, allocating a simple mutex (e.g., `pthread_mutex_t m;`) and then adding a `lock(&m)` at the beginning of the routine and an `unlock(&m)` at the end will solve the problem, ensuring that the code will execute as desired. Unfortunately, as we will see, such an approach is not without problems, in particular with regards to performance. Specifically, as the number of CPUs grows, access to a synchronized shared data structure becomes quite slow.

10.3 One Final Issue: Cache Affinity

One final issue arises in building a multiprocessor cache scheduler, known as **cache affinity** [TTG95]. This notion is simple: a process, when run on a particular CPU, builds up a fair bit of state in the caches (and TLBs) of the CPU. The next time the process runs, it is often advantageous to run it on the same CPU, as it will run faster if some of its state is already present in the caches on that CPU. If, instead, one runs a process on a different CPU each time, the performance of the process will be worse, as it will have to reload the state each time it runs (note it will run correctly on a different CPU thanks to the cache coherence protocols of the hardware). Thus, a multiprocessor scheduler should consider cache affinity when making its scheduling decisions, perhaps preferring to keep a process on the same CPU if at all possible.

10.4 Single-Queue Scheduling

With this background in place, we now discuss how to build a scheduler for a multiprocessor system. The most basic approach is to simply reuse the basic framework for single processor scheduling, by putting all jobs that need to be scheduled into a single queue; we call this **single-queue multiprocessor scheduling** or **SQMS** for short. This approach has the advantage of simplicity; it does not require much work to take an existing policy that picks the best job to run next and adapt it to work on more than one CPU (where it might pick the best two jobs to run, if there are two CPUs, for example).

However, SQMS has obvious shortcomings. The first problem is a lack of **scalability**. To ensure the scheduler works correctly on multiple CPUs, the developers will have inserted some form of **locking** into the code, as described above. Locks ensure that when SQMS code accesses the single queue (say, to find the next job to run), the proper outcome arises.

Locks, unfortunately, can greatly reduce performance, particularly as the number of CPUs in the systems grows [A91]. As contention for such a single lock increases, the system spends more and more time in lock overhead and less time doing the work the system should be doing (note: it would be great to include a real measurement of this in here someday).

The second main problem with SQMS is cache affinity. For example, let us assume we have five jobs to run (A, B, C, D, E) and four processors. Our scheduling queue thus looks like this:

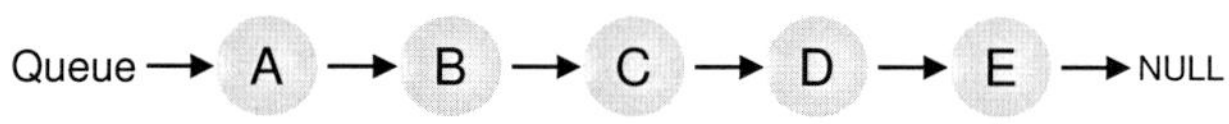

Over time, assuming each job runs for a time slice and then another job is chosen, here is a possible job schedule across CPUs:

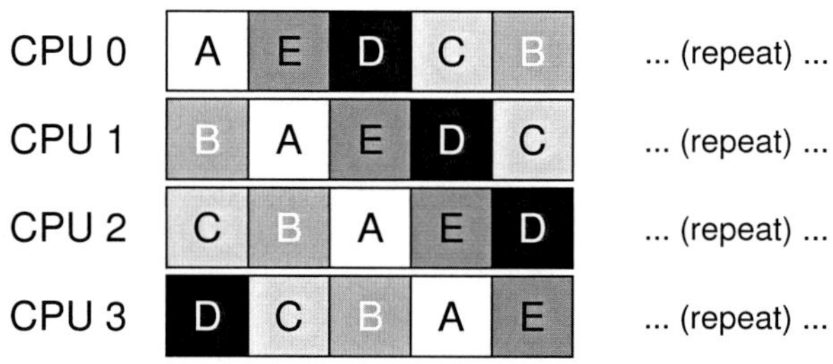

Because each CPU simply picks the next job to run from the globally-shared queue, each job ends up bouncing around from CPU to CPU, thus doing exactly the opposite of what would make sense from the standpoint of cache affinity.

To handle this problem, most SQMS schedulers include some kind of affinity mechanism to try to make it more likely that process will continue to run on the same CPU if possible. Specifically, one might provide affinity for some jobs, but move others around to balance load. For example, imagine the same five jobs scheduled as follows:

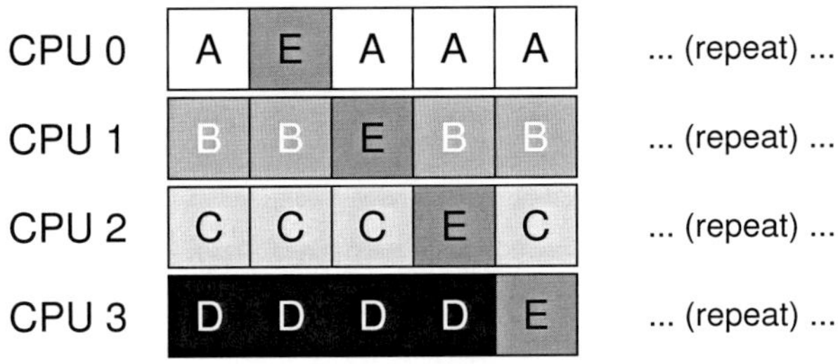

In this arrangement, jobs A through D are not moved across processors, with only job E **migrating** from CPU to CPU, thus preserving affinity for most. You could then decide to migrate a different job the next time through, thus achieving some kind of affinity fairness as well. Implementing such a scheme, however, can be complex.

Thus, we can see the SQMS approach has its strengths and weaknesses. It is straightforward to implement given an existing single-CPU scheduler, which by definition has only a single queue. However, it does not scale well (due to synchronization overheads), and it does not readily preserve cache affinity.

10.5 Multi-Queue Scheduling

Because of the problems caused in single-queue schedulers, some systems opt for multiple queues, e.g., one per CPU. We call this approach **multi-queue multiprocessor scheduling** (or **MQMS**).

In MQMS, our basic scheduling framework consists of multiple scheduling queues. Each queue will likely follow a particular scheduling discipline, such as round robin, though of course any algorithm can be used. When a job enters the system, it is placed on exactly one scheduling queue, according to some heuristic (e.g., random, or picking one with fewer jobs than others). Then it is scheduled essentially independently, thus avoiding the problems of information sharing and synchronization found in the single-queue approach.

For example, assume we have a system where there are just two CPUs (labeled CPU 0 and CPU 1), and some number of jobs enter the system: A, B, C, and D for example. Given that each CPU has a scheduling queue now, the OS has to decide into which queue to place each job. It might do something like this:

Depending on the queue scheduling policy, each CPU now has two jobs to choose from when deciding what should run. For example, with **round robin**, the system might produce a schedule that looks like this:

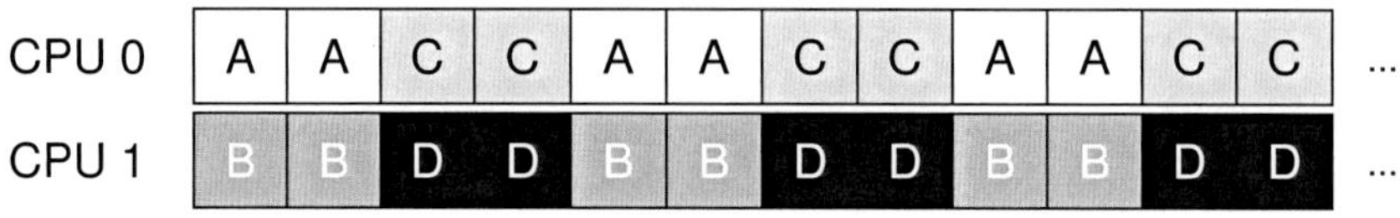

MQMS has a distinct advantage of SQMS in that it should be inherently more scalable. As the number of CPUs grows, so too does the number of queues, and thus lock and cache contention should not become a central problem. In addition, MQMS intrinsically provides cache affinity; jobs stay on the same CPU and thus reap the advantage of reusing cached contents therein.

But, if you've been paying attention, you might see that we have a new problem, which is fundamental in the multi-queue based approach: **load imbalance**. Let's assume we have the same set up as above (four jobs, two CPUs), but then one of the jobs (say C) finishes. We now have the following scheduling queues:

If we then run our round-robin policy on each queue of the system, we will see this resulting schedule:

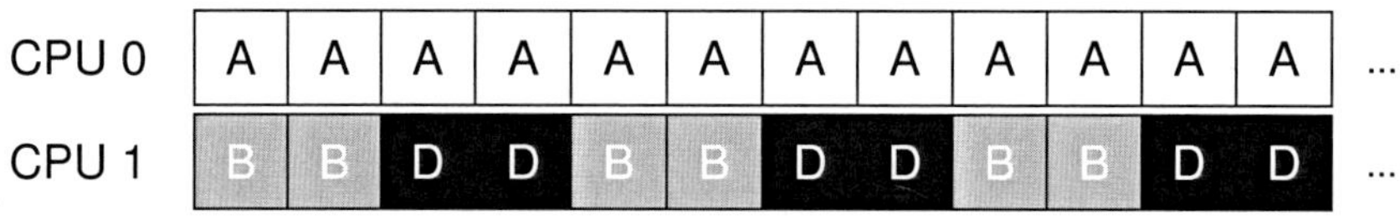

As you can see from this diagram, A gets twice as much CPU as B and D, which is not the desired outcome. Even worse, let's imagine that both A and C finish, leaving just jobs B and D in the system. The two scheduling queues, and resulting timeline, will look like this:

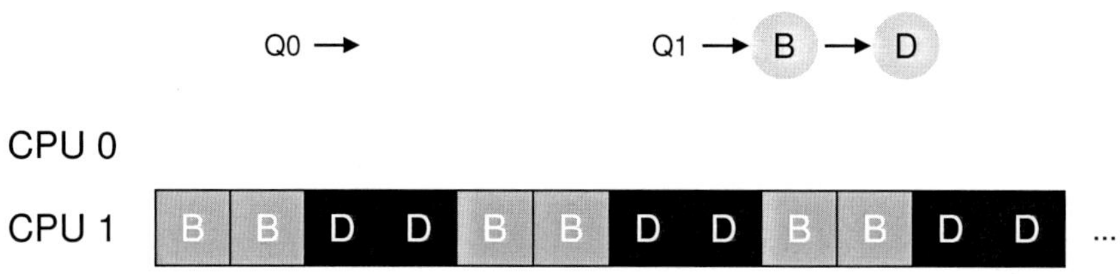

How terrible – CPU 0 is idle! *(insert dramatic and sinister music here)* And thus our CPU usage timeline looks quite sad.

So what should a poor multi-queue multiprocessor scheduler do? How can we overcome the insidious problem of load imbalance and defeat the evil forces of ... the Decepticons[1]? How do we stop asking questions that are hardly relevant to this otherwise wonderful book?

> CRUX: HOW TO DEAL WITH LOAD IMBALANCE
> How should a multi-queue multiprocessor scheduler handle load imbalance, so as to better achieve its desired scheduling goals?

The obvious answer to this query is to move jobs around, a technique which we (once again) refer to as **migration**. By migrating a job from one CPU to another, true load balance can be achieved.

Let's look at a couple of examples to add some clarity. Once again, we have a situation where one CPU is idle and the other has some jobs.

In this case, the desired migration is easy to understand: the OS should simply move one of B or D to CPU 0. The result of this single job migration is evenly balanced load and everyone is happy.

A more tricky case arises in our earlier example, where A was left alone on CPU 0 and B and D were alternating on CPU 1:

In this case, a single migration does not solve the problem. What would you do in this case? The answer, alas, is continuous migration of one or more jobs. One possible solution is to keep switching jobs, as we see in the following timeline. In the figure, first A is alone on CPU 0, and B and D alternate on CPU 1. After a few time slices, B is moved to compete with A on CPU 0, while D enjoys a few time slices alone on CPU 1. And thus load is balanced:

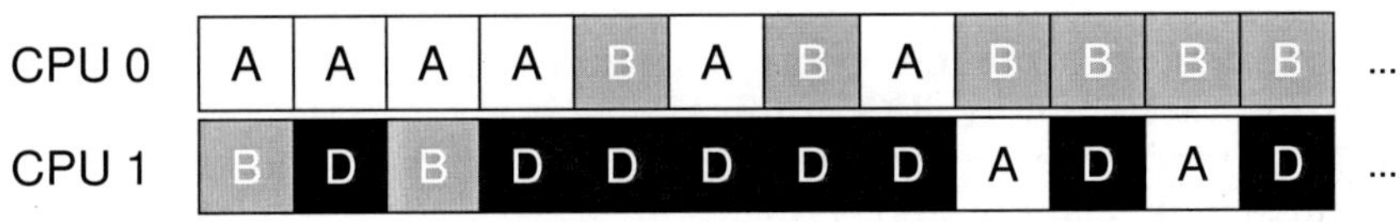

Of course, many other possible migration patterns exist. But now for the tricky part: how should the system decide to enact such a migration?

[1] Little known fact is that the home planet of Cybertron was destroyed by bad CPU scheduling decisions. And now let that be the first and last reference to Transformers in this book, for which we sincerely apologize.

One basic approach is to use a technique known as **work stealing** [FLR98]. With a work-stealing approach, a (source) queue that is low on jobs will occasionally peek at another (target) queue, to see how full it is. If the target queue is (notably) more full than the source queue, the source will "steal" one or more jobs from the target to help balance load.

Of course, there is a natural tension in such an approach. If you look around at other queues too often, you will suffer from high overhead and have trouble scaling, which was the entire purpose of implementing the multiple queue scheduling in the first place! If, on the other hand, you don't look at other queues very often, you are in danger of suffering from severe load imbalances. Finding the right threshold remains, as is common in system policy design, a black art.

10.6 Linux Multiprocessor Schedulers

Interestingly, in the Linux community, no common solution has approached to building a multiprocessor scheduler. Over time, three different schedulers arose: the O(1) scheduler, the Completely Fair Scheduler (CFS), and the BF Scheduler (BFS)[2]. See Meehean's dissertation for an excellent overview of the strengths and weaknesses of said schedulers [M11]; here we just summarize a few of the basics.

Both O(1) and CFS use multiple queues, whereas BFS uses a single queue, showing that both approaches can be successful. Of course, there are many other details which separate these schedulers. For example, the O(1) scheduler is a priority-based scheduler (similar to the MLFQ discussed before), changing a process's priority over time and then scheduling those with highest priority in order to meet various scheduling objectives; interactivity is a particular focus. CFS, in contrast, is a deterministic proportional-share approach (more like Stride scheduling, as discussed earlier). BFS, the only single-queue approach among the three, is also proportional-share, but based on a more complicated scheme known as Earliest Eligible Virtual Deadline First (EEVDF) [SA96]. Read more about these modern algorithms on your own; you should be able to understand how they work now!

10.7 Summary

We have seen various approaches to multiprocessor scheduling. The single-queue approach (SQMS) is rather straightforward to build and balances load well but inherently has difficulty with scaling to many processors and cache affinity. The multiple-queue approach (MQMS) scales better and handles cache affinity well, but has trouble with load imbalance and is more complicated. Whichever approach you take, there is no simple answer: building a general purpose scheduler remains a daunting task, as small code changes can lead to large behavioral differences. Only undertake such an exercise if you know exactly what you are doing, or, at least, are getting paid a large amount of money to do so.

[2] Look up what BF stands for on your own; be forewarned, it is not for the faint of heart.

References

[A90] "The Performance of Spin Lock Alternatives for Shared-Memory Multiprocessors" by Thomas E. Anderson. IEEE TPDS Volume 1:1, January 1990. *A classic paper on how different locking alternatives do and don't scale. By Tom Anderson, very well known researcher in both systems and networking. And author of a very fine OS textbook, we must say.*

[B+10] "An Analysis of Linux Scalability to Many Cores Abstract" by Silas Boyd-Wickizer, Austin T. Clements, Yandong Mao, Aleksey Pesterev, M. Frans Kaashoek, Robert Morris, Nickolai Zeldovich. OSDI '10, Vancouver, Canada, October 2010. *A terrific modern paper on the difficulties of scaling Linux to many cores.*

[CSG99] "Parallel Computer Architecture: A Hardware/Software Approach" by David E. Culler, Jaswinder Pal Singh, and Anoop Gupta. Morgan Kaufmann, 1999. *A treasure filled with details about parallel machines and algorithms. As Mark Hill humorously observes on the jacket, the book contains more information than most research papers.*

[FLR98] "The Implementation of the Cilk-5 Multithreaded Language" by Matteo Frigo, Charles E. Leiserson, Keith Randall. PLDI '98, Montreal, Canada, June 1998. *Cilk is a lightweight language and runtime for writing parallel programs, and an excellent example of the work-stealing paradigm.*

[G83] "Using Cache Memory To Reduce Processor-Memory Traffic" by James R. Goodman. ISCA '83, Stockholm, Sweden, June 1983. *The pioneering paper on how to use bus snooping, i.e., paying attention to requests you see on the bus, to build a cache coherence protocol. Goodman's research over many years at Wisconsin is full of cleverness, this being but one example.*

[M11] "Towards Transparent CPU Scheduling" by Joseph T. Meehean. Doctoral Dissertation at University of Wisconsin—Madison, 2011. *A dissertation that covers a lot of the details of how modern Linux multiprocessor scheduling works. Pretty awesome! But, as co-advisors of Joe's, we may be a bit biased here.*

[SHW11] "A Primer on Memory Consistency and Cache Coherence" by Daniel J. Sorin, Mark D. Hill, and David A. Wood. Synthesis Lectures in Computer Architecture. Morgan and Claypool Publishers, May 2011. *A definitive overview of memory consistency and multiprocessor caching. Required reading for anyone who likes to know way too much about a given topic.*

[SA96] "Earliest Eligible Virtual Deadline First: A Flexible and Accurate Mechanism for Proportional Share Resource Allocation" by Ion Stoica and Hussein Abdel-Wahab. Technical Report TR-95-22, Old Dominion University, 1996. *A tech report on this cool scheduling idea, from Ion Stoica, now a professor at U.C. Berkeley and world expert in networking, distributed systems, and many other things.*

[TTG95] "Evaluating the Performance of Cache-Affinity Scheduling in Shared-Memory Multiprocessors" by Josep Torrellas, Andrew Tucker, Anoop Gupta. Journal of Parallel and Distributed Computing, Volume 24:2, February 1995. *This is not the first paper on the topic, but it has citations to earlier work, and is a more readable and practical paper than some of the earlier queuing-based analysis papers.*

Homework (Simulation)

In this homework, we'll use `multi.py` to simulate a multi-processor CPU scheduler, and learn about some of its details. Read the related README for more information about the simulator and its options.

Questions

1. To start things off, let's learn how to use the simulator to study how to build an effective multi-processor scheduler. The first simulation will run just one job, which has a run-time of 30, and a working-set size of 200. Run this job (called job 'a' here) on one simulated CPU as follows: `./multi.py -n 1 -L a:30:200`. How long will it take to complete? Turn on the `-c` flag to see a final answer, and the `-t` flag to see a tick-by-tick trace of the job and how it is scheduled.

2. Now increase the cache size so as to make the job's working set (size=200) fit into the cache (which, by default, is size=100); for example, run `./multi.py -n 1 -L a:30:200 -M 300`. Can you predict how fast the job will run once it fits in cache? (hint: remember the key parameter of the warm_rate, which is set by the -r flag) Check your answer by running with the solve flag (`-c`) enabled.

3. One cool thing about `multi.py` is that you can see more detail about what is going on with different tracing flags. Run the same simulation as above, but this time with time_left tracing enabled (`-T`). This flag shows both the job that was scheduled on a CPU at each time step, as well as how much run-time that job has left after each tick has run. What do you notice about how that second column decreases?

4. Now add one more bit of tracing, to show the status of each CPU cache for each job, with the `-C` flag. For each job, each cache will either show a blank space (if the cache is cold for that job) or a 'w' (if the cache is warm for that job). At what point does the cache become warm for job 'a' in this simple example? What happens as you change the warmup_time parameter (`-w`) to lower or higher values than the default?

5. At this point, you should have a good idea of how the simulator works for a single job running on a single CPU. But hey, isn't this a multi-processor CPU scheduling chapter? Oh yeah! So let's start working with multiple jobs. Specifically, let's run the following three jobs on a two-CPU system (i.e., type `./multi.py -n 2 -L a:100:100,b:100:50,c:100:50`) Can you predict how long this will take, given a round-robin centralized scheduler? Use `-c` to see if you were right, and then dive down into details with `-t`

to see a step-by-step and then `-C` to see whether caches got warmed effectively for these jobs. What do you notice?

6. Now we'll apply some explicit controls to study **cache affinity**, as described in the chapter. To do this, you'll need the `-A` flag. This flag can be used to limit which CPUs the scheduler can place a particular job upon. In this case, let's use it to place jobs 'b' and 'c' on CPU 1, while restricting 'a' to CPU 0. This magic is accomplished by typing this `./multi.py -n 2 -L a:100:100,b:100:50, c:100:50 -A a:0,b:1,c:1`; don't forget to turn on various tracing options to see what is really happening! Can you predict how fast this version will run? Why does it do better? Will other combinations of 'a', 'b', and 'c' onto the two processors run faster or slower?

7. One interesting aspect of caching multiprocessors is the opportunity for better-than-expected speed up of jobs when using multiple CPUs (and their caches) as compared to running jobs on a single processor. Specifically, when you run on N CPUs, sometimes you can speed up by more than a factor of N, a situation entitled **super-linear speedup**. To experiment with this, use the job description here (`-L a:100:100,b:100:100,c:100:100`) with a small cache (`-M 50`) to create three jobs. Run this on systems with 1, 2, and 3 CPUs (`-n 1`, `-n 2`, `-n 3`). Now, do the same, but with a larger per-CPU cache of size 100. What do you notice about performance as the number of CPUs scales? Use `-c` to confirm your guesses, and other tracing flags to dive even deeper.

8. One other aspect of the simulator worth studying is the per-CPU scheduling option, the `-p` flag. Run with two CPUs again, and this three job configuration (`-L a:100:100,b:100:50,c:100:50`). How does this option do, as opposed to the hand-controlled affinity limits you put in place above? How does performance change as you alter the 'peek interval' (`-P`) to lower or higher values? How does this per-CPU approach work as the number of CPUs scales?

9. Finally, feel free to just generate random workloads and see if you can predict their performance on different numbers of processors, cache sizes, and scheduling options. If you do this, you'll soon be a **multi-processor scheduling master**, which is a pretty awesome thing to be. Good luck!

11

Summary Dialogue on CPU Virtualization

Professor: *So, Student, did you learn anything?*

Student: *Well, Professor, that seems like a loaded question. I think you only want me to say "yes."*

Professor: *That's true. But it's also still an honest question. Come on, give a professor a break, will you?*

Student: *OK, OK. I think I did learn a few things. First, I learned a little about how the OS virtualizes the CPU. There are a bunch of important* ***mechanisms*** *that I had to understand to make sense of this: traps and trap handlers, timer interrupts, and how the OS and the hardware have to carefully save and restore state when switching between processes.*

Professor: *Good, good!*

Student: *All those interactions do seem a little complicated though; how can I learn more?*

Professor: *Well, that's a good question. I think there is no substitute for doing; just reading about these things doesn't quite give you the proper sense. Do the class projects and I bet by the end it will all kind of make sense.*

Student: *Sounds good. What else can I tell you?*

Professor: *Well, did you get some sense of the philosophy of the OS in your quest to understand its basic machinery?*

Student: *Hmm... I think so. It seems like the OS is fairly paranoid. It wants to make sure it stays in charge of the machine. While it wants a program to run as efficiently as possible (and hence the whole reasoning behind* ***limited direct execution****), the OS also wants to be able to say "Ah! Not so fast my friend" in case of an errant or malicious process. Paranoia rules the day, and certainly keeps the OS in charge of the machine. Perhaps that is why we think of the OS as a resource manager.*

Professor: *Yes indeed — sounds like you are starting to put it together! Nice.*

Student: *Thanks.*

Professor: *And what about the policies on top of those mechanisms — any interesting lessons there?*

Student: *Some lessons to be learned there for sure. Perhaps a little obvious, but obvious can be good. Like the notion of bumping short jobs to the front of the queue — I knew that was a good idea ever since the one time I was buying some gum at the store, and the guy in front of me had a credit card that wouldn't work. He was no short job, let me tell you.*

Professor: *That sounds oddly rude to that poor fellow. What else?*

Student: *Well, that you can build a smart scheduler that tries to be like SJF and RR all at once — that MLFQ was pretty neat. Building up a real scheduler seems difficult.*

Professor: *Indeed it is. That's why there is still controversy to this day over which scheduler to use; see the Linux battles between CFS, BFS, and the O(1) scheduler, for example. And no, I will not spell out the full name of BFS.*

Student: *And I won't ask you to! These policy battles seem like they could rage forever; is there really a right answer?*

Professor: *Probably not. After all, even our own metrics are at odds: if your scheduler is good at turnaround time, it's bad at response time, and vice versa. As Lampson said, perhaps the goal isn't to find the best solution, but rather to avoid disaster.*

Student: *That's a little depressing.*

Professor: *Good engineering can be that way. And it can also be uplifting! It's just your perspective on it, really. I personally think being pragmatic is a good thing, and pragmatists realize that not all problems have clean and easy solutions. Anything else that caught your fancy?*

Student: *I really liked the notion of gaming the scheduler; it seems like that might be something to look into when I'm next running a job on Amazon's EC2 service. Maybe I can steal some cycles from some other unsuspecting (and more importantly, OS-ignorant) customer!*

Professor: *It looks like I might have created a monster! Professor Frankenstein is not what I'd like to be called, you know.*

Student: *But isn't that the idea? To get us excited about something, so much so that we look into it on our own? Lighting fires and all that?*

Professor: *I guess so. But I didn't think it would work!*

12

A Dialogue on Memory Virtualization

Student: *So, are we done with virtualization?*

Professor: *No!*

Student: *Hey, no reason to get so excited; I was just asking a question. Students are supposed to do that, right?*

Professor: *Well, professors do always say that, but really they mean this: ask questions, **if** they are good questions, **and** you have actually put a little thought into them.*

Student: *Well, that sure takes the wind out of my sails.*

Professor: *Mission accomplished. In any case, we are not nearly done with virtualization! Rather, you have just seen how to virtualize the CPU, but really there is a big monster waiting in the closet: memory. Virtualizing memory is complicated and requires us to understand many more intricate details about how the hardware and OS interact.*

Student: *That sounds cool. Why is it so hard?*

Professor: *Well, there are a lot of details, and you have to keep them straight in your head to really develop a mental model of what is going on. We'll start simple, with very basic techniques like base/bounds, and slowly add complexity to tackle new challenges, including fun topics like TLBs and multi-level page tables. Eventually, we'll be able to describe the workings of a fully-functional modern virtual memory manager.*

Student: *Neat! Any tips for the poor student, inundated with all of this information and generally sleep-deprived?*

Professor: *For the sleep deprivation, that's easy: sleep more (and party less). For understanding virtual memory, start with this: **every address generated by a user program is a virtual address**. The OS is just providing an illusion to each process, specifically that it has its own large and private memory; with some hardware help, the OS will turn these pretend virtual addresses into real physical addresses, and thus be able to locate the desired information.*

Student: *OK, I think I can remember that... (to self) every address from a user program is virtual, every address from a user program is virtual, every ...*

Professor: *What are you mumbling about?*

Student: *Oh nothing.... (awkward pause) ... Anyway, why does the OS want to provide this illusion again?*

Professor: *Mostly* ***ease of use****: the OS will give each program the view that it has a large contiguous* **address space** *to put its code and data into; thus, as a programmer, you never have to worry about things like "where should I store this variable?" because the virtual address space of the program is large and has lots of room for that sort of thing. Life, for a programmer, becomes much more tricky if you have to worry about fitting all of your code data into a small, crowded memory.*

Student: *Why else?*

Professor: *Well,* **isolation** *and* **protection** *are big deals, too. We don't want one errant program to be able to read, or worse, overwrite, some other program's memory, do we?*

Student: *Probably not. Unless it's a program written by someone you don't like.*

Professor: *Hmmm.... I think we might need to add a class on morals and ethics to your schedule for next semester. Perhaps OS class isn't getting the right message across.*

Student: *Maybe we should. But remember, it's not me who taught us that the proper OS response to errant process behavior is to kill the offending process!*

13

The Abstraction: Address Spaces

In the early days, building computer systems was easy. Why, you ask? Because users didn't expect much. It is those darned users with their expectations of "ease of use", "high performance", "reliability", etc., that really have led to all these headaches. Next time you meet one of those computer users, thank them for all the problems they have caused.

13.1 Early Systems

From the perspective of memory, early machines didn't provide much of an abstraction to users. Basically, the physical memory of the machine looked something like what you see in Figure 131 (page 130).

The OS was a set of routines (a library, really) that sat in memory (starting at physical address 0 in this example), and there would be one running program (a process) that currently sat in physical memory (starting at physical address 64k in this example) and used the rest of memory. There were few illusions here, and the user didn't expect much from the OS. Life was sure easy for OS developers in those days, wasn't it?

13.2 Multiprogramming and Time Sharing

After a time, because machines were expensive, people began to share machines more effectively. Thus the era of **multiprogramming** was born [DV66], in which multiple processes were ready to run at a given time, and the OS would switch between them, for example when one decided to perform an I/O. Doing so increased the effective **utilization** of the CPU. Such increases in **efficiency** were particularly important in those days where each machine cost hundreds of thousands or even millions of dollars (and you thought your Mac was expensive!).

Soon enough, however, people began demanding more of machines, and the era of **time sharing** was born [S59, L60, M62, M83]. Specifically, many realized the limitations of batch computing, particularly on programmers themselves [CV65], who were tired of long (and hence ineffec-

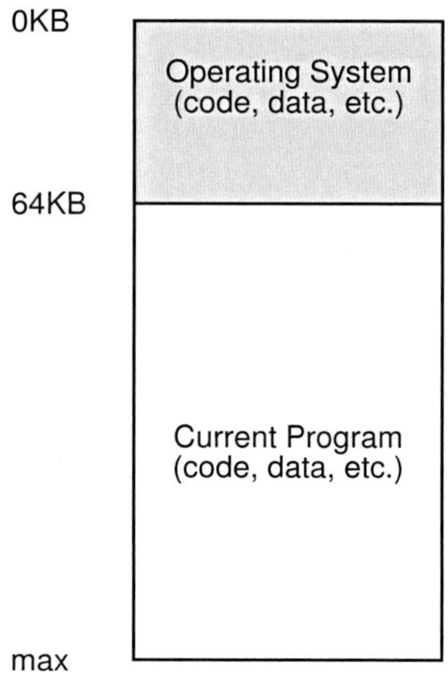

Figure 131: **Operating Systems: The Early Days**

tive) program-debug cycles. The notion of **interactivity** became important, as many users might be concurrently using a machine, each waiting for (or hoping for) a timely response from their currently-executing tasks.

One way to implement time sharing would be to run one process for a short while, giving it full access to all memory (Figure 131), then stop it, save all of its state to some kind of disk (including all of physical memory), load some other process's state, run it for a while, and thus implement some kind of crude sharing of the machine [M+63].

Unfortunately, this approach has a big problem: it is way too slow, particularly as memory grows. While saving and restoring register-level state (the PC, general-purpose registers, etc.) is relatively fast, saving the entire contents of memory to disk is brutally non-performant. Thus, what we'd rather do is leave processes in memory while switching between them, allowing the OS to implement time sharing efficiently (as shown in Figure 132, page 131).

In the diagram, there are three processes (A, B, and C) and each of them have a small part of the 512KB physical memory carved out for them. Assuming a single CPU, the OS chooses to run one of the processes (say A), while the others (B and C) sit in the ready queue waiting to run.

As time sharing became more popular, you can probably guess that new demands were placed on the operating system. In particular, allowing multiple programs to reside concurrently in memory makes **protection** an important issue; you don't want a process to be able to read, or worse, write some other process's memory.

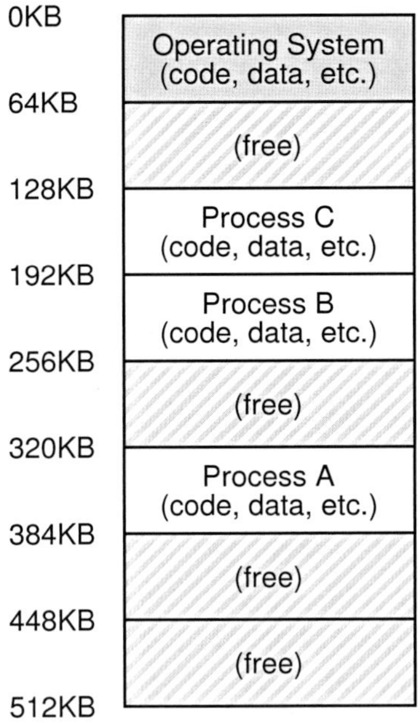

Figure 132: **Three Processes: Sharing Memory**

13.3 The Address Space

However, we have to keep those pesky users in mind, and doing so requires the OS to create an **easy to use** abstraction of physical memory. We call this abstraction the **address space**, and it is the running program's view of memory in the system. Understanding this fundamental OS abstraction of memory is key to understanding how memory is virtualized.

The address space of a process contains all of the memory state of the running program. For example, the **code** of the program (the instructions) have to live in memory somewhere, and thus they are in the address space. The program, while it is running, uses a **stack** to keep track of where it is in the function call chain as well as to allocate local variables and pass parameters and return values to and from routines. Finally, the **heap** is used for dynamically-allocated, user-managed memory, such as that you might receive from a call to `malloc()` in C or `new` in an object-oriented language such as C++ or Java. Of course, there are other things in there too (e.g., statically-initialized variables), but for now let us just assume those three components: code, stack, and heap.

In the example in Figure 133 (page 132), we have a tiny address space (only 16KB)[1]. The program code lives at the top of the address space

[1]We will often use small examples like this because (a) it is a pain to represent a 32-bit address space and (b) the math is harder. We like simple math.

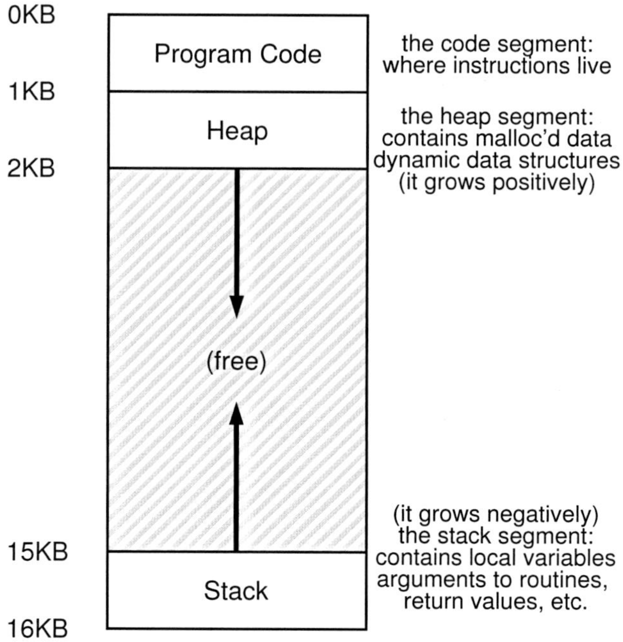

Figure 133: **An Example Address Space**

(starting at 0 in this example, and is packed into the first 1K of the address space). Code is static (and thus easy to place in memory), so we can place it at the top of the address space and know that it won't need any more space as the program runs.

Next, we have the two regions of the address space that may grow (and shrink) while the program runs. Those are the heap (at the top) and the stack (at the bottom). We place them like this because each wishes to be able to grow, and by putting them at opposite ends of the address space, we can allow such growth: they just have to grow in opposite directions. The heap thus starts just after the code (at 1KB) and grows downward (say when a user requests more memory via `malloc()`); the stack starts at 16KB and grows upward (say when a user makes a procedure call). However, this placement of stack and heap is just a convention; you could arrange the address space in a different way if you'd like (as we'll see later, when multiple **threads** co-exist in an address space, no nice way to divide the address space like this works anymore, alas).

Of course, when we describe the address space, what we are describing is the **abstraction** that the OS is providing to the running program. The program really isn't in memory at physical addresses 0 through 16KB; rather it is loaded at some arbitrary physical address(es). Examine processes A, B, and C in Figure 132; there you can see how each process is loaded into memory at a different address. And hence the problem:

THE CRUX: HOW TO VIRTUALIZE MEMORY

How can the OS build this abstraction of a private, potentially large address space for multiple running processes (all sharing memory) on top of a single, physical memory?

When the OS does this, we say the OS is **virtualizing memory**, because the running program thinks it is loaded into memory at a particular address (say 0) and has a potentially very large address space (say 32-bits or 64-bits); the reality is quite different.

When, for example, process A in Figure 132 tries to perform a load at address 0 (which we will call a **virtual address**), somehow the OS, in tandem with some hardware support, will have to make sure the load doesn't actually go to physical address 0 but rather to physical address 320KB (where A is loaded into memory). This is the key to virtualization of memory, which underlies every modern computer system in the world.

13.4 Goals

Thus we arrive at the job of the OS in this set of notes: to virtualize memory. The OS will not only virtualize memory, though; it will do so with style. To make sure the OS does so, we need some goals to guide us. We have seen these goals before (think of the Introduction), and we'll see them again, but they are certainly worth repeating.

One major goal of a virtual memory (VM) system is **transparency**[2]. The OS should implement virtual memory in a way that is invisible to the running program. Thus, the program shouldn't be aware of the fact that memory is virtualized; rather, the program behaves as if it has its own private physical memory. Behind the scenes, the OS (and hardware) does all the work to multiplex memory among many different jobs, and hence implements the illusion.

Another goal of VM is **efficiency**. The OS should strive to make the virtualization as **efficient** as possible, both in terms of time (i.e., not making programs run much more slowly) and space (i.e., not using too much memory for structures needed to support virtualization). In implementing time-efficient virtualization, the OS will have to rely on hardware support, including hardware features such as TLBs (which we will learn about in due course).

Finally, a third VM goal is **protection**. The OS should make sure to **protect** processes from one another as well as the OS itself from pro-

[2]This usage of transparency is sometimes confusing; some students think that "being transparent" means keeping everything out in the open, i.e., what government should be like. Here, it means the opposite: that the illusion provided by the OS should not be visible to applications. Thus, in common usage, a transparent system is one that is hard to notice, not one that responds to requests as stipulated by the Freedom of Information Act.

> TIP: THE PRINCIPLE OF ISOLATION
> Isolation is a key principle in building reliable systems. If two entities are properly isolated from one another, this implies that one can fail without affecting the other. Operating systems strive to isolate processes from each other and in this way prevent one from harming the other. By using memory isolation, the OS further ensures that running programs cannot affect the operation of the underlying OS. Some modern OS's take isolation even further, by walling off pieces of the OS from other pieces of the OS. Such **microkernels** [BH70, R+89, S+03] thus may provide greater reliability than typical monolithic kernel designs.

cesses. When one process performs a load, a store, or an instruction fetch, it should not be able to access or affect in any way the memory contents of any other process or the OS itself (that is, anything *outside* its address space). Protection thus enables us to deliver the property of **isolation** among processes; each process should be running in its own isolated cocoon, safe from the ravages of other faulty or even malicious processes.

In the next chapters, we'll focus our exploration on the basic **mechanisms** needed to virtualize memory, including hardware and operating systems support. We'll also investigate some of the more relevant **policies** that you'll encounter in operating systems, including how to manage free space and which pages to kick out of memory when you run low on space. In doing so, we'll build up your understanding of how a modern virtual memory system really works[3].

13.5 Summary

We have seen the introduction of a major OS subsystem: virtual memory. The VM system is responsible for providing the illusion of a large, sparse, private address space to programs, which hold all of their instructions and data therein. The OS, with some serious hardware help, will take each of these virtual memory references, and turn them into physical addresses, which can be presented to the physical memory in order to fetch the desired information. The OS will do this for many processes at once, making sure to protect programs from one another, as well as protect the OS. The entire approach requires a great deal of mechanism (lots of low-level machinery) as well as some critical policies to work; we'll start from the bottom up, describing the critical mechanisms first. And thus we proceed!

[3] Or, we'll convince you to drop the course. But hold on; if you make it through VM, you'll likely make it all the way!

ASIDE: EVERY ADDRESS YOU SEE IS VIRTUAL

Ever write a C program that prints out a pointer? The value you see (some large number, often printed in hexadecimal), is a **virtual address**. Ever wonder where the code of your program is found? You can print that out too, and yes, if you can print it, it also is a virtual address. In fact, any address you can see as a programmer of a user-level program is a virtual address. It's only the OS, through its tricky techniques of virtualizing memory, that knows where in the physical memory of the machine these instructions and data values lie. So never forget: if you print out an address in a program, it's a virtual one, an illusion of how things are laid out in memory; only the OS (and the hardware) knows the real truth.

Here's a little program (`va.c`) that prints out the locations of the `main()` routine (where code lives), the value of a heap-allocated value returned from `malloc()`, and the location of an integer on the stack:

```
#include <stdio.h>
#include <stdlib.h>
int main(int argc, char *argv[]) {
  printf("location of code : %p\n", main);
  printf("location of heap : %p\n", malloc(100e6));
  int x = 3;
  printf("location of stack: %p\n", &x);
  return x;
}
```

When run on a 64-bit Mac, we get the following output:

```
location of code : 0x1095afe50
location of heap : 0x1096008c0
location of stack: 0x7fff691aea64
```

From this, you can see that code comes first in the address space, then the heap, and the stack is all the way at the other end of this large virtual space. All of these addresses are virtual, and will be translated by the OS and hardware in order to fetch values from their true physical locations.

References

[BH70] "The Nucleus of a Multiprogramming System" by Per Brinch Hansen. Communications of the ACM, 13:4, April 1970. *The first paper to suggest that the OS, or kernel, should be a minimal and flexible substrate for building customized operating systems; this theme is revisited throughout OS research history.*

[CV65] "Introduction and Overview of the Multics System" by F. J. Corbato, V. A. Vyssotsky. Fall Joint Computer Conference, 1965. *A great early Multics paper. Here is the great quote about time sharing: "The impetus for time-sharing first arose from professional programmers because of their constant frustration in debugging programs at batch processing installations. Thus, the original goal was to time-share computers to allow simultaneous access by several persons while giving to each of them the illusion of having the whole machine at his disposal."*

[DV66] "Programming Semantics for Multiprogrammed Computations" by Jack B. Dennis, Earl C. Van Horn. Communications of the ACM, Volume 9, Number 3, March 1966. *An early paper (but not the first) on multiprogramming.*

[L60] "Man-Computer Symbiosis" by J. C. R. Licklider. IRE Transactions on Human Factors in Electronics, HFE-1:1, March 1960. *A funky paper about how computers and people are going to enter into a symbiotic age; clearly well ahead of its time but a fascinating read nonetheless.*

[M62] "Time-Sharing Computer Systems" by J. McCarthy. Management and the Computer of the Future, MIT Press, Cambridge, MA, 1962. *Probably McCarthy's earliest recorded paper on time sharing. In another paper [M83], he claims to have been thinking of the idea since 1957. McCarthy left the systems area and went on to become a giant in Artificial Intelligence at Stanford, including the creation of the LISP programming language. See McCarthy's home page for more info:* `http://www-formal.stanford.edu/jmc/`

[M+63] "A Time-Sharing Debugging System for a Small Computer" by J. McCarthy, S. Boilen, E. Fredkin, J. C. R. Licklider. AFIPS '63 (Spring), New York, NY, May 1963. *A great early example of a system that swapped program memory to the "drum" when the program wasn't running, and then back into "core" memory when it was about to be run.*

[M83] "Reminiscences on the History of Time Sharing" by John McCarthy. 1983. Available: http://www-formal.stanford.edu/jmc/history/timesharing/timesharing.html. *A terrific historical note on where the idea of time-sharing might have come fzshortm, including some doubts towards those who cite Strachey's work [S59] as the by pioneering work in this area..*

[NS07] "Valgrind: A Framework for Heavyweight Dynamic Binary Instrumentation" by N. Nethercote, J. Seward. PLDI 2007, San Diego, California, June 2007. *Valgrind is a lifesaver of a program for those who use unsafe languages like C. Read this paper to learn about its very cool binary instrumentation techniques – it's really quite impressive.*

[R+89] "Mach: A System Software kernel" by R. Rashid, D. Julin, D. Orr, R. Sanzi, R. Baron, A. Forin, D. Golub, M. Jones. COMPCON '89, February 1989. *Although not the first project on microkernels per se, the Mach project at CMU was well-known and influential; it still lives today deep in the bowels of Mac OS X.*

[S59] "Time Sharing in Large Fast Computers" by C. Strachey. Proceedings of the International Conference on Information Processing, UNESCO, June 1959. *One of the earliest references on time sharing.*

[S+03] "Improving the Reliability of Commodity Operating Systems" by M. M. Swift, B. N. Bershad, H. M. Levy. SOSP '03. *The first paper to show how microkernel-like thinking can improve operating system reliability.*

Homework (Code)

In this homework, we'll just learn about a few useful tools to examine virtual memory usage on Linux-based systems. This will only be a brief hint at what is possible; you'll have to dive deeper on your own to truly become an expert (as always!).

Questions

1. The first Linux tool you should check out is the very simple tool `free`. First, type `man free` and read its entire manual page; it's short, don't worry!
2. Now, run `free`, perhaps using some of the arguments that might be useful (e.g., `-m`, to display memory totals in megabytes). How much memory is in your system? How much is free? Do these numbers match your intuition?
3. Next, create a little program that uses a certain amount of memory, called `memory-user.c`. This program should take one command-line argument: the number of megabytes of memory it will use. When run, it should allocate an array, and constantly stream through the array, touching each entry. The program should do this indefinitely, or, perhaps, for a certain amount of time also specified at the command line.
4. Now, while running your `memory-user` program, also (in a different terminal window, but on the same machine) run the `free` tool. How do the memory usage totals change when your program is running? How about when you kill the `memory-user` program? Do the numbers match your expectations? Try this for different amounts of memory usage. What happens when you use really large amounts of memory?
5. Let's try one more tool, known as `pmap`. Spend some time, and read the `pmap` manual page in detail.
6. To use `pmap`, you have to know the **process ID** of the process you're interested in. Thus, first run `ps auxw` to see a list of all processes; then, pick an interesting one, such as a browser. You can also use your `memory-user` program in this case (indeed, you can even have that program call `getpid()` and print out its PID for your convenience).
7. Now run `pmap` on some of these processes, using various flags (like `-X`) to reveal many details about the process. What do you see? How many different entities make up a modern address space, as opposed to our simple conception of code/stack/heap?
8. Finally, let's run `pmap` on your `memory-user` program, with different amounts of used memory. What do you see here? Does the output from `pmap` match your expectations?

14

Interlude: Memory API

In this interlude, we discuss the memory allocation interfaces in UNIX systems. The interfaces provided are quite simple, and hence the chapter is short and to the point[1]. The main problem we address is this:

> CRUX: HOW TO ALLOCATE AND MANAGE MEMORY
>
> In UNIX/C programs, understanding how to allocate and manage memory is critical in building robust and reliable software. What interfaces are commonly used? What mistakes should be avoided?

14.1 Types of Memory

In running a C program, there are two types of memory that are allocated. The first is called **stack** memory, and allocations and deallocations of it are managed *implicitly* by the compiler for you, the programmer; for this reason it is sometimes called **automatic** memory.

Declaring memory on the stack in C is easy. For example, let's say you need some space in a function `func()` for an integer, called `x`. To declare such a piece of memory, you just do something like this:

```
void func() {
  int x; // declares an integer on the stack
  ...
}
```

The compiler does the rest, making sure to make space on the stack when you call into `func()`. When you return from the function, the compiler deallocates the memory for you; thus, if you want some information to live beyond the call invocation, you had better not leave that information on the stack.

[1]Indeed, we hope all chapters are! But this one is shorter and pointier, we think.

It is this need for long-lived memory that gets us to the second type of memory, called **heap** memory, where all allocations and deallocations are *explicitly* handled by you, the programmer. A heavy responsibility, no doubt! And certainly the cause of many bugs. But if you are careful and pay attention, you will use such interfaces correctly and without too much trouble. Here is an example of how one might allocate an integer on the heap:

```
void func() {
  int *x = (int *) malloc(sizeof(int));
  ...
}
```

A couple of notes about this small code snippet. First, you might notice that both stack and heap allocation occur on this line: first the compiler knows to make room for a pointer to an integer when it sees your declaration of said pointer (`int *x`); subsequently, when the program calls `malloc()`, it requests space for an integer on the heap; the routine returns the address of such an integer (upon success, or `NULL` on failure), which is then stored on the stack for use by the program.

Because of its explicit nature, and because of its more varied usage, heap memory presents more challenges to both users and systems. Thus, it is the focus of the remainder of our discussion.

14.2 The `malloc()` Call

The **`malloc()`** call is quite simple: you pass it a size asking for some room on the heap, and it either succeeds and gives you back a pointer to the newly-allocated space, or fails and returns `NULL`[2].

The manual page shows what you need to do to use malloc; type `man malloc` at the command line and you will see:

```
#include <stdlib.h>
...
void *malloc(size_t size);
```

From this information, you can see that all you need to do is include the header file `stdlib.h` to use malloc. In fact, you don't really need to even do this, as the C library, which all C programs link with by default, has the code for `malloc()` inside of it; adding the header just lets the compiler check whether you are calling `malloc()` correctly (e.g., passing the right number of arguments to it, of the right type).

The single parameter `malloc()` takes is of type `size_t` which simply describes how many bytes you need. However, most programmers do not type in a number here directly (such as 10); indeed, it would be considered poor form to do so. Instead, various routines and macros are

[2]Note that `NULL` in C isn't really anything special at all, just a macro for the value zero.

> TIP: WHEN IN DOUBT, TRY IT OUT
> If you aren't sure how some routine or operator you are using behaves, there is no substitute for simply trying it out and making sure it behaves as you expect. While reading the manual pages or other documentation is useful, how it works in practice is what matters. Write some code and test it! That is no doubt the best way to make sure your code behaves as you desire. Indeed, that is what we did to double-check the things we were saying about `sizeof()` were actually true!

utilized. For example, to allocate space for a double-precision floating point value, you simply do this:

```
double *d = (double *) malloc(sizeof(double));
```

Wow, that's lot of `double`-ing! This invocation of `malloc()` uses the `sizeof()` operator to request the right amount of space; in C, this is generally thought of as a *compile-time* operator, meaning that the actual size is known at *compile time* and thus a number (in this case, 8, for a double) is substituted as the argument to `malloc()`. For this reason, `sizeof()` is correctly thought of as an operator and not a function call (a function call would take place at run time).

You can also pass in the name of a variable (and not just a type) to `sizeof()`, but in some cases you may not get the desired results, so be careful. For example, let's look at the following code snippet:

```
int *x = malloc(10 * sizeof(int));
printf("%d\n", sizeof(x));
```

In the first line, we've declared space for an array of 10 integers, which is fine and dandy. However, when we use `sizeof()` in the next line, it returns a small value, such as 4 (on 32-bit machines) or 8 (on 64-bit machines). The reason is that in this case, `sizeof()` thinks we are simply asking how big a *pointer* to an integer is, not how much memory we have dynamically allocated. However, sometimes `sizeof()` does work as you might expect:

```
int x[10];
printf("%d\n", sizeof(x));
```

In this case, there is enough static information for the compiler to know that 40 bytes have been allocated.

Another place to be careful is with strings. When declaring space for a string, use the following idiom: `malloc(strlen(s) + 1)`, which gets the length of the string using the function `strlen()`, and adds 1 to it in order to make room for the end-of-string character. Using `sizeof()` may lead to trouble here.

You might also notice that `malloc()` returns a pointer to type `void`. Doing so is just the way in C to pass back an address and let the programmer decide what to do with it. The programmer further helps out by using what is called a **cast**; in our example above, the programmer casts the return type of `malloc()` to a pointer to a `double`. Casting doesn't really accomplish anything, other than tell the compiler and other programmers who might be reading your code: "yeah, I know what I'm doing." By casting the result of `malloc()`, the programmer is just giving some reassurance; the cast is not needed for the correctness.

14.3 The `free()` Call

As it turns out, allocating memory is the easy part of the equation; knowing when, how, and even if to free memory is the hard part. To free heap memory that is no longer in use, programmers simply call **`free()`**:

```
int *x = malloc(10 * sizeof(int));
...
free(x);
```

The routine takes one argument, a pointer returned by `malloc()`. Thus, you might notice, the size of the allocated region is not passed in by the user, and must be tracked by the memory-allocation library itself.

14.4 Common Errors

There are a number of common errors that arise in the use of `malloc()` and `free()`. Here are some we've seen over and over again in teaching the undergraduate operating systems course. All of these examples compile and run with nary a peep from the compiler; while compiling a C program is necessary to build a correct C program, it is far from sufficient, as you will learn (often in the hard way).

Correct memory management has been such a problem, in fact, that many newer languages have support for **automatic memory management**. In such languages, while you call something akin to `malloc()` to allocate memory (usually **new** or something similar to allocate a new object), you never have to call something to free space; rather, a **garbage collector** runs and figures out what memory you no longer have references to and frees it for you.

Forgetting To Allocate Memory

Many routines expect memory to be allocated before you call them. For example, the routine `strcpy(dst, src)` copies a string from a source pointer to a destination pointer. However, if you are not careful, you might do this:

```
char *src = "hello";
char *dst;          // oops! unallocated
strcpy(dst, src); // segfault and die
```

> TIP: IT COMPILED OR IT RAN ≠ IT IS CORRECT
> Just because a program compiled(!) or even ran once or many times correctly does not mean the program is correct. Many events may have conspired to get you to a point where you believe it works, but then something changes and it stops. A common student reaction is to say (or yell) "But it worked before!" and then blame the compiler, operating system, hardware, or even (dare we say it) the professor. But the problem is usually right where you think it would be, in your code. Get to work and debug it before you blame those other components.

When you run this code, it will likely lead to a **segmentation fault**[3], which is a fancy term for **YOU DID SOMETHING WRONG WITH MEMORY YOU FOOLISH PROGRAMMER AND I AM ANGRY.**

In this case, the proper code might instead look like this:

```
char *src = "hello";
char *dst = (char *) malloc(strlen(src) + 1);
strcpy(dst, src); // work properly
```

Alternately, you could use `strdup()` and make your life even easier. Read the `strdup` man page for more information.

Not Allocating Enough Memory

A related error is not allocating enough memory, sometimes called a **buffer overflow**. In the example above, a common error is to make *almost* enough room for the destination buffer.

```
char *src = "hello";
char *dst = (char *) malloc(strlen(src)); // too small!
strcpy(dst, src); // work properly
```

Oddly enough, depending on how malloc is implemented and many other details, this program will often run seemingly correctly. In some cases, when the string copy executes, it writes one byte too far past the end of the allocated space, but in some cases this is harmless, perhaps overwriting a variable that isn't used anymore. In some cases, these overflows can be incredibly harmful, and in fact are the source of many security vulnerabilities in systems [W06]. In other cases, the malloc library allocated a little extra space anyhow, and thus your program actually doesn't scribble on some other variable's value and works quite fine. In even other cases, the program will indeed fault and crash. And thus we learn another valuable lesson: even though it ran correctly once, doesn't mean it's correct.

[3]Although it sounds arcane, you will soon learn why such an illegal memory access is called a segmentation fault; if that isn't incentive to read on, what is?

Forgetting to Initialize Allocated Memory

With this error, you call `malloc()` properly, but forget to fill in some values into your newly-allocated data type. Don't do this! If you do forget, your program will eventually encounter an **uninitialized read**, where it reads from the heap some data of unknown value. Who knows what might be in there? If you're lucky, some value such that the program still works (e.g., zero). If you're not lucky, something random and harmful.

Forgetting To Free Memory

Another common error is known as a **memory leak**, and it occurs when you forget to free memory. In long-running applications or systems (such as the OS itself), this is a huge problem, as slowly leaking memory eventually leads one to run out of memory, at which point a restart is required. Thus, in general, when you are done with a chunk of memory, you should make sure to free it. Note that using a garbage-collected language doesn't help here: if you still have a reference to some chunk of memory, no garbage collector will ever free it, and thus memory leaks remain a problem even in more modern languages.

In some cases, it may seem like not calling `free()` is reasonable. For example, your program is short-lived, and will soon exit; in this case, when the process dies, the OS will clean up all of its allocated pages and thus no memory leak will take place per se. While this certainly "works" (see the aside on page 145), it is probably a bad habit to develop, so be wary of choosing such a strategy. In the long run, one of your goals as a programmer is to develop good habits; one of those habits is understanding how you are managing memory, and (in languages like C), freeing the blocks you have allocated. Even if you can get away with not doing so, it is probably good to get in the habit of freeing each and every byte you explicitly allocate.

Freeing Memory Before You Are Done With It

Sometimes a program will free memory before it is finished using it; such a mistake is called a **dangling pointer**, and it, as you can guess, is also a bad thing. The subsequent use can crash the program, or overwrite valid memory (e.g., you called `free()`, but then called `malloc()` again to allocate something else, which then recycles the errantly-freed memory).

Freeing Memory Repeatedly

Programs also sometimes free memory more than once; this is known as the **double free**. The result of doing so is undefined. As you can imagine, the memory-allocation library might get confused and do all sorts of weird things; crashes are a common outcome.

ASIDE: WHY NO MEMORY IS LEAKED ONCE YOUR PROCESS EXITS

When you write a short-lived program, you might allocate some space using `malloc()`. The program runs and is about to complete: is there need to call `free()` a bunch of times just before exiting? While it seems wrong not to, no memory will be "lost" in any real sense. The reason is simple: there are really two levels of memory management in the system.

The first level of memory management is performed by the OS, which hands out memory to processes when they run, and takes it back when processes exit (or otherwise die). The second level of management is *within* each process, for example within the heap when you call `malloc()` and `free()`. Even if you fail to call `free()` (and thus leak memory in the heap), the operating system will reclaim *all* the memory of the process (including those pages for code, stack, and, as relevant here, heap) when the program is finished running. No matter what the state of your heap in your address space, the OS takes back all of those pages when the process dies, thus ensuring that no memory is lost despite the fact that you didn't free it.

Thus, for short-lived programs, leaking memory often does not cause any operational problems (though it may be considered poor form). When you write a long-running server (such as a web server or database management system, which never exit), leaked memory is a much bigger issue, and will eventually lead to a crash when the application runs out of memory. And of course, leaking memory is an even larger issue inside one particular program: the operating system itself. Showing us once again: those who write the kernel code have the toughest job of all...

Calling `free()` Incorrectly

One last problem we discuss is the call of `free()` incorrectly. After all, `free()` expects you only to pass to it one of the pointers you received from `malloc()` earlier. When you pass in some other value, bad things can (and do) happen. Thus, such **invalid frees** are dangerous and of course should also be avoided.

Summary

As you can see, there are lots of ways to abuse memory. Because of frequent errors with memory, a whole ecosphere of tools have developed to help find such problems in your code. Check out both **purify** [HJ92] and **valgrind** [SN05]; both are excellent at helping you locate the source of your memory-related problems. Once you become accustomed to using these powerful tools, you will wonder how you survived without them.

14.5 Underlying OS Support

You might have noticed that we haven't been talking about system calls when discussing `malloc()` and `free()`. The reason for this is simple: they are not system calls, but rather library calls. Thus the malloc library manages space within your virtual address space, but itself is built on top of some system calls which call into the OS to ask for more memory or release some back to the system.

One such system call is called `brk`, which is used to change the location of the program's **break**: the location of the end of the heap. It takes one argument (the address of the new break), and thus either increases or decreases the size of the heap based on whether the new break is larger or smaller than the current break. An additional call `sbrk` is passed an increment but otherwise serves a similar purpose.

Note that you should never directly call either `brk` or `sbrk`. They are used by the memory-allocation library; if you try to use them, you will likely make something go (horribly) wrong. Stick to `malloc()` and `free()` instead.

Finally, you can also obtain memory from the operating system via the `mmap()` call. By passing in the correct arguments, `mmap()` can create an **anonymous** memory region within your program — a region which is not associated with any particular file but rather with **swap space**, something we'll discuss in detail later on in virtual memory. This memory can then also be treated like a heap and managed as such. Read the manual page of `mmap()` for more details.

14.6 Other Calls

There are a few other calls that the memory-allocation library supports. For example, `calloc()` allocates memory and also zeroes it before returning; this prevents some errors where you assume that memory is zeroed and forget to initialize it yourself (see the paragraph on "uninitialized reads" above). The routine `realloc()` can also be useful, when you've allocated space for something (say, an array), and then need to add something to it: `realloc()` makes a new larger region of memory, copies the old region into it, and returns the pointer to the new region.

14.7 Summary

We have introduced some of the APIs dealing with memory allocation. As always, we have just covered the basics; more details are available elsewhere. Read the C book [KR88] and Stevens [SR05] (Chapter 7) for more information. For a cool modern paper on how to detect and correct many of these problems automatically, see Novark et al. [N+07]; this paper also contains a nice summary of common problems and some neat ideas on how to find and fix them.

References

[HJ92] "Purify: Fast Detection of Memory Leaks and Access Errors" by R. Hastings, B. Joyce. USENIX Winter '92. *The paper behind the cool Purify tool, now a commercial product.*

[KR88] "The C Programming Language" by Brian Kernighan, Dennis Ritchie. Prentice-Hall 1988. *The C book, by the developers of C. Read it once, do some programming, then read it again, and then keep it near your desk or wherever you program.*

[N+07] "Exterminator: Automatically Correcting Memory Errors with High Probability" by G. Novark, E. D. Berger, B. G. Zorn. PLDI 2007, San Diego, California. *A cool paper on finding and correcting memory errors automatically, and a great overview of many common errors in C and C++ programs. An extended version of this paper is available CACM (Volume 51, Issue 12, December 2008).*

[SN05] "Using Valgrind to Detect Undefined Value Errors with Bit-precision" by J. Seward, N. Nethercote. USENIX '05. *How to use valgrind to find certain types of errors.*

[SR05] "Advanced Programming in the UNIX Environment" by W. Richard Stevens, Stephen A. Rago. Addison-Wesley, 2005. *We've said it before, we'll say it again: read this book many times and use it as a reference whenever you are in doubt. The authors are always surprised at how each time they read something in this book, they learn something new, even after many years of C programming.*

[W06] "Survey on Buffer Overflow Attacks and Countermeasures" by T. Werthman. Available: www.nds.rub.de/lehre/seminar/SS06/Werthmann_BufferOverflow.pdf. *A nice survey of buffer overflows and some of the security problems they cause. Refers to many of the famous exploits.*

Homework (Code)

In this homework, you will gain some familiarity with memory allocation. First, you'll write some buggy programs (fun!). Then, you'll use some tools to help you find the bugs you inserted. Then, you will realize how awesome these tools are and use them in the future, thus making yourself more happy and productive. The tools are the debugger (e.g., `gdb`) and a memory-bug detector called `valgrind` [SN05].

Questions

1. First, write a simple program called `null.c` that creates a pointer to an integer, sets it to `NULL`, and then tries to dereference it. Compile this into an executable called `null`. What happens when you run this program?

2. Next, compile this program with symbol information included (with the `-g` flag). Doing so let's put more information into the executable, enabling the debugger to access more useful information about variable names and the like. Run the program under the debugger by typing `gdb null` and then, once `gdb` is running, typing `run`. What does gdb show you?

3. Finally, use the `valgrind` tool on this program. We'll use the `memcheck` tool that is a part of `valgrind` to analyze what happens. Run this by typing in the following: `valgrind --leak-check=yes null`. What happens when you run this? Can you interpret the output from the tool?

4. Write a simple program that allocates memory using `malloc()` but forgets to free it before exiting. What happens when this program runs? Can you use `gdb` to find any problems with it? How about `valgrind` (again with the `--leak-check=yes` flag)?

5. Write a program that creates an array of integers called `data` of size 100 using `malloc`; then, set `data[100]` to zero. What happens when you run this program? What happens when you run this program using `valgrind`? Is the program correct?

6. Create a program that allocates an array of integers (as above), frees them, and then tries to print the value of one of the elements of the array. Does the program run? What happens when you use `valgrind` on it?

7. Now pass a funny value to free (e.g., a pointer in the middle of the array you allocated above). What happens? Do you need tools to find this type of problem?

8. Try out some of the other interfaces to memory allocation. For example, create a simple vector-like data structure and related routines that use `realloc()` to manage the vector. Use an array to store the vectors elements; when a user adds an entry to the vector, use `realloc()` to allocate more space for it. How well does such a vector perform? How does it compare to a linked list? Use `valgrind` to help you find bugs.

9. Spend more time and read about using `gdb` and `valgrind`. Knowing your tools is critical; spend the time and learn how to become an expert debugger in the UNIX and C environment.

15

Mechanism: Address Translation

In developing the virtualization of the CPU, we focused on a general mechanism known as **limited direct execution** (or **LDE**). The idea behind LDE is simple: for the most part, let the program run directly on the hardware; however, at certain key points in time (such as when a process issues a system call, or a timer interrupt occurs), arrange so that the OS gets involved and makes sure the "right" thing happens. Thus, the OS, with a little hardware support, tries its best to get out of the way of the running program, to deliver an *efficient* virtualization; however, by **interposing** at those critical points in time, the OS ensures that it maintains *control* over the hardware. Efficiency and control together are two of the main goals of any modern operating system.

In virtualizing memory, we will pursue a similar strategy, attaining both efficiency and control while providing the desired virtualization. Efficiency dictates that we make use of hardware support, which at first will be quite rudimentary (e.g., just a few registers) but will grow to be fairly complex (e.g., TLBs, page-table support, and so forth, as you will see). Control implies that the OS ensures that no application is allowed to access any memory but its own; thus, to protect applications from one another, and the OS from applications, we will need help from the hardware here too. Finally, we will need a little more from the VM system, in terms of *flexibility*; specifically, we'd like for programs to be able to use their address spaces in whatever way they would like, thus making the system easier to program. And thus we arrive at the refined crux:

THE CRUX:
HOW TO EFFICIENTLY AND FLEXIBLY VIRTUALIZE MEMORY

How can we build an efficient virtualization of memory? How do we provide the flexibility needed by applications? How do we maintain control over which memory locations an application can access, and thus ensure that application memory accesses are properly restricted? How do we do all of this efficiently?

The generic technique we will use, which you can consider an addition to our general approach of limited direct execution, is something that is referred to as **hardware-based address translation**, or just **address translation** for short. With address translation, the hardware transforms each memory access (e.g., an instruction fetch, load, or store), changing the **virtual** address provided by the instruction to a **physical** address where the desired information is actually located. Thus, on each and every memory reference, an address translation is performed by the hardware to redirect application memory references to their actual locations in memory.

Of course, the hardware alone cannot virtualize memory, as it just provides the low-level mechanism for doing so efficiently. The OS must get involved at key points to set up the hardware so that the correct translations take place; it must thus **manage memory**, keeping track of which locations are free and which are in use, and judiciously intervening to maintain control over how memory is used.

Once again the goal of all of this work is to create a beautiful **illusion**: that the program has its own private memory, where its own code and data reside. Behind that virtual reality lies the ugly physical truth: that many programs are actually sharing memory at the same time, as the CPU (or CPUs) switches between running one program and the next. Through virtualization, the OS (with the hardware's help) turns the ugly machine reality into a useful, powerful, and easy to use abstraction.

15.1 Assumptions

Our first attempts at virtualizing memory will be very simple, almost laughably so. Go ahead, laugh all you want; pretty soon it will be the OS laughing at you, when you try to understand the ins and outs of TLBs, multi-level page tables, and other technical wonders. Don't like the idea of the OS laughing at you? Well, you may be out of luck then; that's just how the OS rolls.

Specifically, we will assume for now that the user's address space must be placed *contiguously* in physical memory. We will also assume, for simplicity, that the size of the address space is not too big; specifically, that it is *less than the size of physical memory*. Finally, we will also assume that each address space is exactly the *same size*. Don't worry if these assumptions sound unrealistic; we will relax them as we go, thus achieving a realistic virtualization of memory.

15.2 An Example

To understand better what we need to do to implement address translation, and why we need such a mechanism, let's look at a simple example. Imagine there is a process whose address space is as indicated in Figure 151. What we are going to examine here is a short code sequence that loads a value from memory, increments it by three, and then stores the value back into memory. You can imagine the C-language representation of this code might look like this:

TIP: INTERPOSITION IS POWERFUL

Interposition is a generic and powerful technique that is often used to great effect in computer systems. In virtualizing memory, the hardware will interpose on each memory access, and translate each virtual address issued by the process to a physical address where the desired information is actually stored. However, the general technique of interposition is much more broadly applicable; indeed, almost any well-defined interface can be interposed upon, to add new functionality or improve some other aspect of the system. One of the usual benefits of such an approach is **transparency**; the interposition often is done without changing the client of the interface, thus requiring no changes to said client.

```
void func() {
    int x = 3000; // thanks, Perry.
    x = x + 3;    // line of code we are interested in
    ...
```

The compiler turns this line of code into assembly, which might look something like this (in x86 assembly). Use `objdump` on Linux or `otool` on a Mac to disassemble it:

```
128: movl 0x0(%ebx), %eax      ;load 0+ebx into eax
132: addl $0x03, %eax          ;add 3 to eax register
135: movl %eax, 0x0(%ebx)      ;store eax back to mem
```

This code snippet is relatively straightforward; it presumes that the address of `x` has been placed in the register `ebx`, and then loads the value at that address into the general-purpose register `eax` using the `movl` instruction (for "longword" move). The next instruction adds 3 to `eax`, and the final instruction stores the value in `eax` back into memory at that same location.

In Figure 151 (page 154), observe how both the code and data are laid out in the process's address space; the three-instruction code sequence is located at address 128 (in the code section near the top), and the value of the variable `x` at address 15 KB (in the stack near the bottom). In the figure, the initial value of `x` is 3000, as shown in its location on the stack.

When these instructions run, from the perspective of the process, the following memory accesses take place.

- Fetch instruction at address 128
- Execute this instruction (load from address 15 KB)
- Fetch instruction at address 132
- Execute this instruction (no memory reference)
- Fetch the instruction at address 135
- Execute this instruction (store to address 15 KB)

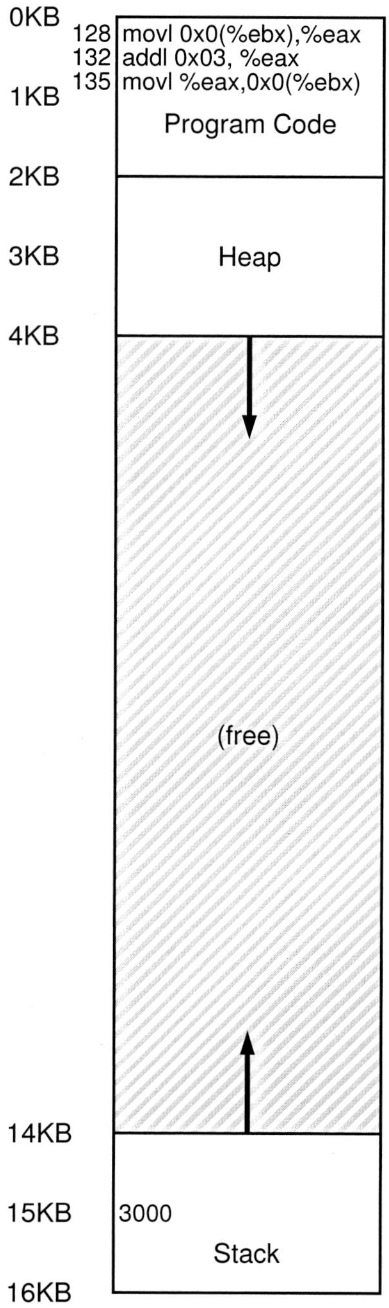

Figure 151: **A Process And Its Address Space**

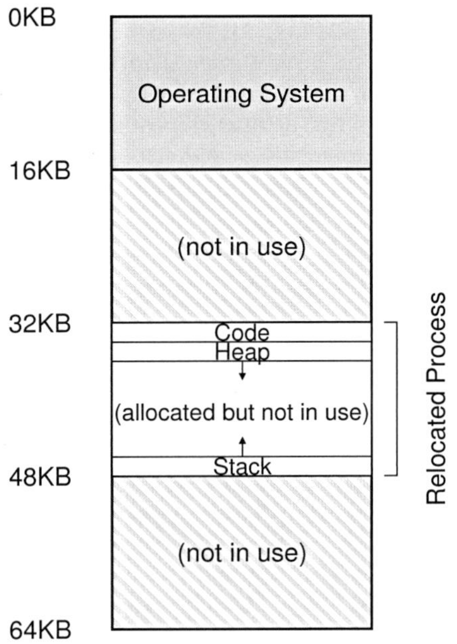

Figure 152: **Physical Memory with a Single Relocated Process**

From the program's perspective, its **address space** starts at address 0 and grows to a maximum of 16 KB; all memory references it generates should be within these bounds. However, to virtualize memory, the OS wants to place the process somewhere else in physical memory, not necessarily at address 0. Thus, we have the problem: how can we **relocate** this process in memory in a way that is **transparent** to the process? How can we provide the illusion of a virtual address space starting at 0, when in reality the address space is located at some other physical address?

An example of what physical memory might look like once this process's address space has been placed in memory is found in Figure 152. In the figure, you can see the OS using the first slot of physical memory for itself, and that it has relocated the process from the example above into the slot starting at physical memory address 32 KB. The other two slots are free (16 KB-32 KB and 48 KB-64 KB).

15.3 Dynamic (Hardware-based) Relocation

To gain some understanding of hardware-based address translation, we'll first discuss its first incarnation. Introduced in the first time-sharing machines of the late 1950's is a simple idea referred to as **base and bounds**; the technique is also referred to as **dynamic relocation**; we'll use both terms interchangeably [SS74].

Specifically, we'll need two hardware registers within each CPU: one is called the **base** register, and the other the **bounds** (sometimes called a **limit** register). This base-and-bounds pair is going to allow us to place the

> ASIDE: SOFTWARE-BASED RELOCATION
>
> In the early days, before hardware support arose, some systems performed a crude form of relocation purely via software methods. The basic technique is referred to as **static relocation**, in which a piece of software known as the **loader** takes an executable that is about to be run and rewrites its addresses to the desired offset in physical memory.
>
> For example, if an instruction was a load from address 1000 into a register (e.g., `movl 1000, %eax`), and the address space of the program was loaded starting at address 3000 (and not 0, as the program thinks), the loader would rewrite the instruction to offset each address by 3000 (e.g., `movl 4000, %eax`). In this way, a simple static relocation of the process's address space is achieved.
>
> However, static relocation has numerous problems. First and most importantly, it does not provide protection, as processes can generate bad addresses and thus illegally access other process's or even OS memory; in general, hardware support is likely needed for true protection [WL+93]. Another negative is that once placed, it is difficult to later relocate an address space to another location [M65].

address space anywhere we'd like in physical memory, and do so while ensuring that the process can only access its own address space.

In this setup, each program is written and compiled as if it is loaded at address zero. However, when a program starts running, the OS decides where in physical memory it should be loaded and sets the base register to that value. In the example above, the OS decides to load the process at physical address 32 KB and thus sets the base register to this value.

Interesting things start to happen when the process is running. Now, when any memory reference is generated by the process, it is **translated** by the processor in the following manner:

```
physical address = virtual address + base
```

Each memory reference generated by the process is a **virtual address**; the hardware in turn adds the contents of the base register to this address and the result is a **physical address** that can be issued to the memory system.

To understand this better, let's trace through what happens when a single instruction is executed. Specifically, let's look at one instruction from our earlier sequence:

```
128: movl 0x0(%ebx), %eax
```

The program counter (PC) is set to 128; when the hardware needs to fetch this instruction, it first adds the value to the base register value of 32 KB (32768) to get a physical address of 32896; the hardware then fetches the instruction from that physical address. Next, the processor begins executing the instruction. At some point, the process then issues

> TIP: HARDWARE-BASED DYNAMIC RELOCATION
> With dynamic relocation, a little hardware goes a long way. Namely, a **base** register is used to transform virtual addresses (generated by the program) into physical addresses. A **bounds** (or **limit**) register ensures that such addresses are within the confines of the address space. Together they provide a simple and efficient virtualization of memory.

the load from virtual address 15 KB, which the processor takes and again adds to the base register (32 KB), getting the final physical address of 47 KB and thus the desired contents.

Transforming a virtual address into a physical address is exactly the technique we refer to as **address translation**; that is, the hardware takes a virtual address the process thinks it is referencing and transforms it into a physical address which is where the data actually resides. Because this relocation of the address happens at runtime, and because we can move address spaces even after the process has started running, the technique is often referred to as **dynamic relocation** [M65].

Now you might be asking: what happened to that bounds (limit) register? After all, isn't this the base *and* bounds approach? Indeed, it is. As you might have guessed, the bounds register is there to help with protection. Specifically, the processor will first check that the memory reference is *within bounds* to make sure it is legal; in the simple example above, the bounds register would always be set to 16 KB. If a process generates a virtual address that is greater than the bounds, or one that is negative, the CPU will raise an exception, and the process will likely be terminated. The point of the bounds is thus to make sure that all addresses generated by the process are legal and within the "bounds" of the process.

We should note that the base and bounds registers are hardware structures kept on the chip (one pair per CPU). Sometimes people call the part of the processor that helps with address translation the **memory management unit (MMU)**; as we develop more sophisticated memory-management techniques, we will be adding more circuitry to the MMU.

A small aside about bound registers, which can be defined in one of two ways. In one way (as above), it holds the *size* of the address space, and thus the hardware checks the virtual address against it first before adding the base. In the second way, it holds the *physical address* of the end of the address space, and thus the hardware first adds the base and then makes sure the address is within bounds. Both methods are logically equivalent; for simplicity, we'll usually assume the former method.

Example Translations

To understand address translation via base-and-bounds in more detail, let's take a look at an example. Imagine a process with an address space of size 4 KB (yes, unrealistically small) has been loaded at physical address 16 KB. Here are the results of a number of address translations:

Virtual Address		Physical Address
0	→	16 KB
1 KB	→	17 KB
3000	→	19384
4400	→	*Fault (out of bounds)*

As you can see from the example, it is easy for you to simply add the base address to the virtual address (which can rightly be viewed as an *offset* into the address space) to get the resulting physical address. Only if the virtual address is "too big" or negative will the result be a fault, causing an exception to be raised.

15.4 Hardware Support: A Summary

Let us now summarize the support we need from the hardware (also see Figure 153, page 159). First, as discussed in the chapter on CPU virtualization, we require two different CPU modes. The OS runs in **privileged mode** (or **kernel mode**), where it has access to the entire machine; applications run in **user mode**, where they are limited in what they can do. A single bit, perhaps stored in some kind of **processor status word**, indicates which mode the CPU is currently running in; upon certain special occasions (e.g., a system call or some other kind of exception or interrupt), the CPU switches modes.

The hardware must also provide the **base and bounds registers** themselves; each CPU thus has an additional pair of registers, part of the **memory management unit** (**MMU**) of the CPU. When a user program is running, the hardware will translate each address, by adding the base value to the virtual address generated by the user program. The hardware must also be able to check whether the address is valid, which is accomplished by using the bounds register and some circuitry within the CPU.

The hardware should provide special instructions to modify the base and bounds registers, allowing the OS to change them when different processes run. These instructions are **privileged**; only in kernel (or privileged) mode can the registers be modified. Imagine the havoc a user process could wreak[1] if it could arbitrarily change the base register while

[1] Is there anything other than "havoc" that can be "wreaked"? [W17]

ASIDE: DATA STRUCTURE — THE FREE LIST

The OS must track which parts of free memory are not in use, so as to be able to allocate memory to processes. Many different data structures can of course be used for such a task; the simplest (which we will assume here) is a **free list**, which simply is a list of the ranges of the physical memory which are not currently in use.

Hardware Requirements	Notes
Privileged mode	*Needed to prevent user-mode processes from executing privileged operations*
Base/bounds registers	*Need pair of registers per CPU to support address translation and bounds checks*
Ability to translate virtual addresses and check if within bounds	*Circuitry to do translations and check limits; in this case, quite simple*
Privileged instruction(s) to update base/bounds	*OS must be able to set these values before letting a user program run*
Privileged instruction(s) to register exception handlers	*OS must be able to tell hardware what code to run if exception occurs*
Ability to raise exceptions	*When processes try to access privileged instructions or out-of-bounds memory*

Figure 153: **Dynamic Relocation: Hardware Requirements**

running. Imagine it! And then quickly flush such dark thoughts from your mind, as they are the ghastly stuff of which nightmares are made.

Finally, the CPU must be able to generate **exceptions** in situations where a user program tries to access memory illegally (with an address that is "out of bounds"); in this case, the CPU should stop executing the user program and arrange for the OS "out-of-bounds" **exception handler** to run. The OS handler can then figure out how to react, in this case likely terminating the process. Similarly, if a user program tries to change the values of the (privileged) base and bounds registers, the CPU should raise an exception and run the "tried to execute a privileged operation while in user mode" handler. The CPU also must provide a method to inform it of the location of these handlers; a few more privileged instructions are thus needed.

15.5 Operating System Issues

Just as the hardware provides new features to support dynamic relocation, the OS now has new issues it must handle; the combination of hardware support and OS management leads to the implementation of a simple virtual memory. Specifically, there are a few critical junctures where the OS must get involved to implement our base-and-bounds version of virtual memory.

First, the OS must take action when a process is created, finding space for its address space in memory. Fortunately, given our assumptions that each address space is (a) smaller than the size of physical memory and (b) the same size, this is quite easy for the OS; it can simply view physical memory as an array of slots, and track whether each one is free or in use. When a new process is created, the OS will have to search a data structure (often called a **free list**) to find room for the new address space and then mark it used. With variable-sized address spaces, life is more complicated, but we will leave that concern for future chapters.

OS Requirements	Notes
Memory management	*Need to allocate memory for new processes;* *Reclaim memory from terminated processes;* *Generally manage memory via* ***free list***
Base/bounds management	*Must set base/bounds properly upon context switch*
Exception handling	*Code to run when exceptions arise;* *likely action is to terminate offending process*

Figure 154: **Dynamic Relocation: Operating System Responsibilities**

Let's look at an example. In Figure 152 (page 155), you can see the OS using the first slot of physical memory for itself, and that it has relocated the process from the example above into the slot starting at physical memory address 32 KB. The other two slots are free (16 KB-32 KB and 48 KB-64 KB); thus, the **free list** should consist of these two entries.

Second, the OS must do some work when a process is terminated (i.e., when it exits gracefully, or is forcefully killed because it misbehaved), reclaiming all of its memory for use in other processes or the OS. Upon termination of a process, the OS thus puts its memory back on the free list, and cleans up any associated data structures as need be.

Third, the OS must also perform a few additional steps when a context switch occurs. There is only one base and bounds register pair on each CPU, after all, and their values differ for each running program, as each program is loaded at a different physical address in memory. Thus, the OS must *save and restore* the base-and-bounds pair when it switches between processes. Specifically, when the OS decides to stop running a process, it must save the values of the base and bounds registers to memory, in some per-process structure such as the **process structure** or **process control block** (PCB). Similarly, when the OS resumes a running process (or runs it the first time), it must set the values of the base and bounds on the CPU to the correct values for this process.

We should note that when a process is stopped (i.e., not running), it is possible for the OS to move an address space from one location in memory to another rather easily. To move a process's address space, the OS first deschedules the process; then, the OS copies the address space from the current location to the new location; finally, the OS updates the saved base register (in the process structure) to point to the new location. When the process is resumed, its (new) base register is restored, and it begins running again, oblivious that its instructions and data are now in a completely new spot in memory.

Fourth, the OS must provide **exception handlers**, or functions to be called, as discussed above; the OS installs these handlers at boot time (via privileged instructions). For example, if a process tries to access memory outside its bounds, the CPU will raise an exception; the OS must be prepared to take action when such an exception arises. The common reaction of the OS will be one of hostility: it will likely terminate the offending process. The OS should be highly protective of the machine it is running, and thus it does not take kindly to a process trying to access memory or

OS @ boot (kernel mode)	Hardware	(No Program Yet)
initialize trap table		
	remember addresses of... system call handler timer handler illegal mem-access handler illegal instruction handler	
start interrupt timer		
	start timer; interrupt after X ms	
initialize process table **initialize free list**		

Figure 155: **Limited Direct Execution (Dynamic Relocation) @ Boot**

execute instructions that it shouldn't. Bye bye, misbehaving process; it's been nice knowing you.

Figures 155 and 156 (page 162) illustrate much of the hardware/OS interaction in a timeline. The first figure shows what the OS does at boot time to ready the machine for use, and the second shows what happens when a process (Process A) starts running; note how its memory translations are handled by the hardware with no OS intervention. At some point (middle of second figure), a timer interrupt occurs, and the OS switches to Process B, which executes a "bad load" (to an illegal memory address); at that point, the OS must get involved, terminating the process and cleaning up by freeing B's memory and removing its entry from the process table. As you can see from the figures, we are still following the basic approach of **limited direct execution**. In most cases, the OS just sets up the hardware appropriately and lets the process run directly on the CPU; only when the process misbehaves does the OS have to become involved.

15.6 Summary

In this chapter, we have extended the concept of limited direct execution with a specific mechanism used in virtual memory, known as **address translation**. With address translation, the OS can control each and every memory access from a process, ensuring the accesses stay within the bounds of the address space. Key to the efficiency of this technique is hardware support, which performs the translation quickly for each access, turning virtual addresses (the process's view of memory) into physical ones (the actual view). All of this is performed in a way that is *transparent* to the process that has been relocated; the process has no idea its memory references are being translated, making for a wonderful illusion.

We have also seen one particular form of virtualization, known as base and bounds or dynamic relocation. Base-and-bounds virtualization is quite *efficient*, as only a little more hardware logic is required to add a

OS @ run (kernel mode)	**Hardware**	**Program (user mode)**
To start process A: allocate entry in process table alloc memory for process set base/bound registers **return-from-trap** (into A)		
	restore registers of A move to **user mode** jump to A's (initial) PC	
		Process A runs Fetch instruction
	translate virtual address perform fetch	
		Execute instruction
	if explicit load/store: ensure address is legal translate virtual address perform load/store	
		(A runs...)
	Timer interrupt move to **kernel mode** jump to handler	
Handle timer decide: stop A, run B call `switch()` routine save regs(A) to proc-struct(A) (including base/bounds) restore regs(B) from proc-struct(B) (including base/bounds) **return-from-trap** (into B)		
	restore registers of B move to **user mode** jump to B's PC	
		Process B runs Execute bad load
	Load is out-of-bounds; move to **kernel mode** jump to trap handler	
Handle the trap decide to kill process B deallocate B's memory free B's entry in process table		

Figure 156: **Limited Direct Execution (Dynamic Relocation) @ Runtime**

base register to the virtual address and check that the address generated by the process is in bounds. Base-and-bounds also offers *protection*; the OS and hardware combine to ensure no process can generate memory references outside its own address space. Protection is certainly one of the most important goals of the OS; without it, the OS could not control the machine (if processes were free to overwrite memory, they could easily do nasty things like overwrite the trap table and take over the system).

Unfortunately, this simple technique of dynamic relocation does have its inefficiencies. For example, as you can see in Figure 152 (page 155), the relocated process is using physical memory from 32 KB to 48 KB; however, because the process stack and heap are not too big, all of the space between the two is simply *wasted*. This type of waste is usually called **internal fragmentation**, as the space *inside* the allocated unit is not all used (i.e., is fragmented) and thus wasted. In our current approach, although there might be enough physical memory for more processes, we are currently restricted to placing an address space in a fixed-sized slot and thus internal fragmentation can arise[2]. Thus, we are going to need more sophisticated machinery, to try to better utilize physical memory and avoid internal fragmentation. Our first attempt will be a slight generalization of base and bounds known as **segmentation**, which we will discuss next.

[2]A different solution might instead place a fixed-sized stack within the address space, just below the code region, and a growing heap below that. However, this limits flexibility by making recursion and deeply-nested function calls challenging, and thus is something we hope to avoid.

References

[M65] "On Dynamic Program Relocation" by W.C. McGee. IBM Systems Journal, Volume 4:3, 1965, pages 184–199. *This paper is a nice summary of early work on dynamic relocation, as well as some basics on static relocation.*

[P90] "Relocating loader for MS-DOS .EXE executable files" by Kenneth D. A. Pillay. Microprocessors & Microsystems archive, Volume 14:7 (September 1990). *An example of a relocating loader for MS-DOS. Not the first one, but just a relatively modern example of how such a system works.*

[SS74] "The Protection of Information in Computer Systems" by J. Saltzer and M. Schroeder. CACM, July 1974. *From this paper: "The concepts of base-and-bound register and hardware-interpreted descriptors appeared, apparently independently, between 1957 and 1959 on three projects with diverse goals. At M.I.T., McCarthy suggested the base-and-bound idea as part of the memory protection system necessary to make time-sharing feasible. IBM independently developed the base-and-bound register as a mechanism to permit reliable multiprogramming of the Stretch (7030) computer system. At Burroughs, R. Barton suggested that hardware-interpreted descriptors would provide direct support for the naming scope rules of higher level languages in the B5000 computer system." We found this quote on Mark Smotherman's cool history pages [S04]; see them for more information.*

[S04] "System Call Support" by Mark Smotherman. May 2004. `people.cs.clemson.edu/~mark/syscall.html`. *A neat history of system call support. Smotherman has also collected some early history on items like interrupts and other fun aspects of computing history. See his web pages for more details.*

[WL+93] "Efficient Software-based Fault Isolation" by Robert Wahbe, Steven Lucco, Thomas E. Anderson, Susan L. Graham. SOSP '93. *A terrific paper about how you can use compiler support to bound memory references from a program, without hardware support. The paper sparked renewed interest in software techniques for isolation of memory references.*

[W17] Answer to footnote: "Is there anything other than havoc that can be wreaked?" by Waciuma Wanjohi. October 2017. *Amazingly, this enterprising reader found the answer via google's Ngram viewing tool (available at the following URL:* `http://books.google.com/ngrams`*). The answer, thanks to Mr. Wanjohi: "It's only since about 1970 that 'wreak havoc' has been more popular than 'wreak vengeance'. In the 1800s, the word wreak was almost always followed by 'his/their vengeance'." Apparently, when you wreak, you are up to no good, but at least wreakers have some options now.*

Homework (Simulation)

The program `relocation.py` allows you to see how address translations are performed in a system with base and bounds registers. See the README for details.

Questions

1. Run with seeds 1, 2, and 3, and compute whether each virtual address generated by the process is in or out of bounds. If in bounds, compute the translation.
2. Run with these flags: `-s 0 -n 10`. What value do you have set `-l` (the bounds register) to in order to ensure that all the generated virtual addresses are within bounds?
3. Run with these flags: `-s 1 -n 10 -l 100`. What is the maximum value that base can be set to, such that the address space still fits into physical memory in its entirety?
4. Run some of the same problems above, but with larger address spaces (`-a`) and physical memories (`-p`).
5. What fraction of randomly-generated virtual addresses are valid, as a function of the value of the bounds register? Make a graph from running with different random seeds, with limit values ranging from 0 up to the maximum size of the address space.

16

Segmentation

So far we have been putting the entire address space of each process in memory. With the base and bounds registers, the OS can easily relocate processes to different parts of physical memory. However, you might have noticed something interesting about these address spaces of ours: there is a big chunk of "free" space right in the middle, between the stack and the heap.

As you can imagine from Figure 161, although the space between the stack and heap is not being used by the process, it is still taking up physical memory when we relocate the entire address space somewhere in physical memory; thus, the simple approach of using a base and bounds register pair to virtualize memory is wasteful. It also makes it quite hard to run a program when the entire address space doesn't fit into memory; thus, base and bounds is not as flexible as we would like. And thus:

> THE CRUX: HOW TO SUPPORT A LARGE ADDRESS SPACE
>
> How do we support a large address space with (potentially) a lot of free space between the stack and the heap? Note that in our examples, with tiny (pretend) address spaces, the waste doesn't seem too bad. Imagine, however, a 32-bit address space (4 GB in size); a typical program will only use megabytes of memory, but still would demand that the entire address space be resident in memory.

16.1 Segmentation: Generalized Base/Bounds

To solve this problem, an idea was born, and it is called **segmentation**. It is quite an old idea, going at least as far back as the very early 1960's [H61, G62]. The idea is simple: instead of having just one base and bounds pair in our MMU, why not have a base and bounds pair per logical **segment** of the address space? A segment is just a contiguous portion of the address space of a particular length, and in our canonical

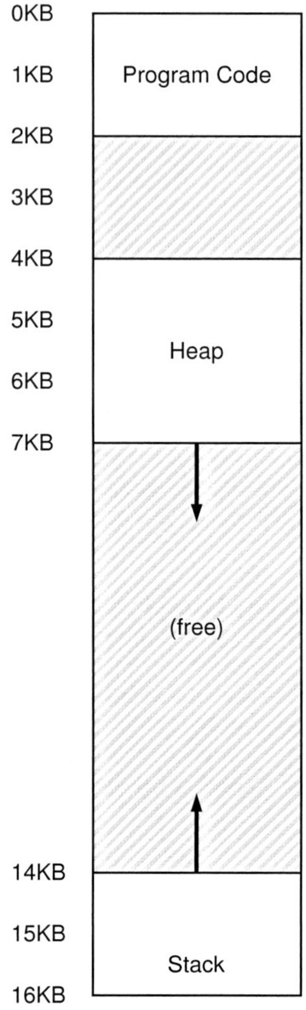

Figure 161: **An Address Space (Again)**

address space, we have three logically-different segments: code, stack, and heap. What segmentation allows the OS to do is to place each one of those segments in different parts of physical memory, and thus avoid filling physical memory with unused virtual address space.

Let's look at an example. Assume we want to place the address space from Figure 161 into physical memory. With a base and bounds pair per segment, we can place each segment *independently* in physical memory. For example, see Figure 162 (page 169); there you see a 64KB physical memory with those three segments in it (and 16KB reserved for the OS).

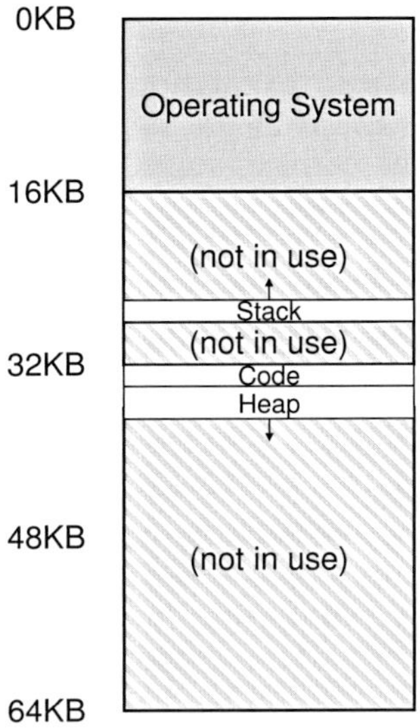

Figure 162: **Placing Segments In Physical Memory**

As you can see in the diagram, only used memory is allocated space in physical memory, and thus large address spaces with large amounts of unused address space (which we sometimes call **sparse address spaces**) can be accommodated.

The hardware structure in our MMU required to support segmentation is just what you'd expect: in this case, a set of three base and bounds register pairs. Figure 163 below shows the register values for the example above; each bounds register holds the size of a segment.

Segment	Base	Size
Code	32K	2K
Heap	34K	3K
Stack	28K	2K

Figure 163: **Segment Register Values**

You can see from the figure that the code segment is placed at physical address 32KB and has a size of 2KB and the heap segment is placed at 34KB and has a size of 3KB. The size segment here is exactly the same as the bounds register introduced previously; it tells the hardware exactly how many bytes are valid in this segment (and thus, enables the hardware to determine when a program has made an illegal access outside of those bounds).

Let's do an example translation, using the address space in Figure 161. Assume a reference is made to virtual address 100 (which is in the code segment, as you can see visually in Figure 161, page 168). When the refer-

ASIDE: THE SEGMENTATION FAULT

The term **segmentation fault** or violation arises from a memory access on a segmented machine to an illegal address. Humorously, the term persists, even on machines with no support for segmentation at all. Or not so humorously, if you can't figure out why your code keeps faulting.

ence takes place (say, on an instruction fetch), the hardware will add the base value to the *offset* into this segment (100 in this case) to arrive at the desired physical address: 100 + 32KB, or 32868. It will then check that the address is within bounds (100 is less than 2KB), find that it is, and issue the reference to physical memory address 32868.

Now let's look at an address in the heap, virtual address 4200 (again refer to Figure 161). If we just add the virtual address 4200 to the base of the heap (34KB), we get a physical address of 39016, which is *not* the correct physical address. What we need to first do is extract the *offset* into the heap, i.e., which byte(s) *in this segment* the address refers to. Because the heap starts at virtual address 4KB (4096), the offset of 4200 is actually 4200 minus 4096, or 104. We then take this offset (104) and add it to the base register physical address (34K) to get the desired result: 34920.

What if we tried to refer to an illegal address (i.e., a virtual address of 7KB or greater), which is beyond the end of the heap? You can imagine what will happen: the hardware detects that the address is out of bounds, traps into the OS, likely leading to the termination of the offending process. And now you know the origin of the famous term that all C programmers learn to dread: the **segmentation violation** or **segmentation fault**.

16.2 Which Segment Are We Referring To?

The hardware uses segment registers during translation. How does it know the offset into a segment, and to which segment an address refers?

One common approach, sometimes referred to as an **explicit** approach, is to chop up the address space into segments based on the top few bits of the virtual address; this technique was used in the VAX/VMS system [LL82]. In our example above, we have three segments; thus we need two bits to accomplish our task. If we use the top two bits of our 14-bit virtual address to select the segment, our virtual address looks like this:

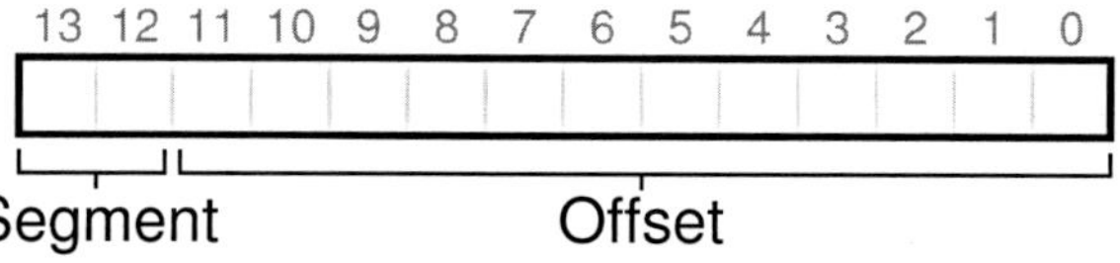

In our example, then, if the top two bits are 00, the hardware knows the virtual address is in the code segment, and thus uses the code base and bounds pair to relocate the address to the correct physical location. If the top two bits are 01, the hardware knows the address is in the heap, and thus uses the heap base and bounds. Let's take our example heap virtual address from above (4200) and translate it, just to make sure this is clear. The virtual address 4200, in binary form, can be seen here:

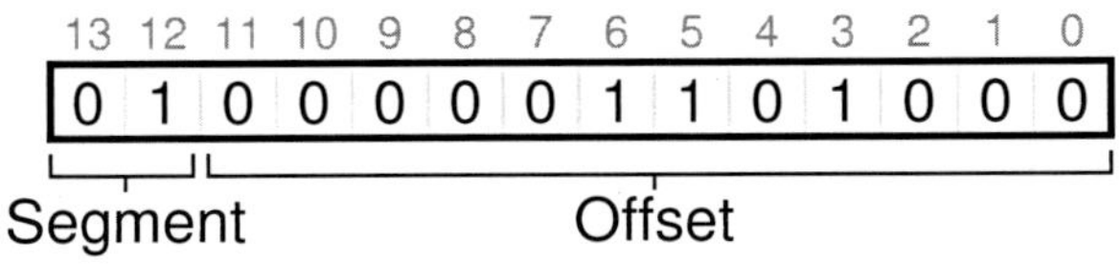

As you can see from the picture, the top two bits (01) tell the hardware which *segment* we are referring to. The bottom 12 bits are the *offset* into the segment: 0000 0110 1000, or hex 0x068, or 104 in decimal. Thus, the hardware simply takes the first two bits to determine which segment register to use, and then takes the next 12 bits as the offset into the segment. By adding the base register to the offset, the hardware arrives at the final physical address. Note the offset eases the bounds check too: we can simply check if the offset is less than the bounds; if not, the address is illegal. Thus, if base and bounds were arrays (with one entry per segment), the hardware would be doing something like this to obtain the desired physical address:

```
// get top 2 bits of 14-bit VA
Segment = (VirtualAddress & SEG_MASK) >> SEG_SHIFT
// now get offset
Offset  = VirtualAddress & OFFSET_MASK
if (Offset >= Bounds[Segment])
    RaiseException(PROTECTION_FAULT)
else
    PhysAddr = Base[Segment] + Offset
    Register = AccessMemory(PhysAddr)
```

In our running example, we can fill in values for the constants above. Specifically, `SEG_MASK` would be set to `0x3000`, `SEG_SHIFT` to `12`, and `OFFSET_MASK` to `0xFFF`.

You may also have noticed that when we use the top two bits, and we only have three segments (code, heap, stack), one segment of the address space goes unused. To fully utilize the virtual address space (and avoid an unused segment), some systems put code in the same segment as the heap and thus use only one bit to select which segment to use [LL82].

Another issue with using the top so many bits to select a segment is that it limits use of the virtual address space. Specifically, each segment is limited to a *maximum size*, which in our example is 4KB (using the top two bits to choose segments implies the 16KB address space gets chopped into four pieces, or 4KB in this example). If a running program wishes to grow a segment (say the heap, or the stack) beyond that maximum, the program is out of luck.

There are other ways for the hardware to determine which segment a particular address is in. In the **implicit** approach, the hardware determines the segment by noticing how the address was formed. If, for example, the address was generated from the program counter (i.e., it was an instruction fetch), then the address is within the code segment; if the address is based off of the stack or base pointer, it must be in the stack segment; any other address must be in the heap.

16.3 What About The Stack?

Thus far, we've left out one important component of the address space: the stack. The stack has been relocated to physical address 28KB in the diagram above, but with one critical difference: *it grows backwards* (i.e., towards lower addresses). In physical memory, it "starts" at 28KB[1] and grows back to 26KB, corresponding to virtual addresses 16KB to 14KB; translation must proceed differently.

The first thing we need is a little extra hardware support. Instead of just base and bounds values, the hardware also needs to know which way the segment grows (a bit, for example, that is set to 1 when the segment grows in the positive direction, and 0 for negative). Our updated view of what the hardware tracks is seen in Figure 164:

Segment	Base	Size (max 4K)	Grows Positive?
Code_{00}	32K	2K	1
Heap_{01}	34K	3K	1
Stack_{11}	28K	2K	0

Figure 164: **Segment Registers (With Negative-Growth Support)**

With the hardware understanding that segments can grow in the negative direction, the hardware must now translate such virtual addresses slightly differently. Let's take an example stack virtual address and translate it to understand the process.

In this example, assume we wish to access virtual address 15KB, which should map to physical address 27KB. Our virtual address, in binary form, thus looks like this: 11 1100 0000 0000 (hex 0x3C00). The hardware uses the top two bits (11) to designate the segment, but then we are left with an offset of 3KB. To obtain the correct negative offset, we must subtract the maximum segment size from 3KB: in this example, a segment can be 4KB, and thus the correct negative offset is 3KB minus 4KB which equals -1KB. We simply add the negative offset (-1KB) to the base (28KB) to arrive at the correct physical address: 27KB. The bounds check can be calculated by ensuring the absolute value of the negative offset is less than or equal to the segment's current size (in this case, 2KB).

---

[1]Although we say, for simplicity, that the stack "starts" at 28KB, this value is actually the byte just *below* the location of the backward growing region; the first valid byte is actually 28KB minus 1. In contrast, forward-growing regions start at the address of the first byte of the segment. We take this approach because it makes the math to compute the physical address straightforward: the physical address is just the base plus the negative offset.

16.4 Support for Sharing

As support for segmentation grew, system designers soon realized that they could realize new types of efficiencies with a little more hardware support. Specifically, to save memory, sometimes it is useful to **share** certain memory segments between address spaces. In particular, **code sharing** is common and still in use in systems today.

To support sharing, we need a little extra support from the hardware, in the form of **protection bits**. Basic support adds a few bits per segment, indicating whether or not a program can read or write a segment, or perhaps execute code that lies within the segment. By setting a code segment to read-only, the same code can be shared across multiple processes, without worry of harming isolation; while each process still thinks that it is accessing its own private memory, the OS is secretly sharing memory which cannot be modified by the process, and thus the illusion is preserved.

An example of the additional information tracked by the hardware (and OS) is shown in Figure 165. As you can see, the code segment is set to read and execute, and thus the same physical segment in memory could be mapped into multiple virtual address spaces.

Segment	Base	Size (max 4K)	Grows Positive?	Protection
$Code_{00}$	32K	2K	1	Read-Execute
$Heap_{01}$	34K	3K	1	Read-Write
$Stack_{11}$	28K	2K	0	Read-Write

Figure 165: **Segment Register Values (with Protection)**

With protection bits, the hardware algorithm described earlier would also have to change. In addition to checking whether a virtual address is within bounds, the hardware also has to check whether a particular access is permissible. If a user process tries to write to a read-only segment, or execute from a non-executable segment, the hardware should raise an exception, and thus let the OS deal with the offending process.

16.5 Fine-grained vs. Coarse-grained Segmentation

Most of our examples thus far have focused on systems with just a few segments (i.e., code, stack, heap); we can think of this segmentation as **coarse-grained**, as it chops up the address space into relatively large, coarse chunks. However, some early systems (e.g., Multics [CV65,DD68]) were more flexible and allowed for address spaces to consist of a large number of smaller segments, referred to as **fine-grained** segmentation.

Supporting many segments requires even further hardware support, with a **segment table** of some kind stored in memory. Such segment tables usually support the creation of a very large number of segments, and thus enable a system to use segments in more flexible ways than we have thus far discussed. For example, early machines like the Burroughs B5000 had support for thousands of segments, and expected a compiler to chop

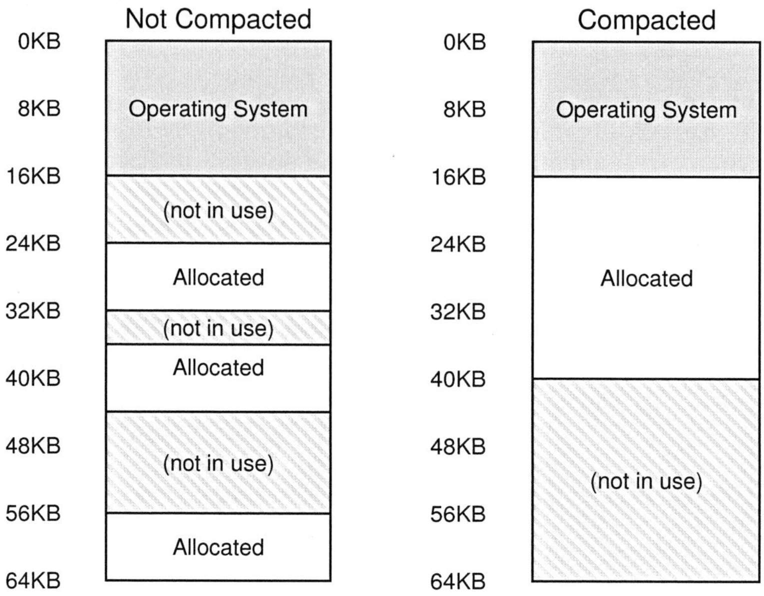

Figure 166: **Non-compacted and Compacted Memory**

code and data into separate segments which the OS and hardware would then support [RK68]. The thinking at the time was that by having fine-grained segments, the OS could better learn about which segments are in use and which are not and thus utilize main memory more effectively.

16.6 OS Support

You now should have a basic idea as to how segmentation works. Pieces of the address space are relocated into physical memory as the system runs, and thus a huge savings of physical memory is achieved relative to our simpler approach with just a single base/bounds pair for the entire address space. Specifically, all the unused space between the stack and the heap need not be allocated in physical memory, allowing us to fit more address spaces into physical memory and support a large and sparse virtual address space per process.

However, segmentation raises a number of new issues for the operating system. The first is an old one: what should the OS do on a context switch? You should have a good guess by now: the segment registers must be saved and restored. Clearly, each process has its own virtual address space, and the OS must make sure to set up these registers correctly before letting the process run again.

The second is OS interaction when segments grow (or perhaps shrink). For example, a program may call `malloc()` to allocate an object. In some cases, the existing heap will be able to service the request, and thus

> TIP: IF 1000 SOLUTIONS EXIST, NO GREAT ONE DOES
> The fact that so many different algorithms exist to try to minimize external fragmentation is indicative of a stronger underlying truth: there is no one "best" way to solve the problem. Thus, we settle for something reasonable and hope it is good enough. The only real solution (as we will see in forthcoming chapters) is to avoid the problem altogether, by never allocating memory in variable-sized chunks.

`malloc()` will find free space for the object and return a pointer to it to the caller. In others, however, the heap segment itself may need to grow. In this case, the memory-allocation library will perform a system call to grow the heap (e.g., the traditional UNIX `sbrk()` system call). The OS will then (usually) provide more space, updating the segment size register to the new (bigger) size, and informing the library of success; the library can then allocate space for the new object and return successfully to the calling program. Do note that the OS could reject the request, if no more physical memory is available, or if it decides that the calling process already has too much.

The last, and perhaps most important, issue is managing free space in physical memory. When a new address space is created, the OS has to be able to find space in physical memory for its segments. Previously, we assumed that each address space was the same size, and thus physical memory could be thought of as a bunch of slots where processes would fit in. Now, we have a number of segments per process, and each segment might be a different size.

The general problem that arises is that physical memory quickly becomes full of little holes of free space, making it difficult to allocate new segments, or to grow existing ones. We call this problem **external fragmentation** [R69]; see Figure 166 (left).

In the example, a process comes along and wishes to allocate a 20KB segment. In that example, there is 24KB free, but not in one contiguous segment (rather, in three non-contiguous chunks). Thus, the OS cannot satisfy the 20KB request. Similar problems could occur when a request to grow a segment arrives; if the next so many bytes of physical space are not available, the OS will have to reject the request, even though there may be free bytes available elsewhere in physical memory.

One solution to this problem would be to **compact** physical memory by rearranging the existing segments. For example, the OS could stop whichever processes are running, copy their data to one contiguous region of memory, change their segment register values to point to the new physical locations, and thus have a large free extent of memory with which to work. By doing so, the OS enables the new allocation request to succeed. However, compaction is expensive, as copying segments is memory-intensive and generally uses a fair amount of processor time;

see Figure 166 (right) for a diagram of compacted physical memory. Compaction also (ironically) makes requests to grow existing segments hard to serve, and may thus cause further rearrangement to accommodate such requests.

A simpler approach might instead be to use a free-list management algorithm that tries to keep large extents of memory available for allocation. There are literally hundreds of approaches that people have taken, including classic algorithms like **best-fit** (which keeps a list of free spaces and returns the one closest in size that satisfies the desired allocation to the requester), **worst-fit**, **first-fit**, and more complex schemes like **buddy algorithm** [K68]. An excellent survey by Wilson et al. is a good place to start if you want to learn more about such algorithms [W+95], or you can wait until we cover some of the basics in a later chapter. Unfortunately, though, no matter how smart the algorithm, external fragmentation will still exist; thus, a good algorithm simply attempts to minimize it.

16.7 Summary

Segmentation solves a number of problems, and helps us build a more effective virtualization of memory. Beyond just dynamic relocation, segmentation can better support sparse address spaces, by avoiding the huge potential waste of memory between logical segments of the address space. It is also fast, as doing the arithmetic segmentation requires is easy and well-suited to hardware; the overheads of translation are minimal. A fringe benefit arises too: code sharing. If code is placed within a separate segment, such a segment could potentially be shared across multiple running programs.

However, as we learned, allocating variable-sized segments in memory leads to some problems that we'd like to overcome. The first, as discussed above, is external fragmentation. Because segments are variable-sized, free memory gets chopped up into odd-sized pieces, and thus satisfying a memory-allocation request can be difficult. One can try to use smart algorithms [W+95] or periodically compact memory, but the problem is fundamental and hard to avoid.

The second and perhaps more important problem is that segmentation still isn't flexible enough to support our fully generalized, sparse address space. For example, if we have a large but sparsely-used heap all in one logical segment, the entire heap must still reside in memory in order to be accessed. In other words, if our model of how the address space is being used doesn't exactly match how the underlying segmentation has been designed to support it, segmentation doesn't work very well. We thus need to find some new solutions. Ready to find them?

References

[CV65] "Introduction and Overview of the Multics System" by F. J. Corbato, V. A. Vyssotsky. Fall Joint Computer Conference, 1965. *One of five papers presented on Multics at the Fall Joint Computer Conference; oh to be a fly on the wall in that room that day!*

[DD68] "Virtual Memory, Processes, and Sharing in Multics" by Robert C. Daley and Jack B. Dennis. Communications of the ACM, Volume 11:5, May 1968. *An early paper on how to perform dynamic linking in Multics, which was way ahead of its time. Dynamic linking finally found its way back into systems about 20 years later, as the large X-windows libraries demanded it. Some say that these large X11 libraries were MIT's revenge for removing support for dynamic linking in early versions of* UNIX*!*

[G62] "Fact Segmentation" by M. N. Greenfield. Proceedings of the SJCC, Volume 21, May 1962. *Another early paper on segmentation; so early that it has no references to other work.*

[H61] "Program Organization and Record Keeping for Dynamic Storage" by A. W. Holt. Communications of the ACM, Volume 4:10, October 1961. *An incredibly early and difficult to read paper about segmentation and some of its uses.*

[I09] "Intel 64 and IA-32 Architectures Software Developer's Manuals" by Intel. 2009. Available: http://www.intel.com/products/processor/manuals. *Try reading about segmentation in here (Chapter 3 in Volume 3a); it'll hurt your head, at least a little bit.*

[K68] "The Art of Computer Programming: Volume I" by Donald Knuth. Addison-Wesley, 1968. *Knuth is famous not only for his early books on the Art of Computer Programming but for his typesetting system TeX which is still a powerhouse typesetting tool used by professionals today, and indeed to typeset this very book. His tomes on algorithms are a great early reference to many of the algorithms that underly computing systems today.*

[L83] "Hints for Computer Systems Design" by Butler Lampson. ACM Operating Systems Review, 15:5, October 1983. *A treasure-trove of sage advice on how to build systems. Hard to read in one sitting; take it in a little at a time, like a fine wine, or a reference manual.*

[LL82] "Virtual Memory Management in the VAX/VMS Operating System" by Henry M. Levy, Peter H. Lipman. IEEE Computer, Volume 15:3, March 1982. *A classic memory management system, with lots of common sense in its design. We'll study it in more detail in a later chapter.*

[RK68] "Dynamic Storage Allocation Systems" by B. Randell and C.J. Kuehner. Communications of the ACM, Volume 11:5, May 1968. *A nice overview of the differences between paging and segmentation, with some historical discussion of various machines.*

[R69] "A note on storage fragmentation and program segmentation" by Brian Randell. Communications of the ACM, Volume 12:7, July 1969. *One of the earliest papers to discuss fragmentation.*

[W+95] "Dynamic Storage Allocation: A Survey and Critical Review" by Paul R. Wilson, Mark S. Johnstone, Michael Neely, David Boles. International Workshop on Memory Management, Scotland, UK, September 1995. *A great survey paper on memory allocators.*

Homework (Simulation)

This program allows you to see how address translations are performed in a system with segmentation. See the README for details.

Questions

1. First let's use a tiny address space to translate some addresses. Here's a simple set of parameters with a few different random seeds; can you translate the addresses?

```
segmentation.py -a 128 -p 512 -b 0 -l 20 -B 512
  -L 20 -s 0
segmentation.py -a 128 -p 512 -b 0 -l 20 -B 512
  -L 20 -s 1
segmentation.py -a 128 -p 512 -b 0 -l 20 -B 512
  -L 20 -s 2
```

2. Now, let's see if we understand this tiny address space we've constructed (using the parameters from the question above). What is the highest legal virtual address in segment 0? What about the lowest legal virtual address in segment 1? What are the lowest and highest *illegal* addresses in this entire address space? Finally, how would you run `segmentation.py` with the `-A` flag to test if you are right?

3. Let's say we have a tiny 16-byte address space in a 128-byte physical memory. What base and bounds would you set up so as to get the simulator to generate the following translation results for the specified address stream: valid, valid, violation, ..., violation, valid, valid? Assume the following parameters:

```
segmentation.py -a 16 -p 128
  -A 0,1,2,3,4,5,6,7,8,9,10,11,12,13,14,15
  --b0 ? --l0 ? --b1 ? --l1 ?
```

4. Assume we want to generate a problem where roughly 90% of the randomly-generated virtual addresses are valid (not segmentation violations). How should you configure the simulator to do so? Which parameters are important to getting this outcome?

5. Can you run the simulator such that no virtual addresses are valid? How?

17

Free-Space Management

In this chapter, we take a small detour from our discussion of virtualizing memory to discuss a fundamental aspect of any memory management system, whether it be a malloc library (managing pages of a process's heap) or the OS itself (managing portions of the address space of a process). Specifically, we will discuss the issues surrounding **free-space management**.

Let us make the problem more specific. Managing free space can certainly be easy, as we will see when we discuss the concept of **paging**. It is easy when the space you are managing is divided into fixed-sized units; in such a case, you just keep a list of these fixed-sized units; when a client requests one of them, return the first entry.

Where free-space management becomes more difficult (and interesting) is when the free space you are managing consists of variable-sized units; this arises in a user-level memory-allocation library (as in `malloc()` and `free()`) and in an OS managing physical memory when using **segmentation** to implement virtual memory. In either case, the problem that exists is known as **external fragmentation**: the free space gets chopped into little pieces of different sizes and is thus fragmented; subsequent requests may fail because there is no single contiguous space that can satisfy the request, even though the total amount of free space exceeds the size of the request.

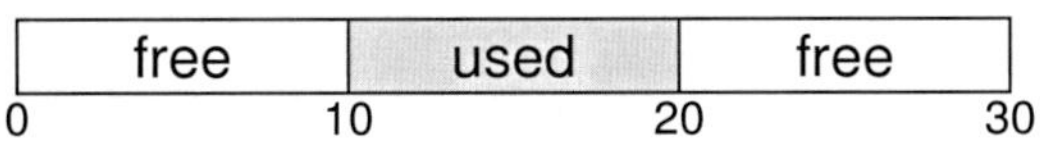

The figure shows an example of this problem. In this case, the total free space available is 20 bytes; unfortunately, it is fragmented into two chunks of size 10 each. As a result, a request for 15 bytes will fail even though there are 20 bytes free. And thus we arrive at the problem addressed in this chapter.

> CRUX: HOW TO MANAGE FREE SPACE
> How should free space be managed, when satisfying variable-sized requests? What strategies can be used to minimize fragmentation? What are the time and space overheads of alternate approaches?

17.1 Assumptions

Most of this discussion will focus on the great history of allocators found in user-level memory-allocation libraries. We draw on Wilson's excellent survey [W+95] but encourage interested readers to go to the source document itself for more details[1].

We assume a basic interface such as that provided by `malloc()` and `free()`. Specifically, `void *malloc(size_t size)` takes a single parameter, `size`, which is the number of bytes requested by the application; it hands back a pointer (of no particular type, or a **void pointer** in C lingo) to a region of that size (or greater). The complementary routine `void free(void *ptr)` takes a pointer and frees the corresponding chunk. Note the implication of the interface: the user, when freeing the space, does not inform the library of its size; thus, the library must be able to figure out how big a chunk of memory is when handed just a pointer to it. We'll discuss how to do this a bit later on in the chapter.

The space that this library manages is known historically as the `heap`, and the generic data structure used to manage free space in the heap is some kind of **free list**. This structure contains references to all of the free chunks of space in the managed region of memory. Of course, this data structure need not be a list *per se*, but just some kind of data structure to track free space.

We further assume that primarily we are concerned with **external fragmentation**, as described above. Allocators could of course also have the problem of **internal fragmentation**; if an allocator hands out chunks of memory bigger than that requested, any unasked for (and thus unused) space in such a chunk is considered *internal* fragmentation (because the waste occurs inside the allocated unit) and is another example of space waste. However, for the sake of simplicity, and because it is the more interesting of the two types of fragmentation, we'll mostly focus on external fragmentation.

We'll also assume that once memory is handed out to a client, it cannot be relocated to another location in memory. For example, if a program calls `malloc()` and is given a pointer to some space within the heap, that memory region is essentially "owned" by the program (and cannot be moved by the library) until the program returns it via a corresponding call to `free()`. Thus, no **compaction** of free space is possible, which

[1] It is nearly 80 pages long; thus, you really have to be interested!

would be useful to combat fragmentation[2]. Compaction could, however, be used in the OS to deal with fragmentation when implementing **segmentation** (as discussed in said chapter on segmentation).

Finally, we'll assume that the allocator manages a contiguous region of bytes. In some cases, an allocator could ask for that region to grow; for example, a user-level memory-allocation library might call into the kernel to grow the heap (via a system call such as `sbrk`) when it runs out of space. However, for simplicity, we'll just assume that the region is a single fixed size throughout its life.

17.2 Low-level Mechanisms

Before delving into some policy details, we'll first cover some common mechanisms used in most allocators. First, we'll discuss the basics of splitting and coalescing, common techniques in most any allocator. Second, we'll show how one can track the size of allocated regions quickly and with relative ease. Finally, we'll discuss how to build a simple list inside the free space to keep track of what is free and what isn't.

Splitting and Coalescing

A free list contains a set of elements that describe the free space still remaining in the heap. Thus, assume the following 30-byte heap:

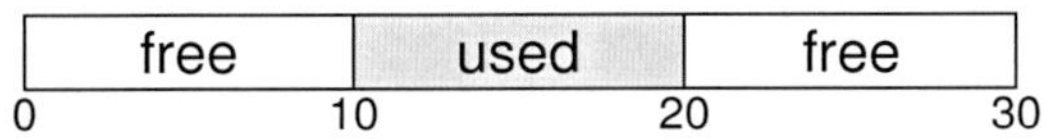

The free list for this heap would have two elements on it. One entry describes the first 10-byte free segment (bytes 0-9), and one entry describes the other free segment (bytes 20-29):

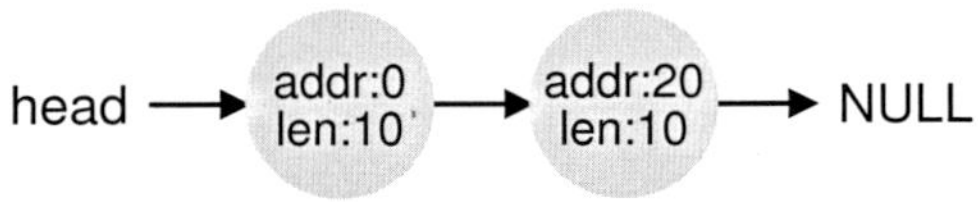

As described above, a request for anything greater than 10 bytes will fail (returning NULL); there just isn't a single contiguous chunk of memory of that size available. A request for exactly that size (10 bytes) could be satisfied easily by either of the free chunks. But what happens if the request is for something *smaller* than 10 bytes?

Assume we have a request for just a single byte of memory. In this case, the allocator will perform an action known as **splitting**: it will find

[2]Once you hand a pointer to a chunk of memory to a C program, it is generally difficult to determine all references (pointers) to that region, which may be stored in other variables or even in registers at a given point in execution. This may not be the case in more strongly-typed, garbage-collected languages, which would thus enable compaction as a technique to combat fragmentation.

a free chunk of memory that can satisfy the request and split it into two. The first chunk it will return to the caller; the second chunk will remain on the list. Thus, in our example above, if a request for 1 byte were made, and the allocator decided to use the second of the two elements on the list to satisfy the request, the call to malloc() would return 20 (the address of the 1-byte allocated region) and the list would end up looking like this:

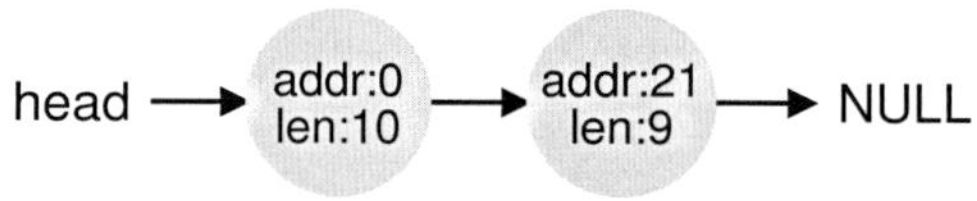

In the picture, you can see the list basically stays intact; the only change is that the free region now starts at 21 instead of 20, and the length of that free region is now just 9[3]. Thus, the split is commonly used in allocators when requests are smaller than the size of any particular free chunk.

A corollary mechanism found in many allocators is known as **coalescing** of free space. Take our example from above once more (free 10 bytes, used 10 bytes, and another free 10 bytes).

Given this (tiny) heap, what happens when an application calls free(10), thus returning the space in the middle of the heap? If we simply add this free space back into our list without too much thinking, we might end up with a list that looks like this:

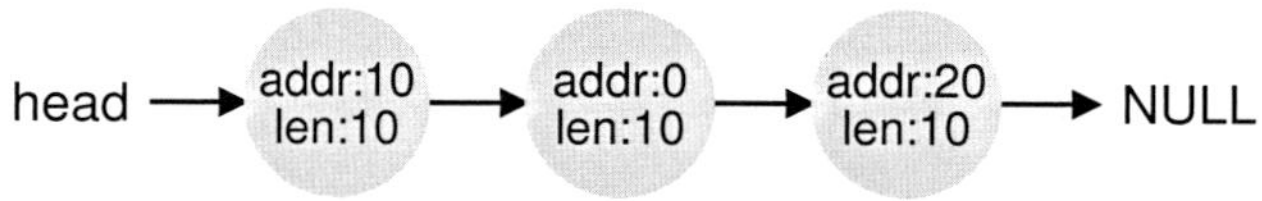

Note the problem: while the entire heap is now free, it is seemingly divided into three chunks of 10 bytes each. Thus, if a user requests 20 bytes, a simple list traversal will not find such a free chunk, and return failure.

What allocators do in order to avoid this problem is coalesce free space when a chunk of memory is freed. The idea is simple: when returning a free chunk in memory, look carefully at the addresses of the chunk you are returning as well as the nearby chunks of free space; if the newly-freed space sits right next to one (or two, as in this example) existing free chunks, merge them into a single larger free chunk. Thus, with coalescing, our final list should look like this:

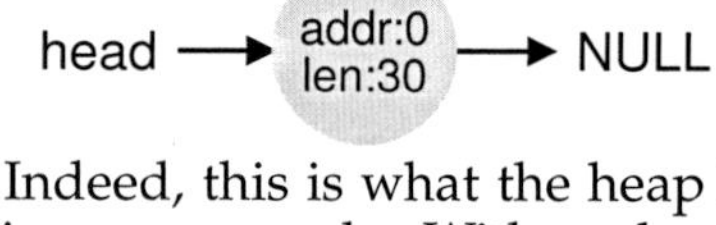

Indeed, this is what the heap list looked like at first, before any allocations were made. With coalescing, an allocator can better ensure that large free extents are available for the application.

[3]This discussion assumes that there are no headers, an unrealistic but simplifying assumption we make for now.

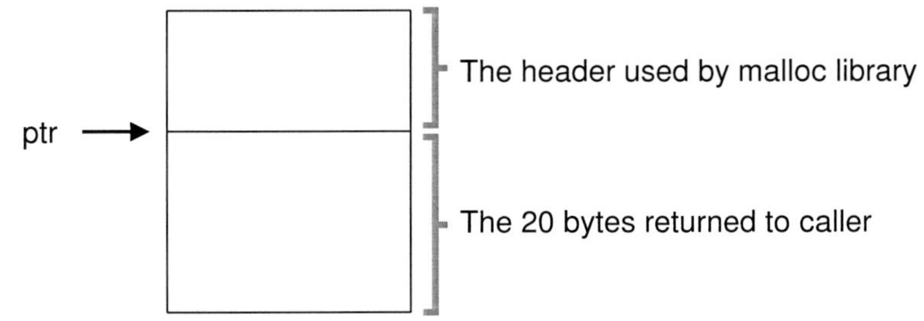

Figure 171: **An Allocated Region Plus Header**

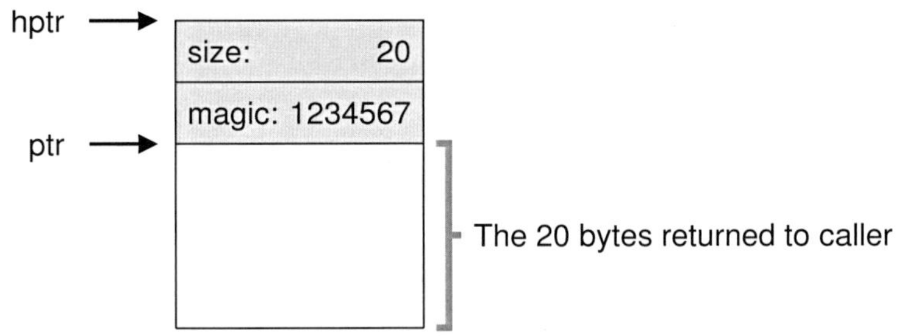

Figure 172: **Specific Contents Of The Header**

Tracking The Size Of Allocated Regions

You might have noticed that the interface to `free(void *ptr)` does not take a size parameter; thus it is assumed that given a pointer, the malloc library can quickly determine the size of the region of memory being freed and thus incorporate the space back into the free list.

To accomplish this task, most allocators store a little bit of extra information in a **header** block which is kept in memory, usually just before the handed-out chunk of memory. Let's look at an example again (Figure 171). In this example, we are examining an allocated block of size 20 bytes, pointed to by `ptr`; imagine the user called `malloc()` and stored the results in `ptr`, e.g., `ptr = malloc(20);`.

The header minimally contains the size of the allocated region (in this case, 20); it may also contain additional pointers to speed up deallocation, a magic number to provide additional integrity checking, and other information. Let's assume a simple header which contains the size of the region and a magic number, like this:

```
typedef struct {
    int size;
    int magic;
} header_t;
```

The example above would look like what you see in Figure 17.2. When the user calls `free(ptr)`, the library then uses simple pointer arithmetic to figure out where the header begins:

```
void free(void *ptr) {
    header_t *hptr = (header_t *) ptr - 1;
    ...
```

After obtaining such a pointer to the header, the library can easily determine whether the magic number matches the expected value as a sanity check (`assert(hptr->magic == 1234567)`) and calculate the total size of the newly-freed region via simple math (i.e., adding the size of the header to size of the region). Note the small but critical detail in the last sentence: the size of the free region is the size of the header plus the size of the space allocated to the user. Thus, when a user requests N bytes of memory, the library does not search for a free chunk of size N; rather, it searches for a free chunk of size N plus the size of the header.

Embedding A Free List

Thus far we have treated our simple free list as a conceptual entity; it is just a list describing the free chunks of memory in the heap. But how do we build such a list inside the free space itself?

In a more typical list, when allocating a new node, you would just call `malloc()` when you need space for the node. Unfortunately, within the memory-allocation library, you can't do this! Instead, you need to build the list *inside* the free space itself. Don't worry if this sounds a little weird; it is, but not so weird that you can't do it!

Assume we have a 4096-byte chunk of memory to manage (i.e., the heap is 4KB). To manage this as a free list, we first have to initialize said list; initially, the list should have one entry, of size 4096 (minus the header size). Here is the description of a node of the list:

```
typedef struct __node_t {
    int              size;
    struct __node_t *next;
} node_t;
```

Now let's look at some code that initializes the heap and puts the first element of the free list inside that space. We are assuming that the heap is built within some free space acquired via a call to the system call `mmap()`; this is not the only way to build such a heap but serves us well in this example. Here is the code:

```
// mmap() returns a pointer to a chunk of free space
node_t *head = mmap(NULL, 4096, PROT_READ|PROT_WRITE,
                    MAP_ANON|MAP_PRIVATE, -1, 0);
head->size   = 4096 - sizeof(node_t);
head->next   = NULL;
```

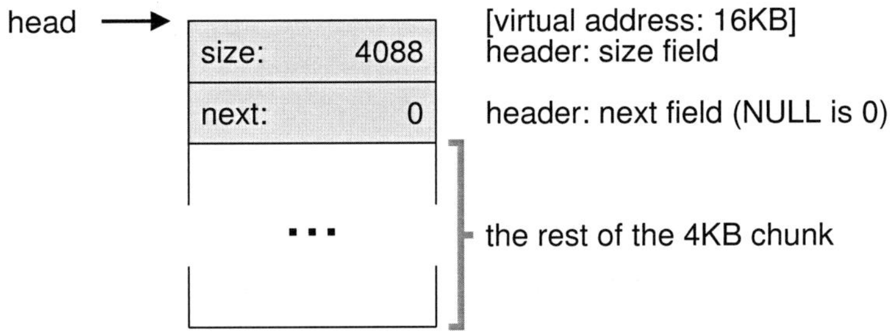

Figure 173: **A Heap With One Free Chunk**

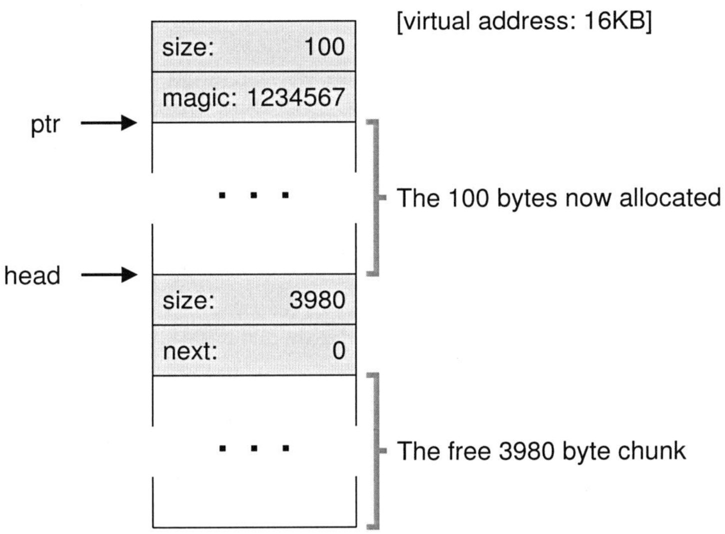

Figure 174: **A Heap: After One Allocation**

After running this code, the status of the list is that it has a single entry, of size 4088. Yes, this is a tiny heap, but it serves as a fine example for us here. The `head` pointer contains the beginning address of this range; let's assume it is 16KB (though any virtual address would be fine). Visually, the heap thus looks like what you see in Figure 173.

Now, let's imagine that a chunk of memory is requested, say of size 100 bytes. To service this request, the library will first find a chunk that is large enough to accommodate the request; because there is only one free chunk (size: 4088), this chunk will be chosen. Then, the chunk will be **split** into two: one chunk big enough to service the request (and header, as described above), and the remaining free chunk. Assuming an 8-byte header (an integer size and an integer magic number), the space in the heap now looks like what you see in Figure 174.

Thus, upon the request for 100 bytes, the library allocated 108 bytes

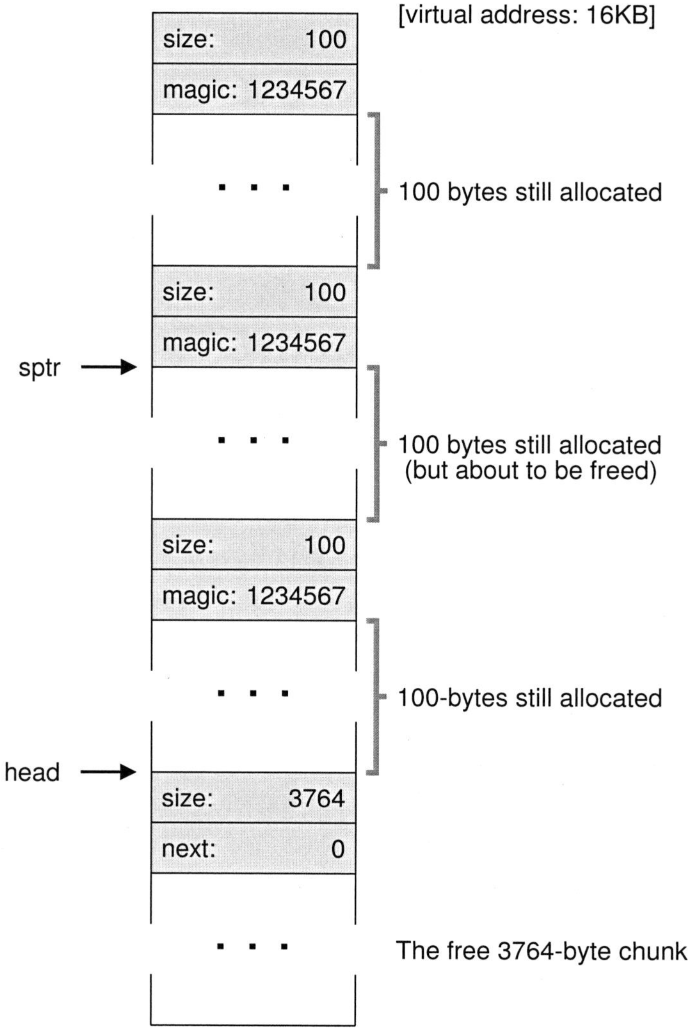

Figure 175: **Free Space With Three Chunks Allocated**

out of the existing one free chunk, returns a pointer (marked `ptr` in the figure above) to it, stashes the header information immediately before the allocated space for later use upon `free()`, and shrinks the one free node in the list to 3980 bytes (4088 minus 108).

Now let's look at the heap when there are three allocated regions, each of 100 bytes (or 108 including the header). A visualization of this heap is shown in Figure 175.

As you can see therein, the first 324 bytes of the heap are now allocated, and thus we see three headers in that space as well as three 100-byte regions being used by the calling program. The free list remains uninteresting: just a single node (pointed to by `head`), but now only 3764

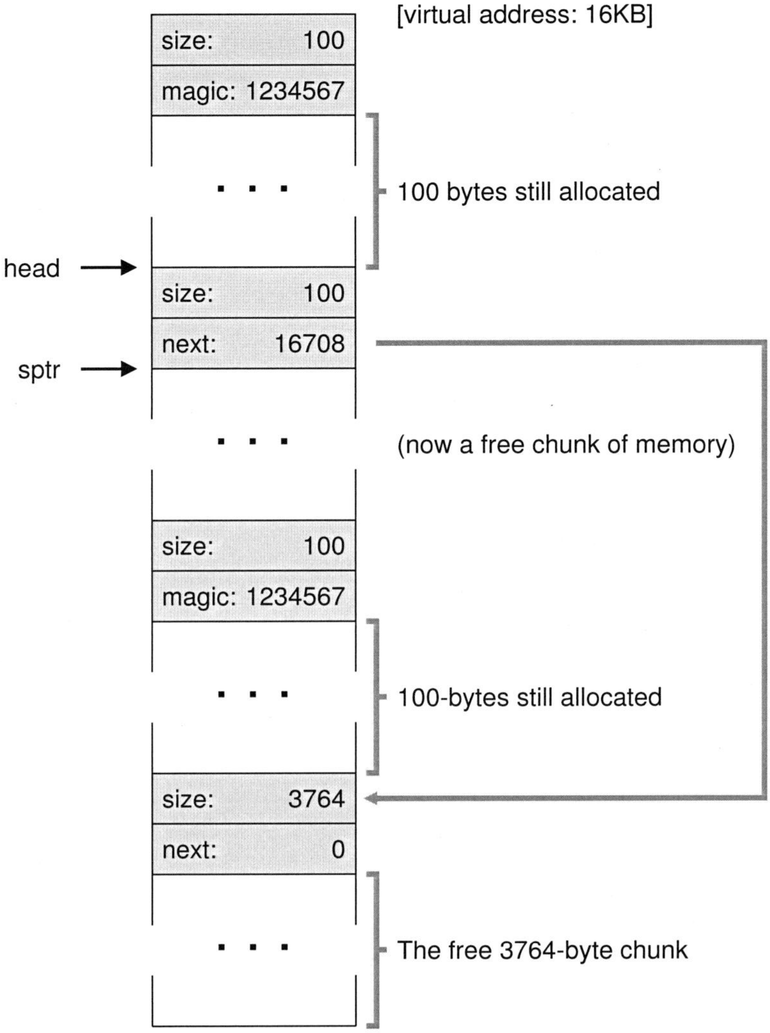

Figure 176: **Free Space With Two Chunks Allocated**

bytes in size after the three splits. But what happens when the calling program returns some memory via `free()`?

In this example, the application returns the middle chunk of allocated memory, by calling `free(16500)` (the value 16500 is arrived upon by adding the start of the memory region, 16384, to the 108 of the previous chunk and the 8 bytes of the header for this chunk). This value is shown in the previous diagram by the pointer `sptr`.

The library immediately figures out the size of the free region, and then adds the free chunk back onto the free list. Assuming we insert at the head of the free list, the space now looks like this (Figure 176).

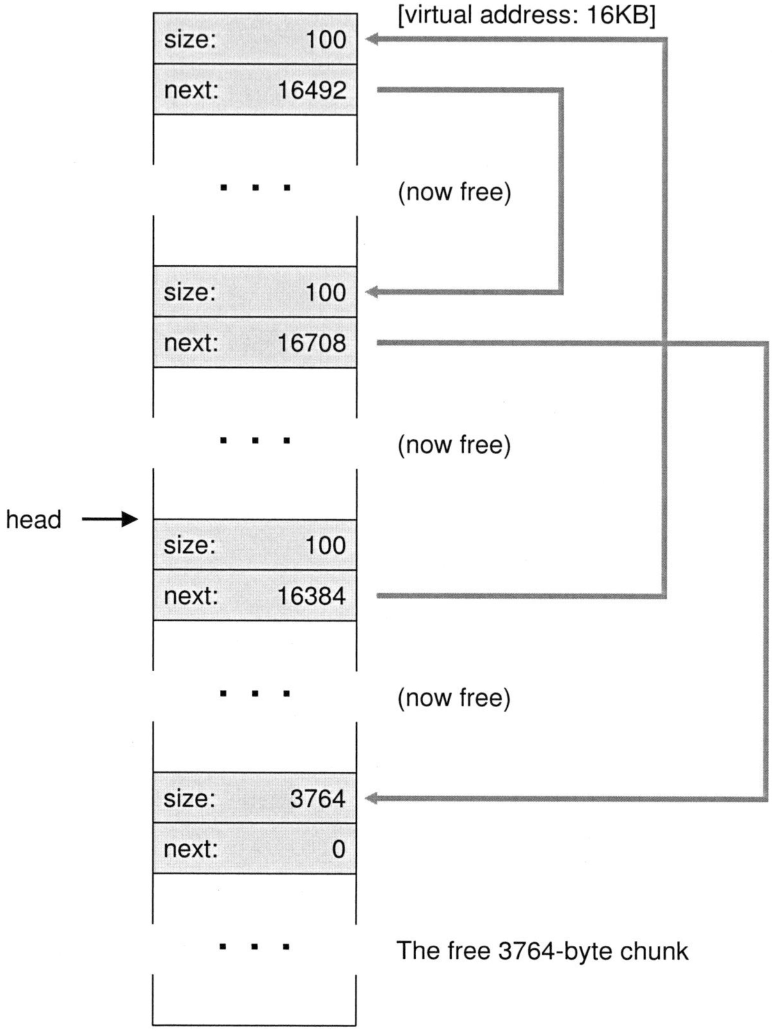

Figure 177: **A Non-Coalesced Free List**

Now we have a list that starts with a small free chunk (100 bytes, pointed to by the head of the list) and a large free chunk (3764 bytes). Our list finally has more than one element on it! And yes, the free space is fragmented, an unfortunate but common occurrence.

One last example: let's assume now that the last two in-use chunks are freed. Without coalescing, you end up with fragmentation (Figure 177).

As you can see from the figure, we now have a big mess! Why? Simple, we forgot to **coalesce** the list. Although all of the memory is free, it is chopped up into pieces, thus appearing as a fragmented memory despite not being one. The solution is simple: go through the list and **merge** neighboring chunks; when finished, the heap will be whole again.

Growing The Heap

We should discuss one last mechanism found within many allocation libraries. Specifically, what should you do if the heap runs out of space? The simplest approach is just to fail. In some cases this is the only option, and thus returning NULL is an honorable approach. Don't feel bad! You tried, and though you failed, you fought the good fight.

Most traditional allocators start with a small-sized heap and then request more memory from the OS when they run out. Typically, this means they make some kind of system call (e.g., `sbrk` in most UNIX systems) to grow the heap, and then allocate the new chunks from there. To service the `sbrk` request, the OS finds free physical pages, maps them into the address space of the requesting process, and then returns the value of the end of the new heap; at that point, a larger heap is available, and the request can be successfully serviced.

17.3 Basic Strategies

Now that we have some machinery under our belt, let's go over some basic strategies for managing free space. These approaches are mostly based on pretty simple policies that you could think up yourself; try it before reading and see if you come up with all of the alternatives (or maybe some new ones!).

The ideal allocator is both fast and minimizes fragmentation. Unfortunately, because the stream of allocation and free requests can be arbitrary (after all, they are determined by the programmer), any particular strategy can do quite badly given the wrong set of inputs. Thus, we will not describe a "best" approach, but rather talk about some basics and discuss their pros and cons.

Best Fit

The **best fit** strategy is quite simple: first, search through the free list and find chunks of free memory that are as big or bigger than the requested size. Then, return the one that is the smallest in that group of candidates; this is the so called best-fit chunk (it could be called smallest fit too). One pass through the free list is enough to find the correct block to return.

The intuition behind best fit is simple: by returning a block that is close to what the user asks, best fit tries to reduce wasted space. However, there is a cost; naive implementations pay a heavy performance penalty when performing an exhaustive search for the correct free block.

Worst Fit

The **worst fit** approach is the opposite of best fit; find the largest chunk and return the requested amount; keep the remaining (large) chunk on the free list. Worst fit tries to thus leave big chunks free instead of lots of small chunks that can arise from a best-fit approach. Once again, however, a full search of free space is required, and thus this approach can be costly. Worse, most studies show that it performs badly, leading to excess fragmentation while still having high overheads.

First Fit

The **first fit** method simply finds the first block that is big enough and returns the requested amount to the user. As before, the remaining free space is kept free for subsequent requests.

First fit has the advantage of speed — no exhaustive search of all the free spaces are necessary — but sometimes pollutes the beginning of the free list with small objects. Thus, how the allocator manages the free list's order becomes an issue. One approach is to use **address-based ordering**; by keeping the list ordered by the address of the free space, coalescing becomes easier, and fragmentation tends to be reduced.

Next Fit

Instead of always beginning the first-fit search at the beginning of the list, the **next fit** algorithm keeps an extra pointer to the location within the list where one was looking last. The idea is to spread the searches for free space throughout the list more uniformly, thus avoiding splintering of the beginning of the list. The performance of such an approach is quite similar to first fit, as an exhaustive search is once again avoided.

Examples

Here are a few examples of the above strategies. Envision a free list with three elements on it, of sizes 10, 30, and 20 (we'll ignore headers and other details here, instead just focusing on how strategies operate):

Assume an allocation request of size 15. A best-fit approach would search the entire list and find that 20 was the best fit, as it is the smallest free space that can accommodate the request. The resulting free list:

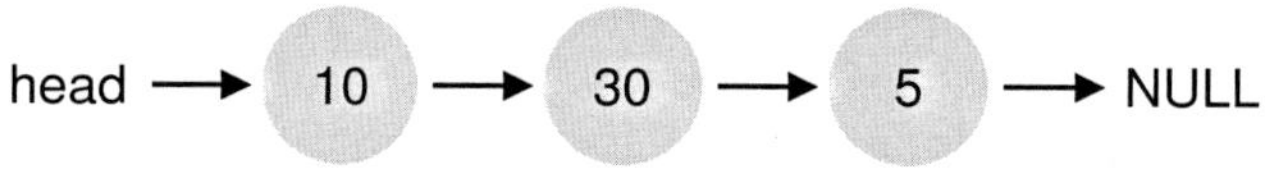

As happens in this example, and often happens with a best-fit approach, a small free chunk is now left over. A worst-fit approach is similar but instead finds the largest chunk, in this example 30. The resulting list:

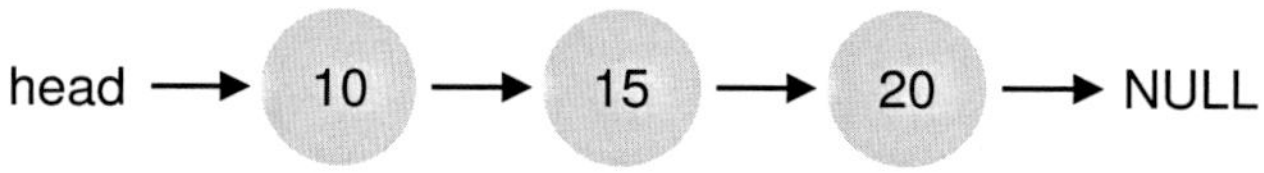

The first-fit strategy, in this example, does the same thing as worst-fit, also finding the first free block that can satisfy the request. The difference is in the search cost; both best-fit and worst-fit look through the entire list; first-fit only examines free chunks until it finds one that fits, thus reducing search cost.

These examples just scratch the surface of allocation policies. More detailed analysis with real workloads and more complex allocator behaviors (e.g., coalescing) are required for a deeper understanding. Perhaps something for a homework section, you say?

17.4 Other Approaches

Beyond the basic approaches described above, there have been a host of suggested techniques and algorithms to improve memory allocation in some way. We list a few of them here for your consideration (i.e., to make you think about a little more than just best-fit allocation).

Segregated Lists

One interesting approach that has been around for some time is the use of **segregated lists**. The basic idea is simple: if a particular application has one (or a few) popular-sized request that it makes, keep a separate list just to manage objects of that size; all other requests are forwarded to a more general memory allocator.

The benefits of such an approach are obvious. By having a chunk of memory dedicated for one particular size of requests, fragmentation is much less of a concern; moreover, allocation and free requests can be served quite quickly when they are of the right size, as no complicated search of a list is required.

Just like any good idea, this approach introduces new complications into a system as well. For example, how much memory should one dedicate to the pool of memory that serves specialized requests of a given size, as opposed to the general pool? One particular allocator, the **slab allocator** by uber-engineer Jeff Bonwick (which was designed for use in the Solaris kernel), handles this issue in a rather nice way [B94].

Specifically, when the kernel boots up, it allocates a number of **object caches** for kernel objects that are likely to be requested frequently (such as locks, file-system inodes, etc.); the object caches thus are each segregated free lists of a given size and serve memory allocation and free requests quickly. When a given cache is running low on free space, it requests some **slabs** of memory from a more general memory allocator (the total amount requested being a multiple of the page size and the object in question). Conversely, when the reference counts of the objects within a given slab all go to zero, the general allocator can reclaim them from the specialized allocator, which is often done when the VM system needs more memory.

ASIDE: GREAT ENGINEERS ARE REALLY GREAT

Engineers like Jeff Bonwick (who not only wrote the slab allocator mentioned herein but also was the lead of an amazing file system, ZFS) are the heart of Silicon Valley. Behind almost any great product or technology is a human (or small group of humans) who are way above average in their talents, abilities, and dedication. As Mark Zuckerberg (of Facebook) says: "Someone who is exceptional in their role is not just a little better than someone who is pretty good. They are 100 times better." This is why, still today, one or two people can start a company that changes the face of the world forever (think Google, Apple, or Facebook). Work hard and you might become such a "100x" person as well. Failing that, work *with* such a person; you'll learn more in a day than most learn in a month. Failing that, feel sad.

The slab allocator also goes beyond most segregated list approaches by keeping free objects on the lists in a pre-initialized state. Bonwick shows that initialization and destruction of data structures is costly [B94]; by keeping freed objects in a particular list in their initialized state, the slab allocator thus avoids frequent initialization and destruction cycles per object and thus lowers overheads noticeably.

Buddy Allocation

Because coalescing is critical for an allocator, some approaches have been designed around making coalescing simple. One good example is found in the **binary buddy allocator** [K65].

In such a system, free memory is first conceptually thought of as one big space of size 2^N. When a request for memory is made, the search for free space recursively divides free space by two until a block that is big enough to accommodate the request is found (and a further split into two would result in a space that is too small). At this point, the requested block is returned to the user. Here is an example of a 64KB free space getting divided in the search for a 7KB block (Figure 178, page 193).

In the example, the leftmost 8KB block is allocated (as indicated by the darker shade of gray) and returned to the user; note that this scheme can suffer from **internal fragmentation**, as you are only allowed to give out power-of-two-sized blocks.

The beauty of buddy allocation is found in what happens when that block is freed. When returning the 8KB block to the free list, the allocator checks whether the "buddy" 8KB is free; if so, it coalesces the two blocks into a 16KB block. The allocator then checks if the buddy of the 16KB block is still free; if so, it coalesces those two blocks. This recursive coalescing process continues up the tree, either restoring the entire free space or stopping when a buddy is found to be in use.

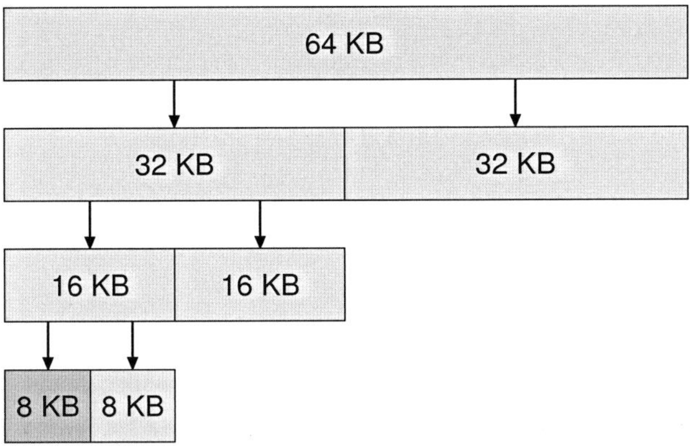

Figure 178: **Example Buddy-managed Heap**

The reason buddy allocation works so well is that it is simple to determine the buddy of a particular block. How, you ask? Think about the addresses of the blocks in the free space above. If you think carefully enough, you'll see that the address of each buddy pair only differs by a single bit; which bit is determined by the level in the buddy tree. And thus you have a basic idea of how binary buddy allocation schemes work. For more detail, as always, see the Wilson survey [W+95].

Other Ideas

One major problem with many of the approaches described above is their lack of **scaling**. Specifically, searching lists can be quite slow. Thus, advanced allocators use more complex data structures to address these costs, trading simplicity for performance. Examples include balanced binary trees, splay trees, or partially-ordered trees [W+95].

Given that modern systems often have multiple processors and run multi-threaded workloads (something you'll learn about in great detail in the section of the book on Concurrency), it is not surprising that a lot of effort has been spent making allocators work well on multiprocessor-based systems. Two wonderful examples are found in Berger et al. [B+00] and Evans [E06]; check them out for the details.

These are but two of the thousands of ideas people have had over time about memory allocators; read on your own if you are curious. Failing that, read about how the glibc allocator works [S15], to give you a sense of what the real world is like.

17.5 Summary

In this chapter, we've discussed the most rudimentary forms of memory allocators. Such allocators exist everywhere, linked into every C program you write, as well as in the underlying OS which is managing memory for its own data structures. As with many systems, there are many trade-offs to be made in building such a system, and the more you know about the exact workload presented to an allocator, the more you could do to tune it to work better for that workload. Making a fast, space-efficient, scalable allocator that works well for a broad range of workloads remains an on-going challenge in modern computer systems.

References

[B+00] "Hoard: A Scalable Memory Allocator for Multithreaded Applications" by Emery D. Berger, Kathryn S. McKinley, Robert D. Blumofe, Paul R. Wilson. ASPLOS-IX, November 2000. *Berger and company's excellent allocator for multiprocessor systems. Beyond just being a fun paper, also used in practice!*

[B94] "The Slab Allocator: An Object-Caching Kernel Memory Allocator" by Jeff Bonwick. USENIX '94. *A cool paper about how to build an allocator for an operating system kernel, and a great example of how to specialize for particular common object sizes.*

[E06] "A Scalable Concurrent malloc(3) Implementation for FreeBSD" by Jason Evans. April, 2006. http://people.freebsd.org/˜jasone/jemalloc/bsdcan2006/jemalloc.pdf. *A detailed look at how to build a real modern allocator for use in multiprocessors. The "jemalloc" allocator is in widespread use today, within FreeBSD, NetBSD, Mozilla Firefox, and within Facebook.*

[K65] "A Fast Storage Allocator" by Kenneth C. Knowlton. Communications of the ACM, Volume 8:10, October 1965. *The common reference for buddy allocation. Random strange fact: Knuth gives credit for the idea not to Knowlton but to Harry Markowitz, a Nobel-prize winning economist. Another strange fact: Knuth communicates all of his emails via a secretary; he doesn't send email himself, rather he tells his secretary what email to send and then the secretary does the work of emailing. Last Knuth fact: he created TeX, the tool used to typeset this book. It is an amazing piece of software*[4].

[S15] "Understanding glibc malloc" by Sploitfun. February, 2015. sploitfun.wordpress.com/2015/02/10/understanding-glibc-malloc/. *A deep dive into how glibc malloc works. Amazingly detailed and a very cool read.*

[W+95] "Dynamic Storage Allocation: A Survey and Critical Review" by Paul R. Wilson, Mark S. Johnstone, Michael Neely, David Boles. International Workshop on Memory Management, Scotland, UK, September 1995. *An excellent and far-reaching survey of many facets of memory allocation. Far too much detail to go into in this tiny chapter!*

[4] Actually we use LaTeX, which is based on Lamport's additions to TeX, but close enough.

Homework (Simulation)

The program, `malloc.py`, lets you explore the behavior of a simple free-space allocator as described in the chapter. See the README for details of its basic operation.

Questions

1. First run with the flags `-n 10 -H 0 -p BEST -s 0` to generate a few random allocations and frees. Can you predict what alloc()/free() will return? Can you guess the state of the free list after each request? What do you notice about the free list over time?
2. How are the results different when using a WORST fit policy to search the free list (`-p WORST`)? What changes?
3. What about when using FIRST fit (`-p FIRST`)? What speeds up when you use first fit?
4. For the above questions, how the list is kept ordered can affect the time it takes to find a free location for some of the policies. Use the different free list orderings (`-l ADDRSORT`, `-l SIZESORT+`, `-l SIZESORT-`) to see how the policies and the list orderings interact.
5. Coalescing of a free list can be quite important. Increase the number of random allocations (say to `-n 1000`). What happens to larger allocation requests over time? Run with and without coalescing (i.e., without and with the `-C` flag). What differences in outcome do you see? How big is the free list over time in each case? Does the ordering of the list matter in this case?
6. What happens when you change the percent allocated fraction `-P` to higher than 50? What happens to allocations as it nears 100? What about as the percent nears 0?
7. What kind of specific requests can you make to generate a highly-fragmented free space? Use the `-A` flag to create fragmented free lists, and see how different policies and options change the organization of the free list.

18

Paging: Introduction

It is sometimes said that the operating system takes one of two approaches when solving most any space-management problem. The first approach is to chop things up into *variable-sized* pieces, as we saw with **segmentation** in virtual memory. Unfortunately, this solution has inherent difficulties. In particular, when dividing a space into different-size chunks, the space itself can become **fragmented**, and thus allocation becomes more challenging over time.

Thus, it may be worth considering the second approach: to chop up space into *fixed-sized* pieces. In virtual memory, we call this idea **paging**, and it goes back to an early and important system, the Atlas [KE+62, L78]. Instead of splitting up a process's address space into some number of variable-sized logical segments (e.g., code, heap, stack), we divide it into fixed-sized units, each of which we call a **page**. Correspondingly, we view physical memory as an array of fixed-sized slots called **page frames**; each of these frames can contain a single virtual-memory page. Our challenge:

> THE CRUX:
> HOW TO VIRTUALIZE MEMORY WITH PAGES
> How can we virtualize memory with pages, so as to avoid the problems of segmentation? What are the basic techniques? How do we make those techniques work well, with minimal space and time overheads?

18.1 A Simple Example And Overview

To help make this approach more clear, let's illustrate it with a simple example. Figure 181 (page 198) presents an example of a tiny address space, only 64 bytes total in size, with four 16-byte pages (virtual pages 0, 1, 2, and 3). Real address spaces are much bigger, of course, commonly 32 bits and thus 4-GB of address space, or even 64 bits[1]; in the book, we'll often use tiny examples to make them easier to digest.

[1] A 64-bit address space is hard to imagine, it is so amazingly large. An analogy might help: if you think of a 32-bit address space as the size of a tennis court, a 64-bit address space is about the size of Europe(!).

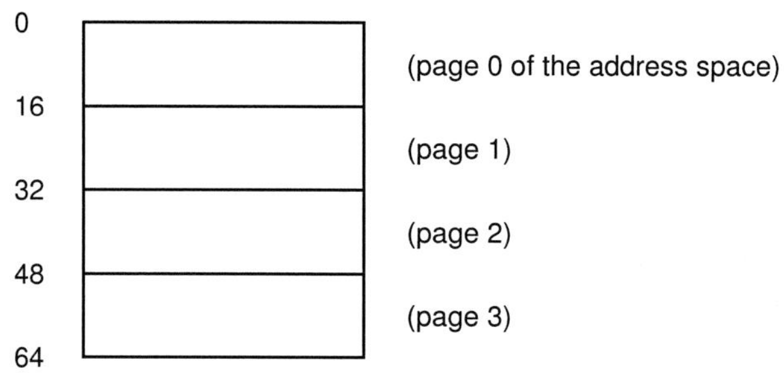

Figure 181: **A Simple 64-byte Address Space**

Physical memory, as shown in Figure 182, also consists of a number of fixed-sized slots, in this case eight page frames (making for a 128-byte physical memory, also ridiculously small). As you can see in the diagram, the pages of the virtual address space have been placed at different locations throughout physical memory; the diagram also shows the OS using some of physical memory for itself.

Paging, as we will see, has a number of advantages over our previous approaches. Probably the most important improvement will be *flexibility*: with a fully-developed paging approach, the system will be able to support the abstraction of an address space effectively, regardless of how a process uses the address space; we won't, for example, make assumptions about the direction the heap and stack grow and how they are used.

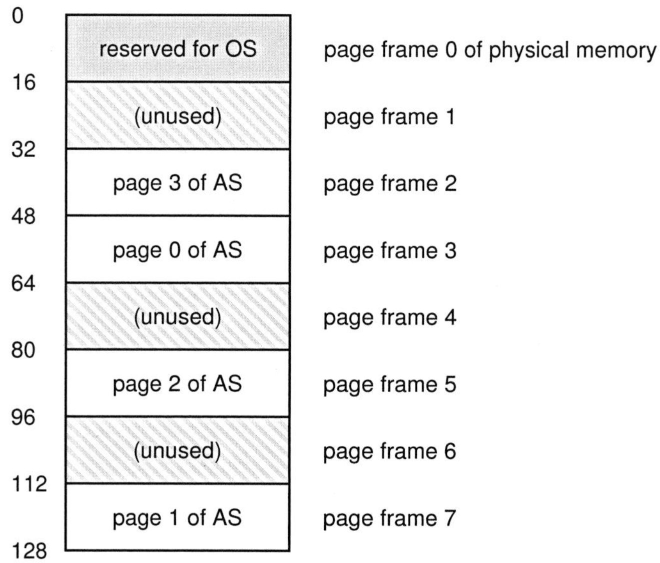

Figure 182: **A 64-Byte Address Space In A 128-Byte Physical Memory**

Another advantage is the *simplicity* of free-space management that paging affords. For example, when the OS wishes to place our tiny 64-byte address space into our eight-page physical memory, it simply finds four free pages; perhaps the OS keeps a **free list** of all free pages for this, and just grabs the first four free pages off of this list. In the example, the OS has placed virtual page 0 of the address space (AS) in physical frame 3, virtual page 1 of the AS in physical frame 7, page 2 in frame 5, and page 3 in frame 2. Page frames 1, 4, and 6 are currently free.

To record where each virtual page of the address space is placed in physical memory, the operating system usually keeps a *per-process* data structure known as a **page table**. The major role of the page table is to store **address translations** for each of the virtual pages of the address space, thus letting us know where in physical memory each page resides. For our simple example (Figure 182, page 198), the page table would thus have the following four entries: (Virtual Page $0 \rightarrow$ Physical Frame 3), (VP $1 \rightarrow$ PF 7), (VP $2 \rightarrow$ PF 5), and (VP $3 \rightarrow$ PF 2).

It is important to remember that this page table is a *per-process* data structure (most page table structures we discuss are per-process structures; an exception we'll touch on is the **inverted page table**). If another process were to run in our example above, the OS would have to manage a different page table for it, as its virtual pages obviously map to *different* physical pages (modulo any sharing going on).

Now, we know enough to perform an address-translation example. Let's imagine the process with that tiny address space (64 bytes) is performing a memory access:

```
movl <virtual address>, %eax
```

Specifically, let's pay attention to the explicit load of the data from address <virtual address> into the register eax (and thus ignore the instruction fetch that must have happened prior).

To **translate** this virtual address that the process generated, we have to first split it into two components: the **virtual page number (VPN)**, and the **offset** within the page. For this example, because the virtual address space of the process is 64 bytes, we need 6 bits total for our virtual address ($2^6 = 64$). Thus, our virtual address can be conceptualized as follows:

Va5	Va4	Va3	Va2	Va1	Va0

In this diagram, Va5 is the highest-order bit of the virtual address, and Va0 the lowest-order bit. Because we know the page size (16 bytes), we can further divide the virtual address as follows:

VPN		offset			
Va5	Va4	Va3	Va2	Va1	Va0

The page size is 16 bytes in a 64-byte address space; thus we need to be able to select 4 pages, and the top 2 bits of the address do just that. Thus, we have a 2-bit virtual page number (VPN). The remaining bits tell us which byte of the page we are interested in, 4 bits in this case; we call this the offset.

When a process generates a virtual address, the OS and hardware must combine to translate it into a meaningful physical address. For example, let us assume the load above was to virtual address 21:

```
movl 21, %eax
```

Turning "21" into binary form, we get "010101", and thus we can examine this virtual address and see how it breaks down into a virtual page number (VPN) and offset:

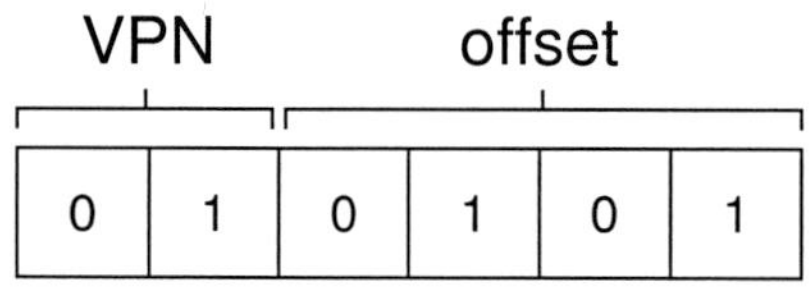

Thus, the virtual address "21" is on the 5th ("0101"th) byte of virtual page "01" (or 1). With our virtual page number, we can now index our page table and find which physical frame virtual page 1 resides within. In the page table above the **physical frame number** (**PFN**) (also sometimes called the **physical page number** or **PPN**) is 7 (binary 111). Thus, we can translate this virtual address by replacing the VPN with the PFN and then issue the load to physical memory (Figure 183).

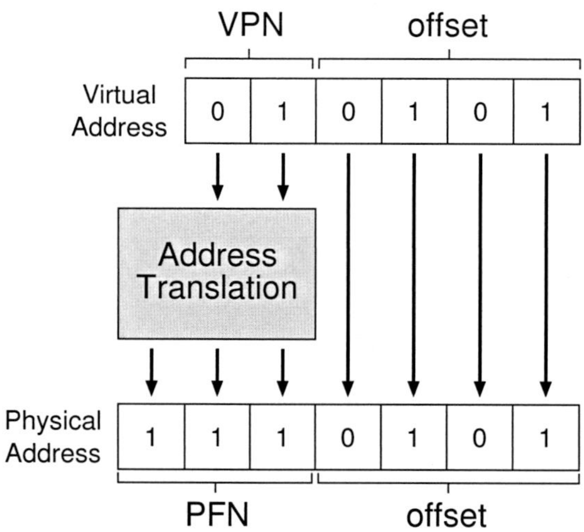

Figure 183: **The Address Translation Process**

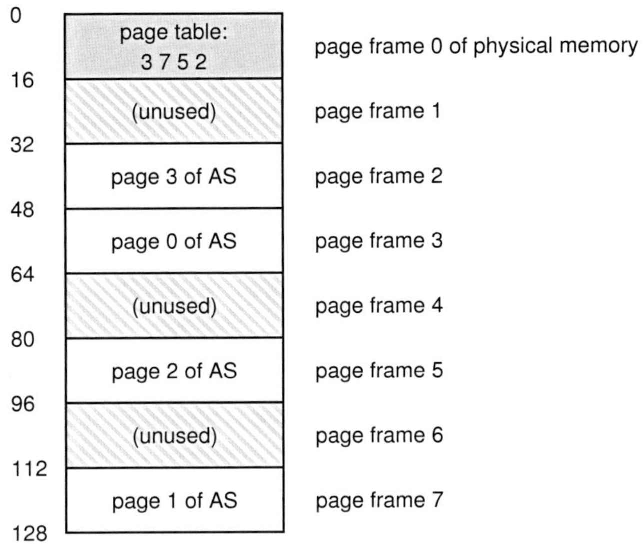

Figure 184: **Example: Page Table in Kernel Physical Memory**

Note the offset stays the same (i.e., it is not translated), because the offset just tells us which byte *within* the page we want. Our final physical address is 1110101 (117 in decimal), and is exactly where we want our load to fetch data from (Figure 182, page 198).

With this basic overview in mind, we can now ask (and hopefully, answer) a few basic questions you may have about paging. For example, where are these page tables stored? What are the typical contents of the page table, and how big are the tables? Does paging make the system (too) slow? These and other beguiling questions are answered, at least in part, in the text below. Read on!

18.2 Where Are Page Tables Stored?

Page tables can get terribly large, much bigger than the small segment table or base/bounds pair we have discussed previously. For example, imagine a typical 32-bit address space, with 4KB pages. This virtual address splits into a 20-bit VPN and 12-bit offset (recall that 10 bits would be needed for a 1KB page size, and just add two more to get to 4KB).

A 20-bit VPN implies that there are 2^{20} translations that the OS would have to manage for each process (that's roughly a million); assuming we need 4 bytes per **page table entry (PTE)** to hold the physical translation plus any other useful stuff, we get an immense 4MB of memory needed for each page table! That is pretty large. Now imagine there are 100 processes running: this means the OS would need 400MB of memory just for all those address translations! Even in the modern era, where

ASIDE: DATA STRUCTURE — THE PAGE TABLE

One of the most important data structures in the memory management subsystem of a modern OS is the **page table**. In general, a page table stores **virtual-to-physical address translations**, thus letting the system know where each page of an address space actually resides in physical memory. Because each address space requires such translations, in general there is one page table per process in the system. The exact structure of the page table is either determined by the hardware (older systems) or can be more flexibly managed by the OS (modern systems).

machines have gigabytes of memory, it seems a little crazy to use a large chunk of it just for translations, no? And we won't even think about how big such a page table would be for a 64-bit address space; that would be too gruesome and perhaps scare you off entirely.

Because page tables are so big, we don't keep any special on-chip hardware in the MMU to store the page table of the currently-running process. Instead, we store the page table for each process in *memory* somewhere. Let's assume for now that the page tables live in physical memory that the OS manages; later we'll see that much of OS memory itself can be virtualized, and thus page tables can be stored in OS virtual memory (and even swapped to disk), but that is too confusing right now, so we'll ignore it. In Figure 184 (page 201) is a picture of a page table in OS memory; see the tiny set of translations in there?

18.3 What's Actually In The Page Table?

Let's talk a little about page table organization. The page table is just a data structure that is used to map virtual addresses (or really, virtual page numbers) to physical addresses (physical frame numbers). Thus, any data structure could work. The simplest form is called a **linear page table**, which is just an array. The OS *indexes* the array by the virtual page number (VPN), and looks up the page-table entry (PTE) at that index in order to find the desired physical frame number (PFN). For now, we will assume this simple linear structure; in later chapters, we will make use of more advanced data structures to help solve some problems with paging.

As for the contents of each PTE, we have a number of different bits in there worth understanding at some level. A **valid bit** is common to indicate whether the particular translation is valid; for example, when a program starts running, it will have code and heap at one end of its address space, and the stack at the other. All the unused space in-between will be marked **invalid**, and if the process tries to access such memory, it will generate a trap to the OS which will likely terminate the process. Thus, the valid bit is crucial for supporting a sparse address space; by simply marking all the unused pages in the address space invalid, we remove the need to allocate physical frames for those pages and thus save a great deal of memory.

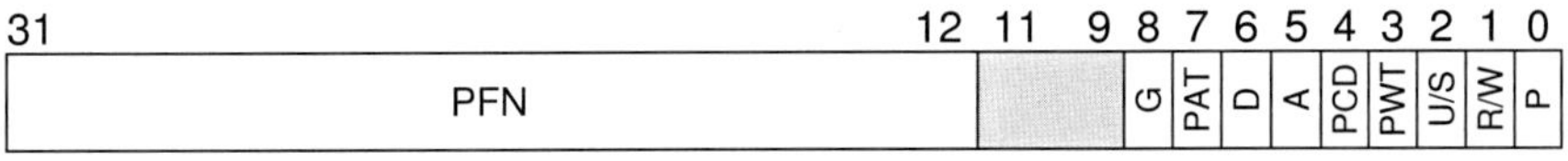

Figure 185: **An x86 Page Table Entry (PTE)**

We also might have **protection bits**, indicating whether the page could be read from, written to, or executed from. Again, accessing a page in a way not allowed by these bits will generate a trap to the OS.

There are a couple of other bits that are important but we won't talk about much for now. A **present bit** indicates whether this page is in physical memory or on disk (i.e., it has been **swapped out**). We will understand this machinery further when we study how to **swap** parts of the address space to disk to support address spaces that are larger than physical memory; swapping allows the OS to free up physical memory by moving rarely-used pages to disk. A **dirty bit** is also common, indicating whether the page has been modified since it was brought into memory.

A **reference bit** (a.k.a. **accessed bit**) is sometimes used to track whether a page has been accessed, and is useful in determining which pages are popular and thus should be kept in memory; such knowledge is critical during **page replacement**, a topic we will study in great detail in subsequent chapters.

Figure 185 shows an example page table entry from the x86 architecture [I09]. It contains a present bit (P); a read/write bit (R/W) which determines if writes are allowed to this page; a user/supervisor bit (U/S) which determines if user-mode processes can access the page; a few bits (PWT, PCD, PAT, and G) that determine how hardware caching works for these pages; an accessed bit (A) and a dirty bit (D); and finally, the page frame number (PFN) itself.

Read the Intel Architecture Manuals [I09] for more details on x86 paging support. Be forewarned, however; reading manuals such as these, while quite informative (and certainly necessary for those who write code to use such page tables in the OS), can be challenging at first. A little patience, and a lot of desire, is required.

ASIDE: WHY NO VALID BIT?

You may notice that in the Intel example, there are no separate valid and present bits, but rather just a present bit (P). If that bit is set (P=1), it means the page is both present and valid. If not (P=0), it means that the page may not be present in memory (but is valid), or may not be valid. An access to a page with P=0 will trigger a trap to the OS; the OS must then use additional structures it keeps to determine whether the page is valid (and thus perhaps should be swapped back in) or not (and thus the program is attempting to access memory illegally). This sort of judiciousness is common in hardware, which often just provide the minimal set of features upon which the OS can build a full service.

18.4 Paging: Also Too Slow

With page tables in memory, we already know that they might be too big. As it turns out, they can slow things down too. For example, take our simple instruction:

```
movl 21, %eax
```

Again, let's just examine the explicit reference to address 21 and not worry about the instruction fetch. In this example, we'll assume the hardware performs the translation for us. To fetch the desired data, the system must first **translate** the virtual address (21) into the correct physical address (117). Thus, before fetching the data from address 117, the system must first fetch the proper page table entry from the process's page table, perform the translation, and then load the data from physical memory.

To do so, the hardware must know where the page table is for the currently-running process. Let's assume for now that a single **page-table base register** contains the physical address of the starting location of the page table. To find the location of the desired PTE, the hardware will thus perform the following functions:

```
VPN     = (VirtualAddress & VPN_MASK) >> SHIFT
PTEAddr = PageTableBaseRegister + (VPN * sizeof(PTE))
```

In our example, VPN_MASK would be set to 0x30 (hex 30, or binary 110000) which picks out the VPN bits from the full virtual address; SHIFT is set to 4 (the number of bits in the offset), such that we move the VPN bits down to form the correct integer virtual page number. For example, with virtual address 21 (010101), and masking turns this value into 010000; the shift turns it into 01, or virtual page 1, as desired. We then use this value as an index into the array of PTEs pointed to by the page table base register.

Once this physical address is known, the hardware can fetch the PTE from memory, extract the PFN, and concatenate it with the offset from the virtual address to form the desired physical address. Specifically, you can think of the PFN being left-shifted by SHIFT, and then bitwise OR'd with the offset to form the final address as follows:

```
offset   = VirtualAddress & OFFSET_MASK
PhysAddr = (PFN << SHIFT) | offset
```

Finally, the hardware can fetch the desired data from memory and put it into register eax. The program has now succeeded at loading a value from memory!

To summarize, we now describe the initial protocol for what happens on each memory reference. Figure 186 (page 205) shows the approach. For every memory reference (whether an instruction fetch or an explicit load or store), paging requires us to perform one extra memory reference in order to first fetch the translation from the page table. That is a lot of

```
// Extract the VPN from the virtual address
VPN = (VirtualAddress & VPN_MASK) >> SHIFT

// Form the address of the page-table entry (PTE)
PTEAddr = PTBR + (VPN * sizeof(PTE))

// Fetch the PTE
PTE = AccessMemory(PTEAddr)

// Check if process can access the page
if (PTE.Valid == False)
    RaiseException(SEGMENTATION_FAULT)
else if (CanAccess(PTE.ProtectBits) == False)
    RaiseException(PROTECTION_FAULT)
else
    // Access is OK: form physical address and fetch it
    offset   = VirtualAddress & OFFSET_MASK
    PhysAddr = (PTE.PFN << PFN_SHIFT) | offset
    Register = AccessMemory(PhysAddr)
```

Figure 186: **Accessing Memory With Paging**

work! Extra memory references are costly, and in this case will likely slow down the process by a factor of two or more.

And now you can hopefully see that there are *two* real problems that we must solve. Without careful design of both hardware and software, page tables will cause the system to run too slowly, as well as take up too much memory. While seemingly a great solution for our memory virtualization needs, these two crucial problems must first be overcome.

18.5 A Memory Trace

Before closing, we now trace through a simple memory access example to demonstrate all of the resulting memory accesses that occur when using paging. The code snippet (in C, in a file called `array.c`) that we are interested in is as follows:

```
int array[1000];
...
for (i = 0; i < 1000; i++)
    array[i] = 0;
```

We compile `array.c` and run it with the following commands:

```
prompt> gcc -o array array.c -Wall -O
prompt> ./array
```

Of course, to truly understand what memory accesses this code snippet (which simply initializes an array) will make, we'll have to know (or assume) a few more things. First, we'll have to **disassemble** the resulting binary (using `objdump` on Linux, or `otool` on a Mac) to see what assembly instructions are used to initialize the array in a loop. Here is the resulting assembly code:

```
1024 movl $0x0,(%edi,%eax,4)
1028 incl %eax
1032 cmpl $0x03e8,%eax
1036 jne  0x1024
```

The code, if you know a little **x86**, is actually quite easy to understand[2]. The first instruction moves the value zero (shown as `$0x0`) into the virtual memory address of the location of the array; this address is computed by taking the contents of `%edi` and adding `%eax` multiplied by four to it. Thus, `%edi` holds the base address of the array, whereas `%eax` holds the array index (`i`); we multiply by four because the array is an array of integers, each of size four bytes.

The second instruction increments the array index held in `%eax`, and the third instruction compares the contents of that register to the hex value `0x03e8`, or decimal 1000. If the comparison shows that two values are not yet equal (which is what the `jne` instruction tests), the fourth instruction jumps back to the top of the loop.

To understand which memory accesses this instruction sequence makes (at both the virtual and physical levels), we'll have to assume something about where in virtual memory the code snippet and array are found, as well as the contents and location of the page table.

For this example, we assume a virtual address space of size 64KB (unrealistically small). We also assume a page size of 1KB.

All we need to know now are the contents of the page table, and its location in physical memory. Let's assume we have a linear (array-based) page table and that it is located at physical address 1KB (1024).

As for its contents, there are just a few virtual pages we need to worry about having mapped for this example. First, there is the virtual page the code lives on. Because the page size is 1KB, virtual address 1024 resides on the second page of the virtual address space (VPN=1, as VPN=0 is the first page). Let's assume this virtual page maps to physical frame 4 (VPN 1 → PFN 4).

Next, there is the array itself. Its size is 4000 bytes (1000 integers), and we assume that it resides at virtual addresses 40000 through 44000 (not including the last byte). The virtual pages for this decimal range are VPN=39 ... VPN=42. Thus, we need mappings for these pages. Let's assume these virtual-to-physical mappings for the example: (VPN 39 → PFN 7), (VPN 40 → PFN 8), (VPN 41 → PFN 9), (VPN 42 → PFN 10).

[2]We are cheating a little bit here, assuming each instruction is four bytes in size for simplicity; in actuality, x86 instructions are variable-sized.

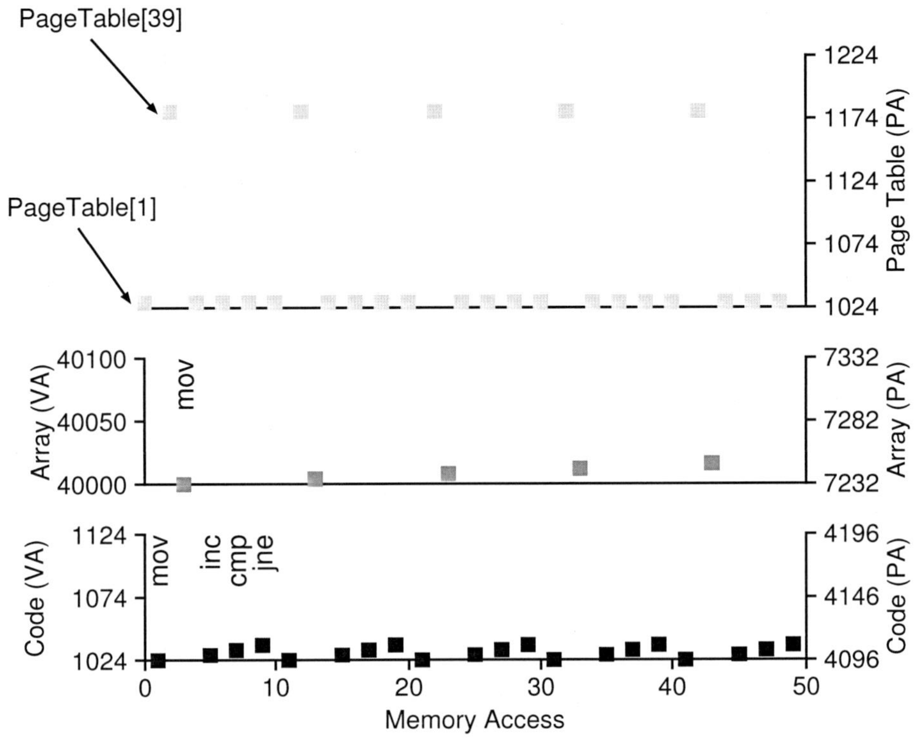

Figure 187: **A Virtual (And Physical) Memory Trace**

We are now ready to trace the memory references of the program. When it runs, each instruction fetch will generate two memory references: one to the page table to find the physical frame that the instruction resides within, and one to the instruction itself to fetch it to the CPU for processing. In addition, there is one explicit memory reference in the form of the `mov` instruction; this adds another page table access first (to translate the array virtual address to the correct physical one) and then the array access itself.

The entire process, for the first five loop iterations, is depicted in Figure 187 (page 207). The bottom most graph shows the instruction memory references on the y-axis in black (with virtual addresses on the left, and the actual physical addresses on the right); the middle graph shows array accesses in dark gray (again with virtual on left and physical on right); finally, the topmost graph shows page table memory accesses in light gray (just physical, as the page table in this example resides in physical memory). The x-axis, for the entire trace, shows memory accesses across the first five iterations of the loop; there are 10 memory accesses per loop, which includes four instruction fetches, one explicit update of memory, and five page table accesses to translate those four fetches and one explicit update.

See if you can make sense of the patterns that show up in this visualization. In particular, what will change as the loop continues to run beyond these first five iterations? Which new memory locations will be accessed? Can you figure it out?

This has just been the simplest of examples (only a few lines of C code), and yet you might already be able to sense the complexity of understanding the actual memory behavior of real applications. Don't worry: it definitely gets worse, because the mechanisms we are about to introduce only complicate this already complex machinery. Sorry[3]!

18.6 Summary

We have introduced the concept of **paging** as a solution to our challenge of virtualizing memory. Paging has many advantages over previous approaches (such as segmentation). First, it does not lead to external fragmentation, as paging (by design) divides memory into fixed-sized units. Second, it is quite flexible, enabling the sparse use of virtual address spaces.

However, implementing paging support without care will lead to a slower machine (with many extra memory accesses to access the page table) as well as memory waste (with memory filled with page tables instead of useful application data). We'll thus have to think a little harder to come up with a paging system that not only works, but works well. The next two chapters, fortunately, will show us how to do so.

[3]We're not really sorry. But, we are sorry about not being sorry, if that makes sense.

References

[KE+62] "One-level Storage System" by T. Kilburn, D.B.G. Edwards, M.J. Lanigan, F.H. Sumner. IRE Trans. EC-11, 2, 1962. Reprinted in Bell and Newell, "Computer Structures: Readings and Examples". McGraw-Hill, New York, 1971. *The Atlas pioneered the idea of dividing memory into fixed-sized pages and in many senses was an early form of the memory-management ideas we see in modern computer systems.*

[I09] "Intel 64 and IA-32 Architectures Software Developer's Manuals" Intel, 2009. Available: http://www.intel.com/products/processor/manuals. *In particular, pay attention to "Volume 3A: System Programming Guide Part 1" and "Volume 3B: System Programming Guide Part 2".*

[L78] "The Manchester Mark I and Atlas: A Historical Perspective" by S. H. Lavington. Communications of the ACM, Volume 21:1, January 1978. *This paper is a great retrospective of some of the history of the development of some important computer systems. As we sometimes forget in the US, many of these new ideas came from overseas.*

Homework (Simulation)

In this homework, you will use a simple program, which is known as `paging-linear-translate.py`, to see if you understand how simple virtual-to-physical address translation works with linear page tables. See the README for details.

Questions

1. Before doing any translations, let's use the simulator to study how linear page tables change size given different parameters. Compute the size of linear page tables as different parameters change. Some suggested inputs are below; by using the `-v flag`, you can see how many page-table entries are filled. First, to understand how linear page table size changes as the address space grows, run with these flags:

   ```
   -P 1k -a 1m -p 512m -v -n 0
   -P 1k -a 2m -p 512m -v -n 0
   -P 1k -a 4m -p 512m -v -n 0
   ```

   Then, to understand how linear page table size changes as page size grows:

   ```
   -P 1k -a 1m -p 512m -v -n 0
   -P 2k -a 1m -p 512m -v -n 0
   -P 4k -a 1m -p 512m -v -n 0
   ```

   Before running any of these, try to think about the expected trends. How should page-table size change as the address space grows? As the page size grows? Why not use big pages in general?

2. Now let's do some translations. Start with some small examples, and change the number of pages that are allocated to the address space with the `-u flag`. For example:

   ```
   -P 1k -a 16k -p 32k -v -u 0
   -P 1k -a 16k -p 32k -v -u 25
   -P 1k -a 16k -p 32k -v -u 50
   -P 1k -a 16k -p 32k -v -u 75
   -P 1k -a 16k -p 32k -v -u 100
   ```

   What happens as you increase the percentage of pages that are allocated in each address space?

3. Now let's try some different random seeds, and some different (and sometimes quite crazy) address-space parameters, for variety:

```
-P 8  -a 32   -p 1024 -v -s 1
-P 8k -a 32k  -p 1m   -v -s 2
-P 1m -a 256m -p 512m -v -s 3
```

Which of these parameter combinations are unrealistic? Why?

4. Use the program to try out some other problems. Can you find the limits of where the program doesn't work anymore? For example, what happens if the address-space size is *bigger* than physical memory?

19

Paging: Faster Translations (TLBs)

Using paging as the core mechanism to support virtual memory can lead to high performance overheads. By chopping the address space into small, fixed-sized units (i.e., pages), paging requires a large amount of mapping information. Because that mapping information is generally stored in physical memory, paging logically requires an extra memory lookup for each virtual address generated by the program. Going to memory for translation information before every instruction fetch or explicit load or store is prohibitively slow. And thus our problem:

> THE CRUX:
> HOW TO SPEED UP ADDRESS TRANSLATION
> How can we speed up address translation, and generally avoid the extra memory reference that paging seems to require? What hardware support is required? What OS involvement is needed?

When we want to make things fast, the OS usually needs some help. And help often comes from the OS's old friend: the hardware. To speed address translation, we are going to add what is called (for historical reasons [CP78]) a **translation-lookaside buffer**, or **TLB** [CG68, C95]. A TLB is part of the chip's **memory-management unit** (**MMU**), and is simply a hardware **cache** of popular virtual-to-physical address translations; thus, a better name would be an **address-translation cache**. Upon each virtual memory reference, the hardware first checks the TLB to see if the desired translation is held therein; if so, the translation is performed (quickly) *without* having to consult the page table (which has all translations). Because of their tremendous performance impact, TLBs in a real sense make virtual memory possible [C95].

```
1  VPN = (VirtualAddress & VPN_MASK) >> SHIFT
2  (Success, TlbEntry) = TLB_Lookup(VPN)
3  if (Success == True)    // TLB Hit
4      if (CanAccess(TlbEntry.ProtectBits) == True)
5          Offset   = VirtualAddress & OFFSET_MASK
6          PhysAddr = (TlbEntry.PFN << SHIFT) | Offset
7          Register = AccessMemory(PhysAddr)
8      else
9          RaiseException(PROTECTION_FAULT)
10 else                    // TLB Miss
11     PTEAddr = PTBR + (VPN * sizeof(PTE))
12     PTE = AccessMemory(PTEAddr)
13     if (PTE.Valid == False)
14         RaiseException(SEGMENTATION_FAULT)
15     else if (CanAccess(PTE.ProtectBits) == False)
16         RaiseException(PROTECTION_FAULT)
17     else
18         TLB_Insert(VPN, PTE.PFN, PTE.ProtectBits)
19         RetryInstruction()
```

Figure 191: **TLB Control Flow Algorithm**

19.1 TLB Basic Algorithm

Figure 191 shows a rough sketch of how hardware might handle a virtual address translation, assuming a simple **linear page table** (i.e., the page table is an array) and a **hardware-managed TLB** (i.e., the hardware handles much of the responsibility of page table accesses; we'll explain more about this below).

The algorithm the hardware follows works like this: first, extract the virtual page number (VPN) from the virtual address (Line 1 in Figure 191), and check if the TLB holds the translation for this VPN (Line 2). If it does, we have a **TLB hit**, which means the TLB holds the translation. Success! We can now extract the page frame number (PFN) from the relevant TLB entry, concatenate that onto the offset from the original virtual address, and form the desired physical address (PA), and access memory (Lines 5–7), assuming protection checks do not fail (Line 4).

If the CPU does not find the translation in the TLB (a **TLB miss**), we have some more work to do. In this example, the hardware accesses the page table to find the translation (Lines 11–12), and, assuming that the virtual memory reference generated by the process is valid and accessible (Lines 13, 15), updates the TLB with the translation (Line 18). These set of actions are costly, primarily because of the extra memory reference needed to access the page table (Line 12). Finally, once the TLB is updated, the hardware retries the instruction; this time, the translation is found in the TLB, and the memory reference is processed quickly.

The TLB, like all caches, is built on the premise that in the common case, translations are found in the cache (i.e., are hits). If so, little overhead is added, as the TLB is found near the processing core and is designed to be quite fast. When a miss occurs, the high cost of paging is incurred; the page table must be accessed to find the translation, and an extra memory reference (or more, with more complex page tables) results. If this happens often, the program will likely run noticeably more slowly; memory accesses, relative to most CPU instructions, are quite costly, and TLB misses lead to more memory accesses. Thus, it is our hope to avoid TLB misses as much as we can.

19.2 Example: Accessing An Array

To make clear the operation of a TLB, let's examine a simple virtual address trace and see how a TLB can improve its performance. In this example, let's assume we have an array of 10 4-byte integers in memory, starting at virtual address 100. Assume further that we have a small 8-bit virtual address space, with 16-byte pages; thus, a virtual address breaks down into a 4-bit VPN (there are 16 virtual pages) and a 4-bit offset (there are 16 bytes on each of those pages).

Figure 192 (page 216) shows the array laid out on the 16 16-byte pages of the system. As you can see, the array's first entry (`a[0]`) begins on (VPN=06, offset=04); only three 4-byte integers fit onto that page. The array continues onto the next page (VPN=07), where the next four entries (`a[3]` ... `a[6]`) are found. Finally, the last three entries of the 10-entry array (`a[7]` ... `a[9]`) are located on the next page of the address space (VPN=08).

Now let's consider a simple loop that accesses each array element, something that would look like this in C:

```
int sum = 0;
for (i = 0; i < 10; i++) {
    sum += a[i];
}
```

For the sake of simplicity, we will pretend that the only memory accesses the loop generates are to the array (ignoring the variables `i` and `sum`, as well as the instructions themselves). When the first array element (`a[0]`) is accessed, the CPU will see a load to virtual address 100. The hardware extracts the VPN from this (VPN=06), and uses that to check the TLB for a valid translation. Assuming this is the first time the program accesses the array, the result will be a TLB miss.

The next access is to `a[1]`, and there is some good news here: a TLB hit! Because the second element of the array is packed next to the first, it lives on the same page; because we've already accessed this page when accessing the first element of the array, the translation is already loaded

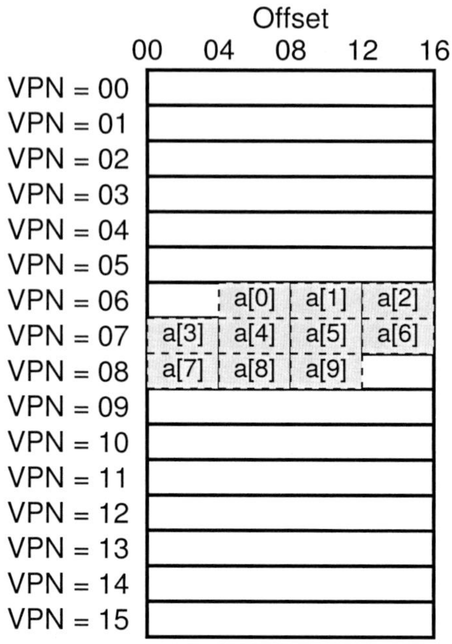

Figure 192: **Example: An Array In A Tiny Address Space**

into the TLB. And hence the reason for our success. Access to `a[2]` encounters similar success (another hit), because it too lives on the same page as `a[0]` and `a[1]`.

Unfortunately, when the program accesses `a[3]`, we encounter another TLB miss. However, once again, the next entries (`a[4]` ... `a[6]`) will hit in the TLB, as they all reside on the same page in memory.

Finally, access to `a[7]` causes one last TLB miss. The hardware once again consults the page table to figure out the location of this virtual page in physical memory, and updates the TLB accordingly. The final two accesses (`a[8]` and `a[9]`) receive the benefits of this TLB update; when the hardware looks in the TLB for their translations, two more hits result.

Let us summarize TLB activity during our ten accesses to the array: **miss**, hit, hit, **miss**, hit, hit, hit, **miss**, hit, hit. Thus, our TLB **hit rate**, which is the number of hits divided by the total number of accesses, is 70%. Although this is not too high (indeed, we desire hit rates that approach 100%), it is non-zero, which may be a surprise. Even though this is the first time the program accesses the array, the TLB improves performance due to **spatial locality**. The elements of the array are packed tightly into pages (i.e., they are close to one another in **space**), and thus only the first access to an element on a page yields a TLB miss.

Also note the role that page size plays in this example. If the page size

> **TIP: USE CACHING WHEN POSSIBLE**
>
> Caching is one of the most fundamental performance techniques in computer systems, one that is used again and again to make the "common-case fast" [HP06]. The idea behind hardware caches is to take advantage of **locality** in instruction and data references. There are usually two types of locality: **temporal locality** and **spatial locality**. With temporal locality, the idea is that an instruction or data item that has been recently accessed will likely be re-accessed soon in the future. Think of loop variables or instructions in a loop; they are accessed repeatedly over time. With spatial locality, the idea is that if a program accesses memory at address x, it will likely soon access memory near x. Imagine here streaming through an array of some kind, accessing one element and then the next. Of course, these properties depend on the exact nature of the program, and thus are not hard-and-fast laws but more like rules of thumb.
>
> Hardware caches, whether for instructions, data, or address translations (as in our TLB) take advantage of locality by keeping copies of memory in small, fast on-chip memory. Instead of having to go to a (slow) memory to satisfy a request, the processor can first check if a nearby copy exists in a cache; if it does, the processor can access it quickly (i.e., in a few CPU cycles) and avoid spending the costly time it takes to access memory (many nanoseconds).
>
> You might be wondering: if caches (like the TLB) are so great, why don't we just make bigger caches and keep all of our data in them? Unfortunately, this is where we run into more fundamental laws like those of physics. If you want a fast cache, it has to be small, as issues like the speed-of-light and other physical constraints become relevant. Any large cache by definition is slow, and thus defeats the purpose. Thus, we are stuck with small, fast caches; the question that remains is how to best use them to improve performance.

had simply been twice as big (32 bytes, not 16), the array access would suffer even fewer misses. As typical page sizes are more like 4KB, these types of dense, array-based accesses achieve excellent TLB performance, encountering only a single miss per page of accesses.

One last point about TLB performance: if the program, soon after this loop completes, accesses the array again, we'd likely see an even better result, assuming that we have a big enough TLB to cache the needed translations: hit, hit, hit, hit, hit, hit, hit, hit, hit, hit. In this case, the TLB hit rate would be high because of **temporal locality**, i.e., the quick re-referencing of memory items in **time**. Like any cache, TLBs rely upon both spatial and temporal locality for success, which are program properties. If the program of interest exhibits such locality (and many programs do), the TLB hit rate will likely be high.

```
1  VPN = (VirtualAddress & VPN_MASK) >> SHIFT
2  (Success, TlbEntry) = TLB_Lookup(VPN)
3  if (Success == True)   // TLB Hit
4      if (CanAccess(TlbEntry.ProtectBits) == True)
5          Offset   = VirtualAddress & OFFSET_MASK
6          PhysAddr = (TlbEntry.PFN << SHIFT) | Offset
7          Register = AccessMemory(PhysAddr)
8      else
9          RaiseException(PROTECTION_FAULT)
10 else                   // TLB Miss
11     RaiseException(TLB_MISS)
```

Figure 193: **TLB Control Flow Algorithm (OS Handled)**

19.3 Who Handles The TLB Miss?

One question that we must answer: who handles a TLB miss? Two answers are possible: the hardware, or the software (OS). In the olden days, the hardware had complex instruction sets (sometimes called **CISC**, for complex-instruction set computers) and the people who built the hardware didn't much trust those sneaky OS people. Thus, the hardware would handle the TLB miss entirely. To do this, the hardware has to know exactly *where* the page tables are located in memory (via a **page-table base register**, used in Line 11 in Figure 191), as well as their *exact format*; on a miss, the hardware would "walk" the page table, find the correct page-table entry and extract the desired translation, update the TLB with the translation, and retry the instruction. An example of an "older" architecture that has **hardware-managed TLBs** is the Intel x86 architecture, which uses a fixed **multi-level page table** (see the next chapter for details); the current page table is pointed to by the CR3 register [I09].

More modern architectures (e.g., MIPS R10k [H93] or Sun's SPARC v9 [WG00], both **RISC** or reduced-instruction set computers) have what is known as a **software-managed TLB**. On a TLB miss, the hardware simply raises an exception (line 11 in Figure 193), which pauses the current instruction stream, raises the privilege level to kernel mode, and jumps to a **trap handler**. As you might guess, this trap handler is code within the OS that is written with the express purpose of handling TLB misses. When run, the code will lookup the translation in the page table, use special "privileged" instructions to update the TLB, and return from the trap; at this point, the hardware retries the instruction (resulting in a TLB hit).

Let's discuss a couple of important details. First, the return-from-trap instruction needs to be a little different than the return-from-trap we saw before when servicing a system call. In the latter case, the return-from-trap should resume execution at the instruction *after* the trap into the OS, just as a return from a procedure call returns to the instruction immediately following the call into the procedure. In the former case, when returning from a TLB miss-handling trap, the hardware must resume execution at the instruction that *caused* the trap; this retry thus lets the in-

ASIDE: RISC VS. CISC

In the 1980's, a great battle took place in the computer architecture community. On one side was the **CISC** camp, which stood for **Complex Instruction Set Computing**; on the other side was **RISC**, for **Reduced Instruction Set Computing** [PS81]. The RISC side was spear-headed by David Patterson at Berkeley and John Hennessy at Stanford (who are also co-authors of some famous books [HP06]), although later John Cocke was recognized with a Turing award for his earliest work on RISC [CM00].

CISC instruction sets tend to have a lot of instructions in them, and each instruction is relatively powerful. For example, you might see a string copy, which takes two pointers and a length and copies bytes from source to destination. The idea behind CISC was that instructions should be high-level primitives, to make the assembly language itself easier to use, and to make code more compact.

RISC instruction sets are exactly the opposite. A key observation behind RISC is that instruction sets are really compiler targets, and all compilers really want are a few simple primitives that they can use to generate high-performance code. Thus, RISC proponents argued, let's rip out as much from the hardware as possible (especially the microcode), and make what's left simple, uniform, and fast.

In the early days, RISC chips made a huge impact, as they were noticeably faster [BC91]; many papers were written; a few companies were formed (e.g., MIPS and Sun). However, as time progressed, CISC manufacturers such as Intel incorporated many RISC techniques into the core of their processors, for example by adding early pipeline stages that transformed complex instructions into micro-instructions which could then be processed in a RISC-like manner. These innovations, plus a growing number of transistors on each chip, allowed CISC to remain competitive. The end result is that the debate died down, and today both types of processors can be made to run fast.

struction run again, this time resulting in a TLB hit. Thus, depending on how a trap or exception was caused, the hardware must save a different PC when trapping into the OS, in order to resume properly when the time to do so arrives.

Second, when running the TLB miss-handling code, the OS needs to be extra careful not to cause an infinite chain of TLB misses to occur. Many solutions exist; for example, you could keep TLB miss handlers in physical memory (where they are **unmapped** and not subject to address translation), or reserve some entries in the TLB for permanently-valid translations and use some of those permanent translation slots for the handler code itself; these **wired** translations always hit in the TLB.

The primary advantage of the software-managed approach is *flexibility*: the OS can use any data structure it wants to implement the page

ASIDE: TLB VALID BIT $\neq$ PAGE TABLE VALID BIT

A common mistake is to confuse the valid bits found in a TLB with those found in a page table. In a page table, when a page-table entry (PTE) is marked invalid, it means that the page has not been allocated by the process, and should not be accessed by a correctly-working program. The usual response when an invalid page is accessed is to trap to the OS, which will respond by killing the process.

A TLB valid bit, in contrast, simply refers to whether a TLB entry has a valid translation within it. When a system boots, for example, a common initial state for each TLB entry is to be set to invalid, because no address translations are yet cached there. Once virtual memory is enabled, and once programs start running and accessing their virtual address spaces, the TLB is slowly populated, and thus valid entries soon fill the TLB.

The TLB valid bit is quite useful when performing a context switch too, as we'll discuss further below. By setting all TLB entries to invalid, the system can ensure that the about-to-be-run process does not accidentally use a virtual-to-physical translation from a previous process.

table, without necessitating hardware change. Another advantage is *simplicity*, as seen in the TLB control flow (line 11 in Figure 193, in contrast to lines 11–19 in Figure 191). The hardware doesn't do much on a miss: just raise an exception and let the OS TLB miss handler do the rest.

19.4 TLB Contents: What's In There?

Let's look at the contents of the hardware TLB in more detail. A typical TLB might have 32, 64, or 128 entries and be what is called **fully associative**. Basically, this just means that any given translation can be anywhere in the TLB, and that the hardware will search the entire TLB in parallel to find the desired translation. A TLB entry might look like this:

VPN | PFN | other bits

Note that both the VPN and PFN are present in each entry, as a translation could end up in any of these locations (in hardware terms, the TLB is known as a **fully-associative** cache). The hardware searches the entries in parallel to see if there is a match.

More interesting are the "other bits". For example, the TLB commonly has a **valid** bit, which says whether the entry has a valid translation or not. Also common are **protection** bits, which determine how a page can be accessed (as in the page table). For example, code pages might be marked *read and execute*, whereas heap pages might be marked *read and write*. There may also be a few other fields, including an **address-space identifier**, a **dirty bit**, and so forth; see below for more information.

19.5 TLB Issue: Context Switches

With TLBs, some new issues arise when switching between processes (and hence address spaces). Specifically, the TLB contains virtual-to-physical translations that are only valid for the currently running process; these translations are not meaningful for other processes. As a result, when switching from one process to another, the hardware or OS (or both) must be careful to ensure that the about-to-be-run process does not accidentally use translations from some previously run process.

To understand this situation better, let's look at an example. When one process (P1) is running, it assumes the TLB might be caching translations that are valid for it, i.e., that come from P1's page table. Assume, for this example, that the 10th virtual page of P1 is mapped to physical frame 100.

In this example, assume another process (P2) exists, and the OS soon might decide to perform a context switch and run it. Assume here that the 10th virtual page of P2 is mapped to physical frame 170. If entries for both processes were in the TLB, the contents of the TLB would be:

VPN	PFN	valid	prot
10	100	1	rwx
—	—	0	—
10	170	1	rwx
—	—	0	—

In the TLB above, we clearly have a problem: VPN 10 translates to either PFN 100 (P1) or PFN 170 (P2), but the hardware can't distinguish which entry is meant for which process. Thus, we need to do some more work in order for the TLB to correctly and efficiently support virtualization across multiple processes. And thus, a crux:

> THE CRUX:
> HOW TO MANAGE TLB CONTENTS ON A CONTEXT SWITCH
> When context-switching between processes, the translations in the TLB for the last process are not meaningful to the about-to-be-run process. What should the hardware or OS do in order to solve this problem?

There are a number of possible solutions to this problem. One approach is to simply **flush** the TLB on context switches, thus emptying it before running the next process. On a software-based system, this can be accomplished with an explicit (and privileged) hardware instruction; with a hardware-managed TLB, the flush could be enacted when the page-table base register is changed (note the OS must change the PTBR on a context switch anyhow). In either case, the flush operation simply sets all valid bits to 0, essentially clearing the contents of the TLB.

By flushing the TLB on each context switch, we now have a working solution, as a process will never accidentally encounter the wrong translations in the TLB. However, there is a cost: each time a process runs, it must incur TLB misses as it touches its data and code pages. If the OS switches between processes frequently, this cost may be high.

To reduce this overhead, some systems add hardware support to enable sharing of the TLB across context switches. In particular, some hardware systems provide an **address space identifier** (**ASID**) field in the TLB. You can think of the ASID as a **process identifier** (**PID**), but usually it has fewer bits (e.g., 8 bits for the ASID versus 32 bits for a PID).

If we take our example TLB from above and add ASIDs, it is clear processes can readily share the TLB: only the ASID field is needed to differentiate otherwise identical translations. Here is a depiction of a TLB with the added ASID field:

VPN	PFN	valid	prot	ASID
10	100	1	rwx	1
—	—	0	—	—
10	170	1	rwx	2
—	—	0	—	—

Thus, with address-space identifiers, the TLB can hold translations from different processes at the same time without any confusion. Of course, the hardware also needs to know which process is currently running in order to perform translations, and thus the OS must, on a context switch, set some privileged register to the ASID of the current process.

As an aside, you may also have thought of another case where two entries of the TLB are remarkably similar. In this example, there are two entries for two different processes with two different VPNs that point to the *same* physical page:

VPN	PFN	valid	prot	ASID
10	101	1	r-x	1
—	—	0	—	—
50	101	1	r-x	2
—	—	0	—	—

This situation might arise, for example, when two processes *share* a page (a code page, for example). In the example above, Process 1 is sharing physical page 101 with Process 2; P1 maps this page into the 10th page of its address space, whereas P2 maps it to the 50th page of its address space. Sharing of code pages (in binaries, or shared libraries) is useful as it reduces the number of physical pages in use, thus reducing memory overheads.

19.6 Issue: Replacement Policy

As with any cache, and thus also with the TLB, one more issue that we must consider is **cache replacement**. Specifically, when we are installing a new entry in the TLB, we have to **replace** an old one, and thus the question: which one to replace?

THE CRUX: HOW TO DESIGN TLB REPLACEMENT POLICY
Which TLB entry should be replaced when we add a new TLB entry? The goal, of course, being to minimize the **miss rate** (or increase **hit rate**) and thus improve performance.

We will study such policies in some detail when we tackle the problem of swapping pages to disk; here we'll just highlight a few typical policies. One common approach is to evict the **least-recently-used** or **LRU** entry. LRU tries to take advantage of locality in the memory-reference stream, assuming it is likely that an entry that has not recently been used is a good candidate for eviction. Another typical approach is to use a **random** policy, which evicts a TLB mapping at random. Such a policy is useful due to its simplicity and ability to avoid corner-case behaviors; for example, a "reasonable" policy such as LRU behaves quite unreasonably when a program loops over $n + 1$ pages with a TLB of size n; in this case, LRU misses upon every access, whereas random does much better.

19.7 A Real TLB Entry

Finally, let's briefly look at a real TLB. This example is from the MIPS R4000 [H93], a modern system that uses software-managed TLBs; a slightly simplified MIPS TLB entry can be seen in Figure 194.

The MIPS R4000 supports a 32-bit address space with 4KB pages. Thus, we would expect a 20-bit VPN and 12-bit offset in our typical virtual address. However, as you can see in the TLB, there are only 19 bits for the VPN; as it turns out, user addresses will only come from half the address space (the rest reserved for the kernel) and hence only 19 bits of VPN are needed. The VPN translates to up to a 24-bit physical frame number (PFN), and hence can support systems with up to 64GB of (physical) main memory (2^{24} 4KB pages).

There are a few other interesting bits in the MIPS TLB. We see a *global* bit (G), which is used for pages that are globally-shared among processes. Thus, if the global bit is set, the ASID is ignored. We also see the 8-bit *ASID*, which the OS can use to distinguish between address spaces (as

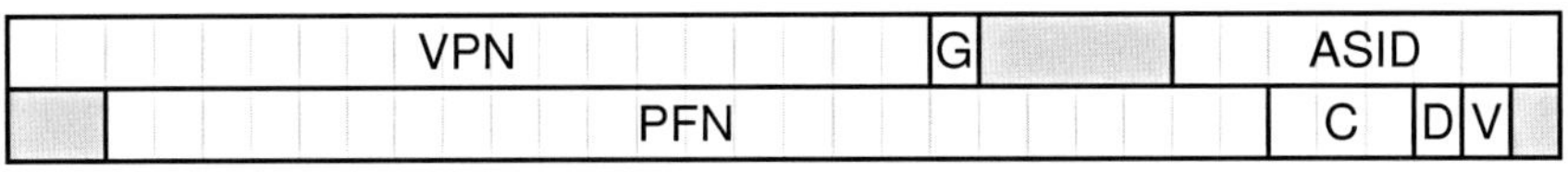

Figure 194: **A MIPS TLB Entry**

> TIP: RAM ISN'T ALWAYS RAM (CULLER'S LAW)
> The term **random-access memory**, or **RAM**, implies that you can access any part of RAM just as quickly as another. While it is generally good to think of RAM in this way, because of hardware/OS features such as the TLB, accessing a particular page of memory may be costly, particularly if that page isn't currently mapped by your TLB. Thus, it is always good to remember the implementation tip: **RAM isn't always RAM**. Sometimes randomly accessing your address space, particularly if the number of pages accessed exceeds the TLB coverage, can lead to severe performance penalties. Because one of our advisors, David Culler, used to always point to the TLB as the source of many performance problems, we name this law in his honor: **Culler's Law**.

described above). One question for you: what should the OS do if there are more than 256 (2^8) processes running at a time? Finally, we see 3 *Coherence* (C) bits, which determine how a page is cached by the hardware (a bit beyond the scope of these notes); a *dirty* bit which is marked when the page has been written to (we'll see the use of this later); a *valid* bit which tells the hardware if there is a valid translation present in the entry. There is also a *page mask* field (not shown), which supports multiple page sizes; we'll see later why having larger pages might be useful. Finally, some of the 64 bits are unused (shaded gray in the diagram).

MIPS TLBs usually have 32 or 64 of these entries, most of which are used by user processes as they run. However, a few are reserved for the OS. A *wired* register can be set by the OS to tell the hardware how many slots of the TLB to reserve for the OS; the OS uses these reserved mappings for code and data that it wants to access during critical times, where a TLB miss would be problematic (e.g., in the TLB miss handler).

Because the MIPS TLB is software managed, there needs to be instructions to update the TLB. The MIPS provides four such instructions: `TLBP`, which probes the TLB to see if a particular translation is in there; `TLBR`, which reads the contents of a TLB entry into registers; `TLBWI`, which replaces a specific TLB entry; and `TLBWR`, which replaces a random TLB entry. The OS uses these instructions to manage the TLB's contents. It is of course critical that these instructions are **privileged**; imagine what a user process could do if it could modify the contents of the TLB (hint: just about anything, including take over the machine, run its own malicious "OS", or even make the Sun disappear).

19.8 Summary

We have seen how hardware can help us make address translation faster. By providing a small, dedicated on-chip TLB as an address-translation cache, most memory references will hopefully be handled *without* having to access the page table in main memory. Thus, in the common case, the performance of the program will be almost as if memory isn't being virtualized at all, an excellent achievement for an operating system, and certainly essential to the use of paging in modern systems.

However, TLBs do not make the world rosy for every program that exists. In particular, if the number of pages a program accesses in a short period of time exceeds the number of pages that fit into the TLB, the program will generate a large number of TLB misses, and thus run quite a bit more slowly. We refer to this phenomenon as exceeding the **TLB coverage**, and it can be quite a problem for certain programs. One solution, as we'll discuss in the next chapter, is to include support for larger page sizes; by mapping key data structures into regions of the program's address space that are mapped by larger pages, the effective coverage of the TLB can be increased. Support for large pages is often exploited by programs such as a **database management system** (a **DBMS**), which have certain data structures that are both large and randomly-accessed.

One other TLB issue worth mentioning: TLB access can easily become a bottleneck in the CPU pipeline, in particular with what is called a **physically-indexed cache**. With such a cache, address translation has to take place *before* the cache is accessed, which can slow things down quite a bit. Because of this potential problem, people have looked into all sorts of clever ways to access caches with *virtual* addresses, thus avoiding the expensive step of translation in the case of a cache hit. Such a **virtually-indexed cache** solves some performance problems, but introduces new issues into hardware design as well. See Wiggins's fine survey for more details [W03].

References

[BC91] "Performance from Architecture: Comparing a RISC and a CISC with Similar Hardware Organization" by D. Bhandarkar and Douglas W. Clark. Communications of the ACM, September 1991. *A great and fair comparison between RISC and CISC. The bottom line: on similar hardware, RISC was about a factor of three better in performance.*

[CM00] "The evolution of RISC technology at IBM" by John Cocke, V. Markstein. IBM Journal of Research and Development, 44:1/2. *A summary of the ideas and work behind the IBM 801, which many consider the first true RISC microprocessor.*

[C95] "The Core of the Black Canyon Computer Corporation" by John Couleur. IEEE Annals of History of Computing, 17:4, 1995. *In this fascinating historical note, Couleur talks about how he invented the TLB in 1964 while working for GE, and the fortuitous collaboration that thus ensued with the Project MAC folks at MIT.*

[CG68] "Shared-access Data Processing System" by John F. Couleur, Edward L. Glaser. Patent 3412382, November 1968. *The patent that contains the idea for an associative memory to store address translations. The idea, according to Couleur, came in 1964.*

[CP78] "The architecture of the IBM System/370" by R.P. Case, A. Padegs. Communications of the ACM. 21:1, 73-96, January 1978. *Perhaps the first paper to use the term* ***translation lookaside buffer****. The name arises from the historical name for a cache, which was a* ***lookaside buffer*** *as called by those developing the Atlas system at the University of Manchester; a cache of address translations thus became a* ***translation lookaside buffer****. Even though the term lookaside buffer fell out of favor, TLB seems to have stuck, for whatever reason.*

[H93] "MIPS R4000 Microprocessor User's Manual". by Joe Heinrich. Prentice-Hall, June 1993. Available: http://cag.csail.mit.edu/raw/ . documents/R4400_Uman_book_Ed2.pdf *A manual, one that is surprisingly readable. Or is it?*

[HP06] "Computer Architecture: A Quantitative Approach" by John Hennessy and David Patterson. Morgan-Kaufmann, 2006. *A great book about computer architecture. We have a particular attachment to the classic first edition.*

[I09] "Intel 64 and IA-32 Architectures Software Developer's Manuals" by Intel, 2009. Available: http://www.intel.com/products/processor/manuals. *In particular, pay attention to "Volume 3A: System Programming Guide" Part 1* and "Volume 3B: System Programming Guide Part 2".

[PS81] "RISC-I: A Reduced Instruction Set VLSI Computer" by D.A. Patterson and C.H. Sequin. ISCA '81, Minneapolis, May 1981. *The paper that introduced the term RISC, and started the avalanche of research into simplifying computer chips for performance.*

[SB92] "CPU Performance Evaluation and Execution Time Prediction Using Narrow Spectrum Benchmarking" by Rafael H. Saavedra-Barrera. EECS Department, University of California, Berkeley. Technical Report No. UCB/CSD-92-684, February 1992.. *A great dissertation about how to predict execution time of applications by breaking them down into constituent pieces and knowing the cost of each piece. Probably the most interesting part that comes out of this work is the tool to measure details of the cache hierarchy (described in Chapter 5). Make sure to check out the wonderful diagrams therein.*

[W03] "A Survey on the Interaction Between Caching, Translation and Protection" by Adam Wiggins. University of New South Wales TR UNSW-CSE-TR-0321, August, 2003. *An excellent survey of how TLBs interact with other parts of the CPU pipeline, namely hardware caches.*

[WG00] "The SPARC Architecture Manual: Version 9" by David L. Weaver and Tom Germond. SPARC International, San Jose, California, September 2000. Available: `www.sparc.org/standards/SPARCV9.pdf`. *Another manual. I bet you were hoping for a more fun citation to end this chapter.*

Homework (Measurement)

In this homework, you are to measure the size and cost of accessing a TLB. The idea is based on work by Saavedra-Barrera [SB92], who developed a simple but beautiful method to measure numerous aspects of cache hierarchies, all with a very simple user-level program. Read his work for more details.

The basic idea is to access some number of pages within a large data structure (e.g., an array) and to time those accesses. For example, let's say the TLB size of a machine happens to be 4 (which would be very small, but useful for the purposes of this discussion). If you write a program that touches 4 or fewer pages, each access should be a TLB hit, and thus relatively fast. However, once you touch 5 pages or more, repeatedly in a loop, each access will suddenly jump in cost, to that of a TLB miss.

The basic code to loop through an array once should look like this:

```
int jump = PAGESIZE / sizeof(int);
for (i = 0; i < NUMPAGES * jump; i += jump)
    a[i] += 1;
```

In this loop, one integer per page of the array `a` is updated, up to the number of pages specified by `NUMPAGES`. By timing such a loop repeatedly (say, a few hundred million times in another loop around this one, or however many loops are needed to run for a few seconds), you can time how long each access takes (on average). By looking for jumps in cost as `NUMPAGES` increases, you can roughly determine how big the first-level TLB is, determine whether a second-level TLB exists (and how big it is if it does), and in general get a good sense of how TLB hits and misses can affect performance.

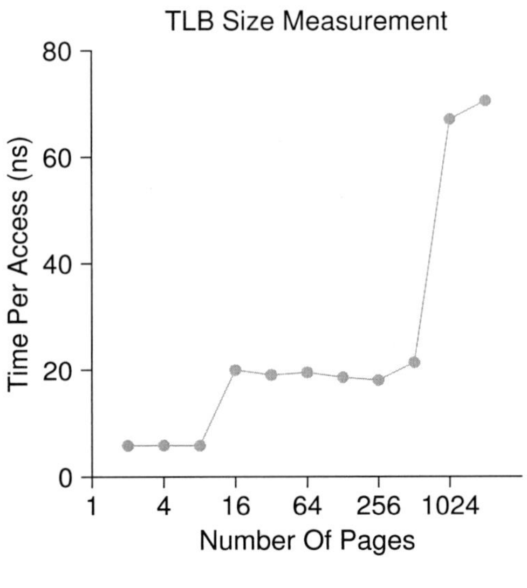

Figure 195: **Discovering TLB Sizes and Miss Costs**

Figure 195 (page 227) shows the average time per access as the number of pages accessed in the loop is increased. As you can see in the graph, when just a few pages are accessed (8 or fewer), the average access time is roughly 5 nanoseconds. When 16 or more pages are accessed, there is a sudden jump to about 20 nanoseconds per access. A final jump in cost occurs at around 1024 pages, at which point each access takes around 70 nanoseconds. From this data, we can conclude that there is a two-level TLB hierarchy; the first is quite small (probably holding between 8 and 16 entries); the second is larger but slower (holding roughly 512 entries). The overall difference between hits in the first-level TLB and misses is quite large, roughly a factor of fourteen. TLB performance matters!

Questions

1. For timing, you'll need to use a timer (e.g., `gettimeofday()`). How precise is such a timer? How long does an operation have to take in order for you to time it precisely? (this will help determine how many times, in a loop, you'll have to repeat a page access in order to time it successfully)
2. Write the program, called `tlb.c`, that can roughly measure the cost of accessing each page. Inputs to the program should be: the number of pages to touch and the number of trials.
3. Now write a script in your favorite scripting language (bash?) to run this program, while varying the number of pages accessed from 1 up to a few thousand, perhaps incrementing by a factor of two per iteration. Run the script on different machines and gather some data. How many trials are needed to get reliable measurements?
4. Next, graph the results, making a graph that looks similar to the one above. Use a good tool like `ploticus` or even `zplot`. Visualization usually makes the data much easier to digest; why do you think that is?
5. One thing to watch out for is compiler optimization. Compilers do all sorts of clever things, including removing loops which increment values that no other part of the program subsequently uses. How can you ensure the compiler does not remove the main loop above from your TLB size estimator?
6. Another thing to watch out for is the fact that most systems today ship with multiple CPUs, and each CPU, of course, has its own TLB hierarchy. To really get good measurements, you have to run your code on just one CPU, instead of letting the scheduler bounce it from one CPU to the next. How can you do that? (hint: look up "pinning a thread" on Google for some clues) What will happen if you don't do this, and the code moves from one CPU to the other?
7. Another issue that might arise relates to initialization. If you don't initialize the array `a` above before accessing it, the first time you access it will be very expensive, due to initial access costs such as demand zeroing. Will this affect your code and its timing? What can you do to counterbalance these potential costs?

20

Paging: Smaller Tables

We now tackle the second problem that paging introduces: page tables are too big and thus consume too much memory. Let's start out with a linear page table. As you might recall[1], linear page tables get pretty big. Assume again a 32-bit address space (2^{32} bytes), with 4KB (2^{12} byte) pages and a 4-byte page-table entry. An address space thus has roughly one million virtual pages in it ($\frac{2^{32}}{2^{12}}$); multiply by the page-table entry size and you see that our page table is 4MB in size. Recall also: we usually have one page table *for every process* in the system! With a hundred active processes (not uncommon on a modern system), we will be allocating hundreds of megabytes of memory just for page tables! As a result, we are in search of some techniques to reduce this heavy burden. There are a lot of them, so let's get going. But not before our crux:

> CRUX: HOW TO MAKE PAGE TABLES SMALLER?
>
> Simple array-based page tables (usually called linear page tables) are too big, taking up far too much memory on typical systems. How can we make page tables smaller? What are the key ideas? What inefficiencies arise as a result of these new data structures?

20.1 Simple Solution: Bigger Pages

We could reduce the size of the page table in one simple way: use bigger pages. Take our 32-bit address space again, but this time assume 16KB pages. We would thus have an 18-bit VPN plus a 14-bit offset. Assuming the same size for each PTE (4 bytes), we now have 2^{18} entries in our linear page table and thus a total size of 1MB per page table, a factor

[1] Or indeed, you might not; this paging thing is getting out of control, no? That said, always make sure you understand the *problem* you are solving before moving onto the solution; indeed, if you understand the problem, you can often derive the solution yourself. Here, the problem should be clear: simple linear (array-based) page tables are too big.

> **ASIDE: MULTIPLE PAGE SIZES**
> As an aside, do note that many architectures (e.g., MIPS, SPARC, x86-64) now support multiple page sizes. Usually, a small (4KB or 8KB) page size is used. However, if a "smart" application requests it, a single large page (e.g., of size 4MB) can be used for a specific portion of the address space, enabling such applications to place a frequently-used (and large) data structure in such a space while consuming only a single TLB entry. This type of large page usage is common in database management systems and other high-end commercial applications. The main reason for multiple page sizes is not to save page table space, however; it is to reduce pressure on the TLB, enabling a program to access more of its address space without suffering from too many TLB misses. However, as researchers have shown [N+02], using multiple page sizes makes the OS virtual memory manager notably more complex, and thus large pages are sometimes most easily used simply by exporting a new interface to applications to request large pages directly.

of four reduction in size of the page table (not surprisingly, the reduction exactly mirrors the factor of four increase in page size).

The major problem with this approach, however, is that big pages lead to waste *within* each page, a problem known as **internal fragmentation** (as the waste is **internal** to the unit of allocation). Applications thus end up allocating pages but only using little bits and pieces of each, and memory quickly fills up with these overly-large pages. Thus, most systems use relatively small page sizes in the common case: 4KB (as in x86) or 8KB (as in SPARCv9). Our problem will not be solved so simply, alas.

20.2 Hybrid Approach: Paging and Segments

Whenever you have two reasonable but different approaches to something in life, you should always examine the combination of the two to see if you can obtain the best of both worlds. We call such a combination a **hybrid**. For example, why eat just chocolate or plain peanut butter when you can instead combine the two in a lovely hybrid known as the Reese's Peanut Butter Cup [M28]?

Years ago, the creators of Multics (in particular Jack Dennis) chanced upon such an idea in the construction of the Multics virtual memory system [M07]. Specifically, Dennis had the idea of combining paging and segmentation in order to reduce the memory overhead of page tables. We can see why this might work by examining a typical linear page table in more detail. Assume we have an address space in which the used portions of the heap and stack are small. For the example, we use a tiny 16KB address space with 1KB pages (Figure 201); the page table for this address space is in Figure 202.

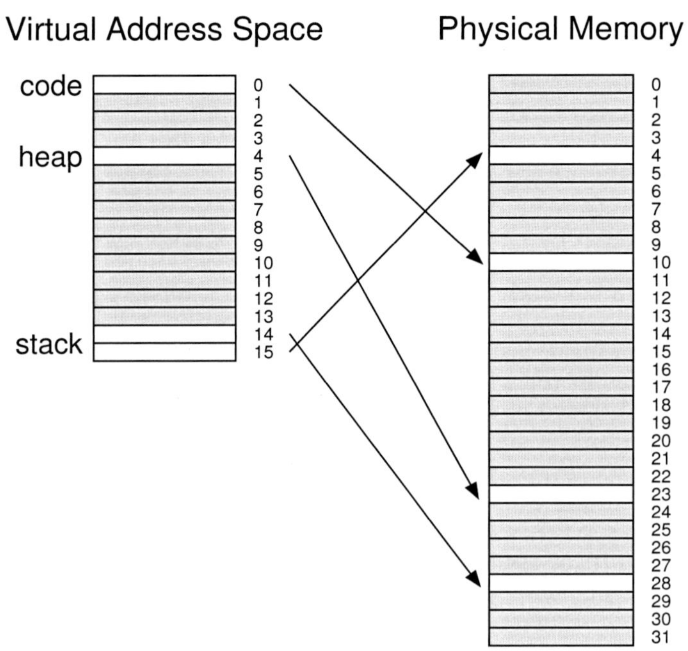

Figure 201: **A 16KB Address Space With 1KB Pages**

PFN	valid	prot	present	dirty
10	1	r-x	1	0
-	0	—	-	-
-	0	—	-	-
-	0	—	-	-
23	1	rw-	1	1
-	0	—	-	-
-	0	—	-	-
-	0	—	-	-
-	0	—	-	-
-	0	—	-	-
-	0	—	-	-
-	0	—	-	-
-	0	—	-	-
-	0	—	-	-
28	1	rw-	1	1
4	1	rw-	1	1

Figure 202: **A Page Table For 16KB Address Space**

This example assumes the single code page (VPN 0) is mapped to physical page 10, the single heap page (VPN 4) to physical page 23, and the two stack pages at the other end of the address space (VPNs 14 and

15) are mapped to physical pages 28 and 4, respectively. As you can see from the picture, *most* of the page table is unused, full of **invalid** entries. What a waste! And this is for a tiny 16KB address space. Imagine the page table of a 32-bit address space and all the potential wasted space in there! Actually, don't imagine such a thing; it's far too gruesome.

Thus, our hybrid approach: instead of having a single page table for the entire address space of the process, why not have one per logical segment? In this example, we might thus have three page tables, one for the code, heap, and stack parts of the address space.

Now, remember with segmentation, we had a **base** register that told us where each segment lived in physical memory, and a **bound** or **limit** register that told us the size of said segment. In our hybrid, we still have those structures in the MMU; here, we use the base not to point to the segment itself but rather to hold the *physical address of the page table* of that segment. The bounds register is used to indicate the end of the page table (i.e., how many valid pages it has).

Let's do a simple example to clarify. Assume a 32-bit virtual address space with 4KB pages, and an address space split into four segments. We'll only use three segments for this example: one for code, one for heap, and one for stack.

To determine which segment an address refers to, we'll use the top two bits of the address space. Let's assume 00 is the unused segment, with 01 for code, 10 for the heap, and 11 for the stack. Thus, a virtual address looks like this:

```
3 3 2 2 2 2 2 2 2 2 2 2 1 1 1 1 1 1 1 1 1 1 0 0 0 0 0 0 0 0 0 0
1 0 9 8 7 6 5 4 3 2 1 0 9 8 7 6 5 4 3 2 1 0 9 8 7 6 5 4 3 2 1 0
|Seg|                VPN                |         Offset        |
```

In the hardware, assume that there are thus three base/bounds pairs, one each for code, heap, and stack. When a process is running, the base register for each of these segments contains the physical address of a linear page table for that segment; thus, each process in the system now has *three* page tables associated with it. On a context switch, these registers must be changed to reflect the location of the page tables of the newly-running process.

On a TLB miss (assuming a hardware-managed TLB, i.e., where the hardware is responsible for handling TLB misses), the hardware uses the segment bits (`SN`) to determine which base and bounds pair to use. The hardware then takes the physical address therein and combines it with the VPN as follows to form the address of the page table entry (PTE):

```
SN           = (VirtualAddress & SEG_MASK) >> SN_SHIFT
VPN          = (VirtualAddress & VPN_MASK) >> VPN_SHIFT
AddressOfPTE = Base[SN] + (VPN * sizeof(PTE))
```

This sequence should look familiar; it is virtually identical to what we saw before with linear page tables. The only difference, of course, is the use of one of three segment base registers instead of the single page table base register.

TIP: USE HYBRIDS

When you have two good and seemingly opposing ideas, you should always see if you can combine them into a **hybrid** that manages to achieve the best of both worlds. Hybrid corn species, for example, are known to be more robust than any naturally-occurring species. Of course, not all hybrids are a good idea; see the Zeedonk (or Zonkey), which is a cross of a Zebra and a Donkey. If you don't believe such a creature exists, look it up, and prepare to be amazed.

The critical difference in our hybrid scheme is the presence of a bounds register per segment; each bounds register holds the value of the maximum valid page in the segment. For example, if the code segment is using its first three pages (0, 1, and 2), the code segment page table will only have three entries allocated to it and the bounds register will be set to 3; memory accesses beyond the end of the segment will generate an exception and likely lead to the termination of the process. In this manner, our hybrid approach realizes a significant memory savings compared to the linear page table; unallocated pages between the stack and the heap no longer take up space in a page table (just to mark them as not valid).

However, as you might notice, this approach is not without problems. First, it still requires us to use segmentation; as we discussed before, segmentation is not quite as flexible as we would like, as it assumes a certain usage pattern of the address space; if we have a large but sparsely-used heap, for example, we can still end up with a lot of page table waste. Second, this hybrid causes external fragmentation to arise again. While most of memory is managed in page-sized units, page tables now can be of arbitrary size (in multiples of PTEs). Thus, finding free space for them in memory is more complicated. For these reasons, people continued to look for better ways to implement smaller page tables.

20.3 Multi-level Page Tables

A different approach doesn't rely on segmentation but attacks the same problem: how to get rid of all those invalid regions in the page table instead of keeping them all in memory? We call this approach a **multi-level page table**, as it turns the linear page table into something like a tree. This approach is so effective that many modern systems employ it (e.g., x86 [BOH10]). We now describe this approach in detail.

The basic idea behind a multi-level page table is simple. First, chop up the page table into page-sized units; then, if an entire page of page-table entries (PTEs) is invalid, don't allocate that page of the page table at all. To track whether a page of the page table is valid (and if valid, where it is in memory), use a new structure, called the **page directory**. The page directory thus either can be used to tell you where a page of the page table is, or that the entire page of the page table contains no valid pages.

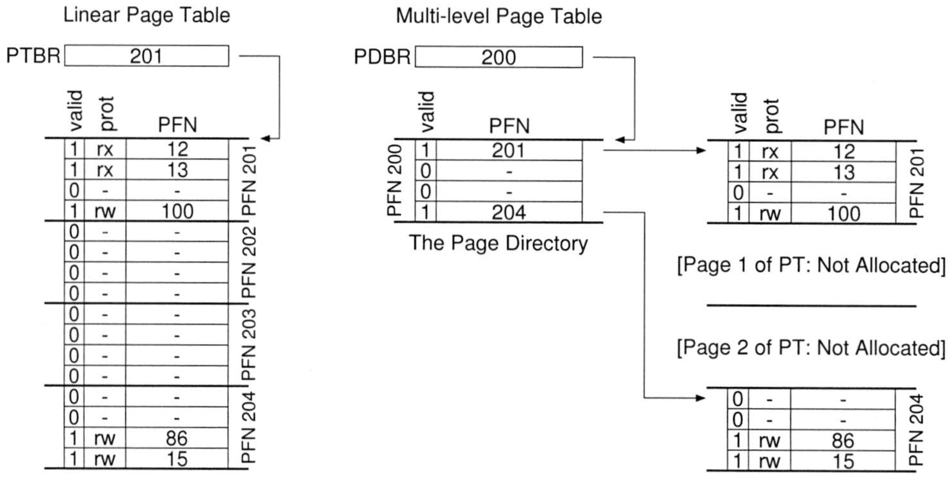

Figure 203: **Linear (Left) And Multi-Level (Right) Page Tables**

Figure 203 shows an example. On the left of the figure is the classic linear page table; even though most of the middle regions of the address space are not valid, we still require page-table space allocated for those regions (i.e., the middle two pages of the page table). On the right is a multi-level page table. The page directory marks just two pages of the page table as valid (the first and last); thus, just those two pages of the page table reside in memory. And thus you can see one way to visualize what a multi-level table is doing: it just makes parts of the linear page table disappear (freeing those frames for other uses), and tracks which pages of the page table are allocated with the page directory.

The page directory, in a simple two-level table, contains one entry per page of the page table. It consists of a number of **page directory entries (PDE)**. A PDE (minimally) has a **valid bit** and a **page frame number** (PFN), similar to a PTE. However, as hinted at above, the meaning of this valid bit is slightly different: if the PDE is valid, it means that at least one of the pages of the page table that the entry points to (via the PFN) is valid, i.e., in at least one PTE on that page pointed to by this PDE, the valid bit in that PTE is set to one. If the PDE is not valid (i.e., equal to zero), the rest of the PDE is not defined.

Multi-level page tables have some obvious advantages over approaches we've seen thus far. First, and perhaps most obviously, the multi-level table only allocates page-table space in proportion to the amount of address space you are using; thus it is generally compact and supports sparse address spaces.

Second, if carefully constructed, each portion of the page table fits neatly within a page, making it easier to manage memory; the OS can simply grab the next free page when it needs to allocate or grow a page

> TIP: UNDERSTAND TIME-SPACE TRADE-OFFS
> When building a data structure, one should always consider **time-space trade-offs** in its construction. Usually, if you wish to make access to a particular data structure faster, you will have to pay a space-usage penalty for the structure.

table. Contrast this to a simple (non-paged) linear page table[2], which is just an array of PTEs indexed by VPN; with such a structure, the entire linear page table must reside contiguously in physical memory. For a large page table (say 4MB), finding such a large chunk of unused contiguous free physical memory can be quite a challenge. With a multi-level structure, we add a **level of indirection** through use of the page directory, which points to pieces of the page table; that indirection allows us to place page-table pages wherever we would like in physical memory.

It should be noted that there is a cost to multi-level tables; on a TLB miss, two loads from memory will be required to get the right translation information from the page table (one for the page directory, and one for the PTE itself), in contrast to just one load with a linear page table. Thus, the multi-level table is a small example of a **time-space trade-off**. We wanted smaller tables (and got them), but not for free; although in the common case (TLB hit), performance is obviously identical, a TLB miss suffers from a higher cost with this smaller table.

Another obvious negative is *complexity*. Whether it is the hardware or OS handling the page-table lookup (on a TLB miss), doing so is undoubtedly more involved than a simple linear page-table lookup. Often we are willing to increase complexity in order to improve performance or reduce overheads; in the case of a multi-level table, we make page-table lookups more complicated in order to save valuable memory.

A Detailed Multi-Level Example

To understand the idea behind multi-level page tables better, let's do an example. Imagine a small address space of size 16KB, with 64-byte pages. Thus, we have a 14-bit virtual address space, with 8 bits for the VPN and 6 bits for the offset. A linear page table would have 2^8 (256) entries, even if only a small portion of the address space is in use. Figure 20.4 (page 236) presents one example of such an address space.

In this example, virtual pages 0 and 1 are for code, virtual pages 4 and 5 for the heap, and virtual pages 254 and 255 for the stack; the rest of the pages of the address space are unused.

To build a two-level page table for this address space, we start with our full linear page table and break it up into page-sized units. Recall our full table (in this example) has 256 entries; assume each PTE is 4 bytes

[2]We are making some assumptions here, i.e., that all page tables reside in their entirety in physical memory (i.e., they are not swapped to disk); we'll soon relax this assumption.

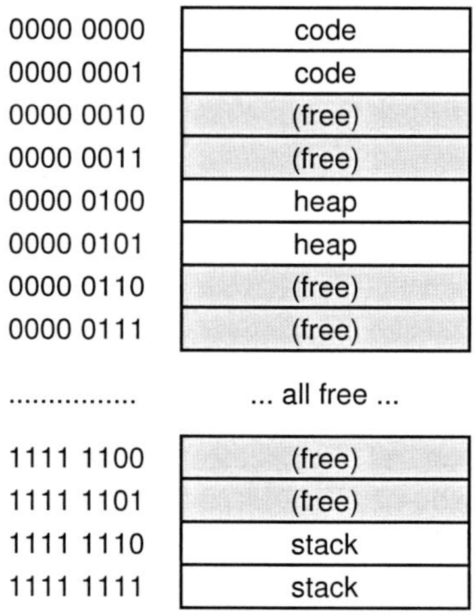

Figure 204: **A 16KB Address Space With 64-byte Pages**

in size. Thus, our page table is 1KB (256 × 4 bytes) in size. Given that we have 64-byte pages, the 1KB page table can be divided into 16 64-byte pages; each page can hold 16 PTEs.

What we need to understand now is how to take a VPN and use it to index first into the page directory and then into the page of the page table. Remember that each is an array of entries; thus, all we need to figure out is how to construct the index for each from pieces of the VPN.

Let's first index into the page directory. Our page table in this example is small: 256 entries, spread across 16 pages. The page directory needs one entry per page of the page table; thus, it has 16 entries. As a result, we need four bits of the VPN to index into the directory; we use the top four bits of the VPN, as follows:

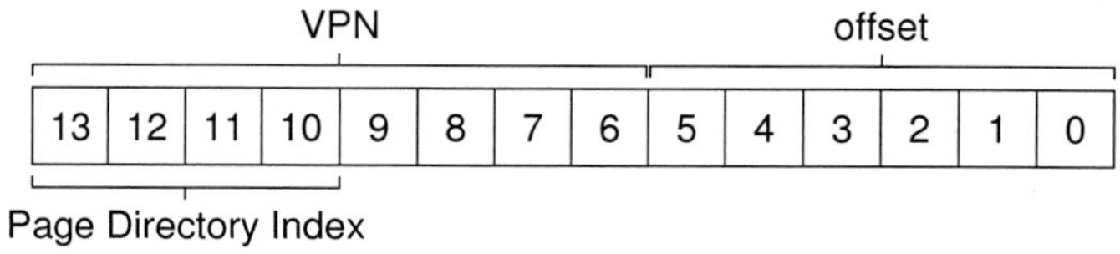

Once we extract the **page-directory index** (`PDIndex` for short) from the VPN, we can use it to find the address of the page-directory entry (PDE) with a simple calculation: `PDEAddr = PageDirBase + (PDIndex * sizeof(PDE))`. This results in our page directory, which we now examine to make further progress in our translation.

If the page-directory entry is marked invalid, we know that the access is invalid, and thus raise an exception. If, however, the PDE is valid, we have more work to do. Specifically, we now have to fetch the page-table entry (PTE) from the page of the page table pointed to by this page-directory entry. To find this PTE, we have to index into the portion of the page table using the remaining bits of the VPN:

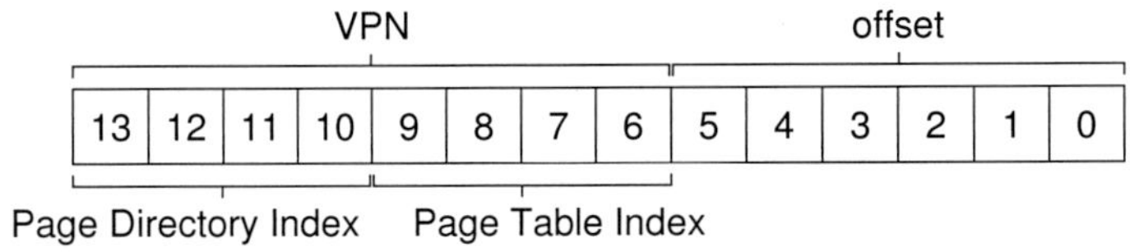

This **page-table index** (`PTIndex` for short) can then be used to index into the page table itself, giving us the address of our PTE:

```
PTEAddr = (PDE.PFN << SHIFT) + (PTIndex * sizeof(PTE))
```

Note that the page-frame number (PFN) obtained from the page-directory entry must be left-shifted into place before combining it with the page-table index to form the address of the PTE.

To see if this all makes sense, we'll now fill in a multi-level page table with some actual values, and translate a single virtual address. Let's begin with the **page directory** for this example (left side of Figure 205).

In the figure, you can see that each page directory entry (PDE) describes something about a page of the page table for the address space. In this example, we have two valid regions in the address space (at the beginning and end), and a number of invalid mappings in-between.

In physical page 100 (the physical frame number of the 0th page of the page table), we have the first page of 16 page table entries for the first 16 VPNs in the address space. See Figure 205 (middle part) for the contents of this portion of the page table.

This page of the page table contains the mappings for the first 16 VPNs; in our example, VPNs 0 and 1 are valid (the code segment), as

Page Directory		**Page of PT (@PFN:100)**			**Page of PT (@PFN:101)**		
PFN	valid?	PFN	valid	prot	PFN	valid	prot
100	1	10	1	r-x	—	0	—
—	0	23	1	r-x	—	0	—
—	0	—	0	—	—	0	—
—	0	—	0	—	—	0	—
—	0	80	1	rw-	—	0	—
—	0	59	1	rw-	—	0	—
—	0	—	0	—	—	0	—
—	0	—	0	—	—	0	—
—	0	—	0	—	—	0	—
—	0	—	0	—	—	0	—
—	0	—	0	—	—	0	—
—	0	—	0	—	—	0	—
—	0	—	0	—	—	0	—
—	0	—	0	—	—	0	—
—	0	—	0	—	55	1	rw-
101	1	—	0	—	45	1	rw-

Figure 205: **A Page Directory, And Pieces Of Page Table**

> TIP: BE WARY OF COMPLEXITY
>
> System designers should be wary of adding complexity into their system. What a good systems builder does is implement the least complex system that achieves the task at hand. For example, if disk space is abundant, you shouldn't design a file system that works hard to use as few bytes as possible; similarly, if processors are fast, it is better to write a clean and understandable module within the OS than perhaps the most CPU-optimized, hand-assembled code for the task at hand. Be wary of needless complexity, in prematurely-optimized code or other forms; such approaches make systems harder to understand, maintain, and debug. As Antoine de Saint-Exupery famously wrote: "Perfection is finally attained not when there is no longer anything to add, but when there is no longer anything to take away." What he didn't write: "It's a lot easier to say something about perfection than to actually achieve it."

are 4 and 5 (the heap). Thus, the table has mapping information for each of those pages. The rest of the entries are marked invalid.

The other valid page of the page table is found inside PFN 101. This page contains mappings for the last 16 VPNs of the address space; see Figure 205 (right) for details.

In the example, VPNs 254 and 255 (the stack) have valid mappings. Hopefully, what we can see from this example is how much space savings are possible with a multi-level indexed structure. In this example, instead of allocating the full *sixteen* pages for a linear page table, we allocate only *three*: one for the page directory, and two for the chunks of the page table that have valid mappings. The savings for large (32-bit or 64-bit) address spaces could obviously be much greater.

Finally, let's use this information in order to perform a translation. Here is an address that refers to the 0th byte of VPN 254: `0x3F80`, or `11 1111 1000 0000` in binary.

Recall that we will use the top 4 bits of the VPN to index into the page directory. Thus, `1111` will choose the last (15th, if you start at the 0th) entry of the page directory above. This points us to a valid page of the page table located at address `101`. We then use the next 4 bits of the VPN (`1110`) to index into that page of the page table and find the desired PTE. 1110 is the next-to-last (14th) entry on the page, and tells us that page 254 of our virtual address space is mapped at physical page 55. By concatenating PFN=55 (or hex `0x37`) with offset=000000, we can thus form our desired physical address and issue the request to the memory system: `PhysAddr = (PTE.PFN << SHIFT) + offset = 00 1101 1100 0000 = 0x0DC0`.

You should now have some idea of how to construct a two-level page table, using a page directory which points to pages of the page table. Unfortunately, however, our work is not done. As we'll now discuss, sometimes two levels of page table is not enough!

More Than Two Levels

In our example thus far, we've assumed that multi-level page tables only have two levels: a page directory and then pieces of the page table. In some cases, a deeper tree is possible (and indeed, needed).

Let's take a simple example and use it to show why a deeper multi-level table can be useful. In this example, assume we have a 30-bit virtual address space, and a small (512 byte) page. Thus our virtual address has a 21-bit virtual page number component and a 9-bit offset.

Remember our goal in constructing a multi-level page table: to make each piece of the page table fit within a single page. Thus far, we've only considered the page table itself; however, what if the page directory gets too big?

To determine how many levels are needed in a multi-level table to make all pieces of the page table fit within a page, we start by determining how many page-table entries fit within a page. Given our page size of 512 bytes, and assuming a PTE size of 4 bytes, you should see that you can fit 128 PTEs on a single page. When we index into a page of the page table, we can thus conclude we'll need the least significant 7 bits ($log_2 128$) of the VPN as an index:

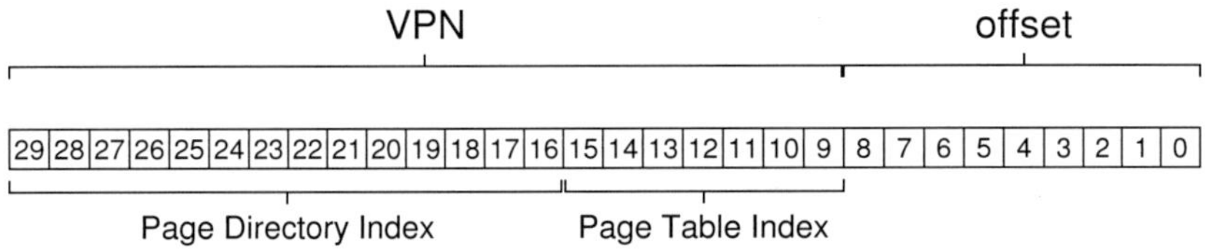

What you also might notice from the diagram above is how many bits are left into the (large) page directory: 14. If our page directory has 2^{14} entries, it spans not one page but 128, and thus our goal of making every piece of the multi-level page table fit into a page vanishes.

To remedy this problem, we build a further level of the tree, by splitting the page directory itself into multiple pages, and then adding another page directory on top of that, to point to the pages of the page directory. We can thus split up our virtual address as follows:

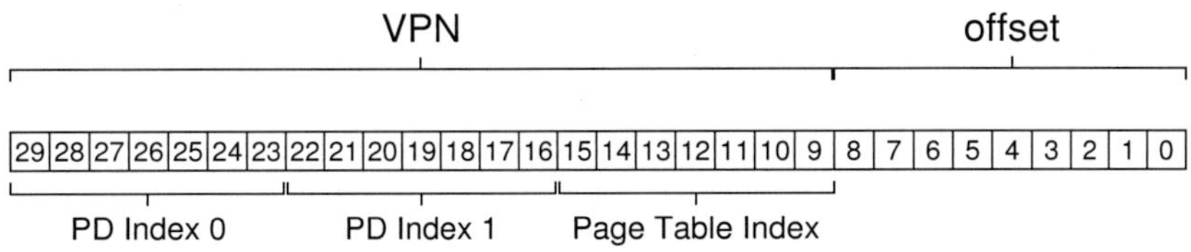

Now, when indexing the upper-level page directory, we use the very top bits of the virtual address (`PD Index 0` in the diagram); this index can be used to fetch the page-directory entry from the top-level page directory. If valid, the second level of the page directory is consulted by combining the physical frame number from the top-level PDE and the

```
VPN = (VirtualAddress & VPN_MASK) >> SHIFT
(Success, TlbEntry) = TLB_Lookup(VPN)
if (Success == True)    // TLB Hit
  if (CanAccess(TlbEntry.ProtectBits) == True)
    Offset   = VirtualAddress & OFFSET_MASK
    PhysAddr = (TlbEntry.PFN << SHIFT) | Offset
    Register = AccessMemory(PhysAddr)
  else
    RaiseException(PROTECTION_FAULT)
else                     // TLB Miss
  // first, get page directory entry
  PDIndex = (VPN & PD_MASK) >> PD_SHIFT
  PDEAddr = PDBR + (PDIndex * sizeof(PDE))
  PDE     = AccessMemory(PDEAddr)
  if (PDE.Valid == False)
    RaiseException(SEGMENTATION_FAULT)
  else
    // PDE is valid: now fetch PTE from page table
    PTIndex = (VPN & PT_MASK) >> PT_SHIFT
    PTEAddr = (PDE.PFN << SHIFT) + (PTIndex * sizeof(PTE))
    PTE     = AccessMemory(PTEAddr)
    if (PTE.Valid == False)
      RaiseException(SEGMENTATION_FAULT)
    else if (CanAccess(PTE.ProtectBits) == False)
      RaiseException(PROTECTION_FAULT)
    else
      TLB_Insert(VPN, PTE.PFN, PTE.ProtectBits)
      RetryInstruction()
```

Figure 206: **Multi-level Page Table Control Flow**

next part of the VPN (`PD Index 1`). Finally, if valid, the PTE address can be formed by using the page-table index combined with the address from the second-level PDE. Whew! That's a lot of work. And all just to look something up in a multi-level table.

The Translation Process: Remember the TLB

To summarize the entire process of address translation using a two-level page table, we once again present the control flow in algorithmic form (Figure 206). The figure shows what happens in hardware (assuming a hardware-managed TLB) upon *every* memory reference.

As you can see from the figure, before any of the complicated multi-level page table access occurs, the hardware first checks the TLB; upon a hit, the physical address is formed directly *without* accessing the page table at all, as before. Only upon a TLB miss does the hardware need to perform the full multi-level lookup. On this path, you can see the cost of our traditional two-level page table: two additional memory accesses to look up a valid translation.

20.4 Inverted Page Tables

An even more extreme space savings in the world of page tables is found with **inverted page tables**. Here, instead of having many page tables (one per process of the system), we keep a single page table that has an entry for each *physical page* of the system. The entry tells us which process is using this page, and which virtual page of that process maps to this physical page.

Finding the correct entry is now a matter of searching through this data structure. A linear scan would be expensive, and thus a hash table is often built over the base structure to speed up lookups. The PowerPC is one example of such an architecture [JM98].

More generally, inverted page tables illustrate what we've said from the beginning: page tables are just data structures. You can do lots of crazy things with data structures, making them smaller or bigger, making them slower or faster. Multi-level and inverted page tables are just two examples of the many things one could do.

20.5 Swapping the Page Tables to Disk

Finally, we discuss the relaxation of one final assumption. Thus far, we have assumed that page tables reside in kernel-owned physical memory. Even with our many tricks to reduce the size of page tables, it is still possible, however, that they may be too big to fit into memory all at once. Thus, some systems place such page tables in **kernel virtual memory**, thereby allowing the system to **swap** some of these page tables to disk when memory pressure gets a little tight. We'll talk more about this in a future chapter (namely, the case study on VAX/VMS), once we understand how to move pages in and out of memory in more detail.

20.6 Summary

We have now seen how real page tables are built; not necessarily just as linear arrays but as more complex data structures. The trade-offs such tables present are in time and space — the bigger the table, the faster a TLB miss can be serviced, as well as the converse — and thus the right choice of structure depends strongly on the constraints of the given environment.

In a memory-constrained system (like many older systems), small structures make sense; in a system with a reasonable amount of memory and with workloads that actively use a large number of pages, a bigger table that speeds up TLB misses might be the right choice. With software-managed TLBs, the entire space of data structures opens up to the delight of the operating system innovator (hint: that's you). What new structures can you come up with? What problems do they solve? Think of these questions as you fall asleep, and dream the big dreams that only operating-system developers can dream.

References

[BOH10] "Computer Systems: A Programmer's Perspective" by Randal E. Bryant and David R. O'Hallaron. Addison-Wesley, 2010. *We have yet to find a good first reference to the multi-level page table. However, this great textbook by Bryant and O'Hallaron dives into the details of x86, which at least is an early system that used such structures. It's also just a great book to have.*

[JM98] "Virtual Memory: Issues of Implementation" by Bruce Jacob, Trevor Mudge. IEEE Computer, June 1998. *An excellent survey of a number of different systems and their approach to virtualizing memory. Plenty of details on x86, PowerPC, MIPS, and other architectures.*

[LL82] "Virtual Memory Management in the VAX/VMS Operating System" by Hank Levy, P. Lipman. IEEE Computer, Vol. 15, No. 3, March 1982. *A terrific paper about a real virtual memory manager in a classic operating system, VMS. So terrific, in fact, that we'll use it to review everything we've learned about virtual memory thus far a few chapters from now.*

[M28] "Reese's Peanut Butter Cups" by Mars Candy Corporation. Published at stores near you. *Apparently these fine confections were invented in 1928 by Harry Burnett Reese, a former dairy farmer and shipping foreman for one Milton S. Hershey. At least, that is what it says on Wikipedia. If true, Hershey and Reese probably hate each other's guts, as any two chocolate barons should.*

[N+02] "Practical, Transparent Operating System Support for Superpages" by Juan Navarro, Sitaram Iyer, Peter Druschel, Alan Cox. OSDI '02, Boston, Massachusetts, October 2002. *A nice paper showing all the details you have to get right to incorporate large pages, or **superpages**, into a modern OS. Not as easy as you might think, alas.*

[M07] "Multics: History" Available: `http://www.multicians.org/history.html`. *This amazing web site provides a huge amount of history on the Multics system, certainly one of the most influential systems in OS history. The quote from therein: "Jack Dennis of MIT contributed influential architectural ideas to the beginning of Multics, especially the idea of combining paging and segmentation." (from Section 1.2.1)*

Homework (Simulation)

This fun little homework tests if you understand how a multi-level page table works. And yes, there is some debate over the use of the term "fun" in the previous sentence. The program is called, perhaps unsurprisingly: `paging-multilevel-translate.py`; see the README for details.

Questions

1. With a linear page table, you need a single register to locate the page table, assuming that hardware does the lookup upon a TLB miss. How many registers do you need to locate a two-level page table? A three-level table?

2. Use the simulator to perform translations given random seeds 0, 1, and 2, and check your answers using the `-c` flag. How many memory references are needed to perform each lookup?

3. Given your understanding of how cache memory works, how do you think memory references to the page table will behave in the cache? Will they lead to lots of cache hits (and thus fast accesses?) Or lots of misses (and thus slow accesses)?

21

Beyond Physical Memory: Mechanisms

Thus far, we've assumed that an address space is unrealistically small and fits into physical memory. In fact, we've been assuming that *every* address space of every running process fits into memory. We will now relax these big assumptions, and assume that we wish to support many concurrently-running large address spaces.

To do so, we require an additional level in the **memory hierarchy**. Thus far, we have assumed that all pages reside in physical memory. However, to support large address spaces, the OS will need a place to stash away portions of address spaces that currently aren't in great demand. In general, the characteristics of such a location are that it should have more capacity than memory; as a result, it is generally slower (if it were faster, we would just use it as memory, no?). In modern systems, this role is usually served by a **hard disk drive**. Thus, in our memory hierarchy, big and slow hard drives sit at the bottom, with memory just above. And thus we arrive at the crux of the problem:

> THE CRUX: HOW TO GO BEYOND PHYSICAL MEMORY
> How can the OS make use of a larger, slower device to transparently provide the illusion of a large virtual address space?

One question you might have: why do we want to support a single large address space for a process? Once again, the answer is convenience and ease of use. With a large address space, you don't have to worry about if there is room enough in memory for your program's data structures; rather, you just write the program naturally, allocating memory as needed. It is a powerful illusion that the OS provides, and makes your life vastly simpler. You're welcome! A contrast is found in older systems that used **memory overlays**, which required programmers to manually move pieces of code or data in and out of memory as they were needed [D97]. Try imagining what this would be like: before calling a function or accessing some data, you need to first arrange for the code or data to be in memory; yuck!

ASIDE: STORAGE TECHNOLOGIES

We'll delve much more deeply into how I/O devices actually work later (see the chapter on I/O devices). So be patient! And of course the slower device need not be a hard disk, but could be something more modern such as a Flash-based SSD. We'll talk about those things too. For now, just assume we have a big and relatively-slow device which we can use to help us build the illusion of a very large virtual memory, even bigger than physical memory itself.

Beyond just a single process, the addition of swap space allows the OS to support the illusion of a large virtual memory for multiple concurrently-running processes. The invention of multiprogramming (running multiple programs "at once", to better utilize the machine) almost demanded the ability to swap out some pages, as early machines clearly could not hold all the pages needed by all processes at once. Thus, the combination of multiprogramming and ease-of-use leads us to want to support using more memory than is physically available. It is something that all modern VM systems do; it is now something we will learn more about.

21.1 Swap Space

The first thing we will need to do is to reserve some space on the disk for moving pages back and forth. In operating systems, we generally refer to such space as **swap space**, because we *swap* pages out of memory to it and *swap* pages into memory from it. Thus, we will simply assume that the OS can read from and write to the swap space, in page-sized units. To do so, the OS will need to remember the **disk address** of a given page.

The size of the swap space is important, as ultimately it determines the maximum number of memory pages that can be in use by a system at a given time. Let us assume for simplicity that it is *very* large for now.

In the tiny example (Figure 211), you can see a little example of a 4-page physical memory and an 8-page swap space. In the example, three processes (Proc 0, Proc 1, and Proc 2) are actively sharing physical memory; each of the three, however, only have some of their valid pages in memory, with the rest located in swap space on disk. A fourth process (Proc 3) has all of its pages swapped out to disk, and thus clearly isn't currently running. One block of swap remains free. Even from this tiny example, hopefully you can see how using swap space allows the system to pretend that memory is larger than it actually is.

We should note that swap space is not the only on-disk location for swapping traffic. For example, assume you are running a program binary (e.g., `ls`, or your own compiled `main` program). The code pages from this binary are initially found on disk, and when the program runs, they are loaded into memory (either all at once when the program starts execution,

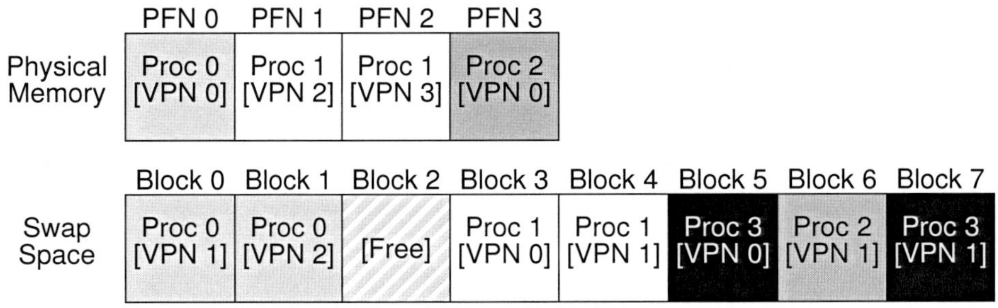

Figure 211: **Physical Memory and Swap Space**

or, as in modern systems, one page at a time when needed). However, if the system needs to make room in physical memory for other needs, it can safely re-use the memory space for these code pages, knowing that it can later swap them in again from the on-disk binary in the file system.

21.2 The Present Bit

Now that we have some space on the disk, we need to add some machinery higher up in the system in order to support swapping pages to and from the disk. Let us assume, for simplicity, that we have a system with a hardware-managed TLB.

Recall first what happens on a memory reference. The running process generates virtual memory references (for instruction fetches, or data accesses), and, in this case, the hardware translates them into physical addresses before fetching the desired data from memory.

Remember that the hardware first extracts the VPN from the virtual address, checks the TLB for a match (a **TLB hit**), and if a hit, produces the resulting physical address and fetches it from memory. This is hopefully the common case, as it is fast (requiring no additional memory accesses).

If the VPN is not found in the TLB (i.e., a **TLB miss**), the hardware locates the page table in memory (using the **page table base register**) and looks up the **page table entry (PTE)** for this page using the VPN as an index. If the page is valid and present in physical memory, the hardware extracts the PFN from the PTE, installs it in the TLB, and retries the instruction, this time generating a TLB hit; so far, so good.

If we wish to allow pages to be swapped to disk, however, we must add even more machinery. Specifically, when the hardware looks in the PTE, it may find that the page is *not present* in physical memory. The way the hardware (or the OS, in a software-managed TLB approach) determines this is through a new piece of information in each page-table entry, known as the **present bit**. If the present bit is set to one, it means the page is present in physical memory and everything proceeds as above; if it is set to zero, the page is *not* in memory but rather on disk somewhere.

ASIDE: SWAPPING TERMINOLOGY AND OTHER THINGS

Terminology in virtual memory systems can be a little confusing and variable across machines and operating systems. For example, a **page fault** more generally could refer to any reference to a page table that generates a fault of some kind: this could include the type of fault we are discussing here, i.e., a page-not-present fault, but sometimes can refer to illegal memory accesses. Indeed, it is odd that we call what is definitely a legal access (to a page mapped into the virtual address space of a process, but simply not in physical memory at the time) a "fault" at all; really, it should be called a **page miss**. But often, when people say a program is "page faulting", they mean that it is accessing parts of its virtual address space that the OS has swapped out to disk.

We suspect the reason that this behavior became known as a "fault" relates to the machinery in the operating system to handle it. When something unusual happens, i.e., when something the hardware doesn't know how to handle occurs, the hardware simply transfers control to the OS, hoping it can make things better. In this case, a page that a process wants to access is missing from memory; the hardware does the only thing it can, which is raise an exception, and the OS takes over from there. As this is identical to what happens when a process does something illegal, it is perhaps not surprising that we term the activity a "fault."

The act of accessing a page that is not in physical memory is commonly referred to as a **page fault**.

Upon a page fault, the OS is invoked to service the page fault. A particular piece of code, known as a **page-fault handler**, runs, and must service the page fault, as we now describe.

21.3 The Page Fault

Recall that with TLB misses, we have two types of systems: hardware-managed TLBs (where the hardware looks in the page table to find the desired translation) and software-managed TLBs (where the OS does). In either type of system, if a page is not present, the OS is put in charge to handle the page fault. The appropriately-named OS **page-fault handler** runs to determine what to do. Virtually all systems handle page faults in software; even with a hardware-managed TLB, the hardware trusts the OS to manage this important duty.

If a page is not present and has been swapped to disk, the OS will need to swap the page into memory in order to service the page fault. Thus, a question arises: how will the OS know where to find the desired page? In many systems, the page table is a natural place to store such information. Thus, the OS could use the bits in the PTE normally used for data such as the PFN of the page for a disk address. When the OS receives a page fault

ASIDE: WHY HARDWARE DOESN'T HANDLE PAGE FAULTS

We know from our experience with the TLB that hardware designers are loathe to trust the OS to do much of anything. So why do they trust the OS to handle a page fault? There are a few main reasons. First, page faults to disk are *slow*; even if the OS takes a long time to handle a fault, executing tons of instructions, the disk operation itself is traditionally so slow that the extra overheads of running software are minimal. Second, to be able to handle a page fault, the hardware would have to understand swap space, how to issue I/Os to the disk, and a lot of other details which it currently doesn't know much about. Thus, for both reasons of performance and simplicity, the OS handles page faults, and even hardware types can be happy.

for a page, it looks in the PTE to find the address, and issues the request to disk to fetch the page into memory.

When the disk I/O completes, the OS will then update the page table to mark the page as present, update the PFN field of the page-table entry (PTE) to record the in-memory location of the newly-fetched page, and retry the instruction. This next attempt may generate a TLB miss, which would then be serviced and update the TLB with the translation (one could alternately update the TLB when servicing the page fault to avoid this step). Finally, a last restart would find the translation in the TLB and thus proceed to fetch the desired data or instruction from memory at the translated physical address.

Note that while the I/O is in flight, the process will be in the **blocked** state. Thus, the OS will be free to run other ready processes while the page fault is being serviced. Because I/O is expensive, this **overlap** of the I/O (page fault) of one process and the execution of another is yet another way a multiprogrammed system can make the most effective use of its hardware.

21.4 What If Memory Is Full?

In the process described above, you may notice that we assumed there is plenty of free memory in which to **page in** a page from swap space. Of course, this may not be the case; memory may be full (or close to it). Thus, the OS might like to first **page out** one or more pages to make room for the new page(s) the OS is about to bring in. The process of picking a page to kick out, or **replace** is known as the **page-replacement policy**.

As it turns out, a lot of thought has been put into creating a good page-replacement policy, as kicking out the wrong page can exact a great cost on program performance. Making the wrong decision can cause a program to run at disk-like speeds instead of memory-like speeds; in current technology that means a program could run 10,000 or 100,000 times

```
1  VPN = (VirtualAddress & VPN_MASK) >> SHIFT
2  (Success, TlbEntry) = TLB_Lookup(VPN)
3  if (Success == True)   // TLB Hit
4      if (CanAccess(TlbEntry.ProtectBits) == True)
5          Offset   = VirtualAddress & OFFSET_MASK
6          PhysAddr = (TlbEntry.PFN << SHIFT) | Offset
7          Register = AccessMemory(PhysAddr)
8      else
9          RaiseException(PROTECTION_FAULT)
10 else                   // TLB Miss
11     PTEAddr = PTBR + (VPN * sizeof(PTE))
12     PTE = AccessMemory(PTEAddr)
13     if (PTE.Valid == False)
14         RaiseException(SEGMENTATION_FAULT)
15     else
16         if (CanAccess(PTE.ProtectBits) == False)
17             RaiseException(PROTECTION_FAULT)
18         else if (PTE.Present == True)
19             // assuming hardware-managed TLB
20             TLB_Insert(VPN, PTE.PFN, PTE.ProtectBits)
21             RetryInstruction()
22         else if (PTE.Present == False)
23             RaiseException(PAGE_FAULT)
```

Figure 212: **Page-Fault Control Flow Algorithm (Hardware)**

slower. Thus, such a policy is something we should study in some detail; indeed, that is exactly what we will do in the next chapter. For now, it is good enough to understand that such a policy exists, built on top of the mechanisms described here.

21.5 Page Fault Control Flow

With all of this knowledge in place, we can now roughly sketch the complete control flow of memory access. In other words, when somebody asks you "what happens when a program fetches some data from memory?", you should have a pretty good idea of all the different possibilities. See the control flow in Figures 212 and 213 for more details; the first figure shows what the hardware does during translation, and the second what the OS does upon a page fault.

From the hardware control flow diagram in Figure 212, notice that there are now three important cases to understand when a TLB miss occurs. First, that the page was both **present** and **valid** (Lines 18–21); in this case, the TLB miss handler can simply grab the PFN from the PTE, retry the instruction (this time resulting in a TLB hit), and thus continue as described (many times) before. In the second case (Lines 22–23), the page fault handler must be run; although this was a legitimate page for

```
PFN = FindFreePhysicalPage()
if (PFN == -1)                 // no free page found
    PFN = EvictPage()          // run replacement algorithm
DiskRead(PTE.DiskAddr, PFN) // sleep (waiting for I/O)
PTE.present = True             // update page table with present
PTE.PFN     = PFN              // bit and translation (PFN)
RetryInstruction()             // retry instruction
```

Figure 213: **Page-Fault Control Flow Algorithm (Software)**

the process to access (it is valid, after all), it is not present in physical memory. Third (and finally), the access could be to an invalid page, due for example to a bug in the program (Lines 13–14). In this case, no other bits in the PTE really matter; the hardware traps this invalid access, and the OS trap handler runs, likely terminating the offending process.

From the software control flow in Figure 213, we can see what the OS roughly must do in order to service the page fault. First, the OS must find a physical frame for the soon-to-be-faulted-in page to reside within; if there is no such page, we'll have to wait for the replacement algorithm to run and kick some pages out of memory, thus freeing them for use here. With a physical frame in hand, the handler then issues the I/O request to read in the page from swap space. Finally, when that slow operation completes, the OS updates the page table and retries the instruction. The retry will result in a TLB miss, and then, upon another retry, a TLB hit, at which point the hardware will be able to access the desired item.

21.6 When Replacements Really Occur

Thus far, the way we've described how replacements occur assumes that the OS waits until memory is entirely full, and only then replaces (evicts) a page to make room for some other page. As you can imagine, this is a little bit unrealistic, and there are many reasons for the OS to keep a small portion of memory free more proactively.

To keep a small amount of memory free, most operating systems thus have some kind of **high watermark** (HW) and **low watermark** (LW) to help decide when to start evicting pages from memory. How this works is as follows: when the OS notices that there are fewer than LW pages available, a background thread that is responsible for freeing memory runs. The thread evicts pages until there are HW pages available. The background thread, sometimes called the **swap daemon** or **page daemon**[1], then goes to sleep, happy that it has freed some memory for running processes and the OS to use.

By performing a number of replacements at once, new performance optimizations become possible. For example, many systems will **cluster**

[1]The word "daemon", usually pronounced "demon", is an old term for a background thread or process that does something useful. Turns out (once again!) that the source of the term is Multics [CS94].

TIP: DO WORK IN THE BACKGROUND

When you have some work to do, it is often a good idea to do it in the **background** to increase efficiency and to allow for grouping of operations. Operating systems often do work in the background; for example, many systems buffer file writes in memory before actually writing the data to disk. Doing so has many possible benefits: increased disk efficiency, as the disk may now receive many writes at once and thus better be able to schedule them; improved latency of writes, as the application thinks the writes completed quite quickly; the possibility of work reduction, as the writes may need never to go to disk (i.e., if the file is deleted); and better use of **idle time**, as the background work may possibly be done when the system is otherwise idle, thus better utilizing the hardware [G+95].

or **group** a number of pages and write them out at once to the swap partition, thus increasing the efficiency of the disk [LL82]; as we will see later when we discuss disks in more detail, such clustering reduces seek and rotational overheads of a disk and thus increases performance noticeably.

To work with the background paging thread, the control flow in Figure 213 should be modified slightly; instead of performing a replacement directly, the algorithm would instead simply check if there are any free pages available. If not, it would inform the background paging thread that free pages are needed; when the thread frees up some pages, it would re-awaken the original thread, which could then page in the desired page and go about its work.

21.7 Summary

In this brief chapter, we have introduced the notion of accessing more memory than is physically present within a system. To do so requires more complexity in page-table structures, as a **present bit** (of some kind) must be included to tell us whether the page is present in memory or not. When not, the operating system **page-fault handler** runs to service the **page fault**, and thus arranges for the transfer of the desired page from disk to memory, perhaps first replacing some pages in memory to make room for those soon to be swapped in.

Recall, importantly (and amazingly!), that these actions all take place **transparently** to the process. As far as the process is concerned, it is just accessing its own private, contiguous virtual memory. Behind the scenes, pages are placed in arbitrary (non-contiguous) locations in physical memory, and sometimes they are not even present in memory, requiring a fetch from disk. While we hope that in the common case a memory access is fast, in some cases it will take multiple disk operations to service it; something as simple as performing a single instruction can, in the worst case, take many milliseconds to complete.

References

[CS94] "Take Our Word For It" by F. Corbato, R. Steinberg. `www.takeourword.com/TOW146` (Page 4). *Richard Steinberg writes: "Someone has asked me the origin of the word daemon as it applies to computing. Best I can tell based on my research, the word was first used by people on your team at Project MAC using the IBM 7094 in 1963." Professor Corbato replies: "Our use of the word daemon was inspired by the Maxwell's daemon of physics and thermodynamics (my background is in physics). Maxwell's daemon was an imaginary agent which helped sort molecules of different speeds and worked tirelessly in the background. We fancifully began to use the word daemon to describe background processes which worked tirelessly to perform system chores."*

[D97] "Before Memory Was Virtual" by Peter Denning. In the Beginning: Recollections of Software Pioneers, Wiley, November 1997. *An excellent historical piece by one of the pioneers of virtual memory and working sets.*

[G+95] "Idleness is not sloth" by Richard Golding, Peter Bosch, Carl Staelin, Tim Sullivan, John Wilkes. USENIX ATC '95, New Orleans, Louisiana. *A fun and easy-to-read discussion of how idle time can be better used in systems, with lots of good examples.*

[LL82] "Virtual Memory Management in the VAX/VMS Operating System" by Hank Levy, P. Lipman. IEEE Computer, Vol. 15, No. 3, March 1982. *Not the first place where page clustering was used, but a clear and simple explanation of how such a mechanism works. We sure cite this paper a lot!*

Homework (Measurement)

This homework introduces you to a new tool, **vmstat**, and how it can be used to understand memory, CPU, and I/O usage. Read the associated README and examine the code in `mem.c` before proceeding to the exercises and questions below.

Questions

1. First, open two separate terminal connections to the *same* machine, so that you can easily run something in one window and the other.

   Now, in one window, run `vmstat 1`, which shows statistics about machine usage every second. Read the man page, the associated README, and any other information you need so that you can understand its output. Leave this window running `vmstat` for the rest of the exercises below.

   Now, we will run the program `mem.c` but with very little memory usage. This can be accomplished by typing `./mem 1` (which uses only 1 MB of memory). How do the CPU usage statistics change when running `mem`? Do the numbers in the `user time` column make sense? How does this change when running more than one instance of `mem` at once?

2. Let's now start looking at some of the memory statistics while running `mem`. We'll focus on two columns: `swpd` (the amount of virtual memory used) and `free` (the amount of idle memory). Run `./mem 1024` (which allocates 1024 MB) and watch how these values change. Then kill the running program (by typing control-c) and watch again how the values change. What do you notice about the values? In particular, how does the `free` column change when the program exits? Does the amount of free memory increase by the expected amount when `mem` exits?

3. We'll next look at the `swap` columns (`si` and `so`), which indicate how much swapping is taking place to and from the disk. Of course, to activate these, you'll need to run `mem` with large amounts of memory. First, examine how much free memory is on your Linux system (for example, by typing `cat /proc/meminfo`; type `man proc` for details on the `/proc` file system and the types of information you can find there). One of the first entries in `/proc/meminfo` is the total amount of memory in your system. Let's assume it's something like 8 GB of memory; if so, start by running `mem 4000` (about 4 GB) and watching the swap in/out columns. Do they ever give non-zero values? Then, try with `5000`, `6000`, etc. What happens to these values as the program enters the second loop (and beyond), as compared to the first loop? How much data (total) are swapped in and out during the second, third, and subsequent loops? (do the numbers make sense?)

4. Do the same experiments as above, but now watch the other statistics (such as CPU utilization, and block I/O statistics). How do they change when `mem` is running?

5. Now let's examine performance. Pick an input for `mem` that comfortably fits in memory (say `4000` if the amount of memory on the system is 8 GB). How long does loop 0 take (and subsequent loops 1, 2, etc.)? Now pick a size comfortably beyond the size of memory (say `12000` again assuming 8 GB of memory). How long do the loops take here? How do the bandwidth numbers compare? How different is performance when constantly swapping versus fitting everything comfortably in memory? Can you make a graph, with the size of memory used by `mem` on the x-axis, and the bandwidth of accessing said memory on the y-axis? Finally, how does the performance of the first loop compare to that of subsequent loops, for both the case where everything fits in memory and where it doesn't?

6. Swap space isn't infinite. You can use the tool `swapon` with the `-s` flag to see how much swap space is available. What happens if you try to run `mem` with increasingly large values, beyond what seems to be available in swap? At what point does the memory allocation fail?

7. Finally, if you're advanced, you can configure your system to use different swap devices using `swapon` and `swapoff`. Read the man pages for details. If you have access to different hardware, see how the performance of swapping changes when swapping to a classic hard drive, a flash-based SSD, and even a RAID array. How much can swapping performance be improved via newer devices? How close can you get to in-memory performance?

22

Beyond Physical Memory: Policies

In a virtual memory manager, life is easy when you have a lot of free memory. A page fault occurs, you find a free page on the free-page list, and assign it to the faulting page. Hey, Operating System, congratulations! You did it again.

Unfortunately, things get a little more interesting when little memory is free. In such a case, this **memory pressure** forces the OS to start **paging out** pages to make room for actively-used pages. Deciding which page (or pages) to **evict** is encapsulated within the **replacement policy** of the OS; historically, it was one of the most important decisions the early virtual memory systems made, as older systems had little physical memory. Minimally, it is an interesting set of policies worth knowing a little more about. And thus our problem:

> THE CRUX: HOW TO DECIDE WHICH PAGE TO EVICT
> How can the OS decide which page (or pages) to evict from memory? This decision is made by the replacement policy of the system, which usually follows some general principles (discussed below) but also includes certain tweaks to avoid corner-case behaviors.

22.1 Cache Management

Before diving into policies, we first describe the problem we are trying to solve in more detail. Given that main memory holds some subset of all the pages in the system, it can rightly be viewed as a **cache** for virtual memory pages in the system. Thus, our goal in picking a replacement policy for this cache is to minimize the number of **cache misses**, i.e., to minimize the number of times that we have to fetch a page from disk. Alternately, one can view our goal as maximizing the number of **cache hits**, i.e., the number of times a page that is accessed is found in memory.

Knowing the number of cache hits and misses let us calculate the **average memory access time** (**AMAT**) for a program (a metric computer architects compute for hardware caches [HP06]). Specifically, given these values, we can compute the AMAT of a program as follows:

$$AMAT = T_M + (P_{Miss} \cdot T_D) \tag{22.1}$$

where T_M represents the cost of accessing memory, T_D the cost of accessing disk, and P_{Miss} the probability of not finding the data in the cache (a miss); P_{Miss} varies from 0.0 to 1.0, and sometimes we refer to a percent miss rate instead of a probability (e.g., a 10% miss rate means $P_{Miss} = 0.10$). Note you always pay the cost of accessing the data in memory; when you miss, however, you must additionally pay the cost of fetching the data from disk.

For example, let us imagine a machine with a (tiny) address space: 4KB, with 256-byte pages. Thus, a virtual address has two components: a 4-bit VPN (the most-significant bits) and an 8-bit offset (the least-significant bits). Thus, a process in this example can access 2^4 or 16 total virtual pages. In this example, the process generates the following memory references (i.e., virtual addresses): 0x000, 0x100, 0x200, 0x300, 0x400, 0x500, 0x600, 0x700, 0x800, 0x900. These virtual addresses refer to the first byte of each of the first ten pages of the address space (the page number being the first hex digit of each virtual address).

Let us further assume that every page except virtual page 3 is already in memory. Thus, our sequence of memory references will encounter the following behavior: hit, hit, hit, miss, hit, hit, hit, hit, hit, hit. We can compute the **hit rate** (the percent of references found in memory): 90%, as 9 out of 10 references are in memory. The **miss rate** is thus 10% ($P_{Miss} = 0.1$). In general, $P_{Hit} + P_{Miss} = 1.0$; hit rate plus miss rate sum to 100%.

To calculate AMAT, we need to know the cost of accessing memory and the cost of accessing disk. Assuming the cost of accessing memory (T_M) is around 100 nanoseconds, and the cost of accessing disk (T_D) is about 10 milliseconds, we have the following AMAT: $100ns + 0.1 \cdot 10ms$, which is $100ns + 1ms$, or 1.0001 ms, or about 1 millisecond. If our hit rate had instead been 99.9% ($P_{miss} = 0.001$), the result is quite different: AMAT is 10.1 microseconds, or roughly 100 times faster. As the hit rate approaches 100%, AMAT approaches 100 nanoseconds.

Unfortunately, as you can see in this example, the cost of disk access is so high in modern systems that even a tiny miss rate will quickly dominate the overall AMAT of running programs. Clearly, we need to avoid as many misses as possible or run slowly, at the rate of the disk. One way to help with this is to carefully develop a smart policy, as we now do.

22.2 The Optimal Replacement Policy

To better understand how a particular replacement policy works, it would be nice to compare it to the best possible replacement policy. As it turns out, such an **optimal** policy was developed by Belady many years ago [B66] (he originally called it MIN). The optimal replacement policy leads to the fewest number of misses overall. Belady showed that a simple (but, unfortunately, difficult to implement!) approach that replaces the page that will be accessed *furthest in the future* is the optimal policy, resulting in the fewest-possible cache misses.

TIP: COMPARING AGAINST OPTIMAL IS USEFUL

Although optimal is not very practical as a real policy, it is incredibly useful as a comparison point in simulation or other studies. Saying that your fancy new algorithm has a 80% hit rate isn't meaningful in isolation; saying that optimal achieves an 82% hit rate (and thus your new approach is quite close to optimal) makes the result more meaningful and gives it context. Thus, in any study you perform, knowing what the optimal is lets you perform a better comparison, showing how much improvement is still possible, and also when you can *stop* making your policy better, because it is close enough to the ideal [AD03].

Hopefully, the intuition behind the optimal policy makes sense. Think about it like this: if you have to throw out some page, why not throw out the one that is needed the furthest from now? By doing so, you are essentially saying that all the other pages in the cache are more important than the one furthest out. The reason this is true is simple: you will refer to the other pages before you refer to the one furthest out.

Let's trace through a simple example to understand the decisions the optimal policy makes. Assume a program accesses the following stream of virtual pages: 0, 1, 2, 0, 1, 3, 0, 3, 1, 2, 1. Figure 221 shows the behavior of optimal, assuming a cache that fits three pages.

In the figure, you can see the following actions. Not surprisingly, the first three accesses are misses, as the cache begins in an empty state; such a miss is sometimes referred to as a **cold-start miss** (or **compulsory miss**). Then we refer again to pages 0 and 1, which both hit in the cache. Finally, we reach another miss (to page 3), but this time the cache is full; a replacement must take place! Which begs the question: which page should we replace? With the optimal policy, we examine the future for each page currently in the cache (0, 1, and 2), and see that 0 is accessed almost immediately, 1 is accessed a little later, and 2 is accessed furthest in the future. Thus the optimal policy has an easy choice: evict page 2, resulting in

Access	Hit/Miss?	Evict	Resulting Cache State
0	Miss		0
1	Miss		0, 1
2	Miss		0, 1, 2
0	Hit		0, 1, 2
1	Hit		0, 1, 2
3	Miss	2	0, 1, 3
0	Hit		0, 1, 3
3	Hit		0, 1, 3
1	Hit		0, 1, 3
2	Miss	3	0, 1, 2
1	Hit		0, 1, 2

Figure 221: **Tracing The Optimal Policy**

> ASIDE: TYPES OF CACHE MISSES
>
> In the computer architecture world, architects sometimes find it useful to characterize misses by type, into one of three categories: compulsory, capacity, and conflict misses, sometimes called the **Three C's** [H87]. A **compulsory miss** (or **cold-start miss** [EF78]) occurs because the cache is empty to begin with and this is the first reference to the item; in contrast, a **capacity miss** occurs because the cache ran out of space and had to evict an item to bring a new item into the cache. The third type of miss (a **conflict miss**) arises in hardware because of limits on where an item can be placed in a hardware cache, due to something known as **set-associativity**; it does not arise in the OS page cache because such caches are always **fully-associative**, i.e., there are no restrictions on where in memory a page can be placed. See H&P for details [HP06].

pages 0, 1, and 3 in the cache. The next three references are hits, but then we get to page 2, which we evicted long ago, and suffer another miss. Here the optimal policy again examines the future for each page in the cache (0, 1, and 3), and sees that as long as it doesn't evict page 1 (which is about to be accessed), we'll be OK. The example shows page 3 getting evicted, although 0 would have been a fine choice too. Finally, we hit on page 1 and the trace completes.

We can also calculate the hit rate for the cache: with 6 hits and 5 misses, the hit rate is $\frac{Hits}{Hits+Misses}$ which is $\frac{6}{6+5}$ or 54.5%. You can also compute the hit rate *modulo* compulsory misses (i.e., ignore the *first* miss to a given page), resulting in a 85.7% hit rate.

Unfortunately, as we saw before in the development of scheduling policies, the future is not generally known; you can't build the optimal policy for a general-purpose operating system[1]. Thus, in developing a real, deployable policy, we will focus on approaches that find some other way to decide which page to evict. The optimal policy will thus serve only as a comparison point, to know how close we are to "perfect".

22.3 A Simple Policy: FIFO

Many early systems avoided the complexity of trying to approach optimal and employed very simple replacement policies. For example, some systems used **FIFO** (first-in, first-out) replacement, where pages were simply placed in a queue when they enter the system; when a replacement occurs, the page on the tail of the queue (the "first-in" page) is evicted. FIFO has one great strength: it is quite simple to implement.

Let's examine how FIFO does on our example reference stream (Figure 222, page 261). We again begin our trace with three compulsory misses to

[1] If you can, let us know! We can become rich together. Or, like the scientists who "discovered" cold fusion, widely scorned and mocked [FP89].

Access	Hit/Miss?	Evict	Resulting Cache State
0	Miss		First-in→ 0
1	Miss		First-in→ 0, 1
2	Miss		First-in→ 0, 1, 2
0	Hit		First-in→ 0, 1, 2
1	Hit		First-in→ 0, 1, 2
3	Miss	0	First-in→ 1, 2, 3
0	Miss	1	First-in→ 2, 3, 0
3	Hit		First-in→ 2, 3, 0
1	Miss	2	First-in→ 3, 0, 1
2	Miss	3	First-in→ 0, 1, 2
1	Hit		First-in→ 0, 1, 2

Figure 22.2: **Tracing The FIFO Policy**

pages 0, 1, and 2, and then hit on both 0 and 1. Next, page 3 is referenced, causing a miss; the replacement decision is easy with FIFO: pick the page that was the "first one" in (the cache state in the figure is kept in FIFO order, with the first-in page on the left), which is page 0. Unfortunately, our next access is to page 0, causing another miss and replacement (of page 1). We then hit on page 3, but miss on 1 and 2, and finally hit on 3.

Comparing FIFO to optimal, FIFO does notably worse: a 36.4% hit rate (or 57.1% excluding compulsory misses). FIFO simply can't determine the importance of blocks: even though page 0 had been accessed a number of times, FIFO still kicks it out, simply because it was the first one brought into memory.

ASIDE: BELADY'S ANOMALY

Belady (of the optimal policy) and colleagues found an interesting reference stream that behaved a little unexpectedly [BNS69]. The memory-reference stream: 1, 2, 3, 4, 1, 2, 5, 1, 2, 3, 4, 5. The replacement policy they were studying was FIFO. The interesting part: how the cache hit rate changed when moving from a cache size of 3 to 4 pages.

In general, you would expect the cache hit rate to *increase* (get better) when the cache gets larger. But in this case, with FIFO, it gets worse! Calculate the hits and misses yourself and see. This odd behavior is generally referred to as **Belady's Anomaly** (to the chagrin of his co-authors).

Some other policies, such as LRU, don't suffer from this problem. Can you guess why? As it turns out, LRU has what is known as a **stack property** [M+70]. For algorithms with this property, a cache of size $N + 1$ naturally includes the contents of a cache of size N. Thus, when increasing the cache size, hit rate will either stay the same or improve. FIFO and Random (among others) clearly do not obey the stack property, and thus are susceptible to anomalous behavior.

Access	Hit/Miss?	Evict	Resulting Cache State
0	Miss		0
1	Miss		0, 1
2	Miss		0, 1, 2
0	Hit		0, 1, 2
1	Hit		0, 1, 2
3	Miss	0	1, 2, 3
0	Miss	1	2, 3, 0
3	Hit		2, 3, 0
1	Miss	3	2, 0, 1
2	Hit		2, 0, 1
1	Hit		2, 0, 1

Figure 223: **Tracing The Random Policy**

22.4 Another Simple Policy: Random

Another similar replacement policy is Random, which simply picks a random page to replace under memory pressure. Random has properties similar to FIFO; it is simple to implement, but it doesn't really try to be too intelligent in picking which blocks to evict. Let's look at how Random does on our famous example reference stream (see Figure 223).

Of course, how Random does depends entirely upon how lucky (or unlucky) Random gets in its choices. In the example above, Random does a little better than FIFO, and a little worse than optimal. In fact, we can run the Random experiment thousands of times and determine how it does in general. Figure 224 shows how many hits Random achieves over 10,000 trials, each with a different random seed. As you can see, sometimes (just over 40% of the time), Random is as good as optimal, achieving 6 hits on the example trace; sometimes it does much worse, achieving 2 hits or fewer. How Random does depends on the luck of the draw.

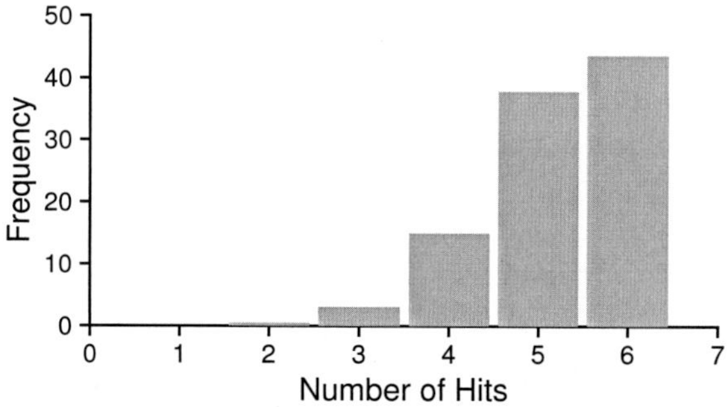

Figure 224: **Random Performance Over 10,000 Trials**

Access	Hit/Miss?	Evict	Resulting Cache State	
0	Miss		LRU→	0
1	Miss		LRU→	0, 1
2	Miss		LRU→	0, 1, 2
0	Hit		LRU→	1, 2, 0
1	Hit		LRU→	2, 0, 1
3	Miss	2	LRU→	0, 1, 3
0	Hit		LRU→	1, 3, 0
3	Hit		LRU→	1, 0, 3
1	Hit		LRU→	0, 3, 1
2	Miss	0	LRU→	3, 1, 2
1	Hit		LRU→	3, 2, 1

Figure 225: **Tracing The LRU Policy**

22.5 Using History: LRU

Unfortunately, any policy as simple as FIFO or Random is likely to have a common problem: it might kick out an important page, one that is about to be referenced again. FIFO kicks out the page that was first brought in; if this happens to be a page with important code or data structures upon it, it gets thrown out anyhow, even though it will soon be paged back in. Thus, FIFO, Random, and similar policies are not likely to approach optimal; something smarter is needed.

As we did with scheduling policy, to improve our guess at the future, we once again lean on the past and use *history* as our guide. For example, if a program has accessed a page in the near past, it is likely to access it again in the near future.

One type of historical information a page-replacement policy could use is **frequency**; if a page has been accessed many times, perhaps it should not be replaced as it clearly has some value. A more commonly-used property of a page is its **recency** of access; the more recently a page has been accessed, perhaps the more likely it will be accessed again.

This family of policies is based on what people refer to as the **principle of locality** [D70], which basically is just an observation about programs and their behavior. What this principle says, quite simply, is that programs tend to access certain code sequences (e.g., in a loop) and data structures (e.g., an array accessed by the loop) quite frequently; we should thus try to use history to figure out which pages are important, and keep those pages in memory when it comes to eviction time.

And thus, a family of simple historically-based algorithms are born. The **Least-Frequently-Used** (**LFU**) policy replaces the least-frequently-used page when an eviction must take place. Similarly, the **Least-Recently-Used** (**LRU**) policy replaces the least-recently-used page. These algorithms are easy to remember: once you know the name, you know exactly what it does, which is an excellent property for a name.

To better understand LRU, let's examine how LRU does on our ex-

> **ASIDE: TYPES OF LOCALITY**
>
> There are two types of locality that programs tend to exhibit. The first is known as **spatial locality**, which states that if a page P is accessed, it is likely the pages around it (say $P - 1$ or $P + 1$) will also likely be accessed. The second is **temporal locality**, which states that pages that have been accessed in the near past are likely to be accessed again in the near future. The assumption of the presence of these types of locality plays a large role in the caching hierarchies of hardware systems, which deploy many levels of instruction, data, and address-translation caching to help programs run fast when such locality exists.
>
> Of course, the **principle of locality**, as it is often called, is no hard-and-fast rule that all programs must obey. Indeed, some programs access memory (or disk) in rather random fashion and don't exhibit much or any locality in their access streams. Thus, while locality is a good thing to keep in mind while designing caches of any kind (hardware or software), it does not *guarantee* success. Rather, it is a heuristic that often proves useful in the design of computer systems.

ample reference stream. Figure 225 (page 263) shows the results. From the figure, you can see how LRU can use history to do better than stateless policies such as Random or FIFO. In the example, LRU evicts page 2 when it first has to replace a page, because 0 and 1 have been accessed more recently. It then replaces page 0 because 1 and 3 have been accessed more recently. In both cases, LRU's decision, based on history, turns out to be correct, and the next references are thus hits. Thus, in our example, LRU does as well as possible, matching optimal in its performance[2].

We should also note that the opposites of these algorithms exist: **Most-Frequently-Used** (**MFU**) and **Most-Recently-Used** (**MRU**). In most cases (not all!), these policies do not work well, as they ignore the locality most programs exhibit instead of embracing it.

22.6 Workload Examples

Let's look at a few more examples in order to better understand how some of these policies behave. Here, we'll examine more complex **workloads** instead of small traces. However, even these workloads are greatly simplified; a better study would include application traces.

Our first workload has no locality, which means that each reference is to a random page within the set of accessed pages. In this simple example, the workload accesses 100 unique pages over time, choosing the next page to refer to at random; overall, 10,000 pages are accessed. In the experiment, we vary the cache size from very small (1 page) to enough to hold all the unique pages (100 page), in order to see how each policy behaves over the range of cache sizes.

[2]OK, we cooked the results. But sometimes cooking is necessary to prove a point.

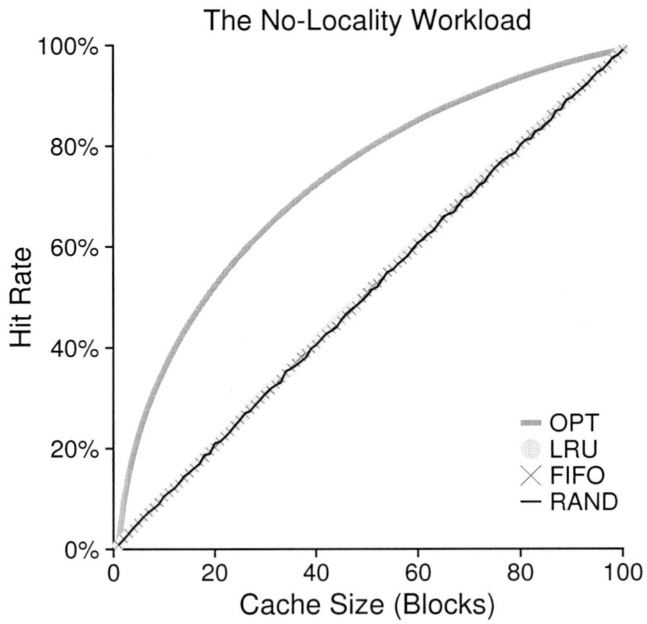

Figure 226: **The No-Locality Workload**

Figure 226 plots the results of the experiment for optimal, LRU, Random, and FIFO. The y-axis of the figure shows the hit rate that each policy achieves; the x-axis varies the cache size as described above.

We can draw a number of conclusions from the graph. First, when there is no locality in the workload, it doesn't matter much which realistic policy you are using; LRU, FIFO, and Random all perform the same, with the hit rate exactly determined by the size of the cache. Second, when the cache is large enough to fit the entire workload, it also doesn't matter which policy you use; all policies (even Random) converge to a 100% hit rate when all the referenced blocks fit in cache. Finally, you can see that optimal performs noticeably better than the realistic policies; peeking into the future, if it were possible, does a much better job of replacement.

The next workload we examine is called the "80-20" workload, which exhibits locality: 80% of the references are made to 20% of the pages (the "hot" pages); the remaining 20% of the references are made to the remaining 80% of the pages (the "cold" pages). In our workload, there are a total 100 unique pages again; thus, "hot" pages are referred to most of the time, and "cold" pages the remainder. Figure 227 (page 266) shows how the policies perform with this workload.

As you can see from the figure, while both random and FIFO do reasonably well, LRU does better, as it is more likely to hold onto the hot pages; as those pages have been referred to frequently in the past, they are likely to be referred to again in the near future. Optimal once again does better, showing that LRU's historical information is not perfect.

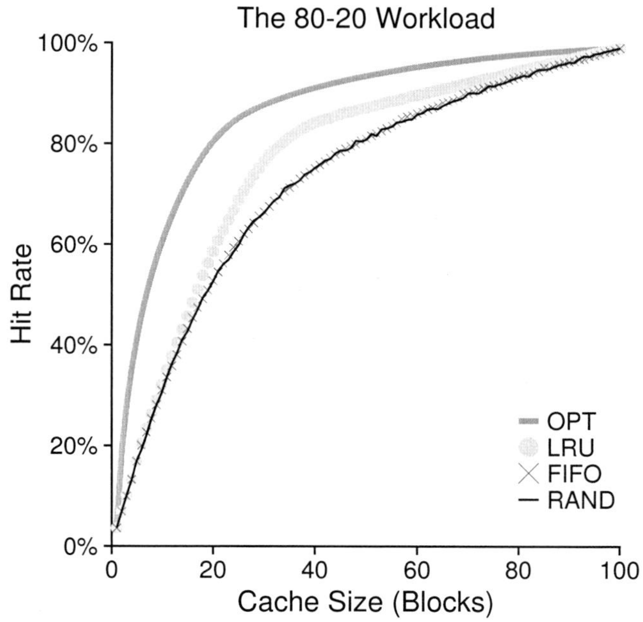

Figure 227: **The 80-20 Workload**

You might now be wondering: is LRU's improvement over Random and FIFO really that big of a deal? The answer, as usual, is "it depends." If each miss is very costly (not uncommon), then even a small increase in hit rate (reduction in miss rate) can make a huge difference on performance. If misses are not so costly, then of course the benefits possible with LRU are not nearly as important.

Let's look at one final workload. We call this one the "looping sequential" workload, as in it, we refer to 50 pages in sequence, starting at 0, then 1, ..., up to page 49, and then we loop, repeating those accesses, for a total of 10,000 accesses to 50 unique pages. The last graph in Figure 228 shows the behavior of the policies under this workload.

This workload, common in many applications (including important commercial applications such as databases [CD85]), represents a worst-case for both LRU and FIFO. These algorithms, under a looping-sequential workload, kick out older pages; unfortunately, due to the looping nature of the workload, these older pages are going to be accessed sooner than the pages that the policies prefer to keep in cache. Indeed, even with a cache of size 49, a looping-sequential workload of 50 pages results in a 0% hit rate. Interestingly, Random fares notably better, not quite approaching optimal, but at least achieving a non-zero hit rate. Turns out that random has some nice properties; one such property is not having weird corner-case behaviors.

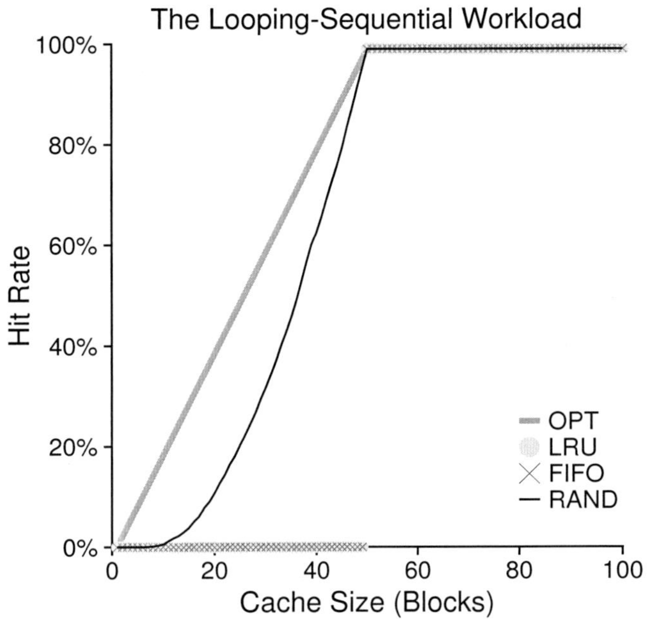

Figure 228: **The Looping Workload**

22.7 Implementing Historical Algorithms

As you can see, an algorithm such as LRU can generally do a better job than simpler policies like FIFO or Random, which may throw out important pages. Unfortunately, historical policies present us with a new challenge: how do we implement them?

Let's take, for example, LRU. To implement it perfectly, we need to do a lot of work. Specifically, upon each *page access* (i.e., each memory access, whether an instruction fetch or a load or store), we must update some data structure to move this page to the front of the list (i.e., the MRU side). Contrast this to FIFO, where the FIFO list of pages is only accessed when a page is *evicted* (by removing the first-in page) or when a new page is added to the list (to the last-in side). To keep track of which pages have been least- and most-recently used, the system has to do some accounting work *on every memory reference.* Clearly, without great care, such accounting could greatly reduce performance.

One method that could help speed this up is to add a little bit of hardware support. For example, a machine could update, on each page access, a time field in memory (for example, this could be in the per-process page table, or just in some separate array in memory, with one entry per physical page of the system). Thus, when a page is accessed, the time field would be set, by hardware, to the current time. Then, when replacing a page, the OS could simply scan all the time fields in the system to find the least-recently-used page.

Unfortunately, as the number of pages in a system grows, scanning a huge array of times just to find the absolute least-recently-used page is prohibitively expensive. Imagine a modern machine with 4GB of memory, chopped into 4KB pages. This machine has 1 million pages, and thus finding the LRU page will take a long time, even at modern CPU speeds. Which begs the question: do we really need to find the absolute oldest page to replace? Can we instead survive with an approximation?

> CRUX: HOW TO IMPLEMENT AN LRU REPLACEMENT POLICY
> Given that it will be expensive to implement perfect LRU, can we approximate it in some way, and still obtain the desired behavior?

22.8 Approximating LRU

As it turns out, the answer is yes: approximating LRU is more feasible from a computational-overhead standpoint, and indeed it is what many modern systems do. The idea requires some hardware support, in the form of a **use bit** (sometimes called the **reference bit**), the first of which was implemented in the first system with paging, the Atlas one-level store [KE+62]. There is one use bit per page of the system, and the use bits live in memory somewhere (they could be in the per-process page tables, for example, or just in an array somewhere). Whenever a page is referenced (i.e., read or written), the use bit is set by hardware to 1. The hardware never clears the bit, though (i.e., sets it to 0); that is the responsibility of the OS.

How does the OS employ the use bit to approximate LRU? Well, there could be a lot of ways, but with the **clock algorithm** [C69], one simple approach was suggested. Imagine all the pages of the system arranged in a circular list. A **clock hand** points to some particular page to begin with (it doesn't really matter which). When a replacement must occur, the OS checks if the currently-pointed to page P has a use bit of 1 or 0. If 1, this implies that page P was recently used and thus is *not* a good candidate for replacement. Thus, the use bit for P set to 0 (cleared), and the clock hand is incremented to the next page ($P + 1$). The algorithm continues until it finds a use bit that is set to 0, implying this page has not been recently used (or, in the worst case, that all pages have been and that we have now searched through the entire set of pages, clearing all the bits).

Note that this approach is not the only way to employ a use bit to approximate LRU. Indeed, any approach which periodically clears the use bits and then differentiates between which pages have use bits of 1 versus 0 to decide which to replace would be fine. The clock algorithm of Corbato's was just one early approach which met with some success, and had the nice property of not repeatedly scanning through all of memory looking for an unused page.

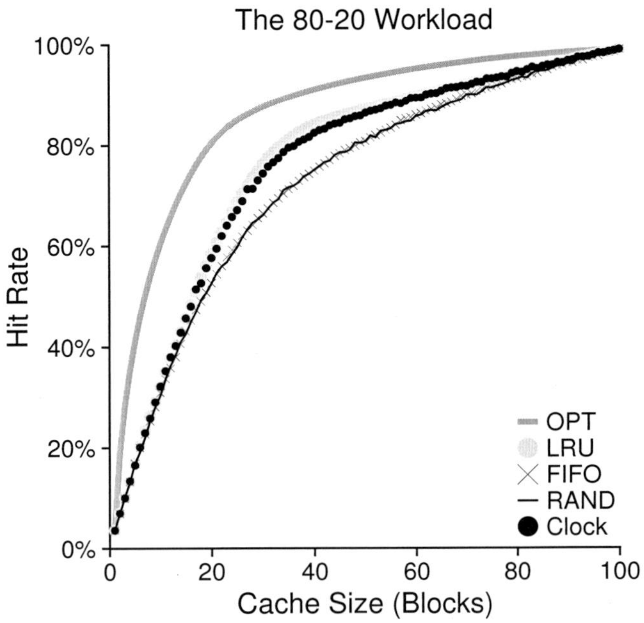

Figure 229: **The 80-20 Workload With Clock**

The behavior of a clock algorithm variant is shown in Figure 229. This variant randomly scans pages when doing a replacement; when it encounters a page with a reference bit set to 1, it clears the bit (i.e., sets it to 0); when it finds a page with the reference bit set to 0, it chooses it as its victim. As you can see, although it doesn't do quite as well as perfect LRU, it does better than approaches that don't consider history at all.

22.9 Considering Dirty Pages

One small modification to the clock algorithm (also originally suggested by Corbato [C69]) that is commonly made is the additional consideration of whether a page has been modified or not while in memory. The reason for this: if a page has been **modified** and is thus **dirty**, it must be written back to disk to evict it, which is expensive. If it has not been modified (and is thus **clean**), the eviction is free; the physical frame can simply be reused for other purposes without additional I/O. Thus, some VM systems prefer to evict clean pages over dirty pages.

To support this behavior, the hardware should include a **modified bit** (a.k.a. **dirty bit**). This bit is set any time a page is written, and thus can be incorporated into the page-replacement algorithm. The clock algorithm, for example, could be changed to scan for pages that are both unused and clean to evict first; failing to find those, then for unused pages that are dirty, and so forth.

22.10 Other VM Policies

Page replacement is not the only policy the VM subsystem employs (though it may be the most important). For example, the OS also has to decide *when* to bring a page into memory. This policy, sometimes called the **page selection** policy (as it was called by Denning [D70]), presents the OS with some different options.

For most pages, the OS simply uses **demand paging**, which means the OS brings the page into memory when it is accessed, "on demand" as it were. Of course, the OS could guess that a page is about to be used, and thus bring it in ahead of time; this behavior is known as **prefetching** and should only be done when there is reasonable chance of success. For example, some systems will assume that if a code page P is brought into memory, that code page $P+1$ will likely soon be accessed and thus should be brought into memory too.

Another policy determines how the OS writes pages out to disk. Of course, they could simply be written out one at a time; however, many systems instead collect a number of pending writes together in memory and write them to disk in one (more efficient) write. This behavior is usually called **clustering** or simply **grouping** of writes, and is effective because of the nature of disk drives, which perform a single large write more efficiently than many small ones.

22.11 Thrashing

Before closing, we address one final question: what should the OS do when memory is simply oversubscribed, and the memory demands of the set of running processes simply exceeds the available physical memory? In this case, the system will constantly be paging, a condition sometimes referred to as **thrashing** [D70].

Some earlier operating systems had a fairly sophisticated set of mechanisms to both detect and cope with thrashing when it took place. For example, given a set of processes, a system could decide not to run a subset of processes, with the hope that the reduced set of processes' **working sets** (the pages that they are using actively) fit in memory and thus can make progress. This approach, generally known as **admission control**, states that it is sometimes better to do less work well than to try to do everything at once poorly, a situation we often encounter in real life as well as in modern computer systems (sadly).

Some current systems take more a draconian approach to memory overload. For example, some versions of Linux run an **out-of-memory killer** when memory is oversubscribed; this daemon chooses a memory-intensive process and kills it, thus reducing memory in a none-too-subtle manner. While successful at reducing memory pressure, this approach can have problems, if, for example, it kills the X server and thus renders any applications requiring the display unusable.

22.12 Summary

We have seen the introduction of a number of page-replacement (and other) policies, which are part of the VM subsystem of all modern operating systems. Modern systems add some tweaks to straightforward LRU approximations like clock; for example, **scan resistance** is an important part of many modern algorithms, such as ARC [MM03]. Scan-resistant algorithms are usually LRU-like but also try to avoid the worst-case behavior of LRU, which we saw with the looping-sequential workload. Thus, the evolution of page-replacement algorithms continues.

However, in many cases the importance of said algorithms has decreased, as the discrepancy between memory-access and disk-access times has increased. Because paging to disk is so expensive, the cost of frequent paging is prohibitive. Thus, the best solution to excessive paging is often a simple (if intellectually unsatisfying) one: buy more memory.

References

[AD03] "Run-Time Adaptation in River" by Remzi H. Arpaci-Dusseau. ACM TOCS, 21:1, February 2003. *A summary of one of the authors' dissertation work on a system named River, where he learned that comparison against the ideal is an important technique for system designers.*

[B66] "A Study of Replacement Algorithms for Virtual-Storage Computer" by Laszlo A. Belady. IBM Systems Journal 5(2): 78-101, 1966. *The paper that introduces the simple way to compute the optimal behavior of a policy (the MIN algorithm).*

[BNS69] "An Anomaly in Space-time Characteristics of Certain Programs Running in a Paging Machine" by L. A. Belady, R. A. Nelson, G. S. Shedler. Communications of the ACM, 12:6, June 1969. *Introduction of the little sequence of memory references known as Belady's Anomaly. How do Nelson and Shedler feel about this name, we wonder?*

[CD85] "An Evaluation of Buffer Management Strategies for Relational Database Systems" by Hong-Tai Chou, David J. DeWitt. VLDB '85, Stockholm, Sweden, August 1985. *A famous database paper on the different buffering strategies you should use under a number of common database access patterns. The more general lesson: if you know something about a workload, you can tailor policies to do better than the general-purpose ones usually found in the OS.*

[C69] "A Paging Experiment with the Multics System" by F.J. Corbato. Included in a Festschrift published in honor of Prof. P.M. Morse. MIT Press, Cambridge, MA, 1969. *The original (and hard to find!) reference to the clock algorithm, though not the first usage of a use bit. Thanks to H. Balakrishnan of MIT for digging up this paper for us.*

[D70] "Virtual Memory" by Peter J. Denning. Computing Surveys, Vol. 2, No. 3, September 1970. *Denning's early and famous survey on virtual memory systems.*

[EF78] "Cold-start vs. Warm-start Miss Ratios" by Malcolm C. Easton, Ronald Fagin. Communications of the ACM, 21:10, October 1978. *A good discussion of cold- vs. warm-start misses.*

[FP89] "Electrochemically Induced Nuclear Fusion of Deuterium" by Martin Fleischmann, Stanley Pons. Journal of Electroanalytical Chemistry, Volume 26, Number 2, Part 1, April, 1989. *The famous paper that would have revolutionized the world in providing an easy way to generate nearly-infinite power from jars of water with a little metal in them. Unfortunately, the results published (and widely publicized) by Pons and Fleischmann were impossible to reproduce, and thus these two well-meaning scientists were discredited (and certainly, mocked). The only guy really happy about this result was Marvin Hawkins, whose name was left off this paper even though he participated in the work, thus avoiding association with one of the biggest scientific goofs of the 20th century.*

[HP06] "Computer Architecture: A Quantitative Approach" by John Hennessy and David Patterson. Morgan-Kaufmann, 2006. *A marvelous book about computer architecture. Read it!*

[H87] "Aspects of Cache Memory and Instruction Buffer Performance" by Mark D. Hill. Ph.D. Dissertation, U.C. Berkeley, 1987. *Mark Hill, in his dissertation work, introduced the Three C's, which later gained wide popularity with its inclusion in H&P [HP06]. The quote from therein: "I have found it useful to partition misses ... into three components intuitively based on the cause of the misses (page 49)."*

[KE+62] "One-level Storage System" by T. Kilburn, D.B.G. Edwards, M.J. Lanigan, F.H. Sumner. IRE Trans. EC-11:2, 1962. *Although Atlas had a use bit, it only had a very small number of pages, and thus the scanning of the use bits in large memories was not a problem the authors solved.*

[M+70] "Evaluation Techniques for Storage Hierarchies" by R. L. Mattson, J. Gecsei, D. R. Slutz, I. L. Traiger. IBM Systems Journal, Volume 9:2, 1970. *A paper that is mostly about how to simulate cache hierarchies efficiently; certainly a classic in that regard, as well for its excellent discussion of some of the properties of various replacement algorithms. Can you figure out why the stack property might be useful for simulating a lot of different-sized caches at once?*

[MM03] "ARC: A Self-Tuning, Low Overhead Replacement Cache" by Nimrod Megiddo and Dharmendra S. Modha. FAST 2003, February 2003, San Jose, California. *An excellent modern paper about replacement algorithms, which includes a new policy, ARC, that is now used in some systems. Recognized in 2014 as a "Test of Time" award winner by the storage systems community at the FAST '14 conference.*

Homework (Simulation)

This simulator, `paging-policy.py`, allows you to play around with different page-replacement policies. See the README for details.

Questions

1. Generate random addresses with the following arguments: `-s 0 -n 10`, `-s 1 -n 10`, and `-s 2 -n 10`. Change the policy from FIFO, to LRU, to OPT. Compute whether each access in said address traces are hits or misses.

2. For a cache of size 5, generate worst-case address reference streams for each of the following policies: FIFO, LRU, and MRU (worst-case reference streams cause the most misses possible. For the worst case reference streams, how much bigger of a cache is needed to improve performance dramatically and approach OPT?

3. Generate a random trace (use python or perl). How would you expect the different policies to perform on such a trace?

4. Now generate a trace with some locality. How can you generate such a trace? How does LRU perform on it? How much better than RAND is LRU? How does CLOCK do? How about CLOCK with different numbers of clock bits?

5. Use a program like `valgrind` to instrument a real application and generate a virtual page reference stream. For example, running `valgrind --tool=lackey --trace-mem=yes ls` will output a nearly-complete reference trace of every instruction and data reference made by the program `ls`. To make this useful for the simulator above, you'll have to first transform each virtual memory reference into a virtual page-number reference (done by masking off the offset and shifting the resulting bits downward). How big of a cache is needed for your application trace in order to satisfy a large fraction of requests? Plot a graph of its working set as the size of the cache increases.

23

Complete Virtual Memory Systems

Before we end our study of virtualizing memory, let us take a closer look at how entire virtual memory systems are put together. We've seen key elements of such systems, including numerous page-table designs, interactions with the TLB (sometimes, even handled by the OS itself), and strategies for deciding which pages to keep in memory and which to kick out. However, there are many other features that comprise a complete virtual memory system, including numerous features for performance, functionality, and security. And thus, our crux:

> THE CRUX: HOW TO BUILD A COMPLETE VM SYSTEM
>
> What features are needed to realize a complete virtual memory system? How do they improve performance, increase security, or otherwise improve the system?

We'll do this by covering two systems. The first is one of the earliest examples of a "modern" virtual memory manager, that found in the **VAX/VMS** operating system [LL82], as developed in the 1970's and early 1980's; a surprising number of techniques and approaches from this system survive to this day, and thus it is well worth studying. Some ideas, even those that are 50 years old, are still worth knowing, a thought that is well known to those in most other fields (e.g., Physics), but has to be stated in technology-driven disciplines (e.g., Computer Science).

The second is that of **Linux**, for reasons that should be obvious. Linux is a widely used system, and runs effectively on systems as small and underpowered as phones to the most scalable multicore systems found in modern datacenters. Thus, its VM system must be flexible enough to run successfully in all of those scenarios. We will discuss each system to illustrate how concepts brought forth in earlier chapters come together in a complete memory manager.

23.1 VAX/VMS Virtual Memory

The VAX-11 minicomputer architecture was introduced in the late 1970's by **Digital Equipment Corporation** (**DEC**). DEC was a massive player in the computer industry during the era of the mini-computer; unfortunately, a series of bad decisions and the advent of the PC slowly (but surely) led to their demise [C03]. The architecture was realized in a number of implementations, including the VAX-11/780 and the less powerful VAX-11/750.

The OS for the system was known as VAX/VMS (or just plain VMS), one of whose primary architects was Dave Cutler, who later led the effort to develop Microsoft's Windows NT [C93]. VMS had the general problem that it would be run on a broad range of machines, including very inexpensive VAXen (yes, that is the proper plural) to extremely high-end and powerful machines in the same architecture family. Thus, the OS had to have mechanisms and policies that worked (and worked well) across this huge range of systems.

As an additional issue, VMS is an excellent example of software innovations used to hide some of the inherent flaws of the architecture. Although the OS often relies on the hardware to build efficient abstractions and illusions, sometimes the hardware designers don't quite get everything right; in the VAX hardware, we'll see a few examples of this, and what the VMS operating system does to build an effective, working system despite these hardware flaws.

Memory Management Hardware

The VAX-11 provided a 32-bit virtual address space per process, divided into 512-byte pages. Thus, a virtual address consisted of a 23-bit VPN and a 9-bit offset. Further, the upper two bits of the VPN were used to differentiate which segment the page resided within; thus, the system was a hybrid of paging and segmentation, as we saw previously.

The lower-half of the address space was known as "process space" and is unique to each process. In the first half of process space (known as `P0`), the user program is found, as well as a heap which grows downward. In the second half of process space (`P1`), we find the stack, which grows upwards. The upper-half of the address space is known as system space (`S`), although only half of it is used. Protected OS code and data reside here, and the OS is in this way shared across processes.

One major concern of the VMS designers was the incredibly small size of pages in the VAX hardware (512 bytes). This size, chosen for historical reasons, has the fundamental problem of making simple linear page tables excessively large. Thus, one of the first goals of the VMS designers was to ensure that VMS would not overwhelm memory with page tables.

The system reduced the pressure page tables place on memory in two ways. First, by segmenting the user address space into two, the VAX-11 provides a page table for each of these regions (`P0` and `P1`) per process;

ASIDE: THE CURSE OF GENERALITY

Operating systems often have a problem known as **the curse of generality**, where they are tasked with general support for a broad class of applications and systems. The fundamental result of the curse is that the OS is not likely to support any one installation very well. In the case of VMS, the curse was very real, as the VAX-11 architecture was realized in a number of different implementations. It is no less real today, where Linux is expected to run well on your phone, a TV set-top box, a laptop computer, desktop computer, and a high-end server running thousands of processes in a cloud-based datacenter.

thus, no page-table space is needed for the unused portion of the address space between the stack and the heap. The base and bounds registers are used as you would expect; a base register holds the address of the page table for that segment, and the bounds holds its size (i.e., number of page-table entries).

Second, the OS reduces memory pressure even further by placing user page tables (for `P0` and `P1`, thus two per process) in kernel virtual memory. Thus, when allocating or growing a page table, the kernel allocates space out of its own virtual memory, in segment `S`. If memory comes under severe pressure, the kernel can swap pages of these page tables out to disk, thus making physical memory available for other uses.

Putting page tables in kernel virtual memory means that address translation is even further complicated. For example, to translate a virtual address in `P0` or `P1`, the hardware has to first try to look up the page-table entry for that page in its page table (the `P0` or `P1` page table for that process); in doing so, however, the hardware may first have to consult the system page table (which lives in physical memory); with that translation complete, the hardware can learn the address of the page of the page table, and then finally learn the address of the desired memory access. All of this, fortunately, is made faster by the VAX's hardware-managed TLBs, which usually (hopefully) circumvent this laborious lookup.

A Real Address Space

One neat aspect of studying VMS is that we can see how a real address space is constructed (Figure 231. Thus far, we have assumed a simple address space of just user code, user data, and user heap, but as we can see above, a real address space is notably more complex.

For example, the code segment never begins at page 0. This page, instead, is marked inaccessible, in order to provide some support for detecting **null-pointer** accesses. Thus, one concern when designing an address space is support for debugging, which the inaccessible zero page provides here in some form.

Perhaps more importantly, the kernel virtual address space (i.e., its data structures and code) is a part of each user address space. On a con-

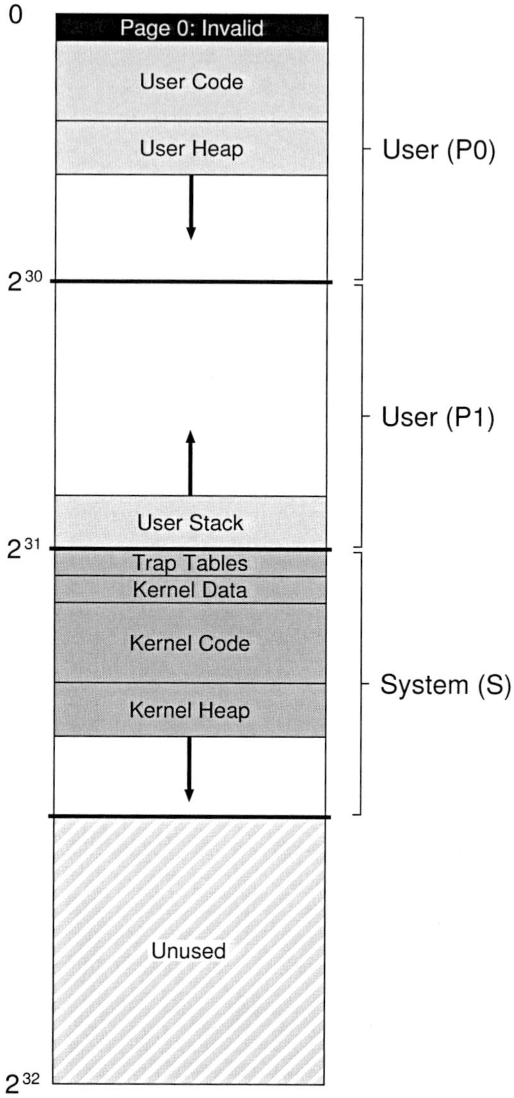

Figure 231: **The VAX/VMS Address Space**

text switch, the OS changes the `P0` and `P1` registers to point to the appropriate page tables of the soon-to-be-run process; however, it does not change the `S` base and bound registers, and as a result the "same" kernel structures are mapped into each user address space.

The kernel is mapped into each address space for a number of reasons. This construction makes life easier for the kernel; when, for example, the OS is handed a pointer from a user program (e.g., on a `write()` system

ASIDE: WHY NULL POINTER ACCESSES CAUSE SEG FAULTS

You should now have a good understanding of exactly what happens on a null-pointer dereference. A process generates a virtual address of 0, by doing something like this:

```
int *p = NULL; // set p = 0
*p = 10;       // try to store 10 to virtual addr 0
```

The hardware tries to look up the VPN (also 0 here) in the TLB, and suffers a TLB miss. The page table is consulted, and the entry for VPN 0 is found to be marked invalid. Thus, we have an invalid access, which transfers control to the OS, which likely terminates the process (on UNIX systems, processes are sent a signal which allows them to react to such a fault; if uncaught, however, the process is killed).

call), it is easy to copy data from that pointer to its own structures. The OS is naturally written and compiled, without worry of where the data it is accessing comes from. If in contrast the kernel were located entirely in physical memory, it would be quite hard to do things like swap pages of the page table to disk; if the kernel were given its own address space, moving data between user applications and the kernel would again be complicated and painful. With this construction (now used widely), the kernel appears almost as a library to applications, albeit a protected one.

One last point about this address space relates to protection. Clearly, the OS does not want user applications reading or writing OS data or code. Thus, the hardware must support different protection levels for pages to enable this. The VAX did so by specifying, in protection bits in the page table, what privilege level the CPU must be at in order to access a particular page. Thus, system data and code are set to a higher level of protection than user data and code; an attempted access to such information from user code will generate a trap into the OS, and (you guessed it) the likely termination of the offending process.

Page Replacement

The page table entry (PTE) in VAX contains the following bits: a valid bit, a protection field (4 bits), a modify (or dirty) bit, a field reserved for OS use (5 bits), and finally a physical frame number (PFN) to store the location of the page in physical memory. The astute reader might note: no **reference bit**! Thus, the VMS replacement algorithm must make do without hardware support for determining which pages are active.

The developers were also concerned about **memory hogs**, programs that use a lot of memory and make it hard for other programs to run. Most of the policies we have looked at thus far are susceptible to such hogging; for example, LRU is a *global* policy that doesn't share memory fairly among processes.

ASIDE: EMULATING REFERENCE BITS

As it turns out, you don't need a hardware reference bit in order to get some notion of which pages are in use in a system. In fact, in the early 1980's, Babaoglu and Joy showed that protection bits on the VAX can be used to emulate reference bits [BJ81]. The basic idea: if you want to gain some understanding of which pages are actively being used in a system, mark all of the pages in the page table as inaccessible (but keep around the information as to which pages are really accessible by the process, perhaps in the "reserved OS field" portion of the page table entry). When a process accesses a page, it will generate a trap into the OS; the OS will then check if the page really should be accessible, and if so, revert the page to its normal protections (e.g., read-only, or read-write). At the time of a replacement, the OS can check which pages remain marked inaccessible, and thus get an idea of which pages have not been recently used.

The key to this "emulation" of reference bits is reducing overhead while still obtaining a good idea of page usage. The OS must not be too aggressive in marking pages inaccessible, or overhead would be too high. The OS also must not be too passive in such marking, or all pages will end up referenced; the OS will again have no good idea which page to evict.

To address these two problems, the developers came up with the **segmented FIFO** replacement policy [RL81]. The idea is simple: each process has a maximum number of pages it can keep in memory, known as its **resident set size** (**RSS**). Each of these pages is kept on a FIFO list; when a process exceeds its RSS, the "first-in" page is evicted. FIFO clearly does not need any support from the hardware, and is thus easy to implement.

Of course, pure FIFO does not perform particularly well, as we saw earlier. To improve FIFO's performance, VMS introduced two **second-chance lists** where pages are placed before getting evicted from memory, specifically a global *clean-page free list* and *dirty-page list*. When a process P exceeds its RSS, a page is removed from its per-process FIFO; if clean (not modified), it is placed on the end of the clean-page list; if dirty (modified), it is placed on the end of the dirty-page list.

If another process Q needs a free page, it takes the first free page off of the global clean list. However, if the original process P faults on that page *before* it is reclaimed, P reclaims it from the free (or dirty) list, thus avoiding a costly disk access. The bigger these global second-chance lists are, the closer the segmented FIFO algorithm performs to LRU [RL81].

Another optimization used in VMS also helps overcome the small page size in VMS. Specifically, with such small pages, disk I/O during swapping could be highly inefficient, as disks do better with large transfers. To make swapping I/O more efficient, VMS adds a number of optimizations, but most important is **clustering**. With clustering, VMS groups large batches of pages together from the global dirty list, and writes them to disk in one fell swoop (thus making them clean). Clustering is used in most modern systems, as the freedom to place pages anywhere within swap space lets the OS group pages, perform fewer and bigger writes, and thus improve performance.

Other Neat Tricks

VMS had two other now-standard tricks: demand zeroing and copy-on-write. We now describe these **lazy** optimizations. One form of laziness in VMS (and most modern systems) is **demand zeroing** of pages. To understand this better, let's consider the example of adding a page to your address space, say in your heap. In a naive implementation, the OS responds to a request to add a page to your heap by finding a page in physical memory, zeroing it (required for security; otherwise you'd be able to see what was on the page from when some other process used it!), and then mapping it into your address space (i.e., setting up the page table to refer to that physical page as desired). But the naive implementation can be costly, particularly if the page does not get used by the process.

With demand zeroing, the OS instead does very little work when the page is added to your address space; it puts an entry in the page table that marks the page inaccessible. If the process then reads or writes the page, a trap into the OS takes place. When handling the trap, the OS notices (usually through some bits marked in the "reserved for OS" portion of the page table entry) that this is actually a demand-zero page; at this point, the OS does the needed work of finding a physical page, zeroing it, and mapping it into the process's address space. If the process never accesses the page, all such work is avoided, and thus the virtue of demand zeroing.

Another cool optimization found in VMS (and again, in virtually every modern OS) is **copy-on-write** (**COW** for short). The idea, which goes at least back to the TENEX operating system [BB+72], is simple: when the OS needs to copy a page from one address space to another, instead of copying it, it can map it into the target address space and mark it read-only in both address spaces. If both address spaces only read the page, no further action is taken, and thus the OS has realized a fast copy without actually moving any data.

If, however, one of the address spaces does indeed try to write to the page, it will trap into the OS. The OS will then notice that the page is a COW page, and thus (lazily) allocate a new page, fill it with the data, and map this new page into the address space of the faulting process. The process then continues and now has its own private copy of the page.

COW is useful for a number of reasons. Certainly any sort of shared library can be mapped copy-on-write into the address spaces of many processes, saving valuable memory space. In UNIX systems, COW is even more critical, due to the semantics of `fork()` and `exec()`. As you might recall, `fork()` creates an exact copy of the address space of the caller; with a large address space, making such a copy is slow and data intensive. Even worse, most of the address space is immediately

> **TIP: BE LAZY**
> Being lazy can be a virtue in both life as well as in operating systems. Laziness can put off work until later, which is beneficial within an OS for a number of reasons. First, putting off work might reduce the latency of the current operation, thus improving responsiveness; for example, operating systems often report that writes to a file succeeded immediately, and only write them to disk later in the background. Second, and more importantly, laziness sometimes obviates the need to do the work at all; for example, delaying a write until the file is deleted removes the need to do the write at all. Laziness is also good in life: for example, by putting off your OS project, you may find that the project specification bugs are worked out by your fellow classmates; however, the class project is unlikely to get canceled, so being too lazy may be problematic, leading to a late project, bad grade, and a sad professor. Don't make professors sad!

over-written by a subsequent call to `exec()`, which overlays the calling process's address space with that of the soon-to-be-exec'd program. By instead performing a copy-on-write `fork()`, the OS avoids much of the needless copying and thus retains the correct semantics while improving performance.

23.2 The Linux Virtual Memory System

We'll now discuss some of the more interesting aspects of the Linux VM system. Linux development has been driven forward by real engineers solving real problems encountered in production, and thus a large number of features have slowly been incorporated into what is now a fully functional, feature-filled virtual memory system.

While we won't be able to discuss *every* aspect of Linux VM, we'll touch on the most important ones, especially where it has gone beyond what is found in classic VM systems such as VAX/VMS. We'll also try to highlight commonalities between Linux and older systems.

For this discussion, we'll focus on Linux for Intel x86. While Linux can and does run on many different processor architectures, Linux on x86 is its most dominant and important deployment, and thus the focus of our attention.

The Linux Address Space

Much like other modern operating systems, and also like VAX/VMS, a Linux virtual address space[1] consists of a user portion (where user

[1]Until recent changes, due to security threats, that is. Read the subsections below about Linux security for details on this modification.

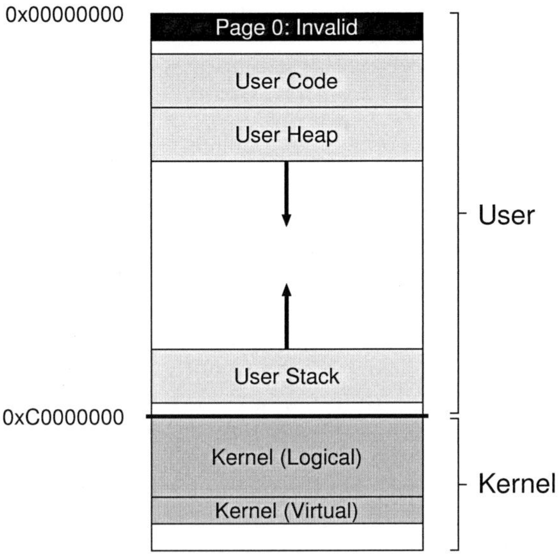

Figure 232: **The Linux Address Space**

program code, stack, heap, and other parts reside) and a kernel portion (where kernel code, stacks, heap, and other parts reside). Like those other systems, upon a context switch, the user portion of the currently-running address space changes; the kernel portion is the same across processes. Like those other systems, a program running in user mode cannot access kernel virtual pages; only by trapping into the kernel and transitioning to privileged mode can such memory be accessed.

In classic 32-bit Linux (i.e., Linux with a 32-bit virtual address space), the split between user and kernel portions of the address space takes place at address `0xC0000000`, or three-quarters of the way through the address space. Thus, virtual addresses `0` through `0xBFFFFFFF` are user virtual addresses; the remaining virtual addresses (`0xC0000000` through `0xFFFFFFFF`) are in the kernel's virtual address space. 64-bit Linux has a similar split but at slightly different points. Figure 232 shows a depiction of a typical (simplified) address space.

One slightly interesting aspect of Linux is that it contains two types of kernel virtual addresses. The first are known as **kernel logical addresses** [O16]. This is what you would consider the normal virtual address space of the kernel; to get more memory of this type, kernel code merely needs to call **`kmalloc`**. Most kernel data structures live here, such as page tables, per-process kernel stacks, and so forth. Unlike most other memory in the system, kernel logical memory *cannot* be swapped to disk.

The most interesting aspect of kernel logical addresses is their connection to physical memory. Specifically, there is a direct mapping between kernel logical addresses and the first portion of physical memory. Thus, kernel logical address `0xC0000000` translates to physical address

0x00000000, 0xC0000FFF to 0x00000FFF, and so forth. This direct mapping has two implications. The first is that it is simple to translate back and forth between kernel logical addresses and physical addresses; as a result, these addresses are often treated as if they are indeed physical. The second is that if a chunk of memory is contiguous in kernel logical address space, it is also contiguous in physical memory. This makes memory allocated in this part of the kernel's address space suitable for operations which need contiguous physical memory to work correctly, such as I/O transfers to and from devices via **directory memory access (DMA)** (something we'll learn about in the third part of this book).

The other type of kernel address is a **kernel virtual address**. To get memory of this type, kernel code calls a different allocator, **`vmalloc`**, which returns a pointer to a virtually contiguous region of the desired size. Unlike kernel logical memory, kernel virtual memory is usually not contiguous; each kernel virtual page may map to non-contiguous physical pages (and is thus not suitable for DMA). However, such memory is easier to allocate as a result, and thus used for large buffers where finding a contiguous large chunk of physical memory would be challenging.

In 32-bit Linux, one other reason for the existence of kernel virtual addresses is that they enable the kernel to address more than (roughly) 1 GB of memory. Years ago, machines had much less memory than this, and enabling access to more than 1 GB was not an issue. However, technology progressed, and soon there was a need to enable the kernel to use larger amounts of memory. Kernel virtual addresses, and their disconnection from a strict one-to-one mapping to physical memory, make this possible. However, with the move to 64-bit Linux, the need is less urgent, because the kernel is not confined to only the last 1 GB of the virtual address space.

Page Table Structure

Because we are focused on Linux for x86, our discussion will center on the type of page-table structure provided by x86, as it determines what Linux can and cannot do. As mentioned before, x86 provides a hardware-managed, multi-level page table structure, with one page table per process; the OS simply sets up mappings in its memory, points a privileged register at the start of the page directory, and the hardware handles the rest. The OS gets involved, as expected, at process creation, deletion, and upon context switches, making sure in each case that the correct page table is being used by the hardware MMU to perform translations.

Probably the biggest change in recent years is the move from 32-bit x86 to 64-bit x86, as briefly mentioned above. As seen in the VAX/VMS system, 32-bit address spaces have been around for a long time, and as technology changed, they were finally starting to become a real limit for programs. Virtual memory makes it easy to program systems, but with modern systems containing many GB of memory, 32 bits were no longer enough to refer to each of them. Thus, the next leap became necessary.

Moving to a 64-bit address affects page table structure in x86 in the expected manner. Because x86 uses a multi-level page table, current 64-bit systems use a four-level table. The full 64-bit nature of the virtual address space is not yet in use, however, rather only the bottom 48 bits. Thus, a virtual address can be viewed as follows:

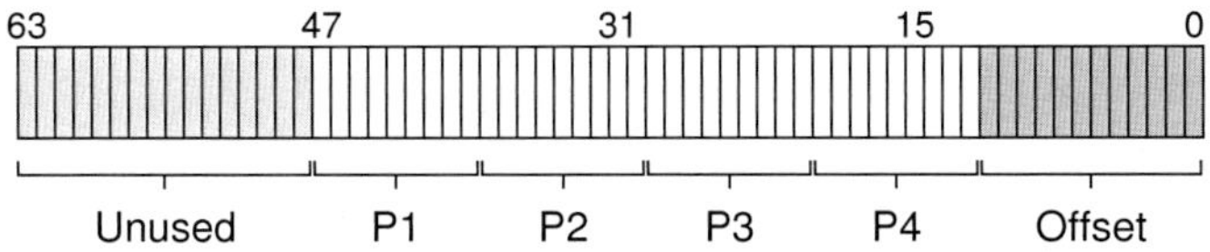

As you can see in the picture, the top 16 bits of a virtual address are unused (and thus play no role in translation), the bottom 12 bits (due to the 4-KB page size) are used as the offset (and hence just used directly, and not translated), leaving the middle 36 bits of virtual address to take part in the translation. The P1 portion of the address is used to index into the topmost page directory, and the translation proceeds from there, one level at a time, until the actual page of the page table is indexed by P4, yielding the desired page table entry.

As system memories grow even larger, more parts of this voluminous address space will become enabled, leading to five-level and eventually six-level page-table tree structures. Imagine that: a simple page table lookup requiring six levels of translation, just to figure out where in memory a certain piece of data resides.

Large Page Support

Intel x86 allows for the use of multiple page sizes, not just the standard 4-KB page. Specifically, recent designs support 2-MB and even 1-GB pages in hardware. Thus, over time, Linux has evolved to allow applications to utilize these **huge pages** (as they are called in the world of Linux).

Using huge pages, as hinted at earlier, leads to numerous benefits. As seen in VAX/VMS, doing so reduces the number of mappings that are needed in the page table; the larger the pages, the fewer the mappings. However, fewer page-table entries is not the driving force behind huge pages; rather, it's better TLB behavior and related performance gains.

When a process actively uses a large amount of memory, it quickly fills up the TLB with translations. If those translations are for 4-KB pages, only a small amount of total memory can be accessed without inducing TLB misses. The result, for modern "big memory" workloads running on machines with many GBs of memory, is a noticeable performance cost; recent research shows that some applications spend 10% of their cycles servicing TLB misses [B+13].

Huge pages allow a process to access a large tract of memory without TLB misses, by using fewer slots in the TLB, and thus is the main advantage. However, there are other benefits to huge pages: there is a shorter TLB-miss path, meaning that when a TLB miss does occur, it is

> **TIP: CONSIDER INCREMENTALISM**
> Many times in life, you are encouraged to be a revolutionary. "Think big!", they say. "Change the world!", they scream. And you can see why it is appealing; in some cases, big changes are needed, and thus pushing hard for them makes a lot of sense. And, if you try it this way, at least they might stop yelling at you.
>
> However, in many cases, a slower, more incremental approach might be the right thing to do. The Linux huge page example in this chapter is an example of engineering incrementalism; instead of taking the stance of a fundamentalist and insisting large pages were the way of the future, developers took the measured approach of first introducing specialized support for it, learning more about its upsides and downsides, and, only when there was real reason for it, adding more generic support for all applications.
>
> Incrementalism, while sometimes scorned, often leads to slow, thoughtful, and sensible progress. When building systems, such an approach might just be the thing you need. Indeed, this may be true in life as well.

serviced more quickly. In addition, allocation can be quite fast (in certain scenarios), a small but sometimes important benefit.

One interesting aspect of Linux support for huge pages is how it was done incrementally. At first, Linux developers knew such support was only important for a few applications, such as large databases with stringent performance demands. Thus, the decision was made to allow applications to explicitly request memory allocations with large pages (either through the `mmap()` or `shmget()` calls). In this way, most applications would be unaffected (and continue to use only 4-KB pages; a few demanding applications would have to be changed to use these interfaces, but for them it would be worth the pain.

More recently, as the need for better TLB behavior is more common among many applications, Linux developers have added **transparent** huge page support. When this feature is enabled, the operating system automatically looks for opportunities to allocate huge pages (usually 2 MB, but on some systems, 1 GB) without requiring application modification.

Huge pages are not without their costs. The biggest potential cost is **internal fragmentation**, i.e., a page that is large but sparsely used. This form of waste can fill memory with large but little used pages. Swapping, if enabled, also does not work well with huge pages, sometimes greatly amplifying the amount of I/O a system does. Overhead of allocation can also be bad (in some other cases). Overall, one thing is clear: the 4-KB page size which served systems so well for so many years is not the universal solution it once was; growing memory sizes demand that we consider large pages and other solutions as part of a necessary evolution of VM systems. Linux's slow adoption of this hardware-based technology is evidence of the coming change.

The Page Cache

To reduce costs of accessing persistent storage (the focus of the third part of this book), most systems use aggressive **caching** subsystems to keep popular data items in memory. Linux, in this regard, is no different than traditional operating systems.

The Linux **page cache** is unified, keeping pages in memory from three primary sources: **memory-mapped files**, file data and metadata from devices (usually accessed by directing `read()` and `write()` calls to the file system), and heap and stack pages that comprise each process (sometimes called **anonymous memory**, because there is no named file underneath of it, but rather swap space). These entities are kept in a **page cache hash table**, allowing for quick lookup when said data is needed.

The page cache tracks if entries are **clean** (read but not updated) or **dirty** (a.k.a., **modified**). Dirty data is periodically written to the backing store (i.e., to a specific file for file data, or to swap space for anonymous regions) by background threads (called `pdflush`), thus ensuring that modified data eventually is written back to persistent storage. This background activity either takes place after a certain time period or if too many pages are considered dirty (both configurable parameters).

In some cases, a system runs low on memory, and Linux has to decide which pages to kick out of memory to free up space. To do so, Linux uses a modified form of **2Q** replacement [JS94], which we describe here.

The basic idea is simple: standard LRU replacement is effective, but can be subverted by certain common access patterns. For example, if a process repeatedly accesses a large file (especially one that is nearly the size of memory, or larger), LRU will kick every other file out of memory. Even worse: retaining portions of this file in memory isn't useful, as they are never re-referenced before getting kicked out of memory.

The Linux version of the 2Q replacement algorithm solves this problem by keeping two lists, and dividing memory between them. When accessed for the first time, a page is placed on one queue (called `A1` in the original paper, but the **inactive list** in Linux); when it is re-referenced, the page is promoted to the other queue (called `Aq` in the original, but the **active list** in Linux). When replacement needs to take place, the candidate for replacement is taken from the inactive list. Linux also periodically moves pages from the bottom of the active list to the inactive list, keeping the active list to about two-thirds of the total page cache size [G04].

Linux would ideally manage these lists in perfect LRU order, but, as discussed in earlier chapters, doing so is costly. Thus, as with many OSes, an approximation of LRU (similar to **clock** replacement) is used.

This 2Q approach generally behaves quite a bit like LRU, but notably handles the case where a cyclic large-file access occurs by confining the pages of that cyclic access to the inactive list. Because said pages are never re-referenced before getting kicked out of memory, they do not flush out other useful pages found in the active list.

ASIDE: THE UBIQUITY OF MEMORY-MAPPING

Memory mapping predates Linux by some years, and is used in many places within Linux and other modern systems. The idea is simple: by calling `mmap()` on an already opened file descriptor, a process is returned a pointer to the beginning of a region of virtual memory where the contents of the file seem to be located. By then using that pointer, a process can access any part of the file with a simple pointer dereference.

Accesses to parts of a memory-mapped file that have not yet been brought into memory trigger **page faults**, at which point the OS will page in the relevant data and make it accessible by updating the page table of the process accordingly (i.e., **demand paging**).

Every regular Linux process uses memory-mapped files, even the code in `main()` does not call `mmap()` directly, because of how Linux loads code from the executable and shared library code into memory. Below is the (highly abbreviated) output of the `pmap` command line tool, which shows what different mapping comprise the virtual address space of a running program (the shell, in this example, `tcsh`). The output shows four columns: the virtual address of the mapping, its size, the protection bits of the region, and the source of the mapping:

```
0000000000400000     372K r-x-- tcsh
00000000019d5000    1780K rw---    [anon ]
00007f4e7cf06000    1792K r-x-- libc-2.23.so
00007f4e7d2d0000      36K r-x-- libcrypt-2.23.so
00007f4e7d508000     148K r-x-- libtinfo.so.5.9
00007f4e7d731000     152K r-x-- ld-2.23.so
00007f4e7d932000      16K rw---    [stack ]
```

As you can see from this output, the code from the `tcsh` binary, as well as code from `libc`, `libcrypt`, `libtinfo`, and code from the dynamic linker itself (`ld.so`) are all mapped into the address space. Also present are two anonymous regions, the heap (the second entry, labeled `anon`) and the stack (labeled `stack`). Memory-mapped files provide a straightforward and efficient way for the OS to construct a modern address space.

Security And Buffer Overflows

Probably the biggest difference between modern VM systems (Linux, Solaris, or one of the BSD variants) and ancient ones (VAX/VMS) is the emphasis on security in the modern era. Protection has always been a serious concern for operating systems, but with machines more interconnected than ever, it is no surprise that developers have implemented a variety of defensive countermeasures to halt those wily hackers from gaining control of systems.

One major threat is found in **buffer overflow** attacks[2], which can be used against normal user programs and even the kernel itself. The idea of these attacks is to find a bug in the target system which lets the attacker inject arbitrary data into the target's address space. Such vulnerabilities sometime arise because the developer assumes (erroneously) that an input will not be overly long, and thus (trustingly) copies the input into a buffer; because the input is in fact too long, it overflows the buffer, thus overwriting memory of the target. Code as innocent as the below can be the source of the problem:

```
int some_function(char *input) {
  char dest_buffer[100];
  strcpy(dest_buffer, input); // oops, unbounded copy!
}
```

In many cases, such an overflow is not catastrophic, e.g., bad input innocently given to a user program or even the OS will probably cause it to crash, but no worse. However, malicious programmers can carefully craft the input that overflows the buffer so as to inject their own code into the targeted system, essentially allowing them to take it over and do their own bidding. If successful upon a network-connected user program, attackers can run arbitrary computations or even rent out cycles on the compromised system; if successful upon the operating system itself, the attack can access even more resources, and is a form of what is called **privilege escalation** (i.e., user code gaining kernel access rights). If you can't guess, these are all Bad Things.

The first and most simple defense against buffer overflow is to prevent execution of any code found within certain regions of an address space (e.g., within the stack). The **NX bit** (for No-eXecute), introduced by AMD into their version of x86 (a similar XD bit is now available on Intel's), is one such defense; it just prevents execution from any page which has this bit set in its corresponding page table entry. The approach prevents code, injected by an attacker into the target's stack, from being executed, and thus mitigates the problem.

However, clever attackers are ... clever, and even when injected code cannot be added explicitly by the attacker, arbitrary code sequences can be executed by malicious code. The idea is known, in its most general form, as a **return-oriented programming** (**ROP**) [S07], and really it is quite brilliant. The observation behind ROP is that there are lots of bits of code (**gadgets**, in ROP terminology) within any program's address space, especially C programs that link with the voluminous C library. Thus, an attacker can overwrite the stack such that the return address in the currently executing function points to a desired malicious instruction (or

[2]See `https://en.wikipedia.org/wiki/Buffer_overflow` for some details and links about this topic, including a reference to the famous article by the security hacker Elias Levy, also known as "Aleph One".

series of instructions), followed by a return instruction. By stringing together a large number of gadgets (i.e., ensuring each return jumps to the next gadget), the attacker can execute arbitrary code. Amazing!

To defend against ROP (including its earlier form, the **return-to-libc attack** [S+04]), Linux (and other systems) add another defense, known as **address space layout randomization** (**ASLR**). Instead of placing code, stack, and the heap at fixed locations within the virtual address space, the OS randomizes their placement, thus making it quite challenging to craft the intricate code sequence required to implement this class of attacks. Most attacks on vulnerable user programs will thus cause crashes, but not be able to gain control of the running program.

Interestingly, you can observe this randomness in practice rather easily. Here's a piece of code that demonstrates it on a modern Linux system:

```
int main(int argc, char *argv[]) {
    int stack = 0;
    printf("%p\n", &stack);
    return 0;
}
```

This code just prints out the (virtual) address of a variable on the stack. In older non-ASLR systems, this value would be the same each time. But, as you can see below, the value changes with each run:

```
prompt> ./random
0x7ffd3e55d2b4
prompt> ./random
0x7ffe1033b8f4
prompt> ./random
0x7ffe45522e94
```

ASLR is such a useful defense for user-level programs that it has also been incorporated into the kernel, in a feature unimaginatively called **kernel address space layout randomization** (**KASLR**). However, it turns out the kernel may have even bigger problems to handle, as we discuss next.

Other Security Problems: Meltdown And Spectre

As we write these words (August, 2018), the world of systems security has been turned upside down by two new and related attacks. The first is called **Meltdown**, and the second **Spectre**. They were discovered at about the same time by four different groups of researchers/engineers, and have led to deep questioning of the fundamental protections offered by computer hardware and the OS above. See `meltdownattack.com` and `spectreattack.com` for papers describing each attack in detail. Spectre is considered the more problematic of the two.

The general weakness exploited in each of these attacks is that the CPUs found in modern systems perform all sorts of crazy behind-the-scenes tricks to improve performance. One class of technique that lies at the core of the problem is called **speculative execution**, in which the CPU guesses which instructions will soon be executed in the future, and starts executing them ahead of time. If the guesses are correct, the program runs faster; if not, the CPU undoes their effects on architectural state (e.g., registers) tries again, this time going down the right path.

The problem with speculation is that it tends to leave traces of its execution in various parts of the system, such as processor caches, branch predictors, etc. And thus the problem: as the authors of the attacks show, such state can make vulnerable the contents of memory, even memory that we thought was protected by the MMU.

One avenue to increasing kernel protection was thus to remove as much of the kernel address space from each user process and instead have a separate kernel page table for most kernel data (called **kernel page-table isolation**, or **KPTI**) [G+17]. Thus, instead of mapping the kernel's code and data structures into each process, only the barest minimum is kept therein; when switching into the kernel, then, a switch to the kernel page table is now needed. Doing so improves security and avoids some attack vectors, but at a cost: performance. Switching page tables is costly. Ah, the costs of security: convenience *and* performance.

Unfortunately, KPTI doesn't solve all of the security problems laid out above, just some of them. And simple solutions, such as turning off speculation, would make little sense, because systems would run thousands of times slower. Thus, it is an interesting time to be alive, if systems security is your thing.

To truly understand these attacks, you'll (likely) have to learn a lot more first. Begin by understanding modern computer architecture, as found in advanced books on the topic, focusing on speculation and all the mechanisms needed to implement it. Definitely read about the Meltdown and Spectre attacks, at the websites mentioned above; they actually also include a useful primer on speculation, so perhaps are not a bad place to start. And study the operating system for further vulnerabilities. Who knows what problems remain?

23.3 Summary

You have now seen a top-to-bottom review of two virtual memory systems. Hopefully, most of the details were easy to follow, as you should have already had a good understanding of the basic mechanisms and policies. More detail on VAX/VMS is available in the excellent (and short) paper by Levy and Lipman [LL82]. We encourage you to read it, as it is a great way to see what the source material behind these chapters is like.

You have also learned a bit about Linux. While a large and complex system, it inherits many good ideas from the past, many of which we have not had room to discuss in detail. For example, Linux performs lazy copy-on-write copying of pages upon `fork()`, thus lowering overheads by avoiding unnecessary copying. Linux also demand zeroes pages (using memory-mapping of the `/dev/zero` device), and has a background swap daemon (**swapd**) that swaps pages to disk to reduce memory pressure. Indeed, the VM is filled with good ideas taken from the past, and also includes many of its own innovations.

To learn more, check out these reasonable (but, alas, outdated) books [BC05,G04]. We encourage you to read them on your own, as we can only provide the merest drop from what is an ocean of complexity. But, you've got to start somewhere. What is any ocean, but a multitude of drops? [M04]

References

[B+13] "Efficient Virtual Memory for Big Memory Servers" by A. Basu, J. Gandhi, J. Chang, M. D. Hill, M. M. Swift. ISCA '13, June 2013, Tel-Aviv, Israel. *A recent work showing that TLBs matter, consuming 10% of cycles for large-memory workloads. The solution: one massive segment to hold large data sets. We go backward, so that we can go forward!*

[BB+72] "TENEX, A Paged Time Sharing System for the PDP-10" by D. G. Bobrow, J. D. Burchfiel, D. L. Murphy, R. S. Tomlinson. CACM, Volume 15, March 1972. *An early time-sharing OS where a number of good ideas came from. Copy-on-write was just one of those; also an inspiration for other aspects of modern systems, including process management, virtual memory, and file systems.*

[BJ81] "Converting a Swap-Based System to do Paging in an Architecture Lacking Page-Reference Bits" by O. Babaoglu, W. N. Joy. SOSP '81, Pacific Grove, California, December 1981. *How to exploit existing protection machinery to emulate reference bits, from a group at Berkeley working on their own version of UNIX: the* ***Berkeley Systems Distribution (BSD)****. The group was influential in the development of virtual memory, file systems, and networking.*

[BC05] "Understanding the Linux Kernel" by D. P. Bovet, M. Cesati. O'Reilly Media, November 2005. *One of the many books you can find on Linux, which are out of date, but still worthwhile.*

[C03] "The Innovator's Dilemma" by Clayton M. Christenson. Harper Paperbacks, January 2003. *A fantastic book about the disk-drive industry and how new innovations disrupt existing ones. A good read for business majors and computer scientists alike. Provides insight on how large and successful companies completely fail.*

[C93] "Inside Windows NT" by H. Custer, D. Solomon. Microsoft Press, 1993. *The book about Windows NT that explains the system top to bottom, in more detail than you might like. But seriously, a pretty good book.*

[G04] "Understanding the Linux Virtual Memory Manager" by M. Gorman. Prentice Hall, 2004. *An in-depth look at Linux VM, but alas a little out of date.*

[G+17] "KASLR is Dead: Long Live KASLR" by D. Gruss, M. Lipp, M. Schwarz, R. Fellner, C. Maurice, S. Mangard. Engineering Secure Software and Systems, 2017. Available: `https://gruss.cc/files/kaiser.pdf` *Excellent info on KASLR, KPTI, and beyond.*

[JS94] "2Q: A Low Overhead High Performance Buffer Management Replacement Algorithm" by T. Johnson, D. Shasha. VLDB '94, Santiago, Chile. *A simple but effective approach to building page replacement.*

[LL82] "Virtual Memory Management in the VAX/VMS Operating System" by H. Levy, P. Lipman. IEEE Computer, Volume 15:3, March 1982. *Read the original source of most of this material. Particularly important if you wish to go to graduate school, where all you do is read papers, work, read some more papers, work more, eventually write a paper, and then work some more.*

[M04] "Cloud Atlas" by D. Mitchell. Random House, 2004. *It's hard to pick a favorite book. There are too many! Each is great in its own unique way. But it'd be hard for these authors not to pick "Cloud Atlas", a fantastic, sprawling epic about the human condition, from where the the last quote of this chapter is lifted. If you are smart – and we think you are – you should stop reading obscure commentary in the references and instead read "Cloud Atlas"; you'll thank us later.*

[O16] "Virtual Memory and Linux" by A. Ott. Embedded Linux Conference, April 2016. https://events.static.linuxfound.org/sites/events/files/slides/elc_2016_mem.pdf . *A useful set of slides which gives an overview of the Linux VM.*

[RL81] "Segmented FIFO Page Replacement" by R. Turner, H. Levy. SIGMETRICS '81, Las Vegas, Nevada, September 1981. *A short paper that shows for some workloads, segmented FIFO can approach the performance of LRU.*

[S07] "The Geometry of Innocent Flesh on the Bone: Return-into-libc without Function Calls (on the x86)" by H. Shacham. CCS '07, October 2007. *A generalization of return-to-libc. Dr. Beth Garner said in Basic Instinct, "She's crazy! She's brilliant!" We might say the same about ROP.*

[S+04] "On the Effectiveness of Address-space Randomization" by H. Shacham, M. Page, B. Pfaff, E. J. Goh, N. Modadugu, D. Boneh. CCS '04, October 2004. *A description of the return-to-libc attack and its limits. Start reading, but be wary: the rabbit hole of systems security is deep...*

24

Summary Dialogue on Memory Virtualization

Student: *(Gulps) Wow, that was a lot of material.*

Professor: *Yes, and?*

Student: *Well, how am I supposed to remember it all? You know, for the exam?*

Professor: *Goodness, I hope that's not why you are trying to remember it.*

Student: *Why should I then?*

Professor: *Come on, I thought you knew better. You're trying to learn something here, so that when you go off into the world, you'll understand how systems actually work.*

Student: *Hmm... can you give an example?*

Professor: *Sure! One time back in graduate school, my friends and I were measuring how long memory accesses took, and once in a while the numbers were way higher than we expected; we thought all the data was fitting nicely into the second-level hardware cache, you see, and thus should have been really fast to access.*

Student: *(nods)*

Professor: *We couldn't figure out what was going on. So what do you do in such a case? Easy, ask a professor! So we went and asked one of our professors, who looked at the graph we had produced, and simply said "TLB". Aha! Of course, TLB misses! Why didn't we think of that? Having a good model of how virtual memory works helps diagnose all sorts of interesting performance problems.*

Student: *I think I see. I'm trying to build these mental models of how things work, so that when I'm out there working on my own, I won't be surprised when a system doesn't quite behave as expected. I should even be able to anticipate how the system will work just by thinking about it.*

Professor: *Exactly. So what have you learned? What's in your mental model of how virtual memory works?*

Student: *Well, I think I now have a pretty good idea of what happens when memory is referenced by a process, which, as you've said many times, happens on each instruction fetch as well as explicit loads and stores.*

Professor: *Sounds good — tell me more.*

Student: *Well, one thing I'll always remember is that the addresses we see in a user program, written in C for example...*

Professor: *What other language is there?*

Student: *(continuing) ... Yes, I know you like C. So do I! Anyhow, as I was saying, I now really know that all addresses that we can observe within a program are virtual addresses; that I, as a programmer, am just given this illusion of where data and code are in memory. I used to think it was cool that I could print the address of a pointer, but now I find it frustrating — it's just a virtual address! I can't see the real physical address where the data lives.*

Professor: *Nope, the OS definitely hides that from you. What else?*

Student: *Well, I think the TLB is a really key piece, providing the system with a small hardware cache of address translations. Page tables are usually quite large and hence live in big and slow memories. Without that TLB, programs would certainly run a great deal more slowly. Seems like the TLB truly makes virtualizing memory possible. I couldn't imagine building a system without one! And I shudder at the thought of a program with a working set that exceeds the coverage of the TLB: with all those TLB misses, it would be hard to watch.*

Professor: *Yes, cover the eyes of the children! Beyond the TLB, what did you learn?*

Student: *I also now understand that the page table is one of those data structures you need to know about; it's just a data structure, though, and that means almost any structure could be used. We started with simple structures, like arrays (a.k.a. linear page tables), and advanced all the way up to multi-level tables (which look like trees), and even crazier things like pageable page tables in kernel virtual memory. All to save a little space in memory!*

Professor: *Indeed.*

Student: *And here's one more important thing: I learned that the address translation structures need to be flexible enough to support what programmers want to do with their address spaces. Structures like the multi-level table are perfect in this sense; they only create table space when the user needs a portion of the address space, and thus there is little waste. Earlier attempts, like the simple base and bounds register, just weren't flexible enough; the structures need to match what users expect and want out of their virtual memory system.*

Professor: *That's a nice perspective. What about all of the stuff we learned about swapping to disk?*

Student: *Well, it's certainly fun to study, and good to know how page replacement works. Some of the basic policies are kind of obvious (like LRU, for example), but building a real virtual memory system seems more interesting, like* *we saw in the VMS case study. But somehow, I found the mechanisms more interesting, and the policies less so.*

Professor: *Oh, why is that?*

Student: *Well, as you said, in the end the best solution to policy problems is simple: buy more memory. But the mechanisms you need to understand to know how stuff really works. Speaking of which...*

Professor: *Yes?*

Student: *Well, my machine is running a little slowly these days... and memory certainly doesn't cost that much...*

Professor: *Oh fine, fine! Here's a few bucks. Go and get yourself some DRAM, cheapskate.*

Student: *Thanks professor! I'll never swap to disk again — or, if I do, at least I'll know what's actually going on!*

Part II

Concurrency

25

A Dialogue on Concurrency

Professor: *And thus we reach the second of our three pillars of operating systems:* ***concurrency****.*

Student: *I thought there were four pillars...?*

Professor: *Nope, that was in an older version of the book.*

Student: *Umm... OK. So what is concurrency, oh wonderful professor?*

Professor: *Well, imagine we have a peach —*

Student: *(interrupting) Peaches again! What is it with you and peaches?*

Professor: *Ever read T.S. Eliot? The Love Song of J. Alfred Prufrock, "Do I dare to eat a peach", and all that fun stuff?*

Student: *Oh yes! In English class in high school. Great stuff! I really liked the part where —*

Professor: *(interrupting) This has nothing to do with that — I just like peaches. Anyhow, imagine there are a lot of peaches on a table, and a lot of people who wish to eat them. Let's say we did it this way: each eater first identifies a peach visually, and then tries to grab it and eat it. What is wrong with this approach?*

Student: *Hmmm... seems like you might see a peach that somebody else also sees. If they get there first, when you reach out, no peach for you!*

Professor: *Exactly! So what should we do about it?*

Student: *Well, probably develop a better way of going about this. Maybe form a line, and when you get to the front, grab a peach and get on with it.*

Professor: *Good! But what's wrong with your approach?*

Student: *Sheesh, do I have to do all the work?*

Professor: *Yes.*

Student: *OK, let me think. Well, we used to have many people grabbing for peaches all at once, which is faster. But in my way, we just go one at a time, which is correct, but quite a bit slower. The best kind of approach would be fast and correct, probably.*

Professor: *You are really starting to impress. In fact, you just told us everything we need to know about concurrency! Well done.*

Student: *I did? I thought we were just talking about peaches. Remember, this is usually the part where you make it about computers again.*

Professor: *Indeed. My apologies! One must never forget the concrete. Well, as it turns out, there are certain types of programs that we call* ***multi-threaded*** *applications; each* ***thread*** *is kind of like an independent agent running around in this program, doing things on the program's behalf. But these threads access memory, and for them, each spot of memory is kind of like one of those peaches. If we don't coordinate access to memory between threads, the program won't work as expected. Make sense?*

Student: *Kind of. But why do we talk about this in an OS class? Isn't that just application programming?*

Professor: *Good question! A few reasons, actually. First, the OS must support multi-threaded applications with primitives such as* ***locks*** *and* ***condition variables****, which we'll talk about soon. Second, the OS itself was the first concurrent program — it must access its own memory very carefully or many strange and terrible things will happen. Really, it can get quite grisly.*

Student: *I see. Sounds interesting. There are more details, I imagine?*

Professor: *Indeed there are...*

26

Concurrency: An Introduction

Thus far, we have seen the development of the basic abstractions that the OS performs. We have seen how to take a single physical CPU and turn it into multiple **virtual CPUs**, thus enabling the illusion of multiple programs running at the same time. We have also seen how to create the illusion of a large, private **virtual memory** for each process; this abstraction of the **address space** enables each program to behave as if it has its own memory when indeed the OS is secretly multiplexing address spaces across physical memory (and sometimes, disk).

In this note, we introduce a new abstraction for a single running process: that of a **thread**. Instead of our classic view of a single point of execution within a program (i.e., a single PC where instructions are being fetched from and executed), a **multi-threaded** program has more than one point of execution (i.e., multiple PCs, each of which is being fetched and executed from). Perhaps another way to think of this is that each thread is very much like a separate process, except for one difference: they *share* the same address space and thus can access the same data.

The state of a single thread is thus very similar to that of a process. It has a program counter (PC) that tracks where the program is fetching instructions from. Each thread has its own private set of registers it uses for computation; thus, if there are two threads that are running on a single processor, when switching from running one (T1) to running the other (T2), a **context switch** must take place. The context switch between threads is quite similar to the context switch between processes, as the register state of T1 must be saved and the register state of T2 restored before running T2. With processes, we saved state to a **process control block (PCB)**; now, we'll need one or more **thread control blocks (TCBs)** to store the state of each thread of a process. There is one major difference, though, in the context switch we perform between threads as compared to processes: the address space remains the same (i.e., there is no need to switch which page table we are using).

One other major difference between threads and processes concerns the stack. In our simple model of the address space of a classic process

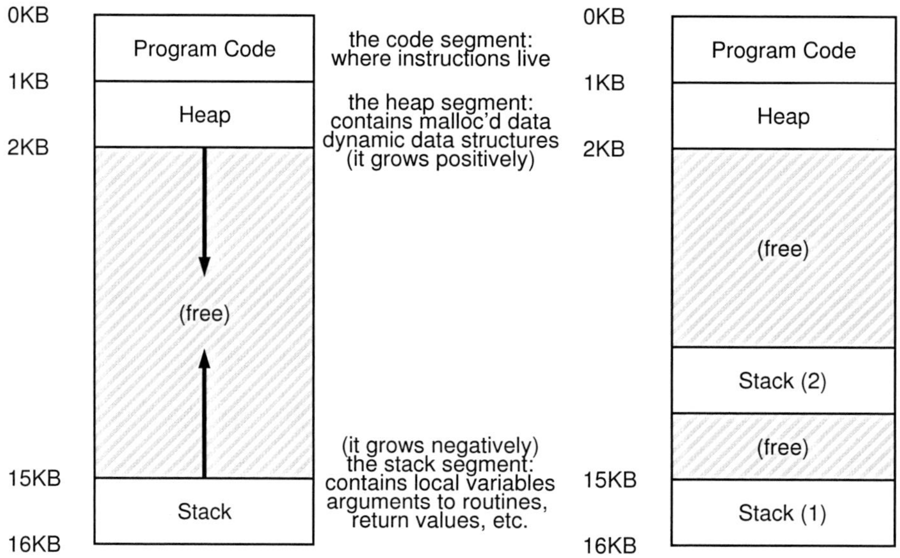

Figure 261: **Single-Threaded And Multi-Threaded Address Spaces**

(which we can now call a **single-threaded** process), there is a single stack, usually residing at the bottom of the address space (Figure 261, left).

However, in a multi-threaded process, each thread runs independently and of course may call into various routines to do whatever work it is doing. Instead of a single stack in the address space, there will be one per thread. Let's say we have a multi-threaded process that has two threads in it; the resulting address space looks different (Figure 261, right).

In this figure, you can see two stacks spread throughout the address space of the process. Thus, any stack-allocated variables, parameters, return values, and other things that we put on the stack will be placed in what is sometimes called **thread-local** storage, i.e., the stack of the relevant thread.

You might also notice how this ruins our beautiful address space layout. Before, the stack and heap could grow independently and trouble only arose when you ran out of room in the address space. Here, we no longer have such a nice situation. Fortunately, this is usually OK, as stacks do not generally have to be very large (the exception being in programs that make heavy use of recursion).

26.1 Why Use Threads?

Before getting into the details of threads and some of the problems you might have in writing multi-threaded programs, let's first answer a more simple question. Why should you use threads at all?

As it turns out, there are at least two major reasons you should use threads. The first is simple: **parallelism**. Imagine you are writing a program that performs operations on very large arrays, for example, adding two large arrays together, or incrementing the value of each element in the array by some amount. If you are running on just a single processor, the task is straightforward: just perform each operation and be done. However, if you are executing the program on a system with multiple processors, you have the potential of speeding up this process considerably by using the processors to each perform a portion of the work. The task of transforming your standard **single-threaded** program into a program that does this sort of work on multiple CPUs is called **parallelization**, and using a thread per CPU to do this work is a natural and typical way to make programs run faster on modern hardware.

The second reason is a bit more subtle: to avoid blocking program progress due to slow I/O. Imagine that you are writing a program that performs different types of I/O: either waiting to send or receive a message, for an explicit disk I/O to complete, or even (implicitly) for a page fault to finish. Instead of waiting, your program may wish to do something else, including utilizing the CPU to perform computation, or even issuing further I/O requests. Using threads is a natural way to avoid getting stuck; while one thread in your program waits (i.e., is blocked waiting for I/O), the CPU scheduler can switch to other threads, which are ready to run and do something useful. Threading enables **overlap** of I/O with other activities *within* a single program, much like **multiprogramming** did for processes *across* programs; as a result, many modern server-based applications (web servers, database management systems, and the like) make use of threads in their implementations.

Of course, in either of the cases mentioned above, you could use multiple *processes* instead of threads. However, threads share an address space and thus make it easy to share data, and hence are a natural choice when constructing these types of programs. Processes are a more sound choice for logically separate tasks where little sharing of data structures in memory is needed.

26.2 An Example: Thread Creation

Let's get into some of the details. Say we wanted to run a program that creates two threads, each of which does some independent work, in this case printing "A" or "B". The code is shown in Figure 262 (page 306).

The main program creates two threads, each of which will run the function `mythread()`, though with different arguments (the string `A` or `B`). Once a thread is created, it may start running right away (depending on the whims of the scheduler); alternately, it may be put in a "ready" but not "running" state and thus not run yet. Of course, on a multiprocessor, the threads could even be running at the same time, but let's not worry about this possibility quite yet.

```
#include <stdio.h>
#include <assert.h>
#include <pthread.h>
#include "common.h"
#include "common_threads.h"

void *mythread(void *arg) {
    printf("%s\n", (char *) arg);
    return NULL;
}

int
main(int argc, char *argv[]) {
    pthread_t p1, p2;
    int rc;
    printf("main: begin\n");
    Pthread_create(&p1, NULL, mythread, "A");
    Pthread_create(&p2, NULL, mythread, "B");
    // join waits for the threads to finish
    Pthread_join(p1, NULL);
    Pthread_join(p2, NULL);
    printf("main: end\n");
    return 0;
}
```

Figure 262: **Simple Thread Creation Code (`t0.c`)**

After creating the two threads (let's call them T1 and T2), the main thread calls `pthread_join()`, which waits for a particular thread to complete. It does so twice, thus ensuring T1 and T2 will run and complete before finally allowing the main thread to run again; when it does, it will print "main: end" and exit. Overall, three threads were employed during this run: the main thread, T1, and T2.

Let us examine the possible execution ordering of this little program. In the execution diagram (Figure 263, page 307), time increases in the downwards direction, and each column shows when a different thread (the main one, or Thread 1, or Thread 2) is running.

Note, however, that this ordering is not the only possible ordering. In fact, given a sequence of instructions, there are quite a few, depending on which thread the scheduler decides to run at a given point. For example, once a thread is created, it may run immediately, which would lead to the execution shown in Figure 264 (page 307).

We also could even see "B" printed before "A", if, say, the scheduler decided to run Thread 2 first even though Thread 1 was created earlier; there is no reason to assume that a thread that is created first will run first. Figure 265 (page 308) shows this final execution ordering, with Thread 2 getting to strut its stuff before Thread 1.

As you might be able to see, one way to think about thread creation

main	Thread 1	Thread2
starts running		
prints "main: begin"		
creates Thread 1		
creates Thread 2		
waits for T1		
	runs	
	prints "A"	
	returns	
waits for T2		
		runs
		prints "B"
		returns
prints "main: end"		

Figure 263: **Thread Trace (1)**

main	Thread 1	Thread2
starts running		
prints "main: begin"		
creates Thread 1		
	runs	
	prints "A"	
	returns	
creates Thread 2		
		runs
		prints "B"
		returns
waits for T1		
returns immediately; T1 is done		
waits for T2		
returns immediately; T2 is done		
prints "main: end"		

Figure 264: **Thread Trace (2)**

is that it is a bit like making a function call; however, instead of first executing the function and then returning to the caller, the system instead creates a new thread of execution for the routine that is being called, and it runs independently of the caller, perhaps before returning from the create, but perhaps much later. What runs next is determined by the OS **scheduler**, and although the scheduler likely implements some sensible algorithm, it is hard to know what will run at any given moment in time.

As you also might be able to tell from this example, threads make life complicated: it is already hard to tell what will run when! Computers are hard enough to understand without concurrency. Unfortunately, with concurrency, it simply gets worse. Much worse.

main	Thread 1	Thread2
starts running		
prints "main: begin"		
creates Thread 1		
creates Thread 2		
		runs
		prints "B"
		returns
waits for T1		
	runs	
	prints "A"	
	returns	
waits for T2		
returns immediately; T2 is done		
prints "main: end"		

Figure 265: **Thread Trace (3)**

26.3 Why It Gets Worse: Shared Data

The simple thread example we showed above was useful in showing how threads are created and how they can run in different orders depending on how the scheduler decides to run them. What it doesn't show you, though, is how threads interact when they access shared data.

Let us imagine a simple example where two threads wish to update a global shared variable. The code we'll study is in Figure 266 (page 309).

Here are a few notes about the code. First, as Stevens suggests [SR05], we wrap the thread creation and join routines to simply exit on failure; for a program as simple as this one, we want to at least notice an error occurred (if it did), but not do anything very smart about it (e.g., just exit). Thus, `Pthread_create()` simply calls `pthread_create()` and makes sure the return code is 0; if it isn't, `Pthread_create()` just prints a message and exits.

Second, instead of using two separate function bodies for the worker threads, we just use a single piece of code, and pass the thread an argument (in this case, a string) so we can have each thread print a different letter before its messages.

Finally, and most importantly, we can now look at what each worker is trying to do: add a number to the shared variable `counter`, and do so 10 million times (1e7) in a loop. Thus, the desired final result is: 20,000,000.

We now compile and run the program, to see how it behaves. Sometimes, everything works how we might expect:

```
prompt> gcc -o main main.c -Wall -pthread; ./main
main: begin (counter = 0)
A: begin
B: begin
A: done
B: done
main: done with both (counter = 20000000)
```

```
#include <stdio.h>
#include <pthread.h>
#include "common.h"
#include "common_threads.h"

static volatile int counter = 0;

// mythread()
//
// Simply adds 1 to counter repeatedly, in a loop
// No, this is not how you would add 10,000,000 to
// a counter, but it shows the problem nicely.
//
void *mythread(void *arg) {
    printf("%s: begin\n", (char *) arg);
    int i;
    for (i = 0; i < 1e7; i++) {
        counter = counter + 1;
    }
    printf("%s: done\n", (char *) arg);
    return NULL;
}

// main()
//
// Just launches two threads (pthread_create)
// and then waits for them (pthread_join)
//
int main(int argc, char *argv[]) {
    pthread_t p1, p2;
    printf("main: begin (counter = %d)\n", counter);
    Pthread_create(&p1, NULL, mythread, "A");
    Pthread_create(&p2, NULL, mythread, "B");

    // join waits for the threads to finish
    Pthread_join(p1, NULL);
    Pthread_join(p2, NULL);
    printf("main: done with both (counter = %d)\n",
            counter);
    return 0;
}
```

Figure 266: **Sharing Data: Uh Oh (`t1.c`)**

Unfortunately, when we run this code, even on a single processor, we don't necessarily get the desired result. Sometimes, we get:

```
prompt> ./main
main: begin (counter = 0)
A: begin
B: begin
A: done
B: done
main: done with both (counter = 19345221)
```

Let's try it one more time, just to see if we've gone crazy. After all, aren't computers supposed to produce **deterministic** results, as you have been taught?! Perhaps your professors have been lying to you? *(gasp)*

```
prompt> ./main
main: begin (counter = 0)
A: begin
B: begin
A: done
B: done
main: done with both (counter = 19221041)
```

Not only is each run wrong, but also yields a *different* result! A big question remains: why does this happen?

TIP: KNOW AND USE YOUR TOOLS

You should always learn new tools that help you write, debug, and understand computer systems. Here, we use a neat tool called a **disassembler.** When you run a disassembler on an executable, it shows you what assembly instructions make up the program. For example, if we wish to understand the low-level code to update a counter (as in our example), we run `objdump` (Linux) to see the assembly code:

```
prompt> objdump -d main
```

Doing so produces a long listing of all the instructions in the program, neatly labeled (particularly if you compiled with the `-g` flag), which includes symbol information in the program. The `objdump` program is just one of many tools you should learn how to use; a debugger like `gdb`, memory profilers like `valgrind` or `purify`, and of course the compiler itself are others that you should spend time to learn more about; the better you are at using your tools, the better systems you'll be able to build.

26.4 The Heart Of The Problem: Uncontrolled Scheduling

To understand why this happens, we must understand the code sequence that the compiler generates for the update to `counter`. In this case, we wish to simply add a number (1) to `counter`. Thus, the code sequence for doing so might look something like this (in x86);

```
mov 0x8049a1c, %eax
add $0x1, %eax
mov %eax, 0x8049a1c
```

This example assumes that the variable `counter` is located at address 0x8049a1c. In this three-instruction sequence, the x86 `mov` instruction is used first to get the memory value at the address and put it into register `eax`. Then, the add is performed, adding 1 (0x1) to the contents of the `eax` register, and finally, the contents of `eax` are stored back into memory at the same address.

Let us imagine one of our two threads (Thread 1) enters this region of code, and is thus about to increment `counter` by one. It loads the value of `counter` (let's say it's 50 to begin with) into its register `eax`. Thus, `eax=50` for Thread 1. Then it adds one to the register; thus `eax=51`. Now, something unfortunate happens: a timer interrupt goes off; thus, the OS saves the state of the currently running thread (its PC, its registers including `eax`, etc.) to the thread's TCB.

Now something worse happens: Thread 2 is chosen to run, and it enters this same piece of code. It also executes the first instruction, getting the value of `counter` and putting it into its `eax` (remember: each thread when running has its own private registers; the registers are **virtualized** by the context-switch code that saves and restores them). The value of `counter` is still 50 at this point, and thus Thread 2 has `eax=50`. Let's then assume that Thread 2 executes the next two instructions, incrementing `eax` by 1 (thus `eax=51`), and then saving the contents of `eax` into `counter` (address 0x8049a1c). Thus, the global variable `counter` now has the value 51.

Finally, another context switch occurs, and Thread 1 resumes running. Recall that it had just executed the `mov` and `add`, and is now about to perform the final `mov` instruction. Recall also that `eax=51`. Thus, the final `mov` instruction executes, and saves the value to memory; the counter is set to 51 again.

Put simply, what has happened is this: the code to increment `counter` has been run twice, but `counter`, which started at 50, is now only equal to 51. A "correct" version of this program should have resulted in the variable `counter` equal to 52.

Let's look at a detailed execution trace to understand the problem better. Assume, for this example, that the above code is loaded at address 100 in memory, like the following sequence (note for those of you used to nice, RISC-like instruction sets: x86 has variable-length instructions; this `mov` instruction takes up 5 bytes of memory, and the `add` only 3):

			(after instruction)		
OS	**Thread 1**	**Thread 2**	**PC**	**eax**	**counter**
	before critical section		100	0	50
	`mov 8049a1c,%eax`		105	**50**	50
	`add $0x1,%eax`		108	**51**	50
interrupt					
save T1					
restore T2			100	0	50
		`mov 8049a1c,%eax`	105	**50**	50
		`add $0x1,%eax`	108	**51**	50
		`mov %eax,8049a1c`	113	51	**51**
interrupt					
save T2					
restore T1			108	51	51
	`mov %eax,8049a1c`		113	51	**51**

Figure 267: **The Problem: Up Close and Personal**

```
100 mov    0x8049a1c, %eax
105 add    $0x1, %eax
108 mov    %eax, 0x8049a1c
```

With these assumptions, what happens is shown in Figure 267 (page 312). Assume the counter starts at value 50, and trace through this example to make sure you understand what is going on.

What we have demonstrated here is called a **race condition** (or, more specifically, a **data race**): the results depend on the timing execution of the code. With some bad luck (i.e., context switches that occur at untimely points in the execution), we get the wrong result. In fact, we may get a different result each time; thus, instead of a nice **deterministic** computation (which we are used to from computers), we call this result **indeterminate**, where it is not known what the output will be and it is indeed likely to be different across runs.

Because multiple threads executing this code can result in a race condition, we call this code a **critical section**. A critical section is a piece of code that accesses a shared variable (or more generally, a shared resource) and must not be concurrently executed by more than one thread.

What we really want for this code is what we call **mutual exclusion**. This property guarantees that if one thread is executing within the critical section, the others will be prevented from doing so.

Virtually all of these terms, by the way, were coined by Edsger Dijkstra, who was a pioneer in the field and indeed won the Turing Award because of this and other work; see his 1968 paper on "Cooperating Sequential Processes" [D68] for an amazingly clear description of the problem. We'll be hearing more about Dijkstra in this section of the book.

> **TIP: USE ATOMIC OPERATIONS**
>
> Atomic operations are one of the most powerful underlying techniques in building computer systems, from the computer architecture, to concurrent code (what we are studying here), to file systems (which we'll study soon enough), database management systems, and even distributed systems [L+93].
>
> The idea behind making a series of actions **atomic** is simply expressed with the phrase "all or nothing"; it should either appear as if all of the actions you wish to group together occurred, or that none of them occurred, with no in-between state visible. Sometimes, the grouping of many actions into a single atomic action is called a **transaction**, an idea developed in great detail in the world of databases and transaction processing [GR92].
>
> In our theme of exploring concurrency, we'll be using synchronization primitives to turn short sequences of instructions into atomic blocks of execution, but the idea of atomicity is much bigger than that, as we will see. For example, file systems use techniques such as journaling or copy-on-write in order to atomically transition their on-disk state, critical for operating correctly in the face of system failures. If that doesn't make sense, don't worry — it will, in some future chapter.

26.5 The Wish For Atomicity

One way to solve this problem would be to have more powerful instructions that, in a single step, did exactly whatever we needed done and thus removed the possibility of an untimely interrupt. For example, what if we had a super instruction that looked like this:

```
memory-add 0x8049a1c, $0x1
```

Assume this instruction adds a value to a memory location, and the hardware guarantees that it executes **atomically**; when the instruction executed, it would perform the update as desired. It could not be interrupted mid-instruction, because that is precisely the guarantee we receive from the hardware: when an interrupt occurs, either the instruction has not run at all, or it has run to completion; there is no in-between state. Hardware can be a beautiful thing, no?

Atomically, in this context, means "as a unit", which sometimes we take as "all or none." What we'd like is to execute the three instruction sequence atomically:

```
mov 0x8049a1c, %eax
add $0x1, %eax
mov %eax, 0x8049a1c
```

As we said, if we had a single instruction to do this, we could just issue that instruction and be done. But in the general case, we won't have such an instruction. Imagine we were building a concurrent B-tree, and wished to update it; would we really want the hardware to support an "atomic update of B-tree" instruction? Probably not, at least in a sane instruction set.

Thus, what we will instead do is ask the hardware for a few useful instructions upon which we can build a general set of what we call **synchronization primitives**. By using this hardware support, in combination with some help from the operating system, we will be able to build multi-threaded code that accesses critical sections in a synchronized and controlled manner, and thus reliably produces the correct result despite the challenging nature of concurrent execution. Pretty awesome, right?

This is the problem we will study in this section of the book. It is a wonderful and hard problem, and should make your mind hurt (a bit). If it doesn't, then you don't understand! Keep working until your head hurts; you then know you're headed in the right direction. At that point, take a break; we don't want your head hurting too much.

THE CRUX: HOW TO SUPPORT SYNCHRONIZATION

What support do we need from the hardware in order to build useful synchronization primitives? What support do we need from the OS? How can we build these primitives correctly and efficiently? How can programs use them to get the desired results?

26.6 One More Problem: Waiting For Another

This chapter has set up the problem of concurrency as if only one type of interaction occurs between threads, that of accessing shared variables and the need to support atomicity for critical sections. As it turns out, there is another common interaction that arises, where one thread must wait for another to complete some action before it continues. This interaction arises, for example, when a process performs a disk I/O and is put to sleep; when the I/O completes, the process needs to be roused from its slumber so it can continue.

Thus, in the coming chapters, we'll be not only studying how to build support for synchronization primitives to support atomicity but also for mechanisms to support this type of sleeping/waking interaction that is common in multi-threaded programs. If this doesn't make sense right now, that is OK! It will soon enough, when you read the chapter on **condition variables**. If it doesn't by then, well, then it is less OK, and you should read that chapter again (and again) until it does make sense.

> **ASIDE: KEY CONCURRENCY TERMS**
> **CRITICAL SECTION, RACE CONDITION,**
> **INDETERMINATE, MUTUAL EXCLUSION**
>
> These four terms are so central to concurrent code that we thought it worth while to call them out explicitly. See some of Dijkstra's early work [D65,D68] for more details.
>
> - A **critical section** is a piece of code that accesses a *shared* resource, usually a variable or data structure.
> - A **race condition** (or **data race** [NM92]) arises if multiple threads of execution enter the critical section at roughly the same time; both attempt to update the shared data structure, leading to a surprising (and perhaps undesirable) outcome.
> - An **indeterminate** program consists of one or more race conditions; the output of the program varies from run to run, depending on which threads ran when. The outcome is thus not **deterministic**, something we usually expect from computer systems.
> - To avoid these problems, threads should use some kind of **mutual exclusion** primitives; doing so guarantees that only a single thread ever enters a critical section, thus avoiding races, and resulting in deterministic program outputs.

26.7 Summary: Why in OS Class?

Before wrapping up, one question that you might have is: why are we studying this in OS class? "History" is the one-word answer; the OS was the first concurrent program, and many techniques were created for use *within* the OS. Later, with multi-threaded processes, application programmers also had to consider such things.

For example, imagine the case where there are two processes running. Assume they both call `write()` to write to the file, and both wish to append the data to the file (i.e., add the data to the end of the file, thus increasing its length). To do so, both must allocate a new block, record in the inode of the file where this block lives, and change the size of the file to reflect the new larger size (among other things; we'll learn more about files in the third part of the book). Because an interrupt may occur at any time, the code that updates these shared structures (e.g., a bitmap for allocation, or the file's inode) are critical sections; thus, OS designers, from the very beginning of the introduction of the interrupt, had to worry about how the OS updates internal structures. An untimely interrupt causes all of the problems described above. Not surprisingly, page tables, process lists, file system structures, and virtually every kernel data structure has to be carefully accessed, with the proper synchronization primitives, to work correctly.

References

[D65] "Solution of a problem in concurrent programming control" by E. W. Dijkstra. Communications of the ACM, 8(9):569, September 1965. *Pointed to as the first paper of Dijkstra's where he outlines the mutual exclusion problem and a solution. The solution, however, is not widely used; advanced hardware and OS support is needed, as we will see in the coming chapters.*

[D68] "Cooperating sequential processes" by Edsger W. Dijkstra. 1968. Available at this site: `http://www.cs.utexas.edu/users/EWD/ewd01xx/EWD123.PDF`. *Dijkstra has an amazing number of his old papers, notes, and thoughts recorded (for posterity) on this website at the last place he worked, the University of Texas. Much of his foundational work, however, was done years earlier while he was at the Technische Hochshule of Eindhoven (THE), including this famous paper on "cooperating sequential processes", which basically outlines all of the thinking that has to go into writing multi-threaded programs. Dijkstra discovered much of this while working on an operating system named after his school: the "THE" operating system (said "T", "H", "E", and not like the word "the").*

[GR92] "Transaction Processing: Concepts and Techniques" by Jim Gray and Andreas Reuter. Morgan Kaufmann, September 1992. *This book is the bible of transaction processing, written by one of the legends of the field, Jim Gray. It is, for this reason, also considered Jim Gray's "brain dump", in which he wrote down everything he knows about how database management systems work. Sadly, Gray passed away tragically a few years back, and many of us lost a friend and great mentor, including the co-authors of said book, who were lucky enough to interact with Gray during their graduate school years.*

[L+93] "Atomic Transactions" by Nancy Lynch, Michael Merritt, William Weihl, Alan Fekete. Morgan Kaufmann, August 1993. *A nice text on some of the theory and practice of atomic transactions for distributed systems. Perhaps a bit formal for some, but lots of good material is found herein.*

[NM92] "What Are Race Conditions? Some Issues and Formalizations" by Robert H. B. Netzer and Barton P. Miller. ACM Letters on Programming Languages and Systems, Volume 1:1, March 1992. *An excellent discussion of the different types of races found in concurrent programs. In this chapter (and the next few), we focus on data races, but later we will broaden to discuss* ***general races*** *as well.*

[SR05] "Advanced Programming in the UNIX Environment" by W. Richard Stevens and Stephen A. Rago. Addison-Wesley, 2005. *As we've said many times, buy this book, and read it, in little chunks, preferably before going to bed. This way, you will actually fall asleep more quickly; more importantly, you learn a little more about how to become a serious UNIX programmer.*

Homework (Simulation)

This program, `x86.py`, allows you to see how different thread interleavings either cause or avoid race conditions. See the README for details on how the program works, then answer the questions below.

Questions

1. Let's examine a simple program, "loop.s". First, just read and understand it. Then, run it with these arguments (`./x86.py -p loop.s -t 1 -i 100 -R dx`) This specifies a single thread, an interrupt every 100 instructions, and tracing of register `%dx`. What will `%dx` be during the run? Use the `-c` flag to check your answers; the answers, on the left, show the value of the register (or memory value) *after* the instruction on the right has run.

2. Same code, different flags: (`./x86.py -p loop.s -t 2 -i 100 -a dx=3,dx=3 -R dx`) This specifies two threads, and initializes each %dx to 3. What values will `%dx` see? Run with `-c` to check. Does the presence of multiple threads affect your calculations? Is there a race in this code?

3. Run this: `./x86.py -p loop.s -t 2 -i 3 -r -a dx=3,dx=3 -R dx` This makes the interrupt interval small/random; use different seeds (`-s`) to see different interleavings. Does the interrupt frequency change anything?

4. Now, a different program, `looping-race-nolock.s`, which accesses a shared variable located at address 2000; we'll call this variable `value`. Run it with a single thread to confirm your understanding: `./x86.py -p looping-race-nolock.s -t 1 -M 2000` What is `value` (i.e., at memory address 2000) throughout the run? Use `-c` to check.

5. Run with multiple iterations/threads: `./x86.py -p looping-race-nolock.s -t 2 -a bx=3 -M 2000` Why does each thread loop three times? What is final value of `value`?

6. Run with random interrupt intervals: `./x86.py -p looping-race-nolock.s -t 2 -M 2000 -i 4 -r -s 0` with different seeds (`-s 1`, `-s 2`, etc.) Can you tell by looking at the thread interleaving what the final value of `value` will be? Does the timing of the interrupt matter? Where can it safely occur? Where not? In other words, where is the critical section exactly?

7. Now examine fixed interrupt intervals: `./x86.py -p looping-race-nolock.s -a bx=1 -t 2 -M 2000 -i 1` What will the final value of the shared variable `value` be? What about when you change `-i 2`, `-i 3`, etc.? For which interrupt intervals does the program give the "correct" answer?

8. Run the same for more loops (e.g., set `-a bx=100`). What interrupt intervals (`-i`) lead to a correct outcome? Which intervals are surprising?

9. One last program: `wait-for-me.s`. Run: `./x86.py -p wait-for-me.s -a ax=1,ax=0 -R ax -M 2000` This sets the `%ax` register to 1 for thread 0, and 0 for thread 1, and watches `%ax` and memory location 2000. How should the code behave? How is the value at location 2000 being used by the threads? What will its final value be?

10. Now switch the inputs: `./x86.py -p wait-for-me.s -a ax=0,ax=1 -R ax -M 2000` How do the threads behave? What is thread 0 doing? How would changing the interrupt interval (e.g., `-i 1000`, or perhaps to use random intervals) change the trace outcome? Is the program efficiently using the CPU?

27

Interlude: Thread API

This chapter briefly covers the main portions of the thread API. Each part will be explained further in the subsequent chapters, as we show how to use the API. More details can be found in various books and online sources [B89, B97, B+96, K+96]. We should note that the subsequent chapters introduce the concepts of locks and condition variables more slowly, with many examples; this chapter is thus better used as a reference.

> CRUX: HOW TO CREATE AND CONTROL THREADS
>
> What interfaces should the OS present for thread creation and control? How should these interfaces be designed to enable ease of use as well as utility?

27.1 Thread Creation

The first thing you have to be able to do to write a multi-threaded program is to create new threads, and thus some kind of thread creation interface must exist. In POSIX, it is easy:

```
#include <pthread.h>
int
pthread_create(pthread_t            *thread,
         const pthread_attr_t *attr,
               void                 *(*start_routine)(void*),
               void                 *arg);
```

This declaration might look a little complex (particularly if you haven't used function pointers in C), but actually it's not too bad. There are four arguments: `thread`, `attr`, `start_routine`, and `arg`. The first, `thread`, is a pointer to a structure of type `pthread_t`; we'll use this structure to interact with this thread, and thus we need to pass it to `pthread_create()` in order to initialize it.

The second argument, `attr`, is used to specify any attributes this thread might have. Some examples include setting the stack size or perhaps information about the scheduling priority of the thread. An attribute is initialized with a separate call to `pthread_attr_init()`; see the manual page for details. However, in most cases, the defaults will be fine; in this case, we will simply pass the value `NULL` in.

The third argument is the most complex, but is really just asking: which function should this thread start running in? In C, we call this a **function pointer**, and this one tells us the following is expected: a function name (`start_routine`), which is passed a single argument of type `void *` (as indicated in the parentheses after `start_routine`), and which returns a value of type `void *` (i.e., a **void pointer**).

If this routine instead required an integer argument, instead of a void pointer, the declaration would look like this:

```
int pthread_create(..., // first two args are the same
                   void *(*start_routine)(int),
                   int  arg);
```

If instead the routine took a void pointer as an argument, but returned an integer, it would look like this:

```
int pthread_create(..., // first two args are the same
                   int (*start_routine)(void *),
                   void *arg);
```

Finally, the fourth argument, `arg`, is exactly the argument to be passed to the function where the thread begins execution. You might ask: why do we need these void pointers? Well, the answer is quite simple: having a void pointer as an argument to the function `start_routine` allows us to pass in *any* type of argument; having it as a return value allows the thread to return *any* type of result.

Let's look at an example in Figure 271. Here we just create a thread that is passed two arguments, packaged into a single type we define ourselves (`myarg_t`). The thread, once created, can simply cast its argument to the type it expects and thus unpack the arguments as desired.

And there it is! Once you create a thread, you really have another live executing entity, complete with its own call stack, running within the *same* address space as all the currently existing threads in the program. The fun thus begins!

27.2 Thread Completion

The example above shows how to create a thread. However, what happens if you want to wait for a thread to complete? You need to do something special in order to wait for completion; in particular, you must call the routine `pthread_join()`.

```
int pthread_join(pthread_t thread, void **value_ptr);
```

```
#include <stdio.h>
#include <pthread.h>

typedef struct {
    int a;
    int b;
} myarg_t;

void *mythread(void *arg) {
    myarg_t *args = (myarg_t *) arg;
    printf("%d %d\n", args->a, args->b);
    return NULL;
}

int main(int argc, char *argv[]) {
    pthread_t p;
    myarg_t args = { 10, 20 };

    int rc = pthread_create(&p, NULL, mythread, &args);
    ...
}
```

Figure 271: **Creating a Thread**

This routine takes two arguments. The first is of type `pthread_t`, and is used to specify which thread to wait for. This variable is initialized by the thread creation routine (when you pass a pointer to it as an argument to `pthread_create()`); if you keep it around, you can use it to wait for that thread to terminate.

The second argument is a pointer to the return value you expect to get back. Because the routine can return anything, it is defined to return a pointer to void; because the `pthread_join()` routine *changes* the value of the passed in argument, you need to pass in a pointer to that value, not just the value itself.

Let's look at another example (Figure 272, page 322). In the code, a single thread is again created, and passed a couple of arguments via the `myarg_t` structure. To return values, the `myret_t` type is used. Once the thread is finished running, the main thread, which has been waiting inside of the `pthread_join()` routine[1], then returns, and we can access the values returned from the thread, namely whatever is in `myret_t`.

A few things to note about this example. First, often times we don't have to do all of this painful packing and unpacking of arguments. For example, if we just create a thread with no arguments, we can pass `NULL` in as an argument when the thread is created. Similarly, we can pass `NULL` into `pthread_join()` if we don't care about the return value.

[1]Note we use wrapper functions here; specifically, we call Malloc(), Pthread_join(), and Pthread_create(), which just call their similarly-named lower-case versions and make sure the

```
typedef struct { int a; int b; } myarg_t;
typedef struct { int x; int y; } myret_t;

void *mythread(void *arg) {
    myret_t *rvals = Malloc(sizeof(myret_t));
    rvals->x = 1;
    rvals->y = 2;
    return (void *) rvals;
}

int main(int argc, char *argv[]) {
    pthread_t p;
    myret_t *rvals;
    myarg_t args = { 10, 20 };
    Pthread_create(&p, NULL, mythread, &args);
    Pthread_join(p, (void **) &rvals);
    printf("returned %d %d\n", rvals->x, rvals->y);
    free(rvals);
    return 0;
}
```

Figure 272: **Waiting for Thread Completion**

Second, if we are just passing in a single value (e.g., a `long long int`), we don't have to package it up as an argument. Figure 273 (page 323) shows an example. In this case, life is a bit simpler, as we don't have to package arguments and return values inside of structures.

Third, we should note that one has to be extremely careful with how values are returned from a thread. Specifically, never return a pointer which refers to something allocated on the thread's call stack. If you do, what do you think will happen? (think about it!) Here is an example of a dangerous piece of code, modified from the example in Figure 272.

```
void *mythread(void *arg) {
    myarg_t *args = (myarg_t *) arg;
    printf("%d %d\n", args->a, args->b);
    myret_t oops; // ALLOCATED ON STACK: BAD!
    oops.x = 1;
    oops.y = 2;
    return (void *) &oops;
}
```

In this case, the variable `oops` is allocated on the stack of `mythread`. However, when it returns, the value is automatically deallocated (that's why the stack is so easy to use, after all!), and thus, passing back a pointer

routines did not return anything unexpected.

```
void *mythread(void *arg) {
    long long int value = (long long int) arg;
    printf("%lld\n", value);
    return (void *) (value + 1);
}

int main(int argc, char *argv[]) {
    pthread_t p;
    long long int rvalue;
    Pthread_create(&p, NULL, mythread, (void *) 100);
    Pthread_join(p, (void **) &rvalue);
    printf("returned %lld\n", rvalue);
    return 0;
}
```

Figure 273: **Simpler Argument Passing to a Thread**

to a now deallocated variable will lead to all sorts of bad results. Certainly, when you print out the values you think you returned, you'll probably (but not necessarily!) be surprised. Try it and find out for yourself[2]!

Finally, you might notice that the use of `pthread_create()` to create a thread, followed by an immediate call to `pthread_join()`, is a pretty strange way to create a thread. In fact, there is an easier way to accomplish this exact task; it's called a **procedure call**. Clearly, we'll usually be creating more than just one thread and waiting for it to complete, otherwise there is not much purpose to using threads at all.

We should note that not all code that is multi-threaded uses the join routine. For example, a multi-threaded web server might create a number of worker threads, and then use the main thread to accept requests and pass them to the workers, indefinitely. Such long-lived programs thus may not need to join. However, a parallel program that creates threads to execute a particular task (in parallel) will likely use join to make sure all such work completes before exiting or moving onto the next stage of computation.

27.3 Locks

Beyond thread creation and join, probably the next most useful set of functions provided by the POSIX threads library are those for providing mutual exclusion to a critical section via **locks**. The most basic pair of routines to use for this purpose is provided by the following:

```
int pthread_mutex_lock(pthread_mutex_t *mutex);
int pthread_mutex_unlock(pthread_mutex_t *mutex);
```

[2]Fortunately the compiler `gcc` will likely complain when you write code like this, which is yet another reason to pay attention to compiler warnings.

The routines should be easy to understand and use. When you have a region of code that is a **critical section**, and thus needs to be protected to ensure correct operation, locks are quite useful. You can probably imagine what the code looks like:

```
pthread_mutex_t lock;
pthread_mutex_lock(&lock);
x = x + 1; // or whatever your critical section is
pthread_mutex_unlock(&lock);
```

The intent of the code is as follows: if no other thread holds the lock when `pthread_mutex_lock()` is called, the thread will acquire the lock and enter the critical section. If another thread does indeed hold the lock, the thread trying to grab the lock will not return from the call until it has acquired the lock (implying that the thread holding the lock has released it via the unlock call). Of course, many threads may be stuck waiting inside the lock acquisition function at a given time; only the thread with the lock acquired, however, should call unlock.

Unfortunately, this code is broken, in two important ways. The first problem is a **lack of proper initialization**. All locks must be properly initialized in order to guarantee that they have the correct values to begin with and thus work as desired when lock and unlock are called.

With POSIX threads, there are two ways to initialize locks. One way to do this is to use `PTHREAD_MUTEX_INITIALIZER`, as follows:

```
pthread_mutex_t lock = PTHREAD_MUTEX_INITIALIZER;
```

Doing so sets the lock to the default values and thus makes the lock usable. The dynamic way to do it (i.e., at run time) is to make a call to `pthread_mutex_init()`, as follows:

```
int rc = pthread_mutex_init(&lock, NULL);
assert(rc == 0); // always check success!
```

The first argument to this routine is the address of the lock itself, whereas the second is an optional set of attributes. Read more about the attributes yourself; passing `NULL` in simply uses the defaults. Either way works, but we usually use the dynamic (latter) method. Note that a corresponding call to `pthread_mutex_destroy()` should also be made, when you are done with the lock; see the manual page for all of details.

The second problem with the code above is that it fails to check error codes when calling lock and unlock. Just like virtually any library routine you call in a UNIX system, these routines can also fail! If your code doesn't properly check error codes, the failure will happen silently, which in this case could allow multiple threads into a critical section. Minimally, use wrappers, which assert that the routine succeeded, as shown in Figure 274 (page 325); more sophisticated (non-toy) programs, which can't simply exit when something goes wrong, should check for failure and do something appropriate when a call does not succeed.

```
// Keeps code clean; only use if exit() OK upon failure
void Pthread_mutex_lock(pthread_mutex_t *mutex) {
    int rc = pthread_mutex_lock(mutex);
    assert(rc == 0);
}
```

Figure 274: **An Example Wrapper**

The lock and unlock routines are not the only routines within the pthreads library to interact with locks. Two other routines of interest:

```
int pthread_mutex_trylock(pthread_mutex_t *mutex);
int pthread_mutex_timedlock(pthread_mutex_t *mutex,
                            struct timespec *abs_timeout);
```

These two calls are used in lock acquisition. The `trylock` version returns failure if the lock is already held; the `timedlock` version of acquiring a lock returns after a timeout or after acquiring the lock, whichever happens first. Thus, the timedlock with a timeout of zero degenerates to the trylock case. Both of these versions should generally be avoided; however, there are a few cases where avoiding getting stuck (perhaps indefinitely) in a lock acquisition routine can be useful, as we'll see in future chapters (e.g., when we study deadlock).

27.4 Condition Variables

The other major component of any threads library, and certainly the case with POSIX threads, is the presence of a **condition variable**. Condition variables are useful when some kind of signaling must take place between threads, if one thread is waiting for another to do something before it can continue. Two primary routines are used by programs wishing to interact in this way:

```
int pthread_cond_wait(pthread_cond_t *cond,
                      pthread_mutex_t *mutex);
int pthread_cond_signal(pthread_cond_t *cond);
```

To use a condition variable, one has to in addition have a lock that is associated with this condition. When calling either of the above routines, this lock should be held.

The first routine, `pthread_cond_wait()`, puts the calling thread to sleep, and thus waits for some other thread to signal it, usually when something in the program has changed that the now-sleeping thread might care about. A typical usage looks like this:

```
pthread_mutex_t lock = PTHREAD_MUTEX_INITIALIZER;
pthread_cond_t  cond = PTHREAD_COND_INITIALIZER;

Pthread_mutex_lock(&lock);
while (ready == 0)
    Pthread_cond_wait(&cond, &lock);
Pthread_mutex_unlock(&lock);
```

In this code, after initialization of the relevant lock and condition[3], a thread checks to see if the variable `ready` has yet been set to something other than zero. If not, the thread simply calls the wait routine in order to sleep until some other thread wakes it.

The code to wake a thread, which would run in some other thread, looks like this:

```
Pthread_mutex_lock(&lock);
ready = 1;
Pthread_cond_signal(&cond);
Pthread_mutex_unlock(&lock);
```

A few things to note about this code sequence. First, when signaling (as well as when modifying the global variable `ready`), we always make sure to have the lock held. This ensures that we don't accidentally introduce a race condition into our code.

Second, you might notice that the wait call takes a lock as its second parameter, whereas the signal call only takes a condition. The reason for this difference is that the wait call, in addition to putting the calling thread to sleep, *releases* the lock when putting said caller to sleep. Imagine if it did not: how could the other thread acquire the lock and signal it to wake up? However, *before* returning after being woken, the `pthread_cond_wait()` re-acquires the lock, thus ensuring that any time the waiting thread is running between the lock acquire at the beginning of the wait sequence, and the lock release at the end, it holds the lock.

One last oddity: the waiting thread re-checks the condition in a while loop, instead of a simple if statement. We'll discuss this issue in detail when we study condition variables in a future chapter, but in general, using a while loop is the simple and safe thing to do. Although it rechecks the condition (perhaps adding a little overhead), there are some pthread implementations that could spuriously wake up a waiting thread; in such a case, without rechecking, the waiting thread will continue thinking that the condition has changed even though it has not. It is safer thus to view waking up as a hint that something might have changed, rather than an absolute fact.

Note that sometimes it is tempting to use a simple flag to signal between two threads, instead of a condition variable and associated lock. For example, we could rewrite the waiting code above to look more like this in the waiting code:

```
while (ready == 0)
    ; // spin
```

The associated signaling code would look like this:

```
ready = 1;
```

[3]One can use `pthread_cond_init()` (and `pthread_cond_destroy()`) instead of the static initializer `PTHREAD_COND_INITIALIZER`. Sound like more work? It is.

Don't ever do this, for the following reasons. First, it performs poorly in many cases (spinning for a long time just wastes CPU cycles). Second, it is error prone. As recent research shows [X+10], it is surprisingly easy to make mistakes when using flags (as above) to synchronize between threads; in that study, roughly half the uses of these *ad hoc* synchronizations were buggy! Don't be lazy; use condition variables even when you think you can get away without doing so.

If condition variables sound confusing, don't worry too much (yet) – we'll be covering them in great detail in a subsequent chapter. Until then, it should suffice to know that they exist and to have some idea how and why they are used.

27.5 Compiling and Running

All of the code examples in this chapter are relatively easy to get up and running. To compile them, you must include the header `pthread.h` in your code. On the link line, you must also explicitly link with the pthreads library, by adding the `-pthread` flag.

For example, to compile a simple multi-threaded program, all you have to do is the following:

```
prompt> gcc -o main main.c -Wall -pthread
```

As long as `main.c` includes the pthreads header, you have now successfully compiled a concurrent program. Whether it works or not, as usual, is a different matter entirely.

27.6 Summary

We have introduced the basics of the pthread library, including thread creation, building mutual exclusion via locks, and signaling and waiting via condition variables. You don't need much else to write robust and efficient multi-threaded code, except patience and a great deal of care!

We now end the chapter with a set of tips that might be useful to you when you write multi-threaded code (see the aside on the following page for details). There are other aspects of the API that are interesting; if you want more information, type `man -k pthread` on a Linux system to see over one hundred APIs that make up the entire interface. However, the basics discussed herein should enable you to build sophisticated (and hopefully, correct and performant) multi-threaded programs. The hard part with threads is not the APIs, but rather the tricky logic of how you build concurrent programs. Read on to learn more.

ASIDE: THREAD API GUIDELINES

There are a number of small but important things to remember when you use the POSIX thread library (or really, any thread library) to build a multi-threaded program. They are:

- **Keep it simple.** Above all else, any code to lock or signal between threads should be as simple as possible. Tricky thread interactions lead to bugs.
- **Minimize thread interactions.** Try to keep the number of ways in which threads interact to a minimum. Each interaction should be carefully thought out and constructed with tried and true approaches (many of which we will learn about in the coming chapters).
- **Initialize locks and condition variables.** Failure to do so will lead to code that sometimes works and sometimes fails in very strange ways.
- **Check your return codes.** Of course, in any C and UNIX programming you do, you should be checking each and every return code, and it's true here as well. Failure to do so will lead to bizarre and hard to understand behavior, making you likely to (a) scream, (b) pull some of your hair out, or (c) both.
- **Be careful with how you pass arguments to, and return values from, threads.** In particular, any time you are passing a reference to a variable allocated on the stack, you are probably doing something wrong.
- **Each thread has its own stack.** As related to the point above, please remember that each thread has its own stack. Thus, if you have a locally-allocated variable inside of some function a thread is executing, it is essentially *private* to that thread; no other thread can (easily) access it. To share data between threads, the values must be in the **heap** or otherwise some locale that is globally accessible.
- **Always use condition variables to signal between threads.** While it is often tempting to use a simple flag, don't do it.
- **Use the manual pages.** On Linux, in particular, the pthread man pages are highly informative and discuss much of the nuances presented here, often in even more detail. Read them carefully!

References

[B89] "An Introduction to Programming with Threads" by Andrew D. Birrell. DEC Technical Report, January, 1989. Available: https://birrell.org/andrew/papers/035-Threads.pdf *A classic but older introduction to threaded programming. Still a worthwhile read, and freely available.*

[B97] "Programming with POSIX Threads" by David R. Butenhof. Addison-Wesley, May 1997. *Another one of these books on threads.*

[B+96] "PThreads Programming: by A POSIX Standard for Better Multiprocessing. " Dick Buttlar, Jacqueline Farrell, Bradford Nichols. O'Reilly, September 1996 *A reasonable book from the excellent, practical publishing house O'Reilly. Our bookshelves certainly contain a great deal of books from this company, including some excellent offerings on Perl, Python, and Javascript (particularly Crockford's "Javascript: The Good Parts".)*

[K+96] "Programming With Threads" by Steve Kleiman, Devang Shah, Bart Smaalders. Prentice Hall, January 1996. *Probably one of the better books in this space. Get it at your local library. Or steal it from your mother. More seriously, just ask your mother for it – she'll let you borrow it, don't worry.*

[X+10] "Ad Hoc Synchronization Considered Harmful" by Weiwei Xiong, Soyeon Park, Jiaqi Zhang, Yuanyuan Zhou, Zhiqiang Ma. OSDI 2010, Vancouver, Canada. *This paper shows how seemingly simple synchronization code can lead to a surprising number of bugs. Use condition variables and do the signaling correctly!*

Homework (Code)

In this section, we'll write some simple multi-threaded programs and use a specific tool, called **helgrind**, to find problems in these programs.

Read the README in the homework download for details on how to build the programs and run `helgrind`.

Questions

1. First build `main-race.c`. Examine the code so you can see the (hopefully obvious) data race in the code. Now run `helgrind` (by typing `valgrind --tool=helgrind main-race`) to see how it reports the race. Does it point to the right lines of code? What other information does it give to you?

2. What happens when you remove one of the offending lines of code? Now add a lock around one of the updates to the shared variable, and then around both. What does `helgrind` report in each of these cases?

3. Now let's look at `main-deadlock.c`. Examine the code. This code has a problem known as **deadlock** (which we discuss in much more depth in a forthcoming chapter). Can you see what problem it might have?

4. Now run `helgrind` on this code. What does `helgrind` report?

5. Now run `helgrind` on `main-deadlock-global.c`. Examine the code; does it have the same problem that `main-deadlock.c` has? Should `helgrind` be reporting the same error? What does this tell you about tools like `helgrind`?

6. Let's next look at `main-signal.c`. This code uses a variable (`done`) to signal that the child is done and that the parent can now continue. Why is this code inefficient? (what does the parent end up spending its time doing, particularly if the child thread takes a long time to complete?)

7. Now run `helgrind` on this program. What does it report? Is the code correct?

8. Now look at a slightly modified version of the code, which is found in `main-signal-cv.c`. This version uses a condition variable to do the signaling (and associated lock). Why is this code preferred to the previous version? Is it correctness, or performance, or both?

9. Once again run `helgrind` on `main-signal-cv`. Does it report any errors?

28

Locks

From the introduction to concurrency, we saw one of the fundamental problems in concurrent programming: we would like to execute a series of instructions atomically, but due to the presence of interrupts on a single processor (or multiple threads executing on multiple processors concurrently), we couldn't. In this chapter, we thus attack this problem directly, with the introduction of something referred to as a **lock**. Programmers annotate source code with locks, putting them around critical sections, and thus ensure that any such critical section executes as if it were a single atomic instruction.

28.1 Locks: The Basic Idea

As an example, assume our critical section looks like this, the canonical update of a shared variable:

```
balance = balance + 1;
```

Of course, other critical sections are possible, such as adding an element to a linked list or other more complex updates to shared structures, but we'll just keep to this simple example for now. To use a lock, we add some code around the critical section like this:

```
lock_t mutex; // some globally-allocated lock 'mutex'
...
lock(&mutex);
balance = balance + 1;
unlock(&mutex);
```

A lock is just a variable, and thus to use one, you must declare a **lock variable** of some kind (such as `mutex` above). This lock variable (or just "lock" for short) holds the state of the lock at any instant in time. It is either **available** (or **unlocked** or **free**) and thus no thread holds the lock, or **acquired** (or **locked** or **held**), and thus exactly one thread holds the lock and presumably is in a critical section. We could store other information in the data type as well, such as which thread holds the lock, or a queue for ordering lock acquisition, but information like that is hidden from the user of the lock.

The semantics of the `lock()` and `unlock()` routines are simple. Calling the routine `lock()` tries to acquire the lock; if no other thread holds the lock (i.e., it is free), the thread will acquire the lock and enter the critical section; this thread is sometimes said to be the **owner** of the lock. If another thread then calls `lock()` on that same lock variable (`mutex` in this example), it will not return while the lock is held by another thread; in this way, other threads are prevented from entering the critical section while the first thread that holds the lock is in there.

Once the owner of the lock calls `unlock()`, the lock is now available (free) again. If no other threads are waiting for the lock (i.e., no other thread has called `lock()` and is stuck therein), the state of the lock is simply changed to free. If there are waiting threads (stuck in `lock()`), one of them will (eventually) notice (or be informed of) this change of the lock's state, acquire the lock, and enter the critical section.

Locks provide some minimal amount of control over scheduling to programmers. In general, we view threads as entities created by the programmer but scheduled by the OS, in any fashion that the OS chooses. Locks yield some of that control back to the programmer; by putting a lock around a section of code, the programmer can guarantee that no more than a single thread can ever be active within that code. Thus locks help transform the chaos that is traditional OS scheduling into a more controlled activity.

28.2 Pthread Locks

The name that the POSIX library uses for a lock is a **mutex**, as it is used to provide **mutual exclusion** between threads, i.e., if one thread is in the critical section, it excludes the others from entering until it has completed the section. Thus, when you see the following POSIX threads code, you should understand that it is doing the same thing as above (we again use our wrappers that check for errors upon lock and unlock):

```
pthread_mutex_t lock = PTHREAD_MUTEX_INITIALIZER;

Pthread_mutex_lock(&lock); // wrapper; exits on failure
balance = balance + 1;
Pthread_mutex_unlock(&lock);
```

You might also notice here that the POSIX version passes a variable to lock and unlock, as we may be using *different* locks to protect different variables. Doing so can increase concurrency: instead of one big lock that is used any time any critical section is accessed (a **coarse-grained** locking strategy), one will often protect different data and data structures with different locks, thus allowing more threads to be in locked code at once (a more **fine-grained** approach).

28.3 Building A Lock

By now, you should have some understanding of how a lock works, from the perspective of a programmer. But how should we build a lock? What hardware support is needed? What OS support? It is this set of questions we address in the rest of this chapter.

> THE CRUX: HOW TO BUILD A LOCK
> How can we build an efficient lock? Efficient locks provide mutual exclusion at low cost, and also might attain a few other properties we discuss below. What hardware support is needed? What OS support?

To build a working lock, we will need some help from our old friend, the hardware, as well as our good pal, the OS. Over the years, a number of different hardware primitives have been added to the instruction sets of various computer architectures; while we won't study how these instructions are implemented (that, after all, is the topic of a computer architecture class), we will study how to use them in order to build a mutual exclusion primitive like a lock. We will also study how the OS gets involved to complete the picture and enable us to build a sophisticated locking library.

28.4 Evaluating Locks

Before building any locks, we should first understand what our goals are, and thus we ask how to evaluate the efficacy of a particular lock implementation. To evaluate whether a lock works (and works well), we should establish some basic criteria. The first is whether the lock does its basic task, which is to provide **mutual exclusion**. Basically, does the lock work, preventing multiple threads from entering a critical section?

The second is **fairness**. Does each thread contending for the lock get a fair shot at acquiring it once it is free? Another way to look at this is by examining the more extreme case: does any thread contending for the lock **starve** while doing so, thus never obtaining it?

The final criterion is **performance**, specifically the time overheads added by using the lock. There are a few different cases that are worth considering here. One is the case of no contention; when a single thread is running and grabs and releases the lock, what is the overhead of doing so? Another is the case where multiple threads are contending for the lock on a single CPU; in this case, are there performance concerns? Finally, how does the lock perform when there are multiple CPUs involved, and threads on each contending for the lock? By comparing these different scenarios, we can better understand the performance impact of using various locking techniques, as described below.

28.5 Controlling Interrupts

One of the earliest solutions used to provide mutual exclusion was to disable interrupts for critical sections; this solution was invented for single-processor systems. The code would look like this:

```
void lock() {
    DisableInterrupts();
}
void unlock() {
    EnableInterrupts();
}
```

Assume we are running on such a single-processor system. By turning off interrupts (using some kind of special hardware instruction) before entering a critical section, we ensure that the code inside the critical section will *not* be interrupted, and thus will execute as if it were atomic. When we are finished, we re-enable interrupts (again, via a hardware instruction) and thus the program proceeds as usual.

The main positive of this approach is its simplicity. You certainly don't have to scratch your head too hard to figure out why this works. Without interruption, a thread can be sure that the code it executes will execute and that no other thread will interfere with it.

The negatives, unfortunately, are many. First, this approach requires us to allow any calling thread to perform a *privileged* operation (turning interrupts on and off), and thus *trust* that this facility is not abused. As you already know, any time we are required to trust an arbitrary program, we are probably in trouble. Here, the trouble manifests in numerous ways: a greedy program could call `lock()` at the beginning of its execution and thus monopolize the processor; worse, an errant or malicious program could call `lock()` and go into an endless loop. In this latter case, the OS never regains control of the system, and there is only one recourse: restart the system. Using interrupt disabling as a general-purpose synchronization solution requires too much trust in applications.

Second, the approach does not work on multiprocessors. If multiple threads are running on different CPUs, and each try to enter the same critical section, it does not matter whether interrupts are disabled; threads will be able to run on other processors, and thus could enter the critical section. As multiprocessors are now commonplace, our general solution will have to do better than this.

Third, turning off interrupts for extended periods of time can lead to interrupts becoming lost, which can lead to serious systems problems. Imagine, for example, if the CPU missed the fact that a disk device has finished a read request. How will the OS know to wake the process waiting for said read?

Finally, and probably least important, this approach can be inefficient. Compared to normal instruction execution, code that masks or unmasks interrupts tends to be executed slowly by modern CPUs.

```
typedef struct __lock_t { int flag; } lock_t;

void init(lock_t *mutex) {
    // 0 -> lock is available, 1 -> held
    mutex->flag = 0;
}

void lock(lock_t *mutex) {
    while (mutex->flag == 1)  // TEST the flag
        ; // spin-wait (do nothing)
    mutex->flag = 1;          // now SET it!
}

void unlock(lock_t *mutex) {
    mutex->flag = 0;
}
```

Figure 281: **First Attempt: A Simple Flag**

For these reasons, turning off interrupts is only used in limited contexts as a mutual-exclusion primitive. For example, in some cases an operating system itself will use interrupt masking to guarantee atomicity when accessing its own data structures, or at least to prevent certain messy interrupt handling situations from arising. This usage makes sense, as the trust issue disappears inside the OS, which always trusts itself to perform privileged operations anyhow.

28.6 A Failed Attempt: Just Using Loads/Stores

To move beyond interrupt-based techniques, we will have to rely on CPU hardware and the instructions it provides us to build a proper lock. Let's first try to build a simple lock by using a single flag variable. In this failed attempt, we'll see some of the basic ideas needed to build a lock, and (hopefully) see why just using a single variable and accessing it via normal loads and stores is insufficient.

In this first attempt (Figure 281), the idea is quite simple: use a simple variable (`flag`) to indicate whether some thread has possession of a lock. The first thread that enters the critical section will call `lock()`, which **tests** whether the flag is equal to 1 (in this case, it is not), and then **sets** the flag to 1 to indicate that the thread now **holds** the lock. When finished with the critical section, the thread calls `unlock()` and clears the flag, thus indicating that the lock is no longer held.

If another thread happens to call `lock()` while that first thread is in the critical section, it will simply **spin-wait** in the while loop for that thread to call `unlock()` and clear the flag. Once that first thread does so, the waiting thread will fall out of the while loop, set the flag to 1 for itself, and proceed into the critical section.

Unfortunately, the code has two problems: one of correctness, and an-

Thread 1	Thread 2
call `lock()`	
while (flag == 1)	
interrupt: switch to Thread 2	
	call `lock()`
	while (flag == 1)
	flag = 1;
	interrupt: switch to Thread 1
flag = 1; // set flag to 1 (too!)	

Figure 282: **Trace: No Mutual Exclusion**

other of performance. The correctness problem is simple to see once you get used to thinking about concurrent programming. Imagine the code interleaving in Figure 282; assume `flag=0` to begin.

As you can see from this interleaving, with timely (untimely?) interrupts, we can easily produce a case where *both* threads set the flag to 1 and both threads are thus able to enter the critical section. This behavior is what professionals call "bad" – we have obviously failed to provide the most basic requirement: providing mutual exclusion.

The performance problem, which we will address more later on, is the fact that the way a thread waits to acquire a lock that is already held: it endlessly checks the value of flag, a technique known as **spin-waiting**. Spin-waiting wastes time waiting for another thread to release a lock. The waste is exceptionally high on a uniprocessor, where the thread that the waiter is waiting for cannot even run (at least, until a context switch occurs)! Thus, as we move forward and develop more sophisticated solutions, we should also consider ways to avoid this kind of waste.

28.7 Building Working Spin Locks with Test-And-Set

Because disabling interrupts does not work on multiple processors, and because simple approaches using loads and stores (as shown above) don't work, system designers started to invent hardware support for locking. The earliest multiprocessor systems, such as the Burroughs B5000 in the early 1960's [M82], had such support; today all systems provide this type of support, even for single CPU systems.

The simplest bit of hardware support to understand is known as a **test-and-set** (or **atomic exchange**[1]) instruction. We define what the test-and-set instruction does via the following C code snippet:

```
int TestAndSet(int *old_ptr, int new) {
    int old = *old_ptr; // fetch old value at old_ptr
    *old_ptr = new;     // store 'new' into old_ptr
    return old;         // return the old value
}
```

[1]Each architecture that supports test-and-set calls it by a different name. On SPARC it is called the load/store unsigned byte instruction (`ldstub`); on x86 it is the locked version of the atomic exchange (`xchg`).

ASIDE: DEKKER'S AND PETERSON'S ALGORITHMS

In the 1960's, Dijkstra posed the concurrency problem to his friends, and one of them, a mathematician named Theodorus Jozef Dekker, came up with a solution [D68]. Unlike the solutions we discuss here, which use special hardware instructions and even OS support, **Dekker's algorithm** uses just loads and stores (assuming they are atomic with respect to each other, which was true on early hardware).

Dekker's approach was later refined by Peterson [P81]. Once again, just loads and stores are used, and the idea is to ensure that two threads never enter a critical section at the same time. Here is **Peterson's algorithm** (for two threads); see if you can understand the code. What are the `flag` and `turn` variables used for?

```
int flag[2];
int turn;

void init() {
    // indicate you intend to hold the lock w/ 'flag'
    flag[0] = flag[1] = 0;
    // whose turn is it? (thread 0 or 1)
    turn = 0;
}
void lock() {
    // 'self' is the thread ID of caller
    flag[self] = 1;
    // make it other thread's turn
    turn = 1 - self;
    while ((flag[1-self] == 1) && (turn == 1 - self))
        ; // spin-wait while it's not your turn
}
void unlock() {
    // simply undo your intent
    flag[self] = 0;
}
```

For some reason, developing locks that work without special hardware support became all the rage for a while, giving theory-types a lot of problems to work on. Of course, this line of work became quite useless when people realized it is much easier to assume a little hardware support (and indeed that support had been around from the earliest days of multiprocessing). Further, algorithms like the ones above don't work on modern hardware (due to relaxed memory consistency models), thus making them even less useful than they were before. Yet more research relegated to the dustbin of history...

```
typedef struct __lock_t {
    int flag;
} lock_t;

void init(lock_t *lock) {
    // 0: lock is available, 1: lock is held
    lock->flag = 0;
}

void lock(lock_t *lock) {
    while (TestAndSet(&lock->flag, 1) == 1)
        ; // spin-wait (do nothing)
}

void unlock(lock_t *lock) {
    lock->flag = 0;
}
```

Figure 283: **A Simple Spin Lock Using Test-and-set**

What the test-and-set instruction does is as follows. It returns the old value pointed to by the `old_ptr`, and simultaneously updates said value to `new`. The key, of course, is that this sequence of operations is performed **atomically**. The reason it is called "test and set" is that it enables you to "test" the old value (which is what is returned) while simultaneously "setting" the memory location to a new value; as it turns out, this slightly more powerful instruction is enough to build a simple **spin lock**, as we now examine in Figure 283. Or better yet: figure it out first yourself!

Let's make sure we understand why this lock works. Imagine first the case where a thread calls `lock()` and no other thread currently holds the lock; thus, `flag` should be 0. When the thread calls `TestAndSet(flag, 1)`, the routine will return the old value of `flag`, which is 0; thus, the calling thread, which is *testing* the value of flag, will not get caught spinning in the while loop and will acquire the lock. The thread will also atomically *set* the value to 1, thus indicating that the lock is now held. When the thread is finished with its critical section, it calls `unlock()` to set the flag back to zero.

The second case we can imagine arises when one thread already has the lock held (i.e., `flag` is 1). In this case, this thread will call `lock()` and then call `TestAndSet(flag, 1)` as well. This time, `TestAndSet()` will return the old value at flag, which is 1 (because the lock is held), while simultaneously setting it to 1 again. As long as the lock is held by another thread, `TestAndSet()` will repeatedly return 1, and thus this thread will spin and spin until the lock is finally released. When the flag is finally set to 0 by some other thread, this thread will call `TestAndSet()` again, which will now return 0 while atomically setting the value to 1 and thus acquire the lock and enter the critical section.

By making both the **test** (of the old lock value) and **set** (of the new

TIP: THINK ABOUT CONCURRENCY AS A MALICIOUS SCHEDULER
From this example, you might get a sense of the approach you need to take to understand concurrent execution. What you should try to do is to pretend you are a **malicious scheduler**, one that interrupts threads at the most inopportune of times in order to foil their feeble attempts at building synchronization primitives. What a mean scheduler you are! Although the exact sequence of interrupts may be *improbable*, it is *possible*, and that is all we need to demonstrate that a particular approach does not work. It can be useful to think maliciously! (at least, sometimes)

value) a single atomic operation, we ensure that only one thread acquires the lock. And that's how to build a working mutual exclusion primitive!

You may also now understand why this type of lock is usually referred to as a **spin lock**. It is the simplest type of lock to build, and simply spins, using CPU cycles, until the lock becomes available. To work correctly on a single processor, it requires a **preemptive scheduler** (i.e., one that will interrupt a thread via a timer, in order to run a different thread, from time to time). Without preemption, spin locks don't make much sense on a single CPU, as a thread spinning on a CPU will never relinquish it.

28.8 Evaluating Spin Locks

Given our basic spin lock, we can now evaluate how effective it is along our previously described axes. The most important aspect of a lock is **correctness**: does it provide mutual exclusion? The answer here is yes: the spin lock only allows a single thread to enter the critical section at a time. Thus, we have a correct lock.

The next axis is **fairness**. How fair is a spin lock to a waiting thread? Can you guarantee that a waiting thread will ever enter the critical section? The answer here, unfortunately, is bad news: spin locks don't provide any fairness guarantees. Indeed, a thread spinning may spin forever, under contention. Simple spin locks (as discussed thus far) are not fair and may lead to starvation.

The final axis is **performance**. What are the costs of using a spin lock? To analyze this more carefully, we suggest thinking about a few different cases. In the first, imagine threads competing for the lock on a single processor; in the second, consider threads spread out across many CPUs.

For spin locks, in the single CPU case, performance overheads can be quite painful; imagine the case where the thread holding the lock is preempted within a critical section. The scheduler might then run every other thread (imagine there are $N - 1$ others), each of which tries to acquire the lock. In this case, each of those threads will spin for the duration of a time slice before giving up the CPU, a waste of CPU cycles.

However, on multiple CPUs, spin locks work reasonably well (if the number of threads roughly equals the number of CPUs). The thinking

```
int CompareAndSwap(int *ptr, int expected, int new) {
    int original = *ptr;
    if (original == expected)
        *ptr = new;
    return original;
}
```

Figure 284: **Compare-and-swap**

goes as follows: imagine Thread A on CPU 1 and Thread B on CPU 2, both contending for a lock. If Thread A (CPU 1) grabs the lock, and then Thread B tries to, B will spin (on CPU 2). However, presumably the critical section is short, and thus soon the lock becomes available, and is acquired by Thread B. Spinning to wait for a lock held on another processor doesn't waste many cycles in this case, and thus can be effective.

28.9 Compare-And-Swap

Another hardware primitive that some systems provide is known as the **compare-and-swap** instruction (as it is called on SPARC, for example), or **compare-and-exchange** (as it called on x86). The C pseudocode for this single instruction is found in Figure 284.

The basic idea is for compare-and-swap to test whether the value at the address specified by `ptr` is equal to `expected`; if so, update the memory location pointed to by `ptr` with the new value. If not, do nothing. In either case, return the original value at that memory location, thus allowing the code calling compare-and-swap to know whether it succeeded or not.

With the compare-and-swap instruction, we can build a lock in a manner quite similar to that with test-and-set. For example, we could just replace the `lock()` routine above with the following:

```
void lock(lock_t *lock) {
    while (CompareAndSwap(&lock->flag, 0, 1) == 1)
        ; // spin
}
```

The rest of the code is the same as the test-and-set example above. This code works quite similarly; it simply checks if the flag is 0 and if so, atomically swaps in a 1 thus acquiring the lock. Threads that try to acquire the lock while it is held will get stuck spinning until the lock is finally released.

If you want to see how to really make a C-callable x86-version of compare-and-swap, the code sequence (from [S05]) might be useful[2].

Finally, as you may have sensed, compare-and-swap is a more powerful instruction than test-and-set. We will make some use of this power in

[2] `github.com/remzi-arpacidusseau/ostep-code/tree/master/threads-locks`

the future when we briefly delve into topics such as **lock-free synchronization** [H91]. However, if we just build a simple spin lock with it, its behavior is identical to the spin lock we analyzed above.

28.10 Load-Linked and Store-Conditional

Some platforms provide a pair of instructions that work in concert to help build critical sections. On the MIPS architecture [H93], for example, the **load-linked** and **store-conditional** instructions can be used in tandem to build locks and other concurrent structures. The C pseudocode for these instructions is as found in Figure 285. Alpha, PowerPC, and ARM provide similar instructions [W09].

The load-linked operates much like a typical load instruction, and simply fetches a value from memory and places it in a register. The key difference comes with the store-conditional, which only succeeds (and updates the value stored at the address just load-linked from) if no intervening store to the address has taken place. In the case of success, the store-conditional returns 1 and updates the value at `ptr` to `value`; if it fails, the value at `ptr` is *not* updated and 0 is returned.

As a challenge to yourself, try thinking about how to build a lock using load-linked and store-conditional. Then, when you are finished, look at the code below which provides one simple solution. Do it! The solution is in Figure 286.

The `lock()` code is the only interesting piece. First, a thread spins waiting for the flag to be set to 0 (and thus indicate the lock is not held). Once so, the thread tries to acquire the lock via the store-conditional; if it succeeds, the thread has atomically changed the flag's value to 1 and thus can proceed into the critical section.

Note how failure of the store-conditional might arise. One thread calls `lock()` and executes the load-linked, returning 0 as the lock is not held. Before it can attempt the store-conditional, it is interrupted and another thread enters the lock code, also executing the load-linked instruction,

```
int LoadLinked(int *ptr) {
    return *ptr;
}

int StoreConditional(int *ptr, int value) {
    if (no update to *ptr since LoadLinked to this address) {
        *ptr = value;
        return 1; // success!
    } else {
        return 0; // failed to update
    }
}
```

Figure 285: **Load-linked And Store-conditional**

```
void lock(lock_t *lock) {
    while (1) {
        while (LoadLinked(&lock->flag) == 1)
            ; // spin until it's zero
        if (StoreConditional(&lock->flag, 1) == 1)
            return; // if set-it-to-1 was a success: all done
                    // otherwise: try it all over again
    }
}

void unlock(lock_t *lock) {
    lock->flag = 0;
}
```

Figure 286: **Using LL/SC To Build A Lock**

and also getting a 0 and continuing. At this point, two threads have each executed the load-linked and each are about to attempt the store-conditional. The key feature of these instructions is that only one of these threads will succeed in updating the flag to 1 and thus acquire the lock; the second thread to attempt the store-conditional will fail (because the other thread updated the value of flag between its load-linked and store-conditional) and thus have to try to acquire the lock again.

In class a few years ago, undergraduate student David Capel suggested a more concise form of the above, for those of you who enjoy short-circuiting boolean conditionals. See if you can figure out why it is equivalent. It certainly is shorter!

```
void lock(lock_t *lock) {
    while (LoadLinked(&lock->flag) ||
          !StoreConditional(&lock->flag, 1))
        ; // spin
}
```

28.11 Fetch-And-Add

One final hardware primitive is the **fetch-and-add** instruction, which atomically increments a value while returning the old value at a particular address. The C pseudocode for the fetch-and-add instruction looks like this:

```
int FetchAndAdd(int *ptr) {
    int old = *ptr;
    *ptr = old + 1;
    return old;
}
```

> TIP: LESS CODE IS BETTER CODE (LAUER'S LAW)
> Programmers tend to brag about how much code they wrote to do something. Doing so is fundamentally broken. What one should brag about, rather, is how *little* code one wrote to accomplish a given task. Short, concise code is always preferred; it is likely easier to understand and has fewer bugs. As Hugh Lauer said, when discussing the construction of the Pilot operating system: "If the same people had twice as much time, they could produce as good of a system in half the code." [L81] We'll call this **Lauer's Law**, and it is well worth remembering. So next time you're bragging about how much code you wrote to finish the assignment, think again, or better yet, go back, rewrite, and make the code as clear and concise as possible.

In this example, we'll use fetch-and-add to build a more interesting **ticket lock**, as introduced by Mellor-Crummey and Scott [MS91]. The lock and unlock code is found in Figure 287 (page 344).

Instead of a single value, this solution uses a ticket and turn variable in combination to build a lock. The basic operation is pretty simple: when a thread wishes to acquire a lock, it first does an atomic fetch-and-add on the ticket value; that value is now considered this thread's "turn" (`myturn`). The globally shared `lock->turn` is then used to determine which thread's turn it is; when `(myturn == turn)` for a given thread, it is that thread's turn to enter the critical section. Unlock is accomplished simply by incrementing the turn such that the next waiting thread (if there is one) can now enter the critical section.

Note one important difference with this solution versus our previous attempts: it ensures progress for all threads. Once a thread is assigned its ticket value, it will be scheduled at some point in the future (once those in front of it have passed through the critical section and released the lock). In our previous attempts, no such guarantee existed; a thread spinning on test-and-set (for example) could spin forever even as other threads acquire and release the lock.

28.12 Too Much Spinning: What Now?

Our simple hardware-based locks are simple (only a few lines of code) and they work (you could even prove that if you'd like to, by writing some code), which are two excellent properties of any system or code. However, in some cases, these solutions can be quite inefficient. Imagine you are running two threads on a single processor. Now imagine that one thread (thread 0) is in a critical section and thus has a lock held, and unfortunately gets interrupted. The second thread (thread 1) now tries to acquire the lock, but finds that it is held. Thus, it begins to spin. And spin. Then it spins some more. And finally, a timer interrupt goes off, thread 0 is run again, which releases the lock, and finally (the next time it runs,

```
typedef struct __lock_t {
    int ticket;
    int turn;
} lock_t;

void lock_init(lock_t *lock) {
    lock->ticket = 0;
    lock->turn   = 0;
}

void lock(lock_t *lock) {
    int myturn = FetchAndAdd(&lock->ticket);
    while (lock->turn != myturn)
        ; // spin
}

void unlock(lock_t *lock) {
    lock->turn = lock->turn + 1;
}
```

Figure 287: **Ticket Locks**

say), thread 1 won't have to spin so much and will be able to acquire the lock. Thus, any time a thread gets caught spinning in a situation like this, it wastes an entire time slice doing nothing but checking a value that isn't going to change! The problem gets worse with N threads contending for a lock; $N - 1$ time slices may be wasted in a similar manner, simply spinning and waiting for a single thread to release the lock. And thus, our next problem:

THE CRUX: HOW TO AVOID SPINNING

How can we develop a lock that doesn't needlessly waste time spinning on the CPU?

Hardware support alone cannot solve the problem. We'll need OS support too! Let's now figure out just how that might work.

28.13 A Simple Approach: Just Yield, Baby

Hardware support got us pretty far: working locks, and even (as with the case of the ticket lock) fairness in lock acquisition. However, we still have a problem: what to do when a context switch occurs in a critical section, and threads start to spin endlessly, waiting for the interrupted (lock-holding) thread to be run again?

Our first try is a simple and friendly approach: when you are going to spin, instead give up the CPU to another thread. As Al Davis might say, "just yield, baby!" [D91]. Figure 288 (page 345) shows the approach.

```
void init() {
    flag = 0;
}

void lock() {
    while (TestAndSet(&flag, 1) == 1)
        yield(); // give up the CPU
}

void unlock() {
    flag = 0;
}
```

Figure 288: **Lock With Test-and-set And Yield**

In this approach, we assume an operating system primitive `yield()` which a thread can call when it wants to give up the CPU and let another thread run. A thread can be in one of three states (running, ready, or blocked); yield is simply a system call that moves the caller from the **running** state to the **ready** state, and thus promotes another thread to running. Thus, the yielding thread essentially **deschedules** itself.

Think about the example with two threads on one CPU; in this case, our yield-based approach works quite well. If a thread happens to call `lock()` and find a lock held, it will simply yield the CPU, and thus the other thread will run and finish its critical section. In this simple case, the yielding approach works well.

Let us now consider the case where there are many threads (say 100) contending for a lock repeatedly. In this case, if one thread acquires the lock and is preempted before releasing it, the other 99 will each call `lock()`, find the lock held, and yield the CPU. Assuming some kind of round-robin scheduler, each of the 99 will execute this run-and-yield pattern before the thread holding the lock gets to run again. While better than our spinning approach (which would waste 99 time slices spinning), this approach is still costly; the cost of a context switch can be substantial, and there is thus plenty of waste.

Worse, we have not tackled the starvation problem at all. A thread may get caught in an endless yield loop while other threads repeatedly enter and exit the critical section. We clearly will need an approach that addresses this problem directly.

28.14 Using Queues: Sleeping Instead Of Spinning

The real problem with our previous approaches is that they leave too much to chance. The scheduler determines which thread runs next; if the scheduler makes a bad choice, a thread runs that must either spin waiting for the lock (our first approach), or yield the CPU immediately (our second approach). Either way, there is potential for waste and no prevention of starvation.

```
typedef struct __lock_t {
    int flag;
    int guard;
    queue_t *q;
} lock_t;

void lock_init(lock_t *m) {
    m->flag  = 0;
    m->guard = 0;
    queue_init(m->q);
}

void lock(lock_t *m) {
    while (TestAndSet(&m->guard, 1) == 1)
        ; //acquire guard lock by spinning
    if (m->flag == 0) {
        m->flag = 1; // lock is acquired
        m->guard = 0;
    } else {
        queue_add(m->q, gettid());
        m->guard = 0;
        park();
    }
}

void unlock(lock_t *m) {
    while (TestAndSet(&m->guard, 1) == 1)
        ; //acquire guard lock by spinning
    if (queue_empty(m->q))
        m->flag = 0; // let go of lock; no one wants it
    else
        unpark(queue_remove(m->q)); // hold lock
                                    // (for next thread!)
    m->guard = 0;
}
```

Figure 289: **Lock With Queues, Test-and-set, Yield, And Wakeup**

Thus, we must explicitly exert some control over which thread next gets to acquire the lock after the current holder releases it. To do this, we will need a little more OS support, as well as a queue to keep track of which threads are waiting to acquire the lock.

For simplicity, we will use the support provided by Solaris, in terms of two calls: `park()` to put a calling thread to sleep, and `unpark(threadID)` to wake a particular thread as designated by `threadID`. These two routines can be used in tandem to build a lock that puts a caller to sleep if it tries to acquire a held lock and wakes it when the lock is free. Let's look at the code in Figure 289 to understand one possible use of such primitives.

ASIDE: MORE REASON TO AVOID SPINNING: PRIORITY INVERSION

One good reason to avoid spin locks is performance: as described in the main text, if a thread is interrupted while holding a lock, other threads that use spin locks will spend a large amount of CPU time just waiting for the lock to become available. However, it turns out there is another interesting reason to avoid spin locks on some systems: correctness. The problem to be wary of is known as **priority inversion**, which unfortunately is an intergalactic scourge, occurring on Earth [M15] and Mars [R97]!

Let's assume there are two threads in a system. Thread 2 (T2) has a high scheduling priority, and Thread 1 (T1) has lower priority. In this example, let's assume that the CPU scheduler will always run T2 over T1, if indeed both are runnable; T1 only runs when T2 is not able to do so (e.g., when T2 is blocked on I/O).

Now, the problem. Assume T2 is blocked for some reason. So T1 runs, grabs a spin lock, and enters a critical section. T2 now becomes unblocked (perhaps because an I/O completed), and the CPU scheduler immediately schedules it (thus descheduling T1). T2 now tries to acquire the lock, and because it can't (T1 holds the lock), it just keeps spinning. Because the lock is a spin lock, T2 spins forever, and the system is hung.

Just avoiding the use of spin locks, unfortunately, does not avoid the problem of inversion (alas). Imagine three threads, T1, T2, and T3, with T3 at the highest priority, and T1 the lowest. Imagine now that T1 grabs a lock. T3 then starts, and because it is higher priority than T1, runs immediately (preempting T1). T3 tries to acquire the lock that T1 holds, but gets stuck waiting, because T1 still holds it. If T2 starts to run, it will have higher priority than T1, and thus it will run. T3, which is higher priority than T2, is stuck waiting for T1, which may never run now that T2 is running. Isn't it sad that the mighty T3 can't run, while lowly T2 controls the CPU? Having high priority just ain't what it used to be.

You can address the priority inversion problem in a number of ways. In the specific case where spin locks cause the problem, you can avoid using spin locks (described more below). More generally, a higher-priority thread waiting for a lower-priority thread can temporarily boost the lower thread's priority, thus enabling it to run and overcoming the inversion, a technique known as **priority inheritance**. A last solution is simplest: ensure all threads have the same priority.

We do a couple of interesting things in this example. First, we combine the old test-and-set idea with an explicit queue of lock waiters to make a more efficient lock. Second, we use a queue to help control who gets the lock next and thus avoid starvation.

You might notice how the guard is used (Figure 289, page 346), basically as a spin-lock around the flag and queue manipulations the lock is using. This approach thus doesn't avoid spin-waiting entirely; a thread might be interrupted while acquiring or releasing the lock, and thus cause other threads to spin-wait for this one to run again. However, the time spent spinning is quite limited (just a few instructions inside the lock and unlock code, instead of the user-defined critical section), and thus this approach may be reasonable.

You might also observe that in `lock()`, when a thread can not acquire the lock (it is already held), we are careful to add ourselves to a queue (by calling the `gettid()` function to get the thread ID of the current thread), set guard to 0, and yield the CPU. A question for the reader: What would happen if the release of the guard lock came *after* the `park()`, and not before? Hint: something bad.

You might further detect that the flag does not get set back to 0 when another thread gets woken up. Why is this? Well, it is not an error, but rather a necessity! When a thread is woken up, it will be as if it is returning from `park()`; however, it does not hold the guard at that point in the code and thus cannot even try to set the flag to 1. Thus, we just pass the lock directly from the thread releasing the lock to the next thread acquiring it; flag is not set to 0 in-between.

Finally, you might notice the perceived race condition in the solution, just before the call to `park()`. With just the wrong timing, a thread will be about to park, assuming that it should sleep until the lock is no longer held. A switch at that time to another thread (say, a thread holding the lock) could lead to trouble, for example, if that thread then released the lock. The subsequent park by the first thread would then sleep forever (potentially), a problem sometimes called the **wakeup/waiting race**.

Solaris solves this problem by adding a third system call: `setpark()`. By calling this routine, a thread can indicate it is *about to* park. If it then happens to be interrupted and another thread calls unpark before park is actually called, the subsequent park returns immediately instead of sleeping. The code modification, inside of `lock()`, is quite small:

```
    queue_add(m->q, gettid());
    setpark(); // new code
    m->guard = 0;
```

A different solution could pass the guard into the kernel. In that case, the kernel could take precautions to atomically release the lock and dequeue the running thread.

28.15 Different OS, Different Support

We have thus far seen one type of support that an OS can provide in order to build a more efficient lock in a thread library. Other OS's provide similar support; the details vary.

For example, Linux provides a **futex** which is similar to the Solaris interface but provides more in-kernel functionality. Specifically, each futex has associated with it a specific physical memory location, as well as a

```
void mutex_lock (int *mutex) {
  int v;
  /* Bit 31 was clear, we got the mutex (the fastpath) */
  if (atomic_bit_test_set (mutex, 31) == 0)
    return;
  atomic_increment (mutex);
  while (1) {
      if (atomic_bit_test_set (mutex, 31) == 0) {
          atomic_decrement (mutex);
          return;
      }
      /* We have to waitFirst make sure the futex value
         we are monitoring is truly negative (locked). */
      v = *mutex;
      if (v >= 0)
        continue;
      futex_wait (mutex, v);
  }
}

void mutex_unlock (int *mutex) {
  /* Adding 0x80000000 to counter results in 0 if and
     only if there are not other interested threads */
  if (atomic_add_zero (mutex, 0x80000000))
    return;

  /* There are other threads waiting for this mutex,
     wake one of them up.  */
  futex_wake (mutex);
}
```

Figure 2810: **Linux-based Futex Locks**

per-futex in-kernel queue. Callers can use futex calls (described below) to sleep and wake as need be.

Specifically, two calls are available. The call to `futex_wait(address, expected)` puts the calling thread to sleep, assuming the value at `address` is equal to `expected`. If it is *not* equal, the call returns immediately. The call to the routine `futex_wake(address)` wakes one thread that is waiting on the queue. The usage of these calls in a Linux mutex is shown in Figure 2810 (page 349).

This code snippet from `lowlevellock.h` in the nptl library (part of the gnu libc library) [L09] is interesting for a few reasons. First, it uses a single integer to track both whether the lock is held or not (the high bit of the integer) and the number of waiters on the lock (all the other bits). Thus, if the lock is negative, it is held (because the high bit is set and that bit determines the sign of the integer).

Second, the code snippet shows how to optimize for the common case, specifically when there is no contention for the lock; with only one thread acquiring and releasing a lock, very little work is done (the atomic bit test-and-set to lock and an atomic add to release the lock).

See if you can puzzle through the rest of this "real-world" lock to understand how it works. Do it and become a master of Linux locking, or at least somebody who listens when a book tells you to do something [3].

28.16 Two-Phase Locks

One final note: the Linux approach has the flavor of an old approach that has been used on and off for years, going at least as far back to Dahm Locks in the early 1960's [M82], and is now referred to as a **two-phase lock**. A two-phase lock realizes that spinning can be useful, particularly if the lock is about to be released. So in the first phase, the lock spins for a while, hoping that it can acquire the lock.

However, if the lock is not acquired during the first spin phase, a second phase is entered, where the caller is put to sleep, and only woken up when the lock becomes free later. The Linux lock above is a form of such a lock, but it only spins once; a generalization of this could spin in a loop for a fixed amount of time before using **futex** support to sleep.

Two-phase locks are yet another instance of a **hybrid** approach, where combining two good ideas may indeed yield a better one. Of course, whether it does depends strongly on many things, including the hardware environment, number of threads, and other workload details. As always, making a single general-purpose lock, good for all possible use cases, is quite a challenge.

28.17 Summary

The above approach shows how real locks are built these days: some hardware support (in the form of a more powerful instruction) plus some operating system support (e.g., in the form of `park()` and `unpark()` primitives on Solaris, or **futex** on Linux). Of course, the details differ, and the exact code to perform such locking is usually highly tuned. Check out the Solaris or Linux code bases if you want to see more details; they are a fascinating read [L09, S09]. Also see David et al.'s excellent work for a comparison of locking strategies on modern multiprocessors [D+13].

[3] Like buy a print copy of OSTEP! Even though the book is available for free online, wouldn't you just love a hard cover for your desk? Or, better yet, ten copies to share with friends and family? And maybe one extra copy to throw at an enemy? (the book *is* heavy, and thus chucking it is surprisingly effective)

References

[D91] "Just Win, Baby: Al Davis and His Raiders" by Glenn Dickey. Harcourt, 1991. *The book about Al Davis and his famous quote. Or, we suppose, the book is more about Al Davis and the Raiders, and not so much the quote. To be clear: we are not recommending this book, we just needed a citation.*

[D+13] "Everything You Always Wanted to Know about Synchronization but Were Afraid to Ask" by Tudor David, Rachid Guerraoui, Vasileios Trigonakis. SOSP '13, Nemacolin Woodlands Resort, Pennsylvania, November 2013. *An excellent paper comparing many different ways to build locks using hardware primitives. Great to see how many ideas work on modern hardware.*

[D68] "Cooperating sequential processes" by Edsger W. Dijkstra. 1968. Available online here: `http://www.cs.utexas.edu/users/EWD/ewd01xx/EWD123.PDF`. *One of the early seminal papers. Discusses how Dijkstra posed the original concurrency problem, and Dekker's solution.*

[H93] "MIPS R4000 Microprocessor User's Manual" by Joe Heinrich. Prentice-Hall, June 1993. Available: http://cag.csail.mit.edu/raw/documents/R4400_Uman_book_Ed2.pdf. *The old MIPS user's manual. Download it while it still exists.*

[H91] "Wait-free Synchronization" by Maurice Herlihy. ACM TOPLAS, Volume 13: 1, January 1991. *A landmark paper introducing a different approach to building concurrent data structures. Because of the complexity involved, some of these ideas have been slow to gain acceptance in deployment.*

[L81] "Observations on the Development of an Operating System" by Hugh Lauer. SOSP '81, Pacific Grove, California, December 1981. *A must-read retrospective about the development of the Pilot OS, an early PC operating system. Fun and full of insights.*

[L09] "glibc 2.9 (include Linux pthreads implementation)" by Many authors.. Available here: `http://ftp.gnu.org/gnu/glibc`. *In particular, take a look at the nptl subdirectory where you will find most of the pthread support in Linux today.*

[M82] "The Architecture of the Burroughs B5000: 20 Years Later and Still Ahead of the Times?" by A. Mayer. 1982. Available: `www.ajwm.net/amayer/papers/B5000.html`. *"It (RDLK) is an indivisible operation which reads from and writes into a memory location." RDLK is thus test-and-set! Dave Dahm created spin locks ("Buzz Locks") and a two-phase lock called "Dahm Locks."*

[M15] "OSSpinLock Is Unsafe" by J. McCall. `mjtsai.com/blog/2015/12/16/osspinlock-is-unsafe`. *Calling OSSpinLock on a Mac is unsafe when using threads of different priorities – you might spin forever! So be careful, Mac fanatics, even your mighty system can be less than perfect...*

[MS91] "Algorithms for Scalable Synchronization on Shared-Memory Multiprocessors" by John M. Mellor-Crummey and M. L. Scott. ACM TOCS, Volume 9, Issue 1, February 1991. *An excellent and thorough survey on different locking algorithms. However, no operating systems support is used, just fancy hardware instructions.*

[P81] "Myths About the Mutual Exclusion Problem" by G.L. Peterson. Information Processing Letters, 12(3), pages 115–116, 1981. *Peterson's algorithm introduced here.*

[R97] "What Really Happened on Mars?" by Glenn E. Reeves. `research.microsoft.com/en-us/um/people/mbj/Mars_Pathfinder/Authoritative_Account.html`. *A description of priority inversion on Mars Pathfinder. Concurrent code correctness matters, especially in space!*

[S05] "Guide to porting from Solaris to Linux on x86" by Ajay Sood, April 29, 2005. Available: `http://www.ibm.com/developerworks/linux/library/l-solar/`.

[S09] "OpenSolaris Thread Library" by Sun.. Code: `src.opensolaris.org/source/xref/onnv/onnv-gate/usr/src/lib/libc/port/threads/synch.c`. *Pretty interesting, although who knows what will happen now that Oracle owns Sun. Thanks to Mike Swift for the pointer.*

[W09] "Load-Link, Store-Conditional" by Many authors.. `en.wikipedia.org/wiki/Load-Link/Store-Conditional`. *Can you believe we referenced Wikipedia? But, we found the information there and it felt wrong not to. Further, it was useful, listing the instructions for the different architectures:* `ldl_l/stl_c` *and* `ldq_l/stq_c` *(Alpha),* `lwarx/stwcx` *(PowerPC),* `ll/sc` *(MIPS), and* `ldrex/strex` *(ARM). Actually Wikipedia is pretty amazing, so don't be so harsh, OK?*

[WG00] "The SPARC Architecture Manual: Version 9" by D. Weaver, T. Germond. SPARC International, 2000. `http://www.sparc.org/standards/SPARCV9.pdf`. *See* `developers.sun.com/solaris/articles/atomic_sparc/` *for more on atomics.*

Homework (Simulation)

This program, `x86.py`, allows you to see how different thread interleavings either cause or avoid race conditions. See the README for details on how the program works and answer the questions below.

Questions

1. Examine `flag.s`. This code "implements" locking with a single memory flag. Can you understand the assembly?
2. When you run with the defaults, does `flag.s` work? Use the `-M` and `-R` flags to trace variables and registers (and turn on `-c` to see their values). Can you predict what value will end up in `flag`?
3. Change the value of the register `%bx` with the `-a` flag (e.g., `-a bx=2,bx=2` if you are running just two threads). What does the code do? How does it change your answer for the question above?
4. Set `bx` to a high value for each thread, and then use the `-i` flag to generate different interrupt frequencies; what values lead to a bad outcomes? Which lead to good outcomes?
5. Now let's look at the program `test-and-set.s`. First, try to understand the code, which uses the `xchg` instruction to build a simple locking primitive. How is the lock acquire written? How about lock release?
6. Now run the code, changing the value of the interrupt interval (`-i`) again, and making sure to loop for a number of times. Does the code always work as expected? Does it sometimes lead to an inefficient use of the CPU? How could you quantify that?
7. Use the `-P` flag to generate specific tests of the locking code. For example, run a schedule that grabs the lock in the first thread, but then tries to acquire it in the second. Does the right thing happen? What else should you test?
8. Now let's look at the code in `peterson.s`, which implements Peterson's algorithm (mentioned in a sidebar in the text). Study the code and see if you can make sense of it.
9. Now run the code with different values of `-i`. What kinds of different behavior do you see? Make sure to set the thread IDs appropriately (using `-a bx=0,bx=1` for example) as the code assumes it.
10. Can you control the scheduling (with the `-P` flag) to "prove" that the code works? What are the different cases you should show hold? Think about mutual exclusion and deadlock avoidance.
11. Now study the code for the ticket lock in `ticket.s`. Does it match the code in the chapter? Then run with the following flags: `-a bx=1000,bx=1000` (causing each thread to loop through the critical section 1000 times). Watch what happens; do the threads spend much time spin-waiting for the lock?
12. How does the code behave as you add more threads?
13. Now examine `yield.s`, in which a `yield` instruction enables one thread to yield control of the CPU (realistically, this would be an OS primitive, but for the simplicity, we assume an instruction does the task). Find a scenario where `test-and-set.s` wastes cycles spinning, but `yield.s` does not. How many instructions are saved? In what scenarios do these savings arise?
14. Finally, examine `test-and-test-and-set.s`. What does this lock do? What kind of savings does it introduce as compared to `test-and-set.s`?

29

Lock-based Concurrent Data Structures

Before moving beyond locks, we'll first describe how to use locks in some common data structures. Adding locks to a data structure to make it usable by threads makes the structure **thread safe**. Of course, exactly how such locks are added determines both the correctness and performance of the data structure. And thus, our challenge:

> CRUX: HOW TO ADD LOCKS TO DATA STRUCTURES
>
> When given a particular data structure, how should we add locks to it, in order to make it work correctly? Further, how do we add locks such that the data structure yields high performance, enabling many threads to access the structure at once, i.e., **concurrently**?

Of course, we will be hard pressed to cover all data structures or all methods for adding concurrency, as this is a topic that has been studied for years, with (literally) thousands of research papers published about it. Thus, we hope to provide a sufficient introduction to the type of thinking required, and refer you to some good sources of material for further inquiry on your own. We found Moir and Shavit's survey to be a great source of information [MS04].

29.1 Concurrent Counters

One of the simplest data structures is a counter. It is a structure that is commonly used and has a simple interface. We define a simple non-concurrent counter in Figure 291.

Simple But Not Scalable

As you can see, the non-synchronized counter is a trivial data structure, requiring a tiny amount of code to implement. We now have our next challenge: how can we make this code **thread safe**? Figure 292 shows how we do so.

```
typedef struct __counter_t {
    int value;
} counter_t;

void init(counter_t *c) {
    c->value = 0;
}

void increment(counter_t *c) {
    c->value++;
}

void decrement(counter_t *c) {
    c->value--;
}

int get(counter_t *c) {
    return c->value;
}
```

Figure 291: **A Counter Without Locks**

This concurrent counter is simple and works correctly. In fact, it follows a design pattern common to the simplest and most basic concurrent data structures: it simply adds a single lock, which is acquired when calling a routine that manipulates the data structure, and is released when returning from the call. In this manner, it is similar to a data structure built with **monitors** [BH73], where locks are acquired and released automatically as you call and return from object methods.

At this point, you have a working concurrent data structure. The problem you might have is performance. If your data structure is too slow, you'll have to do more than just add a single lock; such optimizations, if needed, are thus the topic of the rest of the chapter. Note that if the data structure is *not* too slow, you are done! No need to do something fancy if something simple will work.

To understand the performance costs of the simple approach, we run a benchmark in which each thread updates a single shared counter a fixed number of times; we then vary the number of threads. Figure 295 shows the total time taken, with one to four threads active; each thread updates the counter one million times. This experiment was run upon an iMac with four Intel 2.7 GHz i5 CPUs; with more CPUs active, we hope to get more total work done per unit time.

From the top line in the figure (labeled 'Precise'), you can see that the performance of the synchronized counter scales poorly. Whereas a single thread can complete the million counter updates in a tiny amount of time (roughly 0.03 seconds), having two threads each update the counter one million times concurrently leads to a massive slowdown (taking over 5 seconds!). It only gets worse with more threads.

```
typedef struct __counter_t {
    int             value;
    pthread_mutex_t lock;
} counter_t;

void init(counter_t *c) {
    c->value = 0;
    Pthread_mutex_init(&c->lock, NULL);
}

void increment(counter_t *c) {
    Pthread_mutex_lock(&c->lock);
    c->value++;
    Pthread_mutex_unlock(&c->lock);
}

void decrement(counter_t *c) {
    Pthread_mutex_lock(&c->lock);
    c->value--;
    Pthread_mutex_unlock(&c->lock);
}

int get(counter_t *c) {
    Pthread_mutex_lock(&c->lock);
    int rc = c->value;
    Pthread_mutex_unlock(&c->lock);
    return rc;
}
```

Figure 292: **A Counter With Locks**

Ideally, you'd like to see the threads complete just as quickly on multiple processors as the single thread does on one. Achieving this end is called **perfect scaling**; even though more work is done, it is done in parallel, and hence the time taken to complete the task is not increased.

Scalable Counting

Amazingly, researchers have studied how to build more scalable counters for years [MS04]. Even more amazing is the fact that scalable counters matter, as recent work in operating system performance analysis has shown [B+10]; without scalable counting, some workloads running on Linux suffer from serious scalability problems on multicore machines.

Many techniques have been developed to attack this problem. We'll describe one approach known as an **approximate counter** [C06].

The approximate counter works by representing a single logical counter via numerous *local* physical counters, one per CPU core, as well as a single *global* counter. Specifically, on a machine with four CPUs, there are four

Time	L_1	L_2	L_3	L_4	G
0	0	0	0	0	0
1	0	0	1	1	0
2	1	0	2	1	0
3	2	0	3	1	0
4	3	0	3	2	0
5	4	1	3	3	0
6	$5 \to 0$	1	3	4	5 (from L_1)
7	0	2	4	$5 \to 0$	10 (from L_4)

Figure 293: **Tracing the Approximate Counters**

local counters and one global one. In addition to these counters, there are also locks: one for each local counter[1], and one for the global counter.

The basic idea of approximate counting is as follows. When a thread running on a given core wishes to increment the counter, it increments its local counter; access to this local counter is synchronized via the corresponding local lock. Because each CPU has its own local counter, threads across CPUs can update local counters without contention, and thus updates to the counter are scalable.

However, to keep the global counter up to date (in case a thread wishes to read its value), the local values are periodically transferred to the global counter, by acquiring the global lock and incrementing it by the local counter's value; the local counter is then reset to zero.

How often this local-to-global transfer occurs is determined by a threshold S. The smaller S is, the more the counter behaves like the non-scalable counter above; the bigger S is, the more scalable the counter, but the further off the global value might be from the actual count. One could simply acquire all the local locks and the global lock (in a specified order, to avoid deadlock) to get an exact value, but that is not scalable.

To make this clear, let's look at an example (Figure 293). In this example, the threshold S is set to 5, and there are threads on each of four CPUs updating their local counters L_1 ... L_4. The global counter value (G) is also shown in the trace, with time increasing downward. At each time step, a local counter may be incremented; if the local value reaches the threshold S, the local value is transferred to the global counter and the local counter is reset.

The lower line in Figure 295 (labeled 'Approximate', on page 358) shows the performance of approximate counters with a threshold S of 1024. Performance is excellent; the time taken to update the counter four million times on four processors is hardly higher than the time taken to update it one million times on one processor.

[1]We need the local locks because we assume there may be more than one thread on each core. If, instead, only one thread ran on each core, no local lock would be needed.

```
typedef struct __counter_t {
    int             global;          // global count
    pthread_mutex_t glock;           // global lock
    int             local[NUMCPUS];  // per-CPU count
    pthread_mutex_t llock[NUMCPUS];  // ... and locks
    int             threshold;       // update frequency
} counter_t;

// init: record threshold, init locks, init values
//       of all local counts and global count
void init(counter_t *c, int threshold) {
    c->threshold = threshold;
    c->global = 0;
    pthread_mutex_init(&c->glock, NULL);
    int i;
    for (i = 0; i < NUMCPUS; i++) {
        c->local[i] = 0;
        pthread_mutex_init(&c->llock[i], NULL);
    }
}

// update: usually, just grab local lock and update
// local amount; once local count has risen 'threshold',
// grab global lock and transfer local values to it
void update(counter_t *c, int threadID, int amt) {
    int cpu = threadID % NUMCPUS;
    pthread_mutex_lock(&c->llock[cpu]);
    c->local[cpu] += amt;
    if (c->local[cpu] >= c->threshold) {
        // transfer to global (assumes amt>0)
        pthread_mutex_lock(&c->glock);
        c->global += c->local[cpu];
        pthread_mutex_unlock(&c->glock);
        c->local[cpu] = 0;
    }
    pthread_mutex_unlock(&c->llock[cpu]);
}

// get: just return global amount (approximate)
int get(counter_t *c) {
    pthread_mutex_lock(&c->glock);
    int val = c->global;
    pthread_mutex_unlock(&c->glock);
    return val; // only approximate!
}
```

Figure 294: **Approximate Counter Implementation**

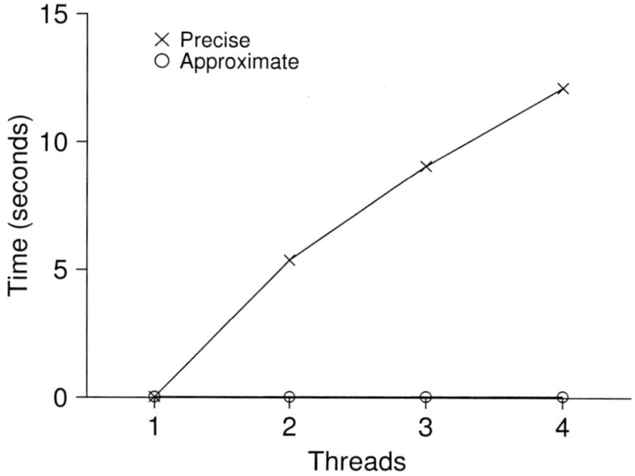

Figure 295: **Performance of Traditional vs. Approximate Counters**

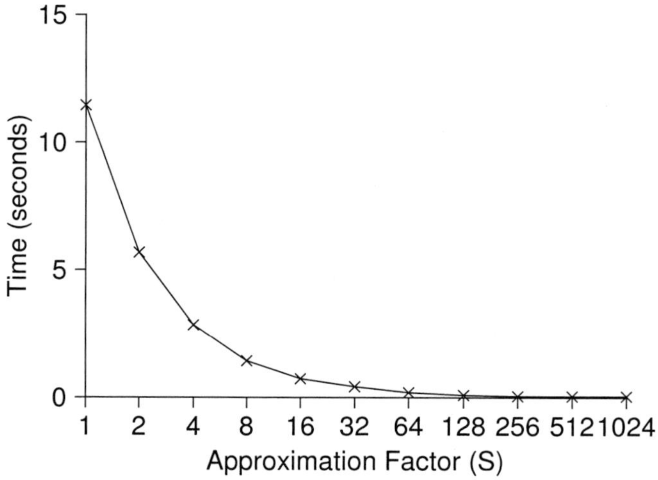

Figure 296: **Scaling Approximate Counters**

Figure 296 shows the importance of the threshold value S, with four threads each incrementing the counter 1 million times on four CPUs. If S is low, performance is poor (but the global count is always quite accurate); if S is high, performance is excellent, but the global count lags (by at most the number of CPUs multiplied by S). This accuracy/performance tradeoff is what approximate counters enable.

A rough version of an approximate counter is found in Figure 294 (page 357). Read it, or better yet, run it yourself in some experiments to better understand how it works.

TIP: MORE CONCURRENCY ISN'T NECESSARILY FASTER
If the scheme you design adds a lot of overhead (for example, by acquiring and releasing locks frequently, instead of once), the fact that it is more concurrent may not be important. Simple schemes tend to work well, especially if they use costly routines rarely. Adding more locks and complexity can be your downfall. All of that said, there is one way to really know: build both alternatives (simple but less concurrent, and complex but more concurrent) and measure how they do. In the end, you can't cheat on performance; your idea is either faster, or it isn't.

29.2 Concurrent Linked Lists

We next examine a more complicated structure, the linked list. Let's start with a basic approach once again. For simplicity, we'll omit some of the obvious routines that such a list would have and just focus on concurrent insert; we'll leave it to the reader to think about lookup, delete, and so forth. Figure 297 shows the code for this rudimentary data structure.

As you can see in the code, the code simply acquires a lock in the insert routine upon entry, and releases it upon exit. One small tricky issue arises if `malloc()` happens to fail (a rare case); in this case, the code must also release the lock before failing the insert.

This kind of exceptional control flow has been shown to be quite error prone; a recent study of Linux kernel patches found that a huge fraction of bugs (nearly 40%) are found on such rarely-taken code paths (indeed, this observation sparked some of our own research, in which we removed all memory-failing paths from a Linux file system, resulting in a more robust system [S+11]).

Thus, a challenge: can we rewrite the insert and lookup routines to remain correct under concurrent insert but avoid the case where the failure path also requires us to add the call to unlock?

The answer, in this case, is yes. Specifically, we can rearrange the code a bit so that the lock and release only surround the actual critical section in the insert code, and that a common exit path is used in the lookup code. The former works because part of the insert actually need not be locked; assuming that `malloc()` itself is thread-safe, each thread can call into it without worry of race conditions or other concurrency bugs. Only when updating the shared list does a lock need to be held. See Figure 298 for the details of these modifications.

As for the lookup routine, it is a simple code transformation to jump out of the main search loop to a single return path. Doing so again reduces the number of lock acquire/release points in the code, and thus decreases the chances of accidentally introducing bugs (such as forgetting to unlock before returning) into the code.

```
// basic node structure
typedef struct __node_t {
    int                key;
    struct __node_t        *next;
} node_t;

// basic list structure (one used per list)
typedef struct __list_t {
    node_t                *head;
    pthread_mutex_t     lock;
} list_t;

void List_Init(list_t *L) {
    L->head = NULL;
    pthread_mutex_init(&L->lock, NULL);
}

int List_Insert(list_t *L, int key) {
    pthread_mutex_lock(&L->lock);
    node_t *new = malloc(sizeof(node_t));
    if (new == NULL) {
        perror("malloc");
        pthread_mutex_unlock(&L->lock);
        return -1; // fail
    }
    new->key  = key;
    new->next = L->head;
    L->head   = new;
    pthread_mutex_unlock(&L->lock);
    return 0; // success
}

int List_Lookup(list_t *L, int key) {
    pthread_mutex_lock(&L->lock);
    node_t *curr = L->head;
    while (curr) {
        if (curr->key == key) {
            pthread_mutex_unlock(&L->lock);
            return 0; // success
        }
        curr = curr->next;
    }
    pthread_mutex_unlock(&L->lock);
    return -1; // failure
}
```

Figure 297: **Concurrent Linked List**

```
void List_Init(list_t *L) {
    L->head = NULL;
    pthread_mutex_init(&L->lock, NULL);
}

void List_Insert(list_t *L, int key) {
    // synchronization not needed
    node_t *new = malloc(sizeof(node_t));
    if (new == NULL) {
        perror("malloc");
        return;
    }
    new->key = key;

    // just lock critical section
    pthread_mutex_lock(&L->lock);
    new->next = L->head;
    L->head   = new;
    pthread_mutex_unlock(&L->lock);
}

int List_Lookup(list_t *L, int key) {
    int rv = -1;
    pthread_mutex_lock(&L->lock);
    node_t *curr = L->head;
    while (curr) {
        if (curr->key == key) {
            rv = 0;
            break;
        }
        curr = curr->next;
    }
    pthread_mutex_unlock(&L->lock);
    return rv; // now both success and failure
}
```

Figure 298: **Concurrent Linked List: Rewritten**

Scaling Linked Lists

Though we again have a basic concurrent linked list, once again we are in a situation where it does not scale particularly well. One technique that researchers have explored to enable more concurrency within a list is something called **hand-over-hand locking** (a.k.a. **lock coupling**) [MS04].

The idea is pretty simple. Instead of having a single lock for the entire list, you instead add a lock per node of the list. When traversing the list, the code first grabs the next node's lock and then releases the current node's lock (which inspires the name hand-over-hand).

> TIP: BE WARY OF LOCKS AND CONTROL FLOW
> A general design tip, which is useful in concurrent code as well as elsewhere, is to be wary of control flow changes that lead to function returns, exits, or other similar error conditions that halt the execution of a function. Because many functions will begin by acquiring a lock, allocating some memory, or doing other similar stateful operations, when errors arise, the code has to undo all of the state before returning, which is error-prone. Thus, it is best to structure code to minimize this pattern.

Conceptually, a hand-over-hand linked list makes some sense; it enables a high degree of concurrency in list operations. However, in practice, it is hard to make such a structure faster than the simple single lock approach, as the overheads of acquiring and releasing locks for each node of a list traversal is prohibitive. Even with very large lists, and a large number of threads, the concurrency enabled by allowing multiple ongoing traversals is unlikely to be faster than simply grabbing a single lock, performing an operation, and releasing it. Perhaps some kind of hybrid (where you grab a new lock every so many nodes) would be worth investigating.

29.3 Concurrent Queues

As you know by now, there is always a standard method to make a concurrent data structure: add a big lock. For a queue, we'll skip that approach, assuming you can figure it out.

Instead, we'll take a look at a slightly more concurrent queue designed by Michael and Scott [MS98]. The data structures and code used for this queue are found in Figure 299 on the following page.

If you study this code carefully, you'll notice that there are two locks, one for the head of the queue, and one for the tail. The goal of these two locks is to enable concurrency of enqueue and dequeue operations. In the common case, the enqueue routine will only access the tail lock, and dequeue only the head lock.

One trick used by Michael and Scott is to add a dummy node (allocated in the queue initialization code); this dummy enables the separation of head and tail operations. Study the code, or better yet, type it in, run it, and measure it, to understand how it works deeply.

Queues are commonly used in multi-threaded applications. However, the type of queue used here (with just locks) often does not completely meet the needs of such programs. A more fully developed bounded queue, that enables a thread to wait if the queue is either empty or overly full, is the subject of our intense study in the next chapter on condition variables. Watch for it!

```
typedef struct __node_t {
    int                 value;
    struct __node_t    *next;
} node_t;

typedef struct __queue_t {
    node_t              *head;
    node_t              *tail;
    pthread_mutex_t     head_lock, tail_lock;
}

void Queue_Init(queue_t *q) {
    node_t *tmp = malloc(sizeof(node_t));
    tmp->next = NULL;
    q->head = q->tail = tmp;
    pthread_mutex_init(&q->head_lock, NULL);
    pthread_mutex_init(&q->tail_lock, NULL);
}

void Queue_Enqueue(queue_t *q, int value) {
    node_t *tmp = malloc(sizeof(node_t));
    assert(tmp != NULL);
    tmp->value = value;
    tmp->next  = NULL;

    pthread_mutex_lock(&q->tail_lock);
    q->tail->next = tmp;
    q->tail = tmp;
    pthread_mutex_unlock(&q->tail_lock);
}

int Queue_Dequeue(queue_t *q, int *value) {
    pthread_mutex_lock(&q->head_lock);
    node_t *tmp = q->head;
    node_t *new_head = tmp->next;
    if (new_head == NULL) {
        pthread_mutex_unlock(&q->head_lock);
        return -1; // queue was empty
    }
    *value = new_head->value;
    q->head = new_head;
    pthread_mutex_unlock(&q->head_lock);
    free(tmp);
    return 0;
}
```

Figure 299: **Michael and Scott Concurrent Queue**

```
#define BUCKETS (101)

typedef struct __hash_t {
    list_t lists[BUCKETS];
} hash_t;

void Hash_Init(hash_t *H) {
    int i;
    for (i = 0; i < BUCKETS; i++)
        List_Init(&H->lists[i]);
}

int Hash_Insert(hash_t *H, int key) {
    return List_Insert(&H->lists[key % BUCKETS], key);
}

int Hash_Lookup(hash_t *H, int key) {
    return List_Lookup(&H->lists[key % BUCKETS], key);
}
```

Figure 2910: **A Concurrent Hash Table**

29.4 Concurrent Hash Table

We end our discussion with a simple and widely applicable concurrent data structure, the hash table. We'll focus on a simple hash table that does not resize; a little more work is required to handle resizing, which we leave as an exercise for the reader (sorry!).

This concurrent hash table (Figure 2910) is straightforward, is built using the concurrent lists we developed earlier, and works incredibly well. The reason for its good performance is that instead of having a single lock for the entire structure, it uses a lock per hash bucket (each of which is represented by a list). Doing so enables many concurrent operations to take place.

Figure 2911 shows the performance of the hash table under concurrent updates (from 10,000 to 50,000 concurrent updates from each of four threads, on the same iMac with four CPUs). Also shown, for the sake of comparison, is the performance of a linked list (with a single lock). As you can see from the graph, this simple concurrent hash table scales magnificently; the linked list, in contrast, does not.

29.5 Summary

We have introduced a sampling of concurrent data structures, from counters, to lists and queues, and finally to the ubiquitous and heavily-used hash table. We have learned a few important lessons along the way: to be careful with acquisition and release of locks around control flow

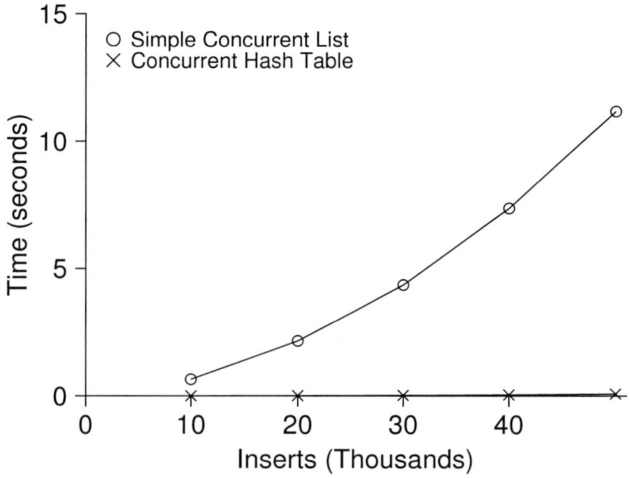

Figure 2911: **Scaling Hash Tables**

changes; that enabling more concurrency does not necessarily increase performance; that performance problems should only be remedied once they exist. This last point, of avoiding **premature optimization**, is central to any performance-minded developer; there is no value in making something faster if doing so will not improve the overall performance of the application.

Of course, we have just scratched the surface of high performance structures. See Moir and Shavit's excellent survey for more information, as well as links to other sources [MS04]. In particular, you might be interested in other structures (such as B-trees); for this knowledge, a database class is your best bet. You also might be interested in techniques that don't use traditional locks at all; such **non-blocking data structures** are something we'll get a taste of in the chapter on common concurrency bugs, but frankly this topic is an entire area of knowledge requiring more study than is possible in this humble book. Find out more on your own if you are interested (as always!).

TIP: AVOID PREMATURE OPTIMIZATION (KNUTH'S LAW)

When building a concurrent data structure, start with the most basic approach, which is to add a single big lock to provide synchronized access. By doing so, you are likely to build a *correct* lock; if you then find that it suffers from performance problems, you can refine it, thus only making it fast if need be. As **Knuth** famously stated, "Premature optimization is the root of all evil."

Many operating systems utilized a single lock when first transitioning to multiprocessors, including Sun OS and Linux. In the latter, this lock even had a name, the **big kernel lock** (**BKL**). For many years, this simple approach was a good one, but when multi-CPU systems became the norm, only allowing a single active thread in the kernel at a time became a performance bottleneck. Thus, it was finally time to add the optimization of improved concurrency to these systems. Within Linux, the more straightforward approach was taken: replace one lock with many. Within Sun, a more radical decision was made: build a brand new operating system, known as Solaris, that incorporates concurrency more fundamentally from day one. Read the Linux and Solaris kernel books for more information about these fascinating systems [BC05, MM00].

References

[B+10] "An Analysis of Linux Scalability to Many Cores" by Silas Boyd-Wickizer, Austin T. Clements, Yandong Mao, Aleksey Pesterev, M. Frans Kaashoek, Robert Morris, Nickolai Zeldovich . OSDI '10, Vancouver, Canada, October 2010. *A great study of how Linux performs on multicore machines, as well as some simple solutions. Includes a neat* ***sloppy counter*** *to solve one form of the scalable counting problem.*

[BH73] "Operating System Principles" by Per Brinch Hansen. Prentice-Hall, 1973. Available: `http://portal.acm.org/citation.cfm?id=540365`. *One of the first books on operating systems; certainly ahead of its time. Introduced monitors as a concurrency primitive.*

[BC05] "Understanding the Linux Kernel (Third Edition)" by Daniel P. Bovet and Marco Cesati. O'Reilly Media, November 2005. *The classic book on the Linux kernel. You should read it.*

[C06] "The Search For Fast, Scalable Counters" by Jonathan Corbet. February 1, 2006. Available: `https://lwn.net/Articles/170003`. *LWN has many wonderful articles about the latest in Linux This article is a short description of scalable approximate counting; read it, and others, to learn more about the latest in Linux.*

[L+13] "A Study of Linux File System Evolution" by Lanyue Lu, Andrea C. Arpaci-Dusseau, Remzi H. Arpaci-Dusseau, Shan Lu. FAST '13, San Jose, CA, February 2013. *Our paper that studies every patch to Linux file systems over nearly a decade. Lots of fun findings in there; read it to see! The work was painful to do though; the poor graduate student, Lanyue Lu, had to look through every single patch by hand in order to understand what they did.*

[MS98] "Nonblocking Algorithms and Preemption-safe Locking on by Multiprogrammed Shared-memory Multiprocessors. " M. Michael, M. Scott. Journal of Parallel and Distributed Computing, Vol. 51, No. 1, 1998 *Professor Scott and his students have been at the forefront of concurrent algorithms and data structures for many years; check out his web page, numerous papers, or books to find out more.*

[MS04] "Concurrent Data Structures" by Mark Moir and Nir Shavit. In Handbook of Data Structures and Applications (Editors D. Metha and S.Sahni). Chapman and Hall/CRC Press, 2004. Available: `www.cs.tau.ac.il/~shanir/concurrent-data-structures.pdf`. *A short but relatively comprehensive reference on concurrent data structures. Though it is missing some of the latest works in the area (due to its age), it remains an incredibly useful reference.*

[MM00] "Solaris Internals: Core Kernel Architecture" by Jim Mauro and Richard McDougall. Prentice Hall, October 2000. *The Solaris book. You should also read this, if you want to learn about something other than Linux.*

[S+11] "Making the Common Case the Only Case with Anticipatory Memory Allocation" by Swaminathan Sundararaman, Yupu Zhang, Sriram Subramanian, Andrea C. Arpaci-Dusseau, Remzi H. Arpaci-Dusseau . FAST '11, San Jose, CA, February 2011. *Our work on removing possibly-failing allocation calls from kernel code paths. By allocating all potentially needed memory before doing any work, we avoid failure deep down in the storage stack.*

Homework (Code)

In this homework, you'll gain some experience with writing concurrent code and measuring its performance. Learning to build code that performs well is a critical skill and thus gaining a little experience here with it is quite worthwhile.

Questions

1. We'll start by redoing the measurements within this chapter. Use the call `gettimeofday()` to measure time within your program. How accurate is this timer? What is the smallest interval it can measure? Gain confidence in its workings, as we will need it in all subsequent questions. You can also look into other timers, such as the cycle counter available on x86 via the `rdtsc` instruction.

2. Now, build a simple concurrent counter and measure how long it takes to increment the counter many times as the number of threads increases. How many CPUs are available on the system you are using? Does this number impact your measurements at all?

3. Next, build a version of the sloppy counter. Once again, measure its performance as the number of threads varies, as well as the threshold. Do the numbers match what you see in the chapter?

4. Build a version of a linked list that uses hand-over-hand locking [MS04], as cited in the chapter. You should read the paper first to understand how it works, and then implement it. Measure its performance. When does a hand-over-hand list work better than a standard list as shown in the chapter?

5. Pick your favorite interesting data structure, such as a B-tree or other slightly more interested structure. Implement it, and start with a simple locking strategy such as a single lock. Measure its performance as the number of concurrent threads increases.

6. Finally, think of a more interesting locking strategy for this favorite data structure of yours. Implement it, and measure its performance. How does it compare to the straightforward locking approach?

30

Condition Variables

Thus far we have developed the notion of a lock and seen how one can be properly built with the right combination of hardware and OS support. Unfortunately, locks are not the only primitives that are needed to build concurrent programs.

In particular, there are many cases where a thread wishes to check whether a **condition** is true before continuing its execution. For example, a parent thread might wish to check whether a child thread has completed before continuing (this is often called a `join()`); how should such a wait be implemented? Let's look at Figure 301.

```
void *child(void *arg) {
    printf("child\n");
    // XXX how to indicate we are done?
    return NULL;
}

int main(int argc, char *argv[]) {
    printf("parent: begin\n");
    pthread_t c;
    Pthread_create(&c, NULL, child, NULL); // create child
    // XXX how to wait for child?
    printf("parent: end\n");
    return 0;
}
```

Figure 301: **A Parent Waiting For Its Child**

What we would like to see here is the following output:

```
parent: begin
child
parent: end
```

We could try using a shared variable, as you see in Figure 302. This solution will generally work, but it is hugely inefficient as the parent spins

```
volatile int done = 0;

void *child(void *arg) {
    printf("child\n");
    done = 1;
    return NULL;
}

int main(int argc, char *argv[]) {
    printf("parent: begin\n");
    pthread_t c;
    Pthread_create(&c, NULL, child, NULL); // create child
    while (done == 0)
        ; // spin
    printf("parent: end\n");
    return 0;
}
```

Figure 302: **Parent Waiting For Child: Spin-based Approach**

and wastes CPU time. What we would like here instead is some way to put the parent to sleep until the condition we are waiting for (e.g., the child is done executing) comes true.

> THE CRUX: HOW TO WAIT FOR A CONDITION
>
> In multi-threaded programs, it is often useful for a thread to wait for some condition to become true before proceeding. The simple approach, of just spinning until the condition becomes true, is grossly inefficient and wastes CPU cycles, and in some cases, can be incorrect. Thus, how should a thread wait for a condition?

30.1 Definition and Routines

To wait for a condition to become true, a thread can make use of what is known as a **condition variable**. A **condition variable** is an explicit queue that threads can put themselves on when some state of execution (i.e., some **condition**) is not as desired (by **waiting** on the condition); some other thread, when it changes said state, can then wake one (or more) of those waiting threads and thus allow them to continue (by **signaling** on the condition). The idea goes back to Dijkstra's use of "private semaphores" [D68]; a similar idea was later named a "condition variable" by Hoare in his work on monitors [H74].

To declare such a condition variable, one simply writes something like this: `pthread_cond_t c;`, which declares `c` as a condition variable (note: proper initialization is also required). A condition variable has two operations associated with it: `wait()` and `signal()`. The `wait()` call is executed when a thread wishes to put itself to sleep; the `signal()` call

```
int done  = 0;
pthread_mutex_t m = PTHREAD_MUTEX_INITIALIZER;
pthread_cond_t c  = PTHREAD_COND_INITIALIZER;

void thr_exit() {
    Pthread_mutex_lock(&m);
    done = 1;
    Pthread_cond_signal(&c);
    Pthread_mutex_unlock(&m);
}

void *child(void *arg) {
    printf("child\n");
    thr_exit();
    return NULL;
}

void thr_join() {
    Pthread_mutex_lock(&m);
    while (done == 0)
        Pthread_cond_wait(&c, &m);
    Pthread_mutex_unlock(&m);
}

int main(int argc, char *argv[]) {
    printf("parent: begin\n");
    pthread_t p;
    Pthread_create(&p, NULL, child, NULL);
    thr_join();
    printf("parent: end\n");
    return 0;
}
```

Figure 30.3: **Parent Waiting For Child: Use A Condition Variable**

is executed when a thread has changed something in the program and thus wants to wake a sleeping thread waiting on this condition. Specifically, the POSIX calls look like this:

```
pthread_cond_wait(pthread_cond_t *c, pthread_mutex_t *m);
pthread_cond_signal(pthread_cond_t *c);
```

We will often refer to these as `wait()` and `signal()` for simplicity. One thing you might notice about the `wait()` call is that it also takes a mutex as a parameter; it assumes that this mutex is locked when `wait()` is called. The responsibility of `wait()` is to release the lock and put the calling thread to sleep (atomically); when the thread wakes up (after some other thread has signaled it), it must re-acquire the lock before returning to the caller. This complexity stems from the desire to prevent certain race conditions from occurring when a thread is trying to put itself to sleep. Let's take a look at the solution to the join problem (Figure 303) to understand this better.

There are two cases to consider. In the first, the parent creates the child thread but continues running itself (assume we have only a single processor) and thus immediately calls into `thr_join()` to wait for the child thread to complete. In this case, it will acquire the lock, check if the child is done (it is not), and put itself to sleep by calling `wait()` (hence releasing the lock). The child will eventually run, print the message "child", and call `thr_exit()` to wake the parent thread; this code just grabs the lock, sets the state variable `done`, and signals the parent thus waking it. Finally, the parent will run (returning from `wait()` with the lock held), unlock the lock, and print the final message "parent: end".

In the second case, the child runs immediately upon creation, sets `done` to 1, calls signal to wake a sleeping thread (but there is none, so it just returns), and is done. The parent then runs, calls `thr_join()`, sees that `done` is 1, and thus does not wait and returns.

One last note: you might observe the parent uses a `while` loop instead of just an `if` statement when deciding whether to wait on the condition. While this does not seem strictly necessary per the logic of the program, it is always a good idea, as we will see below.

To make sure you understand the importance of each piece of the `thr_exit()` and `thr_join()` code, let's try a few alternate implementations. First, you might be wondering if we need the state variable `done`. What if the code looked like the example below? (Figure 304)

Unfortunately this approach is broken. Imagine the case where the child runs immediately and calls `thr_exit()` immediately; in this case, the child will signal, but there is no thread asleep on the condition. When the parent runs, it will simply call wait and be stuck; no thread will ever wake it. From this example, you should appreciate the importance of the state variable `done`; it records the value the threads are interested in knowing. The sleeping, waking, and locking all are built around it.

```
void thr_exit() {
    Pthread_mutex_lock(&m);
    Pthread_cond_signal(&c);
    Pthread_mutex_unlock(&m);
}

void thr_join() {
    Pthread_mutex_lock(&m);
    Pthread_cond_wait(&c, &m);
    Pthread_mutex_unlock(&m);
}
```

Figure 304: **Parent Waiting: No State Variable**

```
void thr_exit() {
    done = 1;
    Pthread_cond_signal(&c);
}

void thr_join() {
    if (done == 0)
        Pthread_cond_wait(&c);
}
```

Figure 305: **Parent Waiting: No Lock**

Here (Figure 305) is another poor implementation. In this example, we imagine that one does not need to hold a lock in order to signal and wait. What problem could occur here? Think about it[1]!

The issue here is a subtle race condition. Specifically, if the parent calls `thr_join()` and then checks the value of `done`, it will see that it is 0 and thus try to go to sleep. But just before it calls wait to go to sleep, the parent is interrupted, and the child runs. The child changes the state variable `done` to 1 and signals, but no thread is waiting and thus no thread is woken. When the parent runs again, it sleeps forever, which is sad.

Hopefully, from this simple join example, you can see some of the basic requirements of using condition variables properly. To make sure you understand, we now go through a more complicated example: the **producer/consumer** or **bounded-buffer** problem.

TIP: ALWAYS HOLD THE LOCK WHILE SIGNALING

Although it is strictly not necessary in all cases, it is likely simplest and best to hold the lock while signaling when using condition variables. The example above shows a case where you *must* hold the lock for correctness; however, there are some other cases where it is likely OK not to, but probably is something you should avoid. Thus, for simplicity, **hold the lock when calling signal**.

The converse of this tip, i.e., hold the lock when calling wait, is not just a tip, but rather mandated by the semantics of wait, because wait always (a) assumes the lock is held when you call it, (b) releases said lock when putting the caller to sleep, and (c) re-acquires the lock just before returning. Thus, the generalization of this tip is correct: **hold the lock when calling signal or wait**, and you will always be in good shape.

[1]Note that this example is not "real" code, because the call to `pthread_cond_wait()` always requires a mutex as well as a condition variable; here, we just pretend that the interface does not do so for the sake of the negative example.

```c
int buffer;
int count = 0; // initially, empty

void put(int value) {
    assert(count == 0);
    count = 1;
    buffer = value;
}

int get() {
    assert(count == 1);
    count = 0;
    return buffer;
}
```

Figure 306: **The Put And Get Routines (v1)**

30.2 The Producer/Consumer (Bounded Buffer) Problem

The next synchronization problem we will confront in this chapter is known as the **producer/consumer** problem, or sometimes as the **bounded buffer** problem, which was first posed by Dijkstra [D72]. Indeed, it was this very producer/consumer problem that led Dijkstra and his co-workers to invent the generalized semaphore (which can be used as either a lock or a condition variable) [D01]; we will learn more about semaphores later.

Imagine one or more producer threads and one or more consumer threads. Producers generate data items and place them in a buffer; consumers grab said items from the buffer and consume them in some way.

This arrangement occurs in many real systems. For example, in a multi-threaded web server, a producer puts HTTP requests into a work queue (i.e., the bounded buffer); consumer threads take requests out of this queue and process them.

A bounded buffer is also used when you pipe the output of one program into another, e.g., `grep foo file.txt | wc -l`. This example runs two processes concurrently; `grep` writes lines from `file.txt` with the string `foo` in them to what it thinks is standard output; the UNIX shell redirects the output to what is called a UNIX pipe (created by the **pipe** system call). The other end of this pipe is connected to the standard input of the process `wc`, which simply counts the number of lines in the input stream and prints out the result. Thus, the `grep` process is the producer; the `wc` process is the consumer; between them is an in-kernel bounded buffer; you, in this example, are just the happy user.

Because the bounded buffer is a shared resource, we must of course require synchronized access to it, lest[2] a race condition arise. To begin to understand this problem better, let us examine some actual code.

The first thing we need is a shared buffer, into which a producer puts data, and out of which a consumer takes data. Let's just use a single

[2] This is where we drop some serious Old English on you, and the subjunctive form.

```
void *producer(void *arg) {
    int i;
    int loops = (int) arg;
    for (i = 0; i < loops; i++) {
        put(i);
    }
}

void *consumer(void *arg) {
    while (1) {
        int tmp = get();
        printf("%d\n", tmp);
    }
}
```

Figure 307: **Producer/Consumer Threads (v1)**

integer for simplicity (you can certainly imagine placing a pointer to a data structure into this slot instead), and the two inner routines to put a value into the shared buffer, and to get a value out of the buffer. See Figure 306 (page 374) for details.

Pretty simple, no? The `put()` routine assumes the buffer is empty (and checks this with an assertion), and then simply puts a value into the shared buffer and marks it full by setting `count` to 1. The `get()` routine does the opposite, setting the buffer to empty (i.e., setting `count` to 0) and returning the value. Don't worry that this shared buffer has just a single entry; later, we'll generalize it to a queue that can hold multiple entries, which will be even more fun than it sounds.

Now we need to write some routines that know when it is OK to access the buffer to either put data into it or get data out of it. The conditions for this should be obvious: only put data into the buffer when `count` is zero (i.e., when the buffer is empty), and only get data from the buffer when `count` is one (i.e., when the buffer is full). If we write the synchronization code such that a producer puts data into a full buffer, or a consumer gets data from an empty one, we have done something wrong (and in this code, an assertion will fire).

This work is going to be done by two types of threads, one set of which we'll call the **producer** threads, and the other set which we'll call **consumer** threads. Figure 307 shows the code for a producer that puts an integer into the shared buffer `loops` number of times, and a consumer that gets the data out of that shared buffer (forever), each time printing out the data item it pulled from the shared buffer.

A Broken Solution

Now imagine that we have just a single producer and a single consumer. Obviously the `put()` and `get()` routines have critical sections within them, as `put()` updates the buffer, and `get()` reads from it. However, putting a lock around the code doesn't work; we need something more.

```
int loops; // must initialize somewhere...
cond_t  cond;
mutex_t mutex;

void *producer(void *arg) {
    int i;
    for (i = 0; i < loops; i++) {
        Pthread_mutex_lock(&mutex);           // p1
        if (count == 1)                       // p2
            Pthread_cond_wait(&cond, &mutex); // p3
        put(i);                               // p4
        Pthread_cond_signal(&cond);           // p5
        Pthread_mutex_unlock(&mutex);         // p6
    }
}

void *consumer(void *arg) {
    int i;
    for (i = 0; i < loops; i++) {
        Pthread_mutex_lock(&mutex);           // c1
        if (count == 0)                       // c2
            Pthread_cond_wait(&cond, &mutex); // c3
        int tmp = get();                      // c4
        Pthread_cond_signal(&cond);           // c5
        Pthread_mutex_unlock(&mutex);         // c6
        printf("%d\n", tmp);
    }
}
```

Figure 308: **Producer/Consumer: Single CV And If Statement**

Not surprisingly, that something more is some condition variables. In this (broken) first try (Figure 308), we have a single condition variable `cond` and associated lock `mutex`.

Let's examine the signaling logic between producers and consumers. When a producer wants to fill the buffer, it waits for it to be empty (p1–p3). The consumer has the exact same logic, but waits for a different condition: fullness (c1–c3).

With just a single producer and a single consumer, the code in Figure 308 works. However, if we have more than one of these threads (e.g., two consumers), the solution has two critical problems. What are they?

... *(pause here to think)* ...

Let's understand the first problem, which has to do with the `if` statement before the wait. Assume there are two consumers (T_{c1} and T_{c2}) and one producer (T_p). First, a consumer (T_{c1}) runs; it acquires the lock (c1), checks if any buffers are ready for consumption (c2), and finding that none are, waits (c3) (which releases the lock).

Then the producer (T_p) runs. It acquires the lock (p1), checks if all

T_{c1}	State	T_{c2}	State	T_p	State	**Count**	*Comment*
c1	Run		Ready		Ready	0	
c2	Run		Ready		Ready	0	
c3	Sleep		Ready		Ready	0	Nothing to get
	Sleep		Ready	p1	Run	0	
	Sleep		Ready	p2	Run	0	
	Sleep		Ready	p4	Run	1	Buffer now full
	Ready		Ready	p5	Run	1	T_{c1} awoken
	Ready		Ready	p6	Run	1	
	Ready		Ready	p1	Run	1	
	Ready		Ready	p2	Run	1	
	Ready		Ready	p3	Sleep	1	Buffer full; sleep
	Ready	c1	Run		Sleep	1	T_{c2} sneaks in ...
	Ready	c2	Run		Sleep	1	
	Ready	c4	Run		Sleep	0	... and grabs data
	Ready	c5	Run		Ready	0	T_p awoken
	Ready	c6	Run		Ready	0	
c4	Run		Ready		Ready	0	Oh oh! No data

Figure 309: **Thread Trace: Broken Solution (v1)**

buffers are full (p2), and finding that not to be the case, goes ahead and fills the buffer (p4). The producer then signals that a buffer has been filled (p5). Critically, this moves the first consumer (T_{c1}) from sleeping on a condition variable to the ready queue; T_{c1} is now able to run (but not yet running). The producer then continues until realizing the buffer is full, at which point it sleeps (p6, p1–p3).

Here is where the problem occurs: another consumer (T_{c2}) sneaks in and consumes the one existing value in the buffer (c1, c2, c4, c5, c6, skipping the wait at c3 because the buffer is full). Now assume T_{c1} runs; just before returning from the wait, it re-acquires the lock and then returns. It then calls `get()` (c4), but there are no buffers to consume! An assertion triggers, and the code has not functioned as desired. Clearly, we should have somehow prevented T_{c1} from trying to consume because T_{c2} snuck in and consumed the one value in the buffer that had been produced. Figure 309 shows the action each thread takes, as well as its scheduler state (Ready, Running, or Sleeping) over time.

The problem arises for a simple reason: after the producer woke T_{c1}, but *before* T_{c1} ever ran, the state of the bounded buffer changed (thanks to T_{c2}). Signaling a thread only wakes them up; it is thus a *hint* that the state of the world has changed (in this case, that a value has been placed in the buffer), but there is no guarantee that when the woken thread runs, the state will *still* be as desired. This interpretation of what a signal means is often referred to as **Mesa semantics**, after the first research that built a condition variable in such a manner [LR80]; the contrast, referred to as

```
int loops;
cond_t  cond;
mutex_t mutex;

void *producer(void *arg) {
    int i;
    for (i = 0; i < loops; i++) {
        Pthread_mutex_lock(&mutex);           // p1
        while (count == 1)                    // p2
            Pthread_cond_wait(&cond, &mutex); // p3
        put(i);                               // p4
        Pthread_cond_signal(&cond);           // p5
        Pthread_mutex_unlock(&mutex);         // p6
    }
}

void *consumer(void *arg) {
    int i;
    for (i = 0; i < loops; i++) {
        Pthread_mutex_lock(&mutex);           // c1
        while (count == 0)                    // c2
            Pthread_cond_wait(&cond, &mutex); // c3
        int tmp = get();                      // c4
        Pthread_cond_signal(&cond);           // c5
        Pthread_mutex_unlock(&mutex);         // c6
        printf("%d\n", tmp);
    }
}
```

Figure 30.10: **Producer/Consumer: Single CV And While**

Hoare semantics, is harder to build but provides a stronger guarantee that the woken thread will run immediately upon being woken [H74]. Virtually every system ever built employs Mesa semantics.

Better, But Still Broken: While, Not If

Fortunately, this fix is easy (Figure 30.10): change the `if` to a `while`. Think about why this works; now consumer T_{c1} wakes up and (with the lock held) immediately re-checks the state of the shared variable (c2). If the buffer is empty at that point, the consumer simply goes back to sleep (c3). The corollary `if` is also changed to a `while` in the producer (p2).

Thanks to Mesa semantics, a simple rule to remember with condition variables is to **always use while loops**. Sometimes you don't have to re-check the condition, but it is always safe to do so; just do it and be happy.

However, this code still has a bug, the second of two problems mentioned above. Can you see it? It has something to do with the fact that there is only one condition variable. Try to figure out what the problem is, before reading ahead. DO IT! *(pause for you to think, or close your eyes...)*

T_{c1}	State	T_{c2}	State	T_p	State	Count	*Comment*
c1	Run		Ready		Ready	0	
c2	Run		Ready		Ready	0	
c3	Sleep		Ready		Ready	0	Nothing to get
	Sleep	c1	Run		Ready	0	
	Sleep	c2	Run		Ready	0	
	Sleep	c3	Sleep		Ready	0	Nothing to get
	Sleep		Sleep	p1	Run	0	
	Sleep		Sleep	p2	Run	0	
	Sleep		Sleep	p4	Run	1	Buffer now full
	Ready		Sleep	p5	Run	1	T_{c1} awoken
	Ready		Sleep	p6	Run	1	
	Ready		Sleep	p1	Run	1	
	Ready		Sleep	p2	Run	1	
	Ready		Sleep	p3	Sleep	1	Must sleep (full)
c2	Run		Sleep		Sleep	1	Recheck condition
c4	Run		Sleep		Sleep	0	T_{c1} grabs data
c5	Run		Ready		Sleep	0	Oops! Woke T_{c2}
c6	Run		Ready		Sleep	0	
c1	Run		Ready		Sleep	0	
c2	Run		Ready		Sleep	0	
c3	Sleep		Ready		Sleep	0	Nothing to get
	Sleep	c2	Run		Sleep	0	
	Sleep	c3	Sleep		Sleep	0	Everyone asleep...

Figure 3011: **Thread Trace: Broken Solution (v2)**

Let's confirm you figured it out correctly, or perhaps let's confirm that you are now awake and reading this part of the book. The problem occurs when two consumers run first (T_{c1} and T_{c2}) and both go to sleep (c3). Then, the producer runs, puts a value in the buffer, and wakes one of the consumers (say T_{c1}). The producer then loops back (releasing and reacquiring the lock along the way) and tries to put more data in the buffer; because the buffer is full, the producer instead waits on the condition (thus sleeping). Now, one consumer is ready to run (T_{c1}), and two threads are sleeping on a condition (T_{c2} and T_p). We are about to cause a problem: things are getting exciting!

The consumer T_{c1} then wakes by returning from `wait()` (c3), re-checks the condition (c2), and finding the buffer full, consumes the value (c4). This consumer then, critically, signals on the condition (c5), waking *only one* thread that is sleeping. However, which thread should it wake?

Because the consumer has emptied the buffer, it clearly should wake the producer. However, if it wakes the consumer T_{c2} (which is definitely possible, depending on how the wait queue is managed), we have a problem. Specifically, the consumer T_{c2} will wake up and find the buffer empty (c2), and go back to sleep (c3). The producer T_p, which has a value

```
cond_t  empty, fill;
mutex_t mutex;

void *producer(void *arg) {
    int i;
    for (i = 0; i < loops; i++) {
        Pthread_mutex_lock(&mutex);
        while (count == 1)
            Pthread_cond_wait(&empty, &mutex);
        put(i);
        Pthread_cond_signal(&fill);
        Pthread_mutex_unlock(&mutex);
    }
}

void *consumer(void *arg) {
    int i;
    for (i = 0; i < loops; i++) {
        Pthread_mutex_lock(&mutex);
        while (count == 0)
            Pthread_cond_wait(&fill, &mutex);
        int tmp = get();
        Pthread_cond_signal(&empty);
        Pthread_mutex_unlock(&mutex);
        printf("%d\n", tmp);
    }
}
```

Figure 3012: **Producer/Consumer: Two CVs And While**

to put into the buffer, is left sleeping. The other consumer thread, T_{c1}, also goes back to sleep. All three threads are left sleeping, a clear bug; see Figure 3011 for the brutal step-by-step of this terrible calamity.

Signaling is clearly needed, but must be more directed. A consumer should not wake other consumers, only producers, and vice-versa.

The Single Buffer Producer/Consumer Solution

The solution here is once again a small one: use *two* condition variables, instead of one, in order to properly signal which type of thread should wake up when the state of the system changes. Figure 3012 shows the resulting code.

In the code, producer threads wait on the condition **empty**, and signals **fill**. Conversely, consumer threads wait on **fill** and signal **empty**. By doing so, the second problem above is avoided by design: a consumer can never accidentally wake a consumer, and a producer can never accidentally wake a producer.

```
int buffer[MAX];
int fill_ptr = 0;
int use_ptr  = 0;
int count    = 0;

void put(int value) {
    buffer[fill_ptr] = value;
    fill_ptr = (fill_ptr + 1) % MAX;
    count++;
}

int get() {
    int tmp = buffer[use_ptr];
    use_ptr = (use_ptr + 1) % MAX;
    count--;
    return tmp;
}
```

Figure 3013: **The Correct Put And Get Routines**

```
cond_t empty, fill;
mutex_t mutex;

void *producer(void *arg) {
    int i;
    for (i = 0; i < loops; i++) {
        Pthread_mutex_lock(&mutex);                // p1
        while (count == MAX)                       // p2
            Pthread_cond_wait(&empty, &mutex);     // p3
        put(i);                                    // p4
        Pthread_cond_signal(&fill);                // p5
        Pthread_mutex_unlock(&mutex);              // p6
    }
}

void *consumer(void *arg) {
    int i;
    for (i = 0; i < loops; i++) {
        Pthread_mutex_lock(&mutex);                // c1
        while (count == 0)                         // c2
            Pthread_cond_wait(&fill, &mutex);      // c3
        int tmp = get();                           // c4
        Pthread_cond_signal(&empty);               // c5
        Pthread_mutex_unlock(&mutex);              // c6
        printf("%d\n", tmp);
    }
}
```

Figure 3014: **The Correct Producer/Consumer Synchronization**

> **TIP: USE WHILE (NOT IF) FOR CONDITIONS**
> When checking for a condition in a multi-threaded program, using a `while` loop is always correct; using an `if` statement only might be, depending on the semantics of signaling. Thus, always use `while` and your code will behave as expected.
> Using while loops around conditional checks also handles the case where **spurious wakeups** occur. In some thread packages, due to details of the implementation, it is possible that two threads get woken up though just a single signal has taken place [L11]. Spurious wakeups are further reason to re-check the condition a thread is waiting on.

The Correct Producer/Consumer Solution

We now have a working producer/consumer solution, albeit not a fully general one. The last change we make is to enable more concurrency and efficiency; specifically, we add more buffer slots, so that multiple values can be produced before sleeping, and similarly multiple values can be consumed before sleeping. With just a single producer and consumer, this approach is more efficient as it reduces context switches; with multiple producers or consumers (or both), it even allows concurrent producing or consuming to take place, thus increasing concurrency. Fortunately, it is a small change from our current solution.

The first change for this correct solution is within the buffer structure itself and the corresponding `put()` and `get()` (Figure 3013). We also slightly change the conditions that producers and consumers check in order to determine whether to sleep or not. We also show the correct waiting and signaling logic (Figure 3014). A producer only sleeps if all buffers are currently filled (p2); similarly, a consumer only sleeps if all buffers are currently empty (c2). And thus we solve the producer/consumer problem; time to sit back and drink a cold one.

30.3 Covering Conditions

We'll now look at one more example of how condition variables can be used. This code study is drawn from Lampson and Redell's paper on Pilot [LR80], the same group who first implemented the **Mesa semantics** described above (the language they used was Mesa, hence the name).

The problem they ran into is best shown via simple example, in this case in a simple multi-threaded memory allocation library. Figure 3015 shows a code snippet which demonstrates the issue.

As you might see in the code, when a thread calls into the memory allocation code, it might have to wait in order for more memory to become free. Conversely, when a thread frees memory, it signals that more memory is free. However, our code above has a problem: which waiting thread (there can be more than one) should be woken up?

```
// how many bytes of the heap are free?
int bytesLeft = MAX_HEAP_SIZE;

// need lock and condition too
cond_t  c;
mutex_t m;

void *
allocate(int size) {
    Pthread_mutex_lock(&m);
    while (bytesLeft < size)
        Pthread_cond_wait(&c, &m);
    void *ptr = ...; // get mem from heap
    bytesLeft -= size;
    Pthread_mutex_unlock(&m);
    return ptr;
}

void free(void *ptr, int size) {
    Pthread_mutex_lock(&m);
    bytesLeft += size;
    Pthread_cond_signal(&c); // whom to signal??
    Pthread_mutex_unlock(&m);
}
```

Figure 3015: **Covering Conditions: An Example**

Consider the following scenario. Assume there are zero bytes free; thread T_a calls `allocate(100)`, followed by thread T_b which asks for less memory by calling `allocate(10)`. Both T_a and T_b thus wait on the condition and go to sleep; there aren't enough free bytes to satisfy either of these requests.

At that point, assume a third thread, T_c, calls `free(50)`. Unfortunately, when it calls signal to wake a waiting thread, it might not wake the correct waiting thread, T_b, which is waiting for only 10 bytes to be freed; T_a should remain waiting, as not enough memory is yet free. Thus, the code in the figure does not work, as the thread waking other threads does not know which thread (or threads) to wake up.

The solution suggested by Lampson and Redell is straightforward: replace the `pthread_cond_signal()` call in the code above with a call to `pthread_cond_broadcast()`, which wakes up *all* waiting threads. By doing so, we guarantee that any threads that should be woken are. The downside, of course, can be a negative performance impact, as we might needlessly wake up many other waiting threads that shouldn't (yet) be awake. Those threads will simply wake up, re-check the condition, and then go immediately back to sleep.

Lampson and Redell call such a condition a **covering condition**, as it covers all the cases where a thread needs to wake up (conservatively); the cost, as we've discussed, is that too many threads might be woken.

The astute reader might also have noticed we could have used this approach earlier (see the producer/consumer problem with only a single condition variable). However, in that case, a better solution was available to us, and thus we used it. In general, if you find that your program only works when you change your signals to broadcasts (but you don't think it should need to), you probably have a bug; fix it! But in cases like the memory allocator above, broadcast may be the most straightforward solution available.

30.4 Summary

We have seen the introduction of another important synchronization primitive beyond locks: condition variables. By allowing threads to sleep when some program state is not as desired, CVs enable us to neatly solve a number of important synchronization problems, including the famous (and still important) producer/consumer problem, as well as covering conditions. A more dramatic concluding sentence would go here, such as "He loved Big Brother" [O49].

References

[D68] "Cooperating sequential processes" by Edsger W. Dijkstra. 1968. Available online here: http://www.cs.utexas.edu/users/EWD/ewd01xx/EWD123.PDF. *Another classic from Dijkstra; reading his early works on concurrency will teach you much of what you need to know.*

[D72] "Information Streams Sharing a Finite Buffer" by E.W. Dijkstra. Information Processing Letters 1: 179–180, 1972. Available: http://www.cs.utexas.edu/users/EWD/ewd03xx/EWD329.PDF *The famous paper that introduced the producer/consumer problem.*

[D01] "My recollections of operating system design" by E.W. Dijkstra. April, 2001. Available: http://www.cs.utexas.edu/users/EWD/ewd13xx/EWD1303.PDF. *A fascinating read for those of you interested in how the pioneers of our field came up with some very basic and fundamental concepts, including ideas like "interrupts" and even "a stack"!*

[H74] "Monitors: An Operating System Structuring Concept" by C.A.R. Hoare. Communications of the ACM, 17:10, pages 549–557, October 1974. *Hoare did a fair amount of theoretical work in concurrency. However, he is still probably most known for his work on Quicksort, the coolest sorting algorithm in the world, at least according to these authors.*

[L11] "Pthread_cond_signal Man Page" by Mysterious author. March, 2011. Available online: http://linux.die.net/man/3/pthread_cond_signal. *The Linux man page shows a nice simple example of why a thread might get a spurious wakeup, due to race conditions within the signal/wakeup code.*

[LR80] "Experience with Processes and Monitors in Mesa" by B.W. Lampson, D.R. Redell. Communications of the ACM. 23:2, pages 105-117, February 1980. *A terrific paper about how to actually implement signaling and condition variables in a real system, leading to the term "Mesa" semantics for what it mzshortns to be woken up; the older semantics, developed by Tony Hoare [H74], then became known as "Hoare" semantics, which is hard to say out loud in class with a straight face.*

[O49] "1984" by George Orwell. Secker and Warburg, 1949. *A little heavy-handed, but of course a must read. That said, we kind of gave away the ending by quoting the last sentence. Sorry! And if the government is reading this, let us just say that we think that the government is "double plus good". Hear that, our pals at the NSA?*

Homework (Code)

This homework lets you explore some real code that uses locks and condition variables to implement various forms of the producer/consumer queue discussed in the chapter. You'll look at the real code, run it in various configurations, and use it to learn about what works and what doesn't, as well as other intricacies. Read the README for details.

Questions

1. Our first question focuses on `main-two-cvs-while.c` (the working solution). First, study the code. Do you think you have an understanding of what should happen when you run the program?

2. Run with one producer and one consumer, and have the producer produce a few values. Start with a buffer (size 1), and then increase it. How does the behavior of the code change with larger buffers? (or does it?) What would you predict `num_full` to be with different buffer sizes (e.g., `-m 10`) and different numbers of produced items (e.g., `-l 100`), when you change the consumer sleep string from default (no sleep) to `-C 0,0,0,0,0,0,1`?

3. If possible, run the code on different systems (e.g., a Mac and Linux). Do you see different behavior across these systems?

4. Let's look at some timings. How long do you think the following execution, with one producer, three consumers, a single-entry shared buffer, and each consumer pausing at point `c3` for a second, will take? `./main-two-cvs-while -p 1 -c 3 -m 1 -C 0,0,0,1,0,0,0:0,0,0,1,0,0,0:0,0,0,1,0,0,0 -l 10 -v -t`

5. Now change the size of the shared buffer to 3 (`-m 3`). Will this make any difference in the total time?

6. Now change the location of the sleep to `c6` (this models a consumer taking something off the queue and then doing something with it), again using a single-entry buffer. What time do you predict in this case? `./main-two-cvs-while -p 1 -c 3 -m 1 -C 0,0,0,0,0,0,1:0,0,0,0,0,0,1:0,0,0,0,0,0,1 -l 10 -v -t`

7. Finally, change the buffer size to 3 again (`-m 3`). What time do you predict now?

8. Now let's look at `main-one-cv-while.c`. Can you configure a sleep string, assuming a single producer, one consumer, and a buffer of size 1, to cause a problem with this code?

9. Now change the number of consumers to two. Can you construct sleep strings for the producer and the consumers so as to cause a problem in the code?

10. Now examine `main-two-cvs-if.c`. Can you cause a problem to happen in this code? Again consider the case where there is only one consumer, and then the case where there is more than one.

11. Finally, examine `main-two-cvs-while-extra-unlock.c`. What problem arises when you release the lock before doing a put or a get? Can you reliably cause such a problem to happen, given the sleep strings? What bad thing can happen?

31

Semaphores

As we know now, one needs both locks and condition variables to solve a broad range of relevant and interesting concurrency problems. One of the first people to realize this years ago was **Edsger Dijkstra** (though it is hard to know the exact history [GR92]), known among other things for his famous "shortest paths" algorithm in graph theory [D59], an early polemic on structured programming entitled "Goto Statements Considered Harmful" [D68a] (what a great title!), and, in the case we will study here, the introduction of a synchronization primitive called the **semaphore** [D68b, D72]. Indeed, Dijkstra and colleagues invented the semaphore as a single primitive for all things related to synchronization; as you will see, one can use semaphores as both locks and condition variables.

> THE CRUX: HOW TO USE SEMAPHORES
>
> How can we use semaphores instead of locks and condition variables? What is the definition of a semaphore? What is a binary semaphore? Is it straightforward to build a semaphore out of locks and condition variables? To build locks and condition variables out of semaphores?

31.1 Semaphores: A Definition

A semaphore is an object with an integer value that we can manipulate with two routines; in the POSIX standard, these routines are `sem_wait()` and `sem_post()`[1]. Because the initial value of the semaphore determines its behavior, before calling any other routine to interact with the semaphore, we must first initialize it to some value, as the code in Figure 311 does.

[1] Historically, `sem_wait()` was called `P()` by Dijkstra and `sem_post()` called `V()`. These shortened forms come from Dutch words; interestingly, *which* Dutch words they supposedly derive from has changed over time. Originally, `P()` came from "passering" (to pass) and `V()` from "vrijgave" (release); later, Dijkstra wrote `P()` was from "prolaag", a contraction of "probeer" (Dutch for "try") and "verlaag" ("decrease"), and `V()` from "verhoog" which means "increase". Sometimes, people call them down and up. Use the Dutch versions to impress your friends, or confuse them, or both. See `https://news.ycombinator.com/item?id=876`) for details.

```
#include <semaphore.h>
sem_t s;
sem_init(&s, 0, 1);
```

Figure 311: **Initializing A Semaphore**

In the figure, we declare a semaphore s and initialize it to the value 1 by passing 1 in as the third argument. The second argument to `sem_init()` will be set to 0 in all of the examples we'll see; this indicates that the semaphore is shared between threads in the same process. See the man page for details on other usages of semaphores (namely, how they can be used to synchronize access across *different* processes), which require a different value for that second argument.

After a semaphore is initialized, we can call one of two functions to interact with it, `sem_wait()` or `sem_post()`. The behavior of these two functions is seen in Figure 312.

For now, we are not concerned with the implementation of these routines, which clearly requires some care; with multiple threads calling into `sem_wait()` and `sem_post()`, there is the obvious need for managing these critical sections. We will now focus on how to *use* these primitives; later we may discuss how they are built.

We should discuss a few salient aspects of the interfaces here. First, we can see that `sem_wait()` will either return right away (because the value of the semaphore was one or higher when we called `sem_wait()`), or it will cause the caller to suspend execution waiting for a subsequent post. Of course, multiple calling threads may call into `sem_wait()`, and thus all be queued waiting to be woken.

Second, we can see that `sem_post()` does not wait for some particular condition to hold like `sem_wait()` does. Rather, it simply increments the value of the semaphore and then, if there is a thread waiting to be woken, wakes one of them up.

Third, the value of the semaphore, when negative, is equal to the number of waiting threads [D68b]. Though the value generally isn't seen by users of the semaphores, this invariant is worth knowing and perhaps can help you remember how a semaphore functions.

```
int sem_wait(sem_t *s) {
    decrement the value of semaphore s by one
    wait if value of semaphore s is negative
}

int sem_post(sem_t *s) {
    increment the value of semaphore s by one
    if there are one or more threads waiting, wake one
}
```

Figure 312: **Semaphore: Definitions Of Wait And Post**

```
sem_t m;
sem_init(&m, 0, X); // initialize to X; what should X be?

sem_wait(&m);
// critical section here
sem_post(&m);
```

Figure 313: **A Binary Semaphore (That Is, A Lock)**

Don't worry (yet) about the seeming race conditions possible within the semaphore; assume that the actions they make are performed atomically. We will soon use locks and condition variables to do just this.

31.2 Binary Semaphores (Locks)

We are now ready to use a semaphore. Our first use will be one with which we are already familiar: using a semaphore as a lock. See Figure 313 for a code snippet; therein, you'll see that we simply surround the critical section of interest with a `sem_wait()`/`sem_post()` pair. Critical to making this work, though, is the initial value of the semaphore `m` (initialized to `X` in the figure). What should `X` be?

... *(Try thinking about it before going on)* ...

Looking back at definition of the `sem_wait()` and `sem_post()` routines above, we can see that the initial value should be 1.

To make this clear, let's imagine a scenario with two threads. The first thread (Thread 0) calls `sem_wait()`; it will first decrement the value of the semaphore, changing it to 0. Then, it will wait only if the value is *not* greater than or equal to 0. Because the value is 0, `sem_wait()` will simply return and the calling thread will continue; Thread 0 is now free to enter the critical section. If no other thread tries to acquire the lock while Thread 0 is inside the critical section, when it calls `sem_post()`, it will simply restore the value of the semaphore to 1 (and not wake a waiting thread, because there are none). Figure 314 shows a trace of this scenario.

A more interesting case arises when Thread 0 "holds the lock" (i.e., it has called `sem_wait()` but not yet called `sem_post()`), and another thread (Thread 1) tries to enter the critical section by calling `sem_wait()`. In this case, Thread 1 will decrement the value of the semaphore to -1, and

Value of Semaphore	Thread 0	Thread 1
1		
1	call `sem_wait()`	
0	`sem_wait()` returns	
0	`(crit sect)`	
0	call `sem_post()`	
1	`sem_post()` returns	

Figure 314: **Thread Trace: Single Thread Using A Semaphore**

Val	Thread 0	State	Thread 1	State
1		Run		Ready
1	call `sem_wait()`	Run		Ready
0	`sem_wait()` returns	Run		Ready
0	`(crit sect begin)`	Run		Ready
0	*Interrupt; Switch→T1*	Ready		Run
0		Ready	call `sem_wait()`	Run
-1		Ready	`decr sem`	Run
-1		Ready	`(sem<0)→sleep`	Sleep
-1		Run	*Switch→T0*	Sleep
-1	`(crit sect end)`	Run		Sleep
-1	call `sem_post()`	Run		Sleep
0	`incr sem`	Run		Sleep
0	`wake(T1)`	Run		Ready
0	`sem_post()` returns	Run		Ready
0	*Interrupt; Switch→T1*	Ready		Run
0		Ready	`sem_wait()` returns	Run
0		Ready	`(crit sect)`	Run
0		Ready	call `sem_post()`	Run
1		Ready	`sem_post()` returns	Run

Figure 315: **Thread Trace: Two Threads Using A Semaphore**

thus wait (putting itself to sleep and relinquishing the processor). When Thread 0 runs again, it will eventually call `sem_post()`, incrementing the value of the semaphore back to zero, and then wake the waiting thread (Thread 1), which will then be able to acquire the lock for itself. When Thread 1 finishes, it will again increment the value of the semaphore, restoring it to 1 again.

Figure 315 shows a trace of this example. In addition to thread actions, the figure shows the **scheduler state** of each thread: Run (the thread is running), Ready (i.e., runnable but not running), and Sleep (the thread is blocked). Note that Thread 1 goes into the sleeping state when it tries to acquire the already-held lock; only when Thread 0 runs again can Thread 1 be awoken and potentially run again.

If you want to work through your own example, try a scenario where multiple threads queue up waiting for a lock. What would the value of the semaphore be during such a trace?

Thus we are able to use semaphores as locks. Because locks only have two states (held and not held), we sometimes call a semaphore used as a lock a **binary semaphore**. Note that if you are using a semaphore only in this binary fashion, it could be implemented in a simpler manner than the generalized semaphores we present here.

31.3 Semaphores For Ordering

Semaphores are also useful to order events in a concurrent program. For example, a thread may wish to wait for a list to become non-empty,

```
sem_t s;

void *child(void *arg) {
    printf("child\n");
    sem_post(&s); // signal here: child is done
    return NULL;
}

int main(int argc, char *argv[]) {
    sem_init(&s, 0, X); // what should X be?
    printf("parent: begin\n");
    pthread_t c;
    Pthread_create(&c, NULL, child, NULL);
    sem_wait(&s); // wait here for child
    printf("parent: end\n");
    return 0;
}
```

Figure 316: **A Parent Waiting For Its Child**

so it can delete an element from it. In this pattern of usage, we often find one thread *waiting* for something to happen, and another thread making that something happen and then *signaling* that it has happened, thus waking the waiting thread. We are thus using the semaphore as an **ordering** primitive (similar to our use of **condition variables** earlier).

A simple example is as follows. Imagine a thread creates another thread and then wants to wait for it to complete its execution (Figure 316). When this program runs, we would like to see the following:

```
parent: begin
child
parent: end
```

The question, then, is how to use a semaphore to achieve this effect; as it turns out, the answer is relatively easy to understand. As you can see in the code, the parent simply calls `sem_wait()` and the child `sem_post()` to wait for the condition of the child finishing its execution to become true. However, this raises the question: what should the initial value of this semaphore be?

(Again, think about it here, instead of reading ahead)

The answer, of course, is that the value of the semaphore should be set to is 0. There are two cases to consider. First, let us assume that the parent creates the child but the child has not run yet (i.e., it is sitting in a ready queue but not running). In this case (Figure 317, page 394), the parent will call `sem_wait()` before the child has called `sem_post()`; we'd like the parent to wait for the child to run. The only way this will happen is if the value of the semaphore is not greater than 0; hence, 0 is the initial value. The parent runs, decrements the semaphore (to -1), then waits (sleeping). When the child finally runs, it will call `sem_post()`, increment the value

Val	Parent	State	Child	State
0	`create(Child)`	Run	*(Child exists, can run)*	Ready
0	call `sem_wait()`	Run		Ready
-1	`decr sem`	Run		Ready
-1	`(sem<0)→sleep`	Sleep		Ready
-1	*Switch→Child*	Sleep	`child runs`	Run
-1		Sleep	call `sem_post()`	Run
0		Sleep	`inc sem`	Run
0		Ready	`wake(Parent)`	Run
0		Ready	`sem_post()` returns	Run
0		Ready	*Interrupt→Parent*	Ready
0	`sem_wait()` returns	Run		Ready

Figure 317: **Thread Trace: Parent Waiting For Child (Case 1)**

Val	Parent	State	Child	State
0	`create(Child)`	Run	*(Child exists; can run)*	Ready
0	*Interrupt→Child*	Ready	`child runs`	Run
0		Ready	call `sem_post()`	Run
1		Ready	`inc sem`	Run
1		Ready	`wake(nobody)`	Run
1		Ready	`sem_post()` returns	Run
1	`parent runs`	Run	*Interrupt→Parent*	Ready
1	call `sem_wait()`	Run		Ready
0	`decrement sem`	Run		Ready
0	`(sem≥0)→awake`	Run		Ready
0	`sem_wait()` returns	Run		Ready

Figure 318: **Thread Trace: Parent Waiting For Child (Case 2)**

of the semaphore to 0, and wake the parent, which will then return from `sem_wait()` and finish the program.

The second case (Figure 318) occurs when the child runs to completion before the parent gets a chance to call `sem_wait()`. In this case, the child will first call `sem_post()`, thus incrementing the value of the semaphore from 0 to 1. When the parent then gets a chance to run, it will call `sem_wait()` and find the value of the semaphore to be 1; the parent will thus decrement the value (to 0) and return from `sem_wait()` without waiting, also achieving the desired effect.

31.4 The Producer/Consumer (Bounded Buffer) Problem

The next problem we will confront in this chapter is known as the **producer/consumer** problem, or sometimes as the **bounded buffer** problem [D72]. This problem is described in detail in the previous chapter on condition variables; see there for details.

> **ASIDE: SETTING THE VALUE OF A SEMAPHORE**
>
> We've now seen two examples of initializing a semaphore. In the first case, we set the value to 1 to use the semaphore as a lock; in the second, to 0, to use the semaphore for ordering. So what's the general rule for semaphore initialization?
>
> One simple way to think about it, thanks to Perry Kivolowitz, is to consider the number of resources you are willing to give away immediately after initialization. With the lock, it was 1, because you are willing to have the lock locked (given away) immediately after initialization. With the ordering case, it was 0, because there is nothing to give away at the start; only when the child thread is done is the resource created, at which point, the value is incremented to 1. Try this line of thinking on future semaphore problems, and see if it helps.

First Attempt

Our first attempt at solving the problem introduces two semaphores, `empty` and `full`, which the threads will use to indicate when a buffer entry has been emptied or filled, respectively. The code for the put and get routines is in Figure 319, and our attempt at solving the producer and consumer problem is in Figure 3110 (page 396).

In this example, the producer first waits for a buffer to become empty in order to put data into it, and the consumer similarly waits for a buffer to become filled before using it. Let us first imagine that `MAX=1` (there is only one buffer in the array), and see if this works.

Imagine again there are two threads, a producer and a consumer. Let us examine a specific scenario on a single CPU. Assume the consumer gets to run first. Thus, the consumer will hit Line C1 in Figure 3110, calling `sem_wait(&full)`. Because full was initialized to the value 0,

```
int buffer[MAX];
int fill = 0;
int use  = 0;

void put(int value) {
    buffer[fill] = value;     // Line F1
    fill = (fill + 1) % MAX; // Line F2
}

int get() {
    int tmp = buffer[use];    // Line G1
    use = (use + 1) % MAX;    // Line G2
    return tmp;
}
```

Figure 319: **The Put And Get Routines**

```
sem_t empty;
sem_t full;

void *producer(void *arg) {
    int i;
    for (i = 0; i < loops; i++) {
        sem_wait(&empty);           // Line P1
        put(i);                     // Line P2
        sem_post(&full);            // Line P3
    }
}

void *consumer(void *arg) {
    int i, tmp = 0;
    while (tmp != -1) {
        sem_wait(&full);            // Line C1
        tmp = get();                // Line C2
        sem_post(&empty);           // Line C3
        printf("%d\n", tmp);
    }
}

int main(int argc, char *argv[]) {
    // ...
    sem_init(&empty, 0, MAX); // MAX are empty
    sem_init(&full, 0, 0);    // 0 are full
    // ...
}
```

Figure 3110: **Adding The Full And Empty Conditions**

the call will decrement `full` (to -1), block the consumer, and wait for another thread to call `sem_post()` on `full`, as desired.

Assume the producer then runs. It will hit Line P1, thus calling the `sem_wait(&empty)` routine. Unlike the consumer, the producer will continue through this line, because `empty` was initialized to the value `MAX` (in this case, 1). Thus, `empty` will be decremented to 0 and the producer will put a data value into the first entry of buffer (Line P2). The producer will then continue on to P3 and call `sem_post(&full)`, changing the value of the `full` semaphore from -1 to 0 and waking the consumer (e.g., move it from blocked to ready).

In this case, one of two things could happen. If the producer continues to run, it will loop around and hit Line P1 again. This time, however, it would block, as the `empty` semaphore's value is 0. If the producer instead was interrupted and the consumer began to run, it would return from `sem_wait(&full)` (Line C1), find that the buffer was full, and consume it. In either case, we achieve the desired behavior.

You can try this same example with more threads (e.g., multiple producers, and multiple consumers). It should still work.

```
void *producer(void *arg) {
    int i;
    for (i = 0; i < loops; i++) {
        sem_wait(&mutex);           // Line P0 (NEW LINE)
        sem_wait(&empty);           // Line P1
        put(i);                     // Line P2
        sem_post(&full);            // Line P3
        sem_post(&mutex);           // Line P4 (NEW LINE)
    }
}

void *consumer(void *arg) {
    int i;
    for (i = 0; i < loops; i++) {
        sem_wait(&mutex);           // Line C0 (NEW LINE)
        sem_wait(&full);            // Line C1
        int tmp = get();            // Line C2
        sem_post(&empty);           // Line C3
        sem_post(&mutex);           // Line C4 (NEW LINE)
        printf("%d\n", tmp);
    }
}
```

Figure 3111: **Adding Mutual Exclusion (Incorrectly)**

Let us now imagine that `MAX` is greater than 1 (say `MAX=10`). For this example, let us assume that there are multiple producers and multiple consumers. We now have a problem: a race condition. Do you see where it occurs? (take some time and look for it) If you can't see it, here's a hint: look more closely at the `put()` and `get()` code.

OK, let's understand the issue. Imagine two producers (Pa and Pb) both calling into `put()` at roughly the same time. Assume producer Pa gets to run first, and just starts to fill the first buffer entry (`fill=0` at Line F1). Before Pa gets a chance to increment the `fill` counter to 1, it is interrupted. Producer Pb starts to run, and at Line F1 it also puts its data into the 0th element of buffer, which means that the old data there is overwritten! This action is a no-no; we don't want any data from the producer to be lost.

A Solution: Adding Mutual Exclusion

As you can see, what we've forgotten here is *mutual exclusion*. The filling of a buffer and incrementing of the index into the buffer is a critical section, and thus must be guarded carefully. So let's use our friend the binary semaphore and add some locks. Figure 3111 shows our attempt.

Now we've added some locks around the entire put()/get() parts of the code, as indicated by the `NEW LINE` comments. That seems like the right idea, but it also doesn't work. Why? Deadlock. Why does deadlock occur? Take a moment to consider it; try to find a case where deadlock arises. What sequence of steps must happen for the program to deadlock?

```
void *producer(void *arg) {
    int i;
    for (i = 0; i < loops; i++) {
        sem_wait(&empty);          // Line P1
        sem_wait(&mutex);          // Line P1.5 (MUTEX HERE)
        put(i);                    // Line P2
        sem_post(&mutex);          // Line P2.5 (AND HERE)
        sem_post(&full);           // Line P3
    }
}

void *consumer(void *arg) {
    int i;
    for (i = 0; i < loops; i++) {
        sem_wait(&full);           // Line C1
        sem_wait(&mutex);          // Line C1.5 (MUTEX HERE)
        int tmp = get();           // Line C2
        sem_post(&mutex);          // Line C2.5 (AND HERE)
        sem_post(&empty);          // Line C3
        printf("%d\n", tmp);
    }
}
```

Figure 3112: **Adding Mutual Exclusion (Correctly)**

Avoiding Deadlock

OK, now that you figured it out, here is the answer. Imagine two threads, one producer and one consumer. The consumer gets to run first. It acquires the mutex (Line C0), and then calls `sem_wait()` on the full semaphore (Line C1); because there is no data yet, this call causes the consumer to block and thus yield the CPU; importantly, though, the consumer still holds the lock.

A producer then runs. It has data to produce and if it were able to run, it would be able to wake the consumer thread and all would be good. Unfortunately, the first thing it does is call `sem_wait()` on the binary mutex semaphore (Line P0). The lock is already held. Hence, the producer is now stuck waiting too.

There is a simple cycle here. The consumer *holds* the mutex and is *waiting* for the someone to signal full. The producer could *signal* full but is *waiting* for the mutex. Thus, the producer and consumer are each stuck waiting for each other: a classic deadlock.

At Last, A Working Solution

To solve this problem, we simply must reduce the scope of the lock. Figure 3112 (page 398) shows the correct solution. As you can see, we simply move the mutex acquire and release to be just around the critical section;

the full and empty wait and signal code is left outside[2]. The result is a simple and working bounded buffer, a commonly-used pattern in multi-threaded programs. Understand it now; use it later. You will thank us for years to come. Or at least, you will thank us when the same question is asked on the final exam, or during a job interview.

31.5 Reader-Writer Locks

Another classic problem stems from the desire for a more flexible locking primitive that admits that different data structure accesses might require different kinds of locking. For example, imagine a number of concurrent list operations, including inserts and simple lookups. While inserts change the state of the list (and thus a traditional critical section makes sense), lookups simply *read* the data structure; as long as we can guarantee that no insert is on-going, we can allow many lookups to proceed concurrently. The special type of lock we will now develop to support this type of operation is known as a **reader-writer lock** [CHP71]. The code for such a lock is available in Figure 3113 (page 400).

The code is pretty simple. If some thread wants to update the data structure in question, it should call the new pair of synchronization operations: `rwlock_acquire_writelock()`, to acquire a write lock, and `rwlock_release_writelock()`, to release it. Internally, these simply use the `writelock` semaphore to ensure that only a single writer can acquire the lock and thus enter the critical section to update the data structure in question.

More interesting is the pair of routines to acquire and release read locks. When acquiring a read lock, the reader first acquires `lock` and then increments the `readers` variable to track how many readers are currently inside the data structure. The important step then taken within `rwlock_acquire_readlock()` occurs when the first reader acquires the lock; in that case, the reader also acquires the write lock by calling `sem_wait()` on the `writelock` semaphore, and then releasing the `lock` by calling `sem_post()`.

Thus, once a reader has acquired a read lock, more readers will be allowed to acquire the read lock too; however, any thread that wishes to acquire the write lock will have to wait until *all* readers are finished; the last one to exit the critical section calls `sem_post()` on "writelock" and thus enables a waiting writer to acquire the lock.

This approach works (as desired), but does have some negatives, especially when it comes to fairness. In particular, it would be relatively easy for readers to starve writers. More sophisticated solutions to this problem exist; perhaps you can think of a better implementation? Hint: think about what you would need to do to prevent more readers from entering the lock once a writer is waiting.

[2]Indeed, it may have been more natural to place the `mutex` acquire/release inside the `put()` and `get()` functions for the purposes of modularity.

```
typedef struct _rwlock_t {
  sem_t lock;      // binary semaphore (basic lock)
  sem_t writelock; // allow ONE writer/MANY readers
  int   readers;   // #readers in critical section
} rwlock_t;

void rwlock_init(rwlock_t *rw) {
  rw->readers = 0;
  sem_init(&rw->lock, 0, 1);
  sem_init(&rw->writelock, 0, 1);
}

void rwlock_acquire_readlock(rwlock_t *rw) {
  sem_wait(&rw->lock);
  rw->readers++;
  if (rw->readers == 1) // first reader gets writelock
    sem_wait(&rw->writelock);
  sem_post(&rw->lock);
}

void rwlock_release_readlock(rwlock_t *rw) {
  sem_wait(&rw->lock);
  rw->readers--;
  if (rw->readers == 0) // last reader lets it go
    sem_post(&rw->writelock);
  sem_post(&rw->lock);
}

void rwlock_acquire_writelock(rwlock_t *rw) {
  sem_wait(&rw->writelock);
}

void rwlock_release_writelock(rwlock_t *rw) {
  sem_post(&rw->writelock);
}
```

Figure 3113: **A Simple Reader-Writer Lock**

Finally, it should be noted that reader-writer locks should be used with some caution. They often add more overhead (especially with more sophisticated implementations), and thus do not end up speeding up performance as compared to just using simple and fast locking primitives [CB08]. Either way, they showcase once again how we can use semaphores in an interesting and useful way.

> TIP: SIMPLE AND DUMB CAN BE BETTER (HILL'S LAW)
> You should never underestimate the notion that the simple and dumb approach can be the best one. With locking, sometimes a simple spin lock works best, because it is easy to implement and fast. Although something like reader/writer locks sounds cool, they are complex, and complex can mean slow. Thus, always try the simple and dumb approach first.
>
> This idea, of appealing to simplicity, is found in many places. One early source is Mark Hill's dissertation [H87], which studied how to design caches for CPUs. Hill found that simple direct-mapped caches worked better than fancy set-associative designs (one reason is that in caching, simpler designs enable faster lookups). As Hill succinctly summarized his work: "Big and dumb is better." And thus we call this similar advice **Hill's Law**.

31.6 The Dining Philosophers

One of the most famous concurrency problems posed, and solved, by Dijkstra, is known as the **dining philosopher's problem** [D71]. The problem is famous because it is fun and somewhat intellectually interesting; however, its practical utility is low. However, its fame forces its inclusion here; indeed, you might be asked about it on some interview, and you'd really hate your OS professor if you miss that question and don't get the job. Conversely, if you get the job, please feel free to send your OS professor a nice note, or some stock options.

The basic setup for the problem is this (as shown in Figure 3114): assume there are five "philosophers" sitting around a table. Between each pair of philosophers is a single fork (and thus, five total). The philosophers each have times where they think, and don't need any forks, and times where they eat. In order to eat, a philosopher needs two forks, both the one on their left and the one on their right. The contention for these forks, and the synchronization problems that ensue, are what makes this a problem we study in concurrent programming.

Here is the basic loop of each philosopher, assuming each has a unique thread identifier p from 0 to 4 (inclusive):

```
while (1) {
    think();
    get_forks(p);
    eat();
    put_forks(p);
}
```

The key challenge, then, is to write the routines `get_forks()` and `put_forks()` such that there is no deadlock, no philosopher starves and

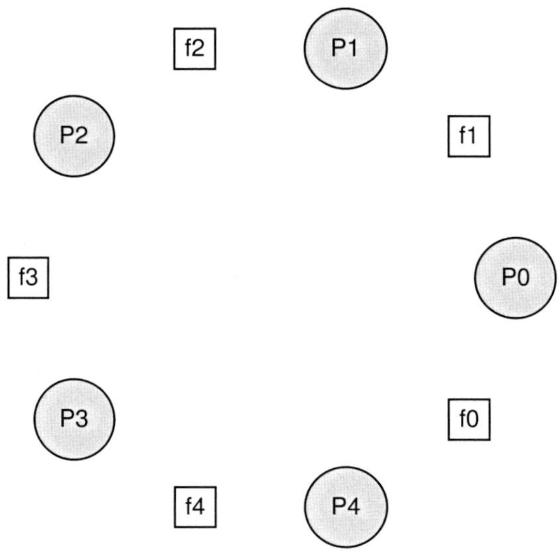

Figure 3114: **The Dining Philosophers**

never gets to eat, and concurrency is high (i.e., as many philosophers can eat at the same time as possible).

Following Downey's solutions [D08], we'll use a few helper functions to get us towards a solution. They are:

```
int left(int p)  { return p; }
int right(int p) { return (p + 1) % 5; }
```

When philosopher `p` wishes to refer to the fork on their left, they simply call `left(p)`. Similarly, the fork on the right of a philosopher `p` is referred to by calling `right(p)`; the modulo operator therein handles the one case where the last philosopher (`p=4`) tries to grab the fork on their right, which is fork 0.

We'll also need some semaphores to solve this problem. Let us assume we have five, one for each fork: `sem_t forks[5]`.

Broken Solution

We attempt our first solution to the problem. Assume we initialize each semaphore (in the `forks` array) to a value of 1. Assume also that each philosopher knows its own number (`p`). We can thus write the `get_forks()` and `put_forks()` routine (Figure 3115, page 403).

The intuition behind this (broken) solution is as follows. To acquire the forks, we simply grab a "lock" on each one: first the one on the left,

```
void get_forks(int p) {
    sem_wait(&forks[left(p)]);
    sem_wait(&forks[right(p)]);
}

void put_forks(int p) {
    sem_post(&forks[left(p)]);
    sem_post(&forks[right(p)]);
}
```

Figure 3115: **The `get_forks()` And `put_forks()` Routines**

```
void get_forks(int p) {
    if (p == 4) {
        sem_wait(&forks[right(p)]);
        sem_wait(&forks[left(p)]);
    } else {
        sem_wait(&forks[left(p)]);
        sem_wait(&forks[right(p)]);
    }
}
```

Figure 3116: **Breaking The Dependency In `get_forks()`**

and then the one on the right. When we are done eating, we release them. Simple, no? Unfortunately, in this case, simple means broken. Can you see the problem that arises? Think about it.

The problem is **deadlock**. If each philosopher happens to grab the fork on their left before any philosopher can grab the fork on their right, each will be stuck holding one fork and waiting for another, forever. Specifically, philosopher 0 grabs fork 0, philosopher 1 grabs fork 1, philosopher 2 grabs fork 2, philosopher 3 grabs fork 3, and philosopher 4 grabs fork 4; all the forks are acquired, and all the philosophers are stuck waiting for a fork that another philosopher possesses. We'll study deadlock in more detail soon; for now, it is safe to say that this is not a working solution.

A Solution: Breaking The Dependency

The simplest way to attack this problem is to change how forks are acquired by at least one of the philosophers; indeed, this is how Dijkstra himself solved the problem. Specifically, let's assume that philosopher 4 (the highest numbered one) gets the forks in a *different* order than the others (Figure 3116); the `put_forks()` code remains the same.

Because the last philosopher tries to grab right before left, there is no situation where each philosopher grabs one fork and is stuck waiting for another; the cycle of waiting is broken. Think through the ramifications of this solution, and convince yourself that it works.

There are other "famous" problems like this one, e.g., the **cigarette smoker's problem** or the **sleeping barber problem**. Most of them are just excuses to think about concurrency; some of them have fascinating names. Look them up if you are interested in learning more, or just getting more practice thinking in a concurrent manner [D08].

31.7 Thread Throttling

One other simple use case for semaphores arises on occasion, and thus we present it here. The specific problem is this: how can a programmer prevent "too many" threads from doing something at once and bogging the system down? Answer: decide upon a threshold for "too many", and then use a semaphore to limit the number of threads concurrently executing the piece of code in question. We call this approach **throttling** [T99], and consider it a form of **admission control**.

Let's consider a more specific example. Imagine that you create hundreds of threads to work on some problem in parallel. However, in a certain part of the code, each thread acquires a large amount of memory to perform part of the computation; let's call this part of the code the *memory-intensive region*. If *all* of the threads enter the memory-intensive region at the same time, the sum of all the memory allocation requests will exceed the amount of physical memory on the machine. As a result, the machine will start thrashing (i.e., swapping pages to and from the disk), and the entire computation will slow to a crawl.

A simple semaphore can solve this problem. By initializing the value of the semaphore to the maximum number of threads you wish to enter the memory-intensive region at once, and then putting a `sem_wait()` and `sem_post()` around the region, a semaphore can naturally throttle the number of threads that are ever concurrently in the dangerous region of the code.

31.8 How To Implement Semaphores

Finally, let's use our low-level synchronization primitives, locks and condition variables, to build our own version of semaphores called ... *(drum roll here)* ... **Zemaphores**. This task is fairly straightforward, as you can see in Figure 3117 (page 405).

In the code above, we use just one lock and one condition variable, plus a state variable to track the value of the semaphore. Study the code for yourself until you really understand it. Do it!

One subtle difference between our Zemaphore and pure semaphores as defined by Dijkstra is that we don't maintain the invariant that the value of the semaphore, when negative, reflects the number of waiting threads; indeed, the value will never be lower than zero. This behavior is easier to implement and matches the current Linux implementation.

```
typedef struct __Zem_t {
    int value;
    pthread_cond_t cond;
    pthread_mutex_t lock;
} Zem_t;

// only one thread can call this
void Zem_init(Zem_t *s, int value) {
    s->value = value;
    Cond_init(&s->cond);
    Mutex_init(&s->lock);
}

void Zem_wait(Zem_t *s) {
    Mutex_lock(&s->lock);
    while (s->value <= 0)
        Cond_wait(&s->cond, &s->lock);
    s->value--;
    Mutex_unlock(&s->lock);
}

void Zem_post(Zem_t *s) {
    Mutex_lock(&s->lock);
    s->value++;
    Cond_signal(&s->cond);
    Mutex_unlock(&s->lock);
}
```

Figure 3117: **Implementing Zemaphores With Locks And CVs**

Curiously, building condition variables out of semaphores is a much trickier proposition. Some highly experienced concurrent programmers tried to do this in the Windows environment, and many different bugs ensued [B04]. Try it yourself, and see if you can figure out why building condition variables out of semaphores is more challenging of a problem than it might appear.

31.9 Summary

Semaphores are a powerful and flexible primitive for writing concurrent programs. Some programmers use them exclusively, shunning locks and condition variables, due to their simplicity and utility.

In this chapter, we have presented just a few classic problems and solutions. If you are interested in finding out more, there are many other materials you can reference. One great (and free reference) is Allen Downey's book on concurrency and programming with semaphores [D08]. This book has lots of puzzles you can work on to improve your understand-

TIP: BE CAREFUL WITH GENERALIZATION

The abstract technique of generalization can thus be quite useful in systems design, where one good idea can be made slightly broader and thus solve a larger class of problems. However, be careful when generalizing; as Lampson warns us "Don't generalize; generalizations are generally wrong" [L83].

One could view semaphores as a generalization of locks and condition variables; however, is such a generalization needed? And, given the difficulty of realizing a condition variable on top of a semaphore, perhaps this generalization is not as general as you might think.

ing of both semaphores in specific and concurrency in general. Becoming a real concurrency expert takes years of effort; going beyond what you learn in this class is undoubtedly the key to mastering such a topic.

References

[B04] "Implementing Condition Variables with Semaphores" by Andrew Birrell. December 2004. *An interesting read on how difficult implementing CVs on top of semaphores really is, and the mistakes the author and co-workers made along the way. Particularly relevant because the group had done a ton of concurrent programming; Birrell, for example, is known for (among other things) writing various thread-programming guides.*

[CB08] "Real-world Concurrency" by Bryan Cantrill, Jeff Bonwick. ACM Queue. Volume 6, No. 5. September 2008. *A nice article by some kernel hackers from a company formerly known as Sun on the real problems faced in concurrent code.*

[CHP71] "Concurrent Control with Readers and Writers" by P.J. Courtois, F. Heymans, D.L. Parnas. Communications of the ACM, 14:10, October 1971. *The introduction of the reader-writer problem, and a simple solution. Later work introduced more complex solutions, skipped here because, well, they are pretty complex.*

[D59] "A Note on Two Problems in Connexion with Graphs" by E. W. Dijkstra. Numerische Mathematik 1, 269–271, 1959. Available: `http://www-m3.ma.tum.de/twiki/pub/MN0506/WebHome/dijkstra.pdf`. *Can you believe people worked on algorithms in 1959? We can't. Even before computers were any fun to use, these people had a sense that they would transform the world...*

[D68a] "Go-to Statement Considered Harmful" by E.W. Dijkstra. CACM, volume 11(3), March 1968. `http://www.cs.utexas.edu/users/EWD/ewd02xx/EWD215.PDF`. *Sometimes thought of as the beginning of the field of software engineering.*

[D68b] "The Structure of the THE Multiprogramming System" by E.W. Dijkstra. CACM, volume 11(5), 1968. *One of the earliest papers to point out that systems work in computer science is an engaging intellectual endeavor. Also argues strongly for modularity in the form of layered systems.*

[D72] "Information Streams Sharing a Finite Buffer" by E.W. Dijkstra. Information Processing Letters 1, 1972. `http://www.cs.utexas.edu/users/EWD/ewd03xx/EWD329.PDF`. *Did Dijkstra invent everything? No, but maybe close. He certainly was the first to clearly write down what the problems were in concurrent code. However, practitioners in OS design knew of many of the problems described by Dijkstra, so perhaps giving him too much credit would be a misrepresentation.*

[D08] "The Little Book of Semaphores" by A.B. Downey. Available at the following site: `http://greenteapress.com/semaphores/`. *A nice (and free!) book about semaphores. Lots of fun problems to solve, if you like that sort of thing.*

[D71] "Hierarchical ordering of sequential processes" by E.W. Dijkstra. Available online here: `http://www.cs.utexas.edu/users/EWD/ewd03xx/EWD310.PDF`. *Presents numerous concurrency problems, including Dining Philosophers. The wikipedia page about this problem is also useful.*

[GR92] "Transaction Processing: Concepts and Techniques" by Jim Gray, Andreas Reuter. Morgan Kaufmann, September 1992. *The exact quote that we find particularly humorous is found on page 485, at the top of Section 8.8: "The first multiprocessors, circa 1960, had test and set instructions ... presumably the OS implementors worked out the appropriate algorithms, although Dijkstra is generally credited with inventing semaphores many years later." Oh, snap!*

[H87] "Aspects of Cache Memory and Instruction Buffer Performance" by Mark D. Hill. Ph.D. Dissertation, U.C. Berkeley, 1987. *Hill's dissertation work, for those obsessed with caching in early systems. A great example of a quantitative dissertation.*

[L83] "Hints for Computer Systems Design" by Butler Lampson. ACM Operating Systems Review, 15:5, October 1983. *Lampson, a famous systems researcher, loved using hints in the design of computer systems. A hint is something that is often correct but can be wrong; in this use, a signal() is telling a waiting thread that it changed the condition that the waiter was waiting on, but not to trust that the condition will be in the desired state when the waiting thread wakes up. In this paper about hints for designing systems, one of Lampson's general hints is that you should use hints. It is not as confusing as it sounds.*

[T99] "Re: NT kernel guy playing with Linux" by Linus Torvalds. June 27, 1999. Available: `https://yarchive.net/comp/linux/semaphores.html`. *A response from Linus himself about the utility of semaphores, including the throttling case we mention in the text. As always, Linus is slightly insulting but quite informative.*

Homework (Code)

In this homework, we'll use semaphores to solve some well-known concurrency problems. Many of these are taken from Downey's excellent "Little Book of Semaphores"[3], which does a good job of pulling together a number of classic problems as well as introducing a few new variants; interested readers should check out the Little Book for more fun.

Each of the following questions provides a code skeleton; your job is to fill in the code to make it work given semaphores. On Linux, you will be using native semaphores; on a Mac (where there is no semaphore support), you'll have to first build an implementation (using locks and condition variables, as described in the chapter). Good luck!

Questions

1. The first problem is just to implement and test a solution to the **fork/join problem**, as described in the text. Even though this solution is described in the text, the act of typing it in on your own is worthwhile; even Bach would rewrite Vivaldi, allowing one soon-to-be master to learn from an existing one. See `fork-join.c` for details. Add the call `sleep(1)` to the child to ensure it is working.
2. Let's now generalize this a bit by investigating the **rendezvous problem**. The problem is as follows: you have two threads, each of which are about to enter the rendezvous point in the code. Neither should exit this part of the code before the other enters it. Consider using two semaphores for this task, and see `rendezvous.c` for details.
3. Now go one step further by implementing a general solution to **barrier synchronization**. Assume there are two points in a sequential piece of code, called P_1 and P_2. Putting a **barrier** between P_1 and P_2 guarantees that all threads will execute P_1 before any one thread executes P_2. Your task: write the code to implement a `barrier()` function that can be used in this manner. It is safe to assume you know N (the total number of threads in the running program) and that all N threads will try to enter the barrier. Again, you should likely use two semaphores to achieve the solution, and some other integers to count things. See `barrier.c` for details.
4. Now let's solve the **reader-writer problem**, also as described in the text. In this first take, don't worry about starvation. See the code in `reader-writer.c` for details. Add `sleep()` calls to your code to demonstrate it works as you expect. Can you show the existence of the starvation problem?
5. Let's look at the reader-writer problem again, but this time, worry about starvation. How can you ensure that all readers and writers eventually make progress? See `reader-writer-nostarve.c` for details.
6. Use semaphores to build a **no-starve mutex**, in which any thread that tries to acquire the mutex will eventually obtain it. See the code in `mutex-nostarve.c` for more information.
7. Liked these problems? See Downey's free text for more just like them. And don't forget, have fun! But, you always do when you write code, no?

[3]Available: `http://greenteapress.com/semaphores/downey08semaphores.pdf`.

32

Common Concurrency Problems

Researchers have spent a great deal of time and effort looking into concurrency bugs over many years. Much of the early work focused on **deadlock**, a topic which we've touched on in the past chapters but will now dive into deeply [C+71]. More recent work focuses on studying other types of common concurrency bugs (i.e., non-deadlock bugs). In this chapter, we take a brief look at some example concurrency problems found in real code bases, to better understand what problems to look out for. And thus our central issue for this chapter:

> CRUX: HOW TO HANDLE COMMON CONCURRENCY BUGS
>
> Concurrency bugs tend to come in a variety of common patterns. Knowing which ones to look out for is the first step to writing more robust, correct concurrent code.

32.1 What Types Of Bugs Exist?

The first, and most obvious, question is this: what types of concurrency bugs manifest in complex, concurrent programs? This question is difficult to answer in general, but fortunately, some others have done the work for us. Specifically, we rely upon a study by Lu et al. [L+08], which analyzes a number of popular concurrent applications in great detail to understand what types of bugs arise in practice.

The study focuses on four major and important open-source applications: MySQL (a popular database management system), Apache (a well-known web server), Mozilla (the famous web browser), and OpenOffice (a free version of the MS Office suite, which some people actually use). In the study, the authors examine concurrency bugs that have been found and fixed in each of these code bases, turning the developers' work into a quantitative bug analysis; understanding these results can help you understand what types of problems actually occur in mature code bases.

Figure 321 shows a summary of the bugs Lu and colleagues studied. From the figure, you can see that there were 105 total bugs, most of which

Application	What it does	Non-Deadlock	Deadlock
MySQL	Database Server	14	9
Apache	Web Server	13	4
Mozilla	Web Browser	41	16
OpenOffice	Office Suite	6	2
Total		74	31

Figure 321: **Bugs In Modern Applications**

were not deadlock (74); the remaining 31 were deadlock bugs. Further, you can see the number of bugs studied from each application; while OpenOffice only had 8 total concurrency bugs, Mozilla had nearly 60.

We now dive into these different classes of bugs (non-deadlock, deadlock) a bit more deeply. For the first class of non-deadlock bugs, we use examples from the study to drive our discussion. For the second class of deadlock bugs, we discuss the long line of work that has been done in either preventing, avoiding, or handling deadlock.

32.2 Non-Deadlock Bugs

Non-deadlock bugs make up a majority of concurrency bugs, according to Lu's study. But what types of bugs are these? How do they arise? How can we fix them? We now discuss the two major types of non-deadlock bugs found by Lu et al.: **atomicity violation** bugs and **order violation** bugs.

Atomicity-Violation Bugs

The first type of problem encountered is referred to as an **atomicity violation**. Here is a simple example, found in MySQL. Before reading the explanation, try figuring out what the bug is. Do it!

```
Thread 1::
if (thd->proc_info) {
  fputs(thd->proc_info, ...);
}

Thread 2::
thd->proc_info = NULL;
```

Figure 322: **Atomicity Violation (`atomicity.c`)**

In the example, two different threads access the field `proc_info` in the structure `thd`. The first thread checks if the value is non-NULL and then prints its value; the second thread sets it to NULL. Clearly, if the first thread performs the check but then is interrupted before the call to `fputs`, the second thread could run in-between, thus setting the pointer to NULL; when the first thread resumes, it will crash, as a NULL pointer will be dereferenced by `fputs`.

The more formal definition of an atomicity violation, according to Lu et al, is this: "The desired serializability among multiple memory accesses is violated (i.e. a code region is intended to be atomic, but the atomicity is not enforced during execution)." In our example above, the code has an *atomicity assumption* (in Lu's words) about the check for non-NULL of `proc_info` and the usage of `proc_info` in the `fputs()` call; when the assumption is incorrect, the code will not work as desired.

Finding a fix for this type of problem is often (but not always) straightforward. Can you think of how to fix the code above?

In this solution (Figure 323), we simply add locks around the shared-variable references, ensuring that when either thread accesses the `proc_info` field, it has a lock held (`proc_info_lock`). Of course, any other code that accesses the structure should also acquire this lock before doing so.

```
pthread_mutex_t proc_info_lock = PTHREAD_MUTEX_INITIALIZER;

Thread 1::
pthread_mutex_lock(&proc_info_lock);
if (thd->proc_info) {
  fputs(thd->proc_info, ...);
}
pthread_mutex_unlock(&proc_info_lock);

Thread 2::
pthread_mutex_lock(&proc_info_lock);
thd->proc_info = NULL;
pthread_mutex_unlock(&proc_info_lock);
```

Figure 323: **Atomicity Violation Fixed (`atomicity_fixed.c`)**

Order-Violation Bugs

Another common type of non-deadlock bug found by Lu et al. is known as an **order violation**. Here is another simple example; once again, see if you can figure out why the code below has a bug in it.

```
Thread 1::
void init() {
   mThread = PR_CreateThread(mMain, ...);
}

Thread 2::
void mMain(...) {
    mState = mThread->State;
}
```

Figure 324: **Ordering Bug (`ordering.c`)**

As you probably figured out, the code in Thread 2 seems to assume that the variable `mThread` has already been initialized (and is not NULL);

```
pthread_mutex_t mtLock  = PTHREAD_MUTEX_INITIALIZER;
pthread_cond_t  mtCond  = PTHREAD_COND_INITIALIZER;
int mtInit              = 0;

Thread 1::
void init() {
   ...
   mThread = PR_CreateThread(mMain, ...);

   // signal that the thread has been created...
   pthread_mutex_lock(&mtLock);
   mtInit = 1;
   pthread_cond_signal(&mtCond);
   pthread_mutex_unlock(&mtLock);
   ...
}

Thread 2::
void mMain(...) {
    ...
    // wait for the thread to be initialized...
    pthread_mutex_lock(&mtLock);
    while (mtInit == 0)
        pthread_cond_wait(&mtCond, &mtLock);
    pthread_mutex_unlock(&mtLock);

    mState = mThread->State;
    ...
}
```

Figure 325: **Fixing The Ordering Violation (`ordering_fixed.c`)**

however, if Thread 2 runs immediately once created, the value of `mThread` will not be set when it is accessed within `mMain()` in Thread 2, and will likely crash with a NULL-pointer dereference. Note that we assume the value of `mThread` is initially NULL; if not, even stranger things could happen as arbitrary memory locations are accessed through the dereference in Thread 2.

The more formal definition of an order violation is the following: "The desired order between two (groups of) memory accesses is flipped (i.e., A should always be executed before B, but the order is not enforced during execution)" [L+08].

The fix to this type of bug is generally to enforce ordering. As discussed previously, using **condition variables** is an easy and robust way to add this style of synchronization into modern code bases. In the example above, we could thus rewrite the code as seen in Figure 325.

In this fixed-up code sequence, we have added a condition variable (`mtCond`) and corresponding lock (`mtLock`), as well as a state variable (mtInit). When the initialization code runs, it sets the state of mtInit to 1 and signals that it has done so. If Thread 2 had run before this point, it will be waiting for this signal and corresponding state change; if it runs later, it will check the state and see that the initialization has already occurred (i.e., mtInit is set to 1), and thus continue as is proper. Note that we could likely use mThread as the state variable itself, but do not do so for the sake of simplicity here. When ordering matters between threads, condition variables (or semaphores) can come to the rescue.

Non-Deadlock Bugs: Summary

A large fraction (97%) of non-deadlock bugs studied by Lu et al. are either atomicity or order violations. Thus, by carefully thinking about these types of bug patterns, programmers can likely do a better job of avoiding them. Moreover, as more automated code-checking tools develop, they should likely focus on these two types of bugs as they constitute such a large fraction of non-deadlock bugs found in deployment.

Unfortunately, not all bugs are as easily fixed as the examples we looked at above. Some require a deeper understanding of what the program is doing, or a larger amount of code or data structure reorganization to fix. Read Lu et al.'s excellent (and readable) paper for more details.

32.3 Deadlock Bugs

Beyond the concurrency bugs mentioned above, a classic problem that arises in many concurrent systems with complex locking protocols is known as **deadlock**. Deadlock occurs, for example, when a thread (say Thread 1) is holding a lock (L1) and waiting for another one (L2); unfortunately, the thread (Thread 2) that holds lock L2 is waiting for L1 to be released. Here is a code snippet that demonstrates such a potential deadlock:

```
Thread 1:                    Thread 2:
pthread_mutex_lock(L1);      pthread_mutex_lock(L2);
pthread_mutex_lock(L2);      pthread_mutex_lock(L1);
```

Figure 326: **Simple Deadlock (deadlock.c)**

Note that if this code runs, deadlock does not necessarily occur; rather, it may occur, if, for example, Thread 1 grabs lock L1 and then a context switch occurs to Thread 2. At that point, Thread 2 grabs L2, and tries to acquire L1. Thus we have a deadlock, as each thread is waiting for the other and neither can run. See Figure 327 for a graphical depiction; the presence of a **cycle** in the graph is indicative of the deadlock.

The figure should make the problem clear. How should programmers write code so as to handle deadlock in some way?

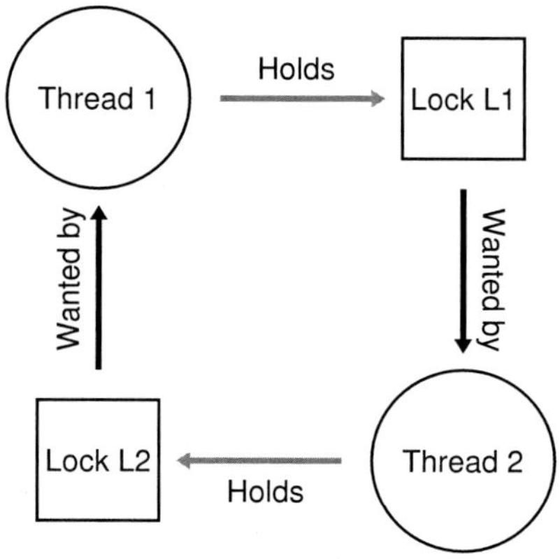

Figure 327: **The Deadlock Dependency Graph**

CRUX: HOW TO DEAL WITH DEADLOCK

How should we build systems to prevent, avoid, or at least detect and recover from deadlock? Is this a real problem in systems today?

Why Do Deadlocks Occur?

As you may be thinking, simple deadlocks such as the one above seem readily avoidable. For example, if Thread 1 and 2 both made sure to grab locks in the same order, the deadlock would never arise. So why do deadlocks happen?

One reason is that in large code bases, complex dependencies arise between components. Take the operating system, for example. The virtual memory system might need to access the file system in order to page in a block from disk; the file system might subsequently require a page of memory to read the block into and thus contact the virtual memory system. Thus, the design of locking strategies in large systems must be carefully done to avoid deadlock in the case of circular dependencies that may occur naturally in the code.

Another reason is due to the nature of **encapsulation**. As software developers, we are taught to hide details of implementations and thus make software easier to build in a modular way. Unfortunately, such modularity does not mesh well with locking. As Jula et al. point out [J+08], some seemingly innocuous interfaces almost invite you to deadlock. For example, take the Java Vector class and the method `AddAll()`. This routine would be called as follows:

```
Vector v1, v2;
v1.AddAll(v2);
```

Internally, because the method needs to be multi-thread safe, locks for both the vector being added to (v1) and the parameter (v2) need to be acquired. The routine acquires said locks in some arbitrary order (say v1 then v2) in order to add the contents of v2 to v1. If some other thread calls `v2.AddAll(v1)` at nearly the same time, we have the potential for deadlock, all in a way that is quite hidden from the calling application.

Conditions for Deadlock

Four conditions need to hold for a deadlock to occur [C+71]:

- **Mutual exclusion:** Threads claim exclusive control of resources that they require (e.g., a thread grabs a lock).
- **Hold-and-wait:** Threads hold resources allocated to them (e.g., locks that they have already acquired) while waiting for additional resources (e.g., locks that they wish to acquire).
- **No preemption:** Resources (e.g., locks) cannot be forcibly removed from threads that are holding them.
- **Circular wait:** There exists a circular chain of threads such that each thread holds one or more resources (e.g., locks) that are being requested by the next thread in the chain.

If any of these four conditions are not met, deadlock cannot occur. Thus, we first explore techniques to *prevent* deadlock; each of these strategies seeks to prevent one of the above conditions from arising and thus is one approach to handling the deadlock problem.

Prevention

Circular Wait

Probably the most practical prevention technique (and certainly one that is frequently employed) is to write your locking code such that you never induce a circular wait. The most straightforward way to do that is to provide a **total ordering** on lock acquisition. For example, if there are only two locks in the system (`L1` and `L2`), you can prevent deadlock by always acquiring `L1` before `L2`. Such strict ordering ensures that no cyclical wait arises; hence, no deadlock.

Of course, in more complex systems, more than two locks will exist, and thus total lock ordering may be difficult to achieve (and perhaps is unnecessary anyhow). Thus, a **partial ordering** can be a useful way to structure lock acquisition so as to avoid deadlock. An excellent real example of partial lock ordering can be seen in the memory mapping code in Linux [T+94] (v5.2); the comment at the top of the source code reveals ten different groups of lock acquisition orders, including simple

TIP: ENFORCE LOCK ORDERING BY LOCK ADDRESS

In some cases, a function must grab two (or more) locks; thus, we know we must be careful or deadlock could arise. Imagine a function that is called as follows: `do_something(mutex_t *m1, mutex_t *m2)`. If the code always grabs `m1` before `m2` (or always `m2` before `m1`), it could deadlock, because one thread could call `do_something(L1, L2)` while another thread could call `do_something(L2, L1)`.

To avoid this particular issue, the clever programmer can use the *address* of each lock as a way of ordering lock acquisition. By acquiring locks in either high-to-low or low-to-high address order, `do_something()` can guarantee that it always acquires locks in the same order, regardless of which order they are passed in. The code would look something like this:

```
if (m1 > m2) { // grab in high-to-low address order
  pthread_mutex_lock(m1);
  pthread_mutex_lock(m2);
} else {
  pthread_mutex_lock(m2);
  pthread_mutex_lock(m1);
}
// Code assumes that m1 != m2 (not the same lock)
```

By using this simple technique, a programmer can ensure a simple and efficient deadlock-free implementation of multi-lock acquisition.

ones such as "`i_mutex` before `i_mmap_rwsem`" and more complex orders such as "`i_mmap_rwsem` before `private_lock` before `swap_lock` before `i_pages lock`".

As you can imagine, both total and partial ordering require careful design of locking strategies and must be constructed with great care. Further, ordering is just a convention, and a sloppy programmer can easily ignore the locking protocol and potentially cause deadlock. Finally, lock ordering requires a deep understanding of the code base, and how various routines are called; just one mistake could result in the "D" word[1].

Hold-and-wait

The hold-and-wait requirement for deadlock can be avoided by acquiring all locks at once, atomically. In practice, this could be achieved as follows:

```
pthread_mutex_lock(prevention);   // begin acquisition
pthread_mutex_lock(L1);
pthread_mutex_lock(L2);
...
pthread_mutex_unlock(prevention); // end
```

[1] Hint: "D" stands for "Deadlock".

By first grabbing the lock `prevention`, this code guarantees that no untimely thread switch can occur in the midst of lock acquisition and thus deadlock can once again be avoided. Of course, it requires that any time any thread grabs a lock, it first acquires the global prevention lock. For example, if another thread was trying to grab locks `L1` and `L2` in a different order, it would be OK, because it would be holding the prevention lock while doing so.

Note that the solution is problematic for a number of reasons. As before, encapsulation works against us: when calling a routine, this approach requires us to know exactly which locks must be held and to acquire them ahead of time. This technique also is likely to decrease concurrency as all locks must be acquired early on (at once) instead of when they are truly needed.

No Preemption

Because we generally view locks as held until unlock is called, multiple lock acquisition often gets us into trouble because when waiting for one lock we are holding another. Many thread libraries provide a more flexible set of interfaces to help avoid this situation. Specifically, the routine `pthread_mutex_trylock()` either grabs the lock (if it is available) and returns success or returns an error code indicating the lock is held; in the latter case, you can try again later if you want to grab that lock.

Such an interface could be used as follows to build a deadlock-free, ordering-robust lock acquisition protocol:

```
top:
  pthread_mutex_lock(L1);
  if (pthread_mutex_trylock(L2) != 0) {
    pthread_mutex_unlock(L1);
    goto top;
  }
```

Note that another thread could follow the same protocol but grab the locks in the other order (`L2` then `L1`) and the program would still be deadlock free. One new problem does arise, however: **livelock**. It is possible (though perhaps unlikely) that two threads could both be repeatedly attempting this sequence and repeatedly failing to acquire both locks. In this case, both systems are running through this code sequence over and over again (and thus it is not a deadlock), but progress is not being made, hence the name livelock. There are solutions to the livelock problem, too: for example, one could add a random delay before looping back and trying the entire thing over again, thus decreasing the odds of repeated interference among competing threads.

One point about this solution: it skirts around the hard parts of using a trylock approach. The first problem that would likely exist again arises due to encapsulation: if one of these locks is buried in some routine that is getting called, the jump back to the beginning becomes more complex to implement. If the code had acquired some resources (other than `L1`) along the way, it must make sure to carefully release them as well; for example, if after acquiring L1, the code had allocated some memory, it would have to release that memory upon failure to acquire L2, before jumping back to the top to try the entire sequence again. However, in limited circumstances (e.g., the Java vector method mentioned earlier), this type of approach could work well.

You might also notice that this approach doesn't really *add* preemption (the forcible action of taking a lock away from a thread that owns it), but rather uses the trylock approach to allow a developer to back out of lock ownership (i.e., preempt their own ownership) in a graceful way. However, it is a practical approach, and thus we include it here, despite its imperfection in this regard.

Mutual Exclusion

The final prevention technique would be to avoid the need for mutual exclusion at all. In general, we know this is difficult, because the code we wish to run does indeed have critical sections. So what can we do?

Herlihy had the idea that one could design various data structures without locks at all [H91, H93]. The idea behind these **lock-free** (and related **wait-free**) approaches here is simple: using powerful hardware instructions, you can build data structures in a manner that does not require explicit locking.

As a simple example, let us assume we have a compare-and-swap instruction, which as you may recall is an atomic instruction provided by the hardware that does the following:

```
int CompareAndSwap(int *address, int expected, int new) {
  if (*address == expected) {
    *address = new;
    return 1; // success
  }
  return 0; // failure
}
```

Imagine we now wanted to atomically increment a value by a certain amount, using compare-and-swap. We could do so with the following simple function:

```
void AtomicIncrement(int *value, int amount) {
  do {
    int old = *value;
  } while (CompareAndSwap(value, old, old + amount) == 0);
}
```

Instead of acquiring a lock, doing the update, and then releasing it, we have instead built an approach that repeatedly tries to update the value to the new amount and uses the compare-and-swap to do so. In this manner, no lock is acquired, and no deadlock can arise (though livelock is still a possibility, and thus a robust solution will be more complex than the simple code snippet above).

Let us consider a slightly more complex example: list insertion. Here is code that inserts at the head of a list:

```
void insert(int value) {
  node_t *n = malloc(sizeof(node_t));
  assert(n != NULL);
  n->value = value;
  n->next  = head;
  head     = n;
}
```

This code performs a simple insertion, but if called by multiple threads at the "same time", has a race condition. Can you figure out why? (draw a picture of what could happen to a list if two concurrent insertions take place, assuming, as always, a malicious scheduling interleaving). Of course, we could solve this by surrounding this code with a lock acquire and release:

```
void insert(int value) {
  node_t *n = malloc(sizeof(node_t));
  assert(n != NULL);
  n->value = value;
  pthread_mutex_lock(listlock);    // begin critical section
  n->next  = head;
  head     = n;
  pthread_mutex_unlock(listlock); // end critical section
}
```

In this solution, we are using locks in the traditional manner[2]. Instead, let us try to perform this insertion in a lock-free manner simply using the compare-and-swap instruction. Here is one possible approach:

```
void insert(int value) {
  node_t *n = malloc(sizeof(node_t));
  assert(n != NULL);
  n->value = value;
  do {
    n->next = head;
  } while (CompareAndSwap(&head, n->next, n) == 0);
}
```

[2]The astute reader might be asking why we grabbed the lock so late, instead of right when entering `insert()`; can you, astute reader, figure out why that is likely correct? What assumptions does the code make, for example, about the call to `malloc()`?

The code here updates the next pointer to point to the current head, and then tries to swap the newly-created node into position as the new head of the list. However, this will fail if some other thread successfully swapped in a new head in the meanwhile, causing this thread to retry again with the new head.

Of course, building a useful list requires more than just a list insert, and not surprisingly building a list that you can insert into, delete from, and perform lookups on in a lock-free manner is non-trivial. Read the rich literature on lock-free and wait-free synchronization to learn more [H01, H91, H93].

Deadlock Avoidance via Scheduling

Instead of deadlock prevention, in some scenarios deadlock **avoidance** is preferable. Avoidance requires some global knowledge of which locks various threads might grab during their execution, and subsequently schedules said threads in a way as to guarantee no deadlock can occur.

For example, assume we have two processors and four threads which must be scheduled upon them. Assume further we know that Thread 1 (T1) grabs locks `L1` and `L2` (in some order, at some point during its execution), T2 grabs `L1` and `L2` as well, T3 grabs just `L2`, and T4 grabs no locks at all. We can show these lock acquisition demands of the threads in tabular form:

	T1	T2	T3	T4
L1	yes	yes	no	no
L2	yes	yes	yes	no

A smart scheduler could thus compute that as long as T1 and T2 are not run at the same time, no deadlock could ever arise. Here is one such schedule:

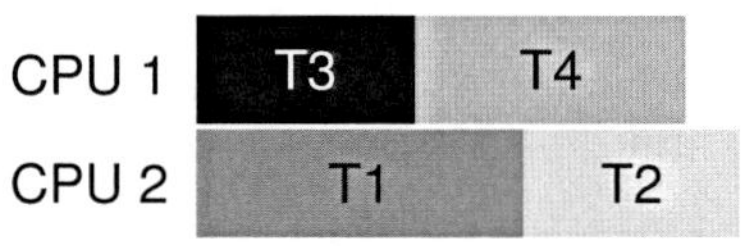

Note that it is OK for (T3 and T1) or (T3 and T2) to overlap. Even though T3 grabs lock `L2`, it can never cause a deadlock by running concurrently with other threads because it only grabs one lock.

Let's look at one more example. In this one, there is more contention for the same resources (again, locks `L1` and `L2`), as indicated by the following contention table:

	T1	T2	T3	T4
L1	yes	yes	yes	no
L2	yes	yes	yes	no

> **TIP: DON'T ALWAYS DO IT PERFECTLY (TOM WEST'S LAW)**
> Tom West, famous as the subject of the classic computer-industry book *Soul of a New Machine* [K81], says famously: "Not everything worth doing is worth doing well", which is a terrific engineering maxim. If a bad thing happens rarely, certainly one should not spend a great deal of effort to prevent it, particularly if the cost of the bad thing occurring is small. If, on the other hand, you are building a space shuttle, and the cost of something going wrong is the space shuttle blowing up, well, perhaps you should ignore this piece of advice.
> Some readers object: "This sounds like you are suggesting mediocrity as a solution!" Perhaps they are right, that we should be careful with advice such as this. However, our experience tells us that in the world of engineering, with pressing deadlines and other real-world concerns, one will always have to decide which aspects of a system to build well and which to put aside for another day. The hard part is knowing which to do when, a bit of insight only gained through experience and dedication to the task at hand.

In particular, threads T1, T2, and T3 all need to grab both locks `L1` and `L2` at some point during their execution. Here is a possible schedule that guarantees that no deadlock could ever occur:

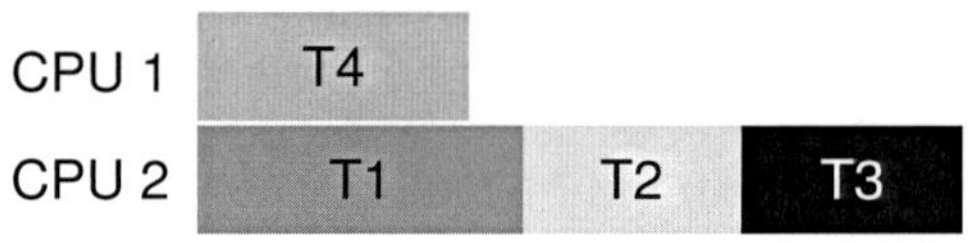

As you can see, static scheduling leads to a conservative approach where T1, T2, and T3 are all run on the same processor, and thus the total time to complete the jobs is lengthened considerably. Though it may have been possible to run these tasks concurrently, the fear of deadlock prevents us from doing so, and the cost is performance.

One famous example of an approach like this is Dijkstra's Banker's Algorithm [D64], and many similar approaches have been described in the literature. Unfortunately, they are only useful in very limited environments, for example, in an embedded system where one has full knowledge of the entire set of tasks that must be run and the locks that they need. Further, such approaches can limit concurrency, as we saw in the second example above. Thus, avoidance of deadlock via scheduling is not a widely-used general-purpose solution.

Detect and Recover

One final general strategy is to allow deadlocks to occasionally occur, and then take some action once such a deadlock has been detected. For example, if an OS froze once a year, you would just reboot it and get happily (or grumpily) on with your work. If deadlocks are rare, such a non-solution is indeed quite pragmatic.

Many database systems employ deadlock detection and recovery techniques. A deadlock detector runs periodically, building a resource graph and checking it for cycles. In the event of a cycle (deadlock), the system needs to be restarted. If more intricate repair of data structures is first required, a human being may be involved to ease the process.

More detail on database concurrency, deadlock, and related issues can be found elsewhere [B+87, K87]. Read these works, or better yet, take a course on databases to learn more about this rich and interesting topic.

32.4 Summary

In this chapter, we have studied the types of bugs that occur in concurrent programs. The first type, non-deadlock bugs, are surprisingly common, but often are easier to fix. They include atomicity violations, in which a sequence of instructions that should have been executed together was not, and order violations, in which the needed order between two threads was not enforced.

We have also briefly discussed deadlock: why it occurs, and what can be done about it. The problem is as old as concurrency itself, and many hundreds of papers have been written about the topic. The best solution in practice is to be careful, develop a lock acquisition order, and thus prevent deadlock from occurring in the first place. Wait-free approaches also have promise, as some wait-free data structures are now finding their way into commonly-used libraries and critical systems, including Linux. However, their lack of generality and the complexity to develop a new wait-free data structure will likely limit the overall utility of this approach. Perhaps the best solution is to develop new concurrent programming models: in systems such as MapReduce (from Google) [GD02], programmers can describe certain types of parallel computations without any locks whatsoever. Locks are problematic by their very nature; perhaps we should seek to avoid using them unless we truly must.

References

[B+87] "Concurrency Control and Recovery in Database Systems" by Philip A. Bernstein, Vassos Hadzilacos, Nathan Goodman. Addison-Wesley, 1987. *The classic text on concurrency in database management systems. As you can tell, understanding concurrency, deadlock, and other topics in the world of databases is a world unto itself. Study it and find out for yourself.*

[C+71] "System Deadlocks" by E.G. Coffman, M.J. Elphick, A. Shoshani. ACM Computing Surveys, 3:2, June 1971. *The classic paper outlining the conditions for deadlock and how you might go about dealing with it. There are certainly some earlier papers on this topic; see the references within this paper for details.*

[D64] "Een algorithme ter voorkoming van de dodelijke omarming" by Edsger Dijkstra. 1964. Available: http://www.cs.utexas.edu/users/EWD/ewd01xx/EWD108.PDF. *Indeed, not only did Dijkstra come up with a number of solutions to the deadlock problem, he was the first to note its existence, at least in written form. However, he called it the "deadly embrace", which (thankfully) did not catch on.*

[GD02] "MapReduce: Simplified Data Processing on Large Clusters" by Sanjay Ghemawhat, Jeff Dean. OSDI '04, San Francisco, CA, October 2004. *The MapReduce paper ushered in the era of large-scale data processing, and proposes a framework for performing such computations on clusters of generally unreliable machines.*

[H01] "A Pragmatic Implementation of Non-blocking Linked-lists" by Tim Harris. International Conference on Distributed Computing (DISC), 2001. *A relatively modern example of the difficulties of building something as simple as a concurrent linked list without locks.*

[H91] "Wait-free Synchronization" by Maurice Herlihy . ACM TOPLAS, 13:1, January 1991. *Herlihy's work pioneers the ideas behind wait-free approaches to writing concurrent programs. These approaches tend to be complex and hard, often more difficult than using locks correctly, probably limiting their success in the real world.*

[H93] "A Methodology for Implementing Highly Concurrent Data Objects" by Maurice Herlihy. ACM TOPLAS, 15:5, November 1993. *A nice overview of lock-free and wait-free structures. Both approaches eschew locks, but wait-free approaches are harder to realize, as they try to ensure than any operation on a concurrent structure will terminate in a finite number of steps (e.g., no unbounded looping).*

[J+08] "Deadlock Immunity: Enabling Systems To Defend Against Deadlocks" by Horatiu Jula, Daniel Tralamazza, Cristian Zamfir, George Candea. OSDI '08, San Diego, CA, December 2008. *An excellent recent paper on deadlocks and how to avoid getting caught in the same ones over and over again in a particular system.*

[K81] "Soul of a New Machine" by Tracy Kidder. Backbay Books, 2000 (reprint of 1980 version). *A must-read for any systems builder or engineer, detailing the early days of how a team inside Data General (DG), led by Tom West, worked to produce a "new machine." Kidder's other books are also excellent, including "Mountains beyond Mountains." Or maybe you don't agree with us, comma?*

[K87] "Deadlock Detection in Distributed Databases" by Edgar Knapp. ACM Computing Surveys, 19:4, December 1987. *An excellent overview of deadlock detection in distributed database systems. Also points to a number of other related works, and thus is a good place to start your reading.*

[L+08] "Learning from Mistakes — A Comprehensive Study on Real World Concurrency Bug Characteristics" by Shan Lu, Soyeon Park, Eunsoo Seo, Yuanyuan Zhou. ASPLOS '08, March 2008, Seattle, Washington. *The first in-depth study of concurrency bugs in real software, and the basis for this chapter. Look at Y.Y. Zhou's or Shan Lu's web pages for many more interesting papers on bugs.*

[T+94] "Linux File Memory Map Code" by Linus Torvalds and many others. Available online at: `http://lxr.free-electrons.com/source/mm/filemap.c`. *Thanks to Michael Walfish (NYU) for pointing out this precious example. The real world, as you can see in this file, can be a bit more complex than the simple clarity found in textbooks...*

Homework (Code)

This homework lets you explore some real code that deadlocks (or avoids deadlock). The different versions of code correspond to different approaches to avoiding deadlock in a simplified `vector_add()` routine. See the README for details on these programs and their common substrate.

Questions

1. First let's make sure you understand how the programs generally work, and some of the key options. Study the code in `vector-deadlock.c`, as well as in `main-common.c` and related files.

   Now, run `./vector-deadlock -n 2 -l 1 -v`, which instantiates two threads (`-n 2`), each of which does one vector add (`-l 1`), and does so in verbose mode (`-v`). Make sure you understand the output. How does the output change from run to run?
2. Now add the `-d` flag, and change the number of loops (`-l`) from 1 to higher numbers. What happens? Does the code (always) deadlock?
3. How does changing the number of threads (`-n`) change the outcome of the program? Are there any values of `-n` that ensure no deadlock occurs?
4. Now examine the code in `vector-global-order.c`. First, make sure you understand what the code is trying to do; do you understand why the code avoids deadlock? Also, why is there a special case in this `vector_add()` routine when the source and destination vectors are the same?
5. Now run the code with the following flags: `-t -n 2 -l 100000 -d`. How long does the code take to complete? How does the total time change when you increase the number of loops, or the number of threads?
6. What happens if you turn on the parallelism flag (`-p`)? How much would you expect performance to change when each thread is working on adding different vectors (which is what `-p` enables) versus working on the same ones?
7. Now let's study `vector-try-wait.c`. First make sure you understand the code. Is the first call to `pthread_mutex_trylock()` really needed?

   Now run the code. How fast does it run compared to the global order approach? How does the number of retries, as counted by the code, change as the number of threads increases?
8. Now let's look at `vector-avoid-hold-and-wait.c`. What is the main problem with this approach? How does its performance compare to the other versions, when running both with `-p` and without it?
9. Finally, let's look at `vector-nolock.c`. This version doesn't use locks at all; does it provide the exact same semantics as the other versions? Why or why not?
10. Now compare its performance to the other versions, both when threads are working on the same two vectors (no `-p`) and when each thread is working on separate vectors (`-p`). How does this no-lock version perform?

33

Event-based Concurrency (Advanced)

Thus far, we've written about concurrency as if the only way to build concurrent applications is to use threads. Like many things in life, this is not completely true. Specifically, a different style of concurrent programming is often used in both GUI-based applications [O96] as well as some types of internet servers [PDZ99]. This style, known as **event-based concurrency**, has become popular in some modern systems, including server-side frameworks such as **node.js** [N13], but its roots are found in C/UNIX systems that we'll discuss below.

The problem that event-based concurrency addresses is two-fold. The first is that managing concurrency correctly in multi-threaded applications can be challenging; as we've discussed, missing locks, deadlock, and other nasty problems can arise. The second is that in a multi-threaded application, the developer has little or no control over what is scheduled at a given moment in time; rather, the programmer simply creates threads and then hopes that the underlying OS schedules them in a reasonable manner across available CPUs. Given the difficulty of building a general-purpose scheduler that works well in all cases for all workloads, sometimes the OS will schedule work in a manner that is less than optimal. And thus, we have ...

> THE CRUX:
> HOW TO BUILD CONCURRENT SERVERS WITHOUT THREADS
> How can we build a concurrent server without using threads, and thus retain control over concurrency as well as avoid some of the problems that seem to plague multi-threaded applications?

33.1 The Basic Idea: An Event Loop

The basic approach we'll use, as stated above, is called **event-based concurrency**. The approach is quite simple: you simply wait for something (i.e., an "event") to occur; when it does, you check what type of event it is and do the small amount of work it requires (which may include issuing I/O requests, or scheduling other events for future handling, etc.). That's it!

Before getting into the details, let's first examine what a canonical event-based server looks like. Such applications are based around a simple construct known as the **event loop**. Pseudocode for an event loop looks like this:

```
while (1) {
    events = getEvents();
    for (e in events)
        processEvent(e);
}
```

It's really that simple. The main loop simply waits for something to do (by calling `getEvents()` in the code above) and then, for each event returned, processes them, one at a time; the code that processes each event is known as an **event handler**. Importantly, when a handler processes an event, it is the only activity taking place in the system; thus, deciding which event to handle next is equivalent to scheduling. This explicit control over scheduling is one of the fundamental advantages of the event-based approach.

But this discussion leaves us with a bigger question: how exactly does an event-based server determine which events are taking place, in particular with regards to network and disk I/O? Specifically, how can an event server tell if a message has arrived for it?

33.2 An Important API: `select()` (or `poll()`)

With that basic event loop in mind, we next must address the question of how to receive events. In most systems, a basic API is available, via either the `select()` or `poll()` system calls.

What these interfaces enable a program to do is simple: check whether there is any incoming I/O that should be attended to. For example, imagine that a network application (such as a web server) wishes to check whether any network packets have arrived, in order to service them. These system calls let you do exactly that.

Take `select()` for example. The manual page (on a Mac) describes the API in this manner:

```
int select(int nfds,
           fd_set *restrict readfds,
           fd_set *restrict writefds,
           fd_set *restrict errorfds,
           struct timeval *restrict timeout);
```

The actual description from the man page: *select() examines the I/O descriptor sets whose addresses are passed in readfds, writefds, and errorfds to see*

> ASIDE: BLOCKING VS. NON-BLOCKING INTERFACES
>
> Blocking (or **synchronous**) interfaces do all of their work before returning to the caller; non-blocking (or **asynchronous**) interfaces begin some work but return immediately, thus letting whatever work that needs to be done get done in the background.
>
> The usual culprit in blocking calls is I/O of some kind. For example, if a call must read from disk in order to complete, it might block, waiting for the I/O request that has been sent to the disk to return.
>
> Non-blocking interfaces can be used in any style of programming (e.g., with threads), but are essential in the event-based approach, as a call that blocks will halt all progress.

if some of their descriptors are ready for reading, are ready for writing, or have an exceptional condition pending, respectively. The first nfds descriptors are checked in each set, i.e., the descriptors from 0 through nfds-1 in the descriptor sets are examined. On return, select() replaces the given descriptor sets with subsets consisting of those descriptors that are ready for the requested operation. select() returns the total number of ready descriptors in all the sets.

A couple of points about `select()`. First, note that it lets you check whether descriptors can be *read* from as well as *written* to; the former lets a server determine that a new packet has arrived and is in need of processing, whereas the latter lets the service know when it is OK to reply (i.e., the outbound queue is not full).

Second, note the timeout argument. One common usage here is to set the timeout to NULL, which causes `select()` to block indefinitely, until some descriptor is ready. However, more robust servers will usually specify some kind of timeout; one common technique is to set the timeout to zero, and thus use the call to `select()` to return immediately.

The `poll()` system call is quite similar. See its manual page, or Stevens and Rago [SR05], for details.

Either way, these basic primitives give us a way to build a non-blocking event loop, which simply checks for incoming packets, reads from sockets with messages upon them, and replies as needed.

33.3 Using `select()`

To make this more concrete, let's examine how to use `select()` to see which network descriptors have incoming messages upon them. Figure 331 shows a simple example.

This code is actually fairly simple to understand. After some initialization, the server enters an infinite loop. Inside the loop, it uses the `FD_ZERO()` macro to first clear the set of file descriptors, and then uses `FD_SET()` to include all of the file descriptors from `minFD` to `maxFD` in

```c
#include <stdio.h>
#include <stdlib.h>
#include <sys/time.h>
#include <sys/types.h>
#include <unistd.h>

int main(void) {
  // open and set up a bunch of sockets (not shown)
  // main loop
  while (1) {
    // initialize the fd_set to all zero
    fd_set readFDs;
    FD_ZERO(&readFDs);

    // now set the bits for the descriptors
    // this server is interested in
    // (for simplicity, all of them from min to max)
    int fd;
    for (fd = minFD; fd < maxFD; fd++)
      FD_SET(fd, &readFDs);

    // do the select
    int rc = select(maxFD+1, &readFDs, NULL, NULL, NULL);

    // check which actually have data using FD_ISSET()
    int fd;
    for (fd = minFD; fd < maxFD; fd++)
      if (FD_ISSET(fd, &readFDs))
        processFD(fd);
  }
}
```

Figure 331: **Simple Code Using `select()`**

the set. This set of descriptors might represent, for example, all of the network sockets to which the server is paying attention. Finally, the server calls `select()` to see which of the connections have data available upon them. By then using `FD_ISSET()` in a loop, the event server can see which of the descriptors have data ready and process the incoming data.

Of course, a real server would be more complicated than this, and require logic to use when sending messages, issuing disk I/O, and many other details. For further information, see Stevens and Rago [SR05] for API information, or Pai et. al or Welsh et al. for a good overview of the general flow of event-based servers [PDZ99, WCB01].

> TIP: DON'T BLOCK IN EVENT-BASED SERVERS
> Event-based servers enable fine-grained control over scheduling of tasks. However, to maintain such control, no call that blocks the execution of the caller can ever be made; failing to obey this design tip will result in a blocked event-based server, frustrated clients, and serious questions as to whether you ever read this part of the book.

33.4 Why Simpler? No Locks Needed

With a single CPU and an event-based application, the problems found in concurrent programs are no longer present. Specifically, because only one event is being handled at a time, there is no need to acquire or release locks; the event-based server cannot be interrupted by another thread because it is decidedly single threaded. Thus, concurrency bugs common in threaded programs do not manifest in the basic event-based approach.

33.5 A Problem: Blocking System Calls

Thus far, event-based programming sounds great, right? You program a simple loop, and handle events as they arise. You don't even need to think about locking! But there is an issue: what if an event requires that you issue a system call that might block?

For example, imagine a request comes from a client into a server to read a file from disk and return its contents to the requesting client (much like a simple HTTP request). To service such a request, some event handler will eventually have to issue an `open()` system call to open the file, followed by a series of `read()` calls to read the file. When the file is read into memory, the server will likely start sending the results to the client.

Both the `open()` and `read()` calls may issue I/O requests to the storage system (when the needed metadata or data is not in memory already), and thus may take a long time to service. With a thread-based server, this is no issue: while the thread issuing the I/O request suspends (waiting for the I/O to complete), other threads can run, thus enabling the server to make progress. Indeed, this natural **overlap** of I/O and other computation is what makes thread-based programming quite natural and straightforward.

With an event-based approach, however, there are no other threads to run: just the main event loop. And this implies that if an event handler issues a call that blocks, the *entire* server will do just that: block until the call completes. When the event loop blocks, the system sits idle, and thus is a huge potential waste of resources. We thus have a rule that must be obeyed in event-based systems: no blocking calls are allowed.

33.6 A Solution: Asynchronous I/O

To overcome this limit, many modern operating systems have introduced new ways to issue I/O requests to the disk system, referred to generically as **asynchronous I/O**. These interfaces enable an application to issue an I/O request and return control immediately to the caller, before the I/O has completed; additional interfaces enable an application to determine whether various I/Os have completed.

For example, let us examine the interface provided on a Mac (other systems have similar APIs). The APIs revolve around a basic structure, the `struct aiocb` or **AIO control block** in common terminology. A simplified version of the structure looks like this (see the manual pages for more information):

```
struct aiocb {
    int                aio_fildes;    // File descriptor
    off_t              aio_offset;    // File offset
    volatile void      *aio_buf;      // Location of buffer
    size_t             aio_nbytes;    // Length of transfer
};
```

To issue an asynchronous read to a file, an application should first fill in this structure with the relevant information: the file descriptor of the file to be read (`aio_fildes`), the offset within the file (`aio_offset`) as well as the length of the request (`aio_nbytes`), and finally the target memory location into which the results of the read should be copied (`aio_buf`).

After this structure is filled in, the application must issue the asynchronous call to read the file; on a Mac, this API is simply the **asynchronous read** API:

```
int aio_read(struct aiocb *aiocbp);
```

This call tries to issue the I/O; if successful, it simply returns right away and the application (i.e., the event-based server) can continue with its work.

There is one last piece of the puzzle we must solve, however. How can we tell when an I/O is complete, and thus that the buffer (pointed to by `aio_buf`) now has the requested data within it?

One last API is needed. On a Mac, it is referred to (somewhat confusingly) as `aio_error()`. The API looks like this:

```
int aio_error(const struct aiocb *aiocbp);
```

This system call checks whether the request referred to by `aiocbp` has completed. If it has, the routine returns success (indicated by a zero); if not, EINPROGRESS is returned. Thus, for every outstanding asynchronous I/O, an application can periodically **poll** the system via a call to `aio_error()` to determine whether said I/O has yet completed.

One thing you might have noticed is that it is painful to check whether an I/O has completed; if a program has tens or hundreds of I/Os issued at a given point in time, should it simply keep checking each of them repeatedly, or wait a little while first, or ... ?

To remedy this issue, some systems provide an approach based on the **interrupt**. This method uses UNIX **signals** to inform applications when an asynchronous I/O completes, thus removing the need to repeatedly ask the system. This polling vs. interrupts issue is seen in devices too, as you will see (or already have seen) in the chapter on I/O devices.

In systems without asynchronous I/O, the pure event-based approach cannot be implemented. However, clever researchers have derived methods that work fairly well in their place. For example, Pai et al. [PDZ99] describe a hybrid approach in which events are used to process network packets, and a thread pool is used to manage outstanding I/Os. Read their paper for details.

33.7 Another Problem: State Management

Another issue with the event-based approach is that such code is generally more complicated to write than traditional thread-based code. The reason is as follows: when an event handler issues an asynchronous I/O, it must package up some program state for the next event handler to use when the I/O finally completes; this additional work is not needed in thread-based programs, as the state the program needs is on the stack of the thread. Adya et al. call this work **manual stack management**, and it is fundamental to event-based programming [A+02].

To make this point more concrete, let's look at a simple example in which a thread-based server needs to read from a file descriptor (`fd`) and, once complete, write the data that it read from the file to a network socket descriptor (`sd`). The code (ignoring error checking) looks like this:

```
int rc = read(fd, buffer, size);
rc = write(sd, buffer, size);
```

As you can see, in a multi-threaded program, doing this kind of work is trivial; when the `read()` finally returns, the code immediately knows which socket to write to because that information is on the stack of the thread (in the variable `sd`).

In an event-based system, life is not so easy. To perform the same task, we'd first issue the read asynchronously, using the AIO calls described above. Let's say we then periodically check for completion of the read using the `aio_error()` call; when that call informs us that the read is complete, how does the event-based server know what to do?

ASIDE: UNIX SIGNALS

A huge and fascinating infrastructure known as **signals** is present in all modern UNIX variants. At its simplest, signals provide a way to communicate with a process. Specifically, a signal can be delivered to an application; doing so stops the application from whatever it is doing to run a **signal handler**, i.e., some code in the application to handle that signal. When finished, the process just resumes its previous behavior.

Each signal has a name, such as **HUP** (hang up), **INT** (interrupt), **SEGV** (segmentation violation), etc.; see the man page for details. Interestingly, sometimes it is the kernel itself that does the signaling. For example, when your program encounters a segmentation violation, the OS sends it a **SIGSEGV** (prepending **SIG** to signal names is common); if your program is configured to catch that signal, you can actually run some code in response to this erroneous program behavior (which is helpful for debugging). When a signal is sent to a process not configured to handle a signal, the default behavior is enacted; for SEGV, the process is killed.

Here is a simple program that goes into an infinite loop, but has first set up a signal handler to catch SIGHUP:

```
void handle(int arg) {
    printf("stop wakin' me up...\n");
}

int main(int argc, char *argv[]) {
    signal(SIGHUP, handle);
    while (1)
        ; // doin' nothin' except catchin' some sigs
    return 0;
}
```

You can send signals to it with the **kill** command line tool (yes, this is an odd and aggressive name). Doing so will interrupt the main while loop in the program and run the handler code `handle()`:

```
prompt> ./main &
[3] 36705
prompt> kill -HUP 36705
stop wakin' me up...
prompt> kill -HUP 36705
stop wakin' me up...
```

There is a lot more to learn about signals, so much that a single chapter, much less a single page, does not nearly suffice. As always, there is one great source: Stevens and Rago [SR05]. Read more if interested.

The solution, as described by Adya et al. [A+02], is to use an old programming language construct known as a **continuation** [FHK84]. Though it sounds complicated, the idea is rather simple: basically, record the needed information to finish processing this event in some data structure; when the event happens (i.e., when the disk I/O completes), look up the needed information and process the event.

In this specific case, the solution would be to record the socket descriptor (`sd`) in some kind of data structure (e.g., a hash table), indexed by the file descriptor (`fd`). When the disk I/O completes, the event handler would use the file descriptor to look up the continuation, which will return the value of the socket descriptor to the caller. At this point (finally), the server can then do the last bit of work to write the data to the socket.

33.8 What Is Still Difficult With Events

There are a few other difficulties with the event-based approach that we should mention. For example, when systems moved from a single CPU to multiple CPUs, some of the simplicity of the event-based approach disappeared. Specifically, in order to utilize more than one CPU, the event server has to run multiple event handlers in parallel; when doing so, the usual synchronization problems (e.g., critical sections) arise, and the usual solutions (e.g., locks) must be employed. Thus, on modern multicore systems, simple event handling without locks is no longer possible.

Another problem with the event-based approach is that it does not integrate well with certain kinds of systems activity, such as **paging**. For example, if an event-handler page faults, it will block, and thus the server will not make progress until the page fault completes. Even though the server has been structured to avoid *explicit* blocking, this type of *implicit* blocking due to page faults is hard to avoid and thus can lead to large performance problems when prevalent.

A third issue is that event-based code can be hard to manage over time, as the exact semantics of various routines changes [A+02]. For example, if a routine changes from non-blocking to blocking, the event handler that calls that routine must also change to accommodate its new nature, by ripping itself into two pieces. Because blocking is so disastrous for event-based servers, a programmer must always be on the lookout for such changes in the semantics of the APIs each event uses.

Finally, though asynchronous disk I/O is now possible on most platforms, it has taken a long time to get there [PDZ99], and it never quite integrates with asynchronous network I/O in as simple and uniform a manner as you might think. For example, while one would simply like to use the `select()` interface to manage all outstanding I/Os, usually some combination of `select()` for networking and the AIO calls for disk I/O are required.

33.9 Summary

We've presented a bare bones introduction to a different style of concurrency based on events. Event-based servers give control of scheduling to the application itself, but do so at some cost in complexity and difficulty of integration with other aspects of modern systems (e.g., paging). Because of these challenges, no single approach has emerged as best; thus, both threads and events are likely to persist as two different approaches to the same concurrency problem for many years to come. Read some research papers (e.g., [A+02, PDZ99, vB+03, WCB01]) or better yet, write some event-based code, to learn more.

References

[A+02] "Cooperative Task Management Without Manual Stack Management" by Atul Adya, Jon Howell, Marvin Theimer, William J. Bolosky, John R. Douceur. USENIX ATC '02, Monterey, CA, June 2002. *This gem of a paper is the first to clearly articulate some of the difficulties of event-based concurrency, and suggests some simple solutions, as well explores the even crazier idea of combining the two types of concurrency management into a single application!*

[FHK84] "Programming With Continuations" by Daniel P. Friedman, Christopher T. Haynes, Eugene E. Kohlbecker. In Program Transformation and Programming Environments, Springer Verlag, 1984. *The classic reference to this old idea from the world of programming languages. Now increasingly popular in some modern languages.*

[N13] "Node.js Documentation" by the folks who built node.js. Available: `nodejs.org/api`. *One of the many cool new frameworks that help you readily build web services and applications. Every modern systems hacker should be proficient in frameworks such as this one (and likely, more than one). Spend the time and do some development in one of these worlds and become an expert.*

[O96] "Why Threads Are A Bad Idea (for most purposes)" by John Ousterhout. Invited Talk at USENIX '96, San Diego, CA, January 1996. *A great talk about how threads aren't a great match for GUI-based applications (but the ideas are more general). Ousterhout formed many of these opinions while he was developing Tcl/Tk, a cool scripting language and toolkit that made it 100x easier to develop GUI-based applications than the state of the art at the time. While the Tk GUI toolkit lives on (in Python for example), Tcl seems to be slowly dying (unfortunately).*

[PDZ99] "Flash: An Efficient and Portable Web Server" by Vivek S. Pai, Peter Druschel, Willy Zwaenepoel. USENIX '99, Monterey, CA, June 1999. *A pioneering paper on how to structure web servers in the then-burgeoning Internet era. Read it to understand the basics as well as to see the authors' ideas on how to build hybrids when support for asynchronous I/O is lacking.*

[SR05] "Advanced Programming in the UNIX Environment" by W. Richard Stevens and Stephen A. Rago. Addison-Wesley, 2005. *Once again, we refer to the classic must-have-on-your-bookshelf book of UNIX systems programming. If there is some detail you need to know, it is in here.*

[vB+03] "Capriccio: Scalable Threads for Internet Services" by Rob von Behren, Jeremy Condit, Feng Zhou, George C. Necula, Eric Brewer. SOSP '03, Lake George, New York, October 2003. *A paper about how to make threads work at extreme scale; a counter to all the event-based work ongoing at the time.*

[WCB01] "SEDA: An Architecture for Well-Conditioned, Scalable Internet Services" by Matt Welsh, David Culler, and Eric Brewer. SOSP '01, Banff, Canada, October 2001. *A nice twist on event-based serving that combines threads, queues, and event-based handling into one streamlined whole. Some of these ideas have found their way into the infrastructures of companies such as Google, Amazon, and elsewhere.*

Homework (Code)

In this (short) homework, you'll gain some experience with event-based code and some of its key concepts. Good luck!

Questions

1. First, write a simple server that can accept and serve TCP connections. You'll have to poke around the Internet a bit if you don't already know how to do this. Build this to serve exactly one request at a time; have each request be very simple, e.g., to get the current time of day.
2. Now, add the `select()` interface. Build a main program that can accept multiple connections, and an event loop that checks which file descriptors have data on them, and then read and process those requests. Make sure to carefully test that you are using `select()` correctly.
3. Next, let's make the requests a little more interesting, to mimic a simple web or file server. Each request should be to read the contents of a file (named in the request), and the server should respond by reading the file into a buffer, and then returning the contents to the client. Use the standard `open()`, `read()`, `close()` system calls to implement this feature. Be a little careful here: if you leave this running for a long time, someone may figure out how to use it to read all the files on your computer!
4. Now, instead of using standard I/O system calls, use the asynchronous I/O interfaces as described in the chapter. How hard was it to incorporate asynchronous interfaces into your program?
5. For fun, add some signal handling to your code. One common use of signals is to poke a server to reload some kind of configuration file, or take some other kind of administrative action. Perhaps one natural way to play around with this is to add a user-level file cache to your server, which stores recently accessed files. Implement a signal handler that clears the cache when the signal is sent to the server process.
6. Finally, we have the hard part: how can you tell if the effort to build an asynchronous, event-based approach are worth it? Can you create an experiment to show the benefits? How much implementation complexity did your approach add?

34

Summary Dialogue on Concurrency

Professor: *So, does your head hurt now?*

Student: *(taking two Motrin tablets) Well, some. It's hard to think about all the ways threads can interleave.*

Professor: *Indeed it is. I am always amazed that when concurrent execution is involved, just a few lines of code can become nearly impossible to understand.*

Student: *Me too! It's kind of embarrassing, as a Computer Scientist, not to be able to make sense of five lines of code.*

Professor: *Oh, don't feel too badly. If you look through the first papers on concurrent algorithms, they are sometimes wrong! And the authors often professors!*

Student: *(gasps) Professors can be ... umm... wrong?*

Professor: *Yes, it is true. Though don't tell anybody — it's one of our trade secrets.*

Student: *I am sworn to secrecy. But if concurrent code is so hard to think about, and so hard to get right, how are we supposed to write correct concurrent code?*

Professor: *Well that is the real question, isn't it? I think it starts with a few simple things. First, keep it simple! Avoid complex interactions between threads, and use well-known and tried-and-true ways to manage thread interactions.*

Student: *Like simple locking, and maybe a producer-consumer queue?*

Professor: *Exactly! Those are common paradigms, and you should be able to produce the working solutions given what you've learned. Second, only use concurrency when absolutely needed; avoid it if at all possible. There is nothing worse than premature optimization of a program.*

Student: *I see — why add threads if you don't need them?*

Professor: *Exactly. Third, if you really need parallelism, seek it in other simplified forms. For example, the Map-Reduce method for writing parallel data analysis code is an excellent example of achieving parallelism without having to handle any of the horrific complexities of locks, condition variables, and the other nasty things we've talked about.*

Student: *Map-Reduce, huh? Sounds interesting — I'll have to read more about it on my own.*

Professor: *Good! You should. In the end, you'll have to do a lot of that, as what we learn together can only serve as the barest introduction to the wealth of knowledge that is out there. Read, read, and read some more! And then try things out, write some code, and then write some more too. And practice more, too; beyond what's in this book, there are plenty of other resources out there*[1]*. As Gladwell talks about in his book "Outliers", you need to put roughly 10,000 hours into something in order to become a real expert. You can't do that all inside of class time!*

Student: *Wow, I'm not sure if that is depressing, or uplifting. But I'll assume the latter, and get to work! Time to write some more concurrent code...*

[1] Here is a link to one, in gamified form: `https://deadlockempire.github.io/`

Part III

Persistence

35

A Dialogue on Persistence

Professor: *And thus we reach the third of our four ... err... three pillars of operating systems:* ***persistence****.*

Student: *Did you say there were three pillars, or four? What is the fourth?*

Professor: *No. Just three, young student, just three. Trying to keep it simple here.*

Student: *OK, fine. But what is persistence, oh fine and noble professor?*

Professor: *Actually, you probably know what it means in the traditional sense, right? As the dictionary would say: "a firm or obstinate continuance in a course of action in spite of difficulty or opposition."*

Student: *It's kind of like taking your class: some obstinance required.*

Professor: *Ha! Yes. But persistence here means something else. Let me explain. Imagine you are outside, in a field, and you pick a —*

Student: *(interrupting) I know! A peach! From a peach tree!*

Professor: *I was going to say apple, from an apple tree. Oh well; we'll do it your way, I guess.*

Student: *(stares blankly)*

Professor: *Anyhow, you pick a peach; in fact, you pick many many peaches, but you want to make them last for a long time. Winter is hard and cruel in Wisconsin, after all. What do you do?*

Student: *Well, I think there are some different things you can do. You can pickle it! Or bake a pie. Or make a jam of some kind. Lots of fun!*

Professor: *Fun? Well, maybe. Certainly, you have to do a lot more work to make the peach* ***persist****. And so it is with information as well; making information persist, despite computer crashes, disk failures, or power outages is a tough and interesting challenge.*

Student: *Nice segue; you're getting quite good at that.*

Professor: *Thanks! A professor can always use a few kind words, you know.*

Student: *I'll try to remember that. I guess it's time to stop talking peaches, and start talking computers?*

Professor: *Yes, it is that time...*

36

I/O Devices

Before delving into the main content of this part of the book (on persistence), we first introduce the concept of an **input/output (I/O) device** and show how the operating system might interact with such an entity. I/O is quite critical to computer systems, of course; imagine a program without any input (it produces the same result each time); now imagine a program with no output (what was the purpose of it running?). Clearly, for computer systems to be interesting, both input and output are required. And thus, our general problem:

> CRUX: HOW TO INTEGRATE I/O INTO SYSTEMS
>
> How should I/O be integrated into systems? What are the general mechanisms? How can we make them efficient?

36.1 System Architecture

To begin our discussion, let's look at a "classical" diagram of a typical system (Figure 361, page 444). The picture shows a single CPU attached to the main memory of the system via some kind of **memory bus** or interconnect. Some devices are connected to the system via a general **I/O bus**, which in many modern systems would be **PCI** (or one of its many derivatives); graphics and some other higher-performance I/O devices might be found here. Finally, even lower down are one or more of what we call a **peripheral bus**, such as **SCSI**, **SATA**, or **USB**. These connect slow devices to the system, including **disks**, **mice**, and **keyboards**.

One question you might ask is: why do we need a hierarchical structure like this? Put simply: physics, and cost. The faster a bus is, the shorter it must be; thus, a high-performance memory bus does not have much room to plug devices and such into it. In addition, engineering a bus for high performance is quite costly. Thus, system designers have adopted this hierarchical approach, where components that demand high performance (such as the graphics card) are nearer the CPU. Lower performance components are further away. The benefits of placing disks and other slow devices on a peripheral bus are manifold; in particular, you can place a large number of devices on it.

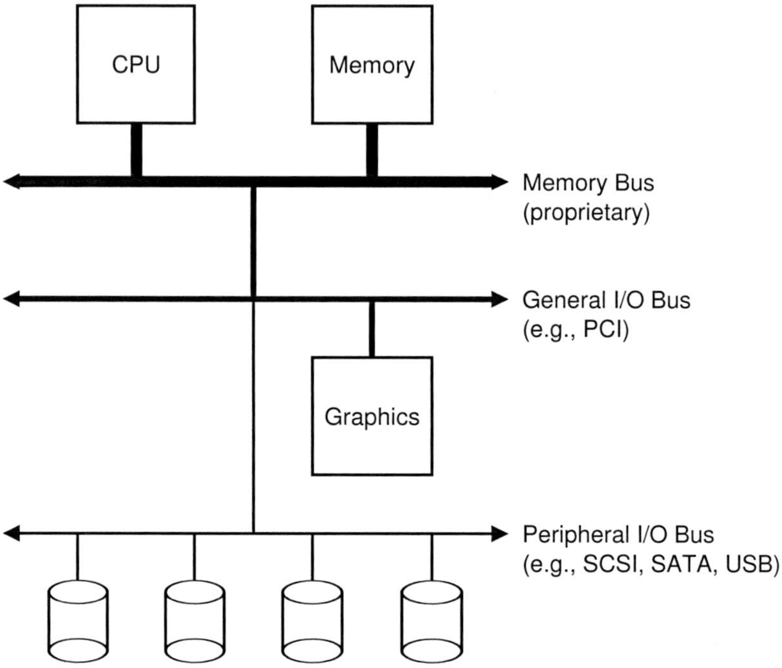

Figure 361: **Prototypical System Architecture**

Of course, modern systems increasingly use specialized chipsets and faster point-to-point interconnects to improve performance. Figure 362 (page 445) shows an approximate diagram of Intel's Z270 Chipset [H17]. Along the top, the CPU connects most closely to the memory system, but also has a high-performance connection to the graphics card (and thus, the display) to enable gaming (oh, the horror!) and other graphics-intensive applications.

The CPU connects to an I/O chip via Intel's proprietary **DMI** (**Direct Media Interface**), and the rest of the devices connect to this chip via a number of different interconnects. On the right, one or more hard drives connect to the system via the **eSATA** interface; **ATA** (the **AT Attachment**, in reference to providing connection to the IBM PC AT), then **SATA** (for **Serial ATA**), and now eSATA (for **external SATA**) represent an evolution of storage interfaces over the past decades, with each step forward increasing performance to keep pace with modern storage devices.

Below the I/O chip are a number of **USB** (**Universal Serial Bus**) connections, which in this depiction enable a keyboard and mouse to be attached to the computer. On many modern systems, USB is used for low performance devices such as these.

Finally, on the left, other higher performance devices can be connected

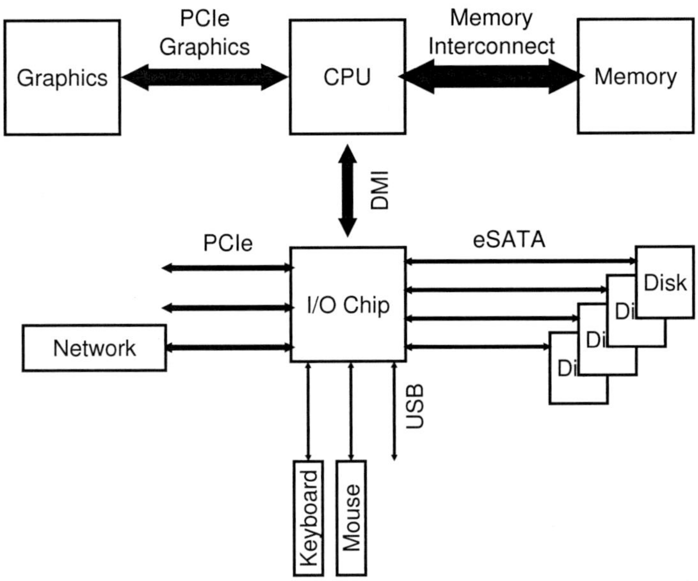

Figure 362: **Modern System Architecture**

to the system via **PCIe** (**Peripheral Component Interconnect Express**). In this diagram, a network interface is attached to the system here; higher performance storage devices (such as **NVMe** persistent storage devices) are often connected here.

36.2 A Canonical Device

Let us now look at a canonical device (not a real one), and use this device to drive our understanding of some of the machinery required to make device interaction efficient. From Figure 363 (page 446), we can see that a device has two important components. The first is the hardware **interface** it presents to the rest of the system. Just like a piece of software, hardware must also present some kind of interface that allows the system software to control its operation. Thus, all devices have some specified interface and protocol for typical interaction.

The second part of any device is its **internal structure**. This part of the device is implementation specific and is responsible for implementing the abstraction the device presents to the system. Very simple devices will have one or a few hardware chips to implement their functionality; more complex devices will include a simple CPU, some general purpose memory, and other device-specific chips to get their job done. For example, modern RAID controllers might consist of hundreds of thousands of lines of **firmware** (i.e., software within a hardware device) to implement its functionality.

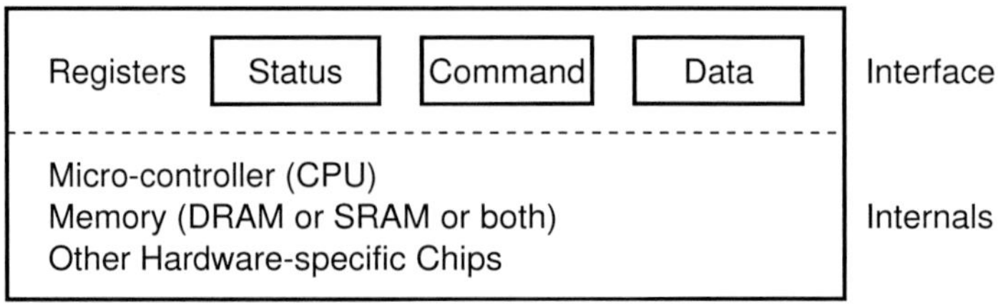

Figure 363: **A Canonical Device**

36.3 The Canonical Protocol

In the picture above, the (simplified) device interface is comprised of three registers: a **status** register, which can be read to see the current status of the device; a **command** register, to tell the device to perform a certain task; and a **data** register to pass data to the device, or get data from the device. By reading and writing these registers, the operating system can control device behavior.

Let us now describe a typical interaction that the OS might have with the device in order to get the device to do something on its behalf. The protocol is as follows:

```
While (STATUS == BUSY)
    ; // wait until device is not busy
Write data to DATA register
Write command to COMMAND register
    (starts the device and executes the command)
While (STATUS == BUSY)
    ; // wait until device is done with your request
```

The protocol has four steps. In the first, the OS waits until the device is ready to receive a command by repeatedly reading the status register; we call this **polling** the device (basically, just asking it what is going on). Second, the OS sends some data down to the data register; one can imagine that if this were a disk, for example, that multiple writes would need to take place to transfer a disk block (say 4KB) to the device. When the main CPU is involved with the data movement (as in this example protocol), we refer to it as **programmed I/O (PIO)**. Third, the OS writes a command to the command register; doing so implicitly lets the device know that both the data is present and that it should begin working on the command. Finally, the OS waits for the device to finish by again polling it in a loop, waiting to see if it is finished (it may then get an error code to indicate success or failure).

This basic protocol has the positive aspect of being simple and working. However, there are some inefficiencies and inconveniences involved. The first problem you might notice in the protocol is that polling seems inefficient; specifically, it wastes a great deal of CPU time just waiting for the (potentially slow) device to complete its activity, instead of switching to another ready process and thus better utilizing the CPU.

> THE CRUX: HOW TO AVOID THE COSTS OF POLLING
> How can the OS check device status without frequent polling, and thus lower the CPU overhead required to manage the device?

36.4 Lowering CPU Overhead With Interrupts

The invention that many engineers came upon years ago to improve this interaction is something we've seen already: the **interrupt**. Instead of polling the device repeatedly, the OS can issue a request, put the calling process to sleep, and context switch to another task. When the device is finally finished with the operation, it will raise a hardware interrupt, causing the CPU to jump into the OS at a predetermined **interrupt service routine (ISR)** or more simply an **interrupt handler**. The handler is just a piece of operating system code that will finish the request (for example, by reading data and perhaps an error code from the device) and wake the process waiting for the I/O, which can then proceed as desired.

Interrupts thus allow for **overlap** of computation and I/O, which is key for improved utilization. This timeline shows the problem:

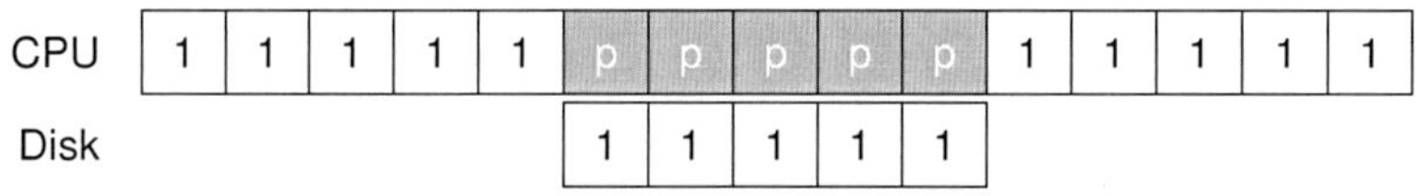

In the diagram, Process 1 runs on the CPU for some time (indicated by a repeated `1` on the CPU line), and then issues an I/O request to the disk to read some data. Without interrupts, the system simply spins, polling the status of the device repeatedly until the I/O is complete (indicated by a `p`). The disk services the request and finally Process 1 can run again.

If instead we utilize interrupts and allow for overlap, the OS can do something else while waiting for the disk:

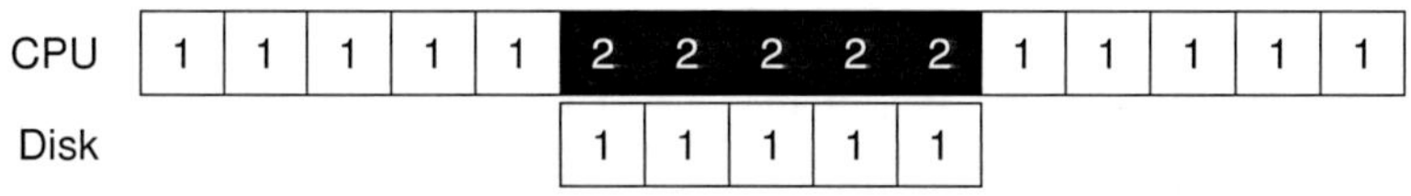

In this example, the OS runs Process 2 on the CPU while the disk services Process 1's request. When the disk request is finished, an interrupt occurs, and the OS wakes up Process 1 and runs it again. Thus, *both* the CPU and the disk are properly utilized during the middle stretch of time.

Note that using interrupts is not *always* the best solution. For example, imagine a device that performs its tasks very quickly: the first poll usually finds the device to be done with task. Using an interrupt in this case will actually *slow down* the system: switching to another process, handling the interrupt, and switching back to the issuing process is expensive. Thus, if a device is fast, it may be best to poll; if it is slow, interrupts, which allow

> TIP: INTERRUPTS NOT ALWAYS BETTER THAN PIO
> Although interrupts allow for overlap of computation and I/O, they only really make sense for slow devices. Otherwise, the cost of interrupt handling and context switching may outweigh the benefits interrupts provide. There are also cases where a flood of interrupts may overload a system and lead it to livelock [MR96]; in such cases, polling provides more control to the OS in its scheduling and thus is again useful.

overlap, are best. If the speed of the device is not known, or sometimes fast and sometimes slow, it may be best to use a **hybrid** that polls for a little while and then, if the device is not yet finished, uses interrupts. This **two-phased** approach may achieve the best of both worlds.

Another reason not to use interrupts arises in networks [MR96]. When a huge stream of incoming packets each generate an interrupt, it is possible for the OS to **livelock**, that is, find itself only processing interrupts and never allowing a user-level process to run and actually service the requests. For example, imagine a web server that experiences a load burst because it became the top-ranked entry on hacker news [H18]. In this case, it is better to occasionally use polling to better control what is happening in the system and allow the web server to service some requests before going back to the device to check for more packet arrivals.

Another interrupt-based optimization is **coalescing**. In such a setup, a device which needs to raise an interrupt first waits for a bit before delivering the interrupt to the CPU. While waiting, other requests may soon complete, and thus multiple interrupts can be coalesced into a single interrupt delivery, thus lowering the overhead of interrupt processing. Of course, waiting too long will increase the latency of a request, a common trade-off in systems. See Ahmad et al. [A+11] for an excellent summary.

36.5 More Efficient Data Movement With DMA

Unfortunately, there is one other aspect of our canonical protocol that requires our attention. In particular, when using programmed I/O (PIO) to transfer a large chunk of data to a device, the CPU is once again overburdened with a rather trivial task, and thus wastes a lot of time and effort that could better be spent running other processes. This timeline illustrates the problem:

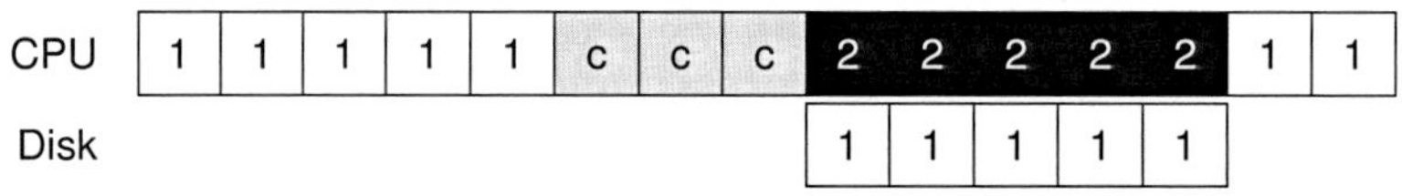

In the timeline, Process 1 is running and then wishes to write some data to the disk. It then initiates the I/O, which must copy the data from memory to the device explicitly, one word at a time (marked `c` in the diagram). When the copy is complete, the I/O begins on the disk and the CPU can finally be used for something else.

> THE CRUX: HOW TO LOWER PIO OVERHEADS
>
> With PIO, the CPU spends too much time moving data to and from devices by hand. How can we offload this work and thus allow the CPU to be more effectively utilized?

The solution to this problem is something we refer to as **Direct Memory Access (DMA)**. A DMA engine is essentially a very specific device within a system that can orchestrate transfers between devices and main memory without much CPU intervention.

DMA works as follows. To transfer data to the device, for example, the OS would program the DMA engine by telling it where the data lives in memory, how much data to copy, and which device to send it to. At that point, the OS is done with the transfer and can proceed with other work. When the DMA is complete, the DMA controller raises an interrupt, and the OS thus knows the transfer is complete. The revised timeline:

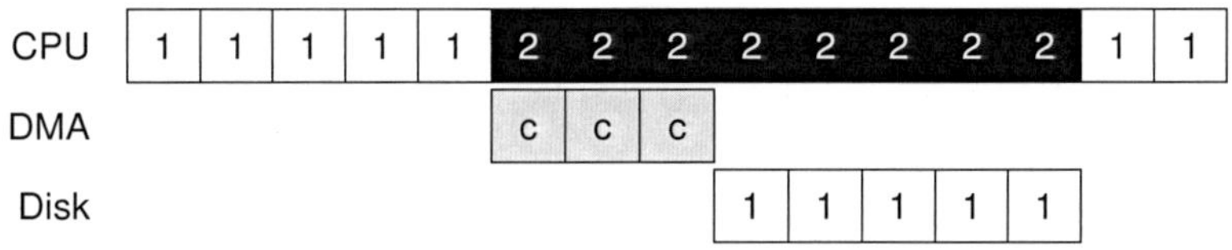

From the timeline, you can see that the copying of data is now handled by the DMA controller. Because the CPU is free during that time, the OS can do something else, here choosing to run Process 2. Process 2 thus gets to use more CPU before Process 1 runs again.

36.6 Methods Of Device Interaction

Now that we have some sense of the efficiency issues involved with performing I/O, there are a few other problems we need to handle to incorporate devices into modern systems. One problem you may have noticed thus far: we have not really said anything about how the OS actually communicates with the device! Thus, the problem:

> THE CRUX: HOW TO COMMUNICATE WITH DEVICES
>
> How should the hardware communicate with a device? Should there be explicit instructions? Or are there other ways to do it?

Over time, two primary methods of device communication have developed. The first, oldest method (used by IBM mainframes for many years) is to have explicit **I/O instructions**. These instructions specify a way for the OS to send data to specific device registers and thus allow the construction of the protocols described above.

For example, on x86, the `in` and `out` instructions can be used to communicate with devices. For example, to send data to a device, the caller specifies a register with the data in it, and a specific *port* which names the device. Executing the instruction leads to the desired behavior.

Such instructions are usually **privileged**. The OS controls devices, and the OS thus is the only entity allowed to directly communicate with them. Imagine if any program could read or write the disk, for example: total chaos (as always), as any user program could use such a loophole to gain complete control over the machine.

The second method to interact with devices is known as **memory-mapped I/O**. With this approach, the hardware makes device registers available as if they were memory locations. To access a particular register, the OS issues a load (to read) or store (to write) the address; the hardware then routes the load/store to the device instead of main memory.

There is not some great advantage to one approach or the other. The memory-mapped approach is nice in that no new instructions are needed to support it, but both approaches are still in use today.

36.7 Fitting Into The OS: The Device Driver

One final problem we will discuss: how to fit devices, each of which have very specific interfaces, into the OS, which we would like to keep as general as possible. For example, consider a file system. We'd like to build a file system that worked on top of SCSI disks, IDE disks, USB keychain drives, and so forth, and we'd like the file system to be relatively oblivious to all of the details of how to issue a read or write request to these different types of drives. Thus, our problem:

THE CRUX: HOW TO BUILD A DEVICE-NEUTRAL OS

How can we keep most of the OS device-neutral, thus hiding the details of device interactions from major OS subsystems?

The problem is solved through the age-old technique of **abstraction**. At the lowest level, a piece of software in the OS must know in detail how a device works. We call this piece of software a **device driver**, and any specifics of device interaction are encapsulated within.

Let us see how this abstraction might help OS design and implementation by examining the Linux file system software stack. Figure 364 is a rough and approximate depiction of the Linux software organization. As you can see from the diagram, a file system (and certainly, an application above) is completely oblivious to the specifics of which disk class it is using; it simply issues block read and write requests to the generic block layer, which routes them to the appropriate device driver, which handles the details of issuing the specific request. Although simplified, the diagram shows how such detail can be hidden from most of the OS.

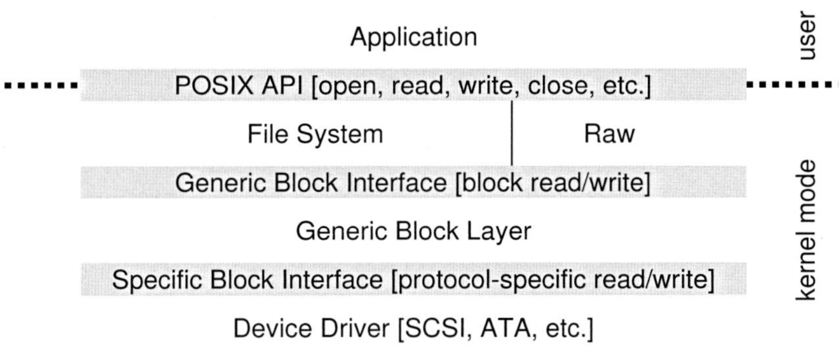

Figure 364: **The File System Stack**

The diagram also shows a **raw interface** to devices, which enables special applications (such as a **file-system checker**, described later [AD14], or a **disk defragmentation** tool) to directly read and write blocks without using the file abstraction. Most systems provide this type of interface to support these low-level storage management applications.

Note that the encapsulation seen above can have its downside as well. For example, if there is a device that has many special capabilities, but has to present a generic interface to the rest of the kernel, those special capabilities will go unused. This situation arises, for example, in Linux with SCSI devices, which have very rich error reporting; because other block devices (e.g., ATA/IDE) have much simpler error handling, all that higher levels of software ever receive is a generic `EIO` (generic IO error) error code; any extra detail that SCSI may have provided is thus lost to the file system [G08].

Interestingly, because device drivers are needed for any device you might plug into your system, over time they have come to represent a huge percentage of kernel code. Studies of the Linux kernel reveal that over 70% of OS code is found in device drivers [C01]; for Windows-based systems, it is likely quite high as well. Thus, when people tell you that the OS has millions of lines of code, what they are really saying is that the OS has millions of lines of device-driver code. Of course, for any given installation, most of that code may not be active (i.e., only a few devices are connected to the system at a time). Perhaps more depressingly, as drivers are often written by "amateurs" (instead of full-time kernel developers), they tend to have many more bugs and thus are a primary contributor to kernel crashes [S03].

36.8 Case Study: A Simple IDE Disk Driver

To dig a little deeper here, let's take a quick look at an actual device: an IDE disk drive [L94]. We summarize the protocol as described in this reference [W10]; we'll also peek at the xv6 source code for a simple example of a working IDE driver [CK+08].

```
Control Register:
  Address 0x3F6 = 0x08 (0000 1RE0): R=reset,
                  E=0 means "enable interrupt"

Command Block Registers:
  Address 0x1F0 = Data Port
  Address 0x1F1 = Error
  Address 0x1F2 = Sector Count
  Address 0x1F3 = LBA low byte
  Address 0x1F4 = LBA mid byte
  Address 0x1F5 = LBA hi  byte
  Address 0x1F6 = 1B1D TOP4LBA: B=LBA, D=drive
  Address 0x1F7 = Command/status

Status Register (Address 0x1F7):
    7      6    5     4    3    2    1     0
   BUSY  READY FAULT SEEK  DRQ  CORR IDDEX ERROR

Error Register (Address 0x1F1): (check when ERROR==1)
    7      6    5     4    3    2    1     0
   BBK    UNC   MC   IDNF  MCR  ABRT T0NF AMNF

   BBK  = Bad Block
   UNC  = Uncorrectable data error
   MC   = Media Changed
   IDNF = ID mark Not Found
   MCR  = Media Change Requested
   ABRT = Command aborted
   T0NF = Track 0 Not Found
   AMNF = Address Mark Not Found
```

Figure 365: **The IDE Interface**

An IDE disk presents a simple interface to the system, consisting of four types of register: control, command block, status, and error. These registers are available by reading or writing to specific "I/O addresses" (such as `0x3F6` below) using (on x86) the `in` and `out` I/O instructions.

The basic protocol to interact with the device is as follows, assuming it has already been initialized.

- **Wait for drive to be ready.** Read Status Register (0x1F7) until drive is READY and not BUSY.
- **Write parameters to command registers.** Write the sector count, logical block address (LBA) of the sectors to be accessed, and drive number (master=0x00 or slave=0x10, as IDE permits just two drives) to command registers (0x1F2-0x1F6).
- **Start the I/O.** by issuing read/write to command register. Write READ—WRITE command to command register (0x1F7).

- **Data transfer (for writes):** Wait until drive status is READY and DRQ (drive request for data); write data to data port.
- **Handle interrupts.** In the simplest case, handle an interrupt for each sector transferred; more complex approaches allow batching and thus one final interrupt when the entire transfer is complete.
- **Error handling.** After each operation, read the status register. If the ERROR bit is on, read the error register for details.

Most of this protocol is found in the xv6 IDE driver (Figure 366), which (after initialization) works through four primary functions. The first is `ide_rw()`, which queues a request (if there are others pending), or issues it directly to the disk (via `ide_start_request()`); in either case, the routine waits for the request to complete and the calling process is put to sleep. The second is `ide_start_request()`, which is used to send a request (and perhaps data, in the case of a write) to the disk; the `in` and `out` x86 instructions are called to read and write device registers, respectively. The start request routine uses the third function, `ide_wait_ready()`, to ensure the drive is ready before issuing a request to it. Finally, `ide_intr()` is invoked when an interrupt takes place; it reads data from the device (if the request is a read, not a write), wakes the process waiting for the I/O to complete, and (if there are more requests in the I/O queue), launches the next I/O via `ide_start_request()`.

36.9 Historical Notes

Before ending, we include a brief historical note on the origin of some of these fundamental ideas. If you are interested in learning more, read Smotherman's excellent summary [S08].

Interrupts are an ancient idea, existing on the earliest of machines. For example, the UNIVAC in the early 1950's had some form of interrupt vectoring, although it is unclear in exactly which year this feature was available [S08]. Sadly, even in its infancy, we are beginning to lose the origins of computing history.

There is also some debate as to which machine first introduced the idea of DMA. For example, Knuth and others point to the DYSEAC (a "mobile" machine, which at the time meant it could be hauled in a trailer), whereas others think the IBM SAGE may have been the first [S08]. Either way, by the mid 50's, systems with I/O devices that communicated directly with memory and interrupted the CPU when finished existed.

The history here is difficult to trace because the inventions are tied to real, and sometimes obscure, machines. For example, some think that the Lincoln Labs TX-2 machine was first with vectored interrupts [S08], but this is hardly clear.

```
static int ide_wait_ready() {
  while (((int r = inb(0x1f7)) & IDE_BSY) || !(r & IDE_DRDY))
    ;  // loop until drive isn't busy
}

static void ide_start_request(struct buf *b) {
  ide_wait_ready();
  outb(0x3f6, 0);                    // generate interrupt
  outb(0x1f2, 1);                    // how many sectors?
  outb(0x1f3, b->sector & 0xff);     // LBA goes here ...
  outb(0x1f4, (b->sector >> 8) & 0xff);    // ... and here
  outb(0x1f5, (b->sector >> 16) & 0xff);   // ... and here!
  outb(0x1f6, 0xe0 | ((b->dev&1)<<4) | ((b->sector>>24)&0x0f));
  if(b->flags & B_DIRTY){
    outb(0x1f7, IDE_CMD_WRITE);      // this is a WRITE
    outsl(0x1f0, b->data, 512/4);    // transfer data too!
  } else {
    outb(0x1f7, IDE_CMD_READ);       // this is a READ (no data)
  }
}

void ide_rw(struct buf *b) {
  acquire(&ide_lock);
  for (struct buf **pp = &ide_queue; *pp; pp=&(*pp)->qnext)
    ;                                // walk queue
  *pp = b;                           // add request to end
  if (ide_queue == b)                // if q is empty
    ide_start_request(b);            // send req to disk
  while ((b->flags & (B_VALID|B_DIRTY)) != B_VALID)
    sleep(b, &ide_lock);             // wait for completion
  release(&ide_lock);
}

void ide_intr() {
  struct buf *b;
  acquire(&ide_lock);
  if (!(b->flags & B_DIRTY) && ide_wait_ready() >= 0)
    insl(0x1f0, b->data, 512/4);     // if READ: get data
  b->flags |= B_VALID;
  b->flags &= ~B_DIRTY;
  wakeup(b);                         // wake waiting process
  if ((ide_queue = b->qnext) != 0)   // start next request
    ide_start_request(ide_queue);    // (if one exists)
  release(&ide_lock);
}
```

Figure 366: **The xv6 IDE Disk Driver (Simplified)**

Because the ideas are relatively obvious — no Einsteinian leap is required to come up with the idea of letting the CPU do something else while a slow I/O is pending — perhaps our focus on "who first?" is misguided. What is certainly clear: as people built these early machines, it became obvious that I/O support was needed. Interrupts, DMA, and related ideas are all direct outcomes of the nature of fast CPUs and slow devices; if you were there at the time, you might have had similar ideas.

36.10 Summary

You should now have a very basic understanding of how an OS interacts with a device. Two techniques, the interrupt and DMA, have been introduced to help with device efficiency, and two approaches to accessing device registers, explicit I/O instructions and memory-mapped I/O, have been described. Finally, the notion of a device driver has been presented, showing how the OS itself can encapsulate low-level details and thus make it easier to build the rest of the OS in a device-neutral fashion.

References

[A+11] "vIC: Interrupt Coalescing for Virtual Machine Storage Device IO" by Irfan Ahmad, Ajay Gulati, Ali Mashtizadeh. USENIX '11. *A terrific survey of interrupt coalescing in traditional and virtualized environments.*

[AD14] "Operating Systems: Three Easy Pieces" (Chapters: Crash Consistency: FSCK and Journaling and Log-Structured File Systems) by Remzi Arpaci-Dusseau and Andrea Arpaci-Dusseau. Arpaci-Dusseau Books, 2014. *A description of a file-system checker and how it works, which requires low-level access to disk devices not normally provided by the file system directly.*

[C01] "An Empirical Study of Operating System Errors" by Andy Chou, Junfeng Yang, Benjamin Chelf, Seth Hallem, Dawson Engler. SOSP '01. *One of the first papers to systematically explore how many bugs are in modern operating systems. Among other neat findings, the authors show that device drivers have something like seven times more bugs than mainline kernel code.*

[CK+08] "The xv6 Operating System" by Russ Cox, Frans Kaashoek, Robert Morris, Nickolai Zeldovich. From: http://pdos.csail.mit.edu/6.828/2008/index.html. *See* `ide.c` *for the IDE device driver, with a few more details therein.*

[D07] "What Every Programmer Should Know About Memory" by Ulrich Drepper. November, 2007. Available: `http://www.akkadia.org/drepper/cpumemory.pdf`. *A fantastic read about modern memory systems, starting at DRAM and going all the way up to virtualization and cache-optimized algorithms.*

[G08] "EIO: Error-handling is Occasionally Correct" by Haryadi Gunawi, Cindy Rubio-Gonzalez, Andrea Arpaci-Dusseau, Remzi Arpaci-Dusseau, Ben Liblit. FAST '08, San Jose, CA, February 2008. *Our own work on building a tool to find code in Linux file systems that does not handle error return properly. We found hundreds and hundreds of bugs, many of which have now been fixed.*

[H17] "Intel Core i7-7700K review: Kaby Lake Debuts for Desktop" by Joel Hruska. January 3, 2017. `www.extremetech.com/extreme/241950-intels-core-i7-7700k-reviewed-kaby-lake-debuts-desktop`. *An in-depth review of a recent Intel chipset, including CPUs and the I/O subsystem.*

[H18] "Hacker News" by Many contributors. Available: https://news.ycombinator.com. *One of the better aggregrators for tech-related stuff. Once back in 2014, this book became a highly-ranked entry, leading to 1 million chapter downloads in just one day! Sadly, we have yet to re-experience such a high.*

[L94] "AT Attachment Interface for Disk Drives" by Lawrence J. Lamers. Reference number: ANSI X3.221, 1994. Available: `ftp://ftp.t10.org/t13/project/d0791r4c-ATA-1.pdf`. *A rather dry document about device interfaces. Read it at your own peril.*

[MR96] "Eliminating Receive Livelock in an Interrupt-driven Kernel" by Jeffrey Mogul, K. K. Ramakrishnan. USENIX '96, San Diego, CA, January 1996. *Mogul and colleagues did a great deal of pioneering work on web server network performance. This paper is but one example.*

[S08] "Interrupts" by Mark Smotherman. July '08. Available: `http://people.cs.clemson.edu/~mark/interrupts.html`. *A treasure trove of information on the history of interrupts, DMA, and related early ideas in computing.*

[S03] "Improving the Reliability of Commodity Operating Systems" by Michael M. Swift, Brian N. Bershad, Henry M. Levy. SOSP '03. *Swift's work revived interest in a more microkernel-like approach to operating systems; minimally, it finally gave some good reasons why address-space based protection could be useful in a modern OS.*

[W10] "Hard Disk Driver" by Washington State Course Homepage. Available online at this site: `http://eecs.wsu.edu/~cs460/cs560/HDdriver.html`. *A nice summary of a simple IDE disk drive's interface and how to build a device driver for it.*

37

Hard Disk Drives

The last chapter introduced the general concept of an I/O device and showed you how the OS might interact with such a beast. In this chapter, we dive into more detail about one device in particular: the **hard disk drive**. These drives have been the main form of persistent data storage in computer systems for decades and much of the development of file system technology (coming soon) is predicated on their behavior. Thus, it is worth understanding the details of a disk's operation before building the file system software that manages it. Many of these details are available in excellent papers by Ruemmler and Wilkes [RW92] and Anderson, Dykes, and Riedel [ADR03].

> CRUX: HOW TO STORE AND ACCESS DATA ON DISK
> How do modern hard-disk drives store data? What is the interface? How is the data actually laid out and accessed? How does disk scheduling improve performance?

37.1 The Interface

Let's start by understanding the interface to a modern disk drive. The basic interface for all modern drives is straightforward. The drive consists of a large number of sectors (512-byte blocks), each of which can be read or written. The sectors are numbered from 0 to $n - 1$ on a disk with n sectors. Thus, we can view the disk as an array of sectors; 0 to $n - 1$ is thus the **address space** of the drive.

Multi-sector operations are possible; indeed, many file systems will read or write 4KB at a time (or more). However, when updating the disk, the only guarantee drive manufacturers make is that a single 512-byte write is **atomic** (i.e., it will either complete in its entirety or it won't complete at all); thus, if an untimely power loss occurs, only a portion of a larger write may complete (sometimes called a **torn write**).

There are some assumptions most clients of disk drives make, but that are not specified directly in the interface; Schlosser and Ganger have

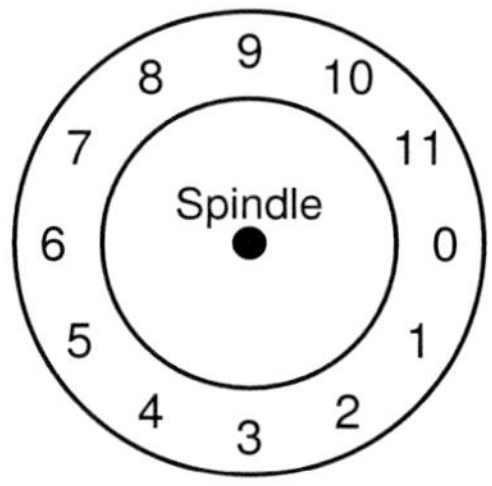

Figure 371: **A Disk With Just A Single Track**

called this the "unwritten contract" of disk drives [SG04]. Specifically, one can usually assume that accessing two blocks[1] near one-another within the drive's address space will be faster than accessing two blocks that are far apart. One can also usually assume that accessing blocks in a contiguous chunk (i.e., a sequential read or write) is the fastest access mode, and usually much faster than any more random access pattern.

37.2 Basic Geometry

Let's start to understand some of the components of a modern disk. We start with a **platter**, a circular hard surface on which data is stored persistently by inducing magnetic changes to it. A disk may have one or more platters; each platter has 2 sides, each of which is called a **surface**. These platters are usually made of some hard material (such as aluminum), and then coated with a thin magnetic layer that enables the drive to persistently store bits even when the drive is powered off.

The platters are all bound together around the **spindle**, which is connected to a motor that spins the platters around (while the drive is powered on) at a constant (fixed) rate. The rate of rotation is often measured in **rotations per minute (RPM)**, and typical modern values are in the 7,200 RPM to 15,000 RPM range. Note that we will often be interested in the time of a single rotation, e.g., a drive that rotates at 10,000 RPM means that a single rotation takes about 6 milliseconds (6 ms).

Data is encoded on each surface in concentric circles of sectors; we call one such concentric circle a **track**. A single surface contains many thousands and thousands of tracks, tightly packed together, with hundreds of tracks fitting into the width of a human hair.

To read and write from the surface, we need a mechanism that allows us to either sense (i.e., read) the magnetic patterns on the disk or to induce a change in (i.e., write) them. This process of reading and writing is accomplished by the **disk head**; there is one such head per surface of the drive. The disk head is attached to a single **disk arm**, which moves across the surface to position the head over the desired track.

[1]We, and others, often use the terms **block** and **sector** interchangeably, assuming the reader will know exactly what is meant per context. Sorry about this!

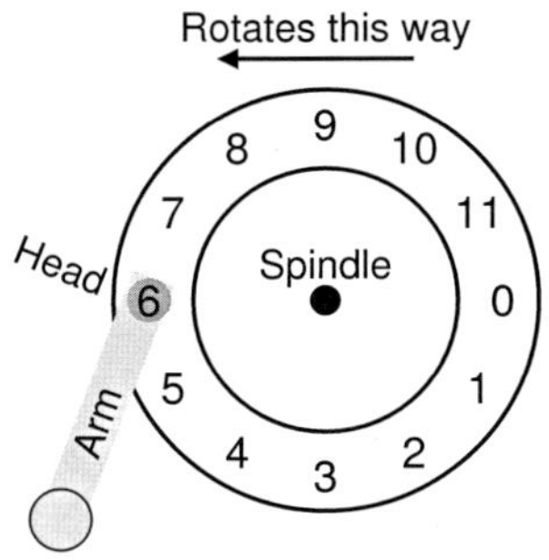

Figure 372: **A Single Track Plus A Head**

37.3 A Simple Disk Drive

Let's understand how disks work by building up a model one track at a time. Assume we have a simple disk with a single track (Figure 371). This track has just 12 sectors, each of which is 512 bytes in size (our typical sector size, recall) and addressed therefore by the numbers 0 through 11. The single platter we have here rotates around the spindle, to which a motor is attached.

Of course, the track by itself isn't too interesting; we want to be able to read or write those sectors, and thus we need a disk head, attached to a disk arm, as we now see (Figure 372). In the figure, the disk head, attached to the end of the arm, is positioned over sector 6, and the surface is rotating counter-clockwise.

Single-track Latency: The Rotational Delay

To understand how a request would be processed on our simple, one-track disk, imagine we now receive a request to read block 0. How should the disk service this request?

In our simple disk, the disk doesn't have to do much. In particular, it must just wait for the desired sector to rotate under the disk head. This wait happens often enough in modern drives, and is an important enough component of I/O service time, that it has a special name: **rotational delay** (sometimes **rotation delay**, though that sounds weird). In the example, if the full rotational delay is R, the disk has to incur a rotational delay of about $\frac{R}{2}$ to wait for 0 to come under the read/write head (if we start at 6). A worst-case request on this single track would be to sector 5, causing nearly a full rotational delay in order to service such a request.

Multiple Tracks: Seek Time

So far our disk just has a single track, which is not too realistic; modern disks of course have many millions. Let's thus look at an ever-so-slightly more realistic disk surface, this one with three tracks (Figure 373, left).

In the figure, the head is currently positioned over the innermost track (which contains sectors 24 through 35); the next track over contains the

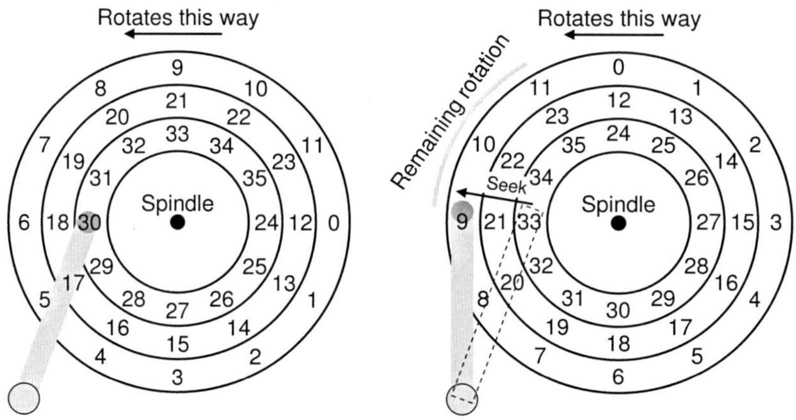

Figure 373: **Three Tracks Plus A Head (Right: With Seek)**

next set of sectors (12 through 23), and the outermost track contains the first sectors (0 through 11).

To understand how the drive might access a given sector, we now trace what would happen on a request to a distant sector, e.g., a read to sector 11. To service this read, the drive has to first move the disk arm to the correct track (in this case, the outermost one), in a process known as a **seek**. Seeks, along with rotations, are one of the most costly disk operations.

The seek, it should be noted, has many phases: first an *acceleration* phase as the disk arm gets moving; then *coasting* as the arm is moving at full speed, then *deceleration* as the arm slows down; finally *settling* as the head is carefully positioned over the correct track. The **settling time** is often quite significant, e.g., 0.5 to 2 ms, as the drive must be certain to find the right track (imagine if it just got close instead!).

After the seek, the disk arm has positioned the head over the right track. A depiction of the seek is found in Figure 373 (right).

As we can see, during the seek, the arm has been moved to the desired track, and the platter of course has rotated, in this case about 3 sectors. Thus, sector 9 is just about to pass under the disk head, and we must only endure a short rotational delay to complete the transfer.

When sector 11 passes under the disk head, the final phase of I/O will take place, known as the **transfer**, where data is either read from or written to the surface. And thus, we have a complete picture of I/O time: first a seek, then waiting for the rotational delay, and finally the transfer.

Some Other Details

Though we won't spend too much time on it, there are some other interesting details about how hard drives operate. Many drives employ some kind of **track skew** to make sure that sequential reads can be properly serviced even when crossing track boundaries. In our simple example disk, this might appear as seen in Figure 374 (page 461).

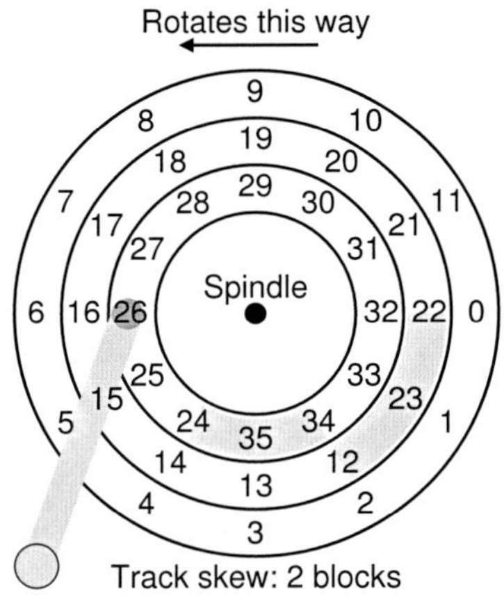

Figure 374: **Three Tracks: Track Skew Of 2**

Sectors are often skewed like this because when switching from one track to another, the disk needs time to reposition the head (even to neighboring tracks). Without such skew, the head would be moved to the next track but the desired next block would have already rotated under the head, and thus the drive would have to wait almost the entire rotational delay to access the next block.

Another reality is that outer tracks tend to have more sectors than inner tracks, which is a result of geometry; there is simply more room out there. These tracks are often referred to as **multi-zoned** disk drives, where the disk is organized into multiple zones, and where a zone is consecutive set of tracks on a surface. Each zone has the same number of sectors per track, and outer zones have more sectors than inner zones.

Finally, an important part of any modern disk drive is its **cache**, for historical reasons sometimes called a **track buffer**. This cache is just some small amount of memory (usually around 8 or 16 MB) which the drive can use to hold data read from or written to the disk. For example, when reading a sector from the disk, the drive might decide to read in all of the sectors on that track and cache them in its memory; doing so allows the drive to quickly respond to any subsequent requests to the same track.

On writes, the drive has a choice: should it acknowledge the write has completed when it has put the data in its memory, or after the write has actually been written to disk? The former is called **write back** caching (or sometimes **immediate reporting**), and the latter **write through**. Write back caching sometimes makes the drive appear "faster", but can be dangerous; if the file system or applications require that data be written to disk in a certain order for correctness, write-back caching can lead to problems (read the chapter on file-system journaling for details).

ASIDE: DIMENSIONAL ANALYSIS

Remember in Chemistry class, how you solved virtually every problem by simply setting up the units such that they canceled out, and somehow the answers popped out as a result? That chemical magic is known by the highfalutin name of **dimensional analysis** and it turns out it is useful in computer systems analysis too.

Let's do an example to see how dimensional analysis works and why it is useful. In this case, assume you have to figure out how long, in milliseconds, a single rotation of a disk takes. Unfortunately, you are given only the **RPM** of the disk, or **rotations per minute**. Let's assume we're talking about a 10K RPM disk (i.e., it rotates 10,000 times per minute). How do we set up the dimensional analysis so that we get time per rotation in milliseconds?

To do so, we start by putting the desired units on the left; in this case, we wish to obtain the time (in milliseconds) per rotation, so that is exactly what we write down: $\frac{Time\ (ms)}{1\ Rotation}$. We then write down everything we know, making sure to cancel units where possible. First, we obtain $\frac{1\ minute}{10{,}000\ Rotations}$ (keeping rotation on the bottom, as that's where it is on the left), then transform minutes into seconds with $\frac{60\ seconds}{1\ minute}$, and then finally transform seconds in milliseconds with $\frac{1000\ ms}{1\ second}$. The final result is the following (with units nicely canceled):

$$\frac{Time\ (ms)}{1\ Rot.} = \frac{1\ \cancel{minute}}{10{,}000\ Rot.} \cdot \frac{60\ \cancel{seconds}}{1\ \cancel{minute}} \cdot \frac{1000\ ms}{1\ \cancel{second}} = \frac{60{,}000\ ms}{10{,}000\ Rot.} = \frac{6\ ms}{Rotation}$$

As you can see from this example, dimensional analysis makes what seems intuitive into a simple and repeatable process. Beyond the RPM calculation above, it comes in handy with I/O analysis regularly. For example, you will often be given the transfer rate of a disk, e.g., 100 MB/second, and then asked: how long does it take to transfer a 512 KB block (in milliseconds)? With dimensional analysis, it's easy:

$$\frac{Time\ (ms)}{1\ Request} = \frac{512\ \cancel{KB}}{1\ Request} \cdot \frac{1\ \cancel{MB}}{1024\ \cancel{KB}} \cdot \frac{1\ \cancel{second}}{100\ \cancel{MB}} \cdot \frac{1000\ ms}{1\ \cancel{second}} = \frac{5\ ms}{Request}$$

37.4 I/O Time: Doing The Math

Now that we have an abstract model of the disk, we can use a little analysis to better understand disk performance. In particular, we can now represent I/O time as the sum of three major components:

$$T_{I/O} = T_{seek} + T_{rotation} + T_{transfer} \tag{37.1}$$

Note that the rate of I/O ($R_{I/O}$), which is often more easily used for

	Cheetah 15K.5	Barracuda
Capacity	300 GB	1 TB
RPM	15,000	7,200
Average Seek	4 ms	9 ms
Max Transfer	125 MB/s	105 MB/s
Platters	4	4
Cache	16 MB	16/32 MB
Connects via	SCSI	SATA

Figure 375: **Disk Drive Specs: SCSI Versus SATA**

comparison between drives (as we will do below), is easily computed from the time. Simply divide the size of the transfer by the time it took:

$$R_{I/O} = \frac{Size_{Transfer}}{T_{I/O}} \tag{37.2}$$

To get a better feel for I/O time, let us perform the following calculation. Assume there are two workloads we are interested in. The first, known as the **random** workload, issues small (e.g., 4KB) reads to random locations on the disk. Random workloads are common in many important applications, including database management systems. The second, known as the **sequential** workload, simply reads a large number of sectors consecutively from the disk, without jumping around. Sequential access patterns are quite common and thus important as well.

To understand the difference in performance between random and sequential workloads, we need to make a few assumptions about the disk drive first. Let's look at a couple of modern disks from Seagate. The first, known as the Cheetah 15K.5 [S09b], is a high-performance SCSI drive. The second, the Barracuda [S09a], is a drive built for capacity. Details on both are found in Figure 375.

As you can see, the drives have quite different characteristics, and in many ways nicely summarize two important components of the disk drive market. The first is the "high performance" drive market, where drives are engineered to spin as fast as possible, deliver low seek times, and transfer data quickly. The second is the "capacity" market, where cost per byte is the most important aspect; thus, the drives are slower but pack as many bits as possible into the space available.

From these numbers, we can start to calculate how well the drives would do under our two workloads outlined above. Let's start by looking at the random workload. Assuming each 4 KB read occurs at a random location on disk, we can calculate how long each such read would take. On the Cheetah:

$$T_{seek} = 4\ ms,\ T_{rotation} = 2\ ms,\ T_{transfer} = 30\ microsecs \tag{37.3}$$

The average seek time (4 milliseconds) is just taken as the average time reported by the manufacturer; note that a full seek (from one end of the

TIP: USE DISKS SEQUENTIALLY

When at all possible, transfer data to and from disks in a sequential manner. If sequential is not possible, at least think about transferring data in large chunks: the bigger, the better. If I/O is done in little random pieces, I/O performance will suffer dramatically. Also, users will suffer. Also, you will suffer, knowing what suffering you have wrought with your careless random I/Os.

surface to the other) would likely take two or three times longer. The average rotational delay is calculated from the RPM directly. 15000 RPM is equal to 250 RPS (rotations per second); thus, each rotation takes 4 ms. On average, the disk will encounter a half rotation and thus 2 ms is the average time. Finally, the transfer time is just the size of the transfer over the peak transfer rate; here it is vanishingly small (30 *microseconds*; note that we need 1000 microseconds just to get 1 millisecond!).

Thus, from our equation above, $T_{I/O}$ for the Cheetah roughly equals 6 ms. To compute the rate of I/O, we just divide the size of the transfer by the average time, and thus arrive at $R_{I/O}$ for the Cheetah under the random workload of about 0.66 MB/s. The same calculation for the Barracuda yields a $T_{I/O}$ of about 13.2 ms, more than twice as slow, and thus a rate of about 0.31 MB/s.

Now let's look at the sequential workload. Here we can assume there is a single seek and rotation before a very long transfer. For simplicity, assume the size of the transfer is 100 MB. Thus, $T_{I/O}$ for the Cheetah and Barracuda is about 800 ms and 950 ms, respectively. The rates of I/O are thus very nearly the peak transfer rates of 125 MB/s and 105 MB/s, respectively. Figure 376 summarizes these numbers.

	Cheetah	Barracuda
$R_{I/O}$ Random	0.66 MB/s	0.31 MB/s
$R_{I/O}$ Sequential	125 MB/s	105 MB/s

Figure 376: **Disk Drive Performance: SCSI Versus SATA**

The figure shows us a number of important things. First, and most importantly, there is a huge gap in drive performance between random and sequential workloads, almost a factor of 200 or so for the Cheetah and more than a factor 300 difference for the Barracuda. And thus we arrive at the most obvious design tip in the history of computing.

A second, more subtle point: there is a large difference in performance between high-end "performance" drives and low-end "capacity" drives. For this reason (and others), people are often willing to pay top dollar for the former while trying to get the latter as cheaply as possible.

ASIDE: COMPUTING THE "AVERAGE" SEEK

In many books and papers, you will see average disk-seek time cited as being roughly one-third of the full seek time. Where does this come from?

Turns out it arises from a simple calculation based on average seek *distance*, not time. Imagine the disk as a set of tracks, from 0 to N. The seek distance between any two tracks x and y is thus computed as the absolute value of the difference between them: $|x - y|$.

To compute the average seek distance, all you need to do is to first add up all possible seek distances:

$$\sum_{x=0}^{N}\sum_{y=0}^{N}|x - y|. \tag{37.4}$$

Then, divide this by the number of different possible seeks: N^2. To compute the sum, we'll just use the integral form:

$$\int_{x=0}^{N}\int_{y=0}^{N}|x - y|\,\mathrm{d}y\,\mathrm{d}x. \tag{37.5}$$

To compute the inner integral, let's break out the absolute value:

$$\int_{y=0}^{x}(x - y)\,\mathrm{d}y + \int_{y=x}^{N}(y - x)\,\mathrm{d}y. \tag{37.6}$$

Solving this leads to $(xy - \frac{1}{2}y^2)\Big|_0^x + (\frac{1}{2}y^2 - xy)\Big|_x^N$ which can be simplified to $(x^2 - Nx + \frac{1}{2}N^2)$. Now we have to compute the outer integral:

$$\int_{x=0}^{N}(x^2 - Nx + \frac{1}{2}N^2)\,\mathrm{d}x, \tag{37.7}$$

which results in:

$$(\frac{1}{3}x^3 - \frac{N}{2}x^2 + \frac{N^2}{2}x)\Big|_0^N = \frac{N^3}{3}. \tag{37.8}$$

Remember that we still have to divide by the total number of seeks (N^2) to compute the average seek distance: $(\frac{N^3}{3})/(N^2) = \frac{1}{3}N$. Thus the average seek distance on a disk, over all possible seeks, is one-third the full distance. And now when you hear that an average seek is one-third of a full seek, you'll know where it came from.

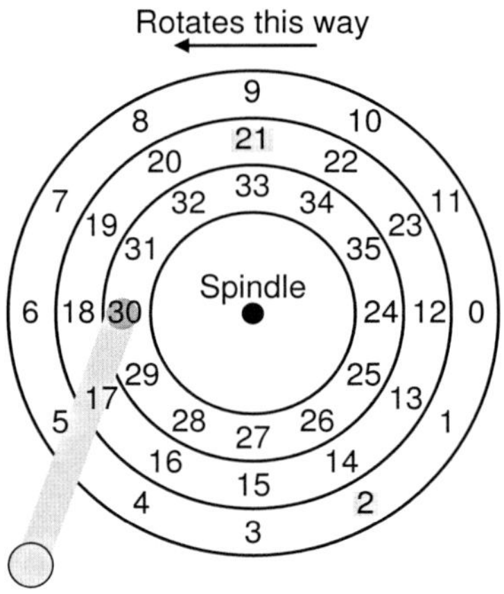

Figure 377: **SSTF: Scheduling Requests 21 And 2**

37.5 Disk Scheduling

Because of the high cost of I/O, the OS has historically played a role in deciding the order of I/Os issued to the disk. More specifically, given a set of I/O requests, the **disk scheduler** examines the requests and decides which one to schedule next [SCO90, JW91].

Unlike job scheduling, where the length of each job is usually unknown, with disk scheduling, we can make a good guess at how long a "job" (i.e., disk request) will take. By estimating the seek and possible rotational delay of a request, the disk scheduler can know how long each request will take, and thus (greedily) pick the one that will take the least time to service first. Thus, the disk scheduler will try to follow the **principle of SJF (shortest job first)** in its operation.

SSTF: Shortest Seek Time First

One early disk scheduling approach is known as **shortest-seek-time-first** (**SSTF**) (also called **shortest-seek-first** or **SSF**). SSTF orders the queue of I/O requests by track, picking requests on the nearest track to complete first. For example, assuming the current position of the head is over the inner track, and we have requests for sectors 21 (middle track) and 2 (outer track), we would then issue the request to 21 first, wait for it to complete, and then issue the request to 2 (Figure 377).

SSTF works well in this example, seeking to the middle track first and then the outer track. However, SSTF is not a panacea, for the following reasons. First, the drive geometry is not available to the host OS; rather, it sees an array of blocks. Fortunately, this problem is rather easily fixed. Instead of SSTF, an OS can simply implement **nearest-block-first** (**NBF**), which schedules the request with the nearest block address next.

The second problem is more fundamental: **starvation**. Imagine in our example above if there were a steady stream of requests to the inner track, where the head currently is positioned. Requests to any other tracks would then be ignored completely by a pure SSTF approach. And thus the crux of the problem:

> CRUX: HOW TO HANDLE DISK STARVATION
> How can we implement SSTF-like scheduling but avoid starvation?

Elevator (a.k.a. SCAN or C-SCAN)

The answer to this query was developed some time ago (see [CKR72] for example), and is relatively straightforward. The algorithm, originally called **SCAN**, simply moves back and forth across the disk servicing requests in order across the tracks. Let's call a single pass across the disk (from outer to inner tracks, or inner to outer) a *sweep*. Thus, if a request comes for a block on a track that has already been serviced on this sweep of the disk, it is not handled immediately, but rather queued until the next sweep (in the other direction).

SCAN has a number of variants, all of which do about the same thing. For example, Coffman et al. introduced **F-SCAN**, which freezes the queue to be serviced when it is doing a sweep [CKR72]; this action places requests that come in during the sweep into a queue to be serviced later. Doing so avoids starvation of far-away requests, by delaying the servicing of late-arriving (but nearer by) requests.

C-SCAN is another common variant, short for **Circular SCAN**. Instead of sweeping in both directions across the disk, the algorithm only sweeps from outer-to-inner, and then resets at the outer track to begin again. Doing so is a bit more fair to inner and outer tracks, as pure back-and-forth SCAN favors the middle tracks, i.e., after servicing the outer track, SCAN passes through the middle twice before coming back to the outer track again.

For reasons that should now be clear, the SCAN algorithm (and its cousins) is sometimes referred to as the **elevator** algorithm, because it behaves like an elevator which is either going up or down and not just servicing requests to floors based on which floor is closer. Imagine how annoying it would be if you were going down from floor 10 to 1, and somebody got on at 3 and pressed 4, and the elevator went up to 4 because it was "closer" than 1! As you can see, the elevator algorithm, when used in real life, prevents fights from taking place on elevators. In disks, it just prevents starvation.

Unfortunately, SCAN and its cousins do not represent the best scheduling technology. In particular, SCAN (or SSTF even) does not actually adhere as closely to the principle of SJF as they could. In particular, they ignore rotation. And thus, another crux:

CRUX: HOW TO ACCOUNT FOR DISK ROTATION COSTS
How can we implement an algorithm that more closely approximates SJF by taking *both* seek and rotation into account?

SPTF: Shortest Positioning Time First

Before discussing **shortest positioning time first** or **SPTF** scheduling (sometimes also called **shortest access time first** or **SATF**), which is the solution to our problem, let us make sure we understand the problem in more detail. Figure 378 presents an example.

In the example, the head is currently positioned over sector 30 on the inner track. The scheduler thus has to decide: should it schedule sector 16 (on the middle track) or sector 8 (on the outer track) for its next request. So which should it service next?

The answer, of course, is "it depends". In engineering, it turns out "it depends" is almost always the answer, reflecting that trade-offs are part of the life of the engineer; such maxims are also good in a pinch, e.g., when you don't know an answer to your boss's question, you might want to try this gem. However, it is almost always better to know *why* it depends, which is what we discuss here.

What it depends on here is the relative time of seeking as compared to rotation. If, in our example, seek time is much higher than rotational delay, then SSTF (and variants) are just fine. However, imagine if seek is quite a bit faster than rotation. Then, in our example, it would make more sense to seek *further* to service request 8 on the outer track than it would to perform the shorter seek to the middle track to service 16, which has to rotate all the way around before passing under the disk head.

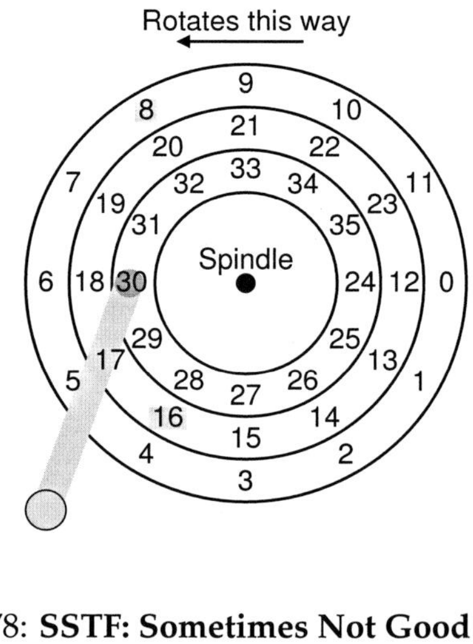

Figure 378: **SSTF: Sometimes Not Good Enough**

> TIP: IT ALWAYS DEPENDS (LIVNY'S LAW)
> Almost any question can be answered with "it depends", as our colleague Miron Livny always says. However, use with caution, as if you answer too many questions this way, people will stop asking you questions altogether. For example, somebody asks: "want to go to lunch?" You reply: "it depends, are *you* coming along?"

On modern drives, as we saw above, both seek and rotation are roughly equivalent (depending, of course, on the exact requests), and thus SPTF is useful and improves performance. However, it is even more difficult to implement in an OS, which generally does not have a good idea where track boundaries are or where the disk head currently is (in a rotational sense). Thus, SPTF is usually performed inside a drive, described below.

Other Scheduling Issues

There are many other issues we do not discuss in this brief description of basic disk operation, scheduling, and related topics. One such issue is this: *where* is disk scheduling performed on modern systems? In older systems, the operating system did all the scheduling; after looking through the set of pending requests, the OS would pick the best one, and issue it to the disk. When that request completed, the next one would be chosen, and so forth. Disks were simpler then, and so was life.

In modern systems, disks can accommodate multiple outstanding requests, and have sophisticated internal schedulers themselves (which can implement SPTF accurately; inside the disk controller, all relevant details are available, including exact head position). Thus, the OS scheduler usually picks what it thinks the best few requests are (say 16) and issues them all to disk; the disk then uses its internal knowledge of head position and detailed track layout information to service said requests in the best possible (SPTF) order.

Another important related task performed by disk schedulers is **I/O merging**. For example, imagine a series of requests to read blocks 33, then 8, then 34, as in Figure 378. In this case, the scheduler should **merge** the requests for blocks 33 and 34 into a single two-block request; any reordering that the scheduler does is performed upon the merged requests. Merging is particularly important at the OS level, as it reduces the number of requests sent to the disk and thus lowers overheads.

One final problem that modern schedulers address is this: how long should the system wait before issuing an I/O to disk? One might naively think that the disk, once it has even a single I/O, should immediately issue the request to the drive; this approach is called **work-conserving**, as the disk will never be idle if there are requests to serve. However, research on **anticipatory disk scheduling** has shown that sometimes it is better to wait for a bit [ID01], in what is called a **non-work-conserving** approach. By waiting, a new and "better" request may arrive at the disk, and thus overall efficiency is increased. Of course, deciding when to wait, and for how long, can be tricky; see the research paper for details, or check out the Linux kernel implementation to see how such ideas are transitioned into practice (if you are the ambitious sort).

37.6 Summary

We have presented a summary of how disks work. The summary is actually a detailed functional model; it does not describe the amazing physics, electronics, and material science that goes into actual drive design. For those interested in even more details of that nature, we suggest a different major (or perhaps minor); for those that are happy with this model, good! We can now proceed to using the model to build more interesting systems on top of these incredible devices.

References

[ADR03] "More Than an Interface: SCSI vs. ATA" by Dave Anderson, Jim Dykes, Erik Riedel. FAST '03, 2003. *One of the best recent-ish references on how modern disk drives really work; a must read for anyone interested in knowing more.*

[CKR72] "Analysis of Scanning Policies for Reducing Disk Seek Times" E.G. Coffman, L.A. Klimko, B. Ryan SIAM Journal of Computing, September 1972, Vol 1. No 3. *Some of the early work in the field of disk scheduling.*

[HK+17] "The Unwritten Contract of Solid State Drives" by Jun He, Sudarsun Kannan, Andrea C. Arpaci-Dusseau, Remzi H. Arpaci-Dusseau. EuroSys '17, Belgrade, Serbia, April 2017. *We take the idea of the unwritten contract, and extend it to SSDs. Using SSDs well seems as complicated than hard drives, and sometimes more so.*

[ID01] "Anticipatory Scheduling: A Disk-scheduling Framework To Overcome Deceptive Idleness In Synchronous I/O" by Sitaram Iyer, Peter Druschel. SOSP '01, October 2001. *A cool paper showing how waiting can improve disk scheduling: better requests may be on their way!*

[JW91] "Disk Scheduling Algorithms Based On Rotational Position" by D. Jacobson, J. Wilkes. Technical Report HPL-CSP-91-7rev1, Hewlett-Packard, February 1991. *A more modern take on disk scheduling. It remains a technical report (and not a published paper) because the authors were scooped by Seltzer et al. [S90].*

[RW92] "An Introduction to Disk Drive Modeling" by C. Ruemmler, J. Wilkes. IEEE Computer, 27:3, March 1994. *A terrific introduction to the basics of disk operation. Some pieces are out of date, but most of the basics remain.*

[SCO90] "Disk Scheduling Revisited" by Margo Seltzer, Peter Chen, John Ousterhout. USENIX 1990. *A paper that talks about how rotation matters too in the world of disk scheduling.*

[SG04] "MEMS-based storage devices and standard disk interfaces: A square peg in a round hole?" Steven W. Schlosser, Gregory R. Ganger FAST '04, pp. 87-100, 2004 *While the MEMS aspect of this paper hasn't yet made an impact, the discussion of the contract between file systems and disks is wonderful and a lasting contribution. We later build on this work to study the "Unwritten Contract of Solid State Drives" [HK+17]*

[S09a] "Barracuda ES.2 data sheet" by Seagate, Inc.. Available at this website, at least, it was: `http://www.seagate.com/docs/pdf/datasheet/disc/ds_barracuda_es.pdf`. *A data sheet; read at your own risk. Risk of what? Boredom.*

[S09b] "Cheetah 15K.5" by Seagate, Inc.. Available at this website, we're pretty sure it is: `http://www.seagate.com/docs/pdf/datasheet/disc/ds-cheetah-15k-5-us.pdf`. *See above commentary on data sheets.*

Homework (Simulation)

This homework uses `disk.py` to familiarize you with how a modern hard drive works. It has a lot of different options, and unlike most of the other simulations, has a graphical animator to show you exactly what happens when the disk is in action. See the README for details.

1. Compute the seek, rotation, and transfer times for the following sets of requests: `-a 0`, `-a 6`, `-a 30`, `-a 7,30,8`, and finally `-a 10,11,12,13`.
2. Do the same requests above, but change the seek rate to different values: `-S 2`, `-S 4`, `-S 8`, `-S 10`, `-S 40`, `-S 0.1`. How do the times change?
3. Do the same requests above, but change the rotation rate: `-R 0.1`, `-R 0.5`, `-R 0.01`. How do the times change?
4. FIFO is not always best, e.g., with the request stream `-a 7,30,8`, what order should the requests be processed in? Run the shortest seek-time first (SSTF) scheduler (`-p SSTF`) on this workload; how long should it take (seek, rotation, transfer) for each request to be served?
5. Now use the shortest access-time first (SATF) scheduler (`-p SATF`). Does it make any difference for `-a 7,30,8` workload? Find a set of requests where SATF outperforms SSTF; more generally, when is SATF better than SSTF?
6. Here is a request stream to try: `-a 10,11,12,13`. What goes poorly when it runs? Try adding track skew to address this problem (`-o skew`). Given the default seek rate, what should the skew be to maximize performance? What about for different seek rates (e.g., `-S 2`, `-S 4`)? In general, could you write a formula to figure out the skew?
7. Specify a disk with different density per zone, e.g., `-z 10,20,30`, which specifies the angular difference between blocks on the outer, middle, and inner tracks. Run some random requests (e.g., `-a -1 -A 5,-1,0`, which specifies that random requests should be used via the `-a -1` flag and that five requests ranging from 0 to the max be generated), and compute the seek, rotation, and transfer times. Use different random seeds. What is the bandwidth (in sectors per unit time) on the outer, middle, and inner tracks?
8. A scheduling window determines how many requests the disk can examine at once. Generate random workloads (e.g., `-A 1000,-1,0`, with different seeds) and see how long the SATF scheduler takes when the scheduling window is changed from 1 up to the number of requests. How big of a window is needed to maximize performance? Hint: use the `-c` flag and don't turn on graphics (`-G`) to run these quickly. When the scheduling window is set to 1, does it matter which policy you are using?
9. Create a series of requests to starve a particular request, assuming an SATF policy. Given that sequence, how does it perform if you use a **bounded SATF (BSATF)** scheduling approach? In this approach, you specify the scheduling window (e.g., `-w 4`); the scheduler only moves onto the next window of requests when *all* requests in the current window have been serviced. Does this solve starvation? How does it perform, as compared to SATF? In general, how should a disk make this trade-off between performance and starvation avoidance?
10. All the scheduling policies we have looked at thus far are **greedy**; they pick the next best option instead of looking for an optimal schedule. Can you find a set of requests in which greedy is not optimal?

38

Redundant Arrays of Inexpensive Disks (RAIDs)

When we use a disk, we sometimes wish it to be faster; I/O operations are slow and thus can be the bottleneck for the entire system. When we use a disk, we sometimes wish it to be larger; more and more data is being put online and thus our disks are getting fuller and fuller. When we use a disk, we sometimes wish for it to be more reliable; when a disk fails, if our data isn't backed up, all that valuable data is gone.

> CRUX: HOW TO MAKE A LARGE, FAST, RELIABLE DISK
> How can we make a large, fast, and reliable storage system? What are the key techniques? What are trade-offs between different approaches?

In this chapter, we introduce the **Redundant Array of Inexpensive Disks** better known as **RAID** [P+88], a technique to use multiple disks in concert to build a faster, bigger, and more reliable disk system. The term was introduced in the late 1980s by a group of researchers at U.C. Berkeley (led by Professors David Patterson and Randy Katz and then student Garth Gibson); it was around this time that many different researchers simultaneously arrived upon the basic idea of using multiple disks to build a better storage system [BG88, K86,K88,PB86,SG86].

Externally, a RAID looks like a disk: a group of blocks one can read or write. Internally, the RAID is a complex beast, consisting of multiple disks, memory (both volatile and non-), and one or more processors to manage the system. A hardware RAID is very much like a computer system, specialized for the task of managing a group of disks.

RAIDs offer a number of advantages over a single disk. One advantage is *performance*. Using multiple disks in parallel can greatly speed up I/O times. Another benefit is *capacity*. Large data sets demand large disks. Finally, RAIDs can improve *reliability*; spreading data across multiple disks (without RAID techniques) makes the data vulnerable to the loss of a single disk; with some form of **redundancy**, RAIDs can tolerate the loss of a disk and keep operating as if nothing were wrong.

TIP: TRANSPARENCY ENABLES DEPLOYMENT

When considering how to add new functionality to a system, one should always consider whether such functionality can be added **transparently**, in a way that demands no changes to the rest of the system. Requiring a complete rewrite of the existing software (or radical hardware changes) lessens the chance of impact of an idea. RAID is a perfect example, and certainly its transparency contributed to its success; administrators could install a SCSI-based RAID storage array instead of a SCSI disk, and the rest of the system (host computer, OS, etc.) did not have to change one bit to start using it. By solving this problem of **deployment**, RAID was made more successful from day one.

Amazingly, RAIDs provide these advantages **transparently** to systems that use them, i.e., a RAID just looks like a big disk to the host system. The beauty of transparency, of course, is that it enables one to simply replace a disk with a RAID and not change a single line of software; the operating system and client applications continue to operate without modification. In this manner, transparency greatly improves the **deployability** of RAID, enabling users and administrators to put a RAID to use without worries of software compatibility.

We now discuss some of the important aspects of RAIDs. We begin with the interface, fault model, and then discuss how one can evaluate a RAID design along three important axes: capacity, reliability, and performance. We then discuss a number of other issues that are important to RAID design and implementation.

38.1 Interface And RAID Internals

To a file system above, a RAID looks like a big, (hopefully) fast, and (hopefully) reliable disk. Just as with a single disk, it presents itself as a linear array of blocks, each of which can be read or written by the file system (or other client).

When a file system issues a *logical I/O* request to the RAID, the RAID internally must calculate which disk (or disks) to access in order to complete the request, and then issue one or more *physical I/Os* to do so. The exact nature of these physical I/Os depends on the RAID level, as we will discuss in detail below. However, as a simple example, consider a RAID that keeps two copies of each block (each one on a separate disk); when writing to such a **mirrored** RAID system, the RAID will have to perform two physical I/Os for every one logical I/O it is issued.

A RAID system is often built as a separate hardware box, with a standard connection (e.g., SCSI, or SATA) to a host. Internally, however, RAIDs are fairly complex, consisting of a microcontroller that runs firmware to direct the operation of the RAID, volatile memory such as DRAM to buffer data blocks as they are read and written, and in some cases, non-volatile memory to buffer writes safely and perhaps even specialized logic to perform parity calculations (useful in some RAID levels, as we will also see below). At a high level, a RAID is very much a specialized computer system: it has a processor, memory, and disks; however, instead of running applications, it runs specialized software designed to operate the RAID.

38.2 Fault Model

To understand RAID and compare different approaches, we must have a fault model in mind. RAIDs are designed to detect and recover from certain kinds of disk faults; thus, knowing exactly which faults to expect is critical in arriving upon a working design.

The first fault model we will assume is quite simple, and has been called the **fail-stop** fault model [S84]. In this model, a disk can be in exactly one of two states: working or failed. With a working disk, all blocks can be read or written. In contrast, when a disk has failed, we assume it is permanently lost.

One critical aspect of the fail-stop model is what it assumes about fault detection. Specifically, when a disk has failed, we assume that this is easily detected. For example, in a RAID array, we would assume that the RAID controller hardware (or software) can immediately observe when a disk has failed.

Thus, for now, we do not have to worry about more complex "silent" failures such as disk corruption. We also do not have to worry about a single block becoming inaccessible upon an otherwise working disk (sometimes called a latent sector error). We will consider these more complex (and unfortunately, more realistic) disk faults later.

38.3 How To Evaluate A RAID

As we will soon see, there are a number of different approaches to building a RAID. Each of these approaches has different characteristics which are worth evaluating, in order to understand their strengths and weaknesses.

Specifically, we will evaluate each RAID design along three axes. The first axis is **capacity**; given a set of N disks each with B blocks, how much useful capacity is available to clients of the RAID? Without redundancy, the answer is $N \cdot B$; in contrast, if we have a system that keeps two copies of each block (called **mirroring**), we obtain a useful capacity of $(N \cdot B)/2$. Different schemes (e.g., parity-based ones) tend to fall in between.

The second axis of evaluation is **reliability**. How many disk faults can the given design tolerate? In alignment with our fault model, we assume only that an entire disk can fail; in later chapters (i.e., on data integrity), we'll think about how to handle more complex failure modes.

Finally, the third axis is **performance**. Performance is somewhat challenging to evaluate, because it depends heavily on the workload presented to the disk array. Thus, before evaluating performance, we will first present a set of typical workloads that one should consider.

We now consider three important RAID designs: RAID Level 0 (striping), RAID Level 1 (mirroring), and RAID Levels 4/5 (parity-based redundancy). The naming of each of these designs as a "level" stems from the pioneering work of Patterson, Gibson, and Katz at Berkeley [P+88].

38.4 RAID Level 0: Striping

The first RAID level is actually not a RAID level at all, in that there is no redundancy. However, RAID level 0, or **striping** as it is better known, serves as an excellent upper-bound on performance and capacity and thus is worth understanding.

The simplest form of striping will **stripe** blocks across the disks of the system as follows (assume here a 4-disk array):

Disk 0	Disk 1	Disk 2	Disk 3
0	1	2	3
4	5	6	7
8	9	10	11
12	13	14	15

Figure 381: **RAID-0: Simple Striping**

From Figure 381, you get the basic idea: spread the blocks of the array across the disks in a round-robin fashion. This approach is designed to extract the most parallelism from the array when requests are made for contiguous chunks of the array (as in a large, sequential read, for example). We call the blocks in the same row a **stripe**; thus, blocks 0, 1, 2, and 3 are in the same stripe above.

In the example, we have made the simplifying assumption that only 1 block (each of say size 4KB) is placed on each disk before moving on to the next. However, this arrangement need not be the case. For example, we could arrange the blocks across disks as in Figure 382:

Disk 0	Disk 1	Disk 2	Disk 3	
0	2	4	6	chunk size:
1	3	5	7	2 blocks
8	10	12	14	
9	11	13	15	

Figure 382: **Striping With A Bigger Chunk Size**

In this example, we place two 4KB blocks on each disk before moving on to the next disk. Thus, the **chunk size** of this RAID array is 8KB, and a stripe thus consists of 4 chunks or 32KB of data.

ASIDE: THE RAID MAPPING PROBLEM

Before studying the capacity, reliability, and performance characteristics of the RAID, we first present an aside on what we call **the mapping problem**. This problem arises in all RAID arrays; simply put, given a logical block to read or write, how does the RAID know exactly which physical disk and offset to access?

For these simple RAID levels, we do not need much sophistication in order to correctly map logical blocks onto their physical locations. Take the first striping example above (chunk size = 1 block = 4KB). In this case, given a logical block address A, the RAID can easily compute the desired disk and offset with two simple equations:

```
Disk   = A % number_of_disks
Offset = A / number_of_disks
```

Note that these are all integer operations (e.g., 4 / 3 = 1 not 1.33333...).

Let's see how these equations work for a simple example. Imagine in the first RAID above that a request arrives for block 14. Given that there are 4 disks, this would mean that the disk we are interested in is (14 % 4 = 2): disk 2. The exact block is calculated as (14 / 4 = 3): block 3. Thus, block 14 should be found on the fourth block (block 3, starting at 0) of the third disk (disk 2, starting at 0), which is exactly where it is.

You can think about how these equations would be modified to support different chunk sizes. Try it! It's not too hard.

Chunk Sizes

Chunk size mostly affects performance of the array. For example, a small chunk size implies that many files will get striped across many disks, thus increasing the parallelism of reads and writes to a single file; however, the positioning time to access blocks across multiple disks increases, because the positioning time for the entire request is determined by the maximum of the positioning times of the requests across all drives.

A big chunk size, on the other hand, reduces such intra-file parallelism, and thus relies on multiple concurrent requests to achieve high throughput. However, large chunk sizes reduce positioning time; if, for example, a single file fits within a chunk and thus is placed on a single disk, the positioning time incurred while accessing it will just be the positioning time of a single disk.

Thus, determining the "best" chunk size is hard to do, as it requires a great deal of knowledge about the workload presented to the disk system [CL95]. For the rest of this discussion, we will assume that the array uses a chunk size of a single block (4KB). Most arrays use larger chunk sizes (e.g., 64 KB), but for the issues we discuss below, the exact chunk size does not matter; thus we use a single block for the sake of simplicity.

Back To RAID-0 Analysis

Let us now evaluate the capacity, reliability, and performance of striping. From the perspective of capacity, it is perfect: given N disks each of size B blocks, striping delivers $N \cdot B$ blocks of useful capacity. From the standpoint of reliability, striping is also perfect, but in the bad way: any disk failure will lead to data loss. Finally, performance is excellent: all disks are utilized, often in parallel, to service user I/O requests.

Evaluating RAID Performance

In analyzing RAID performance, one can consider two different performance metrics. The first is *single-request latency*. Understanding the latency of a single I/O request to a RAID is useful as it reveals how much parallelism can exist during a single logical I/O operation. The second is *steady-state throughput* of the RAID, i.e., the total bandwidth of many concurrent requests. Because RAIDs are often used in high-performance environments, the steady-state bandwidth is critical, and thus will be the main focus of our analyses.

To understand throughput in more detail, we need to put forth some workloads of interest. We will assume, for this discussion, that there are two types of workloads: **sequential** and **random**. With a sequential workload, we assume that requests to the array come in large contiguous chunks; for example, a request (or series of requests) that accesses 1 MB of data, starting at block x and ending at block (x+1 MB), would be deemed sequential. Sequential workloads are common in many environments (think of searching through a large file for a keyword), and thus are considered important.

For random workloads, we assume that each request is rather small, and that each request is to a different random location on disk. For example, a random stream of requests may first access 4KB at logical address 10, then at logical address 550,000, then at 20,100, and so forth. Some important workloads, such as transactional workloads on a database management system (DBMS), exhibit this type of access pattern, and thus it is considered an important workload.

Of course, real workloads are not so simple, and often have a mix of sequential and random-seeming components as well as behaviors in-between the two. For simplicity, we just consider these two possibilities.

As you can tell, sequential and random workloads will result in widely different performance characteristics from a disk. With sequential access, a disk operates in its most efficient mode, spending little time seeking and waiting for rotation and most of its time transferring data. With random access, just the opposite is true: most time is spent seeking and waiting for rotation and relatively little time is spent transferring data. To capture this difference in our analysis, we will assume that a disk can transfer data at S MB/s under a sequential workload, and R MB/s when under a random workload. In general, S is much greater than R (i.e., $S \gg R$).

To make sure we understand this difference, let's do a simple exercise. Specifically, let's calculate S and R given the following disk characteristics. Assume a sequential transfer of size 10 MB on average, and a random transfer of 10 KB on average. Also, assume the following disk characteristics:

Average seek time	7 ms
Average rotational delay	3 ms
Transfer rate of disk	50 MB/s

To compute S, we need to first figure out how time is spent in a typical 10 MB transfer. First, we spend 7 ms seeking, and then 3 ms rotating. Finally, transfer begins; 10 MB @ 50 MB/s leads to 1/5th of a second, or 200 ms, spent in transfer. Thus, for each 10 MB request, we spend 210 ms completing the request. To compute S, we just need to divide:

$$S = \frac{Amount\ of\ Data}{Time\ to\ access} = \frac{10\ MB}{210\ ms} = 47.62\ MB/s$$

As we can see, because of the large time spent transferring data, S is very near the peak bandwidth of the disk (the seek and rotational costs have been amortized).

We can compute R similarly. Seek and rotation are the same; we then compute the time spent in transfer, which is 10 KB @ 50 MB/s, or 0.195 ms.

$$R = \frac{Amount\ of\ Data}{Time\ to\ access} = \frac{10\ KB}{10.195\ ms} = 0.981\ MB/s$$

As we can see, R is less than 1 MB/s, and S/R is almost 50.

Back To RAID-0 Analysis, Again

Let's now evaluate the performance of striping. As we said above, it is generally good. From a latency perspective, for example, the latency of a single-block request should be just about identical to that of a single disk; after all, RAID-0 will simply redirect that request to one of its disks.

From the perspective of steady-state sequential throughput, we'd expect to get the full bandwidth of the system. Thus, throughput equals N (the number of disks) multiplied by S (the sequential bandwidth of a single disk). For a large number of random I/Os, we can again use all of the disks, and thus obtain $N \cdot R$ MB/s. As we will see below, these values are both the simplest to calculate and will serve as an upper bound in comparison with other RAID levels.

38.5 RAID Level 1: Mirroring

Our first RAID level beyond striping is known as RAID level 1, or mirroring. With a mirrored system, we simply make more than one copy of each block in the system; each copy should be placed on a separate disk, of course. By doing so, we can tolerate disk failures.

In a typical mirrored system, we will assume that for each logical block, the RAID keeps two physical copies of it. Here is an example:

Disk 0	Disk 1	Disk 2	Disk 3
0	0	1	1
2	2	3	3
4	4	5	5
6	6	7	7

Figure 383: **Simple RAID-1: Mirroring**

In the example, disk 0 and disk 1 have identical contents, and disk 2 and disk 3 do as well; the data is striped across these mirror pairs. In fact, you may have noticed that there are a number of different ways to place block copies across the disks. The arrangement above is a common one and is sometimes called **RAID-10** or (**RAID 1+0**) because it uses mirrored pairs (RAID-1) and then stripes (RAID-0) on top of them; another common arrangement is **RAID-01** (or **RAID 0+1**), which contains two large striping (RAID-0) arrays, and then mirrors (RAID-1) on top of them. For now, we will just talk about mirroring assuming the above layout.

When reading a block from a mirrored array, the RAID has a choice: it can read either copy. For example, if a read to logical block 5 is issued to the RAID, it is free to read it from either disk 2 or disk 3. When writing a block, though, no such choice exists: the RAID must update *both* copies of the data, in order to preserve reliability. Do note, though, that these writes can take place in parallel; for example, a write to logical block 5 could proceed to disks 2 and 3 at the same time.

RAID-1 Analysis

Let us assess RAID-1. From a capacity standpoint, RAID-1 is expensive; with the mirroring level = 2, we only obtain half of our peak useful capacity. With N disks of B blocks, RAID-1 useful capacity is $(N \cdot B)/2$.

From a reliability standpoint, RAID-1 does well. It can tolerate the failure of any one disk. You may also notice RAID-1 can actually do better than this, with a little luck. Imagine, in the figure above, that disk 0 and disk 2 both failed. In such a situation, there is no data loss! More generally, a mirrored system (with mirroring level of 2) can tolerate 1 disk failure for certain, and up to N/2 failures depending on which disks fail. In practice, we generally don't like to leave things like this to chance; thus most people consider mirroring to be good for handling a single failure.

Finally, we analyze performance. From the perspective of the latency of a single read request, we can see it is the same as the latency on a single disk; all the RAID-1 does is direct the read to one of its copies. A write is a little different: it requires two physical writes to complete before it is done. These two writes happen in parallel, and thus the time will be roughly equivalent to the time of a single write; however, because the logical write must wait for both physical writes to complete, it suffers the worst-case seek and rotational delay of the two requests, and thus (on average) will be slightly higher than a write to a single disk.

ASIDE: THE RAID CONSISTENT-UPDATE PROBLEM

Before analyzing RAID-1, let us first discuss a problem that arises in any multi-disk RAID system, known as the **consistent-update problem** [DAA05]. The problem occurs on a write to any RAID that has to update multiple disks during a single logical operation. In this case, let us assume we are considering a mirrored disk array.

Imagine the write is issued to the RAID, and then the RAID decides that it must be written to two disks, disk 0 and disk 1. The RAID then issues the write to disk 0, but just before the RAID can issue the request to disk 1, a power loss (or system crash) occurs. In this unfortunate case, let us assume that the request to disk 0 completed (but clearly the request to disk 1 did not, as it was never issued).

The result of this untimely power loss is that the two copies of the block are now **inconsistent**; the copy on disk 0 is the new version, and the copy on disk 1 is the old. What we would like to happen is for the state of both disks to change **atomically**, i.e., either both should end up as the new version or neither.

The general way to solve this problem is to use a **write-ahead log** of some kind to first record what the RAID is about to do (i.e., update two disks with a certain piece of data) before doing it. By taking this approach, we can ensure that in the presence of a crash, the right thing will happen; by running a **recovery** procedure that replays all pending transactions to the RAID, we can ensure that no two mirrored copies (in the RAID-1 case) are out of sync.

One last note: because logging to disk on every write is prohibitively expensive, most RAID hardware includes a small amount of non-volatile RAM (e.g., battery-backed) where it performs this type of logging. Thus, consistent update is provided without the high cost of logging to disk.

To analyze steady-state throughput, let us start with the sequential workload. When writing out to disk sequentially, each logical write must result in two physical writes; for example, when we write logical block 0 (in the figure above), the RAID internally would write it to both disk 0 and disk 1. Thus, we can conclude that the maximum bandwidth obtained during sequential writing to a mirrored array is $(\frac{N}{2} \cdot S)$, or half the peak bandwidth.

Unfortunately, we obtain the exact same performance during a sequential read. One might think that a sequential read could do better, because it only needs to read one copy of the data, not both. However, let's use an example to illustrate why this doesn't help much. Imagine we need to read blocks 0, 1, 2, 3, 4, 5, 6, and 7. Let's say we issue the read of 0 to disk 0, the read of 1 to disk 2, the read of 2 to disk 1, and the read of 3 to disk 3. We continue by issuing reads to 4, 5, 6, and 7 to disks 0, 2, 1, and 3, respectively. One might naively think that because we are utilizing all disks, we are achieving the full bandwidth of the array.

To see that this is not (necessarily) the case, however, consider the requests a single disk receives (say disk 0). First, it gets a request for block 0; then, it gets a request for block 4 (skipping block 2). In fact, each disk receives a request for every other block. While it is rotating over the skipped block, it is not delivering useful bandwidth to the client. Thus, each disk will only deliver half its peak bandwidth. And thus, the sequential read will only obtain a bandwidth of ($\frac{N}{2} \cdot S$) MB/s.

Random reads are the best case for a mirrored RAID. In this case, we can distribute the reads across all the disks, and thus obtain the full possible bandwidth. Thus, for random reads, RAID-1 delivers $N \cdot R$ MB/s.

Finally, random writes perform as you might expect: $\frac{N}{2} \cdot R$ MB/s. Each logical write must turn into two physical writes, and thus while all the disks will be in use, the client will only perceive this as half the available bandwidth. Even though a write to logical block x turns into two parallel writes to two different physical disks, the bandwidth of many small requests only achieves half of what we saw with striping. As we will soon see, getting half the available bandwidth is actually pretty good!

38.6 RAID Level 4: Saving Space With Parity

We now present a different method of adding redundancy to a disk array known as **parity**. Parity-based approaches attempt to use less capacity and thus overcome the huge space penalty paid by mirrored systems. They do so at a cost, however: performance.

Disk 0	Disk 1	Disk 2	Disk 3	Disk 4
0	1	2	3	P0
4	5	6	7	P1
8	9	10	11	P2
12	13	14	15	P3

Figure 384: **RAID-4 With Parity**

Here is an example five-disk RAID-4 system (Figure 384). For each stripe of data, we have added a single **parity** block that stores the redundant information for that stripe of blocks. For example, parity block P1 has redundant information that it calculated from blocks 4, 5, 6, and 7.

To compute parity, we need to use a mathematical function that enables us to withstand the loss of any one block from our stripe. It turns out the simple function **XOR** does the trick quite nicely. For a given set of bits, the XOR of all of those bits returns a 0 if there are an even number of 1's in the bits, and a 1 if there are an odd number of 1's. For example:

C0	C1	C2	C3	P
0	0	1	1	XOR(0,0,1,1) = 0
0	1	0	0	XOR(0,1,0,0) = 1

In the first row (0,0,1,1), there are two 1's (C2, C3), and thus XOR of all of those values will be 0 (P); similarly, in the second row there is only one 1 (C1), and thus the XOR must be 1 (P). You can remember this in a simple way: that the number of 1s in any row, including the parity bit, must be an even (not odd) number; that is the **invariant** that the RAID must maintain in order for parity to be correct.

From the example above, you might also be able to guess how parity information can be used to recover from a failure. Imagine the column labeled C2 is lost. To figure out what values must have been in the column, we simply have to read in all the other values in that row (including the XOR'd parity bit) and **reconstruct** the right answer. Specifically, assume the first row's value in column C2 is lost (it is a 1); by reading the other values in that row (0 from C0, 0 from C1, 1 from C3, and 0 from the parity column P), we get the values 0, 0, 1, and 0. Because we know that XOR keeps an even number of 1's in each row, we know what the missing data must be: a 1. And that is how reconstruction works in a XOR-based parity scheme! Note also how we compute the reconstructed value: we just XOR the data bits and the parity bits together, in the same way that we calculated the parity in the first place.

Now you might be wondering: we are talking about XORing all of these bits, and yet from above we know that the RAID places 4KB (or larger) blocks on each disk; how do we apply XOR to a bunch of blocks to compute the parity? It turns out this is easy as well. Simply perform a bitwise XOR across each bit of the data blocks; put the result of each bitwise XOR into the corresponding bit slot in the parity block. For example, if we had blocks of size 4 bits (yes, this is still quite a bit smaller than a 4KB block, but you get the picture), they might look something like this:

Block0	Block1	Block2	Block3	Parity
00	10	11	10	11
10	01	00	01	10

As you can see from the figure, the parity is computed for each bit of each block and the result placed in the parity block.

RAID-4 Analysis

Let us now analyze RAID-4. From a capacity standpoint, RAID-4 uses 1 disk for parity information for every group of disks it is protecting. Thus, our useful capacity for a RAID group is $(N - 1) \cdot B$.

Reliability is also quite easy to understand: RAID-4 tolerates 1 disk failure and no more. If more than one disk is lost, there is simply no way to reconstruct the lost data.

Finally, there is performance. This time, let us start by analyzing steady-state throughput. Sequential read performance can utilize all of the disks except for the parity disk, and thus deliver a peak effective bandwidth of $(N - 1) \cdot S$ MB/s (an easy case).

Disk 0	Disk 1	Disk 2	Disk 3	Disk 4
0	1	2	3	P0
4	5	6	7	P1
8	9	10	11	P2
12	13	14	15	P3

Figure 385: **Full-stripe Writes In RAID-4**

To understand the performance of sequential writes, we must first understand how they are done. When writing a big chunk of data to disk, RAID-4 can perform a simple optimization known as a **full-stripe write**. For example, imagine the case where the blocks 0, 1, 2, and 3 have been sent to the RAID as part of a write request (Figure 385).

In this case, the RAID can simply calculate the new value of P0 (by performing an XOR across the blocks 0, 1, 2, and 3) and then write all of the blocks (including the parity block) to the five disks above in parallel (highlighted in gray in the figure). Thus, full-stripe writes are the most efficient way for RAID-4 to write to disk.

Once we understand the full-stripe write, calculating the performance of sequential writes on RAID-4 is easy; the effective bandwidth is also $(N-1) \cdot S$ MB/s. Even though the parity disk is constantly in use during the operation, the client does not gain performance advantage from it.

Now let us analyze the performance of random reads. As you can also see from the figure above, a set of 1-block random reads will be spread across the data disks of the system but not the parity disk. Thus, the effective performance is: $(N-1) \cdot R$ MB/s.

Random writes, which we have saved for last, present the most interesting case for RAID-4. Imagine we wish to overwrite block 1 in the example above. We could just go ahead and overwrite it, but that would leave us with a problem: the parity block P0 would no longer accurately reflect the correct parity value of the stripe; in this example, P0 must also be updated. How can we update it both correctly and efficiently?

It turns out there are two methods. The first, known as **additive parity**, requires us to do the following. To compute the value of the new parity block, read in all of the other data blocks in the stripe in parallel (in the example, blocks 0, 2, and 3) and XOR those with the new block (1). The result is your new parity block. To complete the write, you can then write the new data and new parity to their respective disks, also in parallel.

The problem with this technique is that it scales with the number of disks, and thus in larger RAIDs requires a high number of reads to compute parity. Thus, the **subtractive parity** method.

For example, imagine this string of bits (4 data bits, one parity):

C0	C1	C2	C3	P
0	0	1	1	XOR(0,0,1,1) = 0

Let's imagine that we wish to overwrite bit C2 with a new value which we will call $C2_{new}$. The subtractive method works in three steps. First, we read in the old data at C2 ($C2_{old}$ = 1) and the old parity (P_{old} = 0). Then, we compare the old data and the new data; if they are the same (e.g., $C2_{new}$ = $C2_{old}$), then we know the parity bit will also remain the same (i.e., P_{new} = P_{old}). If, however, they are different, then we must flip the old parity bit to the opposite of its current state, that is, if (P_{old} == 1), P_{new} will be set to 0; if (P_{old} == 0), P_{new} will be set to 1. We can express this whole mess neatly with XOR (where $\oplus$ is the XOR operator):

$$P_{new} \;=\; (C_{old} \,\oplus\, C_{new}) \,\oplus\, P_{old} \tag{38.1}$$

Because we are dealing with blocks, not bits, we perform this calculation over all the bits in the block (e.g., 4096 bytes in each block multiplied by 8 bits per byte). Thus, in most cases, the new block will be different than the old block and thus the new parity block will too.

You should now be able to figure out when we would use the additive parity calculation and when we would use the subtractive method. Think about how many disks would need to be in the system so that the additive method performs fewer I/Os than the subtractive method; what is the cross-over point?

For this performance analysis, let us assume we are using the subtractive method. Thus, for each write, the RAID has to perform 4 physical I/Os (two reads and two writes). Now imagine there are lots of writes submitted to the RAID; how many can RAID-4 perform in parallel? To understand, let us again look at the RAID-4 layout (Figure 386).

Disk 0	Disk 1	Disk 2	Disk 3	Disk 4
0	1	2	3	P0
*4	5	6	7	+P1
8	9	10	11	P2
12	*13	14	15	+P3

Figure 386: **Example: Writes To 4, 13, And Respective Parity Blocks**

Now imagine there were 2 small writes submitted to the RAID-4 at about the same time, to blocks 4 and 13 (marked with * in the diagram). The data for those disks is on disks 0 and 1, and thus the read and write to data could happen in parallel, which is good. The problem that arises is with the parity disk; both the requests have to read the related parity blocks for 4 and 13, parity blocks 1 and 3 (marked with +). Hopefully, the issue is now clear: the parity disk is a bottleneck under this type of workload; we sometimes thus call this the **small-write problem** for parity-based RAIDs. Thus, even though the data disks could be accessed in parallel, the parity disk prevents any parallelism from materializing; all writes to the system will be serialized because of the parity disk. Because the parity disk has to perform two I/Os (one read, one write) per logical I/O, we can compute the performance of small random writes in RAID-4 by computing the parity disk's performance on those two I/Os, and thus we achieve $(R/2)$ MB/s. RAID-4 throughput under random small writes is terrible; it does not improve as you add disks to the system.

We conclude by analyzing I/O latency in RAID-4. As you now know, a single read (assuming no failure) is just mapped to a single disk, and thus its latency is equivalent to the latency of a single disk request. The latency of a single write requires two reads and then two writes; the reads can happen in parallel, as can the writes, and thus total latency is about twice that of a single disk (with some differences because we have to wait for both reads to complete and thus get the worst-case positioning time, but then the updates don't incur seek cost and thus may be a better-than-average positioning cost).

38.7 RAID Level 5: Rotating Parity

To address the small-write problem (at least, partially), Patterson, Gibson, and Katz introduced RAID-5. RAID-5 works almost identically to RAID-4, except that it **rotates** the parity block across drives (Figure 387).

Disk 0	Disk 1	Disk 2	Disk 3	Disk 4
0	1	2	3	P0
5	6	7	P1	4
10	11	P2	8	9
15	P3	12	13	14
P4	16	17	18	19

Figure 387: **RAID-5 With Rotated Parity**

As you can see, the parity block for each stripe is now rotated across the disks, in order to remove the parity-disk bottleneck for RAID-4.

RAID-5 Analysis

Much of the analysis for RAID-5 is identical to RAID-4. For example, the effective capacity and failure tolerance of the two levels are identical. So are sequential read and write performance. The latency of a single request (whether a read or a write) is also the same as RAID-4.

Random read performance is a little better, because we can now utilize all disks. Finally, random write performance improves noticeably over RAID-4, as it allows for parallelism across requests. Imagine a write to block 1 and a write to block 10; this will turn into requests to disk 1 and disk 4 (for block 1 and its parity) and requests to disk 0 and disk 2 (for block 10 and its parity). Thus, they can proceed in parallel. In fact, we can generally assume that given a large number of random requests, we will be able to keep all the disks about evenly busy. If that is the case, then our total bandwidth for small writes will be $\frac{N}{4} \cdot R$ MB/s. The factor

	RAID-0	RAID-1	RAID-4	RAID-5
Capacity	$N \cdot B$	$(N \cdot B)/2$	$(N-1) \cdot B$	$(N-1) \cdot B$
Reliability	0	1 (for sure) $\frac{N}{2}$ (if lucky)	1	1
Throughput				
Sequential Read	$N \cdot S$	$(N/2) \cdot S$	$(N-1) \cdot S$	$(N-1) \cdot S$
Sequential Write	$N \cdot S$	$(N/2) \cdot S$	$(N-1) \cdot S$	$(N-1) \cdot S$
Random Read	$N \cdot R$	$N \cdot R$	$(N-1) \cdot R$	$N \cdot R$
Random Write	$N \cdot R$	$(N/2) \cdot R$	$\frac{1}{2} \cdot R$	$\frac{N}{4} R$
Latency				
Read	T	T	T	T
Write	T	T	$2T$	$2T$

Figure 388: **RAID Capacity, Reliability, and Performance**

of four loss is due to the fact that each RAID-5 write still generates 4 total I/O operations, which is simply the cost of using parity-based RAID.

Because RAID-5 is basically identical to RAID-4 except in the few cases where it is better, it has almost completely replaced RAID-4 in the marketplace. The only place where it has not is in systems that know they will never perform anything other than a large write, thus avoiding the small-write problem altogether [HLM94]; in those cases, RAID-4 is sometimes used as it is slightly simpler to build.

38.8 RAID Comparison: A Summary

We now summarize our simplified comparison of RAID levels in Figure 388. Note that we have omitted a number of details to simplify our analysis. For example, when writing in a mirrored system, the average seek time is a little higher than when writing to just a single disk, because the seek time is the max of two seeks (one on each disk). Thus, random write performance to two disks will generally be a little less than random write performance of a single disk. Also, when updating the parity disk in RAID-4/5, the first read of the old parity will likely cause a full seek and rotation, but the second write of the parity will only result in rotation.

However, the comparison in Figure 388 does capture the essential differences, and is useful for understanding tradeoffs across RAID levels. For the latency analysis, we simply use T to represent the time that a request to a single disk would take.

To conclude, if you strictly want performance and do not care about reliability, striping is obviously best. If, however, you want random I/O performance and reliability, mirroring is the best; the cost you pay is in lost capacity. If capacity and reliability are your main goals, then RAID-5 is the winner; the cost you pay is in small-write performance. Finally, if you are always doing sequential I/O and want to maximize capacity, RAID-5 also makes the most sense.

38.9 Other Interesting RAID Issues

There are a number of other interesting ideas that one could (and perhaps should) discuss when thinking about RAID. Here are some things we might eventually write about.

For example, there are many other RAID designs, including Levels 2 and 3 from the original taxonomy, and Level 6 to tolerate multiple disk faults [C+04]. There is also what the RAID does when a disk fails; sometimes it has a **hot spare** sitting around to fill in for the failed disk. What happens to performance under failure, and performance during reconstruction of the failed disk? There are also more realistic fault models, to take into account **latent sector errors** or **block corruption** [B+08], and lots of techniques to handle such faults (see the data integrity chapter for details). Finally, you can even build RAID as a software layer: such **software RAID** systems are cheaper but have other problems, including the consistent-update problem [DAA05].

38.10 Summary

We have discussed RAID. RAID transforms a number of independent disks into a large, more capacious, and more reliable single entity; importantly, it does so transparently, and thus hardware and software above is relatively oblivious to the change.

There are many possible RAID levels to choose from, and the exact RAID level to use depends heavily on what is important to the end-user. For example, mirrored RAID is simple, reliable, and generally provides good performance but at a high capacity cost. RAID-5, in contrast, is reliable and better from a capacity standpoint, but performs quite poorly when there are small writes in the workload. Picking a RAID and setting its parameters (chunk size, number of disks, etc.) properly for a particular workload is challenging, and remains more of an art than a science.

References

[B+08] "An Analysis of Data Corruption in the Storage Stack" by Lakshmi N. Bairavasundaram, Garth R. Goodson, Bianca Schroeder, Andrea C. Arpaci-Dusseau, Remzi H. Arpaci-Dusseau. FAST '08, San Jose, CA, February 2008. *Our own work analyzing how often disks actually corrupt your data. Not often, but sometimes! And thus something a reliable storage system must consider.*

[BJ88] "Disk Shadowing" by D. Bitton and J. Gray. VLDB 1988. *One of the first papers to discuss mirroring, therein called "shadowing".*

[CL95] "Striping in a RAID level 5 disk array" by Peter M. Chen and Edward K. Lee. SIGMETRICS 1995. *A nice analysis of some of the important parameters in a RAID-5 disk array.*

[C+04] "Row-Diagonal Parity for Double Disk Failure Correction" by P. Corbett, B. English, A. Goel, T. Grcanac, S. Kleiman, J. Leong, S. Sankar. FAST '04, February 2004. *Though not the first paper on a RAID system with two disks for parity, it is a recent and highly-understandable version of said idea. Read it to learn more.*

[DAA05] "Journal-guided Resynchronization for Software RAID" by Timothy E. Denehy, A. Arpaci-Dusseau, R. Arpaci-Dusseau. FAST 2005. *Our own work on the consistent-update problem. Here we solve it for Software RAID by integrating the journaling machinery of the file system above with the software RAID beneath it.*

[HLM94] "File System Design for an NFS File Server Appliance" by Dave Hitz, James Lau, Michael Malcolm. USENIX Winter 1994, San Francisco, California, 1994. *The sparse paper introducing a landmark product in storage, the write-anywhere file layout or WAFL file system that underlies the NetApp file server.*

[K86] "Synchronized Disk Interleaving" by M.Y. Kim. IEEE Transactions on Computers, Volume C-35: 11, November 1986. *Some of the earliest work on RAID is found here.*

[K88] "Small Disk Arrays – The Emerging Approach to High Performance" by F. Kurzweil. Presentation at Spring COMPCON '88, March 1, 1988, San Francisco, California. *Another early RAID reference.*

[P+88] "Redundant Arrays of Inexpensive Disks" by D. Patterson, G. Gibson, R. Katz. SIGMOD 1988. *This is considered* **the** *RAID paper, written by famous authors Patterson, Gibson, and Katz. The paper has since won many test-of-time awards and ushered in the RAID era, including the name RAID itself!*

[PB86] "Providing Fault Tolerance in Parallel Secondary Storage Systems" by A. Park, K. Balasubramaniam. Department of Computer Science, Princeton, CS-TR-O57-86, November 1986. *Another early work on RAID.*

[SG86] "Disk Striping" by K. Salem, H. Garcia-Molina. IEEE International Conference on Data Engineering, 1986. *And yes, another early RAID work. There are a lot of these, which kind of came out of the woodwork when the RAID paper was published in SIGMOD.*

[S84] "Byzantine Generals in Action: Implementing Fail-Stop Processors" by F.B. Schneider. ACM Transactions on Computer Systems, 2(2):145–154, May 1984. *Finally, a paper that is not about RAID! This paper is actually about how systems fail, and how to make something behave in a fail-stop manner.*

Homework (Simulation)

This section introduces `raid.py`, a simple RAID simulator you can use to shore up your knowledge of how RAID systems work. See the README for details.

Questions

1. Use the simulator to perform some basic RAID mapping tests. Run with different levels (0, 1, 4, 5) and see if you can figure out the mappings of a set of requests. For RAID-5, see if you can figure out the difference between left-symmetric and left-asymmetric layouts. Use some different random seeds to generate different problems than above.
2. Do the same as the first problem, but this time vary the chunk size with `-C`. How does chunk size change the mappings?
3. Do the same as above, but use the `-r` flag to reverse the nature of each problem.
4. Now use the reverse flag but increase the size of each request with the `-S` flag. Try specifying sizes of 8k, 12k, and 16k, while varying the RAID level. What happens to the underlying I/O pattern when the size of the request increases? Make sure to try this with the sequential workload too (`-W sequential`); for what request sizes are RAID-4 and RAID-5 much more I/O efficient?
5. Use the timing mode of the simulator (`-t`) to estimate the performance of 100 random reads to the RAID, while varying the RAID levels, using 4 disks.
6. Do the same as above, but increase the number of disks. How does the performance of each RAID level scale as the number of disks increases?
7. Do the same as above, but use all writes (`-w 100`) instead of reads. How does the performance of each RAID level scale now? Can you do a rough estimate of the time it will take to complete the workload of 100 random writes?
8. Run the timing mode one last time, but this time with a sequential workload (`-W sequential`). How does the performance vary with RAID level, and when doing reads versus writes? How about when varying the size of each request? What size should you write to a RAID when using RAID-4 or RAID-5?

39

Interlude: Files and Directories

Thus far we have seen the development of two key operating system abstractions: the process, which is a virtualization of the CPU, and the address space, which is a virtualization of memory. In tandem, these two abstractions allow a program to run as if it is in its own private, isolated world; as if it has its own processor (or processors); as if it has its own memory. This illusion makes programming the system much easier and thus is prevalent today not only on desktops and servers but increasingly on all programmable platforms including mobile phones and the like.

In this section, we add one more critical piece to the virtualization puzzle: **persistent storage**. A persistent-storage device, such as a classic **hard disk drive** or a more modern **solid-state storage device**, stores information permanently (or at least, for a long time). Unlike memory, whose contents are lost when there is a power loss, a persistent-storage device keeps such data intact. Thus, the OS must take extra care with such a device: this is where users keep data that they really care about.

> CRUX: HOW TO MANAGE A PERSISTENT DEVICE
> How should the OS manage a persistent device? What are the APIs? What are the important aspects of the implementation?

Thus, in the next few chapters, we will explore critical techniques for managing persistent data, focusing on methods to improve performance and reliability. We begin, however, with an overview of the API: the interfaces you'll expect to see when interacting with a UNIX file system.

39.1 Files And Directories

Two key abstractions have developed over time in the virtualization of storage. The first is the **file**. A file is simply a linear array of bytes, each of which you can read or write. Each file has some kind of **low-level name**, usually a number of some kind; often, the user is not aware of

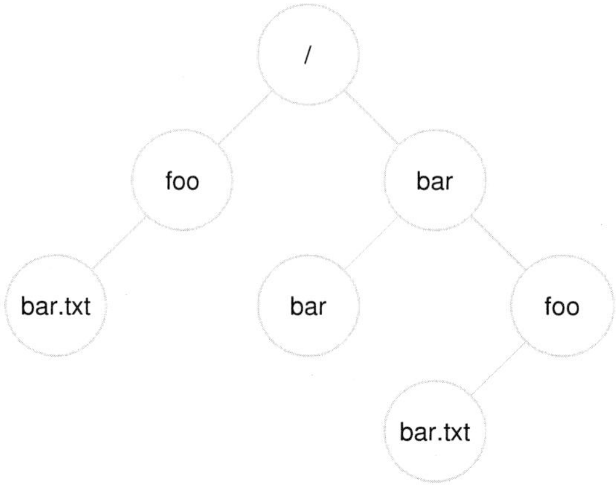

Figure 391: **An Example Directory Tree**

this name (as we will see). For historical reasons, the low-level name of a file is often referred to as its **inode number**. We'll be learning a lot more about inodes in future chapters; for now, just assume that each file has an inode number associated with it.

In most systems, the OS does not know much about the structure of the file (e.g., whether it is a picture, or a text file, or C code); rather, the responsibility of the file system is simply to store such data persistently on disk and make sure that when you request the data again, you get what you put there in the first place. Doing so is not as simple as it seems!

The second abstraction is that of a **directory**. A directory, like a file, also has a low-level name (i.e., an inode number), but its contents are quite specific: it contains a list of (user-readable name, low-level name) pairs. For example, let's say there is a file with the low-level name "10", and it is referred to by the user-readable name of "foo". The directory that "foo" resides in thus would have an entry ("foo", "10") that maps the user-readable name to the low-level name. Each entry in a directory refers to either files or other directories. By placing directories within other directories, users are able to build an arbitrary **directory tree** (or **directory hierarchy**), under which all files and directories are stored.

The directory hierarchy starts at a **root directory** (in UNIX-based systems, the root directory is simply referred to as /) and uses some kind of **separator** to name subsequent **sub-directories** until the desired file or directory is named. For example, if a user created a directory `foo` in the root directory `/`, and then created a file `bar.txt` in the directory `foo`, we could refer to the file by its **absolute pathname**, which in this case would be `/foo/bar.txt`. See Figure 391 for a more complex directory tree; valid directories in the example are `/`, `/foo`, `/bar`, `/bar/bar`, `/bar/foo` and valid files are `/foo/bar.txt` and `/bar/foo/bar.txt`.

> **TIP: THINK CAREFULLY ABOUT NAMING**
> Naming is an important aspect of computer systems [SK09]. In UNIX systems, virtually everything that you can think of is named through the file system. Beyond just files, devices, pipes, and even processes [K84] can be found in what looks like a plain old file system. This uniformity of naming eases your conceptual model of the system, and makes the system simpler and more modular. Thus, whenever creating a system or interface, think carefully about what names you are using.

Directories and files can have the same name as long as they are in different locations in the file-system tree (e.g., there are two files named `bar.txt` in the figure, `/foo/bar.txt` and `/bar/foo/bar.txt`).

You may also notice that the file name in this example often has two parts: `bar` and `txt`, separated by a period. The first part is an arbitrary name, whereas the second part of the file name is usually used to indicate the **type** of the file, e.g., whether it is C code (e.g., `.c`), or an image (e.g., `.jpg`), or a music file (e.g., `.mp3`). However, this is usually just a **convention**: there is usually no enforcement that the data contained in a file named `main.c` is indeed C source code.

Thus, we can see one great thing provided by the file system: a convenient way to **name** all the files we are interested in. Names are important in systems as the first step to accessing any resource is being able to name it. In UNIX systems, the file system thus provides a unified way to access files on disk, USB stick, CD-ROM, many other devices, and in fact many other things, all located under the single directory tree.

39.2 The File System Interface

Let's now discuss the file system interface in more detail. We'll start with the basics of creating, accessing, and deleting files. You may think this is straightforward, but along the way we'll discover the mysterious call that is used to remove files, known as `unlink()`. Hopefully, by the end of this chapter, this mystery won't be so mysterious to you!

39.3 Creating Files

We'll start with the most basic of operations: creating a file. This can be accomplished with the `open` system call; by calling `open()` and passing it the `O_CREAT` flag, a program can create a new file. Here is some example code to create a file called "foo" in the current working directory:

```
int fd = open("foo", O_CREAT|O_WRONLY|O_TRUNC,
              S_IRUSR|S_IWUSR);
```

ASIDE: THE `CREAT()` SYSTEM CALL

The older way of creating a file is to call `creat()`, as follows:

```
// option: add second flag to set permissions
int fd = creat("foo");
```

You can think of `creat()` as `open()` with the following flags: `O_CREAT | O_WRONLY | O_TRUNC`. Because `open()` can create a file, the usage of `creat()` has somewhat fallen out of favor (indeed, it could just be implemented as a library call to `open()`); however, it does hold a special place in UNIX lore. Specifically, when Ken Thompson was asked what he would do differently if he were redesigning UNIX, he replied: "I'd spell creat with an e."

The routine `open()` takes a number of different flags. In this example, the second parameter creates the file (`O_CREAT`) if it does not exist, ensures that the file can only be written to (`O_WRONLY`), and, if the file already exists, truncates it to a size of zero bytes thus removing any existing content (`O_TRUNC`). The third parameter specifies permissions, in this case making the file readable and writable by the owner.

One important aspect of `open()` is what it returns: a **file descriptor**. A file descriptor is just an integer, private per process, and is used in UNIX systems to access files; thus, once a file is opened, you use the file descriptor to read or write the file, assuming you have permission to do so. In this way, a file descriptor is a **capability** [L84], i.e., an opaque handle that gives you the power to perform certain operations. Another way to think of a file descriptor is as a pointer to an object of type file; once you have such an object, you can call other "methods" to access the file, like `read()` and `write()` (we'll see how to do so below).

As stated above, file descriptors are managed by the operating system on a per-process basis. This means some kind of simple structure (e.g., an array) is kept in the `proc` structure on UNIX systems. Here is the relevant piece from the xv6 kernel [CK+08]:

```
struct proc {
  ...
  struct file *ofile[NOFILE]; // Open files
  ...
};
```

A simple array (with a maximum of `NOFILE` open files) tracks which files are opened on a per-process basis. Each entry of the array is actually just a pointer to a `struct file`, which will be used to track information about the file being read or written; we'll discuss this further below.

> **TIP: USE `strace` (AND SIMILAR TOOLS)**
> The `strace` tool provides an awesome way to see what programs are up to. By running it, you can trace which system calls a program makes, see the arguments and return codes, and generally get a very good idea of what is going on.
> The tool also takes some arguments which can be quite useful. For example, `-f` follows any fork'd children too; `-t` reports the time of day at each call; `-e trace=open,close,read,write` only traces calls to those system calls and ignores all others. There are many other flags; read the man pages and find out how to harness this wonderful tool.

39.4 Reading And Writing Files

Once we have some files, of course we might like to read or write them. Let's start by reading an existing file. If we were typing at a command line, we might just use the program `cat` to dump the contents of the file to the screen.

```
prompt> echo hello > foo
prompt> cat foo
hello
prompt>
```

In this code snippet, we redirect the output of the program `echo` to the file `foo`, which then contains the word "hello" in it. We then use `cat` to see the contents of the file. But how does the `cat` program access the file `foo`?

To find this out, we'll use an incredibly useful tool to trace the system calls made by a program. On Linux, the tool is called **strace**; other systems have similar tools (see **dtruss** on a Mac, or **truss** on some older UNIX variants). What `strace` does is trace every system call made by a program while it runs, and dump the trace to the screen for you to see.

Here is an example of using `strace` to figure out what `cat` is doing (some calls removed for readability):

```
prompt> strace cat foo
...
open("foo", O_RDONLY|O_LARGEFILE)          = 3
read(3, "hello\n", 4096)                   = 6
write(1, "hello\n", 6)                     = 6
hello
read(3, "", 4096)                          = 0
close(3)                                   = 0
...
prompt>
```

The first thing that cat does is open the file for reading. A couple of things we should note about this; first, that the file is only opened for reading (not writing), as indicated by the O_RDONLY flag; second, that the 64-bit offset be used (O_LARGEFILE); third, that the call to open() succeeds and returns a file descriptor, which has the value of 3.

Why does the first call to open() return 3, not 0 or perhaps 1 as you might expect? As it turns out, each running process already has three files open, standard input (which the process can read to receive input), standard output (which the process can write to in order to dump information to the screen), and standard error (which the process can write error messages to). These are represented by file descriptors 0, 1, and 2, respectively. Thus, when you first open another file (as cat does above), it will almost certainly be file descriptor 3.

After the open succeeds, cat uses the read() system call to repeatedly read some bytes from a file. The first argument to read() is the file descriptor, thus telling the file system which file to read; a process can of course have multiple files open at once, and thus the descriptor enables the operating system to know which file a particular read refers to. The second argument points to a buffer where the result of the read() will be placed; in the system-call trace above, strace shows the results of the read in this spot ("hello"). The third argument is the size of the buffer, which in this case is 4 KB. The call to read() returns successfully as well, here returning the number of bytes it read (6, which includes 5 for the letters in the word "hello" and one for an end-of-line marker).

At this point, you see another interesting result of the strace: a single call to the write() system call, to the file descriptor 1. As we mentioned above, this descriptor is known as the standard output, and thus is used to write the word "hello" to the screen as the program cat is meant to do. But does it call write() directly? Maybe (if it is highly optimized). But if not, what cat might do is call the library routine printf(); internally, printf() figures out all the formatting details passed to it, and eventually writes to standard output to print the results to the screen.

The cat program then tries to read more from the file, but since there are no bytes left in the file, the read() returns 0 and the program knows that this means it has read the entire file. Thus, the program calls close() to indicate that it is done with the file "foo", passing in the corresponding file descriptor. The file is thus closed, and the reading of it thus complete.

Writing a file is accomplished via a similar set of steps. First, a file is opened for writing, then the write() system call is called, perhaps repeatedly for larger files, and then close(). Use strace to trace writes to a file, perhaps of a program you wrote yourself, or by tracing the dd utility, e.g., dd if=foo of=bar.

> ASIDE: DATA STRUCTURE — THE OPEN FILE TABLE
> Each process maintains an array of file descriptors, each of which refers to an entry in the system-wide **open file table**. Each entry in this table tracks which underlying file the descriptor refers to, the current offset, and other relevant details such as whether the file is readable or writable.

39.5 Reading And Writing, But Not Sequentially

Thus far, we've discussed how to read and write files, but all access has been **sequential**; that is, we have either read a file from the beginning to the end, or written a file out from beginning to end.

Sometimes, however, it is useful to be able to read or write to a specific offset within a file; for example, if you build an index over a text document, and use it to look up a specific word, you may end up reading from some **random** offsets within the document. To do so, we will use the `lseek()` system call. Here is the function prototype:

```
off_t lseek(int fildes, off_t offset, int whence);
```

The first argument is familiar (a file descriptor). The second argument is the `offset`, which positions the **file offset** to a particular location within the file. The third argument, called `whence` for historical reasons, determines exactly how the seek is performed. From the man page:

```
If whence is SEEK_SET, the offset is set to offset bytes.
If whence is SEEK_CUR, the offset is set to its current
  location plus offset bytes.
If whence is SEEK_END, the offset is set to the size of
  the file plus offset bytes.
```

As you can tell from this description, for each file a process opens, the OS tracks a "current" offset, which determines where the next read or write will begin reading from or writing to within the file. Thus, part of the abstraction of an open file is that it has a current offset, which is updated in one of two ways. The first is when a read or write of N bytes takes place, N is added to the current offset; thus each read or write *implicitly* updates the offset. The second is *explicitly* with `lseek`, which changes the offset as specified above.

The offset, as you might have guessed, is kept in that `struct file` we saw earlier, as referenced from the `struct proc`. Here is a (simplified) xv6 definition of the structure:

```
struct file {
  int ref;
  char readable;
  char writable;
  struct inode *ip;
  uint off;
};
```

> **ASIDE: CALLING `LSEEK()` DOES NOT PERFORM A DISK SEEK**
> The poorly-named system call `lseek()` confuses many a student trying to understand disks and how the file systems atop them work. Do not confuse the two! The `lseek()` call simply changes a variable in OS memory that tracks, for a particular process, at which offset its next read or write will start. A disk seek occurs when a read or write issued to the disk is not on the same track as the last read or write, and thus necessitates a head movement. Making this even more confusing is the fact that calling `lseek()` to read or write from/to random parts of a file, and then reading/writing to those random parts, will indeed lead to more disk seeks. Thus, calling `lseek()` can lead to a seek in an upcoming read or write, but absolutely does not cause any disk I/O to occur itself.

As you can see in the structure, the OS can use this to determine whether the opened file is readable or writable (or both), which underlying file it refers to (as pointed to by the `struct inode` pointer `ip`), and the current offset (`off`). There is also a reference count (`ref`), which we will discuss further below.

These file structures represent all of the currently opened files in the system; together, they are sometimes referred to as the **open file table**. The xv6 kernel just keeps these as an array as well, with one lock per entry, as shown here:

```
struct {
  struct spinlock lock;
  struct file file[NFILE];
} ftable;
```

Let's make this a bit clearer with a few examples. First, let's track a process that opens a file (of size 300 bytes) and reads it by calling the `read()` system call repeatedly, each time reading 100 bytes. Here is a trace of the relevant system calls, along with the values returned by each system call, and the value of the current offset in the open file table for this file access:

System Calls	Return Code	Current Offset
`fd = open("file", O_RDONLY);`	3	0
`read(fd, buffer, 100);`	100	100
`read(fd, buffer, 100);`	100	200
`read(fd, buffer, 100);`	100	300
`read(fd, buffer, 100);`	0	300
`close(fd);`	0	–

There are a couple of items of interest to note from the trace. First, you can see how the current offset gets initialized to zero when the file is opened. Next, you can see how it is incremented with each `read()` by the process; this makes it easy for a process to just keep calling `read()` to get the next chunk of the file. Finally, you can see how at the end, an attempted `read()` past the end of the file returns zero, thus indicating to the process that it has read the file in its entirety.

Second, let's trace a process that opens the *same* file twice and issues a read to each of them.

System Calls	Return Code	OFT[10] Current Offset	OFT[11] Current Offset
`fd1 = open("file", O_RDONLY);`	3	0	–
`fd2 = open("file", O_RDONLY);`	4	0	0
`read(fd1, buffer1, 100);`	100	100	0
`read(fd2, buffer2, 100);`	100	100	100
`close(fd1);`	0	–	100
`close(fd2);`	0	–	–

In this example, two file descriptors are allocated (`3` and `4`), and each refers to a *different* entry in the open file table (in this example, entries `10` and `11`, as shown in the table heading; OFT stands for Open File Table). If you trace through what happens, you can see how each current offset is updated independently.

In one final example, a process uses `lseek()` to reposition the current offset before reading; in this case, only a single open file table entry is needed (as with the first example).

System Calls	Return Code	Current Offset
`fd = open("file", O_RDONLY);`	3	0
`lseek(fd, 200, SEEK_SET);`	200	200
`read(fd, buffer, 50);`	50	250
`close(fd);`	0	–

Here, the `lseek()` call first sets the current offset to `200`. The subsequent `read()` then reads the next 50 bytes, and updates the current offset accordingly.

39.6 Shared File Table Entries: `fork()` And `dup()`

In many cases (as in the examples shown above), the mapping of file descriptor to an entry in the open file table is a one-to-one mapping. For example, when a process runs, it might decide to open a file, read it, and then close it; in this example, the file will have a unique entry in the open file table. Even if some other process reads the same file at the same time, each will have its own entry in the open file table. In this way, each logical

```
int main(int argc, char *argv[]) {
    int fd = open("file.txt", O_RDONLY);
    assert(fd >= 0);
    int rc = fork();
    if (rc == 0) {
        rc = lseek(fd, 10, SEEK_SET);
        printf("child: offset %d\n", rc);
    } else if (rc > 0) {
        (void) wait(NULL);
        printf("parent: offset %d\n",
               (int) lseek(fd, 0, SEEK_CUR));
    }
    return 0;
}
```

Figure 392: **Shared Parent/Child File Table Entries (`fork-seek.c`)**

reading or writing of a file is independent, and each has its own current offset while it accesses the given file.

However, there are a few interesting cases where an entry in the open file table is *shared*. One of those cases occurs when a parent process creates a child process with `fork()`. Figure 392 shows a small code snippet in which a parent creates a child and then waits for it to complete. The child adjusts the current offset via a call to `lseek()` and then exits. Finally the parent, after waiting for the child, checks the current offset and prints out its value.

When we run this program, we see the following output:

```
prompt> ./fork-seek
child: offset 10
parent: offset 10
prompt>
```

Figure 393 shows the relationships that connect each process's private descriptor array, the shared open file table entry, and the reference from it to the underlying file-system inode. Note that we finally make use of the **reference count** here. When a file table entry is shared, its reference count is incremented; only when both processes close the file (or exit) will the entry be removed.

Sharing open file table entries across parent and child is occasionally useful. For example, if you create a number of processes that are cooperatively working on a task, they can write to the same output file without any extra coordination. For more on what is shared by processes when `fork()` is called, please see the man pages.

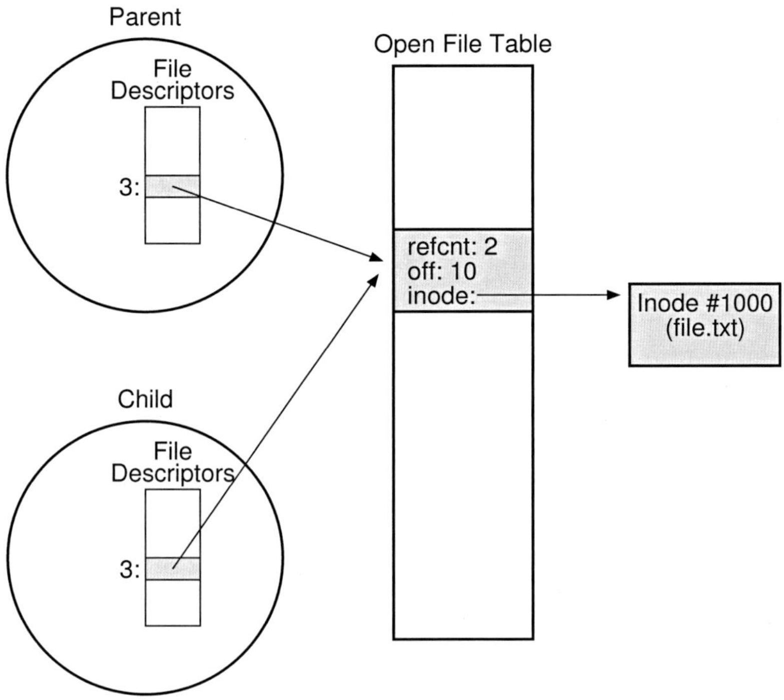

Figure 393: **Processes Sharing An Open File Table Entry**

One other interesting, and perhaps more useful, case of sharing occurs with the **dup()** system call (and its cousins, **dup2()** and **dup3()**).

The `dup()` call allows a process to create a new file descriptor that refers to the same underlying open file as an existing descriptor. Figure 394 shows a small code snippet that shows how `dup()` can be used.

The `dup()` call (and, in particular, `dup2()`) is useful when writing a UNIX shell and performing operations like output redirection; spend some time and think about why! And now, you are thinking: why didn't they tell me this when I was doing the shell project? Oh well, you can't get everything in the right order, even in an incredible book about operating systems. Sorry!

```
int main(int argc, char *argv[]) {
    int fd = open("README", O_RDONLY);
    assert(fd >= 0);
    int fd2 = dup(fd);
    // now fd and fd2 can be used interchangeably
    return 0;
}
```

Figure 394: **Shared File Table Entry With dup() (dup.c)**

39.7 Writing Immediately With `fsync()`

Most times when a program calls `write()`, it is just telling the file system: please write this data to persistent storage, at some point in the future. The file system, for performance reasons, will **buffer** such writes in memory for some time (say 5 seconds, or 30); at that later point in time, the write(s) will actually be issued to the storage device. From the perspective of the calling application, writes seem to complete quickly, and only in rare cases (e.g., the machine crashes after the `write()` call but before the write to disk) will data be lost.

However, some applications require something more than this eventual guarantee. For example, in a database management system (DBMS), development of a correct recovery protocol requires the ability to force writes to disk from time to time.

To support these types of applications, most file systems provide some additional control APIs. In the UNIX world, the interface provided to applications is known as `fsync(int fd)`. When a process calls `fsync()` for a particular file descriptor, the file system responds by forcing all **dirty** (i.e., not yet written) data to disk, for the file referred to by the specified file descriptor. The `fsync()` routine returns once all of these writes are complete.

Here is a simple example of how to use `fsync()`. The code opens the file `foo`, writes a single chunk of data to it, and then calls `fsync()` to ensure the writes are forced immediately to disk. Once the `fsync()` returns, the application can safely move on, knowing that the data has been persisted (if `fsync()` is correctly implemented, that is).

```
int fd = open("foo", O_CREAT|O_WRONLY|O_TRUNC,
              S_IRUSR|S_IWUSR);
assert(fd > -1);
int rc = write(fd, buffer, size);
assert(rc == size);
rc = fsync(fd);
assert(rc == 0);
```

Interestingly, this sequence does not guarantee everything that you might expect; in some cases, you also need to `fsync()` the directory that contains the file `foo`. Adding this step ensures not only that the file itself is on disk, but that the file, if newly created, also is durably a part of the directory. Not surprisingly, this type of detail is often overlooked, leading to many application-level bugs [P+13,P+14].

39.8 Renaming Files

Once we have a file, it is sometimes useful to be able to give a file a different name. When typing at the command line, this is accomplished with `mv` command; in this example, the file `foo` is renamed `bar`:

```
prompt> mv foo bar
```

Using `strace`, we can see that `mv` uses the system call `rename(char *old, char *new)`, which takes precisely two arguments: the original name of the file (`old`) and the new name (`new`).

One interesting guarantee provided by the `rename()` call is that it is (usually) implemented as an **atomic** call with respect to system crashes; if the system crashes during the renaming, the file will either be named the old name or the new name, and no odd in-between state can arise. Thus, `rename()` is critical for supporting certain kinds of applications that require an atomic update to file state.

Let's be a little more specific here. Imagine that you are using a file editor (e.g., emacs), and you insert a line into the middle of a file. The file's name, for the example, is `foo.txt`. The way the editor might update the file to guarantee that the new file has the original contents plus the line inserted is as follows (ignoring error-checking for simplicity):

```
int fd = open("foo.txt.tmp", O_WRONLY|O_CREAT|O_TRUNC,
              S_IRUSR|S_IWUSR);
write(fd, buffer, size); // write out new version of file
fsync(fd);
close(fd);
rename("foo.txt.tmp", "foo.txt");
```

What the editor does in this example is simple: write out the new version of the file under a temporary name (`foo.txt.tmp`), force it to disk with `fsync()`, and then, when the application is certain the new file metadata and contents are on the disk, rename the temporary file to the original file's name. This last step atomically swaps the new file into place, while concurrently deleting the old version of the file, and thus an atomic file update is achieved.

39.9 Getting Information About Files

Beyond file access, we expect the file system to keep a fair amount of information about each file it is storing. We generally call such data about files **metadata**. To see the metadata for a certain file, we can use the `stat()` or `fstat()` system calls. These calls take a pathname (or file descriptor) to a file and fill in a `stat` structure as seen in Figure 395.

You can see that there is a lot of information kept about each file, including its size (in bytes), its low-level name (i.e., inode number), some ownership information, and some information about when the file was accessed or modified, among other things. To see this information, you can use the command line tool `stat`. In this example, we first create a file (called `file`) and then use the `stat` command line tool to learn some things about the file.

```
struct stat {
  dev_t     st_dev;     // ID of device containing file
  ino_t     st_ino;     // inode number
  mode_t    st_mode;    // protection
  nlink_t   st_nlink;   // number of hard links
  uid_t     st_uid;     // user ID of owner
  gid_t     st_gid;     // group ID of owner
  dev_t     st_rdev;    // device ID (if special file)
  off_t     st_size;    // total size, in bytes
  blksize_t st_blksize; // blocksize for filesystem I/O
  blkcnt_t  st_blocks;  // number of blocks allocated
  time_t    st_atime;   // time of last access
  time_t    st_mtime;   // time of last modification
  time_t    st_ctime;   // time of last status change
};
```

Figure 395: **The `stat` structure.**

Here is the output on Linux:

```
prompt> echo hello > file
prompt> stat file
  File: 'file'
  Size: 6   Blocks: 8   IO Block: 4096   regular file
Device: 811h/2065d Inode: 67158084    Links: 1
Access: (0640/-rw-r-----) Uid: (30686/remzi)
  Gid: (30686/remzi)
Access: 2011-05-03 15:50:20.157594748 -0500
Modify: 2011-05-03 15:50:20.157594748 -0500
Change: 2011-05-03 15:50:20.157594748 -0500
```

Each file system usually keeps this type of information in a structure called an **inode**[1]. We'll be learning a lot more about inodes when we talk about file system implementation. For now, you should just think of an inode as a persistent data structure kept by the file system that has information like we see above inside of it. All inodes reside on disk; a copy of active ones are usually cached in memory to speed up access.

39.10 Removing Files

At this point, we know how to create files and access them, either sequentially or not. But how do you delete files? If you've used UNIX, you probably think you know: just run the program `rm`. But what system call does `rm` use to remove a file?

[1]Some file systems call these structures similar, but slightly different, names, such as dnodes; the basic idea is similar however.

Let's use our old friend strace again to find out. Here we remove that pesky file foo:

```
prompt> strace rm foo
...
unlink("foo")                                   = 0
...
```

We've removed a bunch of unrelated cruft from the traced output, leaving just a single call to the mysteriously-named system call unlink(). As you can see, unlink() just takes the name of the file to be removed, and returns zero upon success. But this leads us to a great puzzle: why is this system call named unlink? Why not just remove or delete? To understand the answer to this puzzle, we must first understand more than just files, but also directories.

39.11 Making Directories

Beyond files, a set of directory-related system calls enable you to make, read, and delete directories. Note you can never write to a directory directly. Because the format of the directory is considered file system metadata, the file system considers itself responsible for the integrity of directory data; thus, you can only update a directory indirectly by, for example, creating files, directories, or other object types within it. In this way, the file system makes sure that directory contents are as expected.

To create a directory, a single system call, mkdir(), is available. The eponymous mkdir program can be used to create such a directory. Let's take a look at what happens when we run the mkdir program to make a simple directory called foo:

```
prompt> strace mkdir foo
...
mkdir("foo", 0777)                              = 0
...
prompt>
```

When such a directory is created, it is considered "empty", although it does have a bare minimum of contents. Specifically, an empty directory has two entries: one entry that refers to itself, and one entry that refers to its parent. The former is referred to as the "." (dot) directory, and the latter as ".." (dot-dot). You can see these directories by passing a flag (-a) to the program ls:

```
prompt> ls -a
./  ../
prompt> ls -al
total 8
drwxr-x---  2 remzi remzi    6 Apr 30 16:17 ./
drwxr-x--- 26 remzi remzi 4096 Apr 30 16:17 ../
```

TIP: BE WARY OF POWERFUL COMMANDS

The program rm provides us with a great example of powerful commands, and how sometimes too much power can be a bad thing. For example, to remove a bunch of files at once, you can type something like:

```
prompt> rm *
```

where the * will match all files in the current directory. But sometimes you want to also delete the directories too, and in fact all of their contents. You can do this by telling rm to recursively descend into each directory, and remove its contents too:

```
prompt> rm -rf *
```

Where you get into trouble with this small string of characters is when you issue the command, accidentally, from the root directory of a file system, thus removing every file and directory from it. Oops!

Thus, remember the double-edged sword of powerful commands; while they give you the ability to do a lot of work with a small number of keystrokes, they also can quickly and readily do a great deal of harm.

39.12 Reading Directories

Now that we've created a directory, we might wish to read one too. Indeed, that is exactly what the program ls does. Let's write our own little tool like ls and see how it is done.

Instead of just opening a directory as if it were a file, we instead use a new set of calls. Below is an example program that prints the contents of a directory. The program uses three calls, opendir(), readdir(), and closedir(), to get the job done, and you can see how simple the interface is; we just use a simple loop to read one directory entry at a time, and print out the name and inode number of each file in the directory.

```
int main(int argc, char *argv[]) {
    DIR *dp = opendir(".");
    assert(dp != NULL);
    struct dirent *d;
    while ((d = readdir(dp)) != NULL) {
        printf("%lu %s\n", (unsigned long) d->d_ino,
               d->d_name);
    }
    closedir(dp);
    return 0;
}
```

The declaration below shows the information available within each directory entry in the `struct dirent` data structure:

```
struct dirent {
  char           d_name[256]; // filename
  ino_t          d_ino;       // inode number
  off_t          d_off;       // offset to the next dirent
  unsigned short d_reclen;    // length of this record
  unsigned char  d_type;      // type of file
};
```

Because directories are light on information (basically, just mapping the name to the inode number, along with a few other details), a program may want to call `stat()` on each file to get more information on each, such as its length or other detailed information. Indeed, this is exactly what `ls` does when you pass it the `-l` flag; try `strace` on `ls` with and without that flag to see for yourself.

39.13 Deleting Directories

Finally, you can delete a directory with a call to `rmdir()` (which is used by the program of the same name, `rmdir`). Unlike file deletion, however, removing directories is more dangerous, as you could potentially delete a large amount of data with a single command. Thus, `rmdir()` has the requirement that the directory be empty (i.e., only has "." and ".." entries) before it is deleted. If you try to delete a non-empty directory, the call to `rmdir()` simply will fail.

39.14 Hard Links

We now come back to the mystery of why removing a file is performed via `unlink()`, by understanding a new way to make an entry in the file system tree, through a system call known as `link()`. The `link()` system call takes two arguments, an old pathname and a new one; when you "link" a new file name to an old one, you essentially create another way to refer to the same file. The command-line program `ln` is used to do this, as we see in this example:

```
prompt> echo hello > file
prompt> cat file
hello
prompt> ln file file2
prompt> cat file2
hello
```

Here we created a file with the word "hello" in it, and called the file `file`[2]. We then create a hard link to that file using the `ln` program. After this, we can examine the file by either opening `file` or `file2`.

The way `link()` works is that it simply creates another name in the directory you are creating the link to, and refers it to the *same* inode number (i.e., low-level name) of the original file. The file is not copied in any way; rather, you now just have two human-readable names (`file` and `file2`) that both refer to the same file. We can even see this in the directory itself, by printing out the inode number of each file:

```
prompt> ls -i file file2
67158084 file
67158084 file2
prompt>
```

By passing the `-i` flag to `ls`, it prints out the inode number of each file (as well as the file name). And thus you can see what link really has done: just make a new reference to the same exact inode number (67158084 in this example).

By now you might be starting to see why `unlink()` is called `unlink()`. When you create a file, you are really doing *two* things. First, you are making a structure (the inode) that will track virtually all relevant information about the file, including its size, where its blocks are on disk, and so forth. Second, you are *linking* a human-readable name to that file, and putting that link into a directory.

After creating a hard link to a file, to the file system, there is no difference between the original file name (`file`) and the newly created file name (`file2`); indeed, they are both just links to the underlying metadata about the file, which is found in inode number 67158084.

Thus, to remove a file from the file system, we call `unlink()`. In the example above, we could for example remove the file named `file`, and still access the file without difficulty:

```
prompt> rm file
removed 'file'
prompt> cat file2
hello
```

The reason this works is because when the file system unlinks file, it checks a **reference count** within the inode number. This reference count (sometimes called the **link count**) allows the file system to track how many different file names have been linked to this particular inode. When `unlink()` is called, it removes the "link" between the human-readable

[2]Note again how creative the authors of this book are. We also used to have a cat named "Cat" (true story). However, she died, and we now have a hamster named "Hammy." Update: Hammy is now dead too. The pet bodies are piling up.

name (the file that is being deleted) to the given inode number, and decrements the reference count; only when the reference count reaches zero does the file system also free the inode and related data blocks, and thus truly "delete" the file.

You can see the reference count of a file using `stat()` of course. Let's see what it is when we create and delete hard links to a file. In this example, we'll create three links to the same file, and then delete them. Watch the link count!

```
prompt> echo hello > file
prompt> stat file
... Inode: 67158084     Links: 1 ...
prompt> ln file file2
prompt> stat file
... Inode: 67158084     Links: 2 ...
prompt> stat file2
... Inode: 67158084     Links: 2 ...
prompt> ln file2 file3
prompt> stat file
... Inode: 67158084     Links: 3 ...
prompt> rm file
prompt> stat file2
... Inode: 67158084     Links: 2 ...
prompt> rm file2
prompt> stat file3
... Inode: 67158084     Links: 1 ...
prompt> rm file3
```

39.15 Symbolic Links

There is one other type of link that is really useful, and it is called a **symbolic link** or sometimes a **soft link**. Hard links are somewhat limited: you can't create one to a directory (for fear that you will create a cycle in the directory tree); you can't hard link to files in other disk partitions (because inode numbers are only unique within a particular file system, not across file systems); etc. Thus, a new type of link called the symbolic link was created [MJLF84].

To create such a link, you can use the same program `ln`, but with the `-s` flag. Here is an example:

```
prompt> echo hello > file
prompt> ln -s file file2
prompt> cat file2
hello
```

As you can see, creating a soft link looks much the same, and the original file can now be accessed through the file name `file` as well as the symbolic link name `file2`.

However, beyond this surface similarity, symbolic links are actually quite different from hard links. The first difference is that a symbolic link is actually a file itself, of a different type. We've already talked about regular files and directories; symbolic links are a third type the file system knows about. A `stat` on the symlink reveals all:

```
prompt> stat file
 ... regular file ...
prompt> stat file2
 ... symbolic link ...
```

Running `ls` also reveals this fact. If you look closely at the first character of the long-form of the output from `ls`, you can see that the first character in the left-most column is a `-` for regular files, a `d` for directories, and an `l` for soft links. You can also see the size of the symbolic link (4 bytes in this case) and what the link points to (the file named `file`).

```
prompt> ls -al
drwxr-x---  2 remzi remzi   29 May  3 19:10 ./
drwxr-x--- 27 remzi remzi 4096 May  3 15:14 ../
-rw-r-----  1 remzi remzi    6 May  3 19:10 file
lrwxrwxrwx  1 remzi remzi    4 May  3 19:10 file2 -> file
```

The reason that `file2` is 4 bytes is because the way a symbolic link is formed is by holding the pathname of the linked-to file as the data of the link file. Because we've linked to a file named `file`, our link file `file2` is small (4 bytes). If we link to a longer pathname, our link file would be bigger:

```
prompt> echo hello > alongerfilename
prompt> ln -s alongerfilename file3
prompt> ls -al alongerfilename file3
-rw-r----- 1 remzi remzi  6 May  3 19:17 alongerfilename
lrwxrwxrwx 1 remzi remzi 15 May  3 19:17 file3 ->
                                         alongerfilename
```

Finally, because of the way symbolic links are created, they leave the possibility for what is known as a **dangling reference**:

```
prompt> echo hello > file
prompt> ln -s file file2
prompt> cat file2
hello
prompt> rm file
prompt> cat file2
cat: file2: No such file or directory
```

As you can see in this example, quite unlike hard links, removing the original file named `file` causes the link to point to a pathname that no longer exists.

39.16 Permission Bits And Access Control Lists

The abstraction of a process provided two central virtualizations: of the CPU and of memory. Each of these gave the illusion to a process that it had its own *private* CPU and its own *private* memory; in reality, the OS underneath used various techniques to share limited physical resources among competing entities in a safe and secure manner.

The file system also presents a virtual view of a disk, transforming it from a bunch of raw blocks into much more user-friendly files and directories, as described within this chapter. However, the abstraction is notably different from that of the CPU and memory, in that files are commonly *shared* among different users and processes and are not (always) private. Thus, a more comprehensive set of mechanisms for enabling various degrees of sharing are usually present within file systems.

The first form of such mechanisms is the classic UNIX **permission bits**. To see permissions for a file `foo.txt`, just type:

```
prompt> ls -l foo.txt
-rw-r--r--  1 remzi wheel  0 Aug 24 16:29 foo.txt
```

We'll just pay attention to the first part of this output, namely the `-rw-r--r--`. The first character here just shows the type of the file: `-` for a regular file (which `foo.txt` is), `d` for a directory, `l` for a symbolic link, and so forth; this is (mostly) not related to permissions, so we'll ignore it for now.

We are interested in the permission bits, which are represented by the next nine characters (`rw-r--r--`). These bits determine, for each regular file, directory, and other entities, exactly who can access it and how.

The permissions consist of three groupings: what the **owner** of the file can do to it, what someone in a **group** can do to the file, and finally, what anyone (sometimes referred to as **other**) can do. The abilities the owner, group member, or others can have include the ability to read the file, write it, or execute it.

In the example above, the first three characters of the output of `ls` show that the file is both readable and writable by the owner (`rw-`), and only readable by members of the group `wheel` and also by anyone else in the system (`r--` followed by `r--`).

The owner of the file can readily change these permissions, for example by using the `chmod` command (to change the **file mode**). To remove the ability for anyone except the owner to access the file, you could type:

```
prompt> chmod 600 foo.txt
```

> **ASIDE: SUPERUSER FOR FILE SYSTEMS**
> Which user is allowed to do privileged operations to help administer the file system? For example, if an inactive user's files need to be deleted to save space, who has the rights to do so?
>
> On local file systems, the common default is for there to be some kind of **superuser** (i.e., **root**) who can access all files regardless of privileges. In a distributed file system such as AFS (which has access control lists), a group called `system:administrators` contains users that are trusted to do so. In both cases, these trusted users represent an inherent security risk; if an attacker is able to somehow impersonate such a user, the attacker can access all the information in the system, thus violating expected privacy and protection guarantees.

This command enables the readable bit (4) and writable bit (2) for the owner (OR'ing them together yields the 6 above), but set the group and other permission bits to 0 and 0, respectively, thus setting the permissions to `rw-------`.

The execute bit is particularly interesting. For regular files, its presence determines whether a program can be run or not. For example, if we have a simple shell script called `hello.csh`, we may wish to run it by typing:

```
prompt> ./hello.csh
hello, from shell world.
```

However, if we don't set the execute bit properly for this file, the following happens:

```
prompt> chmod 600 hello.csh
prompt> ./hello.csh
./hello.csh: Permission denied.
```

For directories, the execute bit behaves a bit differently. Specifically, it enables a user (or group, or everyone) to do things like change directories (i.e., `cd`) into the given directory, and, in combination with the writable bit, create files therein. The best way to learn more about this: play around with it yourself! Don't worry, you (probably) won't mess anything up too badly.

Beyond permissions bits, some file systems, such as the distributed file system known as AFS (discussed in a later chapter), include more sophisticated controls. AFS, for example, does this in the form of an **access control list** (**ACL**) per directory. Access control lists are a more general and powerful way to represent exactly who can access a given resource. In a file system, this enables a user to create a very specific list of who can and cannot read a set of files, in contrast to the somewhat limited owner/group/everyone model of permissions bits described above.

For example, here are the access controls for a private directory in one author's AFS account, as shown by the `fs listacl` command:

```
prompt> fs listacl private
Access list for private is
Normal rights:
  system:administrators rlidwka
  remzi rlidwka
```

The listing shows that both the system administrators and the user `remzi` can lookup, insert, delete, and administer files in this directory, as well as read, write, and lock those files.

To allow someone (in this case, the other author) to access to this directory, user `remzi` can just type the following command.

```
prompt> fs setacl private/ andrea rl
```

There goes `remzi`'s privacy! But now you have learned an even more important lesson: there can be no secrets in a good marriage, even within the file system[3].

39.17 Making And Mounting A File System

We've now toured the basic interfaces to access files, directories, and certain types of special types of links. But there is one more topic we should discuss: how to assemble a full directory tree from many underlying file systems. This task is accomplished via first making file systems, and then mounting them to make their contents accessible.

To make a file system, most file systems provide a tool, usually referred to as `mkfs` (pronounced "make fs"), that performs exactly this task. The idea is as follows: give the tool, as input, a device (such as a disk partition, e.g., `/dev/sda1`) and a file system type (e.g., ext3), and it simply writes an empty file system, starting with a root directory, onto that disk partition. And mkfs said, let there be a file system!

However, once such a file system is created, it needs to be made accessible within the uniform file-system tree. This task is achieved via the `mount` program (which makes the underlying system call `mount()` to do the real work). What mount does, quite simply is take an existing directory as a target **mount point** and essentially paste a new file system onto the directory tree at that point.

An example here might be useful. Imagine we have an unmounted ext3 file system, stored in device partition `/dev/sda1`, that has the following contents: a root directory which contains two sub-directories, `a` and `b`, each of which in turn holds a single file named `foo`. Let's say we wish to mount this file system at the mount point `/home/users`. We would type something like this:

[3]Married happily since 1996, if you were wondering. We know, you weren't.

> **TIP: BE WARY OF TOCTTOU**
>
> In 1974, McPhee noticed a problem in computer systems. Specifically, McPhee noted that "... if there exists a time interval between a validity-check and the operation connected with that validity-check, [and,] through multitasking, the validity-check variables can deliberately be changed during this time interval, resulting in an invalid operation being performed by the control program." We today call this the **Time Of Check To Time Of Use (TOCTTOU)** problem, and alas, it still can occur.
>
> A simple example, as described by Bishop and Dilger [BD96], shows how a user can trick a more trusted service and thus cause trouble. Imagine, for example, that a mail service runs as root (and thus has privilege to access all files on a system). This service appends an incoming message to a user's inbox file as follows. First, it calls `lstat()` to get information about the file, specifically ensuring that it is actually just a regular file owned by the target user, and not a link to another file that the mail server should not be updating. Then, after the check succeeds, the server updates the file with the new message.
>
> Unfortunately, the gap between the check and the update leads to a problem: the attacker (in this case, the user who is receiving the mail, and thus has permissions to access the inbox) switches the inbox file (via a call to `rename()`) to point to a sensitive file such as `/etc/passwd` (which holds information about users and their passwords). If this switch happens at just the right time (between the check and the access), the server will blithely update the sensitive file with the contents of the mail. The attacker can now write to the sensitive file by sending an email, an escalation in privilege; by updating `/etc/passwd`, the attacker can add an account with `root` privileges and thus gain control of the system.
>
> There are not any simple and great solutions to the TOCTTOU problem [T+08]. One approach is to reduce the number of services that need root privileges to run, which helps. The `O_NOFOLLOW` flag makes it so that `open()` will fail if the target is a symbolic link, thus avoiding attacks that require said links. More radicial approaches, such as using a **transactional file system** [H+18], would solve the problem, there aren't many transactional file systems in wide deployment. Thus, the usual (lame) advice: careful when you write code that runs with high privileges!

```
prompt> mount -t ext3 /dev/sda1 /home/users
```

If successful, the mount would thus make this new file system available. However, note how the new file system is now accessed. To look at the contents of the root directory, we would use `ls` like this:

```
prompt> ls /home/users/
a b
```

As you can see, the pathname /home/users/ now refers to the root of the newly-mounted directory. Similarly, we could access directories a and b with the pathnames /home/users/a and /home/users/b. Finally, the files named foo could be accessed via /home/users/a/foo and /home/users/b/foo. And thus the beauty of mount: instead of having a number of separate file systems, mount unifies all file systems into one tree, making naming uniform and convenient.

To see what is mounted on your system, and at which points, simply run the mount program. You'll see something like this:

```
/dev/sda1 on / type ext3 (rw)
proc on /proc type proc (rw)
sysfs on /sys type sysfs (rw)
/dev/sda5 on /tmp type ext3 (rw)
/dev/sda7 on /var/vice/cache type ext3 (rw)
tmpfs on /dev/shm type tmpfs (rw)
AFS on /afs type afs (rw)
```

This crazy mix shows that a whole number of different file systems, including ext3 (a standard disk-based file system), the proc file system (a file system for accessing information about current processes), tmpfs (a file system just for temporary files), and AFS (a distributed file system) are all glued together onto this one machine's file-system tree.

39.18 Summary

The file system interface in UNIX systems (and indeed, in any system) is seemingly quite rudimentary, but there is a lot to understand if you wish to master it. Nothing is better, of course, than simply using it (a lot). So please do so! Of course, read more; as always, Stevens [SR05] is the place to begin.

ASIDE: KEY FILE SYSTEM TERMS

- A **file** is an array of bytes which can be created, read, written, and deleted. It has a low-level name (i.e., a number) that refers to it uniquely. The low-level name is often called an **i-number**.
- A **directory** is a collection of tuples, each of which contains a human-readable name and low-level name to which it maps. Each entry refers either to another directory or to a file. Each directory also has a low-level name (i-number) itself. A directory always has two special entries: the `.` entry, which refers to itself, and the `..` entry, which refers to its parent.
- A **directory tree** or **directory hierarchy** organizes all files and directories into a large tree, starting at the **root**.
- To access a file, a process must use a system call (usually, `open()`) to request permission from the operating system. If permission is granted, the OS returns a **file descriptor**, which can then be used for read or write access, as permissions and intent allow.
- Each file descriptor is a private, per-process entity, which refers to an entry in the **open file table**. The entry therein tracks which file this access refers to, the **current offset** of the file (i.e., which part of the file the next read or write will access), and other relevant information.
- Calls to `read()` and `write()` naturally update the current offset; otherwise, processes can use `lseek()` to change its value, enabling random access to different parts of the file.
- To force updates to persistent media, a process must use `fsync()` or related calls. However, doing so correctly while maintaining high performance is challenging [P+14], so think carefully when doing so.
- To have multiple human-readable names in the file system refer to the same underlying file, use **hard links** or **symbolic links**. Each is useful in different circumstances, so consider their strengths and weaknesses before usage. And remember, deleting a file is just performing that one last `unlink()` of it from the directory hierarchy.
- Most file systems have mechanisms to enable and disable sharing. A rudimentary form of such controls are provided by **permissions bits**; more sophisticated **access control lists** allow for more precise control over exactly who can access and manipulate information.

References

[BD96] "Checking for Race Conditions in File Accesses" by Matt Bishop, Michael Dilger. Computing Systems 9:2, 1996. *A great description of the TOCTTOU problem and its presence in file systems.*

[CK+08] "The xv6 Operating System" by Russ Cox, Frans Kaashoek, Robert Morris, Nickolai Zeldovich. From: https://github.com/mit-pdos/xv6-public. *As mentioned before, a cool and simple Unix implementation. We have been using an older version (2012-01-30-1-g1c41342) and hence some examples in the book may not match the latest in the source.*

[H+18] "TxFS: Leveraging File-System Crash Consistency to Provide ACID Transactions" by Y. Hu, Z. Zhu, I. Neal, Y. Kwon, T. Cheng, V. Chidambaram, E. Witchel. USENIX ATC '18, June 2018. *The best paper at USENIX ATC '18, and a good recent place to start to learn about transactional file systems.*

[K84] "Processes as Files" by Tom J. Killian. USENIX, June 1984. *The paper that introduced the /proc file system, where each process can be treated as a file within a pseudo file system. A clever idea that you can still see in modern* UNIX *systems.*

[L84] "Capability-Based Computer Systems" by Henry M. Levy. Digital Press, 1984. Available: http://homes.cs.washington.edu/~levy/capabook. *An excellent overview of early capability-based systems.*

[MJLF84] "A Fast File System for UNIX" by Marshall K. McKusick, William N. Joy, Sam J. Leffler, Robert S. Fabry. ACM TOCS, 2:3, August 1984. *We'll talk about the Fast File System (FFS) explicitly later on. Here, we refer to it because of all the other random fun things it introduced, like long file names and symbolic links. Sometimes, when you are building a system to improve one thing, you improve a lot of other things along the way.*

[P+13] "Towards Efficient, Portable Application-Level Consistency" by Thanumalayan S. Pillai, Vijay Chidambaram, Joo-Young Hwang, Andrea C. Arpaci-Dusseau, and Remzi H. Arpaci-Dusseau. HotDep '13, November 2013. *Our own work that shows how readily applications can make mistakes in committing data to disk; in particular, assumptions about the file system creep into applications and thus make the applications work correctly only if they are running on a specific file system.*

[P+14] "All File Systems Are Not Created Equal: On the Complexity of Crafting Crash-Consistent Applications" by Thanumalayan S. Pillai, Vijay Chidambaram, Ramnatthan Alagappan, Samer Al-Kiswany, Andrea C. Arpaci-Dusseau, and Remzi H. Arpaci-Dusseau. OSDI '14, Broomfield, Colorado, October 2014. *The full conference paper on this topic – with many more details and interesting tidbits than the first workshop paper above.*

[SK09] "Principles of Computer System Design" by Jerome H. Saltzer and M. Frans Kaashoek. Morgan-Kaufmann, 2009. *This tour de force of systems is a must-read for anybody interested in the field. It's how they teach systems at MIT. Read it once, and then read it a few more times to let it all soak in.*

[SR05] "Advanced Programming in the UNIX Environment" by W. Richard Stevens and Stephen A. Rago. Addison-Wesley, 2005. *We have probably referenced this book a few hundred thousand times. It is that useful to you, if you care to become an awesome systems programmer.*

[T+08] "Portably Solving File TOCTTOU Races with Hardness Amplification" by D. Tsafrir, T. Hertz, D. Wagner, D. Da Silva. FAST '08, San Jose, California, 2008. *Not the paper that introduced TOCTTOU, but a recent-ish and well-done description of the problem and a way to solve the problem in a portable manner.*

Homework (Code)

In this homework, we'll just familiarize ourselves with how the APIs described in the chapter work. To do so, you'll just write a few different programs, mostly based on various UNIX utilities.

Questions

1. **Stat:** Write your own version of the command line program `stat`, which simply calls the `stat()` system call on a given file or directory. Print out file size, number of blocks allocated, reference (link) count, and so forth. What is the link count of a directory, as the number of entries in the directory changes? Useful interfaces: `stat()`, naturally.

2. **List Files:** Write a program that lists files in the given directory. When called without any arguments, the program should just print the file names. When invoked with the `-l` flag, the program should print out information about each file, such as the owner, group, permissions, and other information obtained from the `stat()` system call. The program should take one additional argument, which is the directory to read, e.g., `myls -l directory`. If no directory is given, the program should just use the current working directory. Useful interfaces: `stat()`, `opendir()`, `readdir()`, `getcwd()`.

3. **Tail:** Write a program that prints out the last few lines of a file. The program should be efficient, in that it seeks to near the end of the file, reads in a block of data, and then goes backwards until it finds the requested number of lines; at this point, it should print out those lines from beginning to the end of the file. To invoke the program, one should type: `mytail -n file`, where `n` is the number of lines at the end of the file to print. Useful interfaces: `stat()`, `lseek()`, `open()`, `read()`, `close()`.

4. **Recursive Search:** Write a program that prints out the names of each file and directory in the file system tree, starting at a given point in the tree. For example, when run without arguments, the program should start with the current working directory and print its contents, as well as the contents of any sub-directories, etc., until the entire tree, root at the CWD, is printed. If given a single argument (of a directory name), use that as the root of the tree instead. Refine your recursive search with more fun options, similar to the powerful `find` command line tool. Useful interfaces: figure it out.

40

File System Implementation

In this chapter, we introduce a simple file system implementation, known as **vsfs** (the **Very Simple File System**). This file system is a simplified version of a typical UNIX file system and thus serves to introduce some of the basic on-disk structures, access methods, and various policies that you will find in many file systems today.

The file system is pure software; unlike our development of CPU and memory virtualization, we will not be adding hardware features to make some aspect of the file system work better (though we will want to pay attention to device characteristics to make sure the file system works well). Because of the great flexibility we have in building a file system, many different ones have been built, literally from AFS (the Andrew File System) [H+88] to ZFS (Sun's Zettabyte File System) [B07]. All of these file systems have different data structures and do some things better or worse than their peers. Thus, the way we will be learning about file systems is through case studies: first, a simple file system (vsfs) in this chapter to introduce most concepts, and then a series of studies of real file systems to understand how they can differ in practice.

THE CRUX: HOW TO IMPLEMENT A SIMPLE FILE SYSTEM

How can we build a simple file system? What structures are needed on the disk? What do they need to track? How are they accessed?

40.1 The Way To Think

To think about file systems, we usually suggest thinking about two different aspects of them; if you understand both of these aspects, you probably understand how the file system basically works.

The first is the **data structures** of the file system. In other words, what types of on-disk structures are utilized by the file system to organize its data and metadata? The first file systems we'll see (including vsfs below) employ simple structures, like arrays of blocks or other objects, whereas

> **ASIDE: MENTAL MODELS OF FILE SYSTEMS**
> As we've discussed before, mental models are what you are really trying to develop when learning about systems. For file systems, your mental model should eventually include answers to questions like: what on-disk structures store the file system's data and metadata? What happens when a process opens a file? Which on-disk structures are accessed during a read or write? By working on and improving your mental model, you develop an abstract understanding of what is going on, instead of just trying to understand the specifics of some file-system code (though that is also useful, of course!).

more sophisticated file systems, like SGI's XFS, use more complicated tree-based structures [S+96].

The second aspect of a file system is its **access methods**. How does it map the calls made by a process, such as `open()`, `read()`, `write()`, etc., onto its structures? Which structures are read during the execution of a particular system call? Which are written? How efficiently are all of these steps performed?

If you understand the data structures and access methods of a file system, you have developed a good mental model of how it truly works, a key part of the systems mindset. Try to work on developing your mental model as we delve into our first implementation.

40.2 Overall Organization

We now develop the overall on-disk organization of the data structures of the vsfs file system. The first thing we'll need to do is divide the disk into **blocks**; simple file systems use just one block size, and that's exactly what we'll do here. Let's choose a commonly-used size of 4 KB.

Thus, our view of the disk partition where we're building our file system is simple: a series of blocks, each of size 4 KB. The blocks are addressed from 0 to $N-1$, in a partition of size N 4-KB blocks. Assume we have a really small disk, with just 64 blocks:

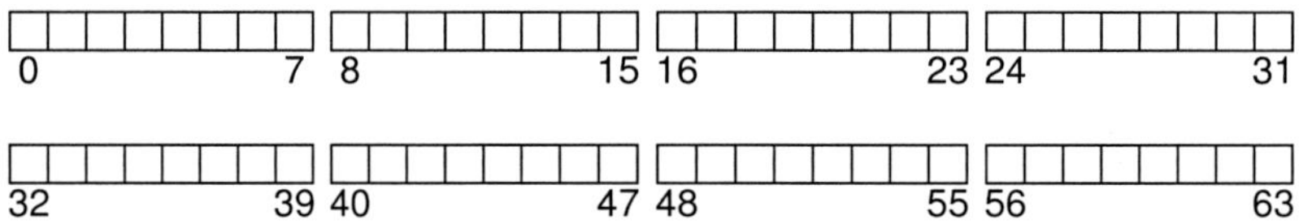

Let's now think about what we need to store in these blocks to build a file system. Of course, the first thing that comes to mind is user data. In fact, most of the space in any file system is (and should be) user data. Let's call the region of the disk we use for user data the **data region**, and, again for simplicity, reserve a fixed portion of the disk for these blocks, say the last 56 of 64 blocks on the disk:

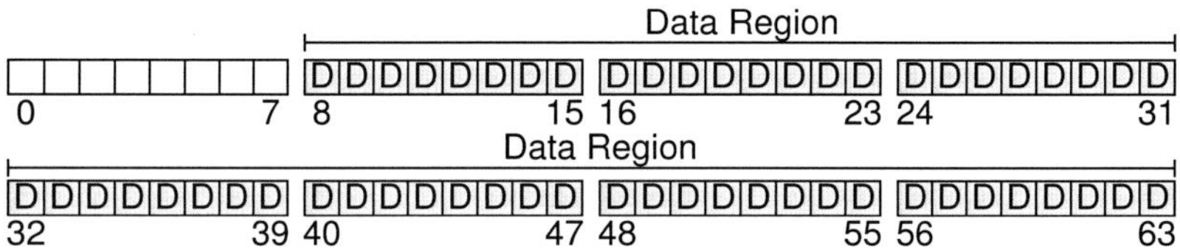

As we learned about (a little) last chapter, the file system has to track information about each file. This information is a key piece of **metadata**, and tracks things like which data blocks (in the data region) comprise a file, the size of the file, its owner and access rights, access and modify times, and other similar kinds of information. To store this information, file systems usually have a structure called an **inode** (we'll read more about inodes below).

To accommodate inodes, we'll need to reserve some space on the disk for them as well. Let's call this portion of the disk the **inode table**, which simply holds an array of on-disk inodes. Thus, our on-disk image now looks like this picture, assuming that we use 5 of our 64 blocks for inodes (denoted by I's in the diagram):

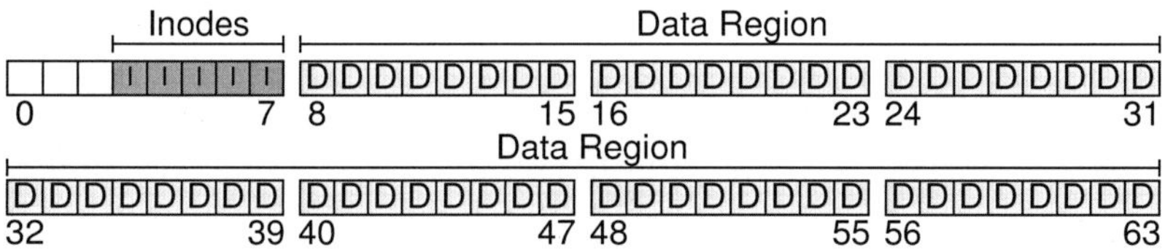

We should note here that inodes are typically not that big, for example 128 or 256 bytes. Assuming 256 bytes per inode, a 4-KB block can hold 16 inodes, and our file system above contains 80 total inodes. In our simple file system, built on a tiny 64-block partition, this number represents the maximum number of files we can have in our file system; however, do note that the same file system, built on a larger disk, could simply allocate a larger inode table and thus accommodate more files.

Our file system thus far has data blocks (D), and inodes (I), but a few things are still missing. One primary component that is still needed, as you might have guessed, is some way to track whether inodes or data blocks are free or allocated. Such **allocation structures** are thus a requisite element in any file system.

Many allocation-tracking methods are possible, of course. For example, we could use a **free list** that points to the first free block, which then points to the next free block, and so forth. We instead choose a simple and popular structure known as a **bitmap**, one for the data region (the **data bitmap**), and one for the inode table (the **inode bitmap**). A bitmap is a simple structure: each bit is used to indicate whether the corresponding object/block is free (0) or in-use (1). And thus our new on-disk layout, with an inode bitmap (i) and a data bitmap (d):

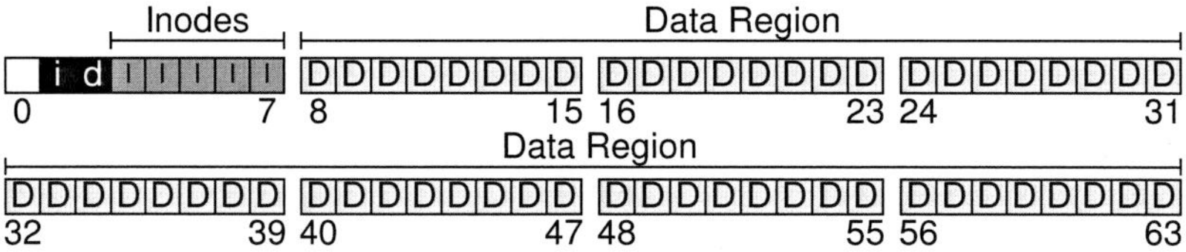

You may notice that it is a bit of overkill to use an entire 4-KB block for these bitmaps; such a bitmap can track whether 32K objects are allocated, and yet we only have 80 inodes and 56 data blocks. However, we just use an entire 4-KB block for each of these bitmaps for simplicity.

The careful reader (i.e., the reader who is still awake) may have noticed there is one block left in the design of the on-disk structure of our very simple file system. We reserve this for the **superblock**, denoted by an S in the diagram below. The superblock contains information about this particular file system, including, for example, how many inodes and data blocks are in the file system (80 and 56, respectively in this instance), where the inode table begins (block 3), and so forth. It will likely also include a magic number of some kind to identify the file system type (in this case, vsfs).

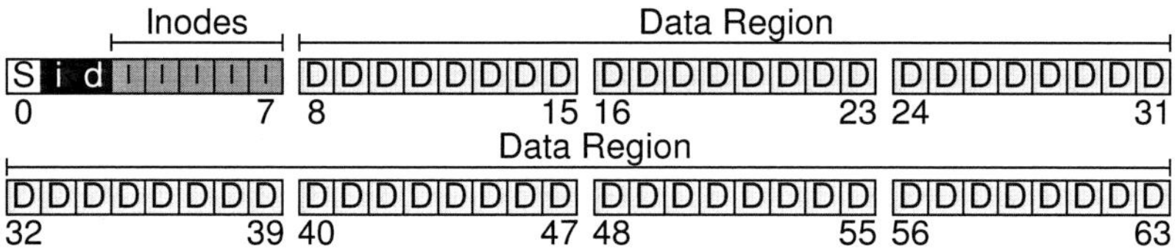

Thus, when mounting a file system, the operating system will read the superblock first, to initialize various parameters, and then attach the volume to the file-system tree. When files within the volume are accessed, the system will thus know exactly where to look for the needed on-disk structures.

40.3 File Organization: The Inode

One of the most important on-disk structures of a file system is the **inode**; virtually all file systems have a structure similar to this. The name inode is short for **index node**, the historical name given to it in UNIX [RT74] and possibly earlier systems, used because these nodes were originally arranged in an array, and the array *indexed* into when accessing a particular inode.

> **ASIDE: DATA STRUCTURE — THE INODE**
>
> The **inode** is the generic name that is used in many file systems to describe the structure that holds the metadata for a given file, such as its length, permissions, and the location of its constituent blocks. The name goes back at least as far as UNIX (and probably further back to Multics if not earlier systems); it is short for **index node**, as the inode number is used to index into an array of on-disk inodes in order to find the inode of that number. As we'll see, design of the inode is one key part of file system design. Most modern systems have some kind of structure like this for every file they track, but perhaps call them different things (such as dnodes, fnodes, etc.).

Each inode is implicitly referred to by a number (called the **i-number**), which we've earlier called the **low-level name** of the file. In vsfs (and other simple file systems), given an i-number, you should directly be able to calculate where on the disk the corresponding inode is located. For example, take the inode table of vsfs as above: 20-KB in size (5 4-KB blocks) and thus consisting of 80 inodes (assuming each inode is 256 bytes); further assume that the inode region starts at 12KB (i.e, the superblock starts at 0KB, the inode bitmap is at address 4KB, the data bitmap at 8KB, and thus the inode table comes right after). In vsfs, we thus have the following layout for the beginning of the file system partition (in closeup view):

The Inode Table (Closeup)

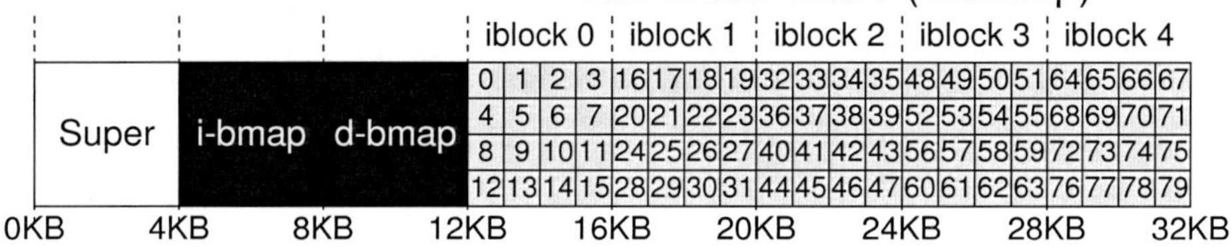

To read inode number 32, the file system would first calculate the offset into the inode region ($32 \cdot sizeof(inode)$ or 8192), add it to the start address of the inode table on disk (`inodeStartAddr` = $12KB$), and thus arrive upon the correct byte address of the desired block of inodes: $20KB$. Recall that disks are not byte addressable, but rather consist of a large number of addressable sectors, usually 512 bytes. Thus, to fetch the block of inodes that contains inode 32, the file system would issue a read to sector $\frac{20 \times 1024}{512}$, or 40, to fetch the desired inode block. More generally, the sector address `sector` of the inode block can be calculated as follows:

```
blk    = (inumber * sizeof(inode_t)) / blockSize;
sector = ((blk * blockSize) + inodeStartAddr) / sectorSize;
```

Inside each inode is virtually all of the information you need about a file: its *type* (e.g., regular file, directory, etc.), its *size*, the number of *blocks* allocated to it, *protection information* (such as who owns the file, as well

Size	Name	What is this inode field for?
2	mode	can this file be read/written/executed?
2	uid	who owns this file?
4	size	how many bytes are in this file?
4	time	what time was this file last accessed?
4	ctime	what time was this file created?
4	mtime	what time was this file last modified?
4	dtime	what time was this inode deleted?
2	gid	which group does this file belong to?
2	links_count	how many hard links are there to this file?
4	blocks	how many blocks have been allocated to this file?
4	flags	how should ext2 use this inode?
4	osd1	an OS-dependent field
60	block	a set of disk pointers (15 total)
4	generation	file version (used by NFS)
4	file_acl	a new permissions model beyond mode bits
4	dir_acl	called access control lists

Figure 401: **Simplified Ext2 Inode**

as who can access it), some *time* information, including when the file was created, modified, or last accessed, as well as information about where its data blocks reside on disk (e.g., pointers of some kind). We refer to all such information about a file as **metadata**; in fact, any information inside the file system that isn't pure user data is often referred to as such. An example inode from ext2 [P09] is shown in Figure 401[1].

One of the most important decisions in the design of the inode is how it refers to where data blocks are. One simple approach would be to have one or more **direct pointers** (disk addresses) inside the inode; each pointer refers to one disk block that belongs to the file. Such an approach is limited: for example, if you want to have a file that is really big (e.g., bigger than the block size multiplied by the number of direct pointers in the inode), you are out of luck.

The Multi-Level Index

To support bigger files, file system designers have had to introduce different structures within inodes. One common idea is to have a special pointer known as an **indirect pointer**. Instead of pointing to a block that contains user data, it points to a block that contains more pointers, each of which point to user data. Thus, an inode may have some fixed number of direct pointers (e.g., 12), and a single indirect pointer. If a file grows large enough, an indirect block is allocated (from the data-block region of the disk), and the inode's slot for an indirect pointer is set to point to it. Assuming 4-KB blocks and 4-byte disk addresses, that adds another 1024 pointers; the file can grow to be $(12 + 1024) \cdot 4K$ or 4144KB.

[1]Type info is kept in the directory entry, and thus is not found in the inode itself.

TIP: CONSIDER EXTENT-BASED APPROACHES

A different approach is to use **extents** instead of pointers. An extent is simply a disk pointer plus a length (in blocks); thus, instead of requiring a pointer for every block of a file, all one needs is a pointer and a length to specify the on-disk location of a file. Just a single extent is limiting, as one may have trouble finding a contiguous chunk of on-disk free space when allocating a file. Thus, extent-based file systems often allow for more than one extent, thus giving more freedom to the file system during file allocation.

In comparing the two approaches, pointer-based approaches are the most flexible but use a large amount of metadata per file (particularly for large files). Extent-based approaches are less flexible but more compact; in particular, they work well when there is enough free space on the disk and files can be laid out contiguously (which is the goal for virtually any file allocation policy anyhow).

Not surprisingly, in such an approach, you might want to support even larger files. To do so, just add another pointer to the inode: the **double indirect pointer**. This pointer refers to a block that contains pointers to indirect blocks, each of which contain pointers to data blocks. A double indirect block thus adds the possibility to grow files with an additional $1024 \cdot 1024$ or 1-million 4KB blocks, in other words supporting files that are over 4GB in size. You may want even more, though, and we bet you know where this is headed: the **triple indirect pointer**.

Overall, this imbalanced tree is referred to as the **multi-level index** approach to pointing to file blocks. Let's examine an example with twelve direct pointers, as well as both a single and a double indirect block. Assuming a block size of 4 KB, and 4-byte pointers, this structure can accommodate a file of just over 4 GB in size (i.e., $(12 + 1024 + 1024^2) \times 4\ KB$). Can you figure out how big of a file can be handled with the addition of a triple-indirect block? (hint: pretty big)

Many file systems use a multi-level index, including commonly-used file systems such as Linux ext2 [P09] and ext3, NetApp's WAFL, as well as the original UNIX file system. Other file systems, including SGI XFS and Linux ext4, use **extents** instead of simple pointers; see the earlier aside for details on how extent-based schemes work (they are akin to segments in the discussion of virtual memory).

You might be wondering: why use an imbalanced tree like this? Why not a different approach? Well, as it turns out, many researchers have studied file systems and how they are used, and virtually every time they find certain "truths" that hold across the decades. One such finding is that *most files are small*. This imbalanced design reflects such a reality; if most files are indeed small, it makes sense to optimize for this case. Thus, with a small number of direct pointers (12 is a typical number), an inode

Most files are small	˜2K is the most common size
Average file size is growing	Almost 200K is the average
Most bytes are stored in large files	A few big files use most of space
File systems contains lots of files	Almost 100K on average
File systems are roughly half full	Even as disks grow, file systems remain ˜50% full
Directories are typically small	Many have few entries; most have 20 or fewer

Figure 402: **File System Measurement Summary**

can directly point to 48 KB of data, needing one (or more) indirect blocks for larger files. See Agrawal et. al [A+07] for a recent-ish study; Figure 402 summarizes those results.

Of course, in the space of inode design, many other possibilities exist; after all, the inode is just a data structure, and any data structure that stores the relevant information, and can query it effectively, is sufficient. As file system software is readily changed, you should be willing to explore different designs should workloads or technologies change.

40.4 Directory Organization

In vsfs (as in many file systems), directories have a simple organization; a directory basically just contains a list of (entry name, inode number) pairs. For each file or directory in a given directory, there is a string and a number in the data block(s) of the directory. For each string, there may also be a length (assuming variable-sized names).

For example, assume a directory `dir` (inode number 5) has three files in it (`foo`, `bar`, and `foobar_is_a_pretty_longname`), with inode numbers 12, 13, and 24 respectively. The on-disk data for `dir` might look like:

```
inum | reclen | strlen | name
  5      12        2     .
  2      12        3     ..
 12      12        4     foo
 13      12        4     bar
 24      36       28     foobar_is_a_pretty_longname
```

In this example, each entry has an inode number, record length (the total bytes for the name plus any left over space), string length (the actual length of the name), and finally the name of the entry. Note that each directory has two extra entries, `.` "dot" and `..` "dot-dot"; the dot directory is just the current directory (in this example, `dir`), whereas dot-dot is the parent directory (in this case, the root).

Deleting a file (e.g., calling `unlink()`) can leave an empty space in the middle of the directory, and hence there should be some way to mark that as well (e.g., with a reserved inode number such as zero). Such a delete is one reason the record length is used: a new entry may reuse an old, bigger entry and thus have extra space within.

> ASIDE: LINKED-BASED APPROACHES
>
> Another simpler approach in designing inodes is to use a **linked list**. Thus, inside an inode, instead of having multiple pointers, you just need one, to point to the first block of the file. To handle larger files, add another pointer at the end of that data block, and so on, and thus you can support large files.
>
> As you might have guessed, linked file allocation performs poorly for some workloads; think about reading the last block of a file, for example, or just doing random access. Thus, to make linked allocation work better, some systems will keep an in-memory table of link information, instead of storing the next pointers with the data blocks themselves. The table is indexed by the address of a data block D; the content of an entry is simply D's next pointer, i.e., the address of the next block in a file which follows D. A null-value could be there too (indicating an end-of-file), or some other marker to indicate that a particular block is free. Having such a table of next pointers makes it so that a linked allocation scheme can effectively do random file accesses, simply by first scanning through the (in memory) table to find the desired block, and then accessing (on disk) it directly.
>
> Does such a table sound familiar? What we have described is the basic structure of what is known as the **file allocation table**, or **FAT** file system. Yes, this classic old Windows file system, before NTFS [C94], is based on a simple linked-based allocation scheme. There are other differences from a standard UNIX file system too; for example, there are no inodes per se, but rather directory entries which store metadata about a file and refer directly to the first block of said file, which makes creating hard links impossible. See Brouwer [B02] for more of the inelegant details.

You might be wondering where exactly directories are stored. Often, file systems treat directories as a special type of file. Thus, a directory has an inode, somewhere in the inode table (with the type field of the inode marked as "directory" instead of "regular file"). The directory has data blocks pointed to by the inode (and perhaps, indirect blocks); these data blocks live in the data block region of our simple file system. Our on-disk structure thus remains unchanged.

We should also note again that this simple linear list of directory entries is not the only way to store such information. As before, any data structure is possible. For example, XFS [S+96] stores directories in B-tree form, making file create operations (which have to ensure that a file name has not been used before creating it) faster than systems with simple lists that must be scanned in their entirety.

> ASIDE: FREE SPACE MANAGEMENT
>
> There are many ways to manage free space; bitmaps are just one way. Some early file systems used **free lists**, where a single pointer in the super block was kept to point to the first free block; inside that block the next free pointer was kept, thus forming a list through the free blocks of the system. When a block was needed, the head block was used and the list updated accordingly.
>
> Modern file systems use more sophisticated data structures. For example, SGI's XFS [S+96] uses some form of a **B-tree** to compactly represent which chunks of the disk are free. As with any data structure, different time-space trade-offs are possible.

40.5 Free Space Management

A file system must track which inodes and data blocks are free, and which are not, so that when a new file or directory is allocated, it can find space for it. Thus **free space management** is important for all file systems. In vsfs, we have two simple bitmaps for this task.

For example, when we create a file, we will have to allocate an inode for that file. The file system will thus search through the bitmap for an inode that is free, and allocate it to the file; the file system will have to mark the inode as used (with a 1) and eventually update the on-disk bitmap with the correct information. A similar set of activities take place when a data block is allocated.

Some other considerations might also come into play when allocating data blocks for a new file. For example, some Linux file systems, such as ext2 and ext3, will look for a sequence of blocks (say 8) that are free when a new file is created and needs data blocks; by finding such a sequence of free blocks, and then allocating them to the newly-created file, the file system guarantees that a portion of the file will be contiguous on the disk, thus improving performance. Such a **pre-allocation** policy is thus a commonly-used heuristic when allocating space for data blocks.

40.6 Access Paths: Reading and Writing

Now that we have some idea of how files and directories are stored on disk, we should be able to follow the flow of operation during the activity of reading or writing a file. Understanding what happens on this **access path** is thus the second key in developing an understanding of how a file system works; pay attention!

For the following examples, let us assume that the file system has been mounted and thus that the superblock is already in memory. Everything else (i.e., inodes, directories) is still on the disk.

	data bitmap	inode bitmap	root inode	foo inode	bar inode	root data	foo data	bar data [0]	bar data [1]	bar data [2]
			read							
						read				
open(bar)				**read**						
							read			
					read					
					read					
read()								**read**		
					write					
					read					
read()									**read**	
					write					
					read					
read()										**read**
					write					

Figure 403: **File Read Timeline (Time Increasing Downward)**

Reading A File From Disk

In this simple example, let us first assume that you want to simply open a file (e.g., `/foo/bar`), read it, and then close it. For this simple example, let's assume the file is just 12KB in size (i.e., 3 blocks).

When you issue an `open("/foo/bar", O_RDONLY)` call, the file system first needs to find the inode for the file `bar`, to obtain some basic information about the file (permissions information, file size, etc.). To do so, the file system must be able to find the inode, but all it has right now is the full pathname. The file system must **traverse** the pathname and thus locate the desired inode.

All traversals begin at the root of the file system, in the **root directory** which is simply called `/`. Thus, the first thing the FS will read from disk is the inode of the root directory. But where is this inode? To find an inode, we must know its i-number. Usually, we find the i-number of a file or directory in its parent directory; the root has no parent (by definition). Thus, the root inode number must be "well known"; the FS must know what it is when the file system is mounted. In most UNIX file systems, the root inode number is 2. Thus, to begin the process, the FS reads in the block that contains inode number 2 (the first inode block).

Once the inode is read in, the FS can look inside of it to find pointers to data blocks, which contain the contents of the root directory. The FS will thus use these on-disk pointers to read through the directory, in this case looking for an entry for `foo`. By reading in one or more directory data blocks, it will find the entry for foo; once found, the FS will also have found the inode number of `foo` (say it is 44) which it will need next.

The next step is to recursively traverse the pathname until the desired inode is found. In this example, the FS reads the block containing the

> ASIDE: READS DON'T ACCESS ALLOCATION STRUCTURES
> We've seen many students get confused by allocation structures such as bitmaps. In particular, many often think that when you are simply reading a file, and not allocating any new blocks, that the bitmap will still be consulted. This is not true! Allocation structures, such as bitmaps, are only accessed when allocation is needed. The inodes, directories, and indirect blocks have all the information they need to complete a read request; there is no need to make sure a block is allocated when the inode already points to it.

inode of `foo` and then its directory data, finally finding the inode number of `bar`. The final step of `open()` is to read `bar`'s inode into memory; the FS then does a final permissions check, allocates a file descriptor for this process in the per-process open-file table, and returns it to the user.

Once open, the program can then issue a `read()` system call to read from the file. The first read (at offset 0 unless `lseek()` has been called) will thus read in the first block of the file, consulting the inode to find the location of such a block; it may also update the inode with a new last-accessed time. The read will further update the in-memory open file table for this file descriptor, updating the file offset such that the next read will read the second file block, etc.

At some point, the file will be closed. There is much less work to be done here; clearly, the file descriptor should be deallocated, but for now, that is all the FS really needs to do. No disk I/Os take place.

A depiction of this entire process is found in Figure 403 (page 529); time increases downward in the figure. In the figure, the open causes numerous reads to take place in order to finally locate the inode of the file. Afterwards, reading each block requires the file system to first consult the inode, then read the block, and then update the inode's last-accessed-time field with a write. Spend some time and understand what is going on.

Also note that the amount of I/O generated by the open is proportional to the length of the pathname. For each additional directory in the path, we have to read its inode as well as its data. Making this worse would be the presence of large directories; here, we only have to read one block to get the contents of a directory, whereas with a large directory, we might have to read many data blocks to find the desired entry. Yes, life can get pretty bad when reading a file; as you're about to find out, writing out a file (and especially, creating a new one) is even worse.

Writing A File To Disk

Writing to a file is a similar process. First, the file must be opened (as above). Then, the application can issue `write()` calls to update the file with new contents. Finally, the file is closed.

Unlike reading, writing to the file may also **allocate** a block (unless the block is being overwritten, for example). When writing out a new file, each write not only has to write data to disk but has to first decide

	data bitmap	inode bitmap	root inode	foo inode	bar inode	root data	foo data	bar data [0]	bar data [1]	bar data [2]
			read							
						read				
				read						
							read			
create (/foo/bar)		**read**								
		write								
							write			
					read					
					write					
				write						
					read					
	read									
write()	**write**									
								write		
					write					
					read					
	read									
write()	**write**									
									write	
					write					
					read					
	read									
write()	**write**									
										write
					write					

Figure 404: **File Creation Timeline (Time Increasing Downward)**

which block to allocate to the file and thus update other structures of the disk accordingly (e.g., the data bitmap and inode). Thus, each write to a file logically generates five I/Os: one to read the data bitmap (which is then updated to mark the newly-allocated block as used), one to write the bitmap (to reflect its new state to disk), two more to read and then write the inode (which is updated with the new block's location), and finally one to write the actual block itself.

The amount of write traffic is even worse when one considers a simple and common operation such as file creation. To create a file, the file system must not only allocate an inode, but also allocate space within the directory containing the new file. The total amount of I/O traffic to do so is quite high: one read to the inode bitmap (to find a free inode), one write to the inode bitmap (to mark it allocated), one write to the new inode itself (to initialize it), one to the data of the directory (to link the high-level name of the file to its inode number), and one read and write to the directory inode to update it. If the directory needs to grow to accommodate the new entry, additional I/Os (i.e., to the data bitmap, and the new directory block) will be needed too. All that just to create a file!

Let's look at a specific example, where the file `/foo/bar` is created, and three blocks are written to it. Figure 404 (page 531) shows what happens during the `open()` (which creates the file) and during each of three 4KB writes.

In the figure, reads and writes to the disk are grouped under which system call caused them to occur, and the rough ordering they might take place in goes from top to bottom of the figure. You can see how much work it is to create the file: 10 I/Os in this case, to walk the pathname and then finally create the file. You can also see that each allocating write costs 5 I/Os: a pair to read and update the inode, another pair to read and update the data bitmap, and then finally the write of the data itself. How can a file system accomplish any of this with reasonable efficiency?

THE CRUX: HOW TO REDUCE FILE SYSTEM I/O COSTS

Even the simplest of operations like opening, reading, or writing a file incurs a huge number of I/O operations, scattered over the disk. What can a file system do to reduce the high costs of doing so many I/Os?

40.7 Caching and Buffering

As the examples above show, reading and writing files can be expensive, incurring many I/Os to the (slow) disk. To remedy what would clearly be a huge performance problem, most file systems aggressively use system memory (DRAM) to cache important blocks.

Imagine the open example above: without caching, every file open would require at least two reads for every level in the directory hierarchy (one to read the inode of the directory in question, and at least one to read its data). With a long pathname (e.g., /1/2/3/ ... /100/file.txt), the file system would literally perform hundreds of reads just to open the file!

Early file systems thus introduced a **fixed-size cache** to hold popular blocks. As in our discussion of virtual memory, strategies such as **LRU** and different variants would decide which blocks to keep in cache. This fixed-size cache would usually be allocated at boot time to be roughly 10% of total memory.

This **static partitioning** of memory, however, can be wasteful; what if the file system doesn't need 10% of memory at a given point in time? With the fixed-size approach described above, unused pages in the file cache cannot be re-purposed for some other use, and thus go to waste.

Modern systems, in contrast, employ a **dynamic partitioning** approach. Specifically, many modern operating systems integrate virtual memory pages and file system pages into a **unified page cache** [S00]. In this way, memory can be allocated more flexibly across virtual memory and file system, depending on which needs more memory at a given time.

Now imagine the file open example with caching. The first open may generate a lot of I/O traffic to read in directory inode and data, but sub-

TIP: UNDERSTAND STATIC VS. DYNAMIC PARTITIONING

When dividing a resource among different clients/users, you can use either **static partitioning** or **dynamic partitioning**. The static approach simply divides the resource into fixed proportions once; for example, if there are two possible users of memory, you can give some fixed fraction of memory to one user, and the rest to the other. The dynamic approach is more flexible, giving out differing amounts of the resource over time; for example, one user may get a higher percentage of disk bandwidth for a period of time, but then later, the system may switch and decide to give a different user a larger fraction of available disk bandwidth.

Each approach has its advantages. Static partitioning ensures each user receives some share of the resource, usually delivers more predictable performance, and is often easier to implement. Dynamic partitioning can achieve better utilization (by letting resource-hungry users consume otherwise idle resources), but can be more complex to implement, and can lead to worse performance for users whose idle resources get consumed by others and then take a long time to reclaim when needed. As is often the case, there is no best method; rather, you should think about the problem at hand and decide which approach is most suitable. Indeed, shouldn't you always be doing that?

sequent file opens of that same file (or files in the same directory) will mostly hit in the cache and thus no I/O is needed.

Let us also consider the effect of caching on writes. Whereas read I/O can be avoided altogether with a sufficiently large cache, write traffic has to go to disk in order to become persistent. Thus, a cache does not serve as the same kind of filter on write traffic that it does for reads. That said, **write buffering** (as it is sometimes called) certainly has a number of performance benefits. First, by delaying writes, the file system can **batch** some updates into a smaller set of I/Os; for example, if an inode bitmap is updated when one file is created and then updated moments later as another file is created, the file system saves an I/O by delaying the write after the first update. Second, by buffering a number of writes in memory, the system can then **schedule** the subsequent I/Os and thus increase performance. Finally, some writes are avoided altogether by delaying them; for example, if an application creates a file and then deletes it, delaying the writes to reflect the file creation to disk **avoids** them entirely. In this case, laziness (in writing blocks to disk) is a virtue.

For the reasons above, most modern file systems buffer writes in memory for anywhere between five and thirty seconds, representing yet another trade-off: if the system crashes before the updates have been propagated to disk, the updates are lost; however, by keeping writes in memory longer, performance can be improved by batching, scheduling, and even avoiding writes.

> **TIP: UNDERSTAND THE DURABILITY/PERFORMANCE TRADE-OFF**
> Storage systems often present a durability/performance trade-off to users. If the user wishes data that is written to be immediately durable, the system must go through the full effort of committing the newly-written data to disk, and thus the write is slow (but safe). However, if the user can tolerate the loss of a little data, the system can buffer writes in memory for some time and write them later to the disk (in the background). Doing so makes writes appear to complete quickly, thus improving perceived performance; however, if a crash occurs, writes not yet committed to disk will be lost, and hence the trade-off. To understand how to make this trade-off properly, it is best to understand what the application using the storage system requires; for example, while it may be tolerable to lose the last few images downloaded by your web browser, losing part of a database transaction that is adding money to your bank account may be less tolerable. Unless you're rich, of course; in that case, why do you care so much about hoarding every last penny?

Some applications (such as databases) don't enjoy this trade-off. Thus, to avoid unexpected data loss due to write buffering, they simply force writes to disk, by calling `fsync()`, by using **direct I/O** interfaces that work around the cache, or by using the **raw disk** interface and avoiding the file system altogether[2]. While most applications live with the trade-offs made by the file system, there are enough controls in place to get the system to do what you want it to, should the default not be satisfying.

40.8 Summary

We have seen the basic machinery required in building a file system. There needs to be some information about each file (metadata), usually stored in a structure called an inode. Directories are just a specific type of file that store name→inode-number mappings. And other structures are needed too; for example, file systems often use a structure such as a bitmap to track which inodes or data blocks are free or allocated.

The terrific aspect of file system design is its freedom; the file systems we explore in the coming chapters each take advantage of this freedom to optimize some aspect of the file system. There are also clearly many policy decisions we have left unexplored. For example, when a new file is created, where should it be placed on disk? This policy and others will also be the subject of future chapters. Or will they?[3]

[2] Take a database class to learn more about old-school databases and their former insistence on avoiding the OS and controlling everything themselves. But watch out! Those database types are always trying to bad mouth the OS. Shame on you, database people. Shame.

[3] Cue mysterious music that gets you even more intrigued about the topic of file systems.

References

[A+07] "A Five-Year Study of File-System Metadata" by Nitin Agrawal, William J. Bolosky, John R. Douceur, Jacob R. Lorch. FAST '07, San Jose, California, February 2007. *An excellent recent analysis of how file systems are actually used. Use the bibliography within to follow the trail of file-system analysis papers back to the early 1980s.*

[B07] "ZFS: The Last Word in File Systems" by Jeff Bonwick and Bill Moore. Available from: `http://www.ostep.org/Citations/zfs_last.pdf`. *One of the most recent important file systems, full of features and awesomeness. We should have a chapter on it, and perhaps soon will.*

[B02] "The FAT File System" by Andries Brouwer. September, 2002. Available online at: `http://www.win.tue.nl/~aeb/linux/fs/fat/fat.html`. *A nice clean description of FAT. The file system kind, not the bacon kind. Though you have to admit, bacon fat probably tastes better.*

[C94] "Inside the Windows NT File System" by Helen Custer. Microsoft Press, 1994. *A short book about NTFS; there are probably ones with more technical details elsewhere.*

[H+88] "Scale and Performance in a Distributed File System" by John H. Howard, Michael L. Kazar, Sherri G. Menees, David A. Nichols, M. Satyanarayanan, Robert N. Sidebotham, Michael J. West.. ACM TOCS, Volume 6:1, February 1988. *A classic distributed file system; we'll be learning more about it later, don't worry.*

[P09] "The Second Extended File System: Internal Layout" by Dave Poirier. 2009. Available: `http://www.nongnu.org/ext2-doc/ext2.html`. *Some details on ext2, a very simple Linux file system based on FFS, the Berkeley Fast File System. We'll be reading about it in the next chapter.*

[RT74] "The UNIX Time-Sharing System" by M. Ritchie, K. Thompson. CACM Volume 17:7, 1974. *The original paper about UNIX. Read it to see the underpinnings of much of modern operating systems.*

[S00] "UBC: An Efficient Unified I/O and Memory Caching Subsystem for NetBSD" by Chuck Silvers. FREENIX, 2000. *A nice paper about NetBSD's integration of file-system buffer caching and the virtual-memory page cache. Many other systems do the same type of thing.*

[S+96] "Scalability in the XFS File System" by Adan Sweeney, Doug Doucette, Wei Hu, Curtis Anderson, Mike Nishimoto, Geoff Peck. USENIX '96, January 1996, San Diego, California. *The first attempt to make scalability of operations, including things like having millions of files in a directory, a central focus. A great example of pushing an idea to the extreme. The key idea behind this file system: everything is a tree. We should have a chapter on this file system too.*

Homework (Simulation)

Use this tool, `vsfs.py`, to study how file system state changes as various operations take place. The file system begins in an empty state, with just a root directory. As the simulation takes place, various operations are performed, thus slowly changing the on-disk state of the file system. See the README for details.

Questions

1. Run the simulator with some different random seeds (say 17, 18, 19, 20), and see if you can figure out which operations must have taken place between each state change.

2. Now do the same, using different random seeds (say 21, 22, 23, 24), except run with the `-r` flag, thus making you guess the state change while being shown the operation. What can you conclude about the inode and data-block allocation algorithms, in terms of which blocks they prefer to allocate?

3. Now reduce the number of data blocks in the file system, to very low numbers (say two), and run the simulator for a hundred or so requests. What types of files end up in the file system in this highly-constrained layout? What types of operations would fail?

4. Now do the same, but with inodes. With very few inodes, what types of operations can succeed? Which will usually fail? What is the final state of the file system likely to be?

41

Locality and The Fast File System

When the UNIX operating system was first introduced, the UNIX wizard himself Ken Thompson wrote the first file system. Let's call that the "old UNIX file system", and it was really simple. Basically, its data structures looked like this on the disk:

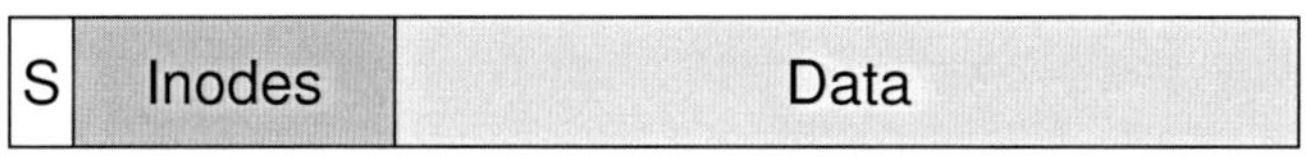

The super block (S) contained information about the entire file system: how big the volume is, how many inodes there are, a pointer to the head of a free list of blocks, and so forth. The inode region of the disk contained all the inodes for the file system. Finally, most of the disk was taken up by data blocks.

The good thing about the old file system was that it was simple, and supported the basic abstractions the file system was trying to deliver: files and the directory hierarchy. This easy-to-use system was a real step forward from the clumsy, record-based storage systems of the past, and the directory hierarchy was a true advance over simpler, one-level hierarchies provided by earlier systems.

41.1 The Problem: Poor Performance

The problem: performance was terrible. As measured by Kirk McKusick and his colleagues at Berkeley [MJLF84], performance started off bad and got worse over time, to the point where the file system was delivering only 2% of overall disk bandwidth!

The main issue was that the old UNIX file system treated the disk like it was a random-access memory; data was spread all over the place without regard to the fact that the medium holding the data was a disk, and thus had real and expensive positioning costs. For example, the data blocks of a file were often very far away from its inode, thus inducing an expensive seek whenever one first read the inode and then the data blocks of a file (a pretty common operation).

Worse, the file system would end up getting quite **fragmented**, as the free space was not carefully managed. The free list would end up pointing to a bunch of blocks spread across the disk, and as files got allocated, they would simply take the next free block. The result was that a logically contiguous file would be accessed by going back and forth across the disk, thus reducing performance dramatically.

For example, imagine the following data block region, which contains four files (A, B, C, and D), each of size 2 blocks:

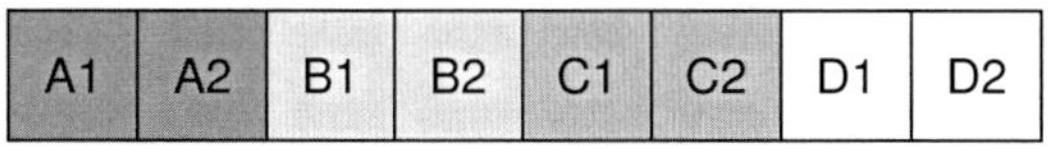

If B and D are deleted, the resulting layout is:

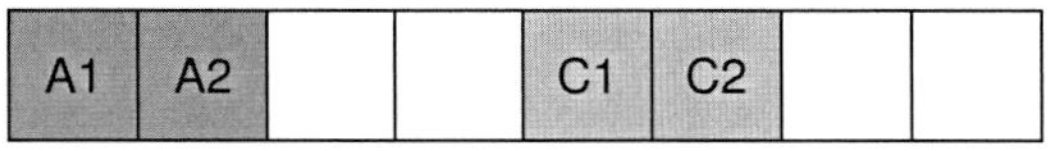

As you can see, the free space is fragmented into two chunks of two blocks, instead of one nice contiguous chunk of four. Let's say you now wish to allocate a file E, of size four blocks:

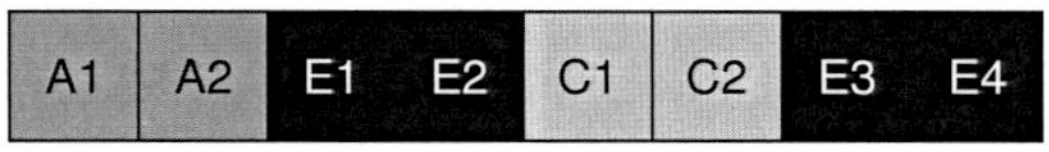

You can see what happens: E gets spread across the disk, and as a result, when accessing E, you don't get peak (sequential) performance from the disk. Rather, you first read E1 and E2, then seek, then read E3 and E4. This fragmentation problem happened all the time in the old UNIX file system, and it hurt performance. A side note: this problem is exactly what disk **defragmentation** tools help with; they reorganize on-disk data to place files contiguously and make free space for one or a few contiguous regions, moving data around and then rewriting inodes and such to reflect the changes.

One other problem: the original block size was too small (512 bytes). Thus, transferring data from the disk was inherently inefficient. Smaller blocks were good because they minimized **internal fragmentation** (waste within the block), but bad for transfer as each block might require a positioning overhead to reach it. Thus, the problem:

THE CRUX:
HOW TO ORGANIZE ON-DISK DATA TO IMPROVE PERFORMANCE

How can we organize file system data structures so as to improve performance? What types of allocation policies do we need on top of those data structures? How do we make the file system "disk aware"?

41.2 FFS: Disk Awareness Is The Solution

A group at Berkeley decided to build a better, faster file system, which they cleverly called the **Fast File System (FFS)**. The idea was to design the file system structures and allocation policies to be "disk aware" and thus improve performance, which is exactly what they did. FFS thus ushered in a new era of file system research; by keeping the same *interface* to the file system (the same APIs, including `open()`, `read()`, `write()`, `close()`, and other file system calls) but changing the internal *implementation*, the authors paved the path for new file system construction, work that continues today. Virtually all modern file systems adhere to the existing interface (and thus preserve compatibility with applications) while changing their internals for performance, reliability, or other reasons.

41.3 Organizing Structure: The Cylinder Group

The first step was to change the on-disk structures. FFS divides the disk into a number of **cylinder groups**. A single **cylinder** is a set of tracks on different surfaces of a hard drive that are the same distance from the center of the drive; it is called a cylinder because of its clear resemblance to the so-called geometrical shape. FFS aggregates N consecutive cylinders into a group, and thus the entire disk can thus be viewed as a collection of cylinder groups. Here is a simple example, showing the four outer most tracks of a drive with six platters, and a cylinder group that consists of three cylinders:

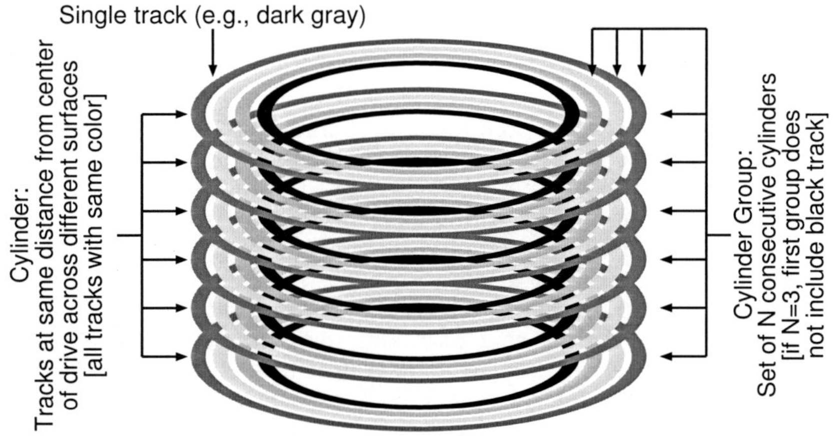

Note that modern drives do not export enough information for the file system to truly understand whether a particular cylinder is in use; as discussed previously [AD14a], disks export a logical address space of blocks and hide details of their geometry from clients. Thus, modern file systems (such as Linux ext2, ext3, and ext4) instead organize the drive into **block groups**, each of which is just a consecutive portion of the disk's address space. The picture below illustrates an example where every 8 blocks are organized into a different block group (note that real groups would consist of many more blocks):

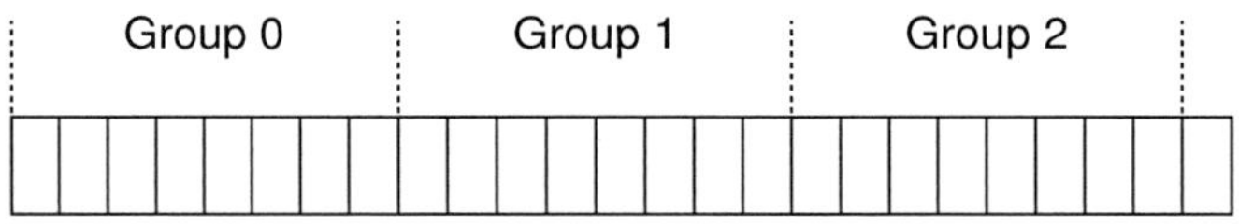

Whether you call them cylinder groups or block groups, these groups are the central mechanism that FFS uses to improve performance. Critically, by placing two files within the same group, FFS can ensure that accessing one after the other will not result in long seeks across the disk.

To use these groups to store files and directories, FFS needs to have the ability to place files and directories into a group, and track all necessary information about them therein. To do so, FFS includes all the structures you might expect a file system to have within each group, e.g., space for inodes, data blocks, and some structures to track whether each of those are allocated or free. Here is a depiction of what FFS keeps within a single cylinder group:

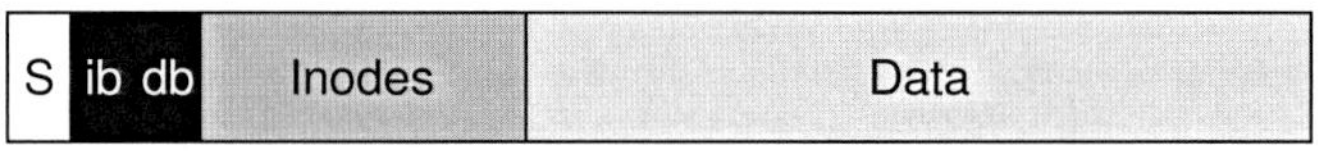

Let's now examine the components of this single cylinder group in more detail. FFS keeps a copy of the **super block** (S) in each group for reliability reasons. The super block is needed to mount the file system; by keeping multiple copies, if one copy becomes corrupt, you can still mount and access the file system by using a working replica.

Within each group, FFS needs to track whether the inodes and data blocks of the group are allocated. A per-group **inode bitmap** (ib) and **data bitmap** (db) serve this role for inodes and data blocks in each group. Bitmaps are an excellent way to manage free space in a file system because it is easy to find a large chunk of free space and allocate it to a file, perhaps avoiding some of the fragmentation problems of the free list in the old file system.

Finally, the **inode** and **data block** regions are just like those in the previous very-simple file system (VSFS). Most of each cylinder group, as usual, is comprised of data blocks.

> ASIDE: FFS FILE CREATION
>
> As an example, think about what data structures must be updated when a file is created; assume, for this example, that the user creates a new file `/foo/bar.txt` and that the file is one block long (4KB). The file is new, and thus needs a new inode; thus, both the inode bitmap and the newly-allocated inode will be written to disk. The file also has data in it and thus it too must be allocated; the data bitmap and a data block will thus (eventually) be written to disk. Hence, at least four writes to the current cylinder group will take place (recall that these writes may be buffered in memory for a while before they take place). But this is not all! In particular, when creating a new file, you must also place the file in the file-system hierarchy, i.e., the directory must be updated. Specifically, the parent directory `foo` must be updated to add the entry for `bar.txt`; this update may fit in an existing data block of `foo` or require a new block to be allocated (with associated data bitmap). The inode of `foo` must also be updated, both to reflect the new length of the directory as well as to update time fields (such as last-modified-time). Overall, it is a lot of work just to create a new file! Perhaps next time you do so, you should be more thankful, or at least surprised that it all works so well.

41.4 Policies: How To Allocate Files and Directories

With this group structure in place, FFS now has to decide how to place files and directories and associated metadata on disk to improve performance. The basic mantra is simple: *keep related stuff together* (and its corollary, *keep unrelated stuff far apart*).

Thus, to obey the mantra, FFS has to decide what is "related" and place it within the same block group; conversely, unrelated items should be placed into different block groups. To achieve this end, FFS makes use of a few simple placement heuristics.

The first is the placement of directories. FFS employs a simple approach: find the cylinder group with a low number of allocated directories (to balance directories across groups) and a high number of free inodes (to subsequently be able to allocate a bunch of files), and put the directory data and inode in that group. Of course, other heuristics could be used here (e.g., taking into account the number of free data blocks).

For files, FFS does two things. First, it makes sure (in the general case) to allocate the data blocks of a file in the same group as its inode, thus preventing long seeks between inode and data (as in the old file system). Second, it places all files that are in the same directory in the cylinder group of the directory they are in. Thus, if a user creates four files, `/a/b`, `/a/c`, `/a/d`, and `b/f`, FFS would try to place the first three near one another (same group) and the fourth far away (in some other group).

Let's look at an example of such an allocation. In the example, assume that there are only 10 inodes and 10 data blocks in each group (both unrealistically small numbers), and that the three directories (the root directory `/`, `/a`, and `/b`) and four files (`/a/c, /a/d, /a/e, /b/f`) are placed within them per the FFS policies. Assume the regular files are each two blocks in size, and that the directories have just a single block of data. For this figure, we use the obvious symbols for each file or directory (i.e., `/` for the root directory, `a` for `/a`, `f` for `/b/f`, and so forth).

```
group inodes     data
    0 /--------- /---------
    1 acde------ accddee---
    2 bf-------- bff-------
    3 ---------- ----------
    4 ---------- ----------
    5 ---------- ----------
    6 ---------- ----------
    7 ---------- ----------
```

Note that the FFS policy does two positive things: the data blocks of each file are near each file's inode, and files in the same directory are near one another (namely, `/a/c`, `/a/d`, and `/a/e` are all in Group 1, and directory `/b` and its file `/b/f` are near one another in Group 2).

In contrast, let's now look at an inode allocation policy that simply spreads inodes across groups, trying to ensure that no group's inode table fills up quickly. The final allocation might thus look something like this:

```
group inodes     data
    0 /--------- /---------
    1 a--------- a---------
    2 b--------- b---------
    3 c--------- cc--------
    4 d--------- dd--------
    5 e--------- ee--------
    6 f--------- ff--------
    7 ---------- ----------
```

As you can see from the figure, while this policy does indeed keep file (and directory) data near its respective inode, files within a directory are arbitrarily spread around the disk, and thus name-based locality is not preserved. Access to files `/a/c`, `/a/d`, and `/a/e` now spans three groups instead of one as per the FFS approach.

The FFS policy heuristics are not based on extensive studies of file-system traffic or anything particularly nuanced; rather, they are based on good old-fashioned **common sense** (isn't that what CS stands for after all?)[1]. Files in a directory *are* often accessed together: imagine compiling a bunch of files and then linking them into a single executable. Be-

[1]Some people refer to common sense as **horse sense**, especially people who work regularly with horses. However, we have a feeling that this idiom may be lost as the "mechanized horse", a.k.a. the car, gains in popularity. What will they invent next? A flying machine??!!

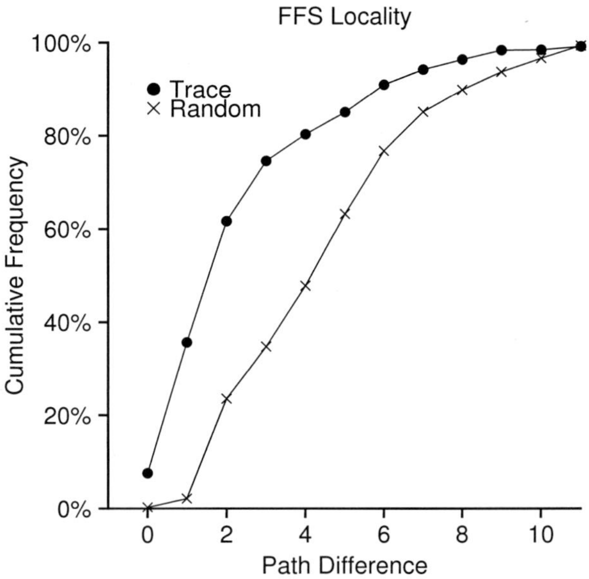

Figure 41.1: **FFS Locality For SEER Traces**

cause such namespace-based locality exists, FFS will often improve performance, making sure that seeks between related files are nice and short.

41.5 Measuring File Locality

To understand better whether these heuristics make sense, let's analyze some traces of file system access and see if indeed there is namespace locality. For some reason, there doesn't seem to be a good study of this topic in the literature.

Specifically, we'll use the SEER traces [K94] and analyze how "far away" file accesses were from one another in the directory tree. For example, if file `f` is opened, and then re-opened next in the trace (before any other files are opened), the distance between these two opens in the directory tree is zero (as they are the same file). If a file `f` in directory `dir` (i.e., `dir/f`) is opened, and followed by an open of file `g` in the same directory (i.e., `dir/g`), the distance between the two file accesses is one, as they share the same directory but are not the same file. Our distance metric, in other words, measures how far up the directory tree you have to travel to find the *common ancestor* of two files; the closer they are in the tree, the lower the metric.

Figure 41.1 shows the locality observed in the SEER traces over all workstations in the SEER cluster over the entirety of all traces. The graph plots the difference metric along the x-axis, and shows the cumulative percentage of file opens that were of that difference along the y-axis. Specifically, for the SEER traces (marked "Trace" in the graph), you can see that about 7% of file accesses were to the file that was opened previously, and that nearly 40% of file accesses were to either the same file or to one in the same directory (i.e., a difference of zero or one). Thus, the FFS locality assumption seems to make sense (at least for these traces).

Interestingly, another 25% or so of file accesses were to files that had a distance of two. This type of locality occurs when the user has structured a set of related directories in a multi-level fashion and consistently jumps between them. For example, if a user has a `src` directory and builds object files (`.o` files) into an `obj` directory, and both of these directories are sub-directories of a main `proj` directory, a common access pattern will be `proj/src/foo.c` followed by `proj/obj/foo.o`. The distance between these two accesses is two, as `proj` is the common ancestor. FFS does *not* capture this type of locality in its policies, and thus more seeking will occur between such accesses.

For comparison, the graph also shows locality for a "Random" trace. The random trace was generated by selecting files from within an existing SEER trace in random order, and calculating the distance metric between these randomly-ordered accesses. As you can see, there is less namespace locality in the random traces, as expected. However, because eventually every file shares a common ancestor (e.g., the root), there is some locality, and thus random is useful as a comparison point.

41.6 The Large-File Exception

In FFS, there is one important exception to the general policy of file placement, and it arises for large files. Without a different rule, a large file would entirely fill the block group it is first placed within (and maybe others). Filling a block group in this manner is undesirable, as it prevents subsequent "related" files from being placed within this block group, and thus may hurt file-access locality.

Thus, for large files, FFS does the following. After some number of blocks are allocated into the first block group (e.g., 12 blocks, or the number of direct pointers available within an inode), FFS places the next "large" chunk of the file (e.g., those pointed to by the first indirect block) in another block group (perhaps chosen for its low utilization). Then, the next chunk of the file is placed in yet another different block group, and so on.

Let's look at some diagrams to understand this policy better. Without the large-file exception, a single large file would place all of its blocks into one part of the disk. We investigate a small example of a file (`/a`) with 30 blocks in an FFS configured with 10 inodes and 40 data blocks per group. Here is the depiction of FFS without the large-file exception:

```
group inodes     data
  0   /a-------- /aaaaaaaaa aaaaaaaaaa aaaaaaaaaa a---------
  1   ---------- ---------- ---------- ---------- ----------
  2   ---------- ---------- ---------- ---------- ----------
```

As you can see in the picture, /a fills up most of the data blocks in Group 0, whereas other groups remain empty. If some other files are now created in the root directory (/), there is not much room for their data in the group.

With the large-file exception (here set to five blocks in each chunk), FFS instead spreads the file spread across groups, and the resulting utilization within any one group is not too high:

```
group inodes      data
  0   /a-------- /aaaaa---- ---------- ---------- ----------
  1   ---------- aaaaa----- ---------- ---------- ----------
  2   ---------- aaaaa----- ---------- ---------- ----------
  3   ---------- aaaaa----- ---------- ---------- ----------
  4   ---------- aaaaa----- ---------- ---------- ----------
  5   ---------- aaaaa----- ---------- ---------- ----------
  6   ---------- ---------- ---------- ---------- ----------
```

The astute reader (that's you) will note that spreading blocks of a file across the disk will hurt performance, particularly in the relatively common case of sequential file access (e.g., when a user or application reads chunks 0 through 29 in order). And you are right, oh astute reader of ours! But you can address this problem by choosing chunk size carefully.

Specifically, if the chunk size is large enough, the file system will spend most of its time transferring data from disk and just a (relatively) little time seeking between chunks of the block. This process of reducing an overhead by doing more work per overhead paid is called **amortization** and is a common technique in computer systems.

Let's do an example: assume that the average positioning time (i.e., seek and rotation) for a disk is 10 ms. Assume further that the disk transfers data at 40 MB/s. If your goal was to spend half our time seeking between chunks and half our time transferring data (and thus achieve 50% of peak disk performance), you would thus need to spend 10 ms transferring data for every 10 ms positioning. So the question becomes: how big does a chunk have to be in order to spend 10 ms in transfer? Easy, just use our old friend, math, in particular the dimensional analysis mentioned in the chapter on disks [AD14a]:

$$\frac{40\ \cancel{MB}}{\cancel{sec}} \cdot \frac{1024\ KB}{1\ \cancel{MB}} \cdot \frac{1\ \cancel{sec}}{1000\ \cancel{ms}} \cdot 10\ \cancel{ms} = 409.6\ KB \tag{41.1}$$

Basically, what this equation says is this: if you transfer data at 40 MB/s, you need to transfer only 409.6KB every time you seek in order to spend half your time seeking and half your time transferring. Similarly, you can compute the size of the chunk you would need to achieve 90% of peak bandwidth (turns out it is about 3.69MB), or even 99% of peak bandwidth (40.6MB!). As you can see, the closer you want to get to peak, the bigger these chunks get (see Figure 412 for a plot of these values).

FFS did not use this type of calculation in order to spread large files across groups, however. Instead, it took a simple approach, based on the

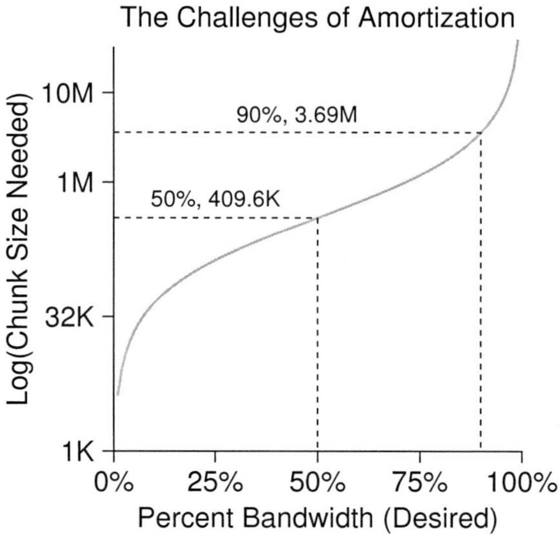

Figure 412: **Amortization: How Big Do Chunks Have To Be?**

structure of the inode itself. The first twelve direct blocks were placed in the same group as the inode; each subsequent indirect block, and all the blocks it pointed to, was placed in a different group. With a block size of 4KB, and 32-bit disk addresses, this strategy implies that every 1024 blocks of the file (4MB) were placed in separate groups, the lone exception being the first 48KB of the file as pointed to by direct pointers.

Note that the trend in disk drives is that transfer rate improves fairly rapidly, as disk manufacturers are good at cramming more bits into the same surface, but the mechanical aspects of drives related to seeks (disk arm speed and the rate of rotation) improve rather slowly [P98]. The implication is that over time, mechanical costs become relatively more expensive, and thus, to amortize said costs, you have to transfer more data between seeks.

41.7 A Few Other Things About FFS

FFS introduced a few other innovations too. In particular, the designers were extremely worried about accommodating small files; as it turned out, many files were 2KB or so in size back then, and using 4KB blocks, while good for transferring data, was not so good for space efficiency. This **internal fragmentation** could thus lead to roughly half the disk being wasted for a typical file system.

The solution the FFS designers hit upon was simple and solved the problem. They decided to introduce **sub-blocks**, which were 512-byte little blocks that the file system could allocate to files. Thus, if you created a small file (say 1KB in size), it would occupy two sub-blocks and thus not

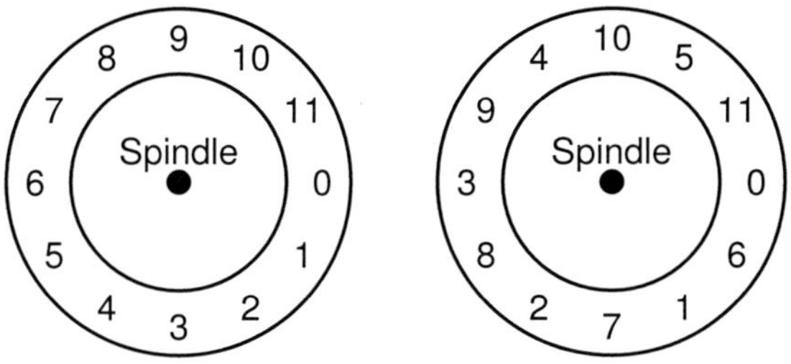

Figure 413: **FFS: Standard Versus Parameterized Placement**

waste an entire 4KB block. As the file grew, the file system will continue allocating 512-byte blocks to it until it acquires a full 4KB of data. At that point, FFS will find a 4KB block, *copy* the sub-blocks into it, and free the sub-blocks for future use.

You might observe that this process is inefficient, requiring a lot of extra work for the file system (in particular, a lot of extra I/O to perform the copy). And you'd be right again! Thus, FFS generally avoided this pessimal behavior by modifying the `libc` library; the library would buffer writes and then issue them in 4KB chunks to the file system, thus avoiding the sub-block specialization entirely in most cases.

A second neat thing that FFS introduced was a disk layout that was optimized for performance. In those times (before SCSI and other more modern device interfaces), disks were much less sophisticated and required the host CPU to control their operation in a more hands-on way. A problem arose in FFS when a file was placed on consecutive sectors of the disk, as on the left in Figure 413.

In particular, the problem arose during sequential reads. FFS would first issue a read to block 0; by the time the read was complete, and FFS issued a read to block 1, it was too late: block 1 had rotated under the head and now the read to block 1 would incur a full rotation.

FFS solved this problem with a different layout, as you can see on the right in Figure 413. By skipping over every other block (in the example), FFS has enough time to request the next block before it went past the disk head. In fact, FFS was smart enough to figure out for a particular disk *how many* blocks it should skip in doing layout in order to avoid the extra rotations; this technique was called **parameterization**, as FFS would figure out the specific performance parameters of the disk and use those to decide on the exact staggered layout scheme.

You might be thinking: this scheme isn't so great after all. In fact, you will only get 50% of peak bandwidth with this type of layout, because you have to go around each track twice just to read each block once. Fortunately, modern disks are much smarter: they internally read the entire track in and buffer it in an internal disk cache (often called a **track buffer** for this very reason). Then, on subsequent reads to the track, the disk will

TIP: MAKE THE SYSTEM USABLE

Probably the most basic lesson from FFS is that not only did it introduce the conceptually good idea of disk-aware layout, but it also added a number of features that simply made the system more usable. Long file names, symbolic links, and a rename operation that worked atomically all improved the utility of a system; while hard to write a research paper about (imagine trying to read a 14-pager about "The Symbolic Link: Hard Link's Long Lost Cousin"), such small features made FFS more useful and thus likely increased its chances for adoption. Making a system usable is often as or more important than its deep technical innovations.

just return the desired data from its cache. File systems thus no longer have to worry about these incredibly low-level details. Abstraction and higher-level interfaces can be a good thing, when designed properly.

Some other usability improvements were added as well. FFS was one of the first file systems to allow for **long file names**, thus enabling more expressive names in the file system instead of the traditional fixed-size approach (e.g., 8 characters). Further, a new concept was introduced called a **symbolic link**. As discussed in a previous chapter [AD14b] , hard links are limited in that they both could not point to directories (for fear of introducing loops in the file system hierarchy) and that they can only point to files within the same volume (i.e., the inode number must still be meaningful). Symbolic links allow the user to create an "alias" to any other file or directory on a system and thus are much more flexible. FFS also introduced an atomic `rename()` operation for renaming files. Usability improvements, beyond the basic technology, also likely gained FFS a stronger user base.

41.8 Summary

The introduction of FFS was a watershed moment in file system history, as it made clear that the problem of file management was one of the most interesting issues within an operating system, and showed how one might begin to deal with that most important of devices, the hard disk. Since that time, hundreds of new file systems have developed, but still today many file systems take cues from FFS (e.g., Linux ext2 and ext3 are obvious intellectual descendants). Certainly all modern systems account for the main lesson of FFS: treat the disk like it's a disk.

References

[AD14a] "Operating Systems: Three Easy Pieces" (Chapter: Hard Disk Drives) by Remzi Arpaci-Dusseau and Andrea Arpaci-Dusseau. Arpaci-Dusseau Books, 2014. *There is no way you should be reading about FFS without having first understood hard drives in some detail. If you try to do so, please instead go directly to jail; do not pass go, and, critically, do not collect 200 much-needed simoleons.*

[AD14b] "Operating Systems: Three Easy Pieces" (Chapter: File System Implementation) by Remzi Arpaci-Dusseau and Andrea Arpaci-Dusseau . Arpaci-Dusseau Books, 2014. *As above, it makes little sense to read this chapter unless you have read (and understood) the chapter on file system implementation. Otherwise, we'll be throwing around terms like "inode" and "indirect block" and you'll be like "huh?" and that is no fun for either of us.*

[K94] "The Design of the SEER Predictive Caching System" by G. H. Kuenning. MOBICOMM '94, Santa Cruz, California, December 1994. *According to Kuenning, this is the best overview of the SEER project, which led to (among other things) the collection of these traces.*

[MJLF84] "A Fast File System for UNIX" by Marshall K. McKusick, William N. Joy, Sam J. Leffler, Robert S. Fabry. ACM TOCS, 2:3, August 1984. *McKusick was recently honored with the IEEE Reynold B. Johnson award for his contributions to file systems, much of which was based on his work building FFS. In his acceptance speech, he discussed the original FFS software: only 1200 lines of code! Modern versions are a little more complex, e.g., the BSD FFS descendant now is in the 50-thousand lines-of-code range.*

[P98] "Hardware Technology Trends and Database Opportunities" by David A. Patterson. Keynote Lecture at SIGMOD '98, June 1998. *A great and simple overview of disk technology trends and how they change over time.*

Homework (Simulation)

This section introduces `ffs.py`, a simple FFS simulator you can use to understand better how FFS-based file and directory allocation work. See the README for details on how to run the simulator.

Questions

1. Examine the file `in.largefile`, and then run the simulator with flag `-f in.largefile` and `-L 4`. The latter sets the large-file exception to 4 blocks. What will the resulting allocation look like? Run with `-c` to check.
2. Now run with `-L 30`. What do you expect to see? Once again, turn on `-c` to see if you were right. You can also use `-S` to see exactly which blocks were allocated to the file `/a`.
3. Now we will compute some statistics about the file. The first is something we call *filespan*, which is the max distance between any two data blocks of the file or between the inode and any data block. Calculate the filespan of `/a`. Run `ffs.py -f in.largefile -L 4 -T -c` to see what it is. Do the same with `-L 100`. What difference do you expect in filespan as the large-file exception parameter changes from low values to high values?
4. Now let's look at a new input file, `in.manyfiles`. How do you think the FFS policy will lay these files out across groups? (you can run with `-v` to see what files and directories are created, or just `cat in.manyfiles`). Run the simulator with `-c` to see if you were right.
5. A metric to evaluate FFS is called *dirspan*. This metric calculates the spread of files within a particular directory, specifically the max distance between the inodes and data blocks of all files in the directory and the inode and data block of the directory itself. Run with `in.manyfiles` and the `-T` flag, and calculate the dirspan of the three directories. Run with `-c` to check. How good of a job does FFS do in minimizing dirspan?
6. Now change the size of the inode table per group to 5 (`-I 5`). How do you think this will change the layout of the files? Run with `-c` to see if you were right. How does it affect the dirspan?
7. Which group should FFS place inode of a new directory in? The default (simulator) policy looks for the group with the most free inodes. A different policy looks for a set of groups with the most free inodes. For example, if you run with `-A 2`, when allocating a new directory, the simulator will look at groups in pairs and pick the best pair for the allocation. Run `./ffs.py -f in.manyfiles -I 5 -A 2 -c` to see how allocation changes with this strategy. How does it affect dirspan? Why might this policy be good?
8. One last policy change we will explore relates to file fragmentation. Run `./ffs.py -f in.fragmented -v` and see if you can predict how the files that remain are allocated. Run with `-c` to confirm your answer. What is interesting about the data layout of file `/i`? Why is it problematic?
9. A new policy, which we call *contiguous allocation* (`-C`), tries to ensure that each file is allocated contiguously. Specifically, with `-C n`, the file system tries to ensure that `n` contiguous blocks are free within a group before allocating a block. Run `./ffs.py -f in.fragmented -v -C 2 -c` to see the difference. How does layout change as the parameter passed to `-C` increases? Finally, how does `-C` affect filespan and dirspan?

42

Crash Consistency: FSCK and Journaling

As we've seen thus far, the file system manages a set of data structures to implement the expected abstractions: files, directories, and all of the other metadata needed to support the basic abstraction that we expect from a file system. Unlike most data structures (for example, those found in memory of a running program), file system data structures must **persist**, i.e., they must survive over the long haul, stored on devices that retain data despite power loss (such as hard disks or flash-based SSDs).

One major challenge faced by a file system is how to update persistent data structures despite the presence of a **power loss** or **system crash**. Specifically, what happens if, right in the middle of updating on-disk structures, someone trips over the power cord and the machine loses power? Or the operating system encounters a bug and crashes? Because of power losses and crashes, updating a persistent data structure can be quite tricky, and leads to a new and interesting problem in file system implementation, known as the **crash-consistency problem**.

This problem is quite simple to understand. Imagine you have to update two on-disk structures, A and B, in order to complete a particular operation. Because the disk only services a single request at a time, one of these requests will reach the disk first (either A or B). If the system crashes or loses power after one write completes, the on-disk structure will be left in an **inconsistent** state. And thus, we have a problem that all file systems need to solve:

> THE CRUX: HOW TO UPDATE THE DISK DESPITE CRASHES
>
> The system may crash or lose power between any two writes, and thus the on-disk state may only partially get updated. After the crash, the system boots and wishes to mount the file system again (in order to access files and such). Given that crashes can occur at arbitrary points in time, how do we ensure the file system keeps the on-disk image in a reasonable state?

In this chapter, we'll describe this problem in more detail, and look at some methods file systems have used to overcome it. We'll begin by examining the approach taken by older file systems, known as **fsck** or the **file system checker**. We'll then turn our attention to another approach, known as **journaling** (also known as **write-ahead logging**), a technique which adds a little bit of overhead to each write but recovers more quickly from crashes or power losses. We will discuss the basic machinery of journaling, including a few different flavors of journaling that Linux ext3 [T98,PAA05] (a relatively modern journaling file system) implements.

42.1 A Detailed Example

To kick off our investigation of journaling, let's look at an example. We'll need to use a **workload** that updates on-disk structures in some way. Assume here that the workload is simple: the append of a single data block to an existing file. The append is accomplished by opening the file, calling `lseek()` to move the file offset to the end of the file, and then issuing a single 4KB write to the file before closing it.

Let's also assume we are using standard simple file system structures on the disk, similar to file systems we have seen before. This tiny example includes an **inode bitmap** (with just 8 bits, one per inode), a **data bitmap** (also 8 bits, one per data block), inodes (8 total, numbered 0 to 7, and spread across four blocks), and data blocks (8 total, numbered 0 to 7). Here is a diagram of this file system:

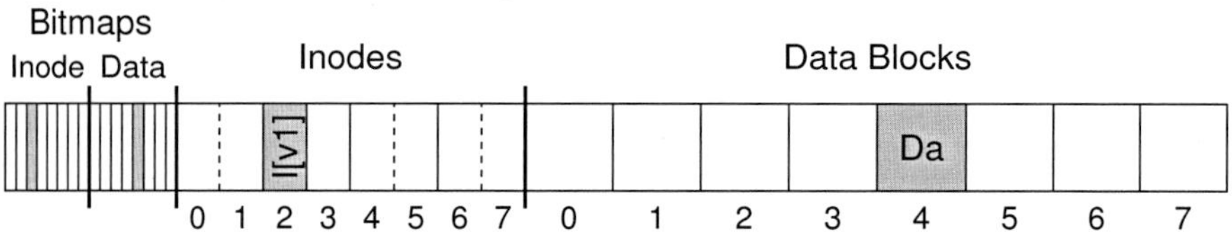

If you look at the structures in the picture, you can see that a single inode is allocated (inode number 2), which is marked in the inode bitmap, and a single allocated data block (data block 4), also marked in the data bitmap. The inode is denoted I[v1], as it is the first version of this inode; it will soon be updated (due to the workload described above).

Let's peek inside this simplified inode too. Inside of I[v1], we see:

```
owner       : remzi
permissions : read-write
size        : 1
pointer     : 4
pointer     : null
pointer     : null
pointer     : null
```

In this simplified inode, the `size` of the file is `1` (it has one block allocated), the first direct pointer points to block `4` (the first data block of the file, Da), and all three other direct pointers are set to `null` (indicating that they are not used). Of course, real inodes have many more fields; see previous chapters for more information.

When we append to the file, we are adding a new data block to it, and thus must update three on-disk structures: the inode (which must point to the new block and record the new larger size due to the append), the new data block Db, and a new version of the data bitmap (call it B[v2]) to indicate that the new data block has been allocated.

Thus, in the memory of the system, we have three blocks which we must write to disk. The updated inode (inode version 2, or I[v2] for short) now looks like this:

```
owner       : remzi
permissions : read-write
size        : 2
pointer     : 4
pointer     : 5
pointer     : null
pointer     : null
```

The updated data bitmap (B[v2]) now looks like this: 00001100. Finally, there is the data block (Db), which is just filled with whatever it is users put into files. Stolen music perhaps?

What we would like is for the final on-disk image of the file system to look like this:

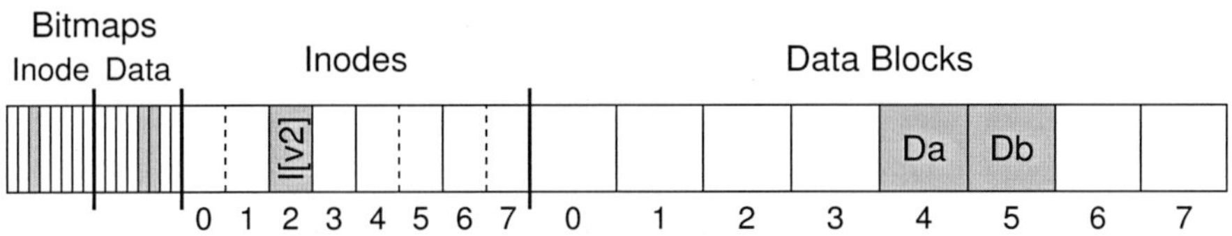

To achieve this transition, the file system must perform three separate writes to the disk, one each for the inode (I[v2]), bitmap (B[v2]), and data block (Db). Note that these writes usually don't happen immediately when the user issues a `write()` system call; rather, the dirty inode, bitmap, and new data will sit in main memory (in the **page cache** or **buffer cache**) for some time first; then, when the file system finally decides to write them to disk (after say 5 seconds or 30 seconds), the file system will issue the requisite write requests to the disk. Unfortunately, a crash may occur and thus interfere with these updates to the disk. In particular, if a crash happens after one or two of these writes have taken place, but not all three, the file system could be left in a funny state.

Crash Scenarios

To understand the problem better, let's look at some example crash scenarios. Imagine only a single write succeeds; there are thus three possible outcomes, which we list here:

- **Just the data block (Db) is written to disk.** In this case, the data is on disk, but there is no inode that points to it and no bitmap that even says the block is allocated. Thus, it is as if the write never occurred. This case is not a problem at all, from the perspective of file-system crash consistency[1].

- **Just the updated inode (I[v2]) is written to disk.** In this case, the inode points to the disk address (5) where Db was about to be written, but Db has not yet been written there. Thus, if we trust that pointer, we will read **garbage** data from the disk (the old contents of disk address 5).

  Further, we have a new problem, which we call a **file-system inconsistency**. The on-disk bitmap is telling us that data block 5 has not been allocated, but the inode is saying that it has. The disagreement between the bitmap and the inode is an inconsistency in the data structures of the file system; to use the file system, we must somehow resolve this problem (more on that below).

- **Just the updated bitmap (B[v2]) is written to disk.** In this case, the bitmap indicates that block 5 is allocated, but there is no inode that points to it. Thus the file system is inconsistent again; if left unresolved, this write would result in a **space leak**, as block 5 would never be used by the file system.

There are also three more crash scenarios in this attempt to write three blocks to disk. In these cases, two writes succeed and the last one fails:

- **The inode (I[v2]) and bitmap (B[v2]) are written to disk, but not data (Db).** In this case, the file system metadata is completely consistent: the inode has a pointer to block 5, the bitmap indicates that 5 is in use, and thus everything looks OK from the perspective of the file system's metadata. But there is one problem: 5 has garbage in it again.

- **The inode (I[v2]) and the data block (Db) are written, but not the bitmap (B[v2]).** In this case, we have the inode pointing to the correct data on disk, but again have an inconsistency between the inode and the old version of the bitmap (B1). Thus, we once again need to resolve the problem before using the file system.

- **The bitmap (B[v2]) and data block (Db) are written, but not the inode (I[v2]).** In this case, we again have an inconsistency between the inode and the data bitmap. However, even though the block was written and the bitmap indicates its usage, we have no idea which file it belongs to, as no inode points to the file.

[1]However, it might be a problem for the user, who just lost some data!

The Crash Consistency Problem

Hopefully, from these crash scenarios, you can see the many problems that can occur to our on-disk file system image because of crashes: we can have inconsistency in file system data structures; we can have space leaks; we can return garbage data to a user; and so forth. What we'd like to do ideally is move the file system from one consistent state (e.g., before the file got appended to) to another **atomically** (e.g., after the inode, bitmap, and new data block have been written to disk). Unfortunately, we can't do this easily because the disk only commits one write at a time, and crashes or power loss may occur between these updates. We call this general problem the **crash-consistency problem** (we could also call it the **consistent-update problem**).

42.2 Solution #1: The File System Checker

Early file systems took a simple approach to crash consistency. Basically, they decided to let inconsistencies happen and then fix them later (when rebooting). A classic example of this lazy approach is found in a tool that does this: **fsck**[2]. `fsck` is a UNIX tool for finding such inconsistencies and repairing them [M86]; similar tools to check and repair a disk partition exist on different systems. Note that such an approach can't fix all problems; consider, for example, the case above where the file system looks consistent but the inode points to garbage data. The only real goal is to make sure the file system metadata is internally consistent.

The tool `fsck` operates in a number of phases, as summarized in McKusick and Kowalski's paper [MK96]. It is run *before* the file system is mounted and made available (`fsck` assumes that no other file-system activity is on-going while it runs); once finished, the on-disk file system should be consistent and thus can be made accessible to users.

Here is a basic summary of what `fsck` does:

- **Superblock:** `fsck` first checks if the superblock looks reasonable, mostly doing sanity checks such as making sure the file system size is greater than the number of blocks that have been allocated. Usually the goal of these sanity checks is to find a suspect (corrupt) superblock; in this case, the system (or administrator) may decide to use an alternate copy of the superblock.
- **Free blocks:** Next, `fsck` scans the inodes, indirect blocks, double indirect blocks, etc., to build an understanding of which blocks are currently allocated within the file system. It uses this knowledge to produce a correct version of the allocation bitmaps; thus, if there is any inconsistency between bitmaps and inodes, it is resolved by trusting the information within the inodes. The same type of check is performed for all the inodes, making sure that all inodes that look like they are in use are marked as such in the inode bitmaps.

[2]Pronounced either "eff-ess-see-kay", "eff-ess-check", or, if you don't like the tool, "eff-suck". Yes, serious professional people use this term.

- **Inode state:** Each inode is checked for corruption or other problems. For example, `fsck` makes sure that each allocated inode has a valid type field (e.g., regular file, directory, symbolic link, etc.). If there are problems with the inode fields that are not easily fixed, the inode is considered suspect and cleared by `fsck`; the inode bitmap is correspondingly updated.
- **Inode links:** `fsck` also verifies the link count of each allocated inode. As you may recall, the link count indicates the number of different directories that contain a reference (i.e., a link) to this particular file. To verify the link count, `fsck` scans through the entire directory tree, starting at the root directory, and builds its own link counts for every file and directory in the file system. If there is a mismatch between the newly-calculated count and that found within an inode, corrective action must be taken, usually by fixing the count within the inode. If an allocated inode is discovered but no directory refers to it, it is moved to the `lost+found` directory.
- **Duplicates:** `fsck` also checks for duplicate pointers, i.e., cases where two different inodes refer to the same block. If one inode is obviously bad, it may be cleared. Alternately, the pointed-to block could be copied, thus giving each inode its own copy as desired.
- **Bad blocks:** A check for bad block pointers is also performed while scanning through the list of all pointers. A pointer is considered "bad" if it obviously points to something outside its valid range, e.g., it has an address that refers to a block greater than the partition size. In this case, `fsck` can't do anything too intelligent; it just removes (clears) the pointer from the inode or indirect block.
- **Directory checks:** `fsck` does not understand the contents of user files; however, directories hold specifically formatted information created by the file system itself. Thus, `fsck` performs additional integrity checks on the contents of each directory, making sure that "." and ".." are the first entries, that each inode referred to in a directory entry is allocated, and ensuring that no directory is linked to more than once in the entire hierarchy.

As you can see, building a working `fsck` requires intricate knowledge of the file system; making sure such a piece of code works correctly in all cases can be challenging [G+08]. However, fsck (and similar approaches) have a bigger and perhaps more fundamental problem: they are *too slow*. With a very large disk volume, scanning the entire disk to find all the allocated blocks and read the entire directory tree may take many minutes or hours. Performance of `fsck`, as disks grew in capacity and RAIDs grew in popularity, became prohibitive (despite recent advances [M+13]).

At a higher level, the basic premise of `fsck` seems just a tad irrational. Consider our example above, where just three blocks are written to the disk; it is incredibly expensive to scan the entire disk to fix problems that occurred during an update of just three blocks. This situation is akin to dropping your keys on the floor in your bedroom, and then commencing a *search-the-entire-house-for-keys* recovery algorithm, starting in the basement and working your way through every room. It works but is wasteful. Thus, as disks (and RAIDs) grew, researchers and practitioners started to look for other solutions.

42.3 Solution #2: Journaling (or Write-Ahead Logging)

Probably the most popular solution to the consistent update problem is to steal an idea from the world of database management systems. That idea, known as **write-ahead logging**, was invented to address exactly this type of problem. In file systems, we usually call write-ahead logging **journaling** for historical reasons. The first file system to do this was Cedar [H87], though many modern file systems use the idea, including Linux ext3 and ext4, reiserfs, IBM's JFS, SGI's XFS, and Windows NTFS.

The basic idea is as follows. When updating the disk, before overwriting the structures in place, first write down a little note (somewhere else on the disk, in a well-known location) describing what you are about to do. Writing this note is the "write ahead" part, and we write it to a structure that we organize as a "log"; hence, write-ahead logging.

By writing the note to disk, you are guaranteeing that if a crash takes places during the update (overwrite) of the structures you are updating, you can go back and look at the note you made and try again; thus, you will know exactly what to fix (and how to fix it) after a crash, instead of having to scan the entire disk. By design, journaling thus adds a bit of work during updates to greatly reduce the amount of work required during recovery.

We'll now describe how **Linux ext3**, a popular journaling file system, incorporates journaling into the file system. Most of the on-disk structures are identical to **Linux ext2**, e.g., the disk is divided into block groups, and each block group contains an inode bitmap, data bitmap, inodes, and data blocks. The new key structure is the journal itself, which occupies some small amount of space within the partition or on another device. Thus, an ext2 file system (without journaling) looks like this:

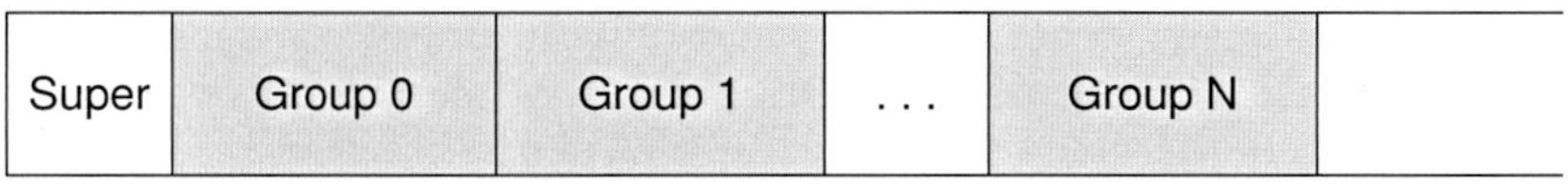

Assuming the journal is placed within the same file system image (though sometimes it is placed on a separate device, or as a file within the file system), an ext3 file system with a journal looks like this:

The real difference is just the presence of the journal, and of course, how it is used.

Data Journaling

Let's look at a simple example to understand how **data journaling** works. Data journaling is available as a mode with the Linux ext3 file system, from which much of this discussion is based.

Say we have our canonical update again, where we wish to write the inode (I[v2]), bitmap (B[v2]), and data block (Db) to disk again. Before writing them to their final disk locations, we are now first going to write them to the log (a.k.a. journal). This is what this will look like in the log:

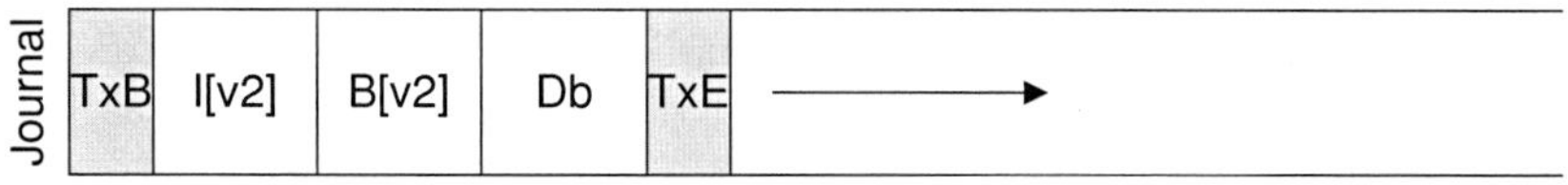

You can see we have written five blocks here. The transaction begin (TxB) tells us about this update, including information about the pending update to the file system (e.g., the final addresses of the blocks I[v2], B[v2], and Db), and some kind of **transaction identifier** (**TID**). The middle three blocks just contain the exact contents of the blocks themselves; this is known as **physical logging** as we are putting the exact physical contents of the update in the journal (an alternate idea, **logical logging**, puts a more compact logical representation of the update in the journal, e.g., "this update wishes to append data block Db to file X", which is a little more complex but can save space in the log and perhaps improve performance). The final block (TxE) is a marker of the end of this transaction, and will also contain the TID.

Once this transaction is safely on disk, we are ready to overwrite the old structures in the file system; this process is called **checkpointing**. Thus, to **checkpoint** the file system (i.e., bring it up to date with the pending update in the journal), we issue the writes I[v2], B[v2], and Db to their disk locations as seen above; if these writes complete successfully, we have successfully checkpointed the file system and are basically done. Thus, our initial sequence of operations:

1. **Journal write:** Write the transaction, including a transaction-begin block, all pending data and metadata updates, and a transaction-end block, to the log; wait for these writes to complete.
2. **Checkpoint:** Write the pending metadata and data updates to their final locations in the file system.

In our example, we would write TxB, I[v2], B[v2], Db, and TxE to the journal first. When these writes complete, we would complete the update by checkpointing I[v2], B[v2], and Db, to their final locations on disk.

Things get a little trickier when a crash occurs during the writes to the journal. Here, we are trying to write the set of blocks in the transaction (e.g., TxB, I[v2], B[v2], Db, TxE) to disk. One simple way to do this would be to issue each one at a time, waiting for each to complete, and then issuing the next. However, this is slow. Ideally, we'd like to issue

> ASIDE: FORCING WRITES TO DISK
>
> To enforce ordering between two disk writes, modern file systems have to take a few extra precautions. In olden times, forcing ordering between two writes, A and B, was easy: just issue the write of A to the disk, wait for the disk to interrupt the OS when the write is complete, and then issue the write of B.
>
> Things got slightly more complex due to the increased use of write caches within disks. With write buffering enabled (sometimes called **immediate reporting**), a disk will inform the OS the write is complete when it simply has been placed in the disk's memory cache, and has not yet reached disk. If the OS then issues a subsequent write, it is not guaranteed to reach the disk after previous writes; thus ordering between writes is not preserved. One solution is to disable write buffering. However, more modern systems take extra precautions and issue explicit **write barriers**; such a barrier, when it completes, guarantees that all writes issued before the barrier will reach disk before any writes issued after the barrier.
>
> All of this machinery requires a great deal of trust in the correct operation of the disk. Unfortunately, recent research shows that some disk manufacturers, in an effort to deliver "higher performing" disks, explicitly ignore write-barrier requests, thus making the disks seemingly run faster but at the risk of incorrect operation [C+13, R+11]. As Kahan said, the fast almost always beats out the slow, even if the fast is wrong.

all five block writes at once, as this would turn five writes into a single sequential write and thus be faster. However, this is unsafe, for the following reason: given such a big write, the disk internally may perform scheduling and complete small pieces of the big write in any order. Thus, the disk internally may (1) write TxB, I[v2], B[v2], and TxE and only later (2) write Db. Unfortunately, if the disk loses power between (1) and (2), this is what ends up on disk:

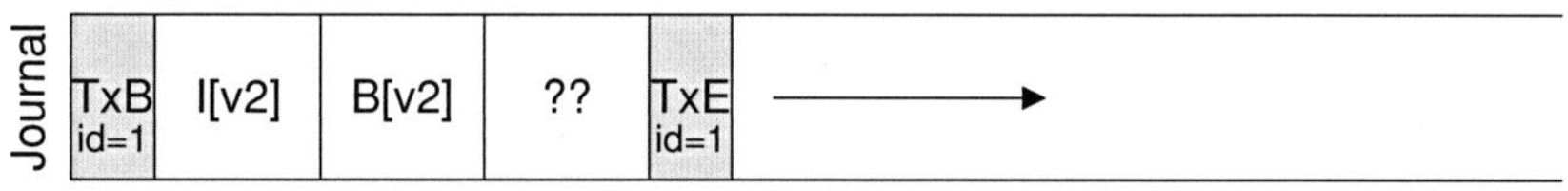

Why is this a problem? Well, the transaction looks like a valid transaction (it has a begin and an end with matching sequence numbers). Further, the file system can't look at that fourth block and know it is wrong; after all, it is arbitrary user data. Thus, if the system now reboots and runs recovery, it will replay this transaction, and ignorantly copy the contents of the garbage block '??' to the location where Db is supposed to live. This is bad for arbitrary user data in a file; it is much worse if it happens to a critical piece of file system, such as the superblock, which could render the file system unmountable.

ASIDE: OPTIMIZING LOG WRITES

You may have noticed a particular inefficiency of writing to the log. Namely, the file system first has to write out the transaction-begin block and contents of the transaction; only after these writes complete can the file system send the transaction-end block to disk. The performance impact is clear, if you think about how a disk works: usually an extra rotation is incurred (think about why).

One of our former graduate students, Vijayan Prabhakaran, had a simple idea to fix this problem [P+05]. When writing a transaction to the journal, include a checksum of the contents of the journal in the begin and end blocks. Doing so enables the file system to write the entire transaction at once, without incurring a wait; if, during recovery, the file system sees a mismatch in the computed checksum versus the stored checksum in the transaction, it can conclude that a crash occurred during the write of the transaction and thus discard the file-system update. Thus, with a small tweak in the write protocol and recovery system, a file system can achieve faster common-case performance; on top of that, the system is slightly more reliable, as any reads from the journal are now protected by a checksum.

This simple fix was attractive enough to gain the notice of Linux file system developers, who then incorporated it into the next generation Linux file system, called (you guessed it!) **Linux ext4**. It now ships on millions of machines worldwide, including the Android handheld platform. Thus, every time you write to disk on many Linux-based systems, a little code developed at Wisconsin makes your system a little faster and more reliable.

To avoid this problem, the file system issues the transactional write in two steps. First, it writes all blocks except the TxE block to the journal, issuing these writes all at once. When these writes complete, the journal will look something like this (assuming our append workload again):

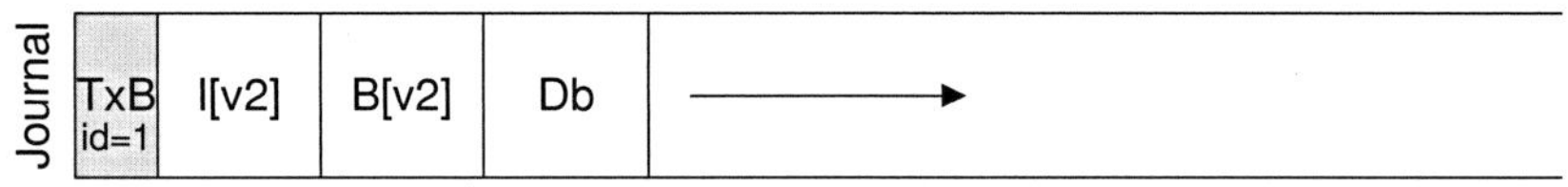

When those writes complete, the file system issues the write of the TxE block, thus leaving the journal in this final, safe state:

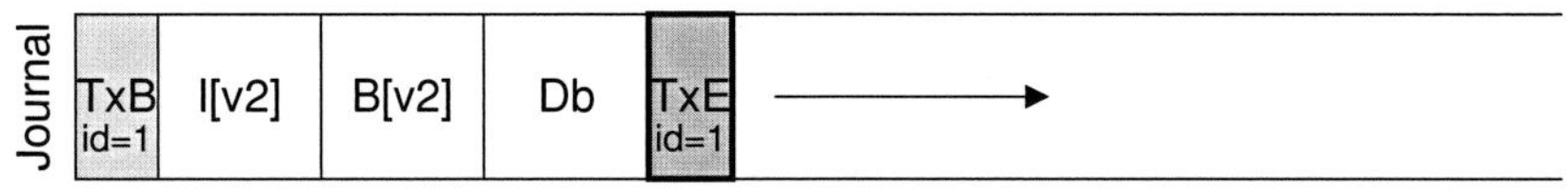

An important aspect of this process is the atomicity guarantee provided by the disk. It turns out that the disk guarantees that any 512-byte write will either happen or not (and never be half-written); thus, to make sure the write of TxE is atomic, one should make it a single 512-byte block. Thus, our current protocol to update the file system, with each of its three phases labeled:

1. **Journal write:** Write the contents of the transaction (including TxB, metadata, and data) to the log; wait for these writes to complete.
2. **Journal commit:** Write the transaction commit block (containing TxE) to the log; wait for write to complete; transaction is said to be **committed**.
3. **Checkpoint:** Write the contents of the update (metadata and data) to their final on-disk locations.

Recovery

Let's now understand how a file system can use the contents of the journal to **recover** from a crash. A crash may happen at any time during this sequence of updates. If the crash happens before the transaction is written safely to the log (i.e., before Step 2 above completes), then our job is easy: the pending update is simply skipped. If the crash happens after the transaction has committed to the log, but before the checkpoint is complete, the file system can **recover** the update as follows. When the system boots, the file system recovery process will scan the log and look for transactions that have committed to the disk; these transactions are thus **replayed** (in order), with the file system again attempting to write out the blocks in the transaction to their final on-disk locations. This form of logging is one of the simplest forms there is, and is called **redo logging**. By recovering the committed transactions in the journal, the file system ensures that the on-disk structures are consistent, and thus can proceed by mounting the file system and readying itself for new requests.

Note that it is fine for a crash to happen at any point during checkpointing, even after some of the updates to the final locations of the blocks have completed. In the worst case, some of these updates are simply performed again during recovery. Because recovery is a rare operation (only taking place after an unexpected system crash), a few redundant writes are nothing to worry about[3].

Batching Log Updates

You might have noticed that the basic protocol could add a lot of extra disk traffic. For example, imagine we create two files in a row, called `file1` and `file2`, in the same directory. To create one file, one has to update a number of on-disk structures, minimally including: the inode bitmap (to allocate a new inode), the newly-created inode of the file,

[3]Unless you worry about everything, in which case we can't help you. Stop worrying so much, it is unhealthy! But now you're probably worried about over-worrying.

the data block of the parent directory containing the new directory entry, and the parent directory inode (which now has a new modification time). With journaling, we logically commit all of this information to the journal for each of our two file creations; because the files are in the same directory, and assuming they even have inodes within the same inode block, this means that if we're not careful, we'll end up writing these same blocks over and over.

To remedy this problem, some file systems do not commit each update to disk one at a time (e.g., Linux ext3); rather, one can buffer all updates into a global transaction. In our example above, when the two files are created, the file system just marks the in-memory inode bitmap, inodes of the files, directory data, and directory inode as dirty, and adds them to the list of blocks that form the current transaction. When it is finally time to write these blocks to disk (say, after a timeout of 5 seconds), this single global transaction is committed containing all of the updates described above. Thus, by buffering updates, a file system can avoid excessive write traffic to disk in many cases.

Making The Log Finite

We thus have arrived at a basic protocol for updating file-system on-disk structures. The file system buffers updates in memory for some time; when it is finally time to write to disk, the file system first carefully writes out the details of the transaction to the journal (a.k.a. write-ahead log); after the transaction is complete, the file system checkpoints those blocks to their final locations on disk.

However, the log is of a finite size. If we keep adding transactions to it (as in this figure), it will soon fill. What do you think happens then?

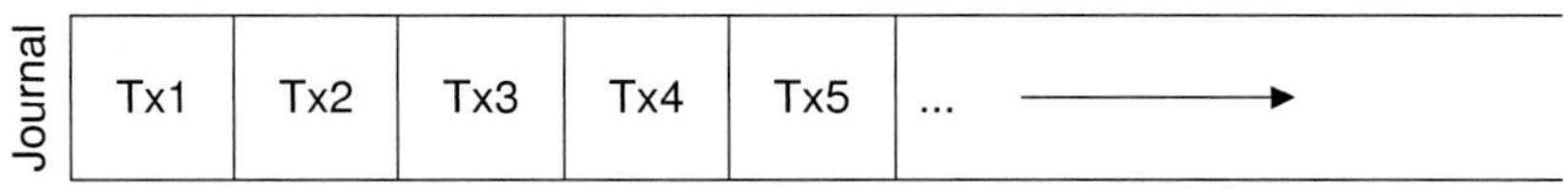

Two problems arise when the log becomes full. The first is simpler, but less critical: the larger the log, the longer recovery will take, as the recovery process must replay all the transactions within the log (in order) to recover. The second is more of an issue: when the log is full (or nearly full), no further transactions can be committed to the disk, thus making the file system "less than useful" (i.e., useless).

To address these problems, journaling file systems treat the log as a circular data structure, re-using it over and over; this is why the journal is sometimes referred to as a **circular log**. To do so, the file system must take action some time after a checkpoint. Specifically, once a transaction has been checkpointed, the file system should free the space it was occupying within the journal, allowing the log space to be reused. There are many ways to achieve this end; for example, you could simply mark the oldest and newest non-checkpointed transactions in the log in a **journal superblock**; all other space is free. Here is a graphical depiction:

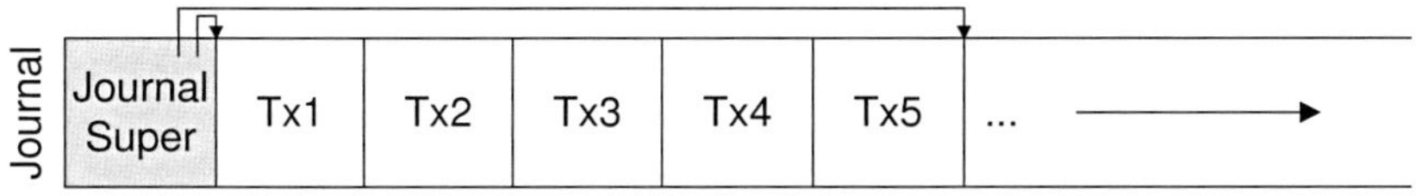

In the journal superblock (not to be confused with the main file system superblock), the journaling system records enough information to know which transactions have not yet been checkpointed, and thus reduces recovery time as well as enables re-use of the log in a circular fashion. And thus we add another step to our basic protocol:

1. **Journal write:** Write the contents of the transaction (containing TxB and the contents of the update) to the log; wait for these writes to complete.
2. **Journal commit:** Write the transaction commit block (containing TxE) to the log; wait for the write to complete; the transaction is now **committed**.
3. **Checkpoint:** Write the contents of the update to their final locations within the file system.
4. **Free:** Some time later, mark the transaction free in the journal by updating the journal superblock.

Thus we have our final data journaling protocol. But there is still a problem: we are writing each data block to the disk *twice*, which is a heavy cost to pay, especially for something as rare as a system crash. Can you figure out a way to retain consistency without writing data twice?

Metadata Journaling

Although recovery is now fast (scanning the journal and replaying a few transactions as opposed to scanning the entire disk), normal operation of the file system is slower than we might desire. In particular, for each write to disk, we are now also writing to the journal first, thus doubling write traffic; this doubling is especially painful during sequential write workloads, which now will proceed at half the peak write bandwidth of the drive. Further, between writes to the journal and writes to the main file system, there is a costly seek, which adds noticeable overhead for some workloads.

Because of the high cost of writing every data block to disk twice, people have tried a few different things in order to speed up performance. For example, the mode of journaling we described above is often called **data journaling** (as in Linux ext3), as it journals all user data (in addition to the metadata of the file system). A simpler (and more common) form of journaling is sometimes called **ordered journaling** (or just **metadata**

journaling), and it is nearly the same, except that user data is *not* written to the journal. Thus, when performing the same update as above, the following information would be written to the journal:

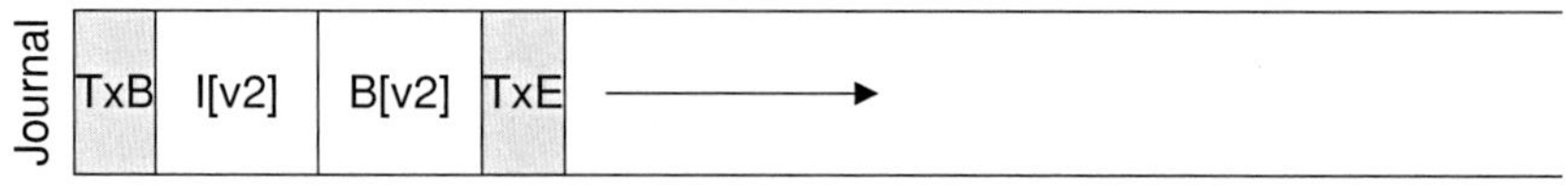

The data block Db, previously written to the log, would instead be written to the file system proper, avoiding the extra write; given that most I/O traffic to the disk is data, not writing data twice substantially reduces the I/O load of journaling. The modification does raise an interesting question, though: when should we write data blocks to disk?

Let's again consider our example append of a file to understand the problem better. The update consists of three blocks: I[v2], B[v2], and Db. The first two are both metadata and will be logged and then checkpointed; the latter will only be written once to the file system. When should we write Db to disk? Does it matter?

As it turns out, the ordering of the data write does matter for metadata-only journaling. For example, what if we write Db to disk *after* the transaction (containing I[v2] and B[v2]) completes? Unfortunately, this approach has a problem: the file system is consistent but I[v2] may end up pointing to garbage data. Specifically, consider the case where I[v2] and B[v2] are written but Db did not make it to disk. The file system will then try to recover. Because Db is *not* in the log, the file system will replay writes to I[v2] and B[v2], and produce a consistent file system (from the perspective of file-system metadata). However, I[v2] will be pointing to garbage data, i.e., at whatever was in the slot where Db was headed.

To ensure this situation does not arise, some file systems (e.g., Linux ext3) write data blocks (of regular files) to the disk *first*, before related metadata is written to disk. Specifically, the protocol is as follows:

1. **Data write:** Write data to final location; wait for completion (the wait is optional; see below for details).
2. **Journal metadata write:** Write the begin block and metadata to the log; wait for writes to complete.
3. **Journal commit:** Write the transaction commit block (containing TxE) to the log; wait for the write to complete; the transaction (including data) is now **committed**.
4. **Checkpoint metadata:** Write the contents of the metadata update to their final locations within the file system.
5. **Free:** Later, mark the transaction free in journal superblock.

By forcing the data write first, a file system can guarantee that a pointer will never point to garbage. Indeed, this rule of "write the pointed-to object before the object that points to it" is at the core of crash consistency, and is exploited even further by other crash consistency schemes [GP94] (see below for details).

In most systems, metadata journaling (akin to ordered journaling of ext3) is more popular than full data journaling. For example, Windows NTFS and SGI's XFS both use some form of metadata journaling. Linux ext3 gives you the option of choosing either data, ordered, or unordered modes (in unordered mode, data can be written at any time). All of these modes keep metadata consistent; they vary in their semantics for data.

Finally, note that forcing the data write to complete (Step 1) before issuing writes to the journal (Step 2) is not required for correctness, as indicated in the protocol above. Specifically, it would be fine to concurrently issue writes to data, the transaction-begin block, and journaled metadata; the only real requirement is that Steps 1 and 2 complete before the issuing of the journal commit block (Step 3).

Tricky Case: Block Reuse

There are some interesting corner cases that make journaling more tricky, and thus are worth discussing. A number of them revolve around block reuse; as Stephen Tweedie (one of the main forces behind ext3) said:

> "What's the hideous part of the entire system? ... It's deleting files. Everything to do with delete is hairy. Everything to do with delete... you have nightmares around what happens if blocks get deleted and then reallocated." [T00]

The particular example Tweedie gives is as follows. Suppose you are using some form of metadata journaling (and thus data blocks for files are *not* journaled). Let's say you have a directory called `foo`. The user adds an entry to `foo` (say by creating a file), and thus the contents of `foo` (because directories are considered metadata) are written to the log; assume the location of the `foo` directory data is block 1000. The log thus contains something like this:

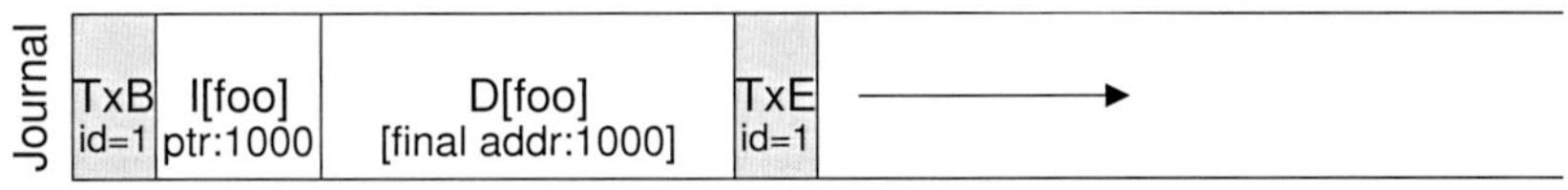

At this point, the user deletes everything in the directory and the directory itself, freeing up block 1000 for reuse. Finally, the user creates a new file (say `bar`), which ends up reusing the same block (1000) that used to belong to `foo`. The inode of `bar` is committed to disk, as is its data; note, however, because metadata journaling is in use, only the inode of `bar` is committed to the journal; the newly-written data in block 1000 in the file `bar` is *not* journaled.

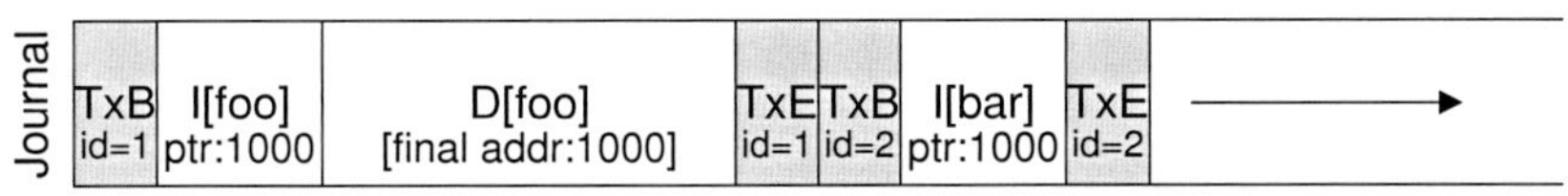

	Journal			File System	
TxB	Contents (metadata)	(data)	TxE	Metadata	Data
issue	**issue**	**issue**			
complete					
	complete				
		complete			
			issue		
			complete		
				issue	**issue**
					complete
				complete	

Figure 421: **Data Journaling Timeline**

Now assume a crash occurs and all of this information is still in the log. During replay, the recovery process simply replays everything in the log, including the write of directory data in block 1000; the replay thus overwrites the user data of current file `bar` with old directory contents! Clearly this is not a correct recovery action, and certainly it will be a surprise to the user when reading the file `bar`.

There are a number of solutions to this problem. One could, for example, never reuse blocks until the delete of said blocks is checkpointed out of the journal. What Linux ext3 does instead is to add a new type of record to the journal, known as a **revoke** record. In the case above, deleting the directory would cause a revoke record to be written to the journal. When replaying the journal, the system first scans for such revoke records; any such revoked data is never replayed, thus avoiding the problem mentioned above.

Wrapping Up Journaling: A Timeline

Before ending our discussion of journaling, we summarize the protocols we have discussed with timelines depicting each of them. Figure 421 shows the protocol when journaling data and metadata, whereas Figure 422 shows the protocol when journaling only metadata.

In each figure, time increases in the downward direction, and each row in the figure shows the logical time that a write can be issued or might complete. For example, in the data journaling protocol (Figure 421), the writes of the transaction begin block (TxB) and the contents of the transaction can logically be issued at the same time, and thus can be completed in any order; however, the write to the transaction end block (TxE) must not be issued until said previous writes complete. Similarly, the checkpointing writes to data and metadata blocks cannot begin until the transaction end block has committed. Horizontal dashed lines show where write-ordering requirements must be obeyed.

A similar timeline is shown for the metadata journaling protocol. Note

TxB	Journal Contents (metadata)	TxE	File System Metadata	File System Data
issue	**issue**			**issue**
				complete
complete				
	complete			
		issue		
		complete		
			issue	
			complete	

Figure 422: **Metadata Journaling Timeline**

that the data write can logically be issued at the same time as the writes to the transaction begin and the contents of the journal; however, it must be issued and complete before the transaction end has been issued.

Finally, note that the time of completion marked for each write in the timelines is arbitrary. In a real system, completion time is determined by the I/O subsystem, which may reorder writes to improve performance. The only guarantees about ordering that we have are those that must be enforced for protocol correctness (and are shown via the horizontal dashed lines in the figures).

42.4 Solution #3: Other Approaches

We've thus far described two options in keeping file system metadata consistent: a lazy approach based on `fsck`, and a more active approach known as journaling. However, these are not the only two approaches. One such approach, known as Soft Updates [GP94], was introduced by Ganger and Patt. This approach carefully orders all writes to the file system to ensure that the on-disk structures are never left in an inconsistent state. For example, by writing a pointed-to data block to disk *before* the inode that points to it, we can ensure that the inode never points to garbage; similar rules can be derived for all the structures of the file system. Implementing Soft Updates can be a challenge, however; whereas the journaling layer described above can be implemented with relatively little knowledge of the exact file system structures, Soft Updates requires intricate knowledge of each file system data structure and thus adds a fair amount of complexity to the system.

Another approach is known as **copy-on-write** (yes, **COW**), and is used in a number of popular file systems, including Sun's ZFS [B07]. This technique never overwrites files or directories in place; rather, it places new updates to previously unused locations on disk. After a number of updates are completed, COW file systems flip the root structure of the file system to include pointers to the newly updated structures. Doing so makes keeping the file system consistent straightforward. We'll be learning more about this technique when we discuss the log-structured file system (LFS) in a future chapter; LFS is an early example of a COW.

Another approach is one we just developed here at Wisconsin. In this technique, entitled **backpointer-based consistency** (or **BBC**), no ordering is enforced between writes. To achieve consistency, an additional **back pointer** is added to every block in the system; for example, each data block has a reference to the inode to which it belongs. When accessing a file, the file system can determine if the file is consistent by checking if the forward pointer (e.g., the address in the inode or direct block) points to a block that refers back to it. If so, everything must have safely reached disk and thus the file is consistent; if not, the file is inconsistent, and an error is returned. By adding back pointers to the file system, a new form of lazy crash consistency can be attained [C+12].

Finally, we also have explored techniques to reduce the number of times a journal protocol has to wait for disk writes to complete. Entitled **optimistic crash consistency** [C+13], this new approach issues as many writes to disk as possible by using a generalized form of the **transaction checksum** [P+05], and includes a few other techniques to detect inconsistencies should they arise. For some workloads, these optimistic techniques can improve performance by an order of magnitude. However, to truly function well, a slightly different disk interface is required [C+13].

42.5 Summary

We have introduced the problem of crash consistency, and discussed various approaches to attacking this problem. The older approach of building a file system checker works but is likely too slow to recover on modern systems. Thus, many file systems now use journaling. Journaling reduces recovery time from O(size-of-the-disk-volume) to O(size-of-the-log), thus speeding recovery substantially after a crash and restart. For this reason, many modern file systems use journaling. We have also seen that journaling can come in many different forms; the most commonly used is ordered metadata journaling, which reduces the amount of traffic to the journal while still preserving reasonable consistency guarantees for both file system metadata and user data. In the end, strong guarantees on user data are probably one of the most important things to provide; oddly enough, as recent research has shown, this area remains a work in progress [P+14].

References

[B07] "ZFS: The Last Word in File Systems" by Jeff Bonwick and Bill Moore. Available online: `http://www.ostep.org/Citations/zfs_last.pdf`. *ZFS uses copy-on-write and journaling, actually, as in some cases, logging writes to disk will perform better.*

[C+12] "Consistency Without Ordering" by Vijay Chidambaram, Tushar Sharma, Andrea C. Arpaci-Dusseau, Remzi H. Arpaci-Dusseau. FAST '12, San Jose, California. *A recent paper of ours about a new form of crash consistency based on back pointers. Read it for the exciting details!*

[C+13] "Optimistic Crash Consistency" by Vijay Chidambaram, Thanu S. Pillai, Andrea C. Arpaci-Dusseau, Remzi H. Arpaci-Dusseau . SOSP '13, Nemacolin Woodlands Resort, PA, November 2013. *Our work on a more optimistic and higher performance journaling protocol. For workloads that call `fsync()` a lot, performance can be greatly improved.*

[GP94] "Metadata Update Performance in File Systems" by Gregory R. Ganger and Yale N. Patt. OSDI '94. *A clever paper about using careful ordering of writes as the main way to achieve consistency. Implemented later in BSD-based systems.*

[G+08] "SQCK: A Declarative File System Checker" by Haryadi S. Gunawi, Abhishek Rajimwale, Andrea C. Arpaci-Dusseau, Remzi H. Arpaci-Dusseau. OSDI '08, San Diego, California. *Our own paper on a new and better way to build a file system checker using SQL queries. We also show some problems with the existing checker, finding numerous bugs and odd behaviors, a direct result of the complexity of `fsck`.*

[H87] "Reimplementing the Cedar File System Using Logging and Group Commit" by Robert Hagmann. SOSP '87, Austin, Texas, November 1987. *The first work (that we know of) that applied write-ahead logging (a.k.a. journaling) to a file system.*

[M+13] "ffsck: The Fast File System Checker" by Ao Ma, Chris Dragga, Andrea C. Arpaci-Dusseau, Remzi H. Arpaci-Dusseau. FAST '13, San Jose, California, February 2013. *A recent paper of ours detailing how to make fsck an order of magnitude faster. Some of the ideas have already been incorporated into the BSD file system checker [MK96] and are deployed today.*

[MK96] "Fsck – The UNIX File System Check Program" by Marshall Kirk McKusick and T. J. Kowalski. Revised in 1996. *Describes the first comprehensive file-system checking tool, the eponymous `fsck`. Written by some of the same people who brought you FFS.*

[MJLF84] "A Fast File System for UNIX" by Marshall K. McKusick, William N. Joy, Sam J. Leffler, Robert S. Fabry. ACM Transactions on Computing Systems, Volume 2:3, August 1984. *You already know enough about FFS, right? But come on, it is OK to re-reference important papers.*

[P+14] "All File Systems Are Not Created Equal: On the Complexity of Crafting Crash-Consistent Applications" by Thanumalayan Sankaranarayana Pillai, Vijay Chidambaram, Ramnatthan Alagappan, Samer Al-Kiswany, Andrea C. Arpaci-Dusseau, Remzi H. Arpaci-Dusseau. OSDI '14, Broomfield, Colorado, October 2014. *A paper in which we study what file systems guarantee after crashes, and show that applications expect something different, leading to all sorts of interesting problems.*

[P+05] "IRON File Systems" by Vijayan Prabhakaran, Lakshmi N. Bairavasundaram, Nitin Agrawal, Haryadi S. Gunawi, Andrea C. Arpaci-Dusseau, Remzi H. Arpaci-Dusseau. SOSP '05, Brighton, England, October 2005. *A paper mostly focused on studying how file systems react to disk failures. Towards the end, we introduce a transaction checksum to speed up logging, which was eventually adopted into Linux ext4.*

[PAA05] "Analysis and Evolution of Journaling File Systems" by Vijayan Prabhakaran, Andrea C. Arpaci-Dusseau, Remzi H. Arpaci-Dusseau. USENIX '05, Anaheim, California, April 2005. *An early paper we wrote analyzing how journaling file systems work.*

[R+11] "Coerced Cache Eviction and Discreet-Mode Journaling" by Abhishek Rajimwale, Vijay Chidambaram, Deepak Ramamurthi, Andrea C. Arpaci-Dusseau, Remzi H. Arpaci-Dusseau. DSN '11, Hong Kong, China, June 2011. *Our own paper on the problem of disks that buffer writes in a memory cache instead of forcing them to disk, even when explicitly told not to do that! Our solution to overcome this problem: if you want A to be written to disk before B, first write A, then send a lot of "dummy" writes to disk, hopefully causing A to be forced to disk to make room for them in the cache. A neat if impractical solution.*

[T98] "Journaling the Linux ext2fs File System" by Stephen C. Tweedie. The Fourth Annual Linux Expo, May 1998. *Tweedie did much of the heavy lifting in adding journaling to the Linux ext2 file system; the result, not surprisingly, is called ext3. Some nice design decisions include the strong focus on backwards compatibility, e.g., you can just add a journaling file to an existing ext2 file system and then mount it as an ext3 file system.*

[T00] "EXT3, Journaling Filesystem" by Stephen Tweedie. Talk at the Ottawa Linux Symposium, July 2000. olstrans.sourceforge.net/release/OLS2000-ext3/OLS2000-ext3.html *A transcript of a talk given by Tweedie on ext3.*

[T01] "The Linux ext2 File System" by Theodore Ts'o, June, 2001.. Available online here: `http://e2fsprogs.sourceforge.net/ext2.html`. *A simple Linux file system based on the ideas found in FFS. For a while it was quite heavily used; now it is really just in the kernel as an example of a simple file system.*

Homework (Simulation)

This section introduces `fsck.py`, a simple simulator you can use to better understand how file system corruptions can be detected (and potentially repaired). Please see the associated README for details on how to run the simulator.

Questions

1. First, run `fsck.py -D`; this flag turns off any corruption, and thus you can use it to generate a random file system, and see if you can determine which files and directories are in there. So, go ahead and do that! Use the `-p` flag to see if you were right. Try this for a few different randomly-generated file systems by setting the seed (`-s`) to different values, like 1, 2, and 3.
2. Now, let's introduce a corruption. Run `fsck.py -S 1` to start. Can you see what inconsistency is introduced? How would you fix it in a real file system repair tool? Use `-c` to check if you were right.
3. Change the seed to `-S 3` or `-S 19`; which inconsistency do you see? Use `-c` to check your answer. What is different in these two cases?
4. Change the seed to `-S 5`; which inconsistency do you see? How hard would it be to fix this problem in an automatic way? Use `-c` to check your answer. Then, introduce a similar inconsistency with `-S 38`; is this harder/possible to detect? Finally, use `-S 642`; is this inconsistency detectable? If so, how would you fix the file system?
5. Change the seed to `-S 6` or `-S 13`; which inconsistency do you see? Use `-c` to check your answer. What is the difference across these two cases? What should the repair tool do when encountering such a situation?
6. Change the seed to `-S 9`; which inconsistency do you see? Use `-c` to check your answer. Which piece of information should a check-and-repair tool trust in this case?
7. Change the seed to `-S 15`; which inconsistency do you see? Use `-c` to check your answer. What can a repair tool do in this case? If no repair is possible, how much data is lost?
8. Change the seed to `-S 10`; which inconsistency do you see? Use `-c` to check your answer. Is there redundancy in the file system structure here that can help a repair?
9. Change the seed to `-S 16` and `-S 20`; which inconsistency do you see? Use `-c` to check your answer. How should the repair tool fix the problem?

43

Log-structured File Systems

In the early 90's, a group at Berkeley led by Professor John Ousterhout and graduate student Mendel Rosenblum developed a new file system known as the log-structured file system [RO91]. Their motivation to do so was based on the following observations:

- **System memories are growing**: As memory gets bigger, more data can be cached in memory. As more data is cached, disk traffic increasingly consists of writes, as reads are serviced by the cache. Thus, file system performance is largely determined by its write performance.
- **There is a large gap between random I/O performance and sequential I/O performance**: Hard-drive transfer bandwidth has increased a great deal over the years [P98]; as more bits are packed into the surface of a drive, the bandwidth when accessing said bits increases. Seek and rotational delay costs, however, have decreased slowly; it is challenging to make cheap and small motors spin the platters faster or move the disk arm more quickly. Thus, if you are able to use disks in a sequential manner, you gain a sizeable performance advantage over approaches that cause seeks and rotations.
- **Existing file systems perform poorly on many common workloads**: For example, FFS [MJLF84] would perform a large number of writes to create a new file of size one block: one for a new inode, one to update the inode bitmap, one to the directory data block that the file is in, one to the directory inode to update it, one to the new data block that is a part of the new file, and one to the data bitmap to mark the data block as allocated. Thus, although FFS places all of these blocks within the same block group, FFS incurs many short seeks and subsequent rotational delays and thus performance falls far short of peak sequential bandwidth.
- **File systems are not RAID-aware**: For example, both RAID-4 and RAID-5 have the **small-write problem** where a logical write to a single block causes 4 physical I/Os to take place. Existing file systems do not try to avoid this worst-case RAID writing behavior.

> **TIP: DETAILS MATTER**
> All interesting systems are comprised of a few general ideas and a number of details. Sometimes, when you are learning about these systems, you think to yourself "Oh, I get the general idea; the rest is just details," and you use this to only half-learn how things really work. Don't do this! Many times, the details are critical. As we'll see with LFS, the general idea is easy to understand, but to really build a working system, you have to think through *all* of the tricky cases.

An ideal file system would thus focus on write performance, and try to make use of the sequential bandwidth of the disk. Further, it would perform well on common workloads that not only write out data but also update on-disk metadata structures frequently. Finally, it would work well on RAIDs as well as single disks.

The new type of file system Rosenblum and Ousterhout introduced was called **LFS**, short for the **Log-structured File System**. When writing to disk, LFS first buffers all updates (including metadata!) in an in-memory **segment**; when the segment is full, it is written to disk in one long, sequential transfer to an unused part of the disk. LFS never overwrites existing data, but rather *always* writes segments to free locations. Because segments are large, the disk (or RAID) is used efficiently, and performance of the file system approaches its zenith.

> **THE CRUX:**
> **HOW TO MAKE ALL WRITES SEQUENTIAL WRITES?**
> How can a file system transform all writes into sequential writes? For reads, this task is impossible, as the desired block to be read may be anywhere on disk. For writes, however, the file system always has a choice, and it is exactly this choice we hope to exploit.

43.1 Writing To Disk Sequentially

We thus have our first challenge: how do we transform all updates to file-system state into a series of sequential writes to disk? To understand this better, let's use a simple example. Imagine we are writing a data block D to a file. Writing the data block to disk might result in the following on-disk layout, with D written at disk address $A0$:

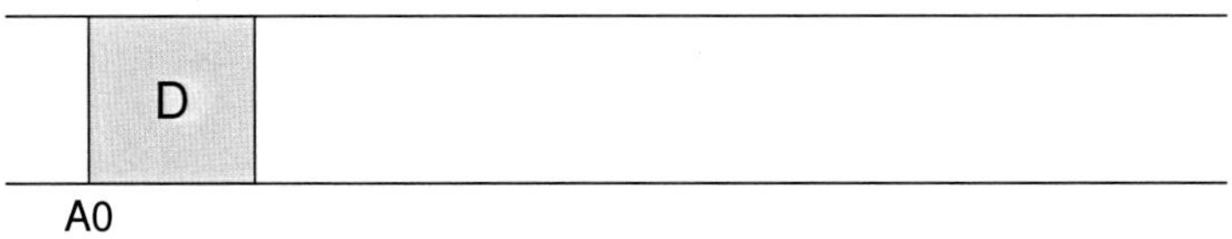

However, when a user writes a data block, it is not only data that gets written to disk; there is also other **metadata** that needs to be updated. In this case, let's also write the **inode** (I) of the file to disk, and have it point to the data block D. When written to disk, the data block and inode would look something like this (note that the inode looks as big as the data block, which generally isn't the case; in most systems, data blocks are 4 KB in size, whereas an inode is much smaller, around 128 bytes):

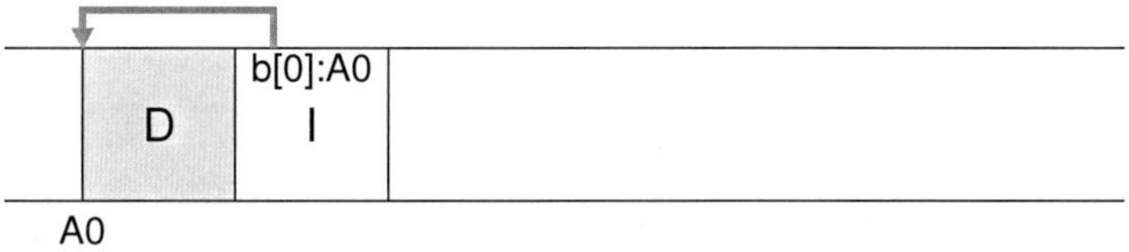

This basic idea, of simply writing all updates (such as data blocks, inodes, etc.) to the disk sequentially, sits at the heart of LFS. If you understand this, you get the basic idea. But as with all complicated systems, the devil is in the details.

43.2 Writing Sequentially And Effectively

Unfortunately, writing to disk sequentially is not (alone) enough to guarantee efficient writes. For example, imagine if we wrote a single block to address A, at time T. We then wait a little while, and write to the disk at address $A + 1$ (the next block address in sequential order), but at time $T + \delta$. In-between the first and second writes, unfortunately, the disk has rotated; when you issue the second write, it will thus wait for most of a rotation before being committed (specifically, if the rotation takes time $T_{rotation}$, the disk will wait $T_{rotation} - \delta$ before it can commit the second write to the disk surface). And thus you can hopefully see that simply writing to disk in sequential order is not enough to achieve peak performance; rather, you must issue a large number of *contiguous* writes (or one large write) to the drive in order to achieve good write performance.

To achieve this end, LFS uses an ancient technique known as **write buffering**[1]. Before writing to the disk, LFS keeps track of updates in memory; when it has received a sufficient number of updates, it writes them to disk all at once, thus ensuring efficient use of the disk.

The large chunk of updates LFS writes at one time is referred to by the name of a **segment**. Although this term is over-used in computer systems, here it just means a large-ish chunk which LFS uses to group writes. Thus, when writing to disk, LFS buffers updates in an in-memory

[1] Indeed, it is hard to find a good citation for this idea, since it was likely invented by many and very early on in the history of computing. For a study of the benefits of write buffering, see Solworth and Orji [SO90]; to learn about its potential harms, see Mogul [M94].

segment, and then writes the segment all at once to the disk. As long as the segment is large enough, these writes will be efficient.

Here is an example, in which LFS buffers two sets of updates into a small segment; actual segments are larger (a few MB). The first update is of four block writes to file j; the second is one block being added to file k. LFS then commits the entire segment of seven blocks to disk at once. The resulting on-disk layout of these blocks is as follows:

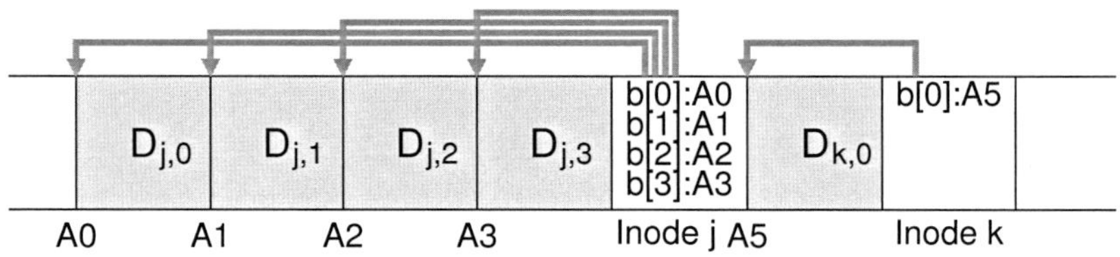

43.3 How Much To Buffer?

This raises the following question: how many updates should LFS buffer before writing to disk? The answer, of course, depends on the disk itself, specifically how high the positioning overhead is in comparison to the transfer rate; see the FFS chapter for a similar analysis.

For example, assume that positioning (i.e., rotation and seek overheads) before each write takes roughly $T_{position}$ seconds. Assume further that the disk transfer rate is R_{peak} MB/s. How much should LFS buffer before writing when running on such a disk?

The way to think about this is that every time you write, you pay a fixed overhead of the positioning cost. Thus, how much do you have to write in order to **amortize** that cost? The more you write, the better (obviously), and the closer you get to achieving peak bandwidth.

To obtain a concrete answer, let's assume we are writing out D MB. The time to write out this chunk of data (T_{write}) is the positioning time $T_{position}$ plus the time to transfer D ($\frac{D}{R_{peak}}$), or:

$$T_{write} = T_{position} + \frac{D}{R_{peak}} \tag{43.1}$$

And thus the effective *rate* of writing ($R_{effective}$), which is just the amount of data written divided by the total time to write it, is:

$$R_{effective} = \frac{D}{T_{write}} = \frac{D}{T_{position} + \frac{D}{R_{peak}}}. \tag{43.2}$$

What we're interested in is getting the effective rate ($R_{effective}$) close to the peak rate. Specifically, we want the effective rate to be some fraction F of the peak rate, where $0 < F < 1$ (a typical F might be 0.9, or 90% of the peak rate). In mathematical form, this means we want $R_{effective} = F \times R_{peak}$.

At this point, we can solve for D:

$$R_{effective} = \frac{D}{T_{position} + \frac{D}{R_{peak}}} = F \times R_{peak} \quad (43.3)$$

$$D = F \times R_{peak} \times (T_{position} + \frac{D}{R_{peak}}) \quad (43.4)$$

$$D = (F \times R_{peak} \times T_{position}) + (F \times R_{peak} \times \frac{D}{R_{peak}}) \quad (43.5)$$

$$D = \frac{F}{1 - F} \times R_{peak} \times T_{position} \quad (43.6)$$

Let's do an example, with a disk with a positioning time of 10 milliseconds and peak transfer rate of 100 MB/s; assume we want an effective bandwidth of 90% of peak ($F = 0.9$). In this case, $D = \frac{0.9}{0.1} \times 100\ MB/s \times 0.01\ seconds = 9\ MB$. Try some different values to see how much we need to buffer in order to approach peak bandwidth. How much is needed to reach 95% of peak? 99%?

43.4 Problem: Finding Inodes

To understand how we find an inode in LFS, let us briefly review how to find an inode in a typical UNIX file system. In a typical file system such as FFS, or even the old UNIX file system, finding inodes is easy, because they are organized in an array and placed on disk at fixed locations.

For example, the old UNIX file system keeps all inodes at a fixed portion of the disk. Thus, given an inode number and the start address, to find a particular inode, you can calculate its exact disk address simply by multiplying the inode number by the size of an inode, and adding that to the start address of the on-disk array; array-based indexing, given an inode number, is fast and straightforward.

Finding an inode given an inode number in FFS is only slightly more complicated, because FFS splits up the inode table into chunks and places a group of inodes within each cylinder group. Thus, one must know how big each chunk of inodes is and the start addresses of each. After that, the calculations are similar and also easy.

In LFS, life is more difficult. Why? Well, we've managed to scatter the inodes all throughout the disk! Worse, we never overwrite in place, and thus the latest version of an inode (i.e., the one we want) keeps moving.

43.5 Solution Through Indirection: The Inode Map

To remedy this, the designers of LFS introduced a **level of indirection** between inode numbers and the inodes through a data structure called the **inode map (imap)**. The imap is a structure that takes an inode number as input and produces the disk address of the most recent version of the

> TIP: USE A LEVEL OF INDIRECTION
>
> People often say that the solution to all problems in Computer Science is simply a **level of indirection**. This is clearly not true; it is just the solution to *most* problems (yes, this is still too strong of a comment, but you get the point). You certainly can think of every virtualization we have studied, e.g., virtual memory, or the notion of a file, as simply a level of indirection. And certainly the inode map in LFS is a virtualization of inode numbers. Hopefully you can see the great power of indirection in these examples, allowing us to freely move structures around (such as pages in the VM example, or inodes in LFS) without having to change every reference to them. Of course, indirection can have a downside too: **extra overhead.** So next time you have a problem, try solving it with indirection, but make sure to think about the overheads of doing so first. As Wheeler famously said, "All problems in computer science can be solved by another level of indirection, except of course for the problem of too many indirections."

inode. Thus, you can imagine it would often be implemented as a simple *array*, with 4 bytes (a disk pointer) per entry. Any time an inode is written to disk, the imap is updated with its new location.

The imap, unfortunately, needs to be kept persistent (i.e., written to disk); doing so allows LFS to keep track of the locations of inodes across crashes, and thus operate as desired. Thus, a question: where should the imap reside on disk?

It could live on a fixed part of the disk, of course. Unfortunately, as it gets updated frequently, this would then require updates to file structures to be followed by writes to the imap, and hence performance would suffer (i.e., there would be more disk seeks, between each update and the fixed location of the imap).

Instead, LFS places chunks of the inode map right next to where it is writing all of the other new information. Thus, when appending a data block to a file k, LFS actually writes the new data block, its inode, and a piece of the inode map all together onto the disk, as follows:

In this picture, the piece of the imap array stored in the block marked *imap* tells LFS that the inode k is at disk address $A1$; this inode, in turn, tells LFS that its data block D is at address $A0$.

43.6 Completing The Solution: The Checkpoint Region

The clever reader (that's you, right?) might have noticed a problem here. How do we find the inode map, now that pieces of it are also now spread across the disk? In the end, there is no magic: the file system must have *some* fixed and known location on disk to begin a file lookup.

LFS has just such a fixed place on disk for this, known as the **checkpoint region (CR)**. The checkpoint region contains pointers to (i.e., addresses of) the latest pieces of the inode map, and thus the inode map pieces can be found by reading the CR first. Note the checkpoint region is only updated periodically (say every 30 seconds or so), and thus performance is not ill-affected. Thus, the overall structure of the on-disk layout contains a checkpoint region (which points to the latest pieces of the inode map); the inode map pieces each contain addresses of the inodes; the inodes point to files (and directories) just like typical UNIX file systems.

Here is an example of the checkpoint region (note it is all the way at the beginning of the disk, at address 0), and a single imap chunk, inode, and data block. A real file system would of course have a much bigger CR (indeed, it would have two, as we'll come to understand later), many imap chunks, and of course many more inodes, data blocks, etc.

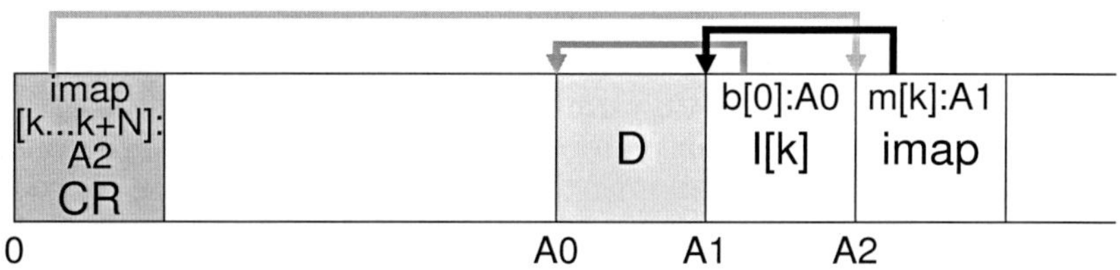

43.7 Reading A File From Disk: A Recap

To make sure you understand how LFS works, let us now walk through what must happen to read a file from disk. Assume we have nothing in memory to begin. The first on-disk data structure we must read is the checkpoint region. The checkpoint region contains pointers (i.e., disk addresses) to the entire inode map, and thus LFS then reads in the entire inode map and caches it in memory. After this point, when given an inode number of a file, LFS simply looks up the inode-number to inode-disk-address mapping in the imap, and reads in the most recent version of the inode. To read a block from the file, at this point, LFS proceeds exactly as a typical UNIX file system, by using direct pointers or indirect pointers or doubly-indirect pointers as need be. In the common case, LFS should perform the same number of I/Os as a typical file system when reading a file from disk; the entire imap is cached and thus the extra work LFS does during a read is to look up the inode's address in the imap.

43.8 What About Directories?

Thus far, we've simplified our discussion a bit by only considering inodes and data blocks. However, to access a file in a file system (such as `/home/remzi/foo`, one of our favorite fake file names), some directories must be accessed too. So how does LFS store directory data?

Fortunately, directory structure is basically identical to classic UNIX file systems, in that a directory is just a collection of (name, inode number) mappings. For example, when creating a file on disk, LFS must both write a new inode, some data, as well as the directory data and its inode that refer to this file. Remember that LFS will do so sequentially on the disk (after buffering the updates for some time). Thus, creating a file `foo` in a directory would lead to the following new structures on disk:

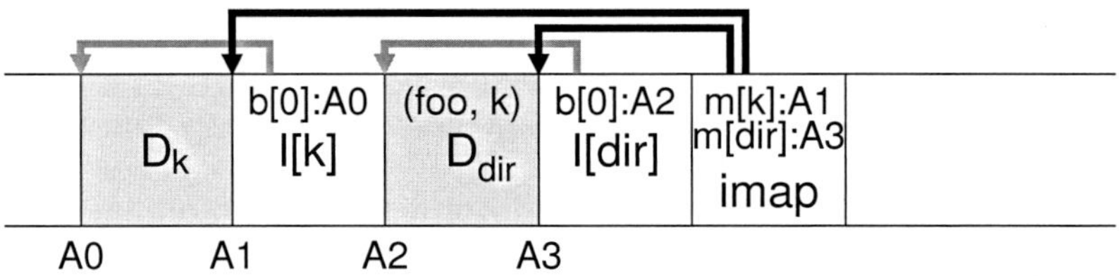

The piece of the inode map contains the information for the location of both the directory file *dir* as well as the newly-created file *f*. Thus, when accessing file `foo` (with inode number *k*), you would first look in the inode map (usually cached in memory) to find the location of the inode of directory *dir* (*A*3); you then read the directory inode, which gives you the location of the directory data (*A*2); reading this data block gives you the name-to-inode-number mapping of (`foo`, *k*). You then consult the inode map again to find the location of inode number *k* (*A*1), and finally read the desired data block at address *A*0.

There is one other serious problem in LFS that the inode map solves, known as the **recursive update problem** [Z+12]. The problem arises in any file system that never updates in place (such as LFS), but rather moves updates to new locations on the disk.

Specifically, whenever an inode is updated, its location on disk changes. If we hadn't been careful, this would have also entailed an update to the directory that points to this file, which then would have mandated a change to the parent of that directory, and so on, all the way up the file system tree.

LFS cleverly avoids this problem with the inode map. Even though the location of an inode may change, the change is never reflected in the directory itself; rather, the imap structure is updated while the directory holds the same name-to-inode-number mapping. Thus, through indirection, LFS avoids the recursive update problem.

43.9 A New Problem: Garbage Collection

You may have noticed another problem with LFS; it repeatedly writes the latest version of a file (including its inode and data) to new locations on disk. This process, while keeping writes efficient, implies that LFS leaves old versions of file structures scattered throughout the disk. We (rather unceremoniously) call these old versions **garbage**.

For example, let's imagine the case where we have an existing file referred to by inode number k, which points to a single data block $D0$. We now update that block, generating both a new inode and a new data block. The resulting on-disk layout of LFS would look something like this (note we omit the imap and other structures for simplicity; a new chunk of imap would also have to be written to disk to point to the new inode):

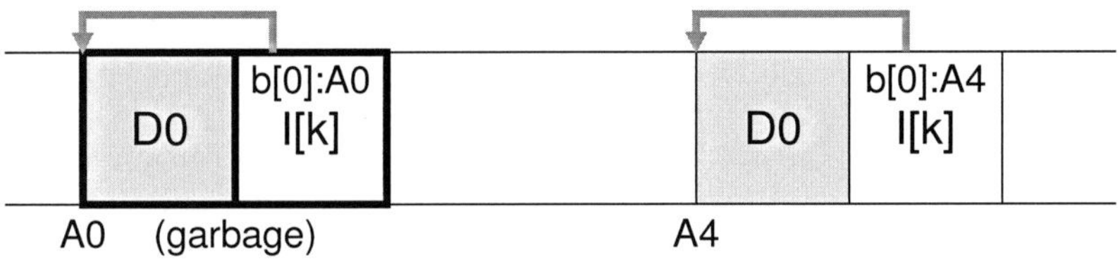

In the diagram, you can see that both the inode and data block have two versions on disk, one old (the one on the left) and one current and thus **live** (the one on the right). By the simple act of (logically) updating a data block, a number of new structures must be persisted by LFS, thus leaving old versions of said blocks on the disk.

As another example, imagine we instead append a block to that original file k. In this case, a new version of the inode is generated, but the old data block is still pointed to by the inode. Thus, it is still live and very much part of the current file system:

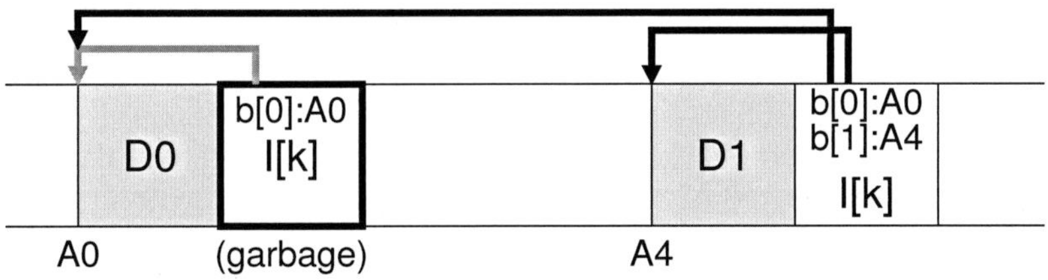

So what should we do with these older versions of inodes, data blocks, and so forth? One could keep those older versions around and allow users to restore old file versions (for example, when they accidentally overwrite or delete a file, it could be quite handy to do so); such a file system is known as a **versioning file system** because it keeps track of the different versions of a file.

However, LFS instead keeps only the latest live version of a file; thus (in the background), LFS must periodically find these old dead versions of file data, inodes, and other structures, and **clean** them; cleaning should thus make blocks on disk free again for use in subsequent writes. Note that the process of cleaning is a form of **garbage collection**, a technique that arises in programming languages that automatically free unused memory for programs.

Earlier we discussed segments as important as they are the mechanism that enables large writes to disk in LFS. As it turns out, they are also quite integral to effective cleaning. Imagine what would happen if the LFS cleaner simply went through and freed single data blocks, inodes, etc., during cleaning. The result: a file system with some number of free **holes** mixed between allocated space on disk. Write performance would drop considerably, as LFS would not be able to find a large contiguous region to write to disk sequentially and with high performance.

Instead, the LFS cleaner works on a segment-by-segment basis, thus clearing up large chunks of space for subsequent writing. The basic cleaning process works as follows. Periodically, the LFS cleaner reads in a number of old (partially-used) segments, determines which blocks are live within these segments, and then write out a new set of segments with just the live blocks within them, freeing up the old ones for writing. Specifically, we expect the cleaner to read in M existing segments, **compact** their contents into N new segments (where $N < M$), and then write the N segments to disk in new locations. The old M segments are then freed and can be used by the file system for subsequent writes.

We are now left with two problems, however. The first is mechanism: how can LFS tell which blocks within a segment are live, and which are dead? The second is policy: how often should the cleaner run, and which segments should it pick to clean?

43.10 Determining Block Liveness

We address the mechanism first. Given a data block D within an on-disk segment S, LFS must be able to determine whether D is live. To do so, LFS adds a little extra information to each segment that describes each block. Specifically, LFS includes, for each data block D, its inode number (which file it belongs to) and its offset (which block of the file this is). This information is recorded in a structure at the head of the segment known as the **segment summary block**.

Given this information, it is straightforward to determine whether a block is live or dead. For a block D located on disk at address A, look in the segment summary block and find its inode number N and offset T. Next, look in the imap to find where N lives and read N from disk (perhaps it is already in memory, which is even better). Finally, using the offset T, look in the inode (or some indirect block) to see where the inode thinks the Tth block of this file is on disk. If it points exactly to disk address A, LFS can conclude that the block D is live. If it points anywhere else, LFS can conclude that D is not in use (i.e., it is dead) and thus know that this version is no longer needed. Here is a pseudocode summary:

```
(N, T) = SegmentSummary[A];
inode  = Read(imap[N]);
if (inode[T] == A)
    // block D is alive
else
    // block D is garbage
```

Here is a diagram depicting the mechanism, in which the segment summary block (marked SS) records that the data block at address $A0$ is actually a part of file k at offset 0. By checking the imap for k, you can find the inode, and see that it does indeed point to that location.

There are some shortcuts LFS takes to make the process of determining liveness more efficient. For example, when a file is truncated or deleted, LFS increases its **version number** and records the new version number in the imap. By also recording the version number in the on-disk segment, LFS can short circuit the longer check described above simply by comparing the on-disk version number with a version number in the imap, thus avoiding extra reads.

43.11 A Policy Question: Which Blocks To Clean, And When?

On top of the mechanism described above, LFS must include a set of policies to determine both when to clean and which blocks are worth cleaning. Determining when to clean is easier; either periodically, during idle time, or when you have to because the disk is full.

Determining which blocks to clean is more challenging, and has been the subject of many research papers. In the original LFS paper [RO91], the authors describe an approach which tries to segregate *hot* and *cold* segments. A hot segment is one in which the contents are being frequently over-written; thus, for such a segment, the best policy is to wait a long time before cleaning it, as more and more blocks are getting over-written (in new segments) and thus being freed for use. A cold segment, in contrast, may have a few dead blocks but the rest of its contents are relatively stable. Thus, the authors conclude that one should clean cold segments sooner and hot segments later, and develop a heuristic that does exactly that. However, as with most policies, this policy isn't perfect; later approaches show how to do better [MR+97].

43.12 Crash Recovery And The Log

One final problem: what happens if the system crashes while LFS is writing to disk? As you may recall in the previous chapter about journaling, crashes during updates are tricky for file systems, and thus something LFS must consider as well.

During normal operation, LFS buffers writes in a segment, and then (when the segment is full, or when some amount of time has elapsed), writes the segment to disk. LFS organizes these writes in a **log**, i.e., the checkpoint region points to a head and tail segment, and each segment points to the next segment to be written. LFS also periodically updates the checkpoint region. Crashes could clearly happen during either of these operations (write to a segment, write to the CR). So how does LFS handle crashes during writes to these structures?

Let's cover the second case first. To ensure that the CR update happens atomically, LFS actually keeps two CRs, one at either end of the disk, and writes to them alternately. LFS also implements a careful protocol when updating the CR with the latest pointers to the inode map and other information; specifically, it first writes out a header (with timestamp), then the body of the CR, and then finally one last block (also with a timestamp). If the system crashes during a CR update, LFS can detect this by seeing an inconsistent pair of timestamps. LFS will always choose to use the most recent CR that has consistent timestamps, and thus consistent update of the CR is achieved.

Let's now address the first case. Because LFS writes the CR every 30 seconds or so, the last consistent snapshot of the file system may be quite old. Thus, upon reboot, LFS can easily recover by simply reading in the checkpoint region, the imap pieces it points to, and subsequent files and directories; however, the last many seconds of updates would be lost.

To improve upon this, LFS tries to rebuild many of those segments through a technique known as **roll forward** in the database community. The basic idea is to start with the last checkpoint region, find the end of the log (which is included in the CR), and then use that to read through the next segments and see if there are any valid updates within it. If there are, LFS updates the file system accordingly and thus recovers much of the data and metadata written since the last checkpoint. See Rosenblum's award-winning dissertation for details [R92].

43.13 Summary

LFS introduces a new approach to updating the disk. Instead of overwriting files in places, LFS always writes to an unused portion of the disk, and then later reclaims that old space through cleaning. This approach, which in database systems is called **shadow paging** [L77] and in file-system-speak is sometimes called **copy-on-write**, enables highly efficient writing, as LFS can gather all updates into an in-memory segment and then write them out together sequentially.

TIP: TURN FLAWS INTO VIRTUES

Whenever your system has a fundamental flaw, see if you can turn it around into a feature or something useful. NetApp's WAFL does this with old file contents; by making old versions available, WAFL no longer has to worry about cleaning quite so often (though it does delete old versions, eventually, in the background), and thus provides a cool feature and removes much of the LFS cleaning problem all in one wonderful twist. Are there other examples of this in systems? Undoubtedly, but you'll have to think of them yourself, because this chapter is over with a capital "O". Over. Done. Kaput. We're out. Peace!

The large writes that LFS generates are excellent for performance on many different devices. On hard drives, large writes ensure that positioning time is minimized; on parity-based RAIDs, such as RAID-4 and RAID-5, they avoid the small-write problem entirely. Recent research has even shown that large I/Os are required for high performance on Flash-based SSDs [H+17]; thus, perhaps surprisingly, LFS-style file systems may be an excellent choice even for these new mediums.

The downside to this approach is that it generates garbage; old copies of the data are scattered throughout the disk, and if one wants to reclaim such space for subsequent usage, one must clean old segments periodically. Cleaning became the focus of much controversy in LFS, and concerns over cleaning costs [SS+95] perhaps limited LFS's initial impact on the field. However, some modern commercial file systems, including NetApp's **WAFL** [HLM94], Sun's **ZFS** [B07], and Linux **btrfs** [R+13], and even modern **flash-based SSDs** [AD14], adopt a similar copy-on-write approach to writing to disk, and thus the intellectual legacy of LFS lives on in these modern file systems. In particular, WAFL got around cleaning problems by turning them into a feature; by providing old versions of the file system via **snapshots**, users could access old files whenever they deleted current ones accidentally.

References

[AD14] "Operating Systems: Three Easy Pieces" (Chapter: Flash-based Solid State Drives) by Remzi Arpaci-Dusseau and Andrea Arpaci-Dusseau. Arpaci-Dusseau Books, 2014. *A bit gauche to refer you to another chapter in this very book, but who are we to judge?*

[B07] "ZFS: The Last Word in File Systems" by Jeff Bonwick and Bill Moore. Copy Available: `http://www.ostep.org/Citations/zfs_last.pdf`. *Slides on ZFS; unfortunately, there is no great ZFS paper (yet). Maybe you will write one, so we can cite it here?*

[H+17] "The Unwritten Contract of of Solid State Drives" by Jun He, Sudarsun Kannan, Andrea C. Arpaci-Dusseau, Remzi H. Arpaci-Dusseau. EuroSys '17, April 2017. *Which unwritten rules one must follow to extract high performance from an SSD? Interestingly, both request scale (large or parallel requests) and locality still matter, even on SSDs. The more things change ...*

[HLM94] "File System Design for an NFS File Server Appliance" by Dave Hitz, James Lau, Michael Malcolm. USENIX Spring '94. *WAFL takes many ideas from LFS and RAID and puts it into a high-speed NFS appliance for the multi-billion dollar storage company NetApp.*

[L77] "Physical Integrity in a Large Segmented Database" by R. Lorie. ACM Transactions on Databases, Volume 2:1, 1977. *The original idea of shadow paging is presented here.*

[MJLF84] "A Fast File System for UNIX" by Marshall K. McKusick, William N. Joy, Sam J. Leffler, Robert S. Fabry. ACM TOCS, Volume 2:3, August 1984. *The original FFS paper; see the chapter on FFS for more details.*

[MR+97] "Improving the Performance of Log-structured File Systems with Adaptive Methods" by Jeanna Neefe Matthews, Drew Roselli, Adam M. Costello, Randolph Y. Wang, Thomas E. Anderson. SOSP 1997, pages 238-251, October, Saint Malo, France. *A more recent paper detailing better policies for cleaning in LFS.*

[M94] "A Better Update Policy" by Jeffrey C. Mogul. USENIX ATC '94, June 1994. *In this paper, Mogul finds that read workloads can be harmed by buffering writes for too long and then sending them to the disk in a big burst. Thus, he recommends sending writes more frequently and in smaller batches.*

[P98] "Hardware Technology Trends and Database Opportunities" by David A. Patterson. ACM SIGMOD '98 Keynote, 1998. Available online here: `http://www.cs.berkeley.edu/~pattrsn/talks/keynote.html`. *A great set of slides on technology trends in computer systems. Hopefully, Patterson will create another of these sometime soon.*

[R+13] "BTRFS: The Linux B-Tree Filesystem" by Ohad Rodeh, Josef Bacik, Chris Mason. ACM Transactions on Storage, Volume 9 Issue 3, August 2013. *Finally, a good paper on BTRFS, a modern take on copy-on-write file systems.*

[RO91] "Design and Implementation of the Log-structured File System" by Mendel Rosenblum and John Ousterhout. SOSP '91, Pacific Grove, CA, October 1991. *The original SOSP paper about LFS, which has been cited by hundreds of other papers and inspired many real systems.*

[R92] "Design and Implementation of the Log-structured File System" by Mendel Rosenblum. http://www.eecs.berkeley.edu/Pubs/TechRpts/1992/CSD-92-696.pdf. *The award-winning dissertation about LFS, with many of the details missing from the paper.*

[SS+95] "File system logging versus clustering: a performance comparison" by Margo Seltzer, Keith A. Smith, Hari Balakrishnan, Jacqueline Chang, Sara McMains, Venkata Padmanabhan. USENIX 1995 Technical Conference, New Orleans, Louisiana, 1995. *A paper that showed the LFS performance sometimes has problems, particularly for workloads with many calls to `fsync()` (such as database workloads). The paper was controversial at the time.*

[SO90] "Write-Only Disk Caches" by Jon A. Solworth, Cyril U. Orji. SIGMOD '90, Atlantic City, New Jersey, May 1990. *An early study of write buffering and its benefits. However, buffering for too long can be harmful: see Mogul [M94] for details.*

[Z+12] "De-indirection for Flash-based SSDs with Nameless Writes" by Yiying Zhang, Leo Prasath Arulraj, Andrea C. Arpaci-Dusseau, Remzi H. Arpaci-Dusseau. FAST '13, San Jose, California, February 2013. *Our paper on a new way to build flash-based storage devices, to avoid redundant mappings in the file system and FTL. The idea is for the device to pick the physical location of a write, and return the address to the file system, which stores the mapping.*

Homework (Simulation)

This section introduces `lfs.py`, a simple LFS simulator you can use to understand better how an LFS-based file system works. Read the README for details on how to run the simulator.

Questions

1. Run `./lfs.py -n 3`, perhaps varying the seed (`-s`). Can you figure out which commands were run to generate the final file system contents? Can you tell which order those commands were issued? Finally, can you determine the liveness of each block in the final file system state? Use `-o` to show which commands were run, and `-c` to show the liveness of the final file system state. How much harder does the task become for you as you increase the number of commands issued (i.e., change `-n 3` to `-n 5`)?

2. If you find the above painful, you can help yourself a little bit by showing the set of updates caused by each specific command. To do so, run `./lfs.py -n 3 -i`. Now see if it is easier to understand what each command must have been. Change the random seed to get different commands to interpret (e.g., `-s 1`, `-s 2`, `-s 3`, etc.).

3. To further test your ability to figure out what updates are made to disk by each command, run the following: `./lfs.py -o -F -s 100` (and perhaps a few other random seeds). This just shows a set of commands and does NOT show you the final state of the file system. Can you reason about what the final state of the file system must be?

4. Now see if you can determine which files and directories are live after a number of file and directory operations. Run `tt ./lfs.py -n 20 -s 1` and then examine the final file system state. Can you figure out which pathnames are valid? Run `tt ./lfs.py -n 20 -s 1 -c -v` to see the results. Run with `-o` to see if your answers match up given the series of random commands. Use different random seeds to get more problems.

5. Now let's issue some specific commands. First, let's create a file and write to it repeatedly. To do so, use the `-L` flag, which lets you specify specific commands to execute. Let's create the file "/foo" and write to it four times:
`-L c,/foo:w,/foo,0,1:w,/foo,1,1:w,/foo,2,1:w,/foo,3,1 -o`. See if you can determine the liveness of the final file system state; use `-c` to check your answers.

6. Now, let's do the same thing, but with a single write operation instead of four. Run `./lfs.py -o -L c,/foo:w,/foo,0,4` to create file "/foo" and write 4 blocks with a single write operation.

Compute the liveness again, and check if you are right with `-c`. What is the main difference between writing a file all at once (as we do here) versus doing it one block at a time (as above)? What does this tell you about the importance of buffering updates in main memory as the real LFS does?

7. Let's do another specific example. First, run the following: `./lfs.py -L c,/foo:w,/foo,0,1`. What does this set of commands do? Now, run `./lfs.py -L c,/foo:w,/foo,7,1`. What does this set of commands do? How are the two different? What can you tell about the `size` field in the inode from these two sets of commands?

8. Now let's look explicitly at file creation versus directory creation. Run simulations `./lfs.py -L c,/foo` and `./lfs.py -L d,/foo` to create a file and then a directory. What is similar about these runs, and what is different?

9. The LFS simulator supports hard links as well. Run the following to study how they work:
`./lfs.py -L c,/foo:l,/foo,/bar:l,/foo,/goo -o -i`.
What blocks are written out when a hard link is created? How is this similar to just creating a new file, and how is it different? How does the reference count field change as links are created?

10. LFS makes many different policy decisions. We do not explore many of them here – perhaps something left for the future – but here is a simple one we do explore: the choice of inode number. First, run `./lfs.py -p c100 -n 10 -o -a s` to show the usual behavior with the "sequential" allocation policy, which tries to use free inode numbers nearest to zero. Then, change to a "random" policy by running `./lfs.py -p c100 -n 10 -o -a r` (the `-p c100` flag ensures 100 percent of the random operations are file creations). What on-disk differences does a random policy versus a sequential policy result in? What does this say about the importance of choosing inode numbers in a real LFS?

11. One last thing we've been assuming is that the LFS simulator always updates the checkpoint region after each update. In the real LFS, that isn't the case: it is updated periodically to avoid long seeks. Run `./lfs.py -N -i -o -s 1000` to see some operations and the intermediate and final states of the file system when the checkpoint region isn't forced to disk. What would happen if the checkpoint region is never updated? What if it is updated periodically? Could you figure out how to recover the file system to the latest state by rolling forward in the log?

44

Flash-based SSDs

After decades of hard-disk drive dominance, a new form of persistent storage device has recently gained significance in the world. Generically referred to as **solid-state storage**, such devices have no mechanical or moving parts like hard drives; rather, they are simply built out of transistors, much like memory and processors. However, unlike typical random-access memory (e.g., DRAM), such a **solid-state storage device** (a.k.a., an **SSD**) retains information despite power loss, and thus is an ideal candidate for use in persistent storage of data.

The technology we'll focus on is known as **flash** (more specifically, **NAND-based flash**), which was created by Fujio Masuoka in the 1980s [M+14]. Flash, as we'll see, has some unique properties. For example, to write to a given chunk of it (i.e., a **flash page**), you first have to erase a bigger chunk (i.e., a **flash block**), which can be quite expensive. In addition, writing too often to a page will cause it to **wear out**. These two properties make construction of a flash-based SSD an interesting challenge:

> CRUX: HOW TO BUILD A FLASH-BASED SSD
>
> How can we build a flash-based SSD? How can we handle the expensive nature of erasing? How can we build a device that lasts a long time, given that repeated overwrite will wear the device out? Will the march of progress in technology ever cease? Or cease to amaze?

44.1 Storing a Single Bit

Flash chips are designed to store one or more bits in a single transistor; the level of charge trapped within the transistor is mapped to a binary value. In a **single-level cell** (**SLC**) flash, only a single bit is stored within a transistor (i.e., 1 or 0); with a **multi-level cell** (**MLC**) flash, two bits are encoded into different levels of charge, e.g., 00, 01, 10, and 11 are represented by low, somewhat low, somewhat high, and high levels. There is even **triple-level cell** (**TLC**) flash, which encodes 3 bits per cell. Overall, SLC chips achieve higher performance and are more expensive.

> **TIP: BE CAREFUL WITH TERMINOLOGY**
> You may have noticed that some terms we have used many times before (blocks, pages) are being used within the context of a flash, but in slightly different ways than before. New terms are not created to make your life harder (although they may be doing just that), but arise because there is no central authority where terminology decisions are made. What is a block to you may be a page to someone else, and vice versa, depending on the context. Your job is simple: to know the appropriate terms within each domain, and use them such that people well-versed in the discipline can understand what you are talking about. It's one of those times where the only solution is simple but sometimes painful: use your memory.

Of course, there are many details as to exactly how such bit-level storage operates, down at the level of device physics. While beyond the scope of this book, you can read more about it on your own [J10].

44.2 From Bits to Banks/Planes

As they say in ancient Greece, storing a single bit (or a few) does not a storage system make. Hence, flash chips are organized into **banks** or **planes** which consist of a large number of cells.

A bank is accessed in two different sized units: **blocks** (sometimes called **erase blocks**), which are typically of size 128 KB or 256 KB, and **pages**, which are a few KB in size (e.g., 4KB). Within each bank there are a large number of blocks; within each block, there are a large number of pages. When thinking about flash, you must remember this new terminology, which is different than the blocks we refer to in disks and RAIDs and the pages we refer to in virtual memory.

Figure 441 shows an example of a flash plane with blocks and pages; there are three blocks, each containing four pages, in this simple example. We'll see below why we distinguish between blocks and pages; it turns out this distinction is critical for flash operations such as reading and writing, and even more so for the overall performance of the device. The most important (and weird) thing you will learn is that to write to a page within a block, you first have to erase the entire block; this tricky detail makes building a flash-based SSD an interesting and worthwhile challenge, and the subject of the second-half of the chapter.

Block:	0				1				2			
Page:	00	01	02	03	04	05	06	07	08	09	10	11
Content:												

Figure 441: **A Simple Flash Chip: Pages Within Blocks**

44.3 Basic Flash Operations

Given this flash organization, there are three low-level operations that a flash chip supports. The **read** command is used to read a page from the flash; **erase** and **program** are used in tandem to write. The details:

- **Read (a page)**: A client of the flash chip can read any page (e.g., 2KB or 4KB), simply by specifying the read command and appropriate page number to the device. This operation is typically quite fast, 10s of microseconds or so, regardless of location on the device, and (more or less) regardless of the location of the previous request (quite unlike a disk). Being able to access any location uniformly quickly means the device is a **random access** device.
- **Erase (a block):** Before writing to a *page* within a flash, the nature of the device requires that you first **erase** the entire *block* the page lies within. Erase, importantly, destroys the contents of the block (by setting each bit to the value 1); therefore, you must be sure that any data you care about in the block has been copied elsewhere (to memory, or perhaps to another flash block) *before* executing the erase. The erase command is quite expensive, taking a few milliseconds to complete. Once finished, the entire block is reset and each page is ready to be programmed.
- **Program (a page):** Once a block has been erased, the program command can be used to change some of the 1's within a page to 0's, and write the desired contents of a page to the flash. Programming a page is less expensive than erasing a block, but more costly than reading a page, usually taking around 100s of microseconds on modern flash chips.

One way to think about flash chips is that each page has a state associated with it. Pages start in an `INVALID` state. By erasing the block that a page resides within, you set the state of the page (and all pages within that block) to `ERASED`, which resets the content of each page in the block but also (importantly) makes them programmable. When you program a page, its state changes to `VALID`, meaning its contents have been set and can be read. Reads do not affect these states (although you should only read from pages that have been programmed). Once a page has been programmed, the only way to change its contents is to erase the entire block within which the page resides. Here is an example of states transition after various erase and program operations within a 4-page block:

		`iiii`	*Initial: pages in block are invalid* (`i`)
Erase()	→	`EEEE`	*State of pages in block set to erased* (`E`)
Program(0)	→	`VEEE`	*Program page 0; state set to valid* (`V`)
Program(0)	→	**error**	*Cannot re-program page after programming*
Program(1)	→	`VVEE`	*Program page 1*
Erase()	→	`EEEE`	*Contents erased; all pages programmable*

A Detailed Example

Because the process of writing (i.e., erasing and programming) is so unusual, let's go through a detailed example to make sure it makes sense. In this example, imagine we have the following four 8-bit pages, within a 4-page block (both unrealistically small sizes, but useful within this example); each page is `VALID` as each has been previously programmed.

Page 0	Page 1	Page 2	Page 3
00011000	11001110	00000001	00111111
VALID	VALID	VALID	VALID

Now say we wish to write to page 0, filling it with new contents. To write any page, we must first erase the entire block. Let's assume we do so, thus leaving the block in this state:

Page 0	Page 1	Page 2	Page 3
11111111	11111111	11111111	11111111
ERASED	ERASED	ERASED	ERASED

Good news! We could now go ahead and program page 0, for example with the contents `00000011`, overwriting the old page 0 (contents `00011000`) as desired. After doing so, our block looks like this:

Page 0	Page 1	Page 2	Page 3
00000011	11111111	11111111	11111111
VALID	ERASED	ERASED	ERASED

And now the bad news: the previous contents of pages 1, 2, and 3 are all gone! Thus, before overwriting any page *within* a block, we must first move any data we care about to another location (e.g., memory, or elsewhere on the flash). The nature of erase will have a strong impact on how we design flash-based SSDs, as we'll soon learn about.

Summary

To summarize, reading a page is easy: just read the page. Flash chips do this quite well, and quickly; in terms of performance, they offer the potential to greatly exceed the random read performance of modern disk drives, which are slow due to mechanical seek and rotation costs.

Writing a page is trickier; the entire block must first be erased (taking care to first move any data we care about to another location), and then the desired page programmed. Not only is this expensive, but frequent repetitions of this program/erase cycle can lead to the biggest reliability problem flash chips have: **wear out**. When designing a storage system with flash, the performance and reliability of writing is a central focus. We'll soon learn more about how modern SSDs attack these issues, delivering excellent performance and reliability despite these limitations.

Device	Read (μs)	Program (μs)	Erase (μs)
SLC	25	200-300	1500-2000
MLC	50	600-900	~3000
TLC	~75	~900-1350	~4500

Figure 442: **Raw Flash Performance Characteristics**

44.4 Flash Performance And Reliability

Because we're interested in building a storage device out of raw flash chips, it is worthwhile to understand their basic performance characteristics. Figure 442 presents a rough summary of some numbers found in the popular press [V12]. Therein, the author presents the basic operation latency of reads, programs, and erases across SLC, MLC, and TLC flash, which store 1, 2, and 3 bits of information per cell, respectively.

As we can see from the table, read latencies are quite good, taking just 10s of microseconds to complete. Program latency is higher and more variable, as low as 200 microseconds for SLC, but higher as you pack more bits into each cell; to get good write performance, you will have to make use of multiple flash chips in parallel. Finally, erases are quite expensive, taking a few milliseconds typically. Dealing with this cost is central to modern flash storage design.

Let's now consider reliability of flash chips. Unlike mechanical disks, which can fail for a wide variety of reasons (including the gruesome and quite physical **head crash**, where the drive head actually makes contact with the recording surface), flash chips are pure silicon and in that sense have fewer reliability issues to worry about. The primary concern is **wear out**; when a flash block is erased and programmed, it slowly accrues a little bit of extra charge. Over time, as that extra charge builds up, it becomes increasingly difficult to differentiate between a 0 and a 1. At the point where it becomes impossible, the block becomes unusable.

The typical lifetime of a block is currently not well known. Manufacturers rate MLC-based blocks as having a 10,000 P/E (Program/Erase) cycle lifetime; that is, each block can be erased and programmed 10,000 times before failing. SLC-based chips, because they store only a single bit per transistor, are rated with a longer lifetime, usually 100,000 P/E cycles. However, recent research has shown that lifetimes are much longer than expected [BD10].

One other reliability problem within flash chips is known as **disturbance**. When accessing a particular page within a flash, it is possible that some bits get flipped in neighboring pages; such bit flips are known as **read disturbs** or **program disturbs**, depending on whether the page is being read or programmed, respectively.

TIP: THE IMPORTANCE OF BACKWARDS COMPATIBILITY

Backwards compatibility is always a concern in layered systems. By defining a stable interface between two systems, one enables innovation on each side of the interface while ensuring continued interoperability. Such an approach has been quite successful in many domains: operating systems have relatively stable APIs for applications, disks provide the same block-based interface to file systems, and each layer in the IP networking stack provides a fixed unchanging interface to the layer above.

Not surprisingly, there can be a downside to such rigidity, as interfaces defined in one generation may not be appropriate in the next. In some cases, it may be useful to think about redesigning the entire system entirely. An excellent example is found in the Sun ZFS file system [B07]; by reconsidering the interaction of file systems and RAID, the creators of ZFS envisioned (and then realized) a more effective integrated whole.

44.5 From Raw Flash to Flash-Based SSDs

Given our basic understanding of flash chips, we now face our next task: how to turn a basic set of flash chips into something that looks like a typical storage device. The standard storage interface is a simple block-based one, where blocks (sectors) of size 512 bytes (or larger) can be read or written, given a block address. The task of the flash-based SSD is to provide that standard block interface atop the raw flash chips inside it.

Internally, an SSD consists of some number of flash chips (for persistent storage). An SSD also contains some amount of volatile (i.e., non-persistent) memory (e.g., SRAM); such memory is useful for caching and buffering of data as well as for mapping tables, which we'll learn about below. Finally, an SSD contains control logic to orchestrate device operation. See Agrawal et. al for details [A+08]; a simplified block diagram is seen in Figure 443 (page 595).

One of the essential functions of this control logic is to satisfy client reads and writes, turning them into internal flash operations as need be. The **flash translation layer**, or **FTL**, provides exactly this functionality. The FTL takes read and write requests on *logical blocks* (that comprise the device interface) and turns them into low-level read, erase, and program commands on the underlying *physical blocks* and *physical pages* (that comprise the actual flash device). The FTL should accomplish this task with the goal of delivering excellent performance and high reliability.

Excellent performance, as we'll see, can be realized through a combination of techniques. One key will be to utilize multiple flash chips in **parallel**; although we won't discuss this technique much further, suffice it to say that all modern SSDs use multiple chips internally to obtain higher performance. Another performance goal will be to reduce **write amplification**, which is defined as the total write traffic (in bytes) issued to the flash chips by the FTL divided by the total write traffic (in bytes) is-

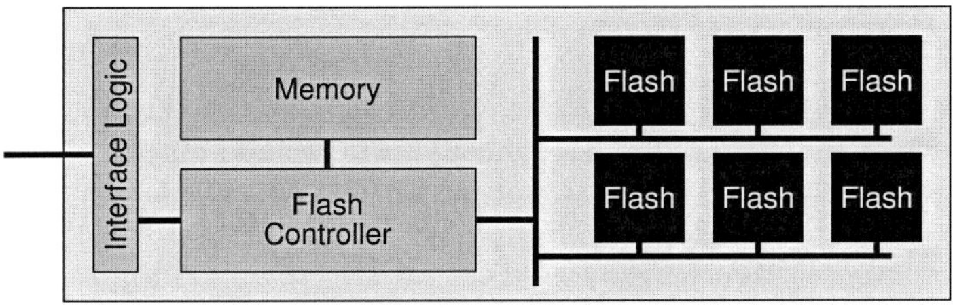

Figure 443: **A Flash-based SSD: Logical Diagram**

sued by the client to the SSD. As we'll see below, naive approaches to FTL construction will lead to high write amplification and low performance.

High reliability will be achieved through the combination of a few different approaches. One main concern, as discussed above, is **wear out**. If a single block is erased and programmed too often, it will become unusable; as a result, the FTL should try to spread writes across the blocks of the flash as evenly as possible, ensuring that all of the blocks of the device wear out at roughly the same time; doing so is called **wear leveling** and is an essential part of any modern FTL.

Another reliability concern is program disturbance. To minimize such disturbance, FTLs will commonly program pages within an erased block *in order*, from low page to high page. This sequential-programming approach minimizes disturbance and is widely utilized.

44.6 FTL Organization: A Bad Approach

The simplest organization of an FTL would be something we call **direct mapped**. In this approach, a read to logical page N is mapped directly to a read of physical page N. A write to logical page N is more complicated; the FTL first has to read in the entire block that page N is contained within; it then has to erase the block; finally, the FTL programs the old pages as well as the new one.

As you can probably guess, the direct-mapped FTL has many problems, both in terms of performance as well as reliability. The performance problems come on each write: the device has to read in the entire block (costly), erase it (quite costly), and then program it (costly). The end result is severe write amplification (proportional to the number of pages in a block) and as a result, terrible write performance, even slower than typical hard drives with their mechanical seeks and rotational delays.

Even worse is the reliability of this approach. If file system metadata or user file data is repeatedly overwritten, the same block is erased and programmed, over and over, rapidly wearing it out and potentially losing data. The direct mapped approach simply gives too much control over wear out to the client workload; if the workload does not spread write load evenly across its logical blocks, the underlying physical blocks containing popular data will quickly wear out. For both reliability and performance reasons, a direct-mapped FTL is a bad idea.

44.7 A Log-Structured FTL

For these reasons, most FTLs today are **log structured**, an idea useful in both storage devices (as we'll see now) and file systems above them (as we'll see in the chapter on **log-structured file systems**). Upon a write to logical block N, the device appends the write to the next free spot in the currently-being-written-to block; we call this style of writing **logging**. To allow for subsequent reads of block N, the device keeps a **mapping table** (in its memory, and persistent, in some form, on the device); this table stores the physical address of each logical block in the system.

Let's go through an example to make sure we understand how the basic log-based approach works. To the client, the device looks like a typical disk, in which it can read and write 512-byte sectors (or groups of sectors). For simplicity, assume that the client is reading or writing 4-KB sized chunks. Let us further assume that the SSD contains some large number of 16-KB sized blocks, each divided into four 4-KB pages; these parameters are unrealistic (flash blocks usually consist of more pages) but will serve our didactic purposes quite well.

Assume the client issues the following sequence of operations:

- Write(100) with contents `a1`
- Write(101) with contents `a2`
- Write(2000) with contents `b1`
- Write(2001) with contents `b2`

These **logical block addresses** (e.g., 100) are used by the client of the SSD (e.g., a file system) to remember where information is located.

Internally, the device must transform these block writes into the erase and program operations supported by the raw hardware, and somehow record, for each logical block address, which **physical page** of the SSD stores its data. Assume that all blocks of the SSD are currently not valid, and must be erased before any page can be programmed. Here we show the initial state of our SSD, with all pages marked `INVALID` (`i`):

Block:	0				1				2			
Page:	00	01	02	03	04	05	06	07	08	09	10	11
Content:												
State:	i	i	i	i	i	i	i	i	i	i	i	i

When the first write is received by the SSD (to logical block 100), the FTL decides to write it to physical block 0, which contains four physical pages: 0, 1, 2, and 3. Because the block is not erased, we cannot write to it yet; the device must first issue an erase command to block 0. Doing so leads to the following state:

Block:	0				1				2			
Page:	00	01	02	03	04	05	06	07	08	09	10	11
Content:												
State:	E	E	E	E	i	i	i	i	i	i	i	i

Block 0 is now ready to be programmed. Most SSDs will write pages in order (i.e., low to high), reducing reliability problems related to **program disturbance**. The SSD then directs the write of logical block 100 into physical page 0:

Block:	0				1				2			
Page:	00	01	02	03	04	05	06	07	08	09	10	11
Content:	a1											
State:	V	E	E	E	i	i	i	i	i	i	i	i

But what if the client wants to *read* logical block 100? How can it find where it is? The SSD must transform a read issued to logical block 100 into a read of physical page 0. To accommodate such functionality, when the FTL writes logical block 100 to physical page 0, it records this fact in an **in-memory mapping table**. We will track the state of this mapping table in the diagrams as well:

Table: 100 → 0 — Memory

Block:	0				1				2				
Page:	00	01	02	03	04	05	06	07	08	09	10	11	Flash
Content:	a1												Chip
State:	V	E	E	E	i	i	i	i	i	i	i	i	

Now you can see what happens when the client writes to the SSD. The SSD finds a location for the write, usually just picking the next free page; it then programs that page with the block's contents, and records the logical-to-physical mapping in its mapping table. Subsequent reads simply use the table to **translate** the logical block address presented by the client into the physical page number required to read the data.

Let's now examine the rest of the writes in our example write stream: 101, 2000, and 2001. After writing these blocks, the state of the device is:

Table: 100 → 0 101 → 1 2000 → 2 2001 → 3 — Memory

Block:	0				1				2				
Page:	00	01	02	03	04	05	06	07	08	09	10	11	Flash
Content:	a1	a2	b1	b2									Chip
State:	V	V	V	V	i	i	i	i	i	i	i	i	

The log-based approach by its nature improves performance (erases only being required once in a while, and the costly read-modify-write of the direct-mapped approach avoided altogether), and greatly enhances reliability. The FTL can now spread writes across all pages, performing what is called **wear leveling** and increasing the lifetime of the device; we'll discuss wear leveling further below.

> **ASIDE: FTL MAPPING INFORMATION PERSISTENCE**
>
> You might be wondering: what happens if the device loses power? Does the in-memory mapping table disappear? Clearly, such information cannot truly be lost, because otherwise the device would not function as a persistent storage device. An SSD must have some means of recovering mapping information.
>
> The simplest thing to do is to record some mapping information with each page, in what is called an **out-of-band** (**OOB**) area. When the device loses power and is restarted, it must reconstruct its mapping table by scanning the OOB areas and reconstructing the mapping table in memory. This basic approach has its problems; scanning a large SSD to find all necessary mapping information is slow. To overcome this limitation, some higher-end devices use more complex **logging** and **checkpointing** techniques to speed up recovery; learn more about logging by reading chapters on crash consistency and log-structured file systems [AD14].

Unfortunately, this basic approach to log structuring has some downsides. The first is that overwrites of logical blocks lead to something we call **garbage**, i.e., old versions of data around the drive and taking up space. The device has to periodically perform **garbage collection** (**GC**) to find said blocks and free space for future writes; excessive garbage collection drives up write amplification and lowers performance. The second is high cost of in-memory mapping tables; the larger the device, the more memory such tables need. We now discuss each in turn.

44.8 Garbage Collection

The first cost of any log-structured approach such as this one is that garbage is created, and therefore **garbage collection** (i.e., dead-block reclamation) must be performed. Let's use our continued example to make sense of this. Recall that logical blocks 100, 101, 2000, and 2001 have been written to the device.

Now, let's assume that blocks 100 and 101 are written to again, with contents `c1` and `c2`. The writes are written to the next free pages (in this case, physical pages 4 and 5), and the mapping table is updated accordingly. Note that the device must have first erased block 1 to make such programming possible:

Table: 100 → 4 101 → 5 2000 → 2 2001 → 3 Memory

Block:	0				1				2				
Page:	00	01	02	03	04	05	06	07	08	09	10	11	Flash Chip
Content:	a1	a2	b1	b2	c1	c2							
State:	V	V	V	V	V	V	E	E	i	i	i	i	

The problem we have now should be obvious: physical pages 0 and 1, although marked `VALID`, have **garbage** in them, i.e., the old versions of blocks 100 and 101. Because of the log-structured nature of the device, overwrites create garbage blocks, which the device must reclaim to provide free space for new writes to take place.

The process of finding garbage blocks (also called **dead blocks**) and reclaiming them for future use is called **garbage collection**, and it is an important component of any modern SSD. The basic process is simple: find a block that contains one or more garbage pages, read in the live (non-garbage) pages from that block, write out those live pages to the log, and (finally) reclaim the entire block for use in writing.

Let's now illustrate with an example. The device decides it wants to reclaim any dead pages within block 0 above. Block 0 has two dead blocks (pages 0 and 1) and two lives blocks (pages 2 and 3, which contain blocks 2000 and 2001, respectively). To do so, the device will:

- Read live data (pages 2 and 3) from block 0
- Write live data to end of the log
- Erase block 0 (freeing it for later usage)

For the garbage collector to function, there must be enough information within each block to enable the SSD to determine whether each page is live or dead. One natural way to achieve this end is to store, at some location within each block, information about which logical blocks are stored within each page. The device can then use the mapping table to determine whether each page within the block holds live data or not.

From our example above (before the garbage collection has taken place), block 0 held logical blocks 100, 101, 2000, 2001. By checking the mapping table (which, before garbage collection, contained `100->4, 101->5, 2000->2, 2001->3`), the device can readily determine whether each of the pages within the SSD block holds live information. For example, 2000 and 2001 clearly are still pointed to by the map; 100 and 101 are not and therefore are candidates for garbage collection.

When this garbage collection process is complete in our example, the state of the device is:

Table: 100 → 4 101 → 5 2000 → 6 2001 → 7 Memory

Block:	0				1				2				
Page:	00	01	02	03	04	05	06	07	08	09	10	11	Flash
Content:					c1	c2	b1	b2					Chip
State:	E	E	E	E	V	V	V	V	i	i	i	i	

As you can see, garbage collection can be expensive, requiring reading and rewriting of live data. The ideal candidate for reclamation is a block that consists of only dead pages; in this case, the block can immediately be erased and used for new data, without expensive data migration.

ASIDE: A NEW STORAGE API KNOWN AS TRIM

When we think of hard drives, we usually just think of the most basic interface to read and write them: read and write (there is also usually some kind of **cache flush** command, ensuring that writes have actually been persisted, but sometimes we omit that for simplicity). With log-structured SSDs, and indeed, any device that keeps a flexible and changing mapping of logical-to-physical blocks, a new interface is useful, known as the **trim** operation.

The trim operation takes an address (and possibly a length) and simply informs the device that the block(s) specified by the address (and length) have been deleted; the device thus no longer has to track any information about the given address range. For a standard hard drive, trim isn't particularly useful, because the drive has a static mapping of block addresses to specific platter, track, and sector(s). For a log-structured SSD, however, it is highly useful to know that a block is no longer needed, as the SSD can then remove this information from the FTL and later reclaim the physical space during garbage collection.

Although we sometimes think of interface and implementation as separate entities, in this case, we see that the implementation shapes the interface. With complex mappings, knowledge of which blocks are no longer needed makes for a more effective implementation.

To reduce GC costs, some SSDs **overprovision** the device [A+08]; by adding extra flash capacity, cleaning can be delayed and pushed to the **background**, perhaps done at a time when the device is less busy. Adding more capacity also increases internal bandwidth, which can be used for cleaning and thus not harm perceived bandwidth to the client. Many modern drives overprovision in this manner, one key to achieving excellent overall performance.

44.9 Mapping Table Size

The second cost of log-structuring is the potential for extremely large mapping tables, with one entry for each 4-KB page of the device. With a large 1-TB SSD, for example, a single 4-byte entry per 4-KB page results in 1 GB of memory needed the device, just for these mappings! Thus, this **page-level** FTL scheme is impractical.

Block-Based Mapping

One approach to reduce the costs of mapping is to only keep a pointer per *block* of the device, instead of per page, reducing the amount of mapping information by a factor of $\frac{Size_{block}}{Size_{page}}$. This **block-level** FTL is akin to having bigger page sizes in a virtual memory system; in that case, you use fewer bits for the VPN and have a larger offset in each virtual address.

Unfortunately, using a block-based mapping inside a log-based FTL does not work very well for performance reasons. The biggest problem arises when a "small write" occurs (i.e., one that is less than the size of a physical block). In this case, the FTL must read a large amount of live data from the old block and copy it into a new one (along with the data from the small write). This data copying increases write amplification greatly and thus decreases performance.

To make this issue more clear, let's look at an example. Assume the client previously wrote out logical blocks 2000, 2001, 2002, and 2003 (with contents, `a`, `b`, `c`, `d`), and that they are located within physical block 1 at physical pages 4, 5, 6, and 7. With per-page mappings, the translation table would have to record four mappings for these logical blocks: 2000→4, 2001→5, 2002→6, 2003→7.

If, instead, we use block-level mapping, the FTL only needs to record a single address translation for all of this data. The address mapping, however, is slightly different than our previous examples. Specifically, we think of the logical address space of the device as being chopped into chunks that are the size of the physical blocks within the flash. Thus, the logical block address consists of two portions: a chunk number and an offset. Because we are assuming four logical blocks fit within each physical block, the offset portion of the logical addresses requires 2 bits; the remaining (most significant) bits form the chunk number.

Logical blocks 2000, 2001, 2002, and 2003 all have the same chunk number (500), and have different offsets (0, 1, 2, and 3, respectively). Thus, with a block-level mapping, the FTL records that chunk 500 maps to block 1 (starting at physical page 4), as shown in this diagram:

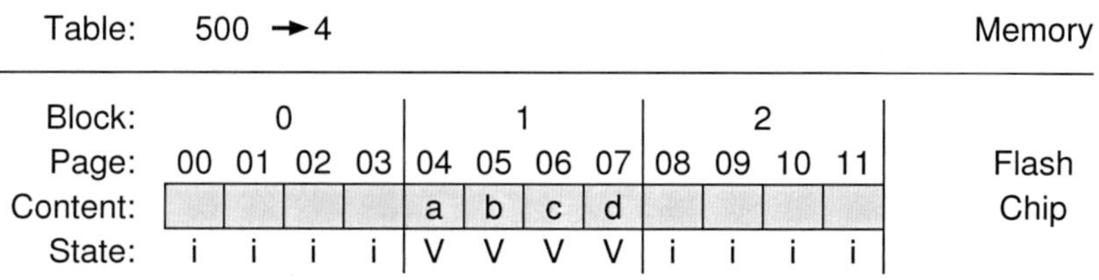

In a block-based FTL, reading is easy. First, the FTL extracts the chunk number from the logical block address presented by the client, by taking the topmost bits out of the address. Then, the FTL looks up the chunk-number to physical-page mapping in the table. Finally, the FTL computes the address of the desired flash page by *adding* the offset from the logical address to the physical address of the block.

For example, if the client issues a read to logical address 2002, the device extracts the logical chunk number (500), looks up the translation in the mapping table (finding 4), and adds the offset from the logical address (2) to the translation (4). The resulting physical-page address (6) is where the data is located; the FTL can then issue the read to that physical address and obtain the desired data (c).

But what if the client writes to logical block 2002 (with contents c')? In this case, the FTL must read in 2000, 2001, and 2003, and then write out all four logical blocks in a new location, updating the mapping table accordingly. Block 1 (where the data used to reside) can then be erased and reused, as shown here.

Table: 500 → 8 Memory

Block:	0				1				2				Flash Chip
Page:	00	01	02	03	04	05	06	07	08	09	10	11	
Content:									a	b	c'	d	
State:	i	i	i	i	E	E	E	E	V	V	V	V	

As you can see from this example, while block level mappings greatly reduce the amount of memory needed for translations, they cause significant performance problems when writes are smaller than the physical block size of the device; as real physical blocks can be 256KB or larger, such writes are likely to happen quite often. Thus, a better solution is needed. Can you sense that this is the part of the chapter where we tell you what that solution is? Better yet, can you figure it out yourself, before reading on?

Hybrid Mapping

To enable flexible writing but also reduce mapping costs, many modern FTLs employ a **hybrid mapping** technique. With this approach, the FTL keeps a few blocks erased and directs all writes to them; these are called **log blocks**. Because the FTL wants to be able to write any page to any location within the log block without all the copying required by a pure block-based mapping, it keeps *per-page* mappings for these log blocks.

The FTL thus logically has two types of mapping table in its memory: a small set of per-page mappings in what we'll call the *log table*, and a larger set of per-block mappings in the *data table*. When looking for a particular logical block, the FTL will first consult the log table; if the logical block's location is not found there, the FTL will then consult the data table to find its location and then access the requested data.

The key to the hybrid mapping strategy is keeping the number of log blocks small. To keep the number of log blocks small, the FTL has to periodically examine log blocks (which have a pointer per page) and *switch* them into blocks that can be pointed to by only a single block pointer. This switch is accomplished by one of three main techniques, based on the contents of the block [KK+02].

For example, let's say the FTL had previously written out logical pages 1000, 1001, 1002, and 1003, and placed them in physical block 2 (physical pages 8, 9, 10, 11); assume the contents of the writes to 1000, 1001, 1002, and 1003 are a, b, c, and d, respectively.

					Memory
Log Table:					
Data Table:	250 → 8				

Block:	0				1				2				
Page:	00	01	02	03	04	05	06	07	08	09	10	11	Flash
Content:									a	b	c	d	Chip
State:	i	i	i	i	i	i	i	i	V	V	V	V	

Now assume that the client overwrites each of these blocks (with data a', b', c', and d'), in the exact same order, in one of the currently available log blocks, say physical block 0 (physical pages 0, 1, 2, and 3). In this case, the FTL will have the following state:

					Memory
Log Table:	1000 → 0	1001 → 1	1002 → 2	1003 → 3	
Data Table:	250 → 8				

Block:	0				1				2				
Page:	00	01	02	03	04	05	06	07	08	09	10	11	Flash
Content:	a'	b'	c'	d'					a	b	c	d	Chip
State:	V	V	V	V	i	i	i	i	V	V	V	V	

Because these blocks have been written exactly in the same manner as before, the FTL can perform what is known as a **switch merge**. In this case, the log block (0) now becomes the storage location for blocks 0, 1, 2, and 3, and is pointed to by a single block pointer; the old block (2) is now erased and used as a log block. In this best case, all the per-page pointers required replaced by a single block pointer.

					Memory
Log Table:					
Data Table:	250 → 0				

Block:	0				1				2				
Page:	00	01	02	03	04	05	06	07	08	09	10	11	Flash
Content:	a'	b'	c'	d'									Chip
State:	V	V	V	V	i	i	i	i	i	i	i	i	

This switch merge is the best case for a hybrid FTL. Unfortunately, sometimes the FTL is not so lucky. Imagine the case where we have the same initial conditions (logical blocks 1000 ... 1003 stored in physical block 2) but then the client overwrites logical blocks 1000 and 1001.

What do you think happens in this case? Why is it more challenging to handle? *(think before looking at the result on the next page)*

Log Table:	1000→0			1001→1									
Data Table:	250 →8												Memory
Block:	0				1				2				
Page:	00	01	02	03	04	05	06	07	08	09	10	11	Flash
Content:	a'	b'							a	b	c	d	Chip
State:	V	V	i	i	i	i	i	i	V	V	V	V	

To reunite the other pages of this physical block, and thus be able to refer to them by only a single block pointer, the FTL performs what is called a **partial merge**. In this operation, logical blocks 1002 and 1003 are read from physical block 2, and then appended to the log. The resulting state of the SSD is the same as the switch merge above; however, in this case, the FTL had to perform extra I/O to achieve its goals, thus increasing write amplification.

The final case encountered by the FTL known as a **full merge**, and requires even more work. In this case, the FTL must pull together pages from many other blocks to perform cleaning. For example, imagine that logical blocks 0, 4, 8, and 12 are written to log block A. To switch this log block into a block-mapped page, the FTL must first create a data block containing logical blocks 0, 1, 2, and 3, and thus the FTL must read 1, 2, and 3 from elsewhere and then write out 0, 1, 2, and 3 together. Next, the merge must do the same for logical block 4, finding 5, 6, and 7 and reconciling them into a single physical block. The same must be done for logical blocks 8 and 12, and then (finally), the log block A can be freed. Frequent full merges, as is not surprising, can seriously harm performance and thus should be avoided when at all possible [GY+09].

Page Mapping Plus Caching

Given the complexity of the hybrid approach above, others have suggested simpler ways to reduce the memory load of page-mapped FTLs. Probably the simplest is just to cache only the active parts of the FTL in memory, thus reducing the amount of memory needed [GY+09].

This approach can work well. For example, if a given workload only accesses a small set of pages, the translations of those pages will be stored in the in-memory FTL, and performance will be excellent without high memory cost. Of course, the approach can also perform poorly. If memory cannot contain the **working set** of necessary translations, each access will minimally require an extra flash read to first bring in the missing mapping before being able to access the data itself. Even worse, to make room for the new mapping, the FTL might have to **evict** an old mapping, and if that mapping is **dirty** (i.e., not yet written to the flash persistently), an extra write will also be incurred. However, in many cases, the workload will display locality, and this caching approach will both reduce memory overheads and keep performance high.

44.10 Wear Leveling

Finally, a related background activity that modern FTLs must implement is **wear leveling**, as introduced above. The basic idea is simple: because multiple erase/program cycles will wear out a flash block, the FTL should try its best to spread that work across all the blocks of the device evenly. In this manner, all blocks will wear out at roughly the same time, instead of a few "popular" blocks quickly becoming unusable.

The basic log-structuring approach does a good initial job of spreading out write load, and garbage collection helps as well. However, sometimes a block will be filled with long-lived data that does not get over-written; in this case, garbage collection will never reclaim the block, and thus it does not receive its fair share of the write load.

To remedy this problem, the FTL must periodically read all the live data out of such blocks and re-write it elsewhere, thus making the block available for writing again. This process of wear leveling increases the write amplification of the SSD, and thus decreases performance as extra I/O is required to ensure that all blocks wear at roughly the same rate. Many different algorithms exist in the literature [A+08, M+14]; read more if you are interested.

44.11 SSD Performance And Cost

Before closing, let's examine the performance and cost of modern SSDs, to better understand how they will likely be used in persistent storage systems. In both cases, we'll compare to classic hard-disk drives (HDDs), and highlight the biggest differences between the two.

Performance

Unlike hard disk drives, flash-based SSDs have no mechanical components, and in fact are in many ways more similar to DRAM, in that they are "random access" devices. The biggest difference in performance, as compared to disk drives, is realized when performing random reads and writes; while a typical disk drive can only perform a few hundred random I/Os per second, SSDs can do much better. Here, we use some data from modern SSDs to see just how much better SSDs perform; we're particularly interested in how well the FTLs hide the performance issues of the raw chips.

Table 444 shows some performance data for three different SSDs and one top-of-the-line hard drive; the data was taken from a few different online sources [S13, T15]. The left two columns show random I/O performance, and the right two columns sequential; the first three rows show data for three different SSDs (from Samsung, Seagate, and Intel), and the last row shows performance for a **hard disk drive** (or **HDD**), in this case a Seagate high-end drive.

We can learn a few interesting facts from the table. First, and most dramatic, is the difference in random I/O performance between the SSDs

Device	Random Reads (MB/s)	Random Writes (MB/s)	Sequential Reads (MB/s)	Sequential Writes (MB/s)
Samsung 840 Pro SSD	103	287	421	384
Seagate 600 SSD	84	252	424	374
Intel SSD 335 SSD	39	222	344	354
Seagate Savvio 15K.3 HDD	2	2	223	223

Figure 444: **SSDs And Hard Drives: Performance Comparison**

and the lone hard drive. While the SSDs obtain tens or even hundreds of MB/s in random I/Os, this "high performance" hard drive has a peak of just a couple MB/s (in fact, we rounded up to get to 2 MB/s). Second, you can see that in terms of sequential performance, there is much less of a difference; while the SSDs perform better, a hard drive is still a good choice if sequential performance is all you need. Third, you can see that SSD random read performance is not as good as SSD random write performance. The reason for such unexpectedly good random-write performance is due to the log-structured design of many SSDs, which transforms random writes into sequential ones and improves performance. Finally, because SSDs exhibit some performance difference between sequential and random I/Os, many of the techniques we will learn in subsequent chapters about how to build file systems for hard drives are still applicable to SSDs; although the magnitude of difference between sequential and random I/Os is smaller, there is enough of a gap to carefully consider how to design file systems to reduce random I/Os.

Cost

As we saw above, the performance of SSDs greatly outstrips modern hard drives, even when performing sequential I/O. So why haven't SSDs completely replaced hard drives as the storage medium of choice? The answer is simple: cost, or more specifically, cost per unit of capacity. Currently [A15], an SSD costs something like $150 for a 250-GB drive; such an SSD costs 60 cents per GB. A typical hard drive costs roughly $50 for 1-TB of storage, which means it costs 5 cents per GB. There is still more than a 10× difference in cost between these two storage media.

These performance and cost differences dictate how large-scale storage systems are built. If performance is the main concern, SSDs are a terrific choice, particularly if random read performance is important. If, on the other hand, you are assembling a large data center and wish to store massive amounts of information, the large cost difference will drive you towards hard drives. Of course, a hybrid approach can make sense – some storage systems are being assembled with both SSDs and hard drives, using a smaller number of SSDs for more popular "hot" data and delivering high performance, while storing the rest of the "colder" (less used) data on hard drives to save on cost. As long as the price gap exists, hard drives are here to stay.

44.12 Summary

Flash-based SSDs are becoming a common presence in laptops, desktops, and servers inside the datacenters that power the world's economy. Thus, you should probably know something about them, right?

Here's the bad news: this chapter (like many in this book) is just the first step in understanding the state of the art. Some places to get some more information about the raw technology include research on actual device performance (such as that by Chen et al. [CK+09] and Grupp et al. [GC+09]), issues in FTL design (including works by Agrawal et al. [A+08], Gupta et al. [GY+09], Huang et al. [H+14], Kim et al. [KK+02], Lee et al. [L+07], and Zhang et al. [Z+12]), and even distributed systems comprised of flash (including Gordon [CG+09] and CORFU [B+12]). And, if we may say so, a really good overview of all the things you need to do to extract high performance from an SSD can be found in a paper on the "unwritten contract" [HK+17].

Don't just read academic papers; also read about recent advances in the popular press (e.g., [V12]). Therein you'll learn more practical (but still useful) information, such as Samsung's use of both TLC and SLC cells within the same SSD to maximize performance (SLC can buffer writes quickly) as well as capacity (TLC can store more bits per cell). And this is, as they say, just the tip of the iceberg. Dive in and learn more about this "iceberg" of research on your own, perhaps starting with Ma et al.'s excellent (and recent) survey [M+14]. Be careful though; icebergs can sink even the mightiest of ships [W15].

ASIDE: KEY SSD TERMS

- A **flash chip** consists of many banks, each of which is organized into **erase blocks** (sometimes just called **blocks**). Each block is further subdivided into some number of **pages**.
- Blocks are large (128KB–2MB) and contain many pages, which are relatively small (1KB–8KB).
- To read from flash, issue a read command with an address and length; this allows a client to read one or more pages.
- Writing flash is more complex. First, the client must **erase** the entire block (which deletes all information within the block). Then, the client can **program** each page exactly once, thus completing the write.
- A new **trim** operation is useful to tell the device when a particular block (or range of blocks) is no longer needed.
- Flash reliability is mostly determined by **wear out**; if a block is erased and programmed too often, it will become unusable.
- A flash-based **solid-state storage device** (**SSD**) behaves as if it were a normal block-based read/write disk; by using a **flash translation layer** (**FTL**), it transforms reads and writes from a client into reads, erases, and programs to underlying flash chips.
- Most FTLs are **log-structured**, which reduces the cost of writing by minimizing erase/program cycles. An in-memory translation layer tracks where logical writes were located within the physical medium.
- One key problem with log-structured FTLs is the cost of **garbage collection**, which leads to **write amplification**.
- Another problem is the size of the mapping table, which can become quite large. Using a **hybrid mapping** or just **caching** hot pieces of the FTL are possible remedies.
- One last problem is **wear leveling**; the FTL must occasionally migrate data from blocks that are mostly read in order to ensure said blocks also receive their share of the erase/program load.

References

[A+08] "Design Tradeoffs for SSD Performance" by N. Agrawal, V. Prabhakaran, T. Wobber, J. D. Davis, M. Manasse, R. Panigrahy. USENIX '08, San Diego California, June 2008. *An excellent overview of what goes into SSD design.*

[AD14] "Operating Systems: Three Easy Pieces" by *Chapters: Crash Consistency: FSCK and Journaling and Log-Structured File Systems.* Remzi Arpaci-Dusseau and Andrea Arpaci-Dusseau. *A lot more detail here about how logging can be used in file systems; some of the same ideas can be applied inside devices too as need be.*

[A15] "Amazon Pricing Study" by Remzi Arpaci-Dusseau. February, 2015. *This is not an actual paper, but rather one of the authors going to Amazon and looking at current prices of hard drives and SSDs. You too can repeat this study, and see what the costs are today. Do it!*

[B+12] "CORFU: A Shared Log Design for Flash Clusters" by M. Balakrishnan, D. Malkhi, V. Prabhakaran, T. Wobber, M. Wei, J. D. Davis. NSDI '12, San Jose, California, April 2012. *A new way to think about designing a high-performance replicated log for clusters using Flash.*

[BD10] "Write Endurance in Flash Drives: Measurements and Analysis" by Simona Boboila, Peter Desnoyers. FAST '10, San Jose, California, February 2010. *A cool paper that reverse engineers flash-device lifetimes. Endurance sometimes far exceeds manufacturer predictions, by up to 100×.*

[B07] "ZFS: The Last Word in File Systems" by Jeff Bonwick and Bill Moore. Available here: `http://www.ostep.org/Citations/zfs_last.pdf`. *Was this the last word in file systems? No, but maybe it's close.*

[CG+09] "Gordon: Using Flash Memory to Build Fast, Power-efficient Clusters for Data-intensive Applications" by Adrian M. Caulfield, Laura M. Grupp, Steven Swanson. ASPLOS '09, Washington, D.C., March 2009. *Early research on assembling flash into larger-scale clusters; definitely worth a read.*

[CK+09] "Understanding Intrinsic Characteristics and System Implications of Flash Memory based Solid State Drives" by Feng Chen, David A. Koufaty, and Xiaodong Zhang. SIGMETRICS/Performance '09, Seattle, Washington, June 2009. *An excellent overview of SSD performance problems circa 2009 (though now a little dated).*

[G14] "The SSD Endurance Experiment" by Geoff Gasior. The Tech Report, September 19, 2014. Available: `http://techreport.com/review/27062`. *A nice set of simple experiments measuring performance of SSDs over time. There are many other similar studies; use google to find more.*

[GC+09] "Characterizing Flash Memory: Anomalies, Observations, and Applications" by L. M. Grupp, A. M. Caulfield, J. Coburn, S. Swanson, E. Yaakobi, P. H. Siegel, J. K. Wolf. IEEE MICRO '09, New York, New York, December 2009. *Another excellent characterization of flash performance.*

[GY+09] "DFTL: a Flash Translation Layer Employing Demand-Based Selective Caching of Page-Level Address Mappings" by Aayush Gupta, Youngjae Kim, Bhuvan Urgaonkar. ASPLOS '09, Washington, D.C., March 2009. *This paper gives an excellent overview of different strategies for cleaning within hybrid SSDs as well as a new scheme which saves mapping table space and improves performance under many workloads.*

[HK+17] "The Unwritten Contract of Solid State Drives" by Jun He, Sudarsun Kannan, Andrea C. Arpaci-Dusseau, Remzi H. Arpaci-Dusseau. EuroSys '17, Belgrade, Serbia, April 2017. *Our own paper which lays out five rules clients should follow in order to get the best performance out of modern SSDs. The rules are request scale, locality, aligned sequentiality, grouping by death time, and uniform lifetime. Read the paper for details!*

[H+14] "An Aggressive Worn-out Flash Block Management Scheme To Alleviate SSD Performance Degradation" by Ping Huang, Guanying Wu, Xubin He, Weijun Xiao. EuroSys '14, 2014. *Recent work showing how to really get the most out of worn-out flash blocks; neat!*

[J10] "Failure Mechanisms and Models for Semiconductor Devices" by Unknown author. Report JEP122F, November 2010. Available on the internet at this exciting so-called web site: `http://www.jedec.org/sites/default/files/docs/JEP122F.pdf`. *A highly detailed discussion of what is going on at the device level and how such devices fail. Only for those not faint of heart. Or physicists. Or both.*

[KK+02] "A Space-Efficient Flash Translation Layer For Compact Flash Systems" by Jesung Kim, Jong Min Kim, Sam H. Noh, Sang Lyul Min, Yookun Cho. IEEE Transactions on Consumer Electronics, Volume 48, Number 2, May 2002. *One of the earliest proposals to suggest hybrid mappings.*

[L+07] "A Log Buffer-Based Flash Translation Layer by Using Fully-Associative Sector Translation. " Sang-won Lee, Tae-Sun Chung, Dong-Ho Lee, Sangwon Park, Ha-Joo Song. ACM Transactions on Embedded Computing Systems, Volume 6, Number 3, July 2007 *A terrific paper about how to build hybrid log/block mappings.*

[M+14] "A Survey of Address Translation Technologies for Flash Memories" by Dongzhe Ma, Jianhua Feng, Guoliang Li. ACM Computing Surveys, Volume 46, Number 3, January 2014. *Probably the best recent survey of flash and related technologies.*

[S13] "The Seagate 600 and 600 Pro SSD Review" by Anand Lal Shimpi. AnandTech, May 7, 2013. Available: `http://www.anandtech.com/show/6935/seagate-600-ssd-review`. *One of many SSD performance measurements available on the internet. Haven't heard of the internet? No problem. Just go to your web browser and type "internet" into the search tool. You'll be amazed at what you can learn.*

[T15] "Performance Charts Hard Drives" by Tom's Hardware. January 2015. Available here: `http://www.tomshardware.com/charts/enterprise-hdd-charts`. *Yet another site with performance data, this time focusing on hard drives.*

[V12] "Understanding TLC Flash" by Kristian Vatto. AnandTech, September, 2012. Available: `http://www.anandtech.com/show/5067/understanding-tlc-nand`. *A short description about TLC flash and its characteristics.*

[W15] "List of Ships Sunk by Icebergs" by Many authors. Available at this location on the "web": `http://en.wikipedia.org/wiki/List_of_ships_sunk_by_icebergs`. *Yes, there is a wikipedia page about ships sunk by icebergs. It is a really boring page and basically everyone knows the only ship the iceberg-sinking-mafia cares about is the Titanic.*

[Z+12] "De-indirection for Flash-based SSDs with Nameless Writes" by Yiying Zhang, Leo Prasath Arulraj, Andrea C. Arpaci-Dusseau, Remzi H. Arpaci-Dusseau. FAST '13, San Jose, California, February 2013. *Our research on a new idea to reduce mapping table space; the key is to re-use the pointers in the file system above to store locations of blocks, instead of adding another level of indirection.*

Homework (Simulation)

This section introduces `ssd.py`, a simple SSD simulator you can use to understand better how SSDs work. Read the README for details on how to run the simulator. It is a long README, so boil a cup of tea (caffeinated likely necessary), put on your reading glasses, let the cat curl up on your lap[1], and get to work.

Questions

1. The homework will mostly focus on the log-structured SSD, which is simulated with the "-T log" flag. We'll use the other types of SSDs for comparison. First, run with flags `-T log -s 1 -n 10 -q`. Can you figure out which operations took place? Use `-c` to check your answers (or just use `-C` instead of `-q -c`). Use different values of `-s` to generate different random workloads.
2. Now just show the commands and see if you can figure out the intermediate states of the Flash. Run with flags `-T log -s 2 -n 10 -C` to show each command. Now, determine the state of the Flash between each command; use `-F` to show the states and see if you were right. Use different random seeds to test your burgeoning expertise.
3. Let's make this problem ever so slightly more interesting by adding the `-r 20` flag. What differences does this cause in the commands? Use `-c` again to check your answers.
4. Performance is determined by the number of erases, programs, and reads (we assume here that trims are free). Run the same workload again as above, but without showing any intermediate states (e.g., `-T log -s 1 -n 10`). Can you estimate how long this workload will take to complete? (default erase time is 1000 microseconds, program time is 40, and read time is 10) Use the `-S` flag to check your answer. You can also change the erase, program, and read times with the `-E, -W, -R` flags.
5. Now, compare performance of the log-structured approach and the (very bad) direct approach (`-T direct` instead of `-T log`). First, estimate how you think the direct approach will perform, then check your answer with the `-S` flag. In general, how much better will the log-structured approach perform than the direct one?
6. Let us next explore the behavior of the garbage collector. To do so, we have to set the high (`-G`) and low (`-g`) watermarks appropriately. First, let's observe what happens when you run a larger workload to the log-structured SSD but without any garbage collection. To do this, run with flags `-T log -n 1000` (the high wa-

[1]Now you might complain, "But I'm a dog person!" To this, we say, too bad! Get a cat, put it on your lap, and do the homework! How else will you learn, if you can't even follow the most basic of instructions?

termark default is 10, so the GC won't run in this configuration). What do you think will happen? Use `-C` and perhaps `-F` to see.

7. To turn on the garbage collector, use lower values. The high watermark (`-G N`) tells the system to start collecting once `N` blocks have been used; the low watermark (`-G M`) tells the system to stop collecting once there are only `M` blocks in use. What watermark values do you think will make for a working system? Use `-C` and `-F` to show the commands and intermediate device states and see.
8. One other useful flag is `-J`, which shows what the collector is doing when it runs. Run with flags `-T log -n 1000 -C -J` to see both the commands and the GC behavior. What do you notice about the GC? The final effect of GC, of course, is performance. Use `-S` to look at final statistics; how many extra reads and writes occur due to garbage collection? Compare this to the ideal SSD (`-T ideal`); how much extra reading, writing, and erasing is there due to the nature of Flash? Compare it also to the `direct` approach; in what way (erases, reads, programs) is the log-structured approach superior?
9. One last aspect to explore is **workload skew**. Adding skew to the workload changes writes such that more writes occur to some smaller fraction of the logical block space. For example, running with `-K 80/20` makes 80% of the writes go to 20% of the blocks. Pick some different skews and perform many randomly-chosen operations (e.g., `-n 1000`), using first `-T direct` to understand the skew, and then `-T log` to see the impact on a log-structured device. What do you expect will happen? One other small skew control to explore is `-k 100`; by adding this flag to a skewed workload, the first 100 writes are not skewed. The idea is to first create a lot of data, but then only update some of it. What impact might that have upon a garbage collector?

45

Data Integrity and Protection

Beyond the basic advances found in the file systems we have studied thus far, a number of features are worth studying. In this chapter, we focus on reliability once again (having previously studied storage system reliability in the RAID chapter). Specifically, how should a file system or storage system ensure that data is safe, given the unreliable nature of modern storage devices?

This general area is referred to as **data integrity** or **data protection**. Thus, we will now investigate techniques used to ensure that the data you put into your storage system is the same when the storage system returns it to you.

> CRUX: HOW TO ENSURE DATA INTEGRITY
>
> How should systems ensure that the data written to storage is protected? What techniques are required? How can such techniques be made efficient, with both low space and time overheads?

45.1 Disk Failure Modes

As you learned in the chapter about RAID, disks are not perfect, and can fail (on occasion). In early RAID systems, the model of failure was quite simple: either the entire disk is working, or it fails completely, and the detection of such a failure is straightforward. This **fail-stop** model of disk failure makes building RAID relatively simple [S90].

What you didn't learn is about all of the other types of failure modes modern disks exhibit. Specifically, as Bairavasundaram et al. studied in great detail [B+07, B+08], modern disks will occasionally seem to be mostly working but have trouble successfully accessing one or more blocks. Specifically, two types of single-block failures are common and worthy of consideration: **latent-sector errors** (**LSEs**) and **block corruption**. We'll now discuss each in more detail.

	Cheap	Costly
LSEs	9.40%	1.40%
Corruption	0.50%	0.05%

Figure 451: **Frequency Of LSEs And Block Corruption**

LSEs arise when a disk sector (or group of sectors) has been damaged in some way. For example, if the disk head touches the surface for some reason (a **head crash**, something which shouldn't happen during normal operation), it may damage the surface, making the bits unreadable. Cosmic rays can also flip bits, leading to incorrect contents. Fortunately, in-disk **error correcting codes** (**ECC**) are used by the drive to determine whether the on-disk bits in a block are good, and in some cases, to fix them; if they are not good, and the drive does not have enough information to fix the error, the disk will return an error when a request is issued to read them.

There are also cases where a disk block becomes **corrupt** in a way not detectable by the disk itself. For example, buggy disk firmware may write a block to the wrong location; in such a case, the disk ECC indicates the block contents are fine, but from the client's perspective the wrong block is returned when subsequently accessed. Similarly, a block may get corrupted when it is transferred from the host to the disk across a faulty bus; the resulting corrupt data is stored by the disk, but it is not what the client desires. These types of faults are particularly insidious because they are **silent faults**; the disk gives no indication of the problem when returning the faulty data.

Prabhakaran et al. describes this more modern view of disk failure as the **fail-partial** disk failure model [P+05]. In this view, disks can still fail in their entirety (as was the case in the traditional fail-stop model); however, disks can also seemingly be working and have one or more blocks become inaccessible (i.e., LSEs) or hold the wrong contents (i.e., corruption). Thus, when accessing a seemingly-working disk, once in a while it may either return an error when trying to read or write a given block (a non-silent partial fault), and once in a while it may simply return the wrong data (a silent partial fault).

Both of these types of faults are somewhat rare, but just how rare? Figure 451 summarizes some of the findings from the two Bairavasundaram studies [B+07,B+08].

The figure shows the percent of drives that exhibited at least one LSE or block corruption over the course of the study (about 3 years, over 1.5 million disk drives). The figure further sub-divides the results into "cheap" drives (usually SATA drives) and "costly" drives (usually SCSI or FibreChannel). As you can see, while buying better drives reduces the frequency of both types of problem (by about an order of magnitude), they still happen often enough that you need to think carefully about how to handle them in your storage system.

Some additional findings about LSEs are:

- Costly drives with more than one LSE are as likely to develop additional errors as cheaper drives
- For most drives, annual error rate increases in year two
- The number of LSEs increase with disk size
- Most disks with LSEs have less than 50
- Disks with LSEs are more likely to develop additional LSEs
- There exists a significant amount of spatial and temporal locality
- Disk scrubbing is useful (most LSEs were found this way)

Some findings about corruption:

- Chance of corruption varies greatly across different drive models within the same drive class
- Age effects are different across models
- Workload and disk size have little impact on corruption
- Most disks with corruption only have a few corruptions
- Corruption is not independent within a disk or across disks in RAID
- There exists spatial locality, and some temporal locality
- There is a weak correlation with LSEs

To learn more about these failures, you should likely read the original papers [B+07,B+08]. But hopefully the main point should be clear: if you really wish to build a reliable storage system, you must include machinery to detect and recover from both LSEs and block corruption.

45.2 Handling Latent Sector Errors

Given these two new modes of partial disk failure, we should now try to see what we can do about them. Let's first tackle the easier of the two, namely latent sector errors.

> CRUX: HOW TO HANDLE LATENT SECTOR ERRORS
> How should a storage system handle latent sector errors? How much extra machinery is needed to handle this form of partial failure?

As it turns out, latent sector errors are rather straightforward to handle, as they are (by definition) easily detected. When a storage system tries to access a block, and the disk returns an error, the storage system should simply use whatever redundancy mechanism it has to return the correct data. In a mirrored RAID, for example, the system should access the alternate copy; in a RAID-4 or RAID-5 system based on parity, the system should reconstruct the block from the other blocks in the parity group. Thus, easily detected problems such as LSEs are readily recovered through standard redundancy mechanisms.

The growing prevalence of LSEs has influenced RAID designs over the years. One particularly interesting problem arises in RAID-4/5 systems when both full-disk faults and LSEs occur in tandem. Specifically, when an entire disk fails, the RAID tries to **reconstruct** the disk (say, onto a hot spare) by reading through all of the other disks in the parity group and recomputing the missing values. If, during reconstruction, an LSE is encountered on any one of the other disks, we have a problem: the reconstruction cannot successfully complete.

To combat this issue, some systems add an extra degree of redundancy. For example, NetApp's **RAID-DP** has the equivalent of two parity disks instead of one [C+04]. When an LSE is discovered during reconstruction, the extra parity helps to reconstruct the missing block. As always, there is a cost, in that maintaining two parity blocks for each stripe is more costly; however, the log-structured nature of the NetApp **WAFL** file system mitigates that cost in many cases [HLM94]. The remaining cost is space, in the form of an extra disk for the second parity block.

45.3 Detecting Corruption: The Checksum

Let's now tackle the more challenging problem, that of silent failures via data corruption. How can we prevent users from getting bad data when corruption arises, and thus leads to disks returning bad data?

CRUX: HOW TO PRESERVE DATA INTEGRITY DESPITE CORRUPTION

Given the silent nature of such failures, what can a storage system do to detect when corruption arises? What techniques are needed? How can one implement them efficiently?

Unlike latent sector errors, *detection* of corruption is a key problem. How can a client tell that a block has gone bad? Once it is known that a particular block is bad, *recovery* is the same as before: you need to have some other copy of the block around (and hopefully, one that is not corrupt!). Thus, we focus here on detection techniques.

The primary mechanism used by modern storage systems to preserve data integrity is called the **checksum**. A checksum is simply the result of a function that takes a chunk of data (say a 4KB block) as input and computes a function over said data, producing a small summary of the contents of the data (say 4 or 8 bytes). This summary is referred to as the checksum. The goal of such a computation is to enable a system to detect if data has somehow been corrupted or altered by storing the checksum with the data and then confirming upon later access that the data's current checksum matches the original storage value.

> TIP: THERE'S NO FREE LUNCH
>
> There's No Such Thing As A Free Lunch, or TNSTAAFL for short, is an old American idiom that implies that when you are seemingly getting something for free, in actuality you are likely paying some cost for it. It comes from the old days when diners would advertise a free lunch for customers, hoping to draw them in; only when you went in, did you realize that to acquire the "free" lunch, you had to purchase one or more alcoholic beverages. Of course, this may not actually be a problem, particularly if you are an aspiring alcoholic (or typical undergraduate student).

Common Checksum Functions

A number of different functions are used to compute checksums, and vary in strength (i.e., how good they are at protecting data integrity) and speed (i.e., how quickly can they be computed). A trade-off that is common in systems arises here: usually, the more protection you get, the costlier it is. There is no such thing as a free lunch.

One simple checksum function that some use is based on exclusive or (XOR). With XOR-based checksums, the checksum is computed by XOR'ing each chunk of the data block being checksummed, thus producing a single value that represents the XOR of the entire block.

To make this more concrete, imagine we are computing a 4-byte checksum over a block of 16 bytes (this block is of course too small to really be a disk sector or block, but it will serve for the example). The 16 data bytes, in hex, look like this:

```
365e c4cd ba14 8a92 ecef 2c3a 40be f666
```

If we view them in binary, we get the following:

```
0011 0110 0101 1110    1100 0100 1100 1101
1011 1010 0001 0100    1000 1010 1001 0010
1110 1100 1110 1111    0010 1100 0011 1010
0100 0000 1011 1110    1111 0110 0110 0110
```

Because we've lined up the data in groups of 4 bytes per row, it is easy to see what the resulting checksum will be: perform an XOR over each column to get the final checksum value:

```
0010 0000 0001 1011    1001 0100 0000 0011
```

The result, in hex, is 0x201b9403.

XOR is a reasonable checksum but has its limitations. If, for example, two bits in the same position within each checksummed unit change, the checksum will not detect the corruption. For this reason, people have investigated other checksum functions.

Another basic checksum function is addition. This approach has the advantage of being fast; computing it just requires performing 2's-complement addition over each chunk of the data, ignoring overflow. It can detect many changes in data, but is not good if the data, for example, is shifted.

A slightly more complex algorithm is known as the **Fletcher checksum**, named (as you might guess) for the inventor, John G. Fletcher [F82]. It is quite simple to compute and involves the computation of two check bytes, $s1$ and $s2$. Specifically, assume a block D consists of bytes $d1$ ... dn; $s1$ is defined as follows: $s1 = (s1 + d_i) \ mod \ 255$ (computed over all d_i); $s2$ in turn is: $s2 = (s2 + s1) \ mod \ 255$ (again over all d_i) [F04]. The Fletcher checksum is almost as strong as the CRC (see below), detecting all single-bit, double-bit errors, and many burst errors [F04].

One final commonly-used checksum is known as a **cyclic redundancy check** (**CRC**). Assume you wish to compute the checksum over a data block D. All you do is treat D as if it is a large binary number (it is just a string of bits after all) and divide it by an agreed upon value (k). The remainder of this division is the value of the CRC. As it turns out, one can implement this binary modulo operation rather efficiently, and hence the popularity of the CRC in networking as well. See elsewhere for more details [M13].

Whatever the method used, it should be obvious that there is no perfect checksum: it is possible two data blocks with non-identical contents will have identical checksums, something referred to as a **collision**. This fact should be intuitive: after all, computing a checksum is taking something large (e.g., 4KB) and producing a summary that is much smaller (e.g., 4 or 8 bytes). In choosing a good checksum function, we are thus trying to find one that minimizes the chance of collisions while remaining easy to compute.

Checksum Layout

Now that you understand a bit about how to compute a checksum, let's next analyze how to use checksums in a storage system. The first question we must address is the layout of the checksum, i.e., how should checksums be stored on disk?

The most basic approach simply stores a checksum with each disk sector (or block). Given a data block D, let us call the checksum over that data $C(D)$. Thus, without checksums, the disk layout looks like this:

D0	D1	D2	D3	D4	D5	D6

With checksums, the layout adds a single checksum for every block:

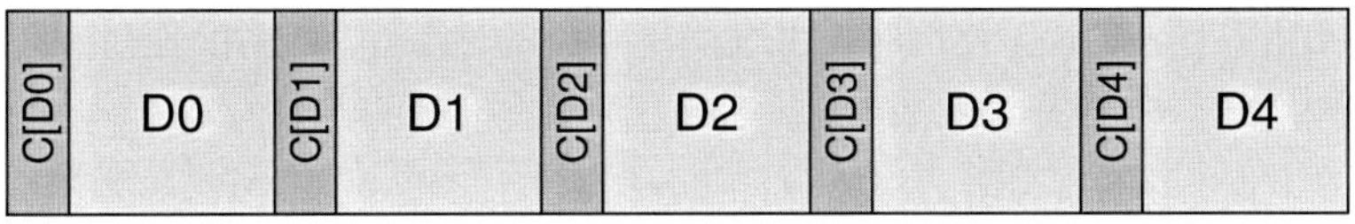

Because checksums are usually small (e.g., 8 bytes), and disks only can write in sector-sized chunks (512 bytes) or multiples thereof, one problem that arises is how to achieve the above layout. One solution employed by drive manufacturers is to format the drive with 520-byte sectors; an extra 8 bytes per sector can be used to store the checksum.

In disks that don't have such functionality, the file system must figure out a way to store the checksums packed into 512-byte blocks. One such possibility is as follows:

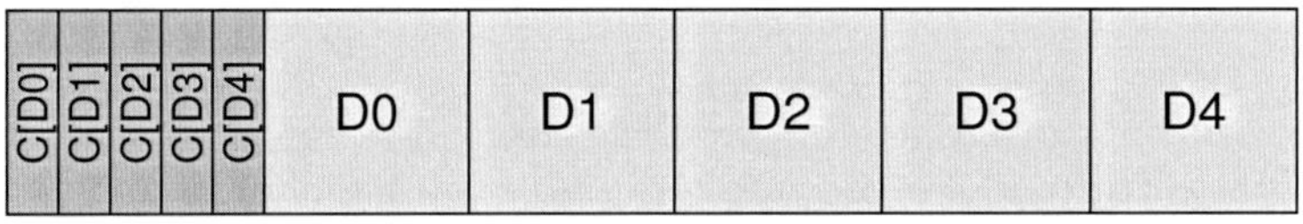

In this scheme, the n checksums are stored together in a sector, followed by n data blocks, followed by another checksum sector for the next n blocks, and so forth. This approach has the benefit of working on all disks, but can be less efficient; if the file system, for example, wants to overwrite block $D1$, it has to read in the checksum sector containing $C(D1)$, update $C(D1)$ in it, and then write out the checksum sector and new data block $D1$ (thus, one read and two writes). The earlier approach (of one checksum per sector) just performs a single write.

45.4 Using Checksums

With a checksum layout decided upon, we can now proceed to actually understand how to *use* the checksums. When reading a block D, the client (i.e., file system or storage controller) also reads its checksum from disk $C_s(D)$, which we call the **stored checksum** (hence the subscript C_s). The client then *computes* the checksum over the retrieved block D, which we call the **computed checksum** $C_c(D)$. At this point, the client compares the stored and computed checksums; if they are equal (i.e., $C_s(D)$ == $C_c(D)$, the data has likely not been corrupted, and thus can be safely returned to the user. If they do *not* match (i.e., $C_s(D)$!= $C_c(D)$), this implies the data has changed since the time it was stored (since the stored checksum reflects the value of the data at that time). In this case, we have a corruption, which our checksum has helped us to detect.

Given a corruption, the natural question is what should we do about it? If the storage system has a redundant copy, the answer is easy: try to use it instead. If the storage system has no such copy, the likely answer is to return an error. In either case, realize that corruption detection is not a magic bullet; if there is no other way to get the non-corrupted data, you are simply out of luck.

45.5 A New Problem: Misdirected Writes

The basic scheme described above works well in the general case of corrupted blocks. However, modern disks have a couple of unusual failure modes that require different solutions.

The first failure mode of interest is called a **misdirected write**. This arises in disk and RAID controllers which write the data to disk correctly, except in the *wrong* location. In a single-disk system, this means that the disk wrote block D_x not to address x (as desired) but rather to address y (thus "corrupting" D_y); in addition, within a multi-disk system, the controller may also write $D_{i,x}$ not to address x of disk i but rather to some other disk j. Thus our question:

> CRUX: HOW TO HANDLE MISDIRECTED WRITES
>
> How should a storage system or disk controller detect misdirected writes? What additional features are required from the checksum?

The answer, not surprisingly, is simple: add a little more information to each checksum. In this case, adding a **physical identifier** (**physical ID**) is quite helpful. For example, if the stored information now contains the checksum $C(D)$ and both the disk and sector numbers of the block, it is easy for the client to determine whether the correct information resides within a particular locale. Specifically, if the client is reading block 4 on disk 10 ($D_{10,4}$), the stored information should include that disk number and sector offset, as shown below. If the information does not match, a misdirected write has taken place, and a corruption is now detected. Here is an example of what this added information would look like on a two-disk system. Note that this figure, like the others before it, is not to scale, as the checksums are usually small (e.g., 8 bytes) whereas the blocks are much larger (e.g., 4 KB or bigger):

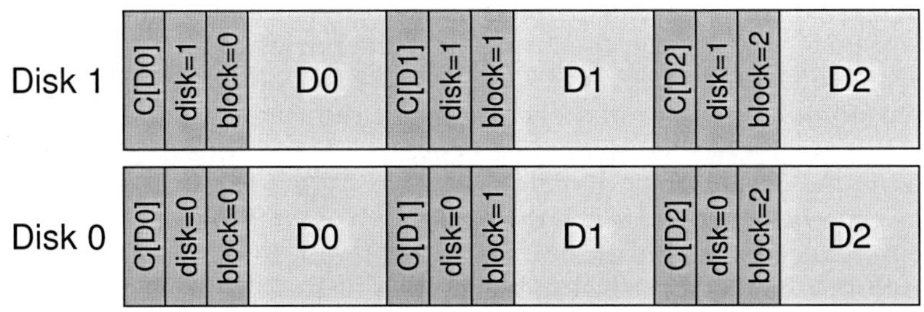

You can see from the on-disk format that there is now a fair amount of redundancy on disk: for each block, the disk number is repeated within each block, and the offset of the block in question is also kept next to the block itself. The presence of redundant information should be no surprise, though; redundancy is the key to error detection (in this case) and recovery (in others). A little extra information, while not strictly needed with perfect disks, can go a long ways in helping detect problematic situations should they arise.

45.6 One Last Problem: Lost Writes

Unfortunately, misdirected writes are not the last problem we will address. Specifically, some modern storage devices also have an issue known as a **lost write**, which occurs when the device informs the upper layer that a write has completed but in fact it never is persisted; thus, what remains is the old contents of the block rather than the updated new contents.

The obvious question here is: do any of our checksumming strategies from above (e.g., basic checksums, or physical identity) help to detect lost writes? Unfortunately, the answer is no: the old block likely has a matching checksum, and the physical ID used above (disk number and block offset) will also be correct. Thus our final problem:

> CRUX: HOW TO HANDLE LOST WRITES
> How should a storage system or disk controller detect lost writes? What additional features are required from the checksum?

There are a number of possible solutions that can help [K+08]. One classic approach [BS04] is to perform a **write verify** or **read-after-write**; by immediately reading back the data after a write, a system can ensure that the data indeed reached the disk surface. This approach, however, is quite slow, doubling the number of I/Os needed to complete a write.

Some systems add a checksum elsewhere in the system to detect lost writes. For example, Sun's **Zettabyte File System** (**ZFS**) includes a checksum in each file system inode and indirect block for every block included within a file. Thus, even if the write to a data block itself is lost, the checksum within the inode will not match the old data. Only if the writes to both the inode and the data are lost simultaneously will such a scheme fail, an unlikely (but unfortunately, possible!) situation.

45.7 Scrubbing

Given all of this discussion, you might be wondering: when do these checksums actually get checked? Of course, some amount of checking occurs when data is accessed by applications, but most data is rarely accessed, and thus would remain unchecked. Unchecked data is problematic for a reliable storage system, as bit rot could eventually affect all copies of a particular piece of data.

To remedy this problem, many systems utilize **disk scrubbing** of various forms [K+08]. By periodically reading through *every* block of the system, and checking whether checksums are still valid, the disk system can reduce the chances that all copies of a certain data item become corrupted. Typical systems schedule scans on a nightly or weekly basis.

45.8 Overheads Of Checksumming

Before closing, we now discuss some of the overheads of using checksums for data protection. There are two distinct kinds of overheads, as is common in computer systems: space and time.

Space overheads come in two forms. The first is on the disk (or other storage medium) itself; each stored checksum takes up room on the disk, which can no longer be used for user data. A typical ratio might be an 8-byte checksum per 4 KB data block, for a 0.19% on-disk space overhead.

The second type of space overhead comes in the memory of the system. When accessing data, there must now be room in memory for the checksums as well as the data itself. However, if the system simply checks the checksum and then discards it once done, this overhead is short-lived and not much of a concern. Only if checksums are kept in memory (for an added level of protection against memory corruption [Z+13]) will this small overhead be observable.

While space overheads are small, the time overheads induced by checksumming can be quite noticeable. Minimally, the CPU must compute the checksum over each block, both when the data is stored (to determine the value of the stored checksum) and when it is accessed (to compute the checksum again and compare it against the stored checksum). One approach to reducing CPU overheads, employed by many systems that use checksums (including network stacks), is to combine data copying and checksumming into one streamlined activity; because the copy is needed anyhow (e.g., to copy the data from the kernel page cache into a user buffer), combined copying/checksumming can be quite effective.

Beyond CPU overheads, some checksumming schemes can induce extra I/O overheads, particularly when checksums are stored distinctly from the data (thus requiring extra I/Os to access them), and for any extra I/O needed for background scrubbing. The former can be reduced by design; the latter can be tuned and thus its impact limited, perhaps by controlling when such scrubbing activity takes place. The middle of the night, when most (not all!) productive workers have gone to bed, may be a good time to perform such scrubbing activity and increase the robustness of the storage system.

45.9 Summary

We have discussed data protection in modern storage systems, focusing on checksum implementation and usage. Different checksums protect against different types of faults; as storage devices evolve, new failure modes will undoubtedly arise. Perhaps such change will force the research community and industry to revisit some of these basic approaches, or invent entirely new approaches altogether. Time will tell. Or it won't. Time is funny that way.

References

[B+07] "An Analysis of Latent Sector Errors in Disk Drives" by L. Bairavasundaram, G. Goodson, S. Pasupathy, J. Schindler. SIGMETRICS '07, San Diego, CA. *The first paper to study latent sector errors in detail. The paper also won the Kenneth C. Sevcik Outstanding Student Paper award, named after a brilliant researcher and wonderful guy who passed away too soon. To show the OSTEP authors it was possible to move from the U.S. to Canada, Ken once sang us the Canadian national anthem, standing up in the middle of a restaurant to do so. We chose the U.S., but got this memory.*

[B+08] "An Analysis of Data Corruption in the Storage Stack" by Lakshmi N. Bairavasundaram, Garth R. Goodson, Bianca Schroeder, Andrea C. Arpaci-Dusseau, Remzi H. Arpaci-Dusseau. FAST '08, San Jose, CA, February 2008. *The first paper to truly study disk corruption in great detail, focusing on how often such corruption occurs over three years for over 1.5 million drives.*

[BS04] "Commercial Fault Tolerance: A Tale of Two Systems" by Wendy Bartlett, Lisa Spainhower. IEEE Transactions on Dependable and Secure Computing, Vol. 1:1, January 2004. *This classic in building fault tolerant systems is an excellent overview of the state of the art from both IBM and Tandem. Another must read for those interested in the area.*

[C+04] "Row-Diagonal Parity for Double Disk Failure Correction" by P. Corbett, B. English, A. Goel, T. Grcanac, S. Kleiman, J. Leong, S. Sankar. FAST '04, San Jose, CA, February 2004. *An early paper on how extra redundancy helps to solve the combined full-disk-failure/partial-disk-failure problem. Also a nice example of how to mix more theoretical work with practical.*

[F04] "Checksums and Error Control" by Peter M. Fenwick. Copy available online here: `http://www.ostep.org/Citations/checksums-03.pdf`. *A great simple tutorial on checksums, available to you for the amazing cost of free.*

[F82] "An Arithmetic Checksum for Serial Transmissions" by John G. Fletcher. IEEE Transactions on Communication, Vol. 30:1, January 1982. *Fletcher's original work on his eponymous checksum. He didn't call it the Fletcher checksum, rather he just didn't call it anything; later, others named it after him. So don't blame old Fletch for this seeming act of braggadocio. This anecdote might remind you of Rubik; Rubik never called it "**Rubik's cube**"; rather, he just called it "my cube."*

[HLM94] "File System Design for an NFS File Server Appliance" by Dave Hitz, James Lau, Michael Malcolm. USENIX Spring '94. *The pioneering paper that describes the ideas and product at the heart of NetApp's core. Based on this system, NetApp has grown into a multi-billion dollar storage company. To learn more about NetApp, read Hitz's autobiography "How to Castrate a Bull" (which is the actual title, no joking). And you thought you could avoid bull castration by going into CS.*

[K+08] "Parity Lost and Parity Regained" by Andrew Krioukov, Lakshmi N. Bairavasundaram, Garth R. Goodson, Kiran Srinivasan, Randy Thelen, Andrea C. Arpaci-Dusseau, Remzi H. Arpaci-Dusseau. FAST '08, San Jose, CA, February 2008. *This work explores how different checksum schemes work (or don't work) in protecting data. We reveal a number of interesting flaws in current protection strategies.*

[M13] "Cyclic Redundancy Checks" by unknown. Available: `http://www.mathpages.com/home/kmath458.htm`. *A super clear and concise description of CRCs. The internet is full of information, as it turns out.*

[P+05] "IRON File Systems" by V. Prabhakaran, L. Bairavasundaram, N. Agrawal, H. Gunawi, A. Arpaci-Dusseau, R. Arpaci-Dusseau. SOSP '05, Brighton, England. *Our paper on how disks have partial failure modes, and a detailed study of how modern file systems react to such failures. As it turns out, rather poorly! We found numerous bugs, design flaws, and other oddities in this work. Some of this has fed back into the Linux community, thus improving file system reliability. You're welcome!*

[RO91] "Design and Implementation of the Log-structured File System" by Mendel Rosenblum and John Ousterhout. SOSP '91, Pacific Grove, CA, October 1991. *So cool we cite it again.*

[S90] "Implementing Fault-Tolerant Services Using The State Machine Approach: A Tutorial" by Fred B. Schneider. ACM Surveys, Vol. 22, No. 4, December 1990. *How to build fault tolerant services. A must read for those building distributed systems.*

[Z+13] "Zettabyte Reliability with Flexible End-to-end Data Integrity" by Y. Zhang, D. Myers, A. Arpaci-Dusseau, R. Arpaci-Dusseau. MSST '13, Long Beach, California, May 2013. *How to add data protection to the page cache of a system. Out of space, otherwise we would write something...*

Homework (Simulation)

In this homework, you'll use `checksum.py` to investigate various aspects of checksums.

Questions

1. First just run `checksum.py` with no arguments. Compute the additive, XOR-based, and Fletcher checksums. Use `-c` to check your answers.
2. Now do the same, but vary the seed (`-s`) to different values.
3. Sometimes the additive and XOR-based checksums produce the same checksum (e.g., if the data value is all zeroes). Can you pass in a 4-byte data value (using the `-D` flag, e.g., `-D a,b,c,d`) that does not contain only zeroes and leads the additive and XOR-based checksum having the same value? In general, when does this occur? Check that you are correct with the `-c` flag.
4. Now pass in a 4-byte value that you know will produce a different checksum values for additive and XOR. In general, when does this occur?
5. Use the simulator to compute checksums twice (once each for a different set of numbers). The two number strings should be different (e.g., `-D a1,b1,c1,d1` the first time and `-D a2,b2,c2,d2` the second) but should produce the same additive checksum. In general, when will the additive checksum be the same, even though the data values are different? Check your specific answer with the `-c` flag.
6. Now do the same for the XOR checksum.
7. Now let's look at a specific set of data values. The first is: `-D 1,2,3,4`. What will the different checksums (additive, XOR, Fletcher) be for this data? Now compare it to computing these checksums over `-D 4,3,2,1`. What do you notice about these three checksums? How does Fletcher compare to the other two? How is Fletcher generally "better" than something like the simple additive checksum?
8. No checksum is perfect. Given a particular input of your choosing, can you find other data values that lead to the same Fletcher checksum? When, in general, does this occur? Start with a simple data string (e.g., `-D 0,1,2,3`) and see if you can replace one of those numbers but end up with the same Fletcher checksum. As always, use `-c` to check your answers.

Homework (Code)

In this part of the homework, you'll write some of your own code to implement various checksums.

Questions

1. Write a short C program (called `check-xor.c`) that computes an XOR-based checksum over an input file, and prints the checksum as output. Use a 8-bit unsigned char to store the (one byte) checksum. Make some test files to see if it works as expected.
2. Now write a short C program (called `check-fletcher.c`) that computes the Fletcher checksum over an input file. Once again, test your program to see if it works.
3. Now compare the performance of both: is one faster than the other? How does performance change as the size of the input file changes? Use internal calls to `gettimeofday` to time the programs. Which should you use if you care about performance? About checking ability?
4. Read about the 16-bit CRC and then implement it. Test it on a number of different inputs to ensure that it works. How is its performance as compared to the simple XOR and Fletcher? How about its checking ability?
5. Now build a tool (`create-csum.c`) that computes a single-byte checksum for every 4KB block of a file, and records the results in an output file (specified on the command line). Build a related tool (`check-csum.c`) that reads a file, computes the checksums over each block, and compares the results to the stored checksums stored in another file. If there is a problem, the program should print that the file has been corrupted. Test the program by manually corrupting the file.

46

Summary Dialogue on Persistence

Student: *Wow, file systems seem interesting(!), and yet complicated.*

Professor: *That's why my spouse and I do our research in this space.*

Student: *Hold on. Are you one of the professors who wrote this book? I thought we were both just fake constructs, used to summarize some main points, and perhaps add a little levity in the study of operating systems.*

Professor: *Uh... er... maybe. And none of your business! And who did you think was writing these things? (sighs) Anyhow, let's get on with it: what did you learn?*

Student: *Well, I think I got one of the main points, which is that it is much harder to manage data for a long time (persistently) than it is to manage data that isn't persistent (like the stuff in memory). After all, if your machines crashes, memory contents disappear! But the stuff in the file system needs to live forever.*

Professor: *Well, as my friend Kevin Hultquist used to say, "Forever is a long time"; while he was talking about plastic golf tees, it's especially true for the garbage that is found in most file systems.*

Student: *Well, you know what I mean! For a long time at least. And even simple things, such as updating a persistent storage device, are complicated, because you have to care what happens if you crash. Recovery, something I had never even thought of when we were virtualizing memory, is now a big deal!*

Professor: *Too true. Updates to persistent storage have always been, and remain, a fun and challenging problem.*

Student: *I also learned about cool things like disk scheduling, and about data protection techniques like RAID and even checksums. That stuff is cool.*

Professor: *I like those topics too. Though, if you really get into it, they can get a little mathematical. Check out some the latest on erasure codes if you want your brain to hurt.*

Student: *I'll get right on that.*

Professor: *(frowns) I think you're being sarcastic. Well, what else did you like?*

Student: *And I also liked all the thought that has gone into building technology-aware systems, like FFS and LFS. Neat stuff! Being disk aware seems cool. But will it matter anymore, with Flash and all the newest, latest technologies?*

Professor: *Good question! And a reminder to get working on that Flash chapter... (scribbles note down to self) ... But yes, even with Flash, all of this stuff is still relevant, amazingly. For example, Flash Translation Layers (FTLs) use log-structuring internally, to improve performance and reliability of Flash-based SSDs. And thinking about locality is always useful. So while the technology may be changing, many of the ideas we have studied will continue to be useful, for a while at least.*

Student: *That's good. I just spent all this time learning it, and I didn't want it to all be for no reason!*

Professor: *Professors wouldn't do that to you, would they?*

47

A Dialogue on Distribution

Professor: *And thus we reach our final little piece in the world of operating systems: distributed systems. Since we can't cover much here, we'll sneak in a little intro here in the section on persistence, and focus mostly on distributed file systems. Hope that is OK!*

Student: *Sounds OK. But what is a distributed system exactly, oh glorious and all-knowing professor?*

Professor: *Well, I bet you know how this is going to go...*

Student: *There's a peach?*

Professor: *Exactly! But this time, it's far away from you, and may take some time to get the peach. And there are a lot of them! Even worse, sometimes a peach becomes rotten. But you want to make sure that when anybody bites into a peach, they will get a mouthful of deliciousness.*

Student: *This peach analogy is working less and less for me.*

Professor: *Come on! It's the last one, just go with it.*

Student: *Fine.*

Professor: *So anyhow, forget about the peaches. Building distributed systems is hard, because things fail all the time. Messages get lost, machines go down, disks corrupt data. It's like the whole world is working against you!*

Student: *But I use distributed systems all the time, right?*

Professor: *Yes! You do. And... ?*

Student: *Well, it seems like they mostly work. After all, when I send a search request to Google, it usually comes back in a snap, with some great results! Same thing when I use Facebook, Amazon, and so forth.*

Professor: *Yes, it is amazing. And that's despite all of those failures taking place! Those companies build a huge amount of machinery into their systems so as to ensure that even though some machines have failed, the entire system stays up and running. They use a lot of techniques to do this: replication, retry, and various other tricks people have developed over time to detect and recover from failures.*

Student: *Sounds interesting. Time to learn something for real?*

Professor: *It does seem so. Let's get to work! But first things first ...*
(bites into peach he has been holding, which unfortunately is rotten)

48

Distributed Systems

Distributed systems have changed the face of the world. When your web browser connects to a web server somewhere else on the planet, it is participating in what seems to be a simple form of a **client/server** distributed system. When you contact a modern web service such as Google or Facebook, you are not just interacting with a single machine, however; behind the scenes, these complex services are built from a large collection (i.e., thousands) of machines, each of which cooperate to provide the particular service of the site. Thus, it should be clear what makes studying distributed systems interesting. Indeed, it is worthy of an entire class; here, we just introduce a few of the major topics.

A number of new challenges arise when building a distributed system. The major one we focus on is **failure**; machines, disks, networks, and software all fail from time to time, as we do not (and likely, will never) know how to build "perfect" components and systems. However, when we build a modern web service, we'd like it to appear to clients as if it never fails; how can we accomplish this task?

> THE CRUX:
> HOW TO BUILD SYSTEMS THAT WORK WHEN COMPONENTS FAIL
> How can we build a working system out of parts that don't work correctly all the time? The basic question should remind you of some of the topics we discussed in RAID storage arrays; however, the problems here tend to be more complex, as are the solutions.

Interestingly, while failure is a central challenge in constructing distributed systems, it also represents an opportunity. Yes, machines fail; but the mere fact that a machine fails does not imply the entire system must fail. By collecting together a set of machines, we can build a system that appears to rarely fail, despite the fact that its components fail regularly. This reality is the central beauty and value of distributed systems, and why they underly virtually every modern web service you use, including Google, Facebook, etc.

> TIP: COMMUNICATION IS INHERENTLY UNRELIABLE
> In virtually all circumstances, it is good to view communication as a fundamentally unreliable activity. Bit corruption, down or non-working links and machines, and lack of buffer space for incoming packets all lead to the same result: packets sometimes do not reach their destination. To build reliable services atop such unreliable networks, we must consider techniques that can cope with packet loss.

Other important issues exist as well. System **performance** is often critical; with a network connecting our distributed system together, system designers must often think carefully about how to accomplish their given tasks, trying to reduce the number of messages sent and further make communication as efficient (low latency, high bandwidth) as possible.

Finally, **security** is also a necessary consideration. When connecting to a remote site, having some assurance that the remote party is who they say they are becomes a central problem. Further, ensuring that third parties cannot monitor or alter an on-going communication between two others is also a challenge.

In this introduction, we'll cover the most basic aspect that is new in a distributed system: **communication**. Namely, how should machines within a distributed system communicate with one another? We'll start with the most basic primitives available, messages, and build a few higher-level primitives on top of them. As we said above, failure will be a central focus: how should communication layers handle failures?

48.1 Communication Basics

The central tenet of modern networking is that communication is fundamentally unreliable. Whether in the wide-area Internet, or a local-area high-speed network such as Infiniband, packets are regularly lost, corrupted, or otherwise do not reach their destination.

There are a multitude of causes for packet loss or corruption. Sometimes, during transmission, some bits get flipped due to electrical or other similar problems. Sometimes, an element in the system, such as a network link or packet router or even the remote host, are somehow damaged or otherwise not working correctly; network cables do accidentally get severed, at least sometimes.

More fundamental however is packet loss due to lack of buffering within a network switch, router, or endpoint. Specifically, even if we could guarantee that all links worked correctly, and that all the components in the system (switches, routers, end hosts) were up and running as expected, loss is still possible, for the following reason. Imagine a packet arrives at a router; for the packet to be processed, it must be placed in memory somewhere within the router. If many such packets arrive at

```
// client code
int main(int argc, char *argv[]) {
  int sd = UDP_Open(20000);
  struct sockaddr_in addrSnd, addrRcv;
  int rc = UDP_FillSockAddr(&addrSnd, "cs.wisc.edu", 10000);
  char message[BUFFER_SIZE];
  sprintf(message, "hello world");
  rc = UDP_Write(sd, &addrSnd, message, BUFFER_SIZE);
  if (rc > 0)
    int rc = UDP_Read(sd, &addrRcv, message, BUFFER_SIZE);
  return 0;
}

// server code
int main(int argc, char *argv[]) {
  int sd = UDP_Open(10000);
  assert(sd > -1);
  while (1) {
    struct sockaddr_in addr;
    char message[BUFFER_SIZE];
    int rc = UDP_Read(sd, &addr, message, BUFFER_SIZE);
    if (rc > 0) {
      char reply[BUFFER_SIZE];
      sprintf(reply, "goodbye world");
      rc = UDP_Write(sd, &addr, reply, BUFFER_SIZE);
    }
  }
  return 0;
}
```

Figure 481: **Example UDP Code (`client.c`, `server.c`)**

once, it is possible that the memory within the router cannot accommodate all of the packets. The only choice the router has at that point is to **drop** one or more of the packets. This same behavior occurs at end hosts as well; when you send a large number of messages to a single machine, the machine's resources can easily become overwhelmed, and thus packet loss again arises.

Thus, packet loss is fundamental in networking. The question thus becomes: how should we deal with it?

48.2 Unreliable Communication Layers

One simple way is this: we don't deal with it. Because some applications know how to deal with packet loss, it is sometimes useful to let them communicate with a basic unreliable messaging layer, an example of the **end-to-end argument** one often hears about (see the **Aside** at end of chapter). One excellent example of such an unreliable layer is found

```
int UDP_Open(int port) {
  int sd;
  if ((sd = socket(AF_INET, SOCK_DGRAM, 0)) == -1)
    return -1;
  struct sockaddr_in myaddr;
  bzero(&myaddr, sizeof(myaddr));
  myaddr.sin_family      = AF_INET;
  myaddr.sin_port        = htons(port);
  myaddr.sin_addr.s_addr = INADDR_ANY;
  if (bind(sd, (struct sockaddr *) &myaddr,
      sizeof(myaddr)) == -1) {
    close(sd);
    return -1;
  }
  return sd;
}

int UDP_FillSockAddr(struct sockaddr_in *addr,
  char *hostname, int port) {
  bzero(addr, sizeof(struct sockaddr_in));
  addr->sin_family = AF_INET;      // host byte order
  addr->sin_port   = htons(port); // network byte order
  struct in_addr *in_addr;
  struct hostent *host_entry;
  if ((host_entry = gethostbyname(hostname)) == NULL)
    return -1;
  in_addr = (struct in_addr *) host_entry->h_addr;
  addr->sin_addr = *in_addr;
  return 0;
}

int UDP_Write(int sd, struct sockaddr_in *addr,
  char *buffer, int n) {
  int addr_len = sizeof(struct sockaddr_in);
  return sendto(sd, buffer, n, 0, (struct sockaddr *)
                addr, addr_len);
}

int UDP_Read(int sd, struct sockaddr_in *addr,
             char *buffer, int n) {
  int len = sizeof(struct sockaddr_in);
  return recvfrom(sd, buffer, n, 0, (struct sockaddr *)
                  addr, (socklen_t *) &len);
}
```

Figure 482: **A Simple UDP Library (udp.c)**

> TIP: USE CHECKSUMS FOR INTEGRITY
>
> Checksums are a commonly-used method to detect corruption quickly and effectively in modern systems. A simple checksum is addition: just sum up the bytes of a chunk of data; of course, many other more sophisticated checksums have been created, including basic cyclic redundancy codes (CRCs), the Fletcher checksum, and many others [MK09].
>
> In networking, checksums are used as follows. Before sending a message from one machine to another, compute a checksum over the bytes of the message. Then send both the message and the checksum to the destination. At the destination, the receiver computes a checksum over the incoming message as well; if this computed checksum matches the sent checksum, the receiver can feel some assurance that the data likely did not get corrupted during transmission.
>
> Checksums can be evaluated along a number of different axes. Effectiveness is one primary consideration: does a change in the data lead to a change in the checksum? The stronger the checksum, the harder it is for changes in the data to go unnoticed. Performance is the other important criterion: how costly is the checksum to compute? Unfortunately, effectiveness and performance are often at odds, meaning that checksums of high quality are often expensive to compute. Life, again, isn't perfect.

in the **UDP/IP** networking stack available today on virtually all modern systems. To use UDP, a process uses the **sockets** API in order to create a **communication endpoint**; processes on other machines (or on the same machine) send UDP **datagrams** to the original process (a datagram is a fixed-sized message up to some max size).

Figures 481 and 482 show a simple client and server built on top of UDP/IP. The client can send a message to the server, which then responds with a reply. With this small amount of code, you have all you need to begin building distributed systems!

UDP is a great example of an unreliable communication layer. If you use it, you will encounter situations where packets get lost (dropped) and thus do not reach their destination; the sender is never thus informed of the loss. However, that does not mean that UDP does not guard against any failures at all. For example, UDP includes a **checksum** to detect some forms of packet corruption.

However, because many applications simply want to send data to a destination and not worry about packet loss, we need more. Specifically, we need reliable communication on top of an unreliable network.

48.3 Reliable Communication Layers

To build a reliable communication layer, we need some new mechanisms and techniques to handle packet loss. Let us consider a simple

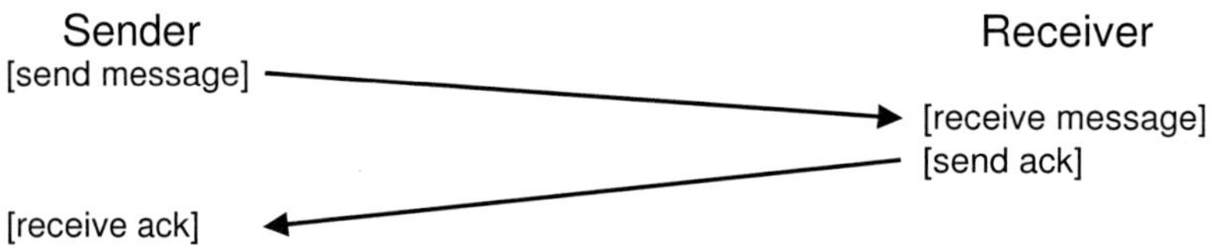

Figure 483: **Message Plus Acknowledgment**

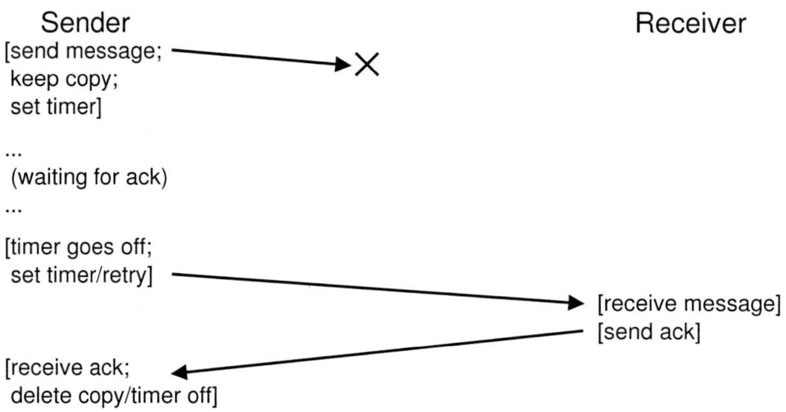

Figure 484: **Message Plus Acknowledgment: Dropped Request**

example in which a client is sending a message to a server over an unreliable connection. The first question we must answer: how does the sender know that the receiver has actually received the message?

The technique that we will use is known as an **acknowledgment**, or **ack** for short. The idea is simple: the sender sends a message to the receiver; the receiver then sends a short message back to *acknowledge* its receipt. Figure 483 depicts the process.

When the sender receives an acknowledgment of the message, it can then rest assured that the receiver did indeed receive the original message. However, what should the sender do if it does not receive an acknowledgment?

To handle this case, we need an additional mechanism, known as a **timeout**. When the sender sends a message, the sender now sets a timer to go off after some period of time. If, in that time, no acknowledgment has been received, the sender concludes that the message has been lost. The sender then simply performs a **retry** of the send, sending the same message again with hopes that this time, it will get through. For this approach to work, the sender must keep a copy of the message around, in case it needs to send it again. The combination of the timeout and the retry have led some to call the approach **timeout/retry**; pretty clever crowd, those networking types, no? Figure 484 shows an example.

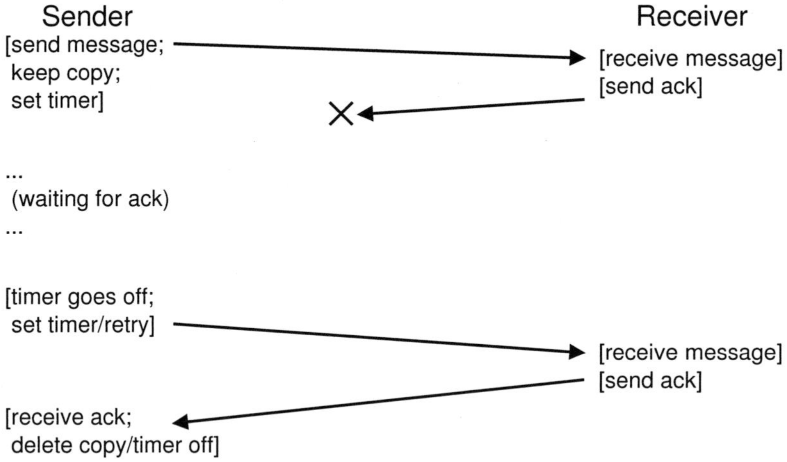

Figure 485: **Message Plus Acknowledgment: Dropped Reply**

Unfortunately, timeout/retry in this form is not quite enough. Figure 485 shows an example of packet loss which could lead to trouble. In this example, it is not the original message that gets lost, but the acknowledgment. From the perspective of the sender, the situation seems the same: no ack was received, and thus a timeout and retry are in order. But from the perspective of the receiver, it is quite different: now the same message has been received twice! While there may be cases where this is OK, in general it is not; imagine what would happen when you are downloading a file and extra packets are repeated inside the download. Thus, when we are aiming for a reliable message layer, we also usually want to guarantee that each message is received **exactly once** by the receiver.

To enable the receiver to detect duplicate message transmission, the sender has to identify each message in some unique way, and the receiver needs some way to track whether it has already seen each message before. When the receiver sees a duplicate transmission, it simply acks the message, but (critically) does *not* pass the message to the application that receives the data. Thus, the sender receives the ack but the message is not received twice, preserving the exactly-once semantics mentioned above.

There are myriad ways to detect duplicate messages. For example, the sender could generate a unique ID for each message; the receiver could track every ID it has ever seen. This approach could work, but it is prohibitively costly, requiring unbounded memory to track all IDs.

A simpler approach, requiring little memory, solves this problem, and the mechanism is known as a **sequence counter**. With a sequence counter, the sender and receiver agree upon a start value (e.g., 1) for a counter that each side will maintain. Whenever a message is sent, the current value of the counter is sent along with the message; this counter value (N) serves as an ID for the message. After the message is sent, the sender then increments the value (to $N + 1$).

TIP: BE CAREFUL SETTING THE TIMEOUT VALUE

As you can probably guess from the discussion, setting the timeout value correctly is an important aspect of using timeouts to retry message sends. If the timeout is too small, the sender will re-send messages needlessly, thus wasting CPU time on the sender and network resources. If the timeout is too large, the sender waits too long to re-send and thus perceived performance at the sender is reduced. The "right" value, from the perspective of a single client and server, is thus to wait just long enough to detect packet loss but no longer.

However, there are often more than just a single client and server in a distributed system, as we will see in future chapters. In a scenario with many clients sending to a single server, packet loss at the server may be an indicator that the server is overloaded. If true, clients might retry in a different adaptive manner; for example, after the first timeout, a client might increase its timeout value to a higher amount, perhaps twice as high as the original value. Such an **exponential back-off** scheme, pioneered in the early Aloha network and adopted in early Ethernet [A70], avoids situations where resources are being overloaded by an excess of re-sends. Robust systems strive to avoid overload of this nature.

The receiver uses its counter value as the expected value for the ID of the incoming message from that sender. If the ID of a received message (N) matches the receiver's counter (also N), it acks the message and passes it up to the application; in this case, the receiver concludes this is the first time this message has been received. The receiver then increments its counter (to $N + 1$), and waits for the next message.

If the ack is lost, the sender will timeout and re-send message N. This time, the receiver's counter is higher ($N+1$), and thus the receiver knows it has already received this message. Thus it acks the message but does *not* pass it up to the application. In this simple manner, sequence counters can be used to avoid duplicates.

The most commonly used reliable communication layer is known as **TCP/IP**, or just **TCP** for short. TCP has a great deal more sophistication than we describe above, including machinery to handle congestion in the network [VJ88], multiple outstanding requests, and hundreds of other small tweaks and optimizations. Read more about it if you're curious; better yet, take a networking course and learn that material well.

48.4 Communication Abstractions

Given a basic messaging layer, we now approach the next question in this chapter: what abstraction of communication should we use when building a distributed system?

The systems community developed a number of approaches over the years. One body of work took OS abstractions and extended them to operate in a distributed environment. For example, **distributed shared memory** (**DSM**) systems enable processes on different machines to share a large, virtual address space [LH89]. This abstraction turns a distributed computation into something that looks like a multi-threaded application; the only difference is that these threads run on different machines instead of different processors within the same machine.

The way most DSM systems work is through the virtual memory system of the OS. When a page is accessed on one machine, two things can happen. In the first (best) case, the page is already local on the machine, and thus the data is fetched quickly. In the second case, the page is currently on some other machine. A page fault occurs, and the page fault handler sends a message to some other machine to fetch the page, install it in the page table of the requesting process, and continue execution.

This approach is not widely in use today for a number of reasons. The largest problem for DSM is how it handles failure. Imagine, for example, if a machine fails; what happens to the pages on that machine? What if the data structures of the distributed computation are spread across the entire address space? In this case, parts of these data structures would suddenly become unavailable. Dealing with failure when parts of your address space go missing is hard; imagine a linked list where a "next" pointer points into a portion of the address space that is gone. Yikes!

A further problem is performance. One usually assumes, when writing code, that access to memory is cheap. In DSM systems, some accesses are inexpensive, but others cause page faults and expensive fetches from remote machines. Thus, programmers of such DSM systems had to be very careful to organize computations such that almost no communication occurred at all, defeating much of the point of such an approach. Though much research was performed in this space, there was little practical impact; nobody builds reliable distributed systems using DSM today.

48.5 Remote Procedure Call (RPC)

While OS abstractions turned out to be a poor choice for building distributed systems, programming language (PL) abstractions make much more sense. The most dominant abstraction is based on the idea of a **remote procedure call**, or **RPC** for short [BN84][1].

Remote procedure call packages all have a simple goal: to make the process of executing code on a remote machine as simple and straightforward as calling a local function. Thus, to a client, a procedure call is made, and some time later, the results are returned. The server simply defines some routines that it wishes to export. The rest of the magic is handled by the RPC system, which in general has two pieces: a **stub generator** (sometimes called a **protocol compiler**), and the **run-time library**. We'll now take a look at each of these pieces in more detail.

[1] In modern programming languages, we might instead say **remote method invocation** (**RMI**), but who likes these languages anyhow, with all of their fancy objects?

Stub Generator

The stub generator's job is simple: to remove some of the pain of packing function arguments and results into messages by automating it. Numerous benefits arise: one avoids, by design, the simple mistakes that occur in writing such code by hand; further, a stub compiler can perhaps optimize such code and thus improve performance.

The input to such a compiler is simply the set of calls a server wishes to export to clients. Conceptually, it could be something as simple as this:

```
interface {
  int func1(int arg1);
  int func2(int arg1, int arg2);
};
```

The stub generator takes an interface like this and generates a few different pieces of code. For the client, a **client stub** is generated, which contains each of the functions specified in the interface; a client program wishing to use this RPC service would link with this client stub and call into it in order to make RPCs.

Internally, each of these functions in the client stub do all of the work needed to perform the remote procedure call. To the client, the code just appears as a function call (e.g., the client calls `func1(x)`); internally, the code in the client stub for `func1()` does this:

- **Create a message buffer.** A message buffer is usually just a contiguous array of bytes of some size.
- **Pack the needed information into the message buffer.** This information includes some kind of identifier for the function to be called, as well as all of the arguments that the function needs (e.g., in our example above, one integer for `func1`). The process of putting all of this information into a single contiguous buffer is sometimes referred to as the **marshaling** of arguments or the **serialization** of the message.
- **Send the message to the destination RPC server.** The communication with the RPC server, and all of the details required to make it operate correctly, are handled by the RPC run-time library, described further below.
- **Wait for the reply.** Because function calls are usually **synchronous**, the call will wait for its completion.
- **Unpack return code and other arguments.** If the function just returns a single return code, this process is straightforward; however, more complex functions might return more complex results (e.g., a list), and thus the stub might need to unpack those as well. This step is also known as **unmarshaling** or **deserialization**.
- **Return to the caller.** Finally, just return from the client stub back into the client code.

For the server, code is also generated. The steps taken on the server are as follows:

- **Unpack the message.** This step, called **unmarshaling** or **deserialization**, takes the information out of the incoming message. The function identifier and arguments are extracted.
- **Call into the actual function.** Finally! We have reached the point where the remote function is actually executed. The RPC runtime calls into the function specified by the ID and passes in the desired arguments.
- **Package the results.** The return argument(s) are marshaled back into a single reply buffer.
- **Send the reply.** The reply is finally sent to the caller.

There are a few other important issues to consider in a stub compiler. The first is complex arguments, i.e., how does one package and send a complex data structure? For example, when one calls the `write()` system call, one passes in three arguments: an integer file descriptor, a pointer to a buffer, and a size indicating how many bytes (starting at the pointer) are to be written. If an RPC package is passed a pointer, it needs to be able to figure out how to interpret that pointer, and perform the correct action. Usually this is accomplished through either well-known types (e.g., a `buffer_t` that is used to pass chunks of data given a size, which the RPC compiler understands), or by annotating the data structures with more information, enabling the compiler to know which bytes need to be serialized.

Another important issue is the organization of the server with regards to concurrency. A simple server just waits for requests in a simple loop, and handles each request one at a time. However, as you might have guessed, this can be grossly inefficient; if one RPC call blocks (e.g., on I/O), server resources are wasted. Thus, most servers are constructed in some sort of concurrent fashion. A common organization is a **thread pool**. In this organization, a finite set of threads are created when the server starts; when a message arrives, it is dispatched to one of these worker threads, which then does the work of the RPC call, eventually replying; during this time, a main thread keeps receiving other requests, and perhaps dispatching them to other workers. Such an organization enables concurrent execution within the server, thus increasing its utilization; the standard costs arise as well, mostly in programming complexity, as the RPC calls may now need to use locks and other synchronization primitives in order to ensure their correct operation.

Run-Time Library

The run-time library handles much of the heavy lifting in an RPC system; most performance and reliability issues are handled herein. We'll now discuss some of the major challenges in building such a run-time layer.

One of the first challenges we must overcome is how to locate a remote service. This problem, of **naming**, is a common one in distributed systems, and in some sense goes beyond the scope of our current discussion. The simplest of approaches build on existing naming systems, e.g., hostnames and port numbers provided by current internet protocols. In such a system, the client must know the hostname or IP address of the machine running the desired RPC service, as well as the port number it is using (a port number is just a way of identifying a particular communication activity taking place on a machine, allowing multiple communication channels at once). The protocol suite must then provide a mechanism to route packets to a particular address from any other machine in the system. For a good discussion of naming, you'll have to look elsewhere, e.g., read about DNS and name resolution on the Internet, or better yet just read the excellent chapter in Saltzer and Kaashoek's book [SK09].

Once a client knows which server it should talk to for a particular remote service, the next question is which transport-level protocol should RPC be built upon. Specifically, should the RPC system use a reliable protocol such as TCP/IP, or be built upon an unreliable communication layer such as UDP/IP?

Naively the choice would seem easy: clearly we would like for a request to be reliably delivered to the remote server, and clearly we would like to reliably receive a reply. Thus we should choose the reliable transport protocol such as TCP, right?

Unfortunately, building RPC on top of a reliable communication layer can lead to a major inefficiency in performance. Recall from the discussion above how reliable communication layers work: with acknowledgments plus timeout/retry. Thus, when the client sends an RPC request to the server, the server responds with an acknowledgment so that the caller knows the request was received. Similarly, when the server sends the reply to the client, the client acks it so that the server knows it was received. By building a request/response protocol (such as RPC) on top of a reliable communication layer, two "extra" messages are sent.

For this reason, many RPC packages are built on top of unreliable communication layers, such as UDP. Doing so enables a more efficient RPC layer, but does add the responsibility of providing reliability to the RPC system. The RPC layer achieves the desired level of responsibility by using timeout/retry and acknowledgments much like we described above. By using some form of sequence numbering, the communication layer can guarantee that each RPC takes place exactly once (in the case of no failure), or at most once (in the case where failure arises).

Other Issues

There are some other issues an RPC run-time must handle as well. For example, what happens when a remote call takes a long time to complete? Given our timeout machinery, a long-running remote call might appear as a failure to a client, thus triggering a retry, and thus the need for some care here. One solution is to use an explicit acknowledgment

Aside: THE END-TO-END ARGUMENT

The **end-to-end argument** makes the case that the highest level in a system, i.e., usually the application at "the end", is ultimately the only locale within a layered system where certain functionality can truly be implemented. In their landmark paper [SRC84], Saltzer et al. argue this through an excellent example: reliable file transfer between two machines. If you want to transfer a file from machine A to machine B, and make sure that the bytes that end up on B are exactly the same as those that began on A, you must have an "end-to-end" check of this; lower-level reliable machinery, e.g., in the network or disk, provides no such guarantee.

The contrast is an approach which tries to solve the reliable-file-transfer problem by adding reliability to lower layers of the system. For example, say we build a reliable communication protocol and use it to build our reliable file transfer. The communication protocol guarantees that every byte sent by a sender will be received in order by the receiver, say using timeout/retry, acknowledgments, and sequence numbers. Unfortunately, using such a protocol does not a reliable file transfer make; imagine the bytes getting corrupted in sender memory before the communication even takes place, or something bad happening when the receiver writes the data to disk. In those cases, even though the bytes were delivered reliably across the network, our file transfer was ultimately not reliable. To build a reliable file transfer, one must include end-to-end checks of reliability, e.g., after the entire transfer is complete, read back the file on the receiver disk, compute a checksum, and compare that checksum to that of the file on the sender.

The corollary to this maxim is that sometimes having lower layers provide extra functionality can indeed improve system performance or otherwise optimize a system. Thus, you should not rule out having such machinery at a lower-level in a system; rather, you should carefully consider the utility of such machinery, given its eventual usage in an overall system or application.

(from the receiver to sender) when the reply isn't immediately generated; this lets the client know the server received the request. Then, after some time has passed, the client can periodically ask whether the server is still working on the request; if the server keeps saying "yes", the client should be happy and continue to wait (after all, sometimes a procedure call can take a long time to finish executing).

The run-time must also handle procedure calls with large arguments, larger than what can fit into a single packet. Some lower-level network protocols provide such sender-side **fragmentation** (of larger packets into a set of smaller ones) and receiver-side **reassembly** (of smaller parts into one larger logical whole); if not, the RPC run-time may have to implement such functionality itself. See Birrell and Nelson's paper for details [BN84].

One issue that many systems handle is that of **byte ordering**. As you may know, some machines store values in what is known as **big endian** ordering, whereas others use **little endian** ordering. Big endian stores bytes (say, of an integer) from most significant to least significant bits, much like Arabic numerals; little endian does the opposite. Both are equally valid ways of storing numeric information; the question here is how to communicate between machines of *different* endianness.

RPC packages often handle this by providing a well-defined endianness within their message formats. In Sun's RPC package, the **XDR** (**eXternal Data Representation**) layer provides this functionality. If the machine sending or receiving a message matches the endianness of XDR, messages are just sent and received as expected. If, however, the machine communicating has a different endianness, each piece of information in the message must be converted. Thus, the difference in endianness can have a small performance cost.

A final issue is whether to expose the asynchronous nature of communication to clients, thus enabling some performance optimizations. Specifically, typical RPCs are made **synchronously**, i.e., when a client issues the procedure call, it must wait for the procedure call to return before continuing. Because this wait can be long, and because the client may have other work it could be doing, some RPC packages enable you to invoke an RPC **asynchronously**. When an asynchronous RPC is issued, the RPC package sends the request and returns immediately; the client is then free to do other work, such as call other RPCs or other useful computation. The client at some point will want to see the results of the asynchronous RPC; it thus calls back into the RPC layer, telling it to wait for outstanding RPCs to complete, at which point return arguments can be accessed.

48.6 Summary

We have seen the introduction of a new topic, distributed systems, and its major issue: how to handle failure which is now a commonplace event. As they say inside of Google, when you have just your desktop machine, failure is rare; when you're in a data center with thousands of machines, failure is happening all the time. The key to any distributed system is how you deal with that failure.

We have also seen that communication forms the heart of any distributed system. A common abstraction of that communication is found in remote procedure call (RPC), which enables clients to make remote calls on servers; the RPC package handles all of the gory details, including timeout/retry and acknowledgment, in order to deliver a service that closely mirrors a local procedure call.

The best way to really understand an RPC package is of course to use one yourself. Sun's RPC system, using the stub compiler `rpcgen`, is an older one; Google's gRPC and Apache Thrift are modern takes on the same. Try one out, and see what all the fuss is about.

References

[A70] "The ALOHA System — Another Alternative for Computer Communications" by Norman Abramson. The 1970 Fall Joint Computer Conference. *The ALOHA network pioneered some basic concepts in networking, including exponential back-off and retransmit, which formed the basis for communication in shared-bus Ethernet networks for years.*

[BN84] "Implementing Remote Procedure Calls" by Andrew D. Birrell, Bruce Jay Nelson. ACM TOCS, Volume 2:1, February 1984. *The foundational RPC system upon which all others build. Yes, another pioneering effort from our friends at Xerox PARC.*

[MK09] "The Effectiveness of Checksums for Embedded Control Networks" by Theresa C. Maxino and Philip J. Koopman. IEEE Transactions on Dependable and Secure Computing, 6:1, January '09. *A nice overview of basic checksum machinery and some performance and robustness comparisons between them.*

[LH89] "Memory Coherence in Shared Virtual Memory Systems" by Kai Li and Paul Hudak. ACM TOCS, 7:4, November 1989. *The introduction of software-based shared memory via virtual memory. An intriguing idea for sure, but not a lasting or good one in the end.*

[SK09] "Principles of Computer System Design" by Jerome H. Saltzer and M. Frans Kaashoek. Morgan-Kaufmann, 2009. *An excellent book on systems, and a must for every bookshelf. One of the few terrific discussions on naming we've seen.*

[SRC84] "End-To-End Arguments in System Design" by Jerome H. Saltzer, David P. Reed, David D. Clark. ACM TOCS, 2:4, November 1984. *A beautiful discussion of layering, abstraction, and where functionality must ultimately reside in computer systems.*

[VJ88] "Congestion Avoidance and Control" by Van Jacobson. SIGCOMM '88 . *A pioneering paper on how clients should adjust to perceived network congestion; definitely one of the key pieces of technology underlying the Internet, and a must read for anyone serious about systems, and for Van Jacobson's relatives because well relatives should read all of your papers.*

Homework (Code)

In this section, we'll write some simple communication code to get you familiar with the task of doing so. Have fun!

Questions

1. Using the code provided in the chapter, build a simple UDP-based server and client. The server should receive messages from the client, and reply with an acknowledgment. In this first attempt, do not add any retransmission or robustness (assume that communication works perfectly). Run this on a single machine for testing; later, run it on two different machines.
2. Turn your code into a **communication library**. Specifically, make your own API, with send and receive calls, as well as other API calls as needed. Rewrite your client and server to use your library instead of raw socket calls.
3. Add reliable communication to your burgeoning communication library, in the form of **timeout/retry**. Specifically, your library should make a copy of any message that it is going to send. When sending it, it should start a timer, so it can track how long it has been since the message was sent. On the receiver, the library should **acknowledge** received messages. The client send should **block** when sending, i.e., it should wait until the message has been acknowledged before returning. It should also be willing to retry sending indefinitely. The maximum message size should be that of the largest single message you can send with UDP. Finally, be sure to perform timeout/retry efficiently by putting the caller to sleep until either an ack arrives or the transmission times out; do *not* spin and waste the CPU!
4. Make your library more efficient and feature-filled. First, add very-large message transfer. Specifically, although the network limit maximum message size, your library should take a message of arbitrarily large size and transfer it from client to server. The client should transmit these large messages in pieces to the server; the server-side library code should assemble received fragments into the contiguous whole, and pass the single large buffer to the waiting server code.
5. Do the above again, but with high performance. Instead of sending each fragment one at a time, you should rapidly send many pieces, thus allowing the network to be much more highly utilized. To do so, carefully mark each piece of the transfer so that the re-assembly on the receiver side does not scramble the message.
6. A final implementation challenge: asynchronous message send with in-order delivery. That is, the client should be able to repeatedly call send to send one message after the other; the receiver should call receive and get each message in order, reliably; many messages from

the sender should be able to be in flight concurrently. Also add a sender-side call that enables a client to wait for all outstanding messages to be acknowledged.

7. Now, one more pain point: measurement. Measure the bandwidth of each of your approaches; how much data can you transfer between two different machines, at what rate? Also measure latency: for single packet send and acknowledgment, how quickly does it finish? Finally, do your numbers look reasonable? What did you expect? How can you better set your expectations so as to know if there is a problem, or that your code is working well?

49

Sun's Network File System (NFS)

One of the first uses of distributed client/server computing was in the realm of distributed file systems. In such an environment, there are a number of client machines and one server (or a few); the server stores the data on its disks, and clients request data through well-formed protocol messages. Figure 491 depicts the basic setup.

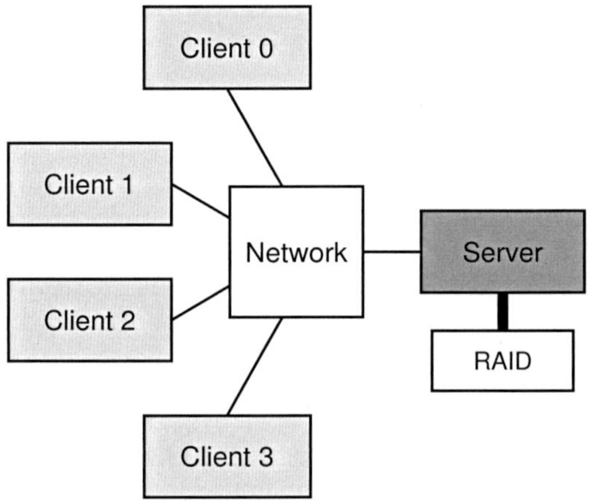

Figure 491: **A Generic Client/Server System**

As you can see from the picture, the server has the disks, and clients send messages across a network to access their directories and files on those disks. Why do we bother with this arrangement? (i.e., why don't we just let clients use their local disks?) Well, primarily this setup allows for easy **sharing** of data across clients. Thus, if you access a file on one machine (Client 0) and then later use another (Client 2), you will have the same view of the file system. Your data is naturally shared across these different machines. A secondary benefit is **centralized administration**; for example, backing up files can be done from the few server machines instead of from the multitude of clients. Another advantage could be **security**; having all servers in a locked machine room prevents certain types of problems from arising.

CRUX: HOW TO BUILD A DISTRIBUTED FILE SYSTEM

How do you build a distributed file system? What are the key aspects to think about? What is easy to get wrong? What can we learn from existing systems?

49.1 A Basic Distributed File System

We now will study the architecture of a simplified distributed file system. A simple client/server distributed file system has more components than the file systems we have studied so far. On the client side, there are client applications which access files and directories through the **client-side file system**. A client application issues **system calls** to the client-side file system (such as `open()`, `read()`, `write()`, `close()`, `mkdir()`, etc.) in order to access files which are stored on the server. Thus, to client applications, the file system does not appear to be any different than a local (disk-based) file system, except perhaps for performance; in this way, distributed file systems provide **transparent** access to files, an obvious goal; after all, who would want to use a file system that required a different set of APIs or otherwise was a pain to use?

The role of the client-side file system is to execute the actions needed to service those system calls. For example, if the client issues a `read()` request, the client-side file system may send a message to the **server-side file system** (or, as it is commonly called, the **file server**) to read a particular block; the file server will then read the block from disk (or its own in-memory cache), and send a message back to the client with the requested data. The client-side file system will then copy the data into the user buffer supplied to the `read()` system call and thus the request will complete. Note that a subsequent `read()` of the same block on the client may be **cached** in client memory or on the client's disk even; in the best such case, no network traffic need be generated.

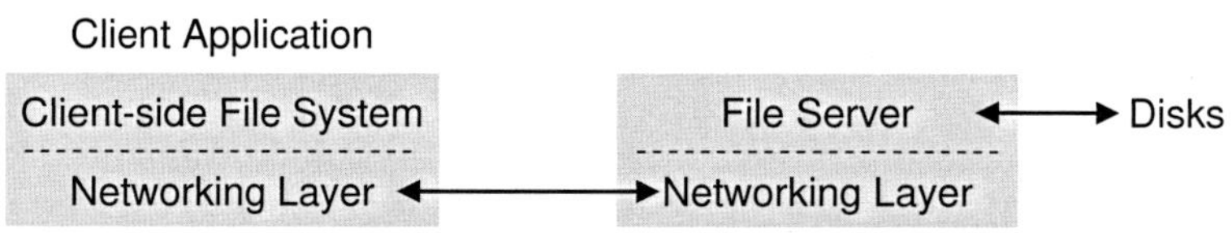

Figure 492: **Distributed File System Architecture**

From this simple overview, you should get a sense that there are two important pieces of software in a client/server distributed file system: the client-side file system and the file server. Together their behavior determines the behavior of the distributed file system. Now it's time to study one particular system: Sun's Network File System (NFS).

> ASIDE: WHY SERVERS CRASH
>
> Before getting into the details of the NFSv2 protocol, you might be wondering: why do servers crash? Well, as you might guess, there are plenty of reasons. Servers may simply suffer from a **power outage** (temporarily); only when power is restored can the machines be restarted. Servers are often comprised of hundreds of thousands or even millions of lines of code; thus, they have **bugs** (even good software has a few bugs per hundred or thousand lines of code), and thus they eventually will trigger a bug that will cause them to crash. They also have memory leaks; even a small memory leak will cause a system to run out of memory and crash. And, finally, in distributed systems, there is a network between the client and the server; if the network acts strangely (for example, if it becomes **partitioned** and clients and servers are working but cannot communicate), it may appear as if a remote machine has crashed, but in reality it is just not currently reachable through the network.

49.2 On To NFS

One of the earliest and quite successful distributed systems was developed by Sun Microsystems, and is known as the Sun Network File System (or NFS) [S86]. In defining NFS, Sun took an unusual approach: instead of building a proprietary and closed system, Sun instead developed an **open protocol** which simply specified the exact message formats that clients and servers would use to communicate. Different groups could develop their own NFS servers and thus compete in an NFS marketplace while preserving interoperability. It worked: today there are many companies that sell NFS servers (including Oracle/Sun, NetApp [HLM94], EMC, IBM, and others), and the widespread success of NFS is likely attributed to this "open market" approach.

49.3 Focus: Simple And Fast Server Crash Recovery

In this chapter, we will discuss the classic NFS protocol (version 2, a.k.a. NFSv2), which was the standard for many years; small changes were made in moving to NFSv3, and larger-scale protocol changes were made in moving to NFSv4. However, NFSv2 is both wonderful and frustrating and thus serves as our focus.

In NFSv2, the main goal in the design of the protocol was *simple and fast server crash recovery*. In a multiple-client, single-server environment, this goal makes a great deal of sense; any minute that the server is down (or unavailable) makes *all* the client machines (and their users) unhappy and unproductive. Thus, as the server goes, so goes the entire system.

49.4 Key To Fast Crash Recovery: Statelessness

This simple goal is realized in NFSv2 by designing what we refer to as a **stateless** protocol. The server, by design, does not keep track of anything about what is happening at each client. For example, the server does not know which clients are caching which blocks, or which files are currently open at each client, or the current file pointer position for a file, etc. Simply put, the server does not track anything about what clients are doing; rather, the protocol is designed to deliver in each protocol request *all the information* that is needed in order to complete the request. If it doesn't now, this stateless approach will make more sense as we discuss the protocol in more detail below.

For an example of a **stateful** (not stateless) protocol, consider the `open()` system call. Given a pathname, `open()` returns a file descriptor (an integer). This descriptor is used on subsequent `read()` or `write()` requests to access various file blocks, as in this application code (note that proper error checking of the system calls is omitted for space reasons):

```
char buffer[MAX];
int fd = open("foo", O_RDONLY); // get descriptor "fd"
read(fd, buffer, MAX);    // read MAX from foo via "fd"
read(fd, buffer, MAX);    // read MAX again
...
read(fd, buffer, MAX);    // read MAX again
close(fd);                // close file
```

Figure 49.3: **Client Code: Reading From A File**

Now imagine that the client-side file system opens the file by sending a protocol message to the server saying "open the file 'foo' and give me back a descriptor". The file server then opens the file locally on its side and sends the descriptor back to the client. On subsequent reads, the client application uses that descriptor to call the `read()` system call; the client-side file system then passes the descriptor in a message to the file server, saying "read some bytes from the file that is referred to by the descriptor I am passing you here".

In this example, the file descriptor is a piece of **shared state** between the client and the server (Ousterhout calls this **distributed state** [O91]). Shared state, as we hinted above, complicates crash recovery. Imagine the server crashes after the first read completes, but before the client has issued the second one. After the server is up and running again, the client then issues the second read. Unfortunately, the server has no idea to which file `fd` is referring; that information was ephemeral (i.e., in memory) and thus lost when the server crashed. To handle this situation, the client and server would have to engage in some kind of **recovery protocol**, where the client would make sure to keep enough information around in its memory to be able to tell the server what it needs to know (in this case, that file descriptor `fd` refers to file `foo`).

It gets even worse when you consider the fact that a stateful server has to deal with client crashes. Imagine, for example, a client that opens a file and then crashes. The `open()` uses up a file descriptor on the server; how can the server know it is OK to close a given file? In normal operation, a client would eventually call `close()` and thus inform the server that the file should be closed. However, when a client crashes, the server never receives a `close()`, and thus has to notice the client has crashed in order to close the file.

For these reasons, the designers of NFS decided to pursue a stateless approach: each client operation contains all the information needed to complete the request. No fancy crash recovery is needed; the server just starts running again, and a client, at worst, might have to retry a request.

49.5 The NFSv2 Protocol

We thus arrive at the NFSv2 protocol definition. Our problem statement is simple:

THE CRUX: HOW TO DEFINE A STATELESS FILE PROTOCOL

How can we define the network protocol to enable stateless operation? Clearly, stateful calls like `open()` can't be a part of the discussion (as it would require the server to track open files); however, the client application will want to call `open()`, `read()`, `write()`, `close()` and other standard API calls to access files and directories. Thus, as a refined question, how do we define the protocol to both be stateless *and* support the POSIX file system API?

One key to understanding the design of the NFS protocol is understanding the **file handle**. File handles are used to uniquely describe the file or directory a particular operation is going to operate upon; thus, many of the protocol requests include a file handle.

You can think of a file handle as having three important components: a *volume identifier*, an *inode number*, and a *generation number*; together, these three items comprise a unique identifier for a file or directory that a client wishes to access. The volume identifier informs the server which file system the request refers to (an NFS server can export more than one file system); the inode number tells the server which file within that partition the request is accessing. Finally, the generation number is needed when reusing an inode number; by incrementing it whenever an inode number is reused, the server ensures that a client with an old file handle can't accidentally access the newly-allocated file.

Here is a summary of some of the important pieces of the protocol; the full protocol is available elsewhere (see Callaghan's book for an excellent and detailed overview of NFS [C00]).

NFSPROC_GETATTR	file handle returns: attributes
NFSPROC_SETATTR	file handle, attributes returns: –
NFSPROC_LOOKUP	directory file handle, name of file/dir to look up returns: file handle
NFSPROC_READ	file handle, offset, count data, attributes
NFSPROC_WRITE	file handle, offset, count, data attributes
NFSPROC_CREATE	directory file handle, name of file, attributes –
NFSPROC_REMOVE	directory file handle, name of file to be removed –
NFSPROC_MKDIR	directory file handle, name of directory, attributes file handle
NFSPROC_RMDIR	directory file handle, name of directory to be removed –
NFSPROC_READDIR	directory handle, count of bytes to read, cookie returns: directory entries, cookie (to get more entries)

Figure 494: **The NFS Protocol: Examples**

We briefly highlight the important components of the protocol. First, the LOOKUP protocol message is used to obtain a file handle, which is then subsequently used to access file data. The client passes a directory file handle and name of a file to look up, and the handle to that file (or directory) plus its attributes are passed back to the client from the server.

For example, assume the client already has a directory file handle for the root directory of a file system (/) (indeed, this would be obtained through the NFS **mount protocol**, which is how clients and servers first are connected together; we do not discuss the mount protocol here for sake of brevity). If an application running on the client opens the file `/foo.txt`, the client-side file system sends a lookup request to the server, passing it the root file handle and the name `foo.txt`; if successful, the file handle (and attributes) for `foo.txt` will be returned.

In case you are wondering, attributes are just the metadata that the file system tracks about each file, including fields such as file creation time, last modification time, size, ownership and permissions information, and so forth, i.e., the same type of information that you would get back if you called `stat()` on a file.

Once a file handle is available, the client can issue READ and WRITE protocol messages on a file to read or write the file, respectively. The READ protocol message requires the protocol to pass along the file handle of the file along with the offset within the file and number of bytes to read. The server then will be able to issue the read (after all, the handle tells the server which volume and which inode to read from, and the offset and count tells it which bytes of the file to read) and return the data to the client (or an error if there was a failure). WRITE is handled similarly, except the data is passed from the client to the server, and just a success code is returned.

One last interesting protocol message is the GETATTR request; given a file handle, it simply fetches the attributes for that file, including the last modified time of the file. We will see why this protocol request is important in NFSv2 below when we discuss caching (can you guess why?).

49.6 From Protocol To Distributed File System

Hopefully you are now getting some sense of how this protocol is turned into a file system across the client-side file system and the file server. The client-side file system tracks open files, and generally translates application requests into the relevant set of protocol messages. The server simply responds to protocol messages, each of which contains all information needed to complete request.

For example, let us consider a simple application which reads a file. In the diagram (Figure 495), we show what system calls the application makes, and what the client-side file system and file server do in responding to such calls.

A few comments about the figure. First, notice how the client tracks all relevant **state** for the file access, including the mapping of the integer file descriptor to an NFS file handle as well as the current file pointer. This enables the client to turn each read request (which you may have noticed do *not* specify the offset to read from explicitly) into a properly-formatted read protocol message which tells the server exactly which bytes from the file to read. Upon a successful read, the client updates the current file position; subsequent reads are issued with the same file handle but a different offset.

Second, you may notice where server interactions occur. When the file is opened for the first time, the client-side file system sends a LOOKUP request message. Indeed, if a long pathname must be traversed (e.g., `/home/remzi/foo.txt`), the client would send three LOOKUPs: one to look up `home` in the directory `/`, one to look up `remzi` in `home`, and finally one to look up `foo.txt` in `remzi`.

Third, you may notice how each server request has all the information needed to complete the request in its entirety. This design point is critical to be able to gracefully recover from server failure, as we will now discuss in more detail; it ensures that the server does not need state to be able to respond to the request.

Client	Server
fd = open("/foo", ...);	
Send LOOKUP (rootdir FH, "foo")	
	Receive LOOKUP request look for "foo" in root dir return foo's FH + attributes
Receive LOOKUP reply allocate file desc in open file table store foo's FH in table store current file position (0) return file descriptor to application	
read(fd, buffer, MAX); Index into open file table with fd get NFS file handle (FH) use current file position as offset Send READ (FH, offset=0, count=MAX)	
	Receive READ request use FH to get volume/inode num read inode from disk (or cache) compute block location (using offset) read data from disk (or cache) return data to client
Receive READ reply update file position (+bytes read) set current file position = MAX return data/error code to app	
read(fd, buffer, MAX); Same except offset=MAX and set current file position = 2*MAX	
read(fd, buffer, MAX); Same except offset=2*MAX and set current file position = 3*MAX	
close(fd); Just need to clean up local structures Free descriptor "fd" in open file table (No need to talk to server)	

Figure 495: **Reading A File: Client-side And File Server Actions**

> TIP: IDEMPOTENCY IS POWERFUL
> **Idempotency** is a useful property when building reliable systems. When an operation can be issued more than once, it is much easier to handle failure of the operation; you can just retry it. If an operation is *not* idempotent, life becomes more difficult.

49.7 Handling Server Failure With Idempotent Operations

When a client sends a message to the server, it sometimes does not receive a reply. There are many possible reasons for this failure to respond. In some cases, the message may be dropped by the network; networks do lose messages, and thus either the request or the reply could be lost and thus the client would never receive a response.

It is also possible that the server has crashed, and thus is not currently responding to messages. After a bit, the server will be rebooted and start running again, but in the meanwhile all requests have been lost. In all of these cases, clients are left with a question: what should they do when the server does not reply in a timely manner?

In NFSv2, a client handles all of these failures in a single, uniform, and elegant way: it simply *retries* the request. Specifically, after sending the request, the client sets a timer to go off after a specified time period. If a reply is received before the timer goes off, the timer is canceled and all is well. If, however, the timer goes off *before* any reply is received, the client assumes the request has not been processed and resends it. If the server replies, all is well and the client has neatly handled the problem.

The ability of the client to simply retry the request (regardless of what caused the failure) is due to an important property of most NFS requests: they are **idempotent**. An operation is called idempotent when the effect of performing the operation multiple times is equivalent to the effect of performing the operation a single time. For example, if you store a value to a memory location three times, it is the same as doing so once; thus "store value to memory" is an idempotent operation. If, however, you increment a counter three times, it results in a different amount than doing so just once; thus, "increment counter" is not idempotent. More generally, any operation that just reads data is obviously idempotent; an operation that updates data must be more carefully considered to determine if it has this property.

The heart of the design of crash recovery in NFS is the idempotency of most common operations. LOOKUP and READ requests are trivially idempotent, as they only read information from the file server and do not update it. More interestingly, WRITE requests are also idempotent. If, for example, a WRITE fails, the client can simply retry it. The WRITE message contains the data, the count, and (importantly) the exact offset to write the data to. Thus, it can be repeated with the knowledge that the outcome of multiple writes is the same as the outcome of a single one.

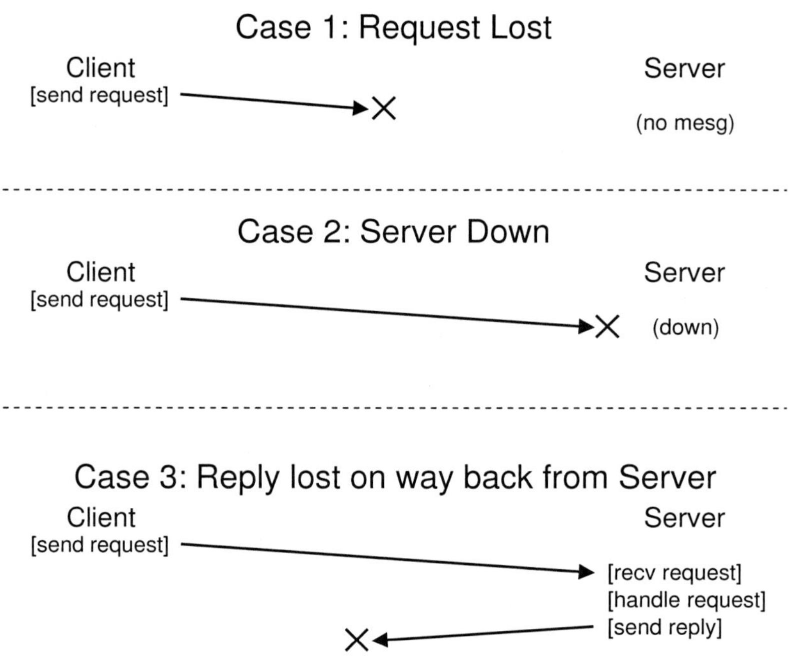

Figure 496: **The Three Types Of Loss**

In this way, the client can handle all timeouts in a unified way. If a WRITE request was simply lost (Case 1 above), the client will retry it, the server will perform the write, and all will be well. The same will happen if the server happened to be down while the request was sent, but back up and running when the second request is sent, and again all works as desired (Case 2). Finally, the server may in fact receive the WRITE request, issue the write to its disk, and send a reply. This reply may get lost (Case 3), again causing the client to re-send the request. When the server receives the request again, it will simply do the exact same thing: write the data to disk and reply that it has done so. If the client this time receives the reply, all is again well, and thus the client has handled both message loss and server failure in a uniform manner. Neat!

A small aside: some operations are hard to make idempotent. For example, when you try to make a directory that already exists, you are informed that the mkdir request has failed. Thus, in NFS, if the file server receives a MKDIR protocol message and executes it successfully but the reply is lost, the client may repeat it and encounter that failure when in fact the operation at first succeeded and then only failed on the retry. Thus, life is not perfect.

TIP: PERFECT IS THE ENEMY OF THE GOOD (VOLTAIRE'S LAW)
Even when you design a beautiful system, sometimes all the corner cases don't work out exactly as you might like. Take the mkdir example above; one could redesign mkdir to have different semantics, thus making it idempotent (think about how you might do so); however, why bother? The NFS design philosophy covers most of the important cases, and overall makes the system design clean and simple with regards to failure. Thus, accepting that life isn't perfect and still building the system is a sign of good engineering. Apparently, this wisdom is attributed to Voltaire, for saying "... a wise Italian says that the best is the enemy of the good" [V72], and thus we call it **Voltaire's Law**.

49.8 Improving Performance: Client-side Caching

Distributed file systems are good for a number of reasons, but sending all read and write requests across the network can lead to a big performance problem: the network generally isn't that fast, especially as compared to local memory or disk. Thus, another problem: how can we improve the performance of a distributed file system?

The answer, as you might guess from reading the big bold words in the sub-heading above, is client-side **caching**. The NFS client-side file system caches file data (and metadata) that it has read from the server in client memory. Thus, while the first access is expensive (i.e., it requires network communication), subsequent accesses are serviced quite quickly out of client memory.

The cache also serves as a temporary buffer for writes. When a client application first writes to a file, the client buffers the data in client memory (in the same cache as the data it read from the file server) before writing the data out to the server. Such **write buffering** is useful because it decouples application `write()` latency from actual write performance, i.e., the application's call to `write()` succeeds immediately (and just puts the data in the client-side file system's cache); only later does the data get written out to the file server.

Thus, NFS clients cache data and performance is usually great and we are done, right? Unfortunately, not quite. Adding caching into any sort of system with multiple client caches introduces a big and interesting challenge which we will refer to as the **cache consistency problem**.

49.9 The Cache Consistency Problem

The cache consistency problem is best illustrated with two clients and a single server. Imagine client C1 reads a file F, and keeps a copy of the file in its local cache. Now imagine a different client, C2, overwrites the file F, thus changing its contents; let's call the new version of the file F

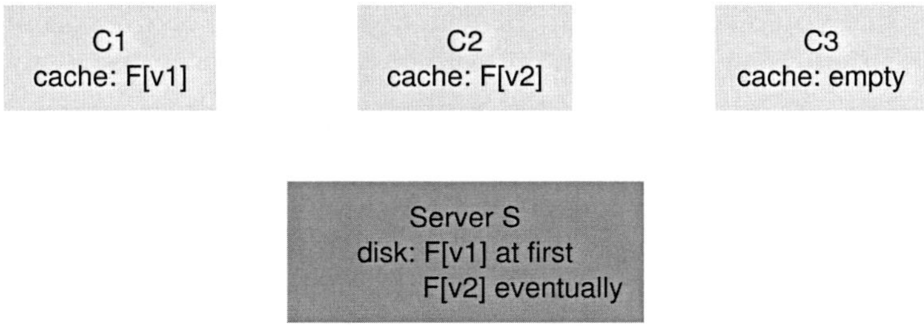

Figure 497: **The Cache Consistency Problem**

(version 2), or F[v2] and the old version F[v1] so we can keep the two distinct (but of course the file has the same name, just different contents). Finally, there is a third client, C3, which has not yet accessed the file F.

You can probably see the problem that is upcoming (Figure 497). In fact, there are two subproblems. The first subproblem is that the client C2 may buffer its writes in its cache for a time before propagating them to the server; in this case, while F[v2] sits in C2's memory, any access of F from another client (say C3) will fetch the old version of the file (F[v1]). Thus, by buffering writes at the client, other clients may get stale versions of the file, which may be undesirable; indeed, imagine the case where you log into machine C2, update F, and then log into C3 and try to read the file, only to get the old copy! Certainly this could be frustrating. Thus, let us call this aspect of the cache consistency problem **update visibility**; when do updates from one client become visible at other clients?

The second subproblem of cache consistency is a **stale cache**; in this case, C2 has finally flushed its writes to the file server, and thus the server has the latest version (F[v2]). However, C1 still has F[v1] in its cache; if a program running on C1 reads file F, it will get a stale version (F[v1]) and not the most recent copy (F[v2]), which is (often) undesirable.

NFSv2 implementations solve these cache consistency problems in two ways. First, to address update visibility, clients implement what is sometimes called **flush-on-close** (a.k.a., **close-to-open**) consistency semantics; specifically, when a file is written to and subsequently closed by a client application, the client flushes all updates (i.e., dirty pages in the cache) to the server. With flush-on-close consistency, NFS ensures that a subsequent open from another node will see the latest file version.

Second, to address the stale-cache problem, NFSv2 clients first check to see whether a file has changed before using its cached contents. Specifically, before using a cached block, the client-side file system will issue a GETATTR request to the server to fetch the file's attributes. The attributes, importantly, include information as to when the file was last modified on the server; if the time-of-modification is more recent than the time that the file was fetched into the client cache, the client **invalidates** the file, thus removing it from the client cache and ensuring that subsequent reads will go to the server and retrieve the latest version of the file. If, on the other hand, the client sees that it has the latest version of the file, it will go ahead and use the cached contents, thus increasing performance.

When the original team at Sun implemented this solution to the stale-cache problem, they realized a new problem; suddenly, the NFS server was flooded with GETATTR requests. A good engineering principle to follow is to design for the **common case**, and to make it work well; here, although the common case was that a file was accessed only from a single client (perhaps repeatedly), the client always had to send GETATTR requests to the server to make sure no one else had changed the file. A client thus bombards the server, constantly asking "has anyone changed this file?", when most of the time no one had.

To remedy this situation (somewhat), an **attribute cache** was added to each client. A client would still validate a file before accessing it, but most often would just look in the attribute cache to fetch the attributes. The attributes for a particular file were placed in the cache when the file was first accessed, and then would timeout after a certain amount of time (say 3 seconds). Thus, during those three seconds, all file accesses would determine that it was OK to use the cached file and thus do so with no network communication with the server.

49.10 Assessing NFS Cache Consistency

A few final words about NFS cache consistency. The flush-on-close behavior was added to "make sense", but introduced a certain performance problem. Specifically, if a temporary or short-lived file was created on a client and then soon deleted, it would still be forced to the server. A more ideal implementation might keep such short-lived files in memory until they are deleted and thus remove the server interaction entirely, perhaps increasing performance.

More importantly, the addition of an attribute cache into NFS made it very hard to understand or reason about exactly what version of a file one was getting. Sometimes you would get the latest version; sometimes you would get an old version simply because your attribute cache hadn't yet timed out and thus the client was happy to give you what was in client memory. Although this was fine most of the time, it would (and still does!) occasionally lead to odd behavior.

And thus we have described the oddity that is NFS client caching. It serves as an interesting example where details of an implementation serve to define user-observable semantics, instead of the other way around.

49.11 Implications On Server-Side Write Buffering

Our focus so far has been on client caching, and that is where most of the interesting issues arise. However, NFS servers tend to be well-equipped machines with a lot of memory too, and thus they have caching concerns as well. When data (and metadata) is read from disk, NFS servers will keep it in memory, and subsequent reads of said data (and metadata) will not go to disk, a potential (small) boost in performance.

More intriguing is the case of write buffering. NFS servers absolutely may *not* return success on a WRITE protocol request until the write has been forced to stable storage (e.g., to disk or some other persistent device). While they can place a copy of the data in server memory, returning success to the client on a WRITE protocol request could result in incorrect behavior; can you figure out why?

The answer lies in our assumptions about how clients handle server failure. Imagine the following sequence of writes as issued by a client:

```
write(fd, a_buffer, size); // fill 1st block with a's
write(fd, b_buffer, size); // fill 2nd block with b's
write(fd, c_buffer, size); // fill 3rd block with c's
```

These writes overwrite the three blocks of a file with a block of a's, then b's, and then c's. Thus, if the file initially looked like this:

```
xxxxxxxxxxxxxxxxxxxxxxxxxxxxxxxxxxxxxxxxxxxx
yyyyyyyyyyyyyyyyyyyyyyyyyyyyyyyyyyyyyyyyyyyy
zzzzzzzzzzzzzzzzzzzzzzzzzzzzzzzzzzzzzzzzzzzz
```

We might expect the final result after these writes to be like this, with the x's, y's, and z's, would be overwritten with a's, b's, and c's, respectively.

```
aaaaaaaaaaaaaaaaaaaaaaaaaaaaaaaaaaaaaaaaaaaa
bbbbbbbbbbbbbbbbbbbbbbbbbbbbbbbbbbbbbbbbbbbb
cccccccccccccccccccccccccccccccccccccccccccc
```

Now let's assume for the sake of the example that these three client writes were issued to the server as three distinct WRITE protocol messages. Assume the first WRITE message is received by the server and issued to the disk, and the client informed of its success. Now assume the second write is just buffered in memory, and the server also reports it success to the client *before* forcing it to disk; unfortunately, the server crashes before writing it to disk. The server quickly restarts and receives the third write request, which also succeeds.

Thus, to the client, all the requests succeeded, but we are surprised that the file contents look like this:

```
aaaaaaaaaaaaaaaaaaaaaaaaaaaaaaaaaaaaaaaaaaaa
yyyyyyyyyyyyyyyyyyyyyyyyyyyyyyyyyyyyyyyyyyyy <--- oops
cccccccccccccccccccccccccccccccccccccccccccc
```

Yikes! Because the server told the client that the second write was successful before committing it to disk, an old chunk is left in the file, which, depending on the application, might be catastrophic.

> ASIDE: INNOVATION BREEDS INNOVATION
>
> As with many pioneering technologies, bringing NFS into the world also required other fundamental innovations to enable its success. Probably the most lasting is the **Virtual File System** (**VFS**) / **Virtual Node** (**vnode**) interface, introduced by Sun to allow different file systems to be readily plugged into the operating system [K86].
>
> The VFS layer includes operations that are done to an entire file system, such as mounting and unmounting, getting file-system wide statistics, and forcing all dirty (not yet written) writes to disk. The vnode layer consists of all operations one can perform on a file, such as open, close, reads, writes, and so forth.
>
> To build a new file system, one simply has to define these "methods"; the framework then handles the rest, connecting system calls to the particular file system implementation, performing generic functions common to all file systems (e.g., caching) in a centralized manner, and thus providing a way for multiple file system implementations to operate simultaneously within the same system.
>
> Although some of the details have changed, many modern systems have some form of a VFS/vnode layer, including Linux, BSD variants, macOS, and even Windows (in the form of the Installable File System). Even if NFS becomes less relevant to the world, some of the necessary foundations beneath it will live on.

To avoid this problem, NFS servers *must* commit each write to stable (persistent) storage before informing the client of success; doing so enables the client to detect server failure during a write, and thus retry until it finally succeeds. Doing so ensures we will never end up with file contents intermingled as in the above example.

The problem that this requirement gives rise to in NFS server implementation is that write performance, without great care, can be *the* major performance bottleneck. Indeed, some companies (e.g., Network Appliance) came into existence with the simple objective of building an NFS server that can perform writes quickly; one trick they use is to first put writes in a battery-backed memory, thus enabling to quickly reply to WRITE requests without fear of losing the data and without the cost of having to write to disk right away; the second trick is to use a file system design specifically designed to write to disk quickly when one finally needs to do so [HLM94, RO91].

49.12 Summary

We have seen the introduction of the NFS distributed file system. NFS is centered around the idea of simple and fast recovery in the face of server failure, and achieves this end through careful protocol design. Idem-

ASIDE: KEY NFS TERMS

- The key to realizing the main goal of fast and simple crash recovery in NFS is in the design of a **stateless** protocol. After a crash, the server can quickly restart and begin serving requests again; clients just **retry** requests until they succeed.
- Making requests **idempotent** is a central aspect of the NFS protocol. An operation is idempotent when the effect of performing it multiple times is equivalent to performing it once. In NFS, idempotency enables client retry without worry, and unifies client lost-message retransmission and how the client handles server crashes.
- Performance concerns dictate the need for client-side **caching** and **write buffering**, but introduces a **cache consistency problem**.
- NFS implementations provide an engineering solution to cache consistency through multiple means: a **flush-on-close** (**close-to-open**) approach ensures that when a file is closed, its contents are forced to the server, enabling other clients to observe the updates to it. An attribute cache reduces the frequency of checking with the server whether a file has changed (via GETATTR requests).
- NFS servers must commit writes to persistent media before returning success; otherwise, data loss can arise.
- To support NFS integration into the operating system, Sun introduced the **VFS/Vnode** interface, enabling multiple file system implementations to coexist in the same operating system.

potency of operations is essential; because a client can safely replay a failed operation, it is OK to do so whether or not the server has executed the request.

We also have seen how the introduction of caching into a multiple-client, single-server system can complicate things. In particular, the system must resolve the cache consistency problem in order to behave reasonably; however, NFS does so in a slightly ad hoc fashion which can occasionally result in observably weird behavior. Finally, we saw how server caching can be tricky: writes to the server must be forced to stable storage before returning success (otherwise data can be lost).

We haven't talked about other issues which are certainly relevant, notably security. Security in early NFS implementations was remarkably lax; it was rather easy for any user on a client to masquerade as other users and thus gain access to virtually any file. Subsequent integration with more serious authentication services (e.g., Kerberos [NT94]) have addressed these obvious deficiencies.

References

[AKW88] "The AWK Programming Language" by Alfred V. Aho, Brian W. Kernighan, Peter J. Weinberger. Pearson, 1988 (1st edition). *A concise, wonderful book about awk. We once had the pleasure of meeting Peter Weinberger; when he introduced himself, he said "I'm Peter Weinberger, you know, the 'W' in awk?" As huge awk fans, this was a moment to savor. One of us (Remzi) then said, "I love awk! I particularly love the book, which makes everything so wonderfully clear." Weinberger replied (crestfallen), "Oh, Kernighan wrote the book."*

[C00] "NFS Illustrated" by Brent Callaghan. Addison-Wesley Professional Computing Series, 2000. *A great NFS reference; incredibly thorough and detailed per the protocol itself.*

[ES03] "New NFS Tracing Tools and Techniques for System Analysis" by Daniel Ellard and Margo Seltzer. LISA '03, San Diego, California. *An intricate, careful analysis of NFS done via passive tracing. By simply monitoring network traffic, the authors show how to derive a vast amount of file system understanding.*

[HLM94] "File System Design for an NFS File Server Appliance" by Dave Hitz, James Lau, Michael Malcolm. USENIX Winter 1994. San Francisco, California, 1994. *Hitz et al. were greatly influenced by previous work on log-structured file systems.*

[K86] "Vnodes: An Architecture for Multiple File System Types in Sun UNIX" by Steve R. Kleiman. USENIX Summer '86, Atlanta, Georgia. *This paper shows how to build a flexible file system architecture into an operating system, enabling multiple different file system implementations to coexist. Now used in virtually every modern operating system in some form.*

[NT94] "Kerberos: An Authentication Service for Computer Networks" by B. Clifford Neuman, Theodore Ts'o. IEEE Communications, 32(9):33-38, September 1994. *Kerberos is an early and hugely influential authentication service. We probably should write a book chapter about it sometime...*

[O91] "The Role of Distributed State" by John K. Ousterhout. 1991. Available at this site: `ftp://ftp.cs.berkeley.edu/ucb/sprite/papers/state.ps`. *A rarely referenced discussion of distributed state; a broader perspective on the problems and challenges.*

[P+94] "NFS Version 3: Design and Implementation" by Brian Pawlowski, Chet Juszczak, Peter Staubach, Carl Smith, Diane Lebel, Dave Hitz. USENIX Summer 1994, pages 137-152. *The small modifications that underlie NFS version 3.*

[P+00] "The NFS version 4 protocol" by Brian Pawlowski, David Noveck, David Robinson, Robert Thurlow. 2nd International System Administration and Networking Conference (SANE 2000). *Undoubtedly the most literary paper on NFS ever written.*

[RO91] "The Design and Implementation of the Log-structured File System" by Mendel Rosenblum, John Ousterhout. Symposium on Operating Systems Principles (SOSP), 1991. *LFS again. No, you can never get enough LFS.*

[S86] "The Sun Network File System: Design, Implementation and Experience" by Russel Sandberg. USENIX Summer 1986. *The original NFS paper; though a bit of a challenging read, it is worthwhile to see the source of these wonderful ideas.*

[Sun89] "NFS: Network File System Protocol Specification" by Sun Microsystems, Inc. Request for Comments: 1094, March 1989. Available: `http://www.ietf.org/rfc/rfc1094.txt`. *The dreaded specification; read it if you must, i.e., you are getting paid to read it. Hopefully, paid a lot. Cash money!*

[V72] "La Begueule" by Francois-Marie Arouet a.k.a. Voltaire. Published in 1772. *Voltaire said a number of clever things, this being but one example. For example, Voltaire also said "If you have two religions in your land, the two will cut each other's throats; but if you have thirty religions, they will dwell in peace." What do you say to that, Democrats and Republicans?*

Homework (Measurement)

In this homework, you'll do a little bit of NFS trace analysis using real traces. The source of these traces is Ellard and Seltzer's effort [ES03]. Make sure to read the related README and download the relevant tarball from the OSTEP homework page (as usual) before starting.

Questions

1. A first question for your trace analysis: using the timestamps found in the first column, determine the period of time the traces were taken from. How long is the period? What day/week/month/year was it? (does this match the hint given in the file name?) Hint: Use the tools `head -1` and `tail -1` to extract the first and last lines of the file, and do the calculation.
2. Now, let's do some operation counts. How many of each type of operation occur in the trace? Sort these by frequency; which operation is most frequent? Does NFS live up to its reputation?
3. Now let's look at some particular operations in more detail. For example, the GETATTR request returns a lot of information about files, including which user ID the request is being performed for, the size of the file, and so forth. Make a distribution of file sizes accessed within the trace; what is the average file size? Also, how many different users access files in the trace? Do a few users dominate traffic, or is it more spread out? What other interesting information is found within GETATTR replies?
4. You can also look at requests to a given file and determine how files are being accessed. For example, is a given file being read or written sequentially? Or randomly? Look at the details of READ and WRITE requests/replies to compute the answer.
5. Traffic comes from many machines and goes to one server (in this trace). Compute a traffic matrix, which shows how many different clients there are in the trace, and how many requests/replies go to each. Do a few machines dominate, or is it more evenly balanced?
6. The timing information, and the per-request/reply unique ID, should allow you to compute the latency for a given request. Compute the latencies of all request/reply pairs, and plot them as a distribution. What is the average? Maximum? Minimum?
7. Sometimes requests are retried, as the request or its reply could be lost or dropped. Can you find any evidence of such retrying in the trace sample?
8. There are many other questions you could answer through more analysis. What questions do you think are important? Suggest them to us, and perhaps we'll add them here!

50

The Andrew File System (AFS)

The Andrew File System was introduced at Carnegie-Mellon University (CMU) [1] in the 1980's [H+88]. Led by the well-known Professor M. Satyanarayanan of Carnegie-Mellon University ("Satya" for short), the main goal of this project was simple: **scale**. Specifically, how can one design a distributed file system such that a server can support as many clients as possible?

Interestingly, there are numerous aspects of design and implementation that affect scalability. Most important is the design of the **protocol** between clients and servers. In NFS, for example, the protocol forces clients to check with the server periodically to determine if cached contents have changed; because each check uses server resources (including CPU and network bandwidth), frequent checks like this will limit the number of clients a server can respond to and thus limit scalability.

AFS also differs from NFS in that from the beginning, reasonable user-visible behavior was a first-class concern. In NFS, cache consistency is hard to describe because it depends directly on low-level implementation details, including client-side cache timeout intervals. In AFS, cache consistency is simple and readily understood: when the file is opened, a client will generally receive the latest consistent copy from the server.

50.1 AFS Version 1

We will discuss two versions of AFS [H+88, S+85]. The first version (which we will call AFSv1, but actually the original system was called the ITC distributed file system [S+85]) had some of the basic design in place, but didn't scale as desired, which led to a re-design and the final protocol (which we will call AFSv2, or just AFS) [H+88]. We now discuss the first version.

[1] Though originally referred to as "Carnegie-Mellon University", CMU later dropped the hyphen, and thus was born the modern form, "Carnegie Mellon University." As AFS derived from work in the early 80's, we refer to CMU in its original fully-hyphenated form. See `https://www.quora.com/When-did-Carnegie-Mellon-University-remove-the-hyphen-in-the-university-name` for more details, if you are into really boring minutiae.

```
TestAuth       Test whether a file has changed
               (used to validate cached entries)
GetFileStat    Get the stat info for a file
Fetch          Fetch the contents of file
Store          Store this file on the server
SetFileStat    Set the stat info for a file
ListDir        List the contents of a directory
```

Figure 501: **AFSv1 Protocol Highlights**

One of the basic tenets of all versions of AFS is **whole-file caching** on the **local disk** of the client machine that is accessing a file. When you `open()` a file, the entire file (if it exists) is fetched from the server and stored in a file on your local disk. Subsequent application `read()` and `write()` operations are redirected to the local file system where the file is stored; thus, these operations require no network communication and are fast. Finally, upon `close()`, the file (if it has been modified) is flushed back to the server. Note the obvious contrasts with NFS, which caches *blocks* (not whole files, although NFS could of course cache every block of an entire file) and does so in client *memory* (not local disk).

Let's get into the details a bit more. When a client application first calls `open()`, the AFS client-side code (which the AFS designers call **Venus**) would send a Fetch protocol message to the server. The Fetch protocol message would pass the entire pathname of the desired file (for example, `/home/remzi/notes.txt`) to the file server (the group of which they called **Vice**), which would then traverse the pathname, find the desired file, and ship the entire file back to the client. The client-side code would then cache the file on the local disk of the client (by writing it to local disk). As we said above, subsequent `read()` and `write()` system calls are strictly *local* in AFS (no communication with the server occurs); they are just redirected to the local copy of the file. Because the `read()` and `write()` calls act just like calls to a local file system, once a block is accessed, it also may be cached in client memory. Thus, AFS also uses client memory to cache copies of blocks that it has in its local disk. Finally, when finished, the AFS client checks if the file has been modified (i.e., that it has been opened for writing); if so, it flushes the new version back to the server with a Store protocol message, sending the entire file and pathname to the server for permanent storage.

The next time the file is accessed, AFSv1 does so much more efficiently. Specifically, the client-side code first contacts the server (using the TestAuth protocol message) in order to determine whether the file has changed. If not, the client would use the locally-cached copy, thus improving performance by avoiding a network transfer. The figure above shows some of the protocol messages in AFSv1. Note that this early version of the protocol only cached file contents; directories, for example, were only kept at the server.

> TIP: MEASURE THEN BUILD (PATTERSON'S LAW)
> One of our advisors, David Patterson (of RISC and RAID fame), used to always encourage us to measure a system and demonstrate a problem *before* building a new system to fix said problem. By using experimental evidence, rather than gut instinct, you can turn the process of system building into a more scientific endeavor. Doing so also has the fringe benefit of making you think about how exactly to measure the system before your improved version is developed. When you do finally get around to building the new system, two things are better as a result: first, you have evidence that shows you are solving a real problem; second, you now have a way to measure your new system in place, to show that it actually improves upon the state of the art. And thus we call this **Patterson's Law**.

50.2 Problems with Version 1

A few key problems with this first version of AFS motivated the designers to rethink their file system. To study the problems in detail, the designers of AFS spent a great deal of time measuring their existing prototype to find what was wrong. Such experimentation is a good thing, because **measurement** is the key to understanding how systems work and how to improve them; obtaining concrete, good data is thus a necessary part of systems construction. In their study, the authors found two main problems with AFSv1:

- **Path-traversal costs are too high**: When performing a Fetch or Store protocol request, the client passes the entire pathname (e.g., `/home/remzi/notes.txt`) to the server. The server, in order to access the file, must perform a full pathname traversal, first looking in the root directory to find `home`, then in `home` to find `remzi`, and so forth, all the way down the path until finally the desired file is located. With many clients accessing the server at once, the designers of AFS found that the server was spending much of its CPU time simply walking down directory paths.
- **The client issues too many TestAuth protocol messages**: Much like NFS and its overabundance of GETATTR protocol messages, AFSv1 generated a large amount of traffic to check whether a local file (or its stat information) was valid with the TestAuth protocol message. Thus, servers spent much of their time telling clients whether it was OK to used their cached copies of a file. Most of the time, the answer was that the file had not changed.

There were actually two other problems with AFSv1: load was not balanced across servers, and the server used a single distinct process per client thus inducing context switching and other overheads. The load imbalance problem was solved by introducing **volumes**, which an administrator could move across servers to balance load; the context-switch problem was solved in AFSv2 by building the server with threads instead of processes. However, for the sake of space, we focus here on the main two protocol problems above that limited the scale of the system.

50.3 Improving the Protocol

The two problems above limited the scalability of AFS; the server CPU became the bottleneck of the system, and each server could only service 20 clients without becoming overloaded. Servers were receiving too many TestAuth messages, and when they received Fetch or Store messages, were spending too much time traversing the directory hierarchy. Thus, the AFS designers were faced with a problem:

THE CRUX: HOW TO DESIGN A SCALABLE FILE PROTOCOL
How should one redesign the protocol to minimize the number of server interactions, i.e., how could they reduce the number of TestAuth messages? Further, how could they design the protocol to make these server interactions efficient? By attacking both of these issues, a new protocol would result in a much more scalable version AFS.

50.4 AFS Version 2

AFSv2 introduced the notion of a **callback** to reduce the number of client/server interactions. A callback is simply a promise from the server to the client that the server will inform the client when a file that the client is caching has been modified. By adding this **state** to the system, the client no longer needs to contact the server to find out if a cached file is still valid. Rather, it assumes that the file is valid until the server tells it otherwise; notice the analogy to **polling** versus **interrupts**.

AFSv2 also introduced the notion of a **file identifier** (**FID**) (similar to the NFS **file handle**) instead of pathnames to specify which file a client was interested in. An FID in AFS consists of a volume identifier, a file identifier, and a "uniquifier" (to enable reuse of the volume and file IDs when a file is deleted). Thus, instead of sending whole pathnames to the server and letting the server walk the pathname to find the desired file, the client would walk the pathname, one piece at a time, caching the results and thus hopefully reducing the load on the server.

For example, if a client accessed the file `/home/remzi/notes.txt`, and `home` was the AFS directory mounted onto / (i.e., / was the local root directory, but `home` and its children were in AFS), the client would first Fetch the directory contents of `home`, put them in the local-disk cache, and set up a callback on `home`. Then, the client would Fetch the directory

Client (C_1)	**Server**
fd = open("/home/remzi/notes.txt", ...);	
Send Fetch (home FID, "remzi")	
	Receive Fetch request
	look for remzi in home dir
	establish callback(C_1) on remzi
	return remzi's content and FID
Receive Fetch reply	
write remzi to local disk cache	
record callback status of remzi	
Send Fetch (remzi FID, "notes.txt")	
	Receive Fetch request
	look for notes.txt in remzi dir
	establish callback(C_1) on notes.txt
	return notes.txt's content and FID
Receive Fetch reply	
write notes.txt to local disk cache	
record callback status of notes.txt	
local `open()` of cached notes.txt	
return file descriptor to application	
read(fd, buffer, MAX);	
perform local `read()` on cached copy	
close(fd);	
do local `close()` on cached copy	
if file has changed, flush to server	
fd = open("/home/remzi/notes.txt", ...);	
Foreach dir (home, remzi)	
if (callback(dir) == VALID)	
use local copy for lookup(dir)	
else	
Fetch (as above)	
if (callback(notes.txt) == VALID)	
open local cached copy	
return file descriptor to it	
else	
Fetch (as above) then open and return fd	

Figure 502: **Reading A File: Client-side And File Server Actions**

`remzi`, put it in the local-disk cache, and set up a callback on `remzi`. Finally, the client would Fetch `notes.txt`, cache this regular file in the local disk, set up a callback, and finally return a file descriptor to the calling application. See Figure 502 for a summary.

The key difference, however, from NFS, is that with each fetch of a directory or file, the AFS client would establish a callback with the server,

> ASIDE: CACHE CONSISTENCY IS NOT A PANACEA
>
> When discussing distributed file systems, much is made of the cache consistency the file systems provide. However, this baseline consistency does not solve all problems with regards to file access from multiple clients. For example, if you are building a code repository, with multiple clients performing check-ins and check-outs of code, you can't simply rely on the underlying file system to do all of the work for you; rather, you have to use explicit **file-level locking** in order to ensure that the "right" thing happens when such concurrent accesses take place. Indeed, any application that truly cares about concurrent updates will add extra machinery to handle conflicts. The baseline consistency described in this chapter and the previous one are useful primarily for casual usage, i.e., when a user logs into a different client, they expect some reasonable version of their files to show up there. Expecting more from these protocols is setting yourself up for failure, disappointment, and tear-filled frustration.

thus ensuring that the server would notify the client of a change in its cached state. The benefit is obvious: although the *first* access to `/home/remzi/notes.txt` generates many client-server messages (as described above), it also establishes callbacks for all the directories as well as the file notes.txt, and thus subsequent accesses are entirely local and require no server interaction at all. Thus, in the common case where a file is cached at the client, AFS behaves nearly identically to a local disk-based file system. If one accesses a file more than once, the second access should be just as fast as accessing a file locally.

50.5 Cache Consistency

When we discussed NFS, there were two aspects of cache consistency we considered: **update visibility** and **cache staleness**. With update visibility, the question is: when will the server be updated with a new version of a file? With cache staleness, the question is: once the server has a new version, how long before clients see the new version instead of an older cached copy?

Because of callbacks and whole-file caching, the cache consistency provided by AFS is easy to describe and understand. There are two important cases to consider: consistency between processes on *different* machines, and consistency between processes on the *same* machine.

Between different machines, AFS makes updates visible at the server and invalidates cached copies at the exact same time, which is when the updated file is closed. A client opens a file, and then writes to it (perhaps repeatedly). When it is finally closed, the new file is flushed to the server (and thus visible). At this point, the server then "breaks" callbacks for any clients with cached copies; the break is accomplished by contacting each client and informing it that the callback it has on the file is no longer

Client$_1$			Client$_2$		Server	*Comments*
P$_1$	**P$_2$**	**Cache**	**P$_3$**	**Cache**	**Disk**	
open(F)		-		-	-	File created
write(A)		A		-	-	
close()		A		-	A	
	open(F)	A		-	A	
	read() → A	A		-	A	
	close()	A		-	A	
open(F)		A		-	A	
write(B)		B		-	A	
	open(F)	B		-	A	Local processes
	read() → B	B		-	A	see writes immediately
	close()	B		-	A	
		B	open(F)	A	A	Remote processes
		B	read() → A	A	A	do not see writes...
		B	close()	A	A	
close()		B		~~A~~	B	... until close()
		B	open(F)	B	B	has taken place
		B	read() → B	B	B	
		B	close()	B	B	
		B	open(F)	B	B	
open(F)		B		B	B	
write(D)		D		B	B	
		D	write(C)	C	B	
		D	close()	C	C	
close()		D		~~C~~	D	
		D	open(F)	D	D	Unfortunately for P$_3$
		D	read() → D	D	D	the last writer wins
		D	close()	D	D	

Figure 503: **Cache Consistency Timeline**

valid. This step ensures that clients will no longer read stale copies of the file; subsequent opens on those clients will require a re-fetch of the new version of the file from the server (and will also serve to reestablish a callback on the new version of the file).

AFS makes an exception to this simple model between processes on the same machine. In this case, writes to a file are immediately visible to other local processes (i.e., a process does not have to wait until a file is closed to see its latest updates). This makes using a single machine behave exactly as you would expect, as this behavior is based upon typical UNIX semantics. Only when switching to a different machine would you be able to detect the more general AFS consistency mechanism.

There is one interesting cross-machine case that is worthy of further discussion. Specifically, in the rare case that processes on different machines are modifying a file at the same time, AFS naturally employs what is known as a **last writer wins** approach (which perhaps should be called **last closer wins**). Specifically, whichever client calls `close()` last will update the entire file on the server last and thus will be the "winning" file, i.e., the file that remains on the server for others to see. The result is a file that was generated in its entirety either by one client or the other. Note the difference from a block-based protocol like NFS: in NFS, writes of individual blocks may be flushed out to the server as each client is updating the file, and thus the final file on the server could end up as a mix of updates from both clients. In many cases, such a mixed file output would not make much sense, i.e., imagine a JPEG image getting modified by two clients in pieces; the resulting mix of writes would not likely constitute a valid JPEG.

A timeline showing a few of these different scenarios can be seen in Figure 503. The columns show the behavior of two processes (P_1 and P_2) on $Client_1$ and its cache state, one process (P_3) on $Client_2$ and its cache state, and the server (Server), all operating on a single file called, imaginatively, `F`. For the server, the figure simply shows the contents of the file after the operation on the left has completed. Read through it and see if you can understand why each read returns the results that it does. A commentary field on the right will help you if you get stuck.

50.6 Crash Recovery

From the description above, you might sense that crash recovery is more involved than with NFS. You would be right. For example, imagine there is a short period of time where a server (S) is not able to contact a client (C1), for example, while the client C1 is rebooting. While C1 is not available, S may have tried to send it one or more callback recall messages; for example, imagine C1 had file F cached on its local disk, and then C2 (another client) updated F, thus causing S to send messages to all clients caching the file to remove it from their local caches. Because C1 may miss those critical messages when it is rebooting, upon rejoining the system, C1 should treat all of its cache contents as suspect. Thus, upon the next access to file F, C1 should first ask the server (with a TestAuth protocol message) whether its cached copy of file F is still valid; if so, C1 can use it; if not, C1 should fetch the newer version from the server.

Server recovery after a crash is also more complicated. The problem that arises is that callbacks are kept in memory; thus, when a server reboots, it has no idea which client machine has which files. Thus, upon server restart, each client of the server must realize that the server has crashed and treat all of their cache contents as suspect, and (as above) reestablish the validity of a file before using it. Thus, a server crash is a big event, as one must ensure that each client is aware of the crash in a timely manner, or risk a client accessing a stale file. There are many ways to implement such recovery; for example, by having the server send a message (saying "don't trust your cache contents!") to each client when it is up and running again, or by having clients check that the server is alive periodically (with a **heartbeat** message, as it is called). As you can see, there is a cost to building a more scalable and sensible caching model; with NFS, clients hardly noticed a server crash.

Workload	NFS	AFS	$\frac{\text{AFS}}{\text{NFS}}$
1. Small file, sequential read	$N_s \cdot L_{net}$	$N_s \cdot L_{net}$	1
2. Small file, sequential re-read	$N_s \cdot L_{mem}$	$N_s \cdot L_{mem}$	1
3. Medium file, sequential read	$N_m \cdot L_{net}$	$N_m \cdot L_{net}$	1
4. Medium file, sequential re-read	$N_m \cdot L_{mem}$	$N_m \cdot L_{mem}$	1
5. Large file, sequential read	$N_L \cdot L_{net}$	$N_L \cdot L_{net}$	1
6. Large file, sequential re-read	$N_L \cdot L_{net}$	$N_L \cdot L_{disk}$	$\frac{L_{disk}}{L_{net}}$
7. Large file, single read	L_{net}	$N_L \cdot L_{net}$	N_L
8. Small file, sequential write	$N_s \cdot L_{net}$	$N_s \cdot L_{net}$	1
9. Large file, sequential write	$N_L \cdot L_{net}$	$N_L \cdot L_{net}$	1
10. Large file, sequential overwrite	$N_L \cdot L_{net}$	$2 \cdot N_L \cdot L_{net}$	2
11. Large file, single write	L_{net}	$2 \cdot N_L \cdot L_{net}$	$2 \cdot N_L$

Figure 504: **Comparison: AFS vs. NFS**

50.7 Scale And Performance Of AFSv2

With the new protocol in place, AFSv2 was measured and found to be much more scalable that the original version. Indeed, each server could support about 50 clients (instead of just 20). A further benefit was that client-side performance often came quite close to local performance, because in the common case, all file accesses were local; file reads usually went to the local disk cache (and potentially, local memory). Only when a client created a new file or wrote to an existing one was there need to send a Store message to the server and thus update the file with new contents.

Let us also gain some perspective on AFS performance by comparing common file-system access scenarios with NFS. Figure 504 (page 675) shows the results of our qualitative comparison.

In the figure, we examine typical read and write patterns analytically, for files of different sizes. Small files have N_s blocks in them; medium files have N_m blocks; large files have N_L blocks. We assume that small and medium files fit into the memory of a client; large files fit on a local disk but not in client memory.

We also assume, for the sake of analysis, that an access across the network to the remote server for a file block takes L_{net} time units. Access to local memory takes L_{mem}, and access to local disk takes L_{disk}. The general assumption is that $L_{net} > L_{disk} > L_{mem}$.

Finally, we assume that the first access to a file does not hit in any caches. Subsequent file accesses (i.e., "re-reads") we assume will hit in caches, if the relevant cache has enough capacity to hold the file.

The columns of the figure show the time a particular operation (e.g., a small file sequential read) roughly takes on either NFS or AFS. The rightmost column displays the ratio of AFS to NFS.

We make the following observations. First, in many cases, the performance of each system is roughly equivalent. For example, when first reading a file (e.g., Workloads 1, 3, 5), the time to fetch the file from the remote server dominates, and is similar on both systems. You might think AFS would be slower in this case, as it has to write the file to local disk; however, those writes are buffered by the local (client-side) file system cache and thus said costs are likely hidden. Similarly, you might think that AFS reads from the local cached copy would be slower, again because AFS stores the cached copy on disk. However, AFS again benefits here from local file system caching; reads on AFS would likely hit in the client-side memory cache, and performance would be similar to NFS.

Second, an interesting difference arises during a large-file sequential re-read (Workload 6). Because AFS has a large local disk cache, it will access the file from there when the file is accessed again. NFS, in contrast, only can cache blocks in client memory; as a result, if a large file (i.e., a file bigger than local memory) is re-read, the NFS client will have to re-fetch the entire file from the remote server. Thus, AFS is faster than NFS in this case by a factor of $\frac{L_{net}}{L_{disk}}$, assuming that remote access is indeed slower than local disk. We also note that NFS in this case increases server load, which has an impact on scale as well.

Third, we note that sequential writes (of new files) should perform similarly on both systems (Workloads 8, 9). AFS, in this case, will write the file to the local cached copy; when the file is closed, the AFS client will force the writes to the server, as per the protocol. NFS will buffer writes in client memory, perhaps forcing some blocks to the server due to client-side memory pressure, but definitely writing them to the server when the file is closed, to preserve NFS flush-on-close consistency. You might think AFS would be slower here, because it writes all data to local disk. However, realize that it is writing to a local file system; those writes are first committed to the page cache, and only later (in the background) to disk, and thus AFS reaps the benefits of the client-side OS memory caching infrastructure to improve performance.

Fourth, we note that AFS performs worse on a sequential file overwrite (Workload 10). Thus far, we have assumed that the workloads that write are also creating a new file; in this case, the file exists, and is then over-written. Overwrite can be a particularly bad case for AFS, because the client first fetches the old file in its entirety, only to subsequently overwrite it. NFS, in contrast, will simply overwrite blocks and thus avoid the initial (useless) read[2].

Finally, workloads that access a small subset of data within large files perform much better on NFS than AFS (Workloads 7, 11). In these cases, the AFS protocol fetches the entire file when the file is opened; unfortunately, only a small read or write is performed. Even worse, if the file is modified, the entire file is written back to the server, doubling the per-

[2]We assume here that NFS writes are block-sized and block-aligned; if they were not, the NFS client would also have to read the block first. We also assume the file was *not* opened with the O_TRUNC flag; if it had been, the initial open in AFS would not fetch the soon to be truncated file's contents.

ASIDE: THE IMPORTANCE OF WORKLOAD

One challenge of evaluating any system is the choice of **workload**. Because computer systems are used in so many different ways, there are a large variety of workloads to choose from. How should the storage system designer decide which workloads are important, in order to make reasonable design decisions?

The designers of AFS, given their experience in measuring how file systems were used, made certain workload assumptions; in particular, they assumed that most files were not frequently shared, and accessed sequentially in their entirety. Given those assumptions, the AFS design makes perfect sense.

However, these assumptions are not always correct. For example, imagine an application that appends information, periodically, to a log. These little log writes, which add small amounts of data to an existing large file, are quite problematic for AFS. Many other difficult workloads exist as well, e.g., random updates in a transaction database.

One place to get some information about what types of workloads are common are through various research studies that have been performed. See any of these studies for good examples of workload analysis [B+91, H+11, R+00, V99], including the AFS retrospective [H+88].

formance impact. NFS, as a block-based protocol, performs I/O that is proportional to the size of the read or write.

Overall, we see that NFS and AFS make different assumptions and not surprisingly realize different performance outcomes as a result. Whether these differences matter is, as always, a question of workload.

50.8 AFS: Other Improvements

Like we saw with the introduction of Berkeley FFS (which added symbolic links and a number of other features), the designers of AFS took the opportunity when building their system to add a number of features that made the system easier to use and manage. For example, AFS provides a true global namespace to clients, thus ensuring that all files were named the same way on all client machines. NFS, in contrast, allows each client to mount NFS servers in any way that they please, and thus only by convention (and great administrative effort) would files be named similarly across clients.

AFS also takes security seriously, and incorporates mechanisms to authenticate users and ensure that a set of files could be kept private if a user so desired. NFS, in contrast, had quite primitive support for security for many years.

AFS also includes facilities for flexible user-managed access control. Thus, when using AFS, a user has a great deal of control over who exactly can access which files. NFS, like most UNIX file systems, has much less support for this type of sharing.

Finally, as mentioned before, AFS adds tools to enable simpler management of servers for the administrators of the system. In thinking about system management, AFS was light years ahead of the field.

50.9 Summary

AFS shows us how distributed file systems can be built quite differently than what we saw with NFS. The protocol design of AFS is particularly important; by minimizing server interactions (through whole-file caching and callbacks), each server can support many clients and thus reduce the number of servers needed to manage a particular site. Many other features, including the single namespace, security, and access-control lists, make AFS quite nice to use. The consistency model provided by AFS is simple to understand and reason about, and does not lead to the occasional weird behavior as one sometimes observes in NFS.

Perhaps unfortunately, AFS is likely on the decline. Because NFS became an open standard, many different vendors supported it, and, along with CIFS (the Windows-based distributed file system protocol), NFS dominates the marketplace. Although one still sees AFS installations from time to time (such as in various educational institutions, including Wisconsin), the only lasting influence will likely be from the ideas of AFS rather than the actual system itself. Indeed, NFSv4 now adds server state (e.g., an "open" protocol message), and thus bears an increasing similarity to the basic AFS protocol.

References

[B+91] "Measurements of a Distributed File System" by Mary Baker, John Hartman, Martin Kupfer, Ken Shirriff, John Ousterhout. SOSP '91, Pacific Grove, California, October 1991. *An early paper measuring how people use distributed file systems. Matches much of the intuition found in AFS.*

[H+11] "A File is Not a File: Understanding the I/O Behavior of Apple Desktop Applications" by Tyler Harter, Chris Dragga, Michael Vaughn, Andrea C. Arpaci-Dusseau, Remzi H. Arpaci-Dusseau. SOSP '11, New York, New York, October 2011. *Our own paper studying the behavior of Apple Desktop workloads; turns out they are a bit different than many of the server-based workloads the systems research community usually focuses upon. Also a good recent reference which points to a lot of related work.*

[H+88] "Scale and Performance in a Distributed File System" by John H. Howard, Michael L. Kazar, Sherri G. Menees, David A. Nichols, M. Satyanarayanan, Robert N. Sidebotham, Michael J. West. ACM Transactions on Computing Systems (ACM TOCS), Volume 6:1, February 1988. *The long journal version of the famous AFS system, still in use in a number of places throughout the world, and also probably the earliest clear thinking on how to build distributed file systems. A wonderful combination of the science of measurement and principled engineering.*

[R+00] "A Comparison of File System Workloads" by Drew Roselli, Jacob R. Lorch, Thomas E. Anderson. USENIX '00, San Diego, California, June 2000. *A more recent set of traces as compared to the Baker paper [B+91], with some interesting twists.*

[S+85] "The ITC Distributed File System: Principles and Design" by M. Satyanarayanan, J.H. Howard, D.A. Nichols, R.N. Sidebotham, A. Spector, M.J. West. SOSP '85, Orcas Island, Washington, December 1985. *The older paper about a distributed file system. Much of the basic design of AFS is in place in this older system, but not the improvements for scale. The name change to "Andrew" is an homage to two people both named Andrew, Andrew Carnegie and Andrew Mellon. These two rich dudes started the Carnegie Institute of Technology and the Mellon Institute of Industrial Research, respectively, which eventually merged to become what is now known as Carnegie Mellon University.*

[V99] "File system usage in Windows NT 4.0" by Werner Vogels. SOSP '99, Kiawah Island Resort, South Carolina, December 1999. *A cool study of Windows workloads, which are inherently different than many of the UNIX-based studies that had previously been done.*

Homework (Simulation)

This section introduces `afs.py`, a simple AFS simulator you can use to shore up your knowledge of how the Andrew File System works. Read the README file for more details.

Questions

1. Run a few simple cases to make sure you can predict what values will be read by clients. Vary the random seed flag (`-s`) and see if you can trace through and predict both intermediate values as well as the final values stored in the files. Also vary the number of files (`-f`), the number of clients (`-C`), and the read ratio (`-r`, from between 0 to 1) to make it a bit more challenging. You might also want to generate slightly longer traces to make for more interesting interactions, e.g., (`-n 2` or higher).
2. Now do the same thing and see if you can predict each callback that the AFS server initiates. Try different random seeds, and make sure to use a high level of detailed feedback (e.g., `-d 3`) to see when callbacks occur when you have the program compute the answers for you (with `-c`). Can you guess exactly when each callback occurs? What is the precise condition for one to take place?
3. Similar to above, run with some different random seeds and see if you can predict the exact cache state at each step. Cache state can be observed by running with `-c` and `-d 7`.
4. Now let's construct some specific workloads. Run the simulation with `-A oa1:w1:c1,oa1:r1:c1` flag. What are different possible values observed by client 1 when it reads the file `a`, when running with the random scheduler? (try different random seeds to see different outcomes)? Of all the possible schedule interleavings of the two clients' operations, how many of them lead to client 1 reading the value 1, and how many reading the value 0?
5. Now let's construct some specific schedules. When running with the `-A oa1:w1:c1,oa1:r1:c1` flag, also run with the following schedules: `-S 01`, `-S 100011`, `-S 011100`, and others of which you can think. What value will client 1 read?
6. Now run with this workload: `-A oa1:w1:c1,oa1:w1:c1`, and vary the schedules as above. What happens when you run with `-S 011100`? What about when you run with `-S 010011`? What is important in determining the final value of the file?

51

Summary Dialogue on Distribution

Student: *Well, that was quick. Too quick, in my opinion!*

Professor: *Yes, distributed systems are complicated and cool and well worth your study; just not in this book (or course).*

Student: *That's too bad; I wanted to learn more! But I did learn a few things.*

Professor: *Like what?*

Student: *Well, everything can fail.*

Professor: *Good start.*

Student: *But by having lots of these things (whether disks, machines, or whatever), you can hide much of the failure that arises.*

Professor: *Keep going!*

Student: *Some basic techniques like retrying are really useful.*

Professor: *That's true.*

Student: *And you have to think carefully about protocols: the exact bits that are exchanged between machines. Protocols can affect everything, including how systems respond to failure and how scalable they are.*

Professor: *You really are getting better at this learning stuff.*

Student: *Thanks! And you're not a bad teacher yourself!*

Professor: *Well thank you very much too.*

Student: *So is this the end of the book?*

Professor: *I'm not sure. They don't tell me anything.*

Student: *Me neither. Let's get out of here.*

Professor: *OK.*

Student: *Go ahead.*

Professor: *No, after you.*

Student: *Please, professors first.*

Professor: *No, please, after you.*

Student: *(exasperated) Fine!*

Professor: *(waiting) ... so why haven't you left?*

Student: *I don't know how. Turns out, the only thing I can do is participate in these dialogues.*

Professor: *Me too. And now you've learned our final lesson...*

General Index

Asides

Tips

Cruces

This book was typeset using the amazing LaTeX typesetting system and the wonderful memoir book-making package. A heartfelt thank you to the legions of programmers who have contributed to this powerful tool over the many years of its development.

All of the graphs and figures in the book were generated using a Python-based version of zplot, a simple and useful tool developed by R. Arpaci-Dusseau to generate graphs in PostScript. The zplot tool arose after many years of frustration with existing graphing tools such as gnuplot (which was limited) and ploticus (which was overly complex though admittedly quite awesome). As a result, R. A-D finally put his years of study of PostScript to good use and developed zplot.